# The Secret History of Star Wars

## The Art of Storytelling and the Making of a Modern Epic

Michael Kaminski

Legacy Books Press

Published by Legacy Books Press
RPO Princess, Box 21031
445 Princess Street
Kingston, Ontario, K7L 5P5
Canada

www.legacybookspress.com

First published in 2008 by Legacy Books Press
2    1

Kaminski, Michael
    The Secret History of Star Wars: The Art of Storytelling and the Making of a Modern Epic
    Includes bibliographical references and index
    ISBN-13: 978-0-9784652-3-0
    1. Performing Arts : Film & Video - Reference 2. Performing Arts : Film & Video - Screenwriting 3. Culture : Star Wars 4. Star Wars

Printed and bound in the United States of America and the United Kingdom.

This book is typeset in a Times New Roman 11-point font.

No Imperial Stormtroopers, Sith, Ewoks, or Jedi were harmed in the writing of this book.

# Table of Contents

Early Transformations
Getting a Screenplay
The Final Draft
The Tragedy of Darth Vader
A Last Hurrah

# Acknowledgments

MUCH of this book was born out of discussion, debate and shared research with other *Star Wars* fans, primarily through online means. To those of you who continue to hold such an interest in the subject matter and to those willing to examine the films with a rational and critical eye, this book is a testament to your efforts. From these sources, special acknowledgment must be made to Noah Henson, Geoffrey McKinney, Chris Olivo and "Toshe_Station," Greg Kirkman, Duane Aubin, and David Furr in this regard, among others. A work as large as this book did not spring into existence without the support and help of countless other individuals I am surely forgetting.

Special mention must also be made to The Starkiller Jedi Bendu Script Site, a site dedicated to preserving and archiving early *Star Wars* drafts and written artifacts, as well as containing a reservoir of various essays and papers exploring the evolution of the *Star Wars* screenplays. Among these, Jan Helander and Bjorn and Brendon Wahlberg's work provided the most useful information, and were often used as convenient reference tools.

Finally, as will become evident upon reading the body of this work, much of this manuscript is comprised of quotations from individuals gleaned from secondary sources. This, in fact, is one of the purposes of this book, to demonstrate that the fractured history of *Star Wars* has remained buried in time over the years and need only to be stitched together into some sort of cohesive explanation—and most importantly, many of these are from as early a time period as could be found, as the history has shifted in its telling as time has transpired. There are too many to even begin to list here—the End Notes section is particularly meticulous to ensure that an accurate record of these sources exists, most of them quoted from magazine and newspaper sources (*Starlog* and *Rolling Stone* in particular being consistently cited, with Kerry O' Quinn's excellent series of interviews which ran from July to September of 1981 in the former being exceptionally illuminating into Lucas' early writing efforts). For those wishing for a good base of full, re-published interviews, the University Press of Mississippi's *George Lucas Interviews* is available, containing many wonderful reprints of vintage interviews.

Dale Pollock's *Skywalking: The Life and Films of George Lucas* continues to remain as the golden standard for an objective analysis of the man and his work, being the only book containing a revealing insight into his early years, and was a source of much information, and of course Laurent Bouzereau's magnificent *The Annotated Screenplays* continues to be upheld as a rare insight into the many X-factors of *Star Wars* history. For those wishing for a journal of the making of *Star Wars*, J.W. Rinzler's authoritative book on the subject is your one-stop source that will forever remain as *the* source of information on the film, and provided invaluable supplemental information. It is mandatory reading for anyone wanting to know about the original film and the origin of the series, and contains mountains of information that has not been included here, including additional insight into the writing process.

Finally, I must also give enormous thanks to my editor, Robert Marks, who believed in this book from day one and has been a great source of encouragement; without his efforts, *The Secret History of Star Wars* would not be in your hands.

# Foreword

ON May 25th, 2005, twenty-eight years to the day that a film called *Star Wars* burst onto cinema screens for the first time, I sat and watched *Revenge of the Sith*, the final piece in a generation-spanning cinematic epic quietly begun all those years ago, and now finally ended. As the curtain closed on the silver screen before me and the celluloid reels spun empty in the projection booth behind me, there was at once the overwhelming feeling of relief, knowing that the decades-long journey of telling this mighty tale had now been finished, but I also felt something much deeper: that an entire generation of viewers was being inaugurated that was largely ignorant to the historic process that led us to this sixth and final film.

The *Star Wars* saga is no ordinary one: told out of order, funded almost exclusively on a private bank account, utilising thousands of artisans and millions of dollars, it comprises the single most successful series of films in movie history. It is a true cultural phenomenon, the scale and scope of which may be unequalled in the world, one that has enthralled hundreds of millions and made its modest creator rich beyond his wildest dreams.

Today, it is unofficially known as *The Tragedy of Darth Vader*—a true epic of mythical proportions that charts the rise, fall and redemption of an iconic character on a scale unrivalled in cinema. So gargantuan is its cultural imprint that it is commonly compared to classic myths of the past. Yet things were not always as they now are. What appeared and enchanted people who first saw and heard the words "Star Wars" is very different to the "Star Wars" that people see and hear today. It was once a tale so unlike its current embodiment that it is no longer viewed under that original groundbreaking configuration, so different that its own creator has even distorted the truth in certain instances, essentially reshaping film and cultural history in the process.

This is "the Secret History of Star Wars." But what exactly do I mean by that? I first became aware that something was amiss sometime in 2002 when it was demonstrated by a fellow fan that Darth Vader, the iconic figure of evil, and Anakin Skywalker, the flawed Jedi who turns to evil and *becomes* Darth Vader, were originally conceived as separate people. Not separate constructs, as they now might be said to exist in the saga "from a certain point of view"—but entirely different characters, totally independent of one another, each existing in some imagined history within the same narrative time and space. Indeed, a cursory evaluation of Lucas' own early notes and script material reveals that Darth Vader and the father of Luke Skywalker were characters that existed *together*, onscreen as separate entities. Clearly, the history of the early story differed drastically from the account in common knowledge, which held that the story had been more or less blueprinted in the mid-1970's.

As my research began to grow I realised that I was embarking on a truly ambitious mission, travelling back in time to uncover the story that once was. A mountain of different sources stood in my way and the process of sifting through all the facts and evidence was itself a daunting task—such is the challenge that has thusfar prevented ardent researchers from composing such a synthesized overview of the series. The history of *Star Wars* is one fractured and broken, disconnected and contradictory, but now, I hope, I have tied it all together, re-constructing the jigsaw puzzle like a sort of cinematic detective. What is presented here is not really "secret" so much as it is an entirely new approach to the films that better reflects their historical reality.

Some people refer to events that shatter all preconceived notions and force the viewer to re-evaluate material in a whole new way as consciousness-raisers. That, I suppose, is what you might characterise this work as: one which will raise the viewer's consciousness about the *Star Wars* series, its genesis, its transformation, and what its current state truly means.

# Introduction

APRIL 17th, 1973 was a chilly Tuesday in San Francisco, USA. Rain peppered the Bay area here and there, springtime not yet disappeared. From the radios of GTOs, Oldsmobiles and Volkswagens the sounds of Deep Purple's Smoke on the Water, David Bowie's Space Oddity and the current hit by Donnie Osmond, The Twelfth of Never, could be heard. The banks open at 9 and a parade of trenchcoats hustles its way through Market Street, newspaper boxes crowded with readers attracted by headlines about President Nixon's first statement before the Senate committee in the Watergate trial. Elsewhere in the city, the San Francisco Giants are getting ready to face the Atlanta Braves later that day after losing their previous game to the Cincinnati Reds.

As all of this is happening, something far more interesting is occurring in a small corner of the suburbs, just outside the city. Medway Avenue, Mill Valley. A small house occupied by a young married couple crests the top of the hill, a white 1967 Camaro in the driveway. Inside, the house is silent, light rainfall pattering against the window panes, and a figure sits at a desk, deep in thought. He is young, only twenty-eight years old. A beard covers his thin face, his eyelids fallen closed behind thick glasses. In front of him is a blue-lined yellow pad of paper. It is blank. Finally, the young man picks up the number two hard-lead pencil that sits on the desk before him and touches its tip to the empty page. His tiny printing scrawls out a simple title: *The Star Wars*.[1]

Four years later, a new film was opening in theatres around the country bearing that very title, written and directed by a man hardly anyone had heard of named George Lucas. No one in the film community had anticipated its arrival but one thing was sure by the time it was released: the world of cinema would never be the same again.

*Star Wars* has undoubtedly become one of the prime mythologies of the twentieth century, a tale so well known that it is studied in university courses alongside Shakespeare and Dostoevsky. It is one which has permeated the culture unto which it was released with such far-reaching influence that it has literally become a religion—on the 2001 UK census, thousands declared their official religion Jedi Knight, leading to its (short-lived) official recognition; according to reports, there were more Jedi than Jews, and the phenomenon spread to Australia where 70,000 proclaimed themselves followers of Jediism.[2] Given that the six films have collectively sold nearly a billion theatrical tickets alone, this should hardly be surprising. If critics may trivialize its study on the grounds that the films are merely juvenile entertainment pieces, the *Star Wars* saga nonetheless remains among the most well known and influential stories of the modern era. Anthropological studies not just of twentieth century culture and entertainment, but of modern folklore, must place *Star Wars* and its five sequels and empire of spin-offs at or near the top of the list of important works.

Perhaps most incredible of all, the entire story of this culture-shaping saga has sprung from a single mind, its first seeds planted that day back in April of 1973. George Lucas has been labelled many things in his day, from the world's greatest storyteller to the world's greatest sell-out; he's been attacked by critics just as often as he has been praised by them. Interest in the creation of the *Star Wars* films has been immense, and indeed, there are few films whose productions are rivaled in public curiosity. For many, *Star Wars'* impossible story and otherworldly visuals were the first realisation that human artists are responsible for the creation of a film.

The story *behind* the story of *Star Wars* was as interesting as the film itself—that of an underdog filmmaker who struggled through many years of toil, crafting a tale too large for even one film to contain. Written from the study of Joseph Campbell and the research of thousands of years of mythology, and fused with the action and adventure of matinee science fiction serials, Lucas had a massive, expensive epic on his hands, and divided the story into three separate films. He had also developed a backstory for his elaborate tale, which together totalled six chapters, and sought to make Episode IV first, due to technical and storytelling reasons. When the film by some miracle went into production, it was beset by problems of all kinds and Lucas was sure it would be a failure—and was shocked when it became the biggest sensation of the year, garnering ten Academy Award nominations and winning seven. With financial independence, George Lucas finally had the freedom to finish the story he had started, the remaining chapters set aside all those years, and thus completed his *Star Wars* saga. This is the accepted story of *Star Wars'* history.

*The accepted story.*

Lucas even tells it in his own words:

> The *Star Wars* series started out as a movie that ended up being so big that I took each act and cut it into its own movie...The original concept really related to a father and a son, and twins—a son and a daughter. It was that relationship that was the core of the story. And it went through a lot of machinations before I even got to the first draft screenplay. And various characters changed shapes and sizes. And it isn't really until it evolved into what is close to what *Star Wars* now is that I began to go back and deal with the stories that evolved to get us to that point...When I first did *Star Wars* I did it as a big piece. It was like a big script. It was way too big to make into a movie. So I took the first third of it, which is basically the first act, and I turned that into what was the original *Star Wars*...after *Star Wars* was successful and I said "Well gee, I can finish this entire script, and I can do the other two parts."[3]

For as long as that beloved trilogy endured—at least two generations—this was the account of its creation. *The Adventures of Luke Skywalker*, as the series was called, and his metamorphosis from wide-eyed farmboy to Jedi master, set alongside the battle between Rebel Alliance and Galactic Empire, divided into three acts. As George Lucas reminded Alan Arnold in 1979, "The *Star Wars* saga is essentially about Luke's background and his destiny."[4] But as the prequels were eventually released and the collective focus of the films changed from Luke Skywalker to Darth Vader, so too in turn changed Lucas' account of its origins:

> You have to remember that originally *Star Wars* was intended to be one movie, Episode IV of a Saturday matinee serial. You never saw what came before or what came after. It was designed to be the tragedy of Darth Vader. It starts with this monster coming through the door, throwing everybody around, then halfway through the movie you realise that the villain of the piece is actually a man and the hero is his son. And so the villain turns into the hero inspired by the son. It was meant to be one movie, but I broke it up because I didn't have the money to do it like that—it would have been five hours long.[5]

Here we have two different accounts of the story behind *Star Wars*. But which one is right? Is the long-held first version correct and Lucas merely exaggerating to include the prequels in the second version, or is the newly-revealed second version correct and Lucas had simply omitted such detail previously? Perhaps a combination of the two is where the truth lies?

What if *neither* version was correct? What if Darth Vader was never written as the father of anyone? What if the story was unknown and revealed to the creator of it at nearly the same rate as it was to the audience?

The real story behind *Star Wars* is much more interesting than the accepted one that Lucas had revealed the entire saga in one piece, as if divinely inspired. Instead, we will see how a documentary cameraman was forced into writing and then stumbled through a three-year scripting effort before arriving at a masterpiece of simplicity, and then gradually added on to this simple story, arriving at ideas through serendipity, accident and necessity, all of which would form and shape the growing mythology of the saga over a period of more than three decades.

*Star Wars* is a film series that has been consumed by its own legend, one with many tall tales and urban myths surrounding it. It is one which has changed to such an extent that, as I shall examine throughout the length of this book, the series that now exists may very well constitute an entirely separate one from that which was unveiled in 1977; this book will hence seek to journey back to the original perspective offered by the first film, uncovering how the story was created, then destroyed and re-configured into what we now call *The Star Wars Saga*. I have attempted to place *Star Wars*, its creation and subsequent transformation, in the context of history, so that a clearer understanding of the processes which formed and shaped its story can be gained.

Of the many reasons that compelled me to compile this book, none was more prominent than the fact that the account of the story's origins promulgated by George Lucas was far from what the case actually was, and often not consistent with what he had expressed in decades prior. Scholars and critics seemed to be ignorant to the fact that buried in time was an entirely different perspective of the birth, growth and maturation of the series; redress of this historic flaw has been in dire need in recent times.

And indeed, before the prequels, Lucas' account of its making was fairly consistent and accepted at face value—but as the films themselves began to shift, subtle hints in Lucas' own telling of the story began to emerge which demonstrated some curious inconsistencies; a new history of *Star Wars* was being written over top of the old one. It was an on-going effort that had been progressing since 1978, when seismic shifts began to be seen in the story of *Star Wars*, and now that Episode III has been released, the prequel trilogy completed and the two trilogies united into the six-episode *Star Wars Saga*, that shifting has finally settled, and the landscape of *Star Wars* only vaguely resembles its original configuration. Like massive continental drifting, *Star Wars* has slowly transformed, perhaps so subtly that we are not even aware of it.

A confounding problem to the version of history presented within this book, especially with respect to the formation of the character of Darth Vader, perhaps the linchpin on which now rests the entire storyline, is that viewers tend to read into the earlier material and writings aspects which reinforce the later storyline which simply aren't there when viewing the material on its own. A main feature of this book is the examination of how the more contemporary facets of the *Star Wars* saga, most notably the notion of Anakin Skywalker and his fall to the dark side and subsequent redemption by his son Luke, were totally absent from the earliest versions of 1977's *Star Wars*—even the finished film itself. From the "historical background" established in that first film, George Lucas combined characters and concepts and retroactively altered those in that film with revelations in the subsequent films, building, movie by movie, a series that, by 2005 when said "revelations" were complete, had absolutely no relation to the story contained in the initial 1977 film but still used its content and plot in the construction of the new storyline.

It is a fascinating development and a unique example in both cinema and popular storytelling, one which was made doubly so by the backwards process in which "prequels" were made and joined to the original three films and which solidified this newly-created storyline concerning a redeemed galactic messiah. What is more, this process appears to still be going on, with a seventh *Star Wars* feature film already released in 2008 heralding the animated *Clone War* series, which will then be followed by a live-action series; while these are considered outside the "canon" of the episodic saga, the *Star Wars* storytelling process nonetheless continues.

Before we proceed any further though, I am going to ask of you something which may seem bizarre and even a little difficult to do—I want you to forget everything you know about the *Star Wars* "Saga." But this goes beyond just the prequels. I want you to momentarily erase *Empire Strikes Back* and *Return of the Jedi* from your mind. I ask this of you so that you can look at *Star Wars* with fresh eyes, with the same eyes that gazed transfixedly at silver screens in 1977—it will soon become apparent that the film has not been viewed in the same light since its release. And I also recommend this self-induced hypnosis so that you can view the content of this book with objectivity, for large sections of it, particularly the first half, defy accepted knowledge of the behind-the-scenes workings of the films. The *Star Wars* story remains entrenched in the consciousness of the moviegoing public, an entrenchment which has been dug in for over thirty years, and for many readers some of the realities I ultimately unearthed in the writing of this book may be controversial. Certainly so for anyone who has read anything about the origins of the films—which, I am assuming, are well known by anyone interested enough to be reading this book. In any case, I urge the reader to keep an objective point of view and look at the evolving story as a chronologically-built entity.

Now, I want to take you back to the beginning. May 25th, 1977. *Star Wars* has been released. No, there is no "Episode IV," there is no "A New Hope"—those are additions in the years to come. For now, there is only *Star Wars*, a magical fairy tale about a young farm boy who fights an evil Empire and rescues a beautiful princess, along with the help of his wizard mentor, loyal droid servants, pirate friend and a cowardly lion. A mysterious power known as "The Force" aids the hero with the strength to vanquish the forces of evil and destroy the battle station Death Star, while the menacing black knight of the Empire, Darth Vader, survives the battle; the conflict between good and evil will continue another day. Ending the tale, the heroes are bestowed medals of honour in light of their heroic deeds which stand to "restore freedom to the galaxy," just as the opening scroll promised.

Do you remember that movie? It is hard to nowadays imagine *Star Wars* as simply "*Star Wars*, the movie." While today, *Star Wars* has become an epic saga, filled with melodrama and a scope which spans the forty-year rise and fall of Anakin Skywalker, it is surprising to look back on the magical simplicity of that first film way back in 1977. Indeed, it would be as strange as looking at a "*Wizard of Oz* Saga," instead of merely "*Wizard of Oz*, the movie," magical and timeless as we remember it.* Audiences today are largely unaware of how differently the first *Star Wars* film was perceived—and most importantly, presented—way back then. A swashbuckling fairy tale, filled with humour, adventure and simple mythology, with good guys on one side and bad guys on the other. It was

---

* There actually are many *Wizard of Oz* tales, from the original series of books written by L. Frank Baum, which totaled thirteen, as well as countless sequels by subsequent authors which have produced well over twenty additional books, plus the many cinema versions, such as Walter Murch's sequel to the 1939 film, *Return to Oz*, which Lucas himself helped finance, as well as the many Broadway and animated spin-offs.

a romantic story in its idealised and heroic depiction of chivalry and adventure, a perfect fusion of old-fashioned storytelling and modern technology, all told with the most sophisticated of cinematic technique. It was pure and simple, and anyone could watch it, young or old, man or woman.

When one looks back at that film, it is surprising to find how much the story has changed. George Lucas has said the prequels will alter our perception of the original trilogy, but before that the sequels alone altered the original film as well. The Emperor was not a wicked sorcerer but a crooked politician, modelled after Richard Nixon. Yoda did not train Ben Kenobi, because we didn't know Yoda existed, and Princess Leia was not Luke's sister.

The plot thickens with the mere mention of an iconic name: Darth Vader. Remember, Anakin Skywalker does not exist, so far as the audience is concerned. Darth Vader is the name of a man, a seemingly robotic henchman of the Empire, who was once a student of Obi Wan's but betrayed him long ago and murdered Luke's father. He was labeled in the publicity materials and novels as a "Dark Lord of the Sith"—but for all audiences of the time knew, "Sith" could have been a race or an Imperial rank; in fact he is stated as a Sith *Lord*, presumably one of many, who also serve the Emperor, and it was not clear that Darth was even human.

Yes, it was a very different galaxy.

So how then did we get to a six-episode saga of Biblical scope? How did we get to Anakin and Leia Skywalker, Darth Sidious and Master Yoda? Well, first we have to go back to the beginning.

# Chapter I: The Beginning

GEORGE Lucas' original vision was basically "cowboys in space," a swash-buckling adventure with heroes and bad guys, set in a science fiction world. In an interview conducted after the release of *American Graffiti*, Lucas was asked what his next project will be—"I'm working on a western movie set in outer space," he replied. The interviewer and other guests looked at each other uneasily. "Uh, okay George..." But Lucas laughed their apprehension off. "Don't worry," he said, "Ten year old boys will love it."

Born in 1944, Lucas had a rather normal, middle-class upbringing in a north California small town, the only son of a Republican Methodist father who owned a small stationery business. He found a closer bond with his two older sisters Anne and Katherine, and especially his younger sister Wendy, as well as his mother. "I was as normal as you can get," Lucas recalled of his childhood in an interview for *American Film*. "I wanted a car and hated school. I was a poor student. I lived for summer vacations and got into trouble a lot shooting out windows with my BB gun."[1]

Modesto was a small town with flat, dusty roads, located centrally in the state of California, miles away from anything resembling civilization—an Earth-bound Tatooine. Its population when young Lucas was born was less than twenty thousand, and it was this quaint "Norman Rockwell" environment, as he once described it, that the young Lucas grew up in, a safe, traditional-values post-war small town.

For a filmmaker who would grow up to make his life's work about fathers and sons, his own relationship with his father should naturally be a point of interest. A stern, old-fashioned man, one gets the impression that Lucas' father felt that George never quite measured up to his ideals of what a good son should be. His father, George Lucas Sr., was the only son of a roughneck oil-worker who died when George Sr. was only fifteen; George Sr. became head of the family, thrusting responsibility upon him and molding him into a self-made man, a responsibility that was made even harder on the struggling family when the Great Depression hit. He met his wife Dorothy, whom he married two years later, on the first day of high school upon settling in the small town of Modesto, California in 1929.

He eventually began working for a stationery store called L.M. Morris, named after its owner; the elderly Morris had no son of his own, and with George Sr. not having a father the two naturally bonded and George Sr. eventually took over the business.[2] When World War II hit the homefront he volunteered but was rejected for his married status. On May 14th, 1944, his first son was born—George Lucas Jr. Naturally, George Lucas Sr. was a stern parent with tough expectations from his own son, especially since his other children were all girls. He often disapproved of his son's interests, such as his affection for comic books and the arts; he felt George was wasting his time with trivial and silly things. In the summer he would shave off George's hair, leading to young Lucas being nicknamed Butch. "He was the boss; he was the one you feared," Lucas recalled of his father in Dale Pollock's *Skywalking*.[3] "I've always had a basic dislike of authority figures, a fear and resentment of grown-ups."[4] Naturally, no authority was more significant than his own father.

When George turned eighteen his father expected him to accept his offer to take over the stationery business—but George refused, hoping instead to go to college to study art. The incident escalated into an enormous argument that for many years created a rift between the two. "It was one of the few times I can remember really yelling at my father, screaming at him, telling him that no matter what he said, I wasn't going into the business."

"Well, you'll be back in a few years," his father smugly replied.

"I'll never be back," George shouted, and then added, "And as a matter of fact, I'm going to be a millionaire before I'm thirty!"[5]

But his father was no tyrant—he was strict but fair. He instilled in his son a strong sense of discipline and a notorious work ethic—George Sr. had to struggle and work hard for everything he had and so too would his son. George also learned the value of money, as his father was quick to pass on to him the lessons he learned from the days of the Depression, and indeed,

Lucas would be notoriously cautious with his earnings, but also a smart businessman like his father. It is not hard to pinpoint the theme of Luke Skywalker fearing he would become like his father, Darth Vader, as stemming from Lucas' issues with his own. The two Lucases are perhaps more alike than the filmmaker would wish. "I'm the son of a small town businessman," Lucas told *Playboy* in 1997. "He was conservative, and I'm very conservative, always have been."[6]

"A scrawny little devil," his father recalled, as a child Lucas was often a target for neighbourhood bullies, who would pick on him and throw his shoes into the sprinkler, leaving his younger sister Wendy to chase them away.[7] A poor student, Wendy would sometimes get up at five in the morning to correct his English papers misspellings. "He never listened to me," George Sr. remarked to *Time*'s Gerald Clarke in 1983. "He was his mother's pet. If he wanted a camera, or this or that, he got it. He was hard to understand. He was always dreaming up things."[8]

Escaping his dull Modesto life, young Lucas found comfort in fantasy, and comic books ruled his imagination. He became obsessed with them until he was introduced to television, amassing such a collection that his father had to house them in a shed he built in the backyard. "I've always been interested in the fantastic, and have always been prone to imagining a different kind of world from the here and now, and creating fantasies," Lucas said.[9] Whenever he or Wendy got a dollar, they would head down to the drugstore and buy ten comic books, which they would read in the shed behind their Ramona Avenue house. When Lucas was ten years old, the family finally got a television and his comic book obsession was replaced, spending Saturday mornings watching cartoons.

As a child he also frequently played war games. "I loved the war," said Lucas, who grew up in the patriotic shadow of the World War II victory. "It was a big deal when I was growing up. It was on all the coffee tables in the form of books, and on TV with things like 'Victory at Sea.' I was inundated by these war things."[10]

With a childhood in the 1950's, cowboy films naturally took centre stage. "I liked westerns," he said in a 1999 interview. "Westerns were very big when I was growing up. When we finally got a television there was a whole run of westerns on television. John Wayne films, directed by John Ford, before I knew who John Ford was. I think those were very influential in my enjoyment of movies."[11]

In addition to comic books, Lucas also began devouring science fiction magazines such as *Amazing* and *Astounding Tales*, which were the regular homes of science fiction gurus like Robert Heinlein and E.E. Smith. "As a kid, I read a lot of science fiction," Lucas recalled in 1977. "But instead of reading technical, hard-science writers like Isaac Asimov, I was interested in Harry Harrison and a fantastic, surreal approach to the genre."[12] He has also cited *Metropolis* and *Forbidden Planet* as impressive films in the fantasy field. "They stand out in my mind."[13]

It is no surprise, then, that a staple of young Lucas' childhood became watching the old science fiction and adventure serials on television. *Adventure Theater*, a 1956 television show, re-broadcast episodes of vintage serials, with tales involving pirates and swashbucklers and filled with action and adventure. In 1954, *Flash Gordon* was revived in a new series, and the older, 1930s and 40s serial episodes were re-discovered. Similarly, *Buck Rogers* was revived in a 1950 television series. The quick-paced world of television and the serials ingrained in Lucas a short attention span, and he was quick to change the channel if there wasn't enough action and excitement onscreen. "The way I see things, the way I interpret things, is influenced by television," Lucas admits in *Skywalking*. "Visual conception, fast pace, quick cuts. I can't help it. I'm a product of the television age."[14] He told *Starlog* magazine in 1981:

> One of my favourite things were Republic serials and things like *Flash Gordon*. I'd watch them and say, "This is fantastic!" There was a television program called "Adventure Theater" at 6:00 every night. We didn't have a TV set, so I used to go over to a friends house, and we watched it religiously every night. It was a twenty minute serial chapter, and the left over minutes of the half-hour was filled with "Crusader Rabbit." I loved it... And I loved *Amazing Stories* and those other science fiction pulps that were around at the time.[15]

He soon developed an affinity for visuals and graphics, having skills as an illustrator, painter, and photographer. Lucas discussed his early influences with Alan Arnold in 1979:

> George Lucas: I wasn't much that much of a reader. It wasn't until I went to college that I started to read seriously. I liked novels of exploration and works about and by the great explorers.

> Alan Arnold: Did comic strips play a part in your early life?

> GL: Yes. The "Flash Gordon" strip was in our local newspaper and I followed it. In the comic book area I liked adventures in outer space, particularly "Tommy Tomorrow" but movie serials were the real stand-out event. I especially loved the "Flash Gordon" serials. Thinking back on what I really enjoyed as a kid, it was those serials, that bizarre way of looking at things. Of course I realise now how crude and badly done they were.

AA: Do you think the enjoyment you got from those serials led you eventually to make the *Star Wars* pictures?

GL: Well, loving them that much when they were so awful, I began to wonder what would happen if they were done really well. Surely, kids would love them even more.

AA: How old were you when "Flash Gordon" and the other serials fascinated you?

GL: Nine and ten.

AA: The term "comic strip" is a bit misleading. Comics are seldom comic, are they?

GL: Originally, they were comic but the comic strip is now a sophisticated medium. It's storytelling through pictures. I was naturally drawn to the form through an interest in painting and drawing. Comic strips are also sociologically interesting, an indication of what a culture is all about. To me, Uncle Scrooge in the "Donald Duck" strip is a perfect indicator of the American psyche.

AA: So you're not offended when someone calls your work animated comic strip?

GL: No. I'm a fan of comic art. I collect it. It *is* a kind of art, a more significant kind sociologically than some fine art. It says more about our time, which is what fine art should do...There are quite a few [contemporary] illustrators in the science-fiction and science-fantasy modes I like very much. I like them because their designs and imaginations are so vivid. Illustrators like Frazetta, Druillet and Moebius are quite sophisticated in their style.[16]

Lucas' love of comic books and adventure serials did not surprise critics in 1977, who hailed *Star Wars* as a comic book come to life and a throwback to the adventure films of cinema's golden age. Lucas was such an aficionado that he even co-owned a comic book store in New York in the 1970s, one of the very first in the world and one that treated the subject as "Art" and not disposable schlock—the legendary Supersnipe Comic Emporium, famous for its comic art gallery.

## *Flights of Fancy*

The *Buck Rogers* comic strip was launched in 1929 as the first science fiction comic strip, although *Flash Gordon* is often remembered as being the originator since it was this series that first reached silver screens. *Buck Rogers* followed the adventures of its title character, a US Air Service pilot who awakens five-hundred years in the future and must save the galaxy from evil forces. Author Kristen Brennan wrote of the strip's origins:

> Buck Rogers first appeared in a novella called *Armageddon-2419 A.D.* by Philip Francis Nowlan, in the August 1928 issue of *Amazing Stories* magazine. It was John Flint Dille, president of the National Newspaper Service syndicate, who had the inspiration to make the first science fiction comic strip. He hired Nowlan to write scripts based on his Buck Rogers novel, and artist Richard Calkins to illustrate them. The spaceships and most gadgets in the Buck Rogers strip were strongly influenced by the paintings of Frank Paul, house illustrator for *Amazing Stories Magazine* from 1926 through 1929. Paul's vision was most responsible for creating the public perception of what a spaceship would look like from 1926-1966: a brightly-colored cross between a rocket and a submarine.[17]

In 1934, five years after the *Buck Rogers* strip was first published, writer and illustrator Alex Raymond launched the *Flash Gordon* comic strip. The vernacular of *Flash Gordon* was the same as *Buck Rogers*—capes, ray guns, spaceships, aliens and gadgets. However, the true source of inspiration for Raymond came from Edgar Rice Burroughs' John Carter of Mars novels, released over twenty years earlier starting in 1912, whose action-packed plots were natural precursors to comics and serials. Kristen Brennan explained:

> Burroughs' first novel was *A Princess of Mars* (1912), which was really the first swashbuckling, wish-fulfillment science fiction novel: The hero is magically transported to Mars, which is filled with beautiful, forever-youthful women who wear elaborate jewelry but no clothes. Men are valued solely on their combat ability, and the reader's alter-ego, being from the higher-gravity world of Earth, is many times stronger than Martians. This series routinely falls out of the public's memory, because the literati don't care for science fiction and the science fiction community takes great pains to distance ourselves from such 'juvenile fantasies' in (futile) hopes of convincing the literati to take us seriously. It's a shame this book isn't better-known, because if you can look past the silliness (which is no worse than any *James Bond* movie), *Princess* is one of the most exciting, imaginative and well-crafted adventure stories of all time, in the same league as *Star Wars*...Like many early science fiction

adventure writers, Burroughs borrowed ideas from H.G. Wells, Westerns, H.
Rider Haggard and the other usual sources, but he seems to have also broken
convention by importing into fiction ideas from 19th century psychics, in
particular Helena Blavatsky (1831-1891) and Edgar Cayce (1877-1945).[18]

Alex Raymond's *Flash Gordon* strip followed a trio of heroes—Flash
Gordon and his companions Dale Arden and Dr. Hans Zarkov. The story
begins when Dr. Zarkov invents a rocketship which transports the three of
them to planet Mongo, where they find themselves stranded. Mongo
contains a number of different alien races who have all fallen captive to the
tyrannical rule of Ming the Merciless, and soon the trio get caught up in the
great rebellion to vanquish Ming. The series had a very distinctive look and
style, with medieval costumes, architecture and swords mixing with high
technology like spaceships and ray guns, along with a good balance of
improbable fantasy. Although these were precursed by *Buck Rogers*, it was
*Flash Gordon* that added the more fanciful elements and gave them heavier
stylisation.

The *Flash Gordon* comic strip was released in America at the height of
the Great Depression. With many living under such impoverished and
gloomy conditions, the escapist adventure of *Flash Gordon* was welcomed
with open arms, and the more sophisticated writing and illustrating of Alex
Raymond made the strip outshadow its precursor, *Buck Rogers*. It was at
this time that the motion picture serials were also reaching their height.

The motion picture sound serials belonged to the era of the Saturday
Matinee, when kids bought a half pound of candy for a few pennies, paid
the ten cent theater admission and were delighted to a handful of cartoon
shorts, a two-reeler, a B western and a serial episode. The serials were
crudely produced and simplistically fashioned adventures, typically running
ten to twenty minutes in length and lasting roughly a dozen episodes, with
each episode ending in a cliffhanger to ensure the audience returned the
following week for the next instalment—essentially, a prototype form of
television. They were jam-packed with action, suspense and excitement,
with nary a moment to let the audience catch their breath (or ponder the
dubious construction of the films themselves). The characters were all one-
dimensional: you immediately knew exactly who the villain was, and he
was uncompromisingly bad, while the square-jawed hero was instantly
recognizable to the audience—dashing, brave and incorruptibly good.
Characters bounded from one predicament to the next, always escaping
certain doom in the nick of time, leaving the villain to remain at large and
swear to catch them next time. There was the hero, the heroine, often a
sidekick, a villain—usually not battled until the last chapter, preferring to

strike from a distance—and his henchman, a proxy for the villain and often caped and/or masked and bearing names such as The Scorpion and The Lightning.

The disposable, escapist fun that the serial offered for young people was the perfect solution to the terrible depression the nation was enduring at that time. The first of the sound serials were the westerns, giving John Wayne his first roles in *Shadow of the Eagle* and *Hurricane Express*, both in 1932; aviation and jungle series soon followed, such as *The Phantom of the Air* in 1932 and *Tailspin Tommy* in 1934, the first serial based off a comic strip, while serial legend Larry "Buster" Crabbe got his start with 1933's *Tarzan the Fearless*. 1934's *The Lost Jungle* and 1937's *The Jungle Menace* continued to popularize the jungle serials, which were helped by the success of the ultimate jungle adventure film, *King Kong*, a few years earlier. 1935's *The Phantom Empire* proved to be one of the most influential serials, a surreal amalgamation of westerns and science fiction in which singing cowboy Gene Autry discovers a long-lost advanced civilization living miles underneath his ranch, featuring robots, mad scientists, oversized laboratories and ray guns, yet with the inhabitants using swords and dressing in medieval costume. *The Phantom Empire* was produced by Mascot pictures which soon merged with other studios to become Republic pictures, often regarded as the king of the serials, and quickly put out two serials that were virtually identical to *Phantom Empire*, one set in a jungle (*The Darkest Africa*) and one set underwater (*Undersea Kingdom*), both in 1936. This all naturally set the stage for the serial adaptation of *Flash Gordon*.

When *Flash Gordon* made its way to the silver screen in a twelve-parter in 1936, it represented a peak in the genre, and is the most remembered and beloved of all the sound serial films cranked out between 1930 and 1950. Produced by Universal, it had a budget many times higher than the ordinary serial, reused expensive sets from *The Mummy*, *Bride of Frankenstein* and *Phantom of the Opera*, and starred Buster Crabbe in the title role. *Flash Gordon* was immediately popular, especially since the comic strip was still going strong. It was followed by two sequels, *Flash Gordon's Trip to Mars* in 1938, and *Flash Gordon Conquers the Universe* in 1941. The enormous success of the *Flash Gordon* adaptation made studios realise that comic books were natural sources for the simple, fast-paced, heroic adventure fantasy of the serials, and soon *The Adventures of Captain Marvel*, *Batman*, *Superman*, *Dick Tracy*, *The Shadow*, *The Green Hornet* and *The Lone Ranger* were all plundered and put on the big screen in weekly installments.

When the first *Flash Gordon* serial ended, not only did Universal eventually bring it back for two sequels, they also adapted *Buck Rogers* in 1939—naturally, it starred Flash Gordon himself, Buster Crabbe. Because the characters were already so similar, they were, in effect, blurred into one.

The serials died out in the late 1940s as times changed and audiences grew tired of the repetitive plots and formulaic structure. However the explosive growth of television in the 1950s represented the perfect opportunity for the serials to return—now as episodes of television series. The twenty-minute running time was perfectly suited to the thirty-minute time slots when padded with a cartoon short and commercials, and the cliffhanger endings ensured that audiences returned next week. *Buck Rogers* and *Flash Gordon* became television favourites, and just as had happened in the 1930s, comic books were adapted as the medium became popular, from early efforts like 1949s *The Lone Ranger* and 1950s *Dick Tracy*, to later efforts such as 1966s *The Green Hornet* and the most memorable of all the television serials, Adam West's immortal turn as the title character in 1966s *Batman*, with the cliffhanger voiceover urging viewers to tune in next week, "same Bat-time, same Bat-channel!" With the level of camp reached by *Batman*, the television adventure serial died once again, replaced with soap operas and more serious dramas.

The swashbuckler adventure movies would meet their end around the same time as the serials: Errol Flynn had entranced young audiences in the 30s and 40s in films such as *The Adventures of Robin Hood*, *The Sea Hawk* and *Captain Blood*, always the charming hero who defied tyrants, rescued the girl, swung in on a rope with a sword in his hand and saved the day, whether he was a 17th century pirate of the Caribbean seas or an 19th century calvary officer charging into canon fire. But as scandal and old age caught up with him in the 1950s he had stopped making those films. The special effects of fantasy auteur Ray Harryhausen continued the flame of adventure in the '50s and '60s, wowing kids with his stop-motion visions of cyclopes and dragons, but by the time Lucas had grown up these too would be dying off.

### Modesto Part II

When Lucas turned fifteen, the family moved to a walnut ranch on the dusty outskirts of Modesto. Desolate and remote from anything, the family ranch made Lucas feel even more isolated, far away from friends and settlements. It is no wonder that Lucas became preoccupied with the only means of temporary escape—cars.

As a teenager Lucas had been obsessed with automobiles, initially hoping to be a race car driver, until his life nearly ended in a terrible crash the day before graduating from high school. His specially-built racing seatbelt ripped in two, throwing his body through the window of the car as it rolled over and over—an act that saved his life as the car wrapped itself around a walnut tree (on his own property, no less). If he remained in the car he would have surely been killed. Lucas cannot recall the crash, but remembers waking up in the hospital days later. "They thought I was dead," he reported. "I wasn't breathing and I had no heartbeat. I had two broken bones and crushed lungs."[19]

The event made Lucas reconsider his life and what he was doing with it. "I wasn't *just* in an accident, I was in an accident that by all logic I should have been killed," he told *60 Minutes*. "And you go through kind of an experience like that you say 'How did I survive? *Why* did I survive?'"[20] He elaborated in a 1981 *Starlog* interview:

> I spent some time in the hospital, and I realised that it probably wouldn't be smart for me to be a race driver—especially after this accident. Before that accident you are very oblivious to the danger because you don't realise how close to the edge you are. But once you've gone over the edge and you realise what's on the other side, it changes your perspective. I was in a club with a lot of guys who were race drivers—one of 'em went on and drove in LeMans—and he eventually quit too because of the same thing. You see what the future is there, and you realise that you'll probably end up being dead. That's where most of them end up; it's inevitable, because the odds are if you stay with it long enough that's what will happen to you. And I just decided that maybe that wasn't for me. I decided I'd settle down and go to school.[21]

After the accident, the academically below-average Lucas began to apply himself in his education, attending Modesto Junior College where he studied social sciences to surprising success. If the combined ingredients of his childhood formed the basis for *Star Wars*, it may be argued that the deeper and more subtextual elements of *Star Wars* fell into place here. In his first year of junior college, his major was in anthropology.

"Well, I started out in anthropology," he told *The Boston Globe*, "so to me how society works, how people put themselves together and make things work, has always been a big interest. Which is where mythology comes from, where religion comes from, where social structure comes from."[22] At that time it was also the mid-'60s and the United States space program was in full swing as the space race reached its peak. Unmanned satellites were being launched and the once unconquerable frontier of outer space was finally being explored after centuries of speculation. Lucas recounted to John Seabrook a realisation that would help form the shaping of *Star Wars*:

> When I was in college, for two years I studied anthropology—that was basically all I did…Myths, stories from other cultures. It seemed to me that there was no longer a lot of mythology in our society—the kind of stories we tell ourselves and our children, which is the way our heritage is passed down. Westerns used to provide that, but there weren't westerns anymore. I wanted to find a new form. So I looked around, and I tried to figure out where myth comes from. It comes from the borders of society, from out there, from places of mystery—the wide Sargasso Sea. And I thought, space. Because back then space was a source of great mystery.[23]

But being a beatnik or an artist was the cool new thing at the time, and Lucas began to consider pursuing a future in his more creative interests instead. "What I really wanted to do was go to art school," he explained to author Alan Arnold. "My father, however, was very much against it. He didn't want me to become a painter. He said you can go to art school, but you'll have to pay your own way. Aware, I think, that I'm basically a lazy person, he knew I wouldn't go to art school if I had to work my way through. In the meantime, I had been getting more involved in still photography."[24] At the suggestion of his childhood friend John Plummer, he applied to the University of Southern California's film program, knowing they had camera courses. He told *Hollywood Reporter*:

> I went to junior college in Modesto and got very involved in social sciences, (and) I was going to go to San Francisco State to get my degree in anthropology. I was also trying to get into Art Center College of Design (in Pasadena) to become an illustrator and photographer. (Meanwhile,) a friend of mine was going to USC and thought they had a cinematography school; I applied, got in and was surprised to see there was a film school—I didn't even know there was such a thing.[25]

Indeed, USC was home to one of the earliest film schools, which were just beginning to spring up in the early '60s. Back then, nobody *got into* the film industry—you were either born into it or you didn't get in. If your father was a cameraman then you could become an assistant cameraman, or if your father was an editor then you could become an assistant editor; Hollywood was an impenetrable fortress. The '60s saw the creation of "film schools," where film theory and criticism was taught and low-budget equipment was made available for students to learn on—but this was not thought of as a stepping stone to Hollywood. Film students went on to make corporate or industrial films, or perhaps do documentary and news crew work. Hollywood was the last thing film schools were made for, and the term "independent filmmaking" did not yet exist in America.

At the same time Lucas was applying to USC, he was finally beginning to be exposed to films outside of the standard domestic fare. Although Lucas likes to give the impression that all he knew was Hollywood cinema before film school, in truth he was very much into the San Francisco underground filmmaking scene, where auteurs such as Jordan Belson and Bruce Conner were mesmerising art students and beatniks with their experimental cinema, as poets and painters began using army surplus 16mm film cameras to create their own movies and give birth to the west coast indie scene. Lucas would regularly venture up to the city with John Plummer to attend the screenings and festivals that were popular there. "Once I started driving, I'd go up to San Francisco on the weekends and occasionally see a foreign film or other kinds of film," Lucas recalled in Marcus Hearn's *The Cinema of George Lucas*. "There was a group called Canyon Cinema, which did avant-garde, underground movies. There were a few little theatres where they'd hang a sheet on a wall and project a 16mm movie onto it. I liked the more avant-garde films, the ones that were more abstract in nature."[26]

Steve Silberman described the San Francisco scene during Lucas' filmic awakening in the 1960s:

> A filmmaker named Bruce Baillie tacked up a bedsheet in his backyard in 1960 to screen the work of indie pioneers like Jordan Belson, who crafted footage of exploding galaxies in his North Beach studio, saying that he made films so life on Earth could be seen through the eyes of a god. Filmmakers Stan Brakhage and Bruce Conner had equally transcendent ambitions for the emerging medium: Brakhage painted directly on film and juxtaposed images of childbirth and solar flares, while Conner made mash-ups of stock footage to produce slapstick visions of the apocalypse. For the next few years, Baillie's series, dubbed Canyon Cinema, toured local coffeehouses, where art films shared the stage with folksingers and stand-up comedians.
>
> These events became a magnet for the teenage Lucas and his boyhood friend John Plummer. As their peers cruised Modesto's Tenth Street in the rites of passage immortalized in *American Graffiti*, the 19-year-olds began slipping away to San Francisco to hang out in jazz clubs and find news of Canyon Cinema screenings in flyers at the City Lights bookstore. Already a promising photographer, Lucas embraced these films with the enthusiasm of a suburban goth discovering the Velvet Underground.

"That's when George really started exploring," Plummer recalls. "We went to a theater on Union Street that showed art movies, we drove up to San Francisco State for a film festival, and there was an old beatnik coffeehouse in Cow Hollow with shorts that were really out there."[27]

Lucas and Plummer then began migrating south to the New Art Cinema in Santa Monica where European art house films were being screened—films like Goddard's *Breathless* and Trauffaut's *Jules et Jim*, films which delivered stories that were unlike anything seen through the stale filter of Hollywood at that time, showcasing off-the-wall editing and handheld cinematography.[28]

It was this sense of counterculture experimentation that would form Lucas' earliest cinematic influences, instilling in him a natural inclination for unusual documentary and self-made filmmaking.

Still fascinated with machines and cars, Lucas had been working as a mechanic, and while photographing cars on a race track met Haskell Wexler, one of California's best cameramen and early American pioneer of the "cinéma vérité" documentary style, whose car was being fixed by Lucas' boss. Noticing Lucas' camera, the two started talking and quickly became friends, sharing their mutual love of racing. Cinéma vérité, meaning "cinema of truth," was a documentary style characterised by its natural, unobtrusive "fly on the wall" style of observation, which became popular in the 1950s and '60s in the US in dramatised films, where it was also known as "direct cinema," employing a natural, documentary-like approach to the story. Wexler was the first of Lucas' role models, shaping him towards cinematography and documentary work. Wexler tried to get him into one of the film unions but the notoriously closed-door system wouldn't budge. Lucas applied to San Francisco State in the hopes of studying anthropology, as he had in junior college, before awaiting his rejection from USC—but miraculously he was accepted. Legend states that it was Wexler's recommendation that gained him admission, but, as author Dale Pollock showed, Lucas did it on his own.[29]

"USC was a good school, but it needed people," Lucas recalled of the film program's lenient standards. "So we all got in. The way USC was organized at the time was that if you had the drive to make a film, then you got to make a film."[30] George Sr. however was still unhappy about it, viewing Hollywood as a corrupt cesspool. "I fought him," the elder Lucas said. "I didn't want him to go into that damn movie business."[31]

Lucas recalls the life-shaping years in a 1981 interview with *Starlog*:

I still had all my friends in racing; I was still interested in racing, so I started doing a lot of photography at the races—rather than driving or being a pit crew. I had always been interested in art, and I'd been very good at it. My father didn't see much of a career in being an artist, so he discouraged me from doing that whole thing. When I went to junior college I got very interested in the social sciences—psychology, sociology, anthropology—that area. But it was really by fluke that I ended up going to the University of Southern California and getting into the film business.

I had been interested in photography and art, and a very close friend of mine, whom I grew up with ever since I was four-years-old was going to USC and asked me to take the test with him. I was going to San Francisco State and become an anthropology major or something like that. And he said, "They've got a film school down there, and it's great 'cause you can do photography." So I said, "Well, all right, but it's a long shot 'cause my grades are not good enough to get into a school like that." So I went and I took the test and I passed. I got accepted!

At about that time, I had been working on a race car for Haskell Wexler, and I met him, and he influenced me in the direction of cinematography—being a cameraman. So the idea wasn't remote. I said, "Yeah, I know a cinematographer, and I like photography, and maybe that wouldn't be a bad thing to get into." But I didn't know anything about the movies at that point. Just what I saw on television, and going to the movies once a week.[32]

### Adventures in Filmmaking

At USC's film school program, the world of foreign and experimental films opened up to Lucas, who had already been fascinated with alternative cinema in his ventures to the San Francisco scene. The documentaries and animated shorts produced by the National Film Board of Canada made a strong impression on him, such as Norman McLaren's combination of live-action and animation, or Claude Jutra's Goddardian use of documentary-like camerawork. Arthur Lipsett's esoteric documentary *21-87* affected him the most. Lipsett was a Montreal filmmaker who worked as an animator at the National Film Board of Canada but would later be known for his experimental short films—he used bits and scraps of footage that others had thrown away, crafting together an exhilarating montage of bizarre images and sounds, juxtaposed to create emotion without any hint of plot or character. He later went mad and committed suicide in 1986. "I said, '*That's* the kind of movie I want to make—a very off-the-wall, abstract kind of film,'" Lucas remarked to Dale Pollock. "It was really where I was at, and I think that's one reason I started calling most of my [college] movies by numbers. I saw that film twenty or thirty times."[33]

*21-87* would be influential on Lucas first feature, the abstract *THX 1138*, and it also clearly inspired Lucas' very first short film, a montage of sounds and images called *Look at Life*.

Lucas' visual aesthetic would be influenced by legendary Japanese director Akira Kurosawa, which his classmate John Milius first introduced him to. He explains in an interview conducted for *Hidden Fortress'* DVD release:

> I grew up in a small town. Central California. And the movie theaters there didn't show much beyond *Bridge on the River Kwai* and *The Blob*. So I didn't really experience foreign films until I found my way into film school. And at that point is actually when I was exposed to Kurosawa...The first one I saw was *Seven Samurai*, and after that I was completely hooked...It's really his visual style to me that is so strong and unique, and again, a very, very powerful element in how he tells his stories. I think he comes from a generation of filmmakers that were still influenced by silent films, which is something that I've been very interested in from having come from film school...he uses long lenses, which I happen to like a lot. It isolates the characters from the backgrounds in a lot of cases. So you'll see a lot of stuff where there's big wide shots, lots of depth, and then he'll come in and isolate the characters from the background and you'll only really focus on the characters...you can't help but be influenced by his use of camera.[34]

Very clearly, Lucas was someone whose strengths and interests lay in images—plot and character were still alien to him. He was in his element with machines and gizmos, where the controls and levers of editing machines and cameras replaced the automobile engines he had been so intimate with in his previous life, lending him a natural talent for visual communication. His first venture into creative writing would be made during his tour of duty at USC; Lucas discussed his early writing in a 1981 interview:

> No [I hadn't done any writing before film school]. I mean, I had taken some creative writing classes, normal English, and all the things you end up taking—and if I had gone to San Francisco State I might have become an English major. But I had no intention of becoming a writer. I was always terrible in English...I don't think I am a good writer now. I think I'm a *terrible* writer. The whole writing thing is something I was very bad at—I can barely spell my own name, let alone form a sentence—and I struggled through English classes. I went to USC as a photographer—I wanted to be a cameraman—but obviously at film school you have to do everything: cinematography, editing and script writing. Well, I did terrible in script writing. I hated stories, and I

hated plot, and I wanted to make visual films that had nothing to do with telling a story.

I was a difficult student. I got into a lot of trouble all the time because of that attitude. I felt I could make a movie about *anything*; I mean, give me the phonebook, and I'll make a movie out of it. I didn't want to know about stories and plot and characters and all that stuff. And that's what I did. My first films were very abstract—tone poems, visual.[35]

His early attitude is especially amusing given *Star Wars'* focus on elaborate plotting and multiple characters, one of the reasons he would struggle so much with the material. He said in 1974:

I'm not a good writer. It's very, very hard for me. I don't feel I have a natural talent for it—as opposed to camera, which I could always just *do*. It was a natural. And the same thing for editing. I've always been able to just sit down and cut.

But I don't have a natural talent for writing. When I sit down I bleed on the page, and it's just awful. Writing just doesn't flow in a creative surge the way other things do.[36]

Lucas' first film, *Look at Life*, was made in an animation class of all places.

The first class I had was an animation class. It wasn't a production class. And in the animation class they gave us one minute of film to put onto the animation camera to operate it, to see how you could move left, move right, make it go up and down. They had certain requirements that you had to do…It was a test. I took that one minute of film and made it into a movie, and it was a movie that won about 25 awards in every film festival in the world, and kind of changed the whole animation department.[37]

Following that, Lucas made an impressive total of eight short films during his time at USC, all with his trademark affection for graphics, visual juxtaposition, non-narrative structure, prominent audio design and off-beat editing, culminating with *THX 1138 4: EB*, a visual-based tale of a man on the run in a futuristic world, containing virtually no conventional character or narrative elements and featuring unusual editing and sound design. At a party at Herb Kossower's House (an instructor in the animation department), Lucas mentioned the idea of a futuristic "Big Brother" type of film that could be made with existing locations. "The idea had been floating in my mind for a long time," he said. "It was based on the concept that we live in the future and that you could make a futuristic film using existing stuff."[38] Lucas' USC classmates Walter Murch and Matthew

Robbins had already written a two-page treatment called "Breakout" and gave the story to Lucas.

Lucas had already graduated from USC by that time, leaving the university in 1966 with a Bachelors of Fine Arts. The Vietnam war hung over young Americans like a dark cloud and Lucas knew that he would be drafted once he finished college. USC had a large military population on campus, and air and navy students being taught documentary techniques told Lucas he could easily get a job as an officer in the photography unit. Lucas tried to join the Air Force but was rejected because of the many speeding tickets from his Modesto days. "I was just doing it out of desperation," he admitted.[39] He briefly considered fleeing to Canada with friends like Matthew Robbins but USC students warned him he would be homesick. He inevitably would be rejected from the draft once his medical exam revealed he had diabetes.

With his major background in camera and editing, he suddenly found himself on his own in the independent world of film production, taking any work he could get, even as a grip, and as an assistant and animation camera operator for graphic designer Saul Bass; he later applied for a job at the Hanna-Barbara animation studio but was rejected.[40] An aspiring documentary cameraman, Lucas would later do freelance documentary camerawork, being one of the cameramen on the *Woodstock* documentary of 1970 and the Rolling Stones' infamous 1969 concert at the Altamont Speedway where an audience member was stabbed to death. "I loved shooting *cinema verite* and I thought I would become a documentary filmmaker. Of course, being a student in the sixties, I wanted to make socially relevant films, you know, tell it like it is."[41] Lucas eventually returned to USC a short time after graduating, in 1967, for their graduate program, also becoming a teaching assistant for night classes where he taught cinematography to navy students, with his emphasis on using available light. It was here, in this class, that he filmed *THX 1138: 4EB*, having access to a plethora of futuristic-looking navy equipment and a ready crew of students, using the project as a sort of teaching exercise. Light years ahead of any student film being made at the time, it was an enormous hit at student film festivals.

This led to him being invited to a student documentary competition sponsored by Columbia Pictures for the film *Mackennan's Gold*—along with other student filmmakers, they were to each make a documentary on the production, which was shooting on location in Utah and Arizona, with the intention of using the documentaries as promos for the film. While the others had made more standard documentaries in the vérité tradition, Lucas' was a more poetic and esoteric exploration that barely even paid notice to the production. Instead, it focussed on the desert that the studio had descended upon for filming, showing the crew as ants in the distance while desert life continued on after the film abandoned the location. It impressed producer Carl Foreman. Lucas won another scholarship program (narrowly edging out classmate Walter Murch), this time with Warner Brothers, eventually landing on Francis Ford Coppola's movie *Finian's Rainbow* as a student observer in 1967. Lucas was more interested in the Warners animation department (birthplace of *Looney Tunes*) but the department was closed down as the studio underwent a massive re-structuring after being sold by Jack Warner to Seven Arts Productions, and the only sign of life on the studio lot was Coppola's production.

Francis Ford Coppola was a film school legend—a graduate of UCLA, he began his career as a successful screenwriter before making the jump to directing. "Francis Coppola had directed his first picture as a UCLA student and now, Jesus, he's got a feature to direct!" Lucas recalled in *Skywalking*. "It sent shock waves through the student film world because nobody else had ever done that. It was a big event."[42]

*Finian's Rainbow* was a corny musical starring Fred Astaire that was made almost entirely on the studio backlot—Coppola hated it but went along with it because it was an opportunity never before bestowed upon a former film student. Ironically, it would be the antithesis of all that he would later stand for. It represented the very last of the Old Hollywood type of films, before the new Seven Arts regime change would allow *Easy Rider* to throw open the doors for young filmmakers like Lucas and Coppola to lay this type of film to rest.

In the summer of 1967, Lucas aimlessly wandered onto Coppola's set. "I was working on the show and there was this skinny kid, watching for the second day in a row," Coppola remembered. "You always feel uncomfortable when there's a stranger watching you, so I went up to him and asked who he was."[43] Being the only young people on a crew where the average age was fifty, the two naturally bonded and became good friends, and Lucas became his personal assistant for the film. In Coppola, Lucas found a mentor, a big, boisterous older brother who complimented his quiet, reserved nature and before long Lucas began sporting his trademark beard in mimicry of his older teacher. Lucas shadowed him as a one-man documentary crew for Coppola's next film, *The Rain People*, creating a documentary entitled *Filmmaker*. *Rain People* was shot on the road with a very small crew, a low budget and little planning, the atmosphere reminiscent of the student film days at USC; it was a type of production that was gaining in prominence across the country, culminating with 1969's

*Easy Rider*, released the very same year. In *The Cinema of George Lucas* he recalled the radical concept:

> Francis said, "I've had it with these big Hollywood movies, I don't want to do this. I've got this plan to do a tiny movie with just a small group of people, a bit like making a student film. I'm going to start in New York, get in a truck and drive across the United States, making a movie as I go. No planning, no nothing—just do it."[44]

Lucas shot his *Rain People* documentary while also writing the feature-length script of *THX 1138*. "I wanted George also to make a film, and George wanted to make a feature version of *THX 1138*," Coppola explained. "And so I said, 'Well, you know, we could get money in the budget for you to do a documentary on the making of the film, but really you could be writing your script.'"[45]

This is where we come to the most earliest and primitive beginnings of what would eventually become *Star Wars*. *THX 1138 4:EB*—the student film—had been written by Lucas' USC friends (and soon to be fellow Zoetrope employees) Walter Murch and Matthew Robbins, but once Lucas began making professional films it was at Coppola's insistence that he picked up a pen.

"I come from experimental cinema; it's my specialty," Lucas said in a 1977 interview. "My friendship and my association with Coppola compelled me to write. His specialty is 'literature,' traditional writing. He studied theater, text; he's a lot more oriented towards 'play writing' than I am: mis en scene, editing, the structured film. He told me, 'you have to learn to write, to structure.' So it's because of him that I got into it. He forced me."[46]

Lucas was lucky to have such a mentor: Coppola came from a very literary background, already having an impressive resume of screenplays behind him, and could practically write in his sleep; in fact, around this time he was co-writing *Patton*, which would bring him his first Oscar. Lucas recalls Coppola's advice: "He said, 'Look, when you write a script, just go as fast as you can. Just get it done. Don't ever read what you've written. Try to get it done in a week or two, then go back and fix it—you keep fixing it. But if you try to get each page perfect, you'll never get beyond page ten!'"[47]

But, in setting out to develop *THX 1138*, Lucas still hoped to hire others to script the film. Lucas told Kerry O' Quinn in a 1981 interview:

Francis's main areas of expertise were directing actors and writing—and mine was primarily in camera and editing. So we interfaced very well and complimented each other. I became his assistant, and I helped him with the editing, and I'd go around with the Polaroid and shoot angles, and that sort of thing.

In the meantime I was trying to get a movie off the ground, because Carl Foreman had been impressed with the [documentary] movie I'd made for him, so I was talking to him about this other project I wanted to do which was based on a short subject I did in film school—*THX-1138*. So Francis heard about that too, and he said, 'Well look, I'll do it for you.' He said he'd get me a deal to write the screenplay. I said 'I can't write a screenplay. I'm not a writer. I can't possibly write!'

And he said, "Look—if you're going to make it in this industry, you've got to learn how to write. You can't direct without knowing how to write. So you're going to sit down, and you're going to learn how to write!"

So they chained me to my desk and I wrote this screenplay. Agonizing experience! It always is. I finished it, read it and said, "This is awful." I said, "Francis, I'm not a writer. This is a terrible script." He read it and said, "You're right. This is a terrible script." So he and I sat down together and re-wrote it, and it still was a pretty bad script. I said, "Look, we've got to get a writer." So we hired a writer to work on the project—a playwright who'd written some stuff for films [Oliver Hailey]. I worked with him and gave him the screenplay, and we talked about it, and he wrote a script, and it was all right—it just wasn't anything at all what I wanted the movie to be... You know I had this idea and I just couldn't express it. I tried to express it to the writer, and he tried to give it back to me, but his script was just not what I wanted. It was worse than what I'd done. So after that experience I realized that if the script was going to be written the way I wanted it, I was going to have to write it myself. So a friend of mine from film school, Walter Murch, sat down with me, and we wrote the screenplay... Francis talked Warner Brothers into going with it, and that's really how I got into writing.[48]

In 1968, Lucas took a few days off the production of *Rain People* to substitute for Coppola as a panelist at a convention of English teachers in San Francisco, where he met John Korty. Korty was an independent filmmaker in the area, making movies on his own for pocket change and operating his production company out of a barn in Stinson Beach. It was proof that the dream of independence was possible, and Lucas immediately put him on the phone to Coppola, who visited Korty shortly after and an alliance was made.[49]

What resulted was the infamous American Zoetrope production company, an idealistic commune of filmmakers who strove for artistic independence from movie studios. While Coppola took a trip to Europe to sample the latest editing machines, he also discovered an independent production company in Denmark that laid the foundation for Coppola's Zoetrope philosophy. "They had like a big mansion out by the sea," Coppola remembered, "and of course they had made all the bedrooms into editing rooms, and the garage was a big mix studio, and they would have lunch together in the garden. And there were all these beautiful Danish girls there with the boys, working together. And I said—'This is what we want!'"[50] Coppola returned to California with excitement. "I told young George Lucas about having this house in the country, and there'll be all these young people working together, and we'll be independent."[51] Coppola found a countryside estate near San Francisco, but its cost was too high—he had already spent more money than he had on the editing equipment. Lucas, however, would not forget this.

Instead, an industrial building near downtown San Francisco would become the new home to the dozen or so indie filmmakers involved in the company, complete with such bohemian frills as a pool table and espresso machine. It became a hangout for young artists stopping by the area, which at one time or another included Woody Allen, Sidney Poitier, Ken Kesey and Jerry Garcia,[52] no doubt wandering in from the fledgling office of *Rolling Stone* just around the corner. "We used to have these parties and we'd dance and drink and carry on," filmmaker Carroll Ballard remembered, "and in the middle of the party somebody would show up—one time *Kurosawa* showed up!"[53] John Milius remembers its legendary grand-opening party: "At that party you could go around to different floors, and all kinds of things were going on. There was a lot dope being smoked, a lot of sex; it was great."[54] Proving that they weren't just a collection of pot-smoking hippies but could deliver a product, the just-arrived European editing machines were put to use and *Rain People* was cut, with Lucas' girlfriend Marcia Griffin assistant editing and Walter Murch mixing sound. "The clatter of film was heard twenty-four hours a day," Murch said.[55]

Coppola had made a deal to develop pictures from the company for Warner Brothers, who were looking to scoop up a fresh pool of young talent after *Easy Rider* turned the industry on its head. The first film to be made at American Zoetrope was to be produced by Coppola and was also Lucas' directorial debut—the feature-length adaptation of his student film, *THX 1138*.

Warner Brothers' acceptance of the abstract and countercultural *THX 1138* was due to the imminent explosion of the American New Wave, or "New Hollywood." Cultural revolutions had been happening around the world in the 1960s, and in the cinema they had taken place as well—in all places of the globe except in Hollywood. Although the American cultural revolution had already made its mark on the country by the time the 1960s were fading, it was mysteriously absent from one particular art form, motion pictures, which were controlled by old-timer executives.

In the late 1960s the last of the studio heads from Hollywood's so-called Golden Era—people like Darryl Zanuck and Jack Warner—clung to their backlots like captains of a sinking ship, all of them in their seventies and older and incredulous to the youth counterculture taking over the country. In the meantime, the films being churned out by the studios were tired and outdated, the box office was doing terrible business and theatre attendance was at record lows. The movies were dying. Most of the studios were sold off—legend states that Lucas' first day on the lot of Warner Brothers when he won his scholarship was the day Jack Warner left,[56] and the once-majestic compound was turned into a ghost-town. In the meantime, *Bonnie and Clyde* was released in 1967, followed by entries such as *The Wild Bunch*, *Night of the Living Dead* and *The Graduate*—films that finally began to break down the conventions typically regarded by movie studios, exploring risqué, violent and more socially relevant subject matter. When *Easy Rider* burst on to the scene in 1969, it was a revolution in American cinema. With its nudity, language, drug-use and existentialist outlook, it represented a turning point when young people began to make films about young people, films that were real and defied conservatism. The advent of cheaper and lighter film equipment allowed *Easy Rider* to be made on the road, without stars, without studio representatives and without much money—an *independent* film. It was a sensation in theatres.

Studio executives were left in freefall. They didn't understand this new wave of films and why audiences were flocking to them—but they knew that it was the only market left for the endangered species that was Hollywood cinema. In 1970 and 1971, suddenly a barrage of youth-oriented films were put into production—the stranger the better.

"Because of the catastrophic crisis of '69, '70, and '71, when the industry imploded, the door was wide open and you could just waltz in and have these meetings and propose whatever," said Paul Schrader, writer of *Taxi Driver*, who was then film critic for LA underground newspaper *Free Press*.[57] Hollywood was in chaos and young people were taking over. "If you were young or you came out of film school, or you made a little experimental film up in San Francisco, *that* was the ticket into the system," added Peter Guber, who was head of Columbia Pictures in the 1970s.[58] Warner Brothers in particular was interested in hiring hip, young directors who could make more of these types of pictures for them and were desperate for fresh films. In this environment, two young, bearded men from San Francisco—George Lucas and Francis Coppola—were given just under a million dollars by Warner Brothers to make an artsy science fiction film called *THX 1138*.

Ned Tanen, executive at Universal who would later green-light *American Graffiti* and reject *Star Wars*, recalls in Peter Biskind's *Easy Riders, Raging Bulls*:

> [Studios] said to kids who could not have gotten an appointment on the lot two weeks earlier, "It's your movie, don't come back to us with your problems, we don't even want to know about them." These were not movies where the studio was dealing with someone they trusted. They were dealing with kids whom they didn't trust, didn't like their arrogant behavior, didn't like the way they dressed, didn't want to see ponytails and sandals in the commissary while they were eating. They viewed them with absolute dread. Beyond dread. It was like they just wanted to send them to a concentration camp. But the studio left them alone because they thought they'd screw it up if they interfered, and the movies didn't cost anything. They realised that there was a fountain of talent. That's how, in the late 60s, early 70s, it became a director's medium.[59]

In this light, *THX 1138* was truly the product of an auteur, an esoteric film that could never have been made at any other time. The twenty-six year-old Lucas had lucked out, landing in Coppola's hands immediately after film school and was being pushed through open doors at an alarming rate, now finding himself heading an art-house film without studio interference.

Stanley Kubrick's watershed *2001: A Space Odyssey* had come out just before Lucas began writing the film, showcasing not only the first realistic, tangible conception of space travel, but also the first serious depiction of science fiction in film and the same avant-garde form Lucas was obsessed with. "To see somebody actually do it, to make a visual film, was hugely inspirational to me," Lucas says. "If [Kubrick] did it, I can do it."[60]

The student film of *THX* had lacked any plot and was simply a visual montage of a man running through underground corridors while high-tech surveillance technicians studied him from their control rooms—in his attempt to surround this set piece with a plot for the feature version, Lucas took influence from George Orwell's *1984* and Aldous Huxley's *Brave New World*, novels published in 1949 and 1932 respectively which told downbeat stories of a dystopic future where the populace is bleakly oppressed by its government, who control all forms of emotion, sexuality and individuality, and where drug use, torture and manipulation sedate opposition.[61]

Expanding on the student film, *THX 1138* is a typical example of its era, containing sex, nudity and drug use (futuristic as it may be), violence and abstract structure, as well as heavy social commentary, portraying the public as complacent consumers and the government as violent fascists. This type of content was still very risqué at that point in time—the MPAA was created in 1968 to deal with this new influx of filmmaking, making the R-rating only three years old. Documentaries were all Lucas knew and so naturally that is how he approached the film. He described *THX 1138* as a "documentary film of the future";[62] it was filmed by documentary cameraman (among them, Haskell Wexler), shot almost exclusively on location in San Francisco, using only available light and with hardly any rehearsals—an extension of the method used in Lucas' student version. So involved with the photography of the picture was Lucas that when *American Cinematographer*, the industry trade magazine, covered the shoot in 1971 it was Lucas who wrote an article for the magazine on the technical photographic aspects of the film, revealing that he served as the unofficial director of photography. "I was playing off the fact that it was a documentary, but I wasn't doing the shaky camera and all that kind of stuff," Lucas recalled to author Marcus Hearn. "I was doing an extremely stylized look with no camera movement to speak of. The only camera movement occurred if an object moved—I would pan with it. Sometimes, I'd shoot people and let them go off camera, or let them get halfway off camera, and I would adjust the frame."[63]

The film purposefully did not explain the unusual futuristic world—it was a science fiction story completely devoid of exposition, something of a first in any medium. As Walter Murch explained, it was an idea culled from Lucas' love of Japanese cinema. "Japanese films are interesting to us because they were made by a culture for itself. The problem that George and I found with science fiction films that we saw is that they felt that they had to explain these strange rituals to you, whereas a Japanese film would just have the ritual and you'd have to figure it out for yourself."[64]

Lucas even entertained the idea of filming the movie in Japan before budgetary demands forced him to keep the production in the United States.[65] "Sometimes we'd only have about two hours to shoot in a particular place," Lucas recalled. "There were a lot of things that made it seem like a street film—we would get in there, get our shots before the police came, and then run away as fast as we could."[66] After a short production period of a mere thirty-five days, Lucas edited the picture in the attic of his house with his wife Marcia.

Lucas had met Marcia Griffin while making his way as an editing assistant after graduating from USC. They married in 1969 and bought a small house in Mill Valley, just on the outskirts of San Francisco. A professional editor herself with years of experience in the world of commercials by the time they met, Marcia would be responsible for the picture cutting of nearly all of her husband's films, and unbeknownst to most, would be one of the prime influences in the shape of the *Star Wars* films during their writing and editing. "I always felt I was an optimist because I'm extroverted," Marcia reflected. "And I always thought George was more introverted, quiet, and pessimistic."[67] It has often been said that the two were a pair of opposites that complemented each other: "I say black, she says white," Lucas commented in *Skywalking*. "We want to complete ourselves so we look for someone who is strong where we're weak."[68] Bold and assertive, she was one of the few who could go toe to toe with Lucas in an argument and occasionally emerge victorious. "Marcia was very opinionated, and had very good opinions about things, and would not put up if she thought George was going in the wrong direction," Walter Murch remembered in a 2001 interview for *Biography*. "There were heated creative arguments between them—for the good."[69] Being concerned more with character and emotion, she complemented George's more technical and intellectual interests. Perhaps unsurprisingly, she was not very pleased with *THX 1138* because she felt it did not engage the audience, left them cold.

When *THX 1138* was finally done, Warner Brothers was left aghast. Far from the hip and edgy youth-oriented project they thought it would be, they had an abstract science fiction documentary in the vein of the San Francisco and Canadian experimentalists like Bruce Conner and Arthur Lipsett. They trimmed off a few minutes of material in a desperate attempt to shorten the film and dumped it into cinemas, advertising it as a futuristic love story. Not only did the film bomb, but Warners cancelled the American Zoetrope deal (in effect, robbing themselves of *The Conversation* and *Apocalypse Now*), leaving American Zoetrope bankrupt and Coppola and Lucas without money or jobs. *Apocalypse Now* was to be their second project, a low-budget film about the Vietnam war, but with the Warner deal collapsed and both of them nearly ruined they sought out more commercial projects to dig them out of their hole.

The deletion of a few minutes worth of material from the film traumatized Lucas, and only reinforced his distaste for authority. He would endure the same experience on *American Graffiti*, forging a lifelong complex for absolute control of his material. He told *Film Quarterly*:

There was no reason for the cutting...it was just arbitrary. You do a film like *American Graffiti* or *THX*—it takes two years of your life, you get paid hardly anything at all, and you sweat blood. You write it, you slave over it, you stay up twenty-eight nights getting cold and sick. Then you put it together, and you've *lived* with it. It's exactly like raising a kid. You raise a kid for two or three years, you struggle with it, then somebody comes along and says "Well, it's a very nice kid, but I think we ought to cut off one of its fingers." So they take their little axe and chop off one of the fingers. They say "Don't worry. Nobody will notice. She'll live, everything will be all right." But I mean, it *hurts* a great deal.[70]

After *THX*, Lucas wanted to make a film about the Vietnam war—which was still going on at that point. He recruited his friend John Milius to write the script, an avid fan of the military and all things machismo, and who was also rejected from the Vietnam draft due to medical conditions. He told *Starlog* in 1981:

My second project was *Apocalypse Now* which John Milius and I had been working on in school, and we got a deal with Francis to develop that project. So I said, "This is great; I love John Milius; he's a terrific writer." I was going to get a screenplay, and I wasn't going to have to write it. Finally, I had someone better than me.[71]

Lucas' vision of *Apocalypse Now* is one of the most fascinating entries in filmdom's "what could have been."* Coppola all but did away with Lucas' version, instead adapting Joseph Conrad's novel *Heart of Darkness* into a sepulchral tale of madness—an infamous effort that consumed 16 months of filming and had many costly disasters. Lucas' vision was altogether different, a darkly satirical look at the war, filled with comic-book-like characters and done in the style of a documentary.** He told *Rolling Stone*:

---

* Although Coppola would ultimately make the film, Lucas would fulfill his desire through a 16mm Vietnam combat sequence for *More American Graffiti* in 1979, made with the comic satire and documentary look that Lucas originally envisioned.

** John Baxter (p. 86) surmises that Lucas' approach was inspired by Haskell Wexler's documentary-like film *Medium Cool*, which had experimentally mixed reality and fiction by placing actors in a real-life riot.

I was doing it much more as a documentary in the style of *Dr. Strangelove*. It was going to be shot in 16mm. That's how John and I originally pitched it to Francis. Until he made it [in 1979], though, you couldn't do a film about the Vietnam War. That's what we discovered. No one would even have anything to do with it…Most of the things in the film were things the public didn't know about yet. Nobody had any idea that people were taking drugs over there. Nobody had any idea how crazy it was. None of that had come out. The film at that time was vaguely an exposé, vaguely a satire and vaguely a story about angry young men.[72]

With American Zoetrope all but folded, *Apocalypse Now* was shelved when Lucas decided to make a more commercial film about small-town teenage cruising, mostly due to his troubling financial woes. The themes, visuals and storytelling devices Lucas would implement in *Star Wars* can be seen through all his films, and they are just as prominent in *THX 1138*; it is here that *Star Wars* began to bubble up from his subconscious.

Lalo Schifrin, the film's composer, supposedly has said that Lucas confided in him as far back as 1969 that he wanted to make a *Flash Gordon* type of film. The first issue of *Bantha Tracks*, the *Star Wars* Fan Club newsletter, stated that "as early as 1971 [Lucas] wanted to make a space fantasy film."[73] It was an idea planted in Lucas' head during film school, as he would later reveal,[74] one that had been forming, essentially, since his childhood. "I think that damn movie was whirring through the editing machine in George's head on the day we met," Marcia Lucas said with characteristic irreverence. "He never doubted it would get made. Even when he was a film student at USC, he spent a lot of his time thinking of ways to get those spaceships and creatures on the screen."[75]

As Lucas took his first steps into the world of professional filmmaking, he still had in his mind the memories of comic books, pulp science fiction novels and adventure serials, swirling together to form a growing vision. Mona Skager, Zoetrope associate and script supervisor of *The Rain People*, had typed up his *THX* script as he wrote it and remembers the first hints of Lucas' grander ambitions: "George was watching television—and all of a sudden he started talking about holograms, spaceships and the wave of the future."[76] Tellingly, *THX 1138* would begin with a clip of Buster Crabbe portraying Buck Rogers. Lucas reveals in a 1999 interview:

I conceived [*Star Wars*] at about the same time I finished *THX*, which was my first film. I was getting a lot of pressure from my peers to do something other than these artsy character movies; they said I should move into a more socially-acceptable medium. I was thinking of something that I could get excited about that would be a little less esoteric. I came up with the idea for *American*

*Graffiti*. At the same time, I came up with the idea of doing a sort of modern mythology, like Saturday morning serials for kids. I came up with two ideas: one was *Indiana Jones* and the other was *Star Wars*.[77]

But first Lucas would make *American Graffiti*, a low-budget coming-of-age comedy with a rock and roll soundtrack, inspired by his teenage years cruising the streets of Modesto. Lucas had personally paid to enter *THX 1138* in the prestigious Cannes film festival that May, and with their last two thousand dollars, George and Marcia headed to France with backpacks. Lucas remembered the troubled time in an interview with *Rolling Stone*:

> Francis had borrowed all this money from Warner Brothers to set [American Zoetrope] up, and when the studio saw a rough cut of *THX* and the scripts of the movies we wanted to make, they said "This is all junk. You have to pay back the money you owe us." Which is why Francis did *Godfather*. He was so much in debt he didn't have any choice.
>
> ...I was left high and dry. *THX* had taken three years to make and I hadn't made any money. Marcia was still supporting us, and I thought, "Well, I'll do the rock and roll movie—that's commercial." [*smiling*] Besides, I was getting a lot of razz from Francis and a bunch of friends who said that everyone said I was cold and weird and why didn't I do something warm and human. I thought "You want warm and human, I'll give you warm and human." So I went to Gloria [Katz] and Willard Huyck and they developed the idea for *American Graffiti*, and I took the twelve-page treatment around...And it got turned down by every studio in town. The situation was pretty grim. Then I got invited to the Cannes Film Festival, because *THX* had been chosen by some radical directors' group. But Warner Brothers wouldn't pay my way. So, with our last $2000, we bought a Eurail Pass, got backpacks and went to Cannes.[78]

It was here, at Cannes in 1971, that Lucas finally got a development deal for his future—United Artists was interested in the offbeat Lucas and he proposed to them two ideas: one a quirky coming-of-age film titled *American Graffiti* and the other a swashbuckling space adventure that he was calling *The Star Wars*, for which he hadn't yet developed any story or content but rather the concept of a *Flash Gordon*-esque space opera. "I decided to stop in New York on the way to [Cannes] and make David Picker, who was then head of United Artists, have a meeting with me," Lucas remembered in a *Rolling Stone* article. "I told him about my rock and roll movie. We flew off to England and he called and said, 'Okay, I'll take a chance.' I met him at his giant suite at the Carlton Hotel in Cannes and we made a two-picture deal for *American Graffiti* and *Star Wars*."[79]

### Second Chance

United Artists signed the deal at the Carlton Hotel, and *American Graffiti* was to be made first. As he had done on *THX 1138*, Lucas wrote the script himself—after the original planned writers, his husband-and-wife friends Gloria Katz and Willard Huyck, became unavailable. Richard Walter initially wrote a draft but Lucas discarded it because it was nothing at all like his life in Modesto, instead being more in the vein of the hot-rod exploitation flicks popular at the time. "I'm a Jew from New York. What do I know about Modesto? We didn't have cars. We rode the subway, or bicycles," Walter remarked.[80] Lucas was forced to write it himself. Listening to his old rock and roll 45's, Lucas delved into his memories of being a teenager in Modesto and quickly churned out a screenplay after a few weeks. Eventually, the final draft would be re-written by the Huycks, a process which would occur on *Star Wars* as well. Lucas explained to Larry Sturhahn:

> Originally I wasn't going to write it at all because I don't like writing and only do it if I have to. But Bill [Huyck] and I went to USC Film School together. I had read all of his screenplays and loved them and thought he was a brilliant writer, so when I had the idea for the film about four guys who cruise around and do all this stuff on the last night of summer, I sat down with Bill and Gloria (they're husband and wife) and together we hacked out this idea about four characters who do this, that, and the other thing.
>
> Then it took me about a year to get the money because I wasn't the hottest thing in Hollywood. By that time and with the miniscule amount to write the screenplay, Bill had gotten the chance to direct a picture and wasn't available, so I sat down and wrote the original screenplay.
>
> Then I got the deal to make the film based on the screenplay, but I wasn't happy with it because I don't have a lot of confidence in my screen-writing ability. By that time—and due to begin shooting in two months—Bill was available, so I suggested they come in and re-write it. They didn't change the structure; what they did was improve the dialog, make it funnier, more human, truer... the scenes are mine, the dialog is theirs.[81]

Lucas met Gary Kurtz around this time, another pivotal player in Lucas' early days who would be regarded as his personal manager (though his creative involvement is sometimes exaggerated). Lucas told Alan Arnold:

> We met when I was cutting *THX*. I had shot the film in Techniscope and was cutting it on a Steenbeck editing machine which was then still fairly rare in the

US. Gary came up from LA with Monte Hellman (director of *Two-Lane Blacktop*) because they were thinking about shooting *Two Lane Blacktop* in Techniscope. They wanted to see what the process was like, and to see the Steenbeck which was in the attic of my house in Mill Valley.

Gary and I found that we had a lot in common, including the background of USC. Francis Coppola thought Gary might be the right person to be the line producer for my next film, *Apocalypse Now*, as it was a war film and Gary had been a sergeant in the Marines. So, we started to do *Apocalypse* together, but as it happened Francis couldn't get the financing and I had to put it aside.

It was after I'd talked to United Artists in Cannes and thought that I'd made the deal for *Graffiti* that I told Gary that I wasn't going to do *Apocalypse* but *Graffiti*, a sort of hot-rod movie. As he'd just done a hot-rod movie (*Two-Lane Blacktop*), I asked if he would like to work for me, and he agreed.[82]

Lucas recounted the tumultuous period of scripting *Graffiti* in this interview with *Rolling Stone*:

Bill and Gloria had a chance to direct their own movie, so I hired another friend to write the script. The first draft wasn't at all what I wanted. It was a desperate situation. I asked Marcia to support us some more. I was borrowing money from friends and relatives. I wrote the script in three weeks, turned it in to UA, and they said, "Not interested."…Then Universal said they might be interested if I could get a movie star. I said no. Universal said that even a name producer might do, and they gave me a list of names and Francis was on the list. See, *Godfather* was about to be released, and the whole town was abuzz. Universal, being what it is, was trying to cash in on this real quick.

…[But] Universal wouldn't give us our first check. Francis came very close to financing *American Graffiti* himself. Finally, Universal mellowed…at the bleakest point in all of this, I got an offer to direct. I was writing every day, which I hate, so there was a temptation, but I said no. It went on until the price was $100,000 and points. The most I had ever been paid to direct a movie was $15,000. I said no. It was a real turning point…[the film was] *Lady Ice*, starring Donald Sutherland. It was a disaster. If I had done that movie, it would have been the end of my career.[83]

Filming *American Graffiti* was difficult, shooting almost exclusively at night on location and made in twenty-eight days on a budget of less than eight-hundred thousand dollars—conditions even more constrained than Lucas' first film. Haskell Wexler graciously stepped in to photograph the film after a rocky first few days—as Lucas was, initially, playing the role of director of photography as well. Being a cameraman himself, Lucas was more interested in the technical matters and hired a drama coach to help the actors.[84] Coppola said, "He had to shoot so fast that there wasn't any time for any directing. He stood 'em up and shot 'em, and [the actors] were so talented, they—it was just lucky."[85]

Once again, Lucas approached the film the only way he knew how to: "I shot the film very much like a documentary...I would set the scene up, talk to the actors about what was going to happen, where they were going to go and what they were going to do, set the cameras up with long lenses, and let the actors run through the scenes with each other."[86]

The shoot was trying on everyone and Lucas became ill, while producer Gary Kurtz threw his back out and required a cane for a number of months. "I'm not really a 'night person,' and making a film in that short a time with all sorts of cars—it was a very complicated thing," Lucas said. "Directing is very difficult because you're making a thousand decisions—there are no hard fast answers—and you're dealing with *people*, sometimes very difficult people, emotional people—I just didn't enjoy it."[87] Lucas began to grow tired of the wearisome effort of directing motion pictures—his real passion had been in camerawork and editing—and says he planned on retiring from directing. But he had "long dreamed of making a space movie that would evoke the *Flash Gordon* and *Buck Rogers* serials he had watched on TV as a child," according to biographer Dale Pollock, and was determined to somehow realise this.[88] The images of duelling swashbucklers and spacecraft dog-fights continued to swell in his mind.

Lucas financially survived through his wife Marcia. Being a professional editor herself, the years it took Lucas to make *THX 1138* and *American Graffiti* were ones in which Marcia was the sole supporter for the two of them, even as they sank deeper in debt—in fact, they were dead broke at the time *American Graffiti* was made. Marcia was involved in all of George's projects, and even in those of his friends—she was assistant editor on *Rain People* and Haskell Wexler's directorial debut that same year, *Medium Cool*, and her first editing credit was on Lucas' documentary, *Filmmaker*. After *THX 1138* she would go on to edit *American Graffiti* and all three *Star Wars* films, winning an Oscar for the first one, as well as being picture cutter on Martin Scorsese's peak period of *Alice Doesn't Live Here Anymore*, *Taxi Driver* and *New York, New York*. She was as much a part of the American New Wave as supporting players John Milius and Walter Murch, perhaps more so, and her influence not only on *Star Wars* but on cinema in general is often forgotten. In *Mythmaker* John Milius raved:

> She was a stunning editor...Maybe the best editor I've ever known, in many ways. She'd come in and look at the films we'd made—like *The Wind and the Lion*, for instance—and she'd say, "Take this scene and move it over here,"

and it worked. And it did what I wanted the film to do, and I would have never thought of it. And she did that to everybody's films: to George's, to Steven [Spielberg]'s, to mine, and Scorsese in particular.[89]

George and Marcia had moved into a small house in Mill Valley, just outside of San Francisco, with George hoping to become part of the independent scene that had nonetheless started developing there in the wake of Zoetrope's collapse. Marcia, on the other hand, would have been content to stay in Los Angeles and go the secure union route, where she had steady work. "Marcia's career was in Los Angeles and I respected that," Lucas said. "I didn't want her to give it up and have me drag her to San Francisco."[90] But Marcia liked San Francisco and was happy to move there, but became disappointed when work didn't immediately find her way. Marcia was ready to have a baby, but George wasn't. "He didn't want the extra responsibility at that time because he might be forced into taking a job he didn't want to take," Marcia said.[91] Soon enough, however, she would find herself one of the pre-eminent editors in the budding locale.

"Slowly but surely, a film community is being developed here," Lucas said of the burgeoning San Francisco scene in 1974. "Michael Ritchie lives up here now, John Korty lives up here, I live up here, Francis lives up here. They are all close friends of mine, and we are continuing to make movies up here. We sort of support each other. My wife worked as an editor on *The Candidate*, and she's also worked for John Korty to get us through these little tough spots between movies. Phil Kaufman moved up here, and a couple more of my friends are thinking seriously about moving here. So there's community here, a very small one, and we all exchange ideas. It's not something you can create overnight."[92]

Marcia was assistant-editing Michael Ritchie's *The Candidate* while Lucas was licking his wounds from *American Graffiti*, sure it would be another flop. It was here that Lucas began developing his space opera film into more than just an idea floating within his mind, as he explained to *Starlog* magazine:

When I finished *American Graffiti* again I was broke. I had got paid twice what I made for *THX*—$20, 000 for *Graffiti*, but it took me two years to do it, so when you take taxes out there was not much left. So by the time I was finished, I was out of money again. My wife was working, and we were trying to make ends meet, so I said "I've got to get another picture going here—just to survive." So that's when I decided that I wanted to do a children's film.

It was a very eccentric idea at the time. Everyone said, "Why don't you make another *THX*? Why don't you make some kind of *Taxi Driver* movie? Some kind of important movie?" But I said, "No, no—I think I'll just go off in a completely different direction." My first movie had been made in the streets, using absolutely nothing, and I thought before I retire I want to make one real movie—you know, on sound stages with sets, the way they used to make movies.

I'd had this idea for doing a space adventure. In the process of going through film school you end up with a little stack of ideas for great movies that you'd love to make, and I picked one off and said, "This space epic is the one I want to do." Like *American Graffiti*, it was such an *obvious* thing that I was just amazed nobody had ever done it before.[93]

# Chapter II: The Star Wars

"GEORGE and I had dinner one night, and we were looking through the paper while we were editing *American Graffiti*," Gary Kurtz remembered in a 2002 interview with *IGN Film Force*. "We were looking through the newspaper, looking at the film listings to see if there was anything out there worth going to see. And, there wasn't. Discussion came around to *Flash Gordon*, and wouldn't it be great to have a *Flash Gordon* kind of science fiction movie–that would be great. We'd love to see that. That's sort of the gestation of *Star Wars*–and that was based on something that we wanted to see, that we would pay to go see! And no one was making it."[1]

It was during the making of *American Graffiti* that Lucas took his initial steps to making his *Flash Gordon* film a reality. Lucas had first proposed the film to United Artists in 1971 as a two-picture deal with *American Graffiti* but only as a broad concept of making some kind of "space opera" type of adventure film—now he was actually making it real. The title "The Star Wars" had been registered by United Artists with the MPAA on August 1st, 1971[2] but it sat unproduced as only a vague, indistinct vision in Lucas' head of capes and swords, ray guns and spaceships.

"I had thought about doing what became *Star Wars* long before *THX 1138*," Lucas has said.[3] Lucas had, in fact, attempted to purchase the rights to remake *Flash Gordon* on a whim while in New York with Coppola in

May, 1971.[4]* On his way to Cannes, Lucas briefly visited the city to convince United Artists to give him money to make *American Graffiti*, but he also used the opportunity to check in on the *Flash Gordon* copyright holders to see if they would part with the trademark. Lucas was unsuccessful—King Features owned the rights and demanded more money than he had. Famed Italian producer Dino DeLaurentis had beat him to it and was in the process of courting Federico Fellini to direct a feature film version. "I remember having lunch with George at the Palm restaurant in New York," Coppola remembered, "and he was very depressed because he had just come back and they wouldn't sell him *Flash Gordon*. And he says, 'Well, I'll just invent my own.'"[5]

Thus was born "The Star Wars." When Lucas met United Artists president David Picker at the Carleton Hotel in Cannes a day or two later he didn't have *Flash Gordon* but he had something just as good—his own version. Lucas was only supposed to be securing a deal for *American Graffiti* but he was able to also get backing for his childhood dream of making a heroic space fantasy, which he now had to create from scratch. Lucas told *American Film* in 1977:

> I loved the *Flash Gordon* comic books...I loved the Universal serials with Buster Crabbe. After *THX 1138* I wanted to do Flash Gordon and tried to buy the rights to it from King Features, but they wanted a lot of money for it, more than I could afford then. They didn't want to part with their rights—they wanted Fellini to do *Flash Gordon*.

---

* The dating of this incident is somewhat ambiguous; accounts place it anywhere from 1973 all the way back to before *THX 1138*, and even Jonathan Rinzler, in *The Making of Star Wars*, is very tactful not to assign it to any specific time period. Most likely Lucas had tried to purchase *Flash Gordon* while visiting United Artists in New York on his way to Cannes in 1971; the Cannes film festival occurred in May that year. Rinzler states that, on this visit, Lucas stayed with Coppola. Coppola actually was there filming *The Godfather* on location (the film was shot between March and August 1971). This would explain how, after Lucas' offer was rejected, he proceeded to have lunch with Coppola at the Palm restaurant. This must mean that Lucas originally planned on proposing the two-picture deal of *American Graffiti* and *Flash Gordon* to United Artists when he got to Cannes. Arriving in France without *Flash Gordon*, he instead started calling it "The Star Wars" and decided he would create the story himself.

> I realized that *I* could make up a character as easily as Alex Raymond, who took his character from Edgar Rice Burroughs. It's your basic superhero in outer space. I realised that what I really wanted to do was a contemporary action fantasy.[6]

Two years later, in 1973, Lucas finally started figuring out what, exactly, "The Star Wars" was. "When I made the deal I had to give it a name," he said, "but it wasn't until I finished *Graffiti* in '73 that I started writing it."[7] He took the basic charm of *Flash Gordon*—good guys who fight a never ending battle against villains, always finding themselves in new adventures and unlikely danger, and who inhabit a setting with a strange mix of magic and technology—and began making it into his own. In place of Emperor Ming, he would place the aptly-named Emperor, and eventually in later drafts his henchman Darth Vader. Laser swords, ray guns, capes and medieval garb, sorcerers, rocket ships and space battles would all stem from the *Flash Gordon* and *Buck Rogers* episodes Lucas grew up with. The film needed to be filled with impressive visuals and constant peril and excitement, a non-stop action film with lots of explosions and graphics. "One of the key visions I had of the film when I started was of a dogfight in outer space with spaceships," Lucas said in *The Making of Star Wars*. "I said, 'I want to make that movie. I want to *see* that.'"[8] According to the first issue of *Bantha Tracks*, the official *Star Wars* fan club newsletter, Lucas also researched where Alex Raymond, the author and illustrator of the 1930s *Flash Gordon* comic strip, got his inspiration from, which led him to the John Carter of Mars novels by Edgar Rice Burroughs, which were similar in style and design.[*]

After making the dark and dismal *THX 1138*, a film which had a disastrous release, Lucas had learned that an audience responded much more to hope and optimism than to bleak cynicism. Lucas said in 1974:

> I realised after *THX* that people don't care about how the country's being ruined. All that movie did was make people more pessimistic, more depressed, and less willing to get involved in trying to make the world better. So I decided that this time I would make a more optimistic film that makes people feel positive about their fellow human beings. It's too easy to make films about Watergate. And it's hard to be optimistic when everything tells you to be pessimistic and cynical. I'm a very bad cynic. But we've got to regenerate optimism. Maybe kids will walk out of this film and for a second they'll feel

---

[*] Further research, the issue reports, led him to discover that the John Carter of Mars books were inspired by Edwin Arnold's *Gulliver of Mars*, published in 1905.

"We could really make something out of this country, or we could really make something out of ourselves." It's all that hokey stuff about being a good neighbor, and the American spirit and all that crap. There *is* something in it.[9]

Lucas was speaking of *American Graffiti* but it was a lesson that would be carried over to *Star Wars* with even more prominence, though the screenplay would morph through various incarnations before this emerged with the significance with which it carries in the final film. Lucas began outlining *Star Wars* even before *Graffiti* was released, and when *Graffiti* finally was it only reinforced his beliefs, as he told *Bantha Tracks* in 1980:

> After seeing the effect *Graffiti* had on high-school kids...I started thinking about ten and twelve year olds...I saw that kids that age don't have the fantasy life we had as kids. They don't have westerns; they don't have pirate movies; they don't have all that stupid serial fantasy life that we used to believe in. They also don't have heroes. I had been a big fan of Flash Gordon and a believer in the exploration of space. I felt, then, that *Star Wars* would be a natural and give kids a fantasy life that they really needed to have.[10]

Lucas is quick to admit he hates writing, and at every opportunity he had tried to get friends to write his scripts for him—usually with complicated results: writers deserting (*American Graffiti*), drafts unsatisfactory (*THX 1138*), and projects shelved (*Apocalypse Now*). "*Star Wars* was a little bit different," he told *Starlog* magazine in 1981, "because by that time I'd decided that it was useless to try to get someone else to write my screenplays...I finally gave up!"[11]

### "My Little Space Thing"

The *Star Wars* Souvenir program states that Lucas began working on story material in January of 1973, which would be just around the time *American Graffiti* was having its first audience screening at San Francisco's Northpoint Theater (on January 28th).[12] In fact, Lucas may have began writing immediately afterwards—the screening audience loved *Graffiti* but Universal head Ned Tanen hated the film and called it "unreleasable," perhaps fuelling Lucas to begin his next project. Lucas stated to *Rolling Stone*:

> It was January 1973. I had been paid $20,000 for *Graffiti*, it had taken two years, I was $15,000 in debt and Universal hated the film so much they were contemplating selling it as a TV Movie of the Week. I had to start paying back

some of this movie so I thought, "I'll whip up that treatment, my second deal at United Artists, my little space thing."[13]

Creating an entire space fantasy from scratch was no easy task though. He wanted to have a comic-book-like feel to the story that recalled the great pulp space opera works like E.E. Smith's *Skylark of Space*, but had trouble devising an actual story. To jog his mind, he began by brainstorming exotic names that he could use for characters and planets, almost in a free-association manner, simply to develop the sort of bizarre atmosphere and far-out style that he was looking for. The first name is "Emperor Ford Xerxes XII" (Xerxes being a Persian king who invaded ancient Greece), which was followed by "Xenos, Thorpe, Roland, Monroe, Lars, Kane, Hayden, Crispin, Leila, Zena, Owen, Mace, Wan, Star, Bail, Biggs, Bligh, Cain, Clegg, Fleet, Valorum."[14] He then started combining first and last names and fleshing out their purpose and characterisation: Alexander Xerxes XII is the "Emperor of Decarte," Owen Lars is an "Imperial General," Han Solo is "leader of the Hubble people," Mace Windy a "Jedi-Bendu," C.2. Thorpe is a space pilot, while Anakin Starkiller is "King of Bebers" and Luke Skywalker "Prince of Bebers." He came up with planets such as "Yoshiro" and "Aquilae" the desert planets, "Norton III" an ice planet, and "Yavin" is a jungle world with its native eight-foot-tall Wookies.

Having bombarded himself with such an exotically alien ambiance he finally attempted to construct a story. What he ended up with was a vague two pages of a hand-written plot summary with the curious title *Journal of the Whills*. It opened with the convoluted line, "This is the story of Mace Windy, a revered Jedi-Bendu of Opuchi, as related to us by C.J. Thorpe, padawaan learner to the famed Jedi." In the brief plot outline, Mace Windy is a "Jedi-Bendu" or "Jedi-Templer," a vague sci-fi adaptation of a space superhero crossed with a samurai. Windy takes on an apprentice, C.J. Thorpe, who narrates the story retrospectively in the first person. The tale is uncharacteristically literary in prose, and is divided into two parts, headed with "I" and "II" respectively, Part I being Thrope's training and Part II being his greatest mission. J.W. Rinzler described it:

> The initials *C.J.* or *C.2.* (it switches back and forth) stand for "Chuiee Two Thorpe of Kissel. My father is Han Dardell Thorpe, chief pilot of the renown galactic cruiser *Tarnack*." At the age of sixteen Chuiee enters the "exalted Intersystems Academy to train as a potential Jedi-Templer. It is here that I became padawaan learner to the great Mace Windy... at that time, Warlord to the Chairman of the Alliance of Independent Systems... Some felt that he was

more powerful than the Imperial leader of the Galactic Empire... Ironically, it was his own comrades' fear... that led to his replacement... and expulsion from the royal forces."

After Windy's dismissal, Chuiee begs to stay in his service "until I had finished my education." *Part II* takes up the story: "It was four years later that our greatest adventure began. We were guardians on a shipment of fusion portables to Yavin, when we were summoned to the desolate second planet of Yoshiro by a mysterious courier from the Chairman of the Alliance." At this point Lucas's first space-fantasy narrative trails off... [15]

This plot summary has little relation to the final product, but contains a few elements which would be later incorporated into the screenplays, such as the phonetics of "Chuiee" ("Chewie"), a pilot named Han, a galactic Empire, a space academy, and intergalactic superheroes named Jedi. Much of it recalls the space opera works of E.E. Smith and his Lensmen series, with its intergalactic space commandos, far-fetched comic-book style plotting and exotic names.

Lucas took this summary to his agent, Jeff Berg, for an opinion—unsurprisingly, Berg was left utterly confounded at the incomprehensible story and recommended Lucas try something simpler, later saying: "I knew more about the story based on what George had told me than what was in that brief treatment."[16] Frustrated, Lucas began anew.

It seems coming up with an original story was harder than Lucas realised—despite claiming that he was determined to make his own "superhero in outer space" adventure, he would end up *adapting* another story for his first proper story synopsis, completed after the disastrous *Journal of the Whills* attempt. Aside from *Flash Gordon*, the other main influence, at least for Lucas' initial conception of *Star Wars*, is the Japanese samurai films of Akira Kurosawa, but in particular 1958's *The Hidden Fortress*. Lucas discovered Kurosawa at the recommendation of John Milius while attending film school and quickly fell in love with Kurosawa's films.

Akira Kurosawa had a prolific, successful but sometimes tumultuous career—at the time Lucas was developing *Star Wars* in 1973, the Japanese director was considered a has-been and attempted committing suicide after he proved unable to find any work. He began his career in the 1930s as an Assistant Director, becoming Toho studios' top AD and a protégé to director Kajiro Yamamoto before finally making his directorial debut in 1943 with *Sugata Sanshiro*, or *Judo Saga*, based on Tsuneo Tomita's novel about a martial arts student who comes to learn the meaning of life through the study of judo. Though Kurosawa frequently depicted contemporary

Japan, he is best known for his "jidai geki," or period films, portraying the stoic samurai warriors of Japan's past. Kurosawa wrote nearly all of his films—over thirty, and usually in collaboration with a team of his usual writing partners—but rarely were the stories original creations. He often adapted Shakespeare, remaking *King Lear* in 1985 as *Ran* and *Macbeth* in 1957 as *Throne of Blood*, and frequently sourced folk tales and novels as the basis for many of his stories, such as in *Red Beard, Dersu Uzala, The Idiot, Rashomon* and *Hidden Fortress* itself. Like Lucas, and some would argue the best storytellers, very little of Kurosawa's stories were "original." Indeed, even Shakespeare could be regarded as a literary thief if originality is the basis for our appraisal. In fact, this is one of the largest misconceptions of the creative process—a misconception usually asserted by those ignorant of the process. Artists take from what they know and what they've seen and combine them in new ways, and it is this unique sum of influences that gives us creative variation when they are combined with the particularities of the artist.

Lucas even extended this creative synthesis to the visual design: "I'm trying to make everything look very natural, a casual almost I've-seen-this-before look," he said in 1975. "You look at that painting of Tusken Raiders and the banthas, and you say, 'Oh yeah, Bedouins...' Then you look at it some more and say, 'Wait a minute, that's not right. Those aren't Bedouins, and what are those creatures back there?' Like the X-wing and TIE fighter battle, you say, 'I've seen that, it's World War II—but wait a minute—that isn't any kind of jet I've ever seen before.' I want the whole film to have that quality!"[17]

So, in the tracing of the *plot* of *Star Wars* we come to Akira Kurosawa, and more specifically a 1958 film entitled *The Hidden Fortress*. More than any other of Kurosawa's films, *The Hidden Fortress* is a fairy tale, a fast-paced adventure film aimed at a much younger and broader audience than his usual complicated and dark subject matter. Lucas has admitted to borrowing the two bickering peasants from whose perspective the story is told and turning them into R2-D2 and C-3P0—but in fact, not only were the droids not robots but human, literal adaptations of the bickering peasants in his initial treatment, Lucas "borrowed" nearly all of *The Hidden Fortress* for the first treatment, so much that he even contemplated purchasing the rights to the film.[18] He flat-out *remade* it. The first proper version[*] of *"The*

---

[*] Because *Journal of the Whills* is so distinct from the progression that began with *The Star Wars*, I often consider it as a separate entity, a proto-*Star-Wars* that was abandoned; it contains super-commandos named Jedi, but otherwise is not

*Star Wars"* takes the form of a fourteen-page story synopsis, also called a treatment or outline in filmmaking terms, which essentially is *The Hidden Fortress* set on another planet. There are no Jedi or Sith, or even the Force—these were dressings that Lucas later added to his initial plot base, which fundamentally is an adaptation of Kurosawa's film and which includes practically every scene from it.

Without the advantage of home video, Lucas relied on a plot summary of Kurosawa's film, copying entire passages from *Hidden Fortress'* synopsis in Donald Richie's authoritative book *The Films of Akira Kurosawa*, first published in 1965. Although the final film transformed and shifted more than enough to qualify it as a unique work unto itself by the time it reached the silver screen, its plot remains similar to its very incarnation in the 1973 treatment, at its most basic, a "re-imagined" version of *The Hidden Fortress*.

"*Hidden Fortress* was an influence on *Star Wars* right from the beginning," Lucas said in *The Making of Star Wars*. "I was searching around for a story. I had some scenes—the cantina scene and the space battle scene—but I couldn't think of a basic plot. Originally, the film was a good concept in search of a story. And then I thought of *Hidden Fortress*, which I'd seen again in 1972 or '73, and so the first plots were very much like it."[19]

*Journal of the Whills* was overly complicated and too strange to translate into audience friendly terms, but Kurosawa was a master at understanding how to entertain the masses in broad, simple strokes. "A film should appeal to sophisticated, profound-thinking people while at the same time entertaining simplistic people," Kurosawa once said.[20] "A truly good movie is really enjoyable too. There's nothing complicated about it. A truly good movie is interesting and easy to understand."[21]

*The Hidden Fortress* opens with two bickering peasants, Tahei and Matashichi, wandering the desert landscape, cursing their "lot in life." It is a period of civil war, and the various clans of Japan are all at battle with one another. The two peasants bicker until they split up, each wandering in a different direction—they are both individually found by the enemy and placed in a slave-camp, where they are miraculously reunited to each others

---

directly related to the entity which began with the *Star Wars* treatment and is conceptually quite different, whereas the *Star Wars* treatment is related to the first draft, and that draft to the next draft, and so on. That *Journal of the Whills* has a separate title helps differentiate it. When I speak of "the treatment" or synopsis, I will be referring to the May fourteen-page version.

delight. After an uprising in the prison camp allows them to escape, they stumble upon a gold bar hidden inside a piece of wood, and soon find themselves intertwined with a duo of strangers—a beautiful peasant girl and her roughneck companion. In reality these two are Princess Yuki and General Rokurota Makabe, the two peasants having stumbled across the hidden fortress in which they are hiding, for a reward has been posted for the princess' capture. The gold bar hidden inside the stick is one of hundreds, and is the secret royal treasure, which the enemy is also seeking. General Makabe is attempting to escort the princess through the dangerous enemy territory, and the two peasants find themselves helping them in exchange for a share of the gold. Together, the four of them embark on a treacherous quest through enemy lands, dodging soldiers and evading enemy forces, somehow surviving close-call after close-call. Along the way, after an exciting horseback chase, General Makabe duels his arch opponent who later helps them escape after they are captured. They reach friendly territory, and the General and princess are revealed in all their true glory, much to the bafflement of the two peasants who stumble away realising they have been adventuring with demigods.

On April 17th, 1973, Lucas began writing a new story.[22] Handwritten at ten pages and typed at fourteen, the *Star Wars* treatment was completed in the first week of May, 1973.[23] There is some interesting debate as to what and when Lucas first wrote, and it has also been frequently erroneously reported that Lucas began writing in 1972; for an in-depth look at the holy grail of *Star Wars* lore, the *Journal of the Whills* (a document conceptually separate from Lucas' attempted plot summary of that same name), see Appendix A. But to simplify things, it is accurate to say that *Star Wars* was officially born on the first week of May, 1973, with the completion of the fourteen-page synopsis, which was begun following Lucas' failed *Journal of the Whills* summary of late January of that year. It was titled *The Star Wars*, and told the adventurous tale of a General who leads a princess on a dangerous escape route through enemy lands, a sci-fantasy remake of *The Hidden Fortress*.

Jan Helander, in his authoritative essay "The Development of Star Wars as Seen Through the Scripts by George Lucas," describes the synopsis as follows:

> The galaxy is plagued by a civil war between an evil Empire and rebel forces. Two bickering Imperial bureaucrats try to flee from a space fortress which is under attack, and crash land on the planet of Aquilae. A wanted rebel princess and her relentless general Luke Skywalker, on their way to a space port in order to get the princess to safety, find and capture them and after a hazardous

journey the group make it to a religious temple where they discover a band of young boy rebels. The boys decide to follow them across the wasteland in spite of the general's reluctance, and they soon reach a shabby cantina near the space port where the general is forced to use his "lazer sword" to kill a bully who is taunting one of the boys.

The group, pursued by Imperial troops, must steal a fighter ship in order to escape and after a long chase they manage to hide in an asteroid field. However, the rebels' ship is damaged and they are forced to jettison towards the forbidden planet of Yavin with rocket packs. On Yavin, they travel on "jet-sticks" made from their rocket packs, until they are attacked by giant furry aliens who capture the princess and the bureaucrats and sell them to an Imperial platoon. Skywalker is almost killed, but one of the aliens helps to take him to an old farmer who knows where the Imperial outpost is. After an attack on the outpost, the general and the boys learn that the princess has been taken to Alderaan, a "city-planet" and the capitol of the Empire. After rigorous training, Skywalker and the young rebels man a squadron of fighter ships, and disguised as Imperial rangers they manage to reach the prison complex of Alderaan. They free the princess, but an alarm goes off and a few of the boys are killed before the group is able to escape to the friendly planet of Ophuchi. There, everyone (including the bureaucrats) are rewarded at a ceremony, as the princess reveals her true goddess-like self.[24]

## *Influences*

A summation of the treatment does not reveal the full impact of *Hidden Fortress*—a reading of the actual document itself reveals nearly a scene-by-scene remake of Kurosawa's film.

From Lucas' synopsis:

> It is the thirty-third century, a period of civil wars in the galaxy. A rebel princess, with her family, her retainers, and the clan treasure, is being pursued. If they can cross territory controlled by the Empire and reach a friendly planet, they will be saved. The Sovereign knows this, and posts a reward for the capture of the princess.

Versus Kurosawa's film: It is the sixteenth century, a period of civil wars. A princess, with her family, her retainers, and the clan treasure is being pursued. If they can cross enemy territory and reach a friendly province they will be saved. The enemy knows this and posts a reward for the capture of the princess.

From Lucas' synopsis:

She is being guarded by one of her generals, (Luke Skywalker) and it is he who leads her on the long and dangerous journey that follows. They take along with them two hundred pounds of the greatly treasured "aura spice", and also two Imperial bureaucrats, whom the general has captured.

Versus Kurosawa's film: She is being guarded by one of her generals, (Rokurota Makabe) and it is he who leads her on the long and dangerous journey that follows. They take along with them two hundred pounds of the greatly treasured royal gold and also two peasants, whom the general has captured.

From Lucas' synopsis:

The two terrified, bickering bureaucrats crash land on Aquilae while trying to flee the battle of the space fortress. They accidentally discover a small container of the priceless "aura spice" and are rummaging around the rocks pushing and pulling each other trying to find more when they are discovered by Luke Skywalker and taken to his camp.

Versus Kurosawa's film: The two terrified, bickering peasants stumble upon the hidden fortress while trying to flee the battle of the prison camp. They accidentally discover a small piece of wood containing the priceless royal gold and are rummaging around the rocks pushing and pulling each other trying to find more when they are discovered by Rokurota Makabe and taken to his camp.

From Lucas' synopsis:

The princess and the general are disguised as farmers, and the bureaucrats join their party with the intention of stealing their "land speeder" and "aura spice." It doesn't take them too long to realize the general isn't a farmer and that they are captives about to embark on a dangerous mission. The two bureaucrats are essentially comic relief inserted among the general seriousness of the adventure.

Versus Kurosawa's film: The princess and the general are disguised as farmers, and the peasants join their party with the intention of stealing their horses and royal treasure. It doesn't take them too long to realise the general isn't a farmer and that they are captives about to embark on a dangerous mission. The two peasants are essentially comic relief inserted among the general seriousness of the adventure.

From Lucas' synopsis:

The small group in their sleek, white, two-man 'land speeders' travel across the wastelands of Aquilae, headed for the space port city of Gordon, where they hope to get a spacecraft that will take them to the friendly planet of Ophuchi.

At a desolate rest stop, the rebels are stopped and questioned by an Imperial patrol. Apparently satisfied, the captain lets the group continue on their way, but a short distance into the wilderness, they are attacked by the patrol. The Imperial patrol of twelve men is no match for the incredibly skilled and powerful general, who makes short work of the enemy.

Versus Kurosawa's film: The small group and their horses travel across the wastelands of Yamana, ending up in a small town, where they get a cart that will help them take the gold to the friendly province of Hayakawa. At a desolate rest stop, they are stopped and questioned by an Imperial patrol. Apparently satisfied, the captain lets the group continue on their way, but a short distance into the wilderness, they are attacked by the patrol. The Imperial patrol of four men is no match for the incredibly skilled and powerful general, who makes short work of the enemy.

As you can see, 1973's *The Star Wars* was indeed a remake of *Hidden Fortress*, although the later sections of Lucas' synopsis add scenes beyond the scope of Kurosawa's story, most notably the last third where primitive aliens and young boys help the General free the princess. Kurosawa's films had often been the target of western pilfering—*Seven Samurai* was remade as *Magnificent Seven* in 1960, *Rashomon* as *The Outrage* in 1964 and *Yojimbo* as Sergio Leone's *Fistful of Dollars* in 1964. Leone's film became an international hit, which brought it to the attention of Kurosawa—who sued Leone.

Jan Helander made the following observation:

This thirteen page synopsis bears little resemblance to the 1977 *Star Wars* picture. The space opera feel of old science fiction films like *The Forbidden Planet* is present, and the laser weapons and the constant action were trademarks of the Flash Gordon serials Lucas had seen in his childhood...The similarity between *The Star Wars* and *The Hidden Fortress* is evident if one compares Lucas's outline with a plot summary from Donald Richie's 1965 biography *The Films of Akira Kurosawa*:

The Star Wars:
"It is the thirty-third century, a period of civil wars in the galaxy. A rebel princess, with her family, her retainers, and the clan treasure, is being pursued. If they can cross territory controlled by the Empire and reach a friendly planet, they will be saved. The Sovereign knows this, and posts a reward for the capture of the princess."

The Hidden Fortress:

"It is the sixteenth century, a period of civil wars. A princess, with her family, her retainers, and the clan treasure is being pursued. If they can cross enemy territory and reach a friendly province they will be saved. The enemy knows this and posts a reward for the capture of the princess."

This transcription-like example is not representative of Lucas's entire synopsis, but it gives a good insight into the influence of *The Hidden Fortress* as well as Lucas's struggle to get his own ideas down on paper. Both *The Star Wars* and *The Hidden Fortress* contain a journey across enemy lands, but while Kurosawa's characters mount horses, Lucas lets the general, the princess and the bureaucrats travel in 'land speeders'. The rebel princess's clan treasure is two hundred pounds of 'aura spice', while Kurosawa's princess brings sixteen hundred pounds of gold with her. A horse chase in the Japanese film has been adapted to a scene where the rebels, on their jetsticks, are being pursued by the furry aliens, riding bird-like creatures much like those in the *John Carter on Mars* books by Edgar Rice Burroughs. General Skywalker is challenged by one of the aliens to a spear fight, a duel which also is present in *The Hidden Fortress*.[25]

Kurosawa biographer Donald Richie described *Hidden Fortress* as a "romantic", "mythic", "adventurous" and "operatic" "fairy-tale,"[26] five of the most common words used to describe *Star Wars*.

It has been said that *Hidden Fortress* was Kurosawa's attempt to remake an earlier film of his own with the extravagance and scope he had always wanted but never quite achieved[27]—that earlier film was 1945's *They Who Tread on the Tiger's Tail*, based on a medieval legend which forms the basis for both the Noh drama *Ataka* and the Kabuki play *Kanjincho*.[28]

*They Who Tread on the Tiger's Tail* is a sixty-minute film about a feudal Lord in medieval Japan who is on the run from the enemy along with his loyal bodyguards. Escaping through a forest to avoid the enemy, they disguise themselves as priests in order to pass through a border crossing. Kurosawa took this from one of the Kabuki theatre's most famous plays, *Kanjincho*, first performed in 1845, which is about two famous warriors (Benkei and Yoshitsune) disguised as priests in medieval Japan who attempt to pass through an enemy border crossing (the Ataka gate) being guarded by a soldier named Togashi. The play's title comes from a famous moment where Benkei and Yoshitsune, in order to pass through the Ataka gate, claim they are monks collecting donations for a Buddhist temple, and the guard Togashi demands they show him the kanjincho, or subscription list of those who have donated.

*Kanjincho* was a Kabuki version of a play from the medieval Noh style of Japanese theatre, *Ataka*, written by Kanze Kojiro Nobumitsu, who lived from 1435-1516. The characters in *Ataka* (and by extension *Kanjincho* and Kurosawa's film) were real-life historical people who lived in the 12th century: the famous samurai-warlord Minamoto Yoshitsune and his servant Benkei, who fought through the great civil wars that broke out in that century. By the time *Ataka* was written, Yoshitsune had been dead for two hundred years and was already mythologized in Japanese folklore, such as in the literary epic *Tale of the Heike* (or the *Heike monogatari*), which is described as being "to the Japanese what *The Iliad* is to the western world."[29] *Tale of the Heike*, which relates specifically about the great Genpei war from 1180-1185, was not set down in writing until around 1220 and was completed by many authors in episodic fashion over a period of a hundred years,[30] and was originally an oral tradition sung by travelling monks.

Minamoto Yoshitsune lived from 1159 to 1189, and is one of the most popular characters in Japanese history. His older brother was Minamoto Yoritomo, who created Japan's first military administration, or shogunate. Yoshitsune's father, Minamoto Yoshitomo, and two of his brothers were killed in an unsuccessful uprising in 1160 when they attempted to usurp the rival Taira (or Heike) clan in what is known as The Heiji Rebellion. During the Siege of Sanjo Palace, the Minamoto clan and its allies (a force of roughly five-hundred men) kidnapped the Emperor and sacked the palace, but after much fighting the Taira clan defeated them. Young Minamoto Yoshitsune, only an infant, was decreed banished by the Taira clan, and was imprisoned in a monastery. In 1180, now a young man, he escaped and joined a rebellion that his brother Yoritomo, now head of the clan, had organized. Prince Mochihito, the son of the Emperor that the Minamoto clan had captured in the Heiji Rebellion, had turned against the Taira clan because he believed they were attempting to take the throne, and supplied the Minamoto clan with an army, beginning the Genpei wars. Over the next several years Yoshitsune became a great warrior and led the Minamoto army to victory in many battles, defeating the Taira clan. Eventually, tensions developed between Yoshitsune and his brother Yoritomo, and they fought at the Battle of Koromogawa, where Yoshitsune was defeated and his retainer Benkei was killed heroically defending him. Fleeing north, Yoshitsune and his family committed suppuku, or ritual suicide.

So, if we follow the rabbit hole deep enough then, this mythologized historical character, who lived nearly a millennia ago in Japan, is in some distant way responsible for *Star Wars* existing as it does.

A point of distinction to make about the characters of *The Star Wars* is that although General Luke Skywalker in the treatment bears the same name as the protagonist of the final film, his character has more in common with Obi Wan, that of an elderly Jedi master—although the Jedi do not yet exist in the story development, with the character instead being a mere General, a port of the General Makabe character from Kurosawa's film. Lucas would make this character a secondary one in the next draft, with the protagonist in that draft essentially one of the young boys in training. The Luke Skywalker of the final film does not exist yet, nor does Darth Vader. Neither of them were any part of Lucas' original concept. Nor are the Jedi, Sith or even the Force—his original story was simply a futuristic adventure tale, a self-contained story about an elderly General leading a princess to safety and a rebellion against a dictatorship. It was, at its most basic roots, an elaborated version of Kurosawa's *Hidden Fortress* set in outer space.

Despite the fact that Lucas now claims to have had the whole story pre-decided in his head, he was much more accurate in this quote from 1977's theatre souvenir program:

> I had the *Star Wars* project in mind even before I started my last picture, *American Graffiti*, and as soon as I finished I began writing *Star Wars* in January 1973...In fact, I wrote four entirely different screenplays for *Star Wars*, searching for just the right ingredients, characters and storyline. It's always been what you might call a good idea in search of a story.[31]

Being a college student in the mid-'60s and living in the liberal Bay-area of San Francisco, the growing political and social climate had a shaping influence on Lucas' life as well, which would be reflected in all of his work, including *Star Wars*. "The sixties were amazing," he told Alan Arnold in 1979. "I was in college and was just the right age. I guess everybody who lived through that period felt a very strong sense that something special was happening."[32] But unlike many of his contemporaries who grew up in L.A. and New York, Lucas' quaint small-town roots instilled a certain naiveté in his childhood, where Errol Flynn and Buster Crabbe captured his imagination—a quality of work that was no longer being made by the cynical and "serious" American New Wave.

Although his more contemporary statements on the matter play up the mythological aspect of the film, his comments during its release concentrate on what was the film's true audience hook—its escapist fantasy fun, the counterargument to the more gritty, serious and pessimistic films being made in the 1970s, such as *French Connection*, *Dirty Harry* and *Taxi Driver*. It had little to do with creating a complicated saga or a "modern mythology," as the 1973 synopsis shows. It was about reviving the traditional adventure genre, about revitalising the imagination of an increasingly-bleak generation of kids with an action-packed sci-fi swashbuckler (but also one with a certain warm, fairy-tale-like charm, which is why *Hidden Fortress* was so perfectly suited). "Some of my friends are more concerned about art and being considered a Fellini or an Orson Wells," Lucas said back in 1974 when he first began work on the project. "I'm more drawn to Flash Gordon. I like action adventure, chases, things blowing up, and I have strong feelings about science fiction and comic books and that sort of world."[33] Rejecting the self-aggrandising seriousness he felt in the work of some of his contemporaries, he went on to state: "I don't care if I make a piece of art or a piece of shit."[34] He said in 1977:

> My main reason for making it was to give young people an honest, wholesome fantasy life, the kind my generation had. We had westerns, pirate movies, all kinds of great things. Now they have *The Six Million Dollar Man* and *Kojak*. Where are the romance, the adventure, and the fun that used to be in practically every movie made?[35]

In *Star Wars* we also see the residual remains of his first two films. *THX 1138*, also a science fiction piece with heavy Japanese influences, contains many visual similarities, and in effect *THX 1138* can be seen as a sort of low-tech precursor in many ways. The robotic police men became the stormtroopers, the car chase would become the speeder chases in later films, proto-Jawa's appear as "shell dwellers," there are holograms, gritty yet futuristic hardware (a "used universe" as the term was later coined), a mysterious cloaked spectre who bears more than a passing resemblance to the Emperor, and the prevalent themes of man versus machine and of the underdog fighting back against an oppressive system. The film even opens with a vintage clip from the *Buck Rogers* serials. Like *THX 1138*, *Star Wars* also did little to explain the fantastic world, plunging the audience into the midst of the story and providing little in the way of exposition.

If *THX 1138* provided the visual reference and mis-en-scene, *American Graffiti* would provide the characters, telling the tale of a young man's first initiation into the world and the all-important act of leaving home—though this would not come to prominence until a few more years, with the second draft screenplay. "[*Star Wars* was] my next movie after *American Graffiti*,"

Lucas said in 2004, "and in a way the subject and everything is young people, and it's a subject that is the very same subject that *American Graffiti* is about. It's about a young boy leaving his world and going off into the unknown to a great adventure. *American Graffiti* focuses on that final night when that decision is made. *Star Wars* carries that story on to what happens after you leave."[36] Amusingly, a hot-shot racer appears in *Graffiti* as well, played by Harrison Ford ("A lot of the elements of Han Solo are a lot like Bob Falfa in *American Graffiti*. But I don't—I hope—they're not the same person," Ford commented in 1977[37]). Even Lucas' never-filmed war project, *Apocalypse Now*, later transformed into a film by Coppola, contained much of the same themes, such as ill-equipped humans overcoming technological oppression. Walter Murch offers the opinion that *Apocalypse Now* essentially transformed into *Star Wars*. "*Star Wars* is George's version of *Apocalypse Now*, rewritten in an otherworldly context," Murch explained. "The Rebels in *Star Wars* are the Vietnamese, and the Empire is the United States."[38]

This transformation can even be read into the first treatment, in which a group of rebels strike out from a jungle and topple an empire, and this theme would swell in importance in the subtext of the eventual screenplay. "A lot of my interest in *Apocalypse Now* was carried over into *Star Wars*," Lucas admitted in *The Making of Star Wars*. "I figured that I couldn't make that film because it was about the Vietnam War, so I would essentially deal with some of the same interesting concepts that I was going to use and convert them into space fantasy, so you'd have essentially a large technological empire going after a small group of freedom fighters or human beings."[39]

Influences other than Kurosawa and *Flash Gordon* are peppered in this synopsis, the primary one being the work of Frank Herbert, most specifically his novel *Dune*.

Frank Herbert was one of the most popular contemporary science fiction writers at the time Lucas was writing *Star Wars*. His epic novel *Dune* had been released in 1965 (after being serialised in *Analog* magazine in two parts in 1963 and 1965) and was an instant hit in science fiction circles, marking a milestone in the genre—many have compared its context in science fiction to *Lord of the Rings*' context in the fantasy genre.

The story of *Dune* concerns an intergalactic empire made up of three regional Houses, the largest of which is the Imperial House Corrino, which controls the lesser two fiefdoms, House Harkonnen and House Atreides; the plot is propelled by the political struggles between these three Houses. The protagonist of the novel is young Paul Atreides, son of Duke Leto Atreides and heir to the dukedom—due to his noble status, he receives special martial arts training, as well as the mystical powers of the Bene Gesserit sisterhood cult. House Atreides becomes seen as a threat, and so the Corrino Emperor Shaddam IV decides that it must be destroyed. The Emperor cannot wipe out House Atreides with an open attack, and so he employs subterfuge, granting the Atreides control of the treacherous desert planet Arakis, also known as Dune, an inhospitable world coveted for its spice Melange which increases one's lifespan and which had previously been controlled by House Harkonnen. The Emperor's scheme culminates when he sends an army dressed as Harkonnens to Dune to wipe out the royal family, but Paul and his mother escape into the desert wilderness. Here they meet a roaming desert band of fighters known as Fremen. With Paul's developing abilities, he begins training the band of rebels, later becoming known as demigod military leader Paul Muad'Dib. He and his army quickly overwhelm the Imperial forces with their mystical skills and Paul becomes the head of the Imperial throne.

Many have observed the desert setting of *Dune* as being an obvious inspiration for Tatooine, although the planet does not exist in the synopsis. The 1973 synopsis, however, does indeed bear a strong *Dune* influence, and that is the latter half, where it drifts from the Kurosawa source material. The subplot involving the band of rebel boys might stem from two sources, one of them being *Dune*. In Frank Herbert's novel, Paul Atreides comes across a band of rebels, and in order to finally assault the Empire he will need their help; he comes to lead them, and with his small army he attacks the Imperial fortress and topples the Empire. In the *Star Wars* treatment, General Skywalker comes across a band of rebels, and in order to finally assault the Empire to free the captured princess he realises he needs their help; he begins training them and they attack the Imperial stronghold and rescue the princess. The use of coveted "spice" in the synopsis is evidence of *Dune*'s influence.

The second influence from where the rebel subplot stems is yet another Kurosawa film. General Skywalker encounters a group of young boys who are eager to attack the Imperial outposts—Skywalker overhears their boastful plan and laughs at them. They turn to see him walking into their hideout, scratching himself, looking down on them as the block-headed young fools that they are. They can see that he is a real General, a great warrior, and beg to join him but the General refuses and commands them to return to their homes; they plead that they have no where else to go and instead follow the General on his mission. This sequence is straight out of an early scene in Kurosawa's 1962 film *Sanjuro*, where Toshiro Mifune's scruffy, cynical samurai character encounters a group of young boys who plan on attacking a corrupt superintendant who has imprisoned the uncle of the leader of the boys. They beg the samurai to help them but he refuses and tells them to go home—realising that at the mercy of the corrupt superintendant they have no future, the samurai finally joins forces with them.

In Lucas' treatment they eventually make their way to a cantina, where one of the boys is taunted by a bully—Skywalker draws his lightsaber and in an instant the bully's arm lies on the ground (this scene survived all the drafts). This is taken from Kurosawa's *Yojimbo*, from 1961, which *Sanjuro* was a sequel to.

Other influences on the *Star Wars* treatment is the work of Edward Elmer Smith (aka E.E. "Doc" Smith), who is known as one of the greatest science fiction writers of all time, and is credited with inventing the "space opera" genre with his story *The Skylark of Space*, published in 1928 as a serial in *Amazing Stories* (though it was actually written in 1919). His direct influence on the initial treatment is minimal but his series of Lensmen tales would come to mold the coming drafts Lucas would write.

The section where Skywalker encounters the "furry" aliens on the jungle planet is also deviant from *Hidden Fortress*, although the jet-stick chase and spear fight appear in Kurosawa's film. These creatures have been thought to have been taken from H. Beam Piper's *Fuzzy* stories, the first and most famous of which was published in 1962, which revolved around a forest-dwelling race of primitive furry creatures. Piper was a noted space opera author whose work was often published in magazines such as *Astounding Science Fiction*.[40]

Finally, Isaac Asimov is one of the most influential science fiction writers, though unlike most of Lucas' influences was more of an intellectual rather than action oriented writer. His *Foundation* series has been said to have had an impact on *Star Wars*, though its influence is minimal on the 1973 synopsis. Asimov initially wrote three *Foundation* novels between 1951 and 1953 which formed a trilogy; the first novel, however, was a collection of four short stories which had been published in *Astounding* magazine between 1942 and 1944. The *Foundation* series is notable in relation to *Star Wars* for charting the rise and fall of an interplanetary civilization known as The Empire.

The *Foundation* novels are sometimes erroneously attributed to Lucas' very first treatment, although they are influential on the subsequent drafts where Lucas fashioned an environment that was more unique and developed. There is but one instance where Asimov's work may be cited in the synopsis, which is the "city-planet" Alderaan which is home to the Empire, which parallels Asimov's "city-planet" Trantor, home to the

Empire (though such a generic concept could arguably boil down to coincidence).

For whatever reasons, however, the story of the 1973 synopsis did not entirely satisfy Lucas. Unlike any of Lucas' other stories, this one does not tell the tale of someone, especially a youngster, taking their first steps into some kind of larger world, a theme running throughout all of Lucas' works, and perhaps Lucas felt that the Kurosawa source material restricted his imagination from the more outrageous and space opera-esque concepts milling about in his mind, the ones he had attempted to put down on paper with his *Journal of the Whills*. He began thinking about ways to transform the story into something more complicated and interesting, surrounding it with more prevalent comic-book influences and truly making it into a "superhero in outer space" adventure tale.

### The Screenplay Begins

Since Lucas had written the outline in May, *American Graffiti* had been released in August—and to everyone's surprise it was a hit! Made for well under a million dollars, the film would eventually gross over $100 million, making it the most profitable film in history. It was released at a time when independent filmmaking was beginning to dethrone the immovable studio system—*Easy Rider* had paved the way in 1969, giving the world a gritty and realistic film made for young people by young people, shot on the road for pennies (and often under the influence of drugs). Universal hoped to catch some of the market that had been created in *Easy Rider*'s wake, resulting in a handful of films made for under a million dollars and aimed at young adults, of which *American Graffiti* was a part of.* With its mega-success Lucas was hailed as the savior of independent filmmaking, being one of the few post-*Easy Rider* indie films to truly break into the mainstream, and in the aftermath of *American Graffiti* and *Godfather* (released the year before) a new wave of moviemaking finally broke open to popularity, such as Friedkin's *The Exorcist* and Scorsese's *Mean Streets* in 1973—it was an *American* New Wave (or "New Hollywood" as the press had labelled it).

---

* Other films in this production series were *The Hired Hand* (1971), *The Last Movie* (1971), *Taking Off* (1971), and *Silent Running* (1972), though the last title had a fairly substantial budget.

With the release of *American Graffiti* in August of 1973, Lucas was suddenly a known name in the film community and it is around here that the first published record of Lucas' *Star Wars* concept appears, this one way back to when he first began work on the project in 1973, in the midst of beginning work on the rough draft screenplay. Lucas said in the fall of 1973:

> *Star Wars* is a mixture of *Lawrence of Arabia*, the James Bond films and *2001*. The space aliens are the heroes, and the Homo Sapiens naturally the villains. Nobody has ever done anything like this since *Flash Gordon Conquers the Universe* in 1942.[41]*

United Artists passed on *Star Wars* when Lucas approached them with it in the summer of 1973, since it had been part of the initial deal made at Cannes in 1971, as did Universal, who had made *American Graffiti* but not yet released it.[42]** Lucas was fed up with the way Universal was bulldozing him with the troubled release negotiations for *Graffiti* and feared that they would accept *Star Wars*, as they had contractual first rights after United Artists. "We did not want to go with Universal," Lucas' lawyer Tom Pollock said.[43] Universal asked for more time to make its decision, but when the ten day waiting period was over Lucas was released of his obligation and sought another home for his film. Ten days after Universal passed, Twentieth Century Fox took on *Star Wars*. Lucas' bizarre fourteen-

---

* Lucas' description of it here shows how much more outrageous and comic-book-like he was making it.

** Although it is often thought that UA and Universal hated and did not understand Lucas' concept, this is not the case. In their rejection letter, UA states that "The innocence of the story, plus the sophistication of the world [Lucas] will depict makes for the best kind of motion picture. It is truly a film for children of all ages," but surmises that "There seems to be too much cost involved for this kind of juvenile story," and concluded it to be "a risky project." Universal concludes in its internal rejection memo "If the movie works, we might have a wonderful, humorous and exciting adventure-fantasy, an artistic and very commercial venture. Most of what we need is here. The question, in the end, is how much faith we have in Mr Lucas's ability to pull it all off." In other words, the script was well-liked but considered a risky project, and since Lucas' only film had bombed it was one the studios were not confident enough to take.

page outline had miraculously found a home due to the conviction of Alan Ladd jr., who had been smuggled an advance print of *American Graffiti*. Amazingly, the very synopsis Ladd signed on for could not possibly have been filmed—Lucas didn't tell him that it was a remake of *Hidden Fortress* and that he hadn't secured the rights from Toho studios. Luckily, by this point Lucas was developing an alternate storyline of his own. Ladd understood little of Lucas' obscure story but felt that he was talented. "When he said, 'This sequence is going to be like *The Sea Hawk* or this like *Captain Blood* or this like *Flash Gordon*,' I knew exactly what he was saying," Ladd told Dale Pollock. "That gave me confidence that he was going to pull it off."[44]

Ladd's decision proved very wise when *American Graffiti* was released three weeks later. In June of 1973, the *Star Wars* deal was closed, giving Lucas $50,000 to write and $100,000 to direct, more money than he had seen in his life, plus control of merchandising and sequel rights, and Gary Kurtz $50,000 for producing. The stunning success of *Graffiti* when it was released later in August finally gave George and Marcia true wealth, turning them into overnight millionaires. In the fall of that year they sold their tiny Mill Valley home and moved into a much larger one, and soon bought a Victorian house to use as an office in the nearby district of San Anselmo, 52 Parkway. "It was a house in itself, on an isolated piece of property," Gary Kurtz recalled in John Baxter's *Mythmaker*. "We could rent out rooms to other pictures, but it was only local; it wasn't a matter of advertising in the Hollywood trades for clients. First of all, it was always dubious whether we could legally have that as an office, since it was zoned as a single family residence, so we just didn't tell anybody. And nobody cared, really. San Anselmo is kind of lackadaisical about that kind of thing."[45] Lucasfilm had been created in 1971 at the suggestion of Lucas' lawyer Tom Pollock in order to legally protect Lucas, but now it was taking its first steps towards becoming an actual film company. The first employees were hired—Gary Kurtz' sister-in-law Bunny Alsup became Lucas' personal secretary, and Lucy Wilson became his financial book-keeper.[46] Michael Ritchie, Hal Barwood and Matthew Robbins rented space in the large house, which soon resembled a casual, Zoetrope-like atmosphere.

"George rented out rooms in his house to various filmmakers," Hal Barwood said in *The Making of Star Wars*. "And George of course had his offices there. He was living in another little house down in San Anselmo. And we would all stroll down the hill and walk off to various venues in San Anselmo and have lunch. And it was just a wonderful way, through enthusiastic conversation, to keep our interest in the movie business alive.

Because the movie business is very difficult for most of us; we don't usually get a majority of our projects to completion. Most of our dreams turn into screenplays, but they stall out at that stage. So it was a great way for us to encourage each other."[47]

Shortly after Lucas moved in, someone bought nearby property and built houses close to Lucas' property line. "He didn't like the fact that they were built," Kurtz told John Baxter. "And he bought them, just to keep them out of peoples hands. We used them for offices and editing rooms for a while. We used the garages for storing posters and film clips, and the houses for meeting rooms."[48] It was the beginnings of Lucas' empire-aspirations that would eventually become Skywalker Ranch.

"When I was writing *Star Wars*, for the first year, there was an infinite number of distractions," Lucas remembered in Rinzler's *Making of*. "*Graffiti* was a huge hit, plus I was restoring my office at the same time. Building a screening room kept me going for nine, ten months."[49]

Around September of 1973, Lucas began thoroughly reworking his synopsis into an actual script,[50] and had even begun preliminary work on it during a vacation he took after *Graffiti* was released[51] (likely sketching out the complex world he was creating), drifting away from Kurosawa and towards more outrageous space fantasy material.

The struggle to script *Star Wars* is legendary for its complications and evolutions—plot points, themes and characters changed and transformed with each draft to such an extent that an entire volume could be dedicated to exploring this aspect of *Star Wars'* history. Jan Helander provides the best assessment in his paper "The Development of Star Wars as Seen Through the Scripts of George Lucas." I will not delve into less relevant information but instead offer more abbreviated versions of the content.

Basically, there were four versions of the script, plus the initial treatment, totalling five, all written by Lucas (though one may count the initial *Journal of the Whills* summary as a sixth, and some of the script synopses may be viewed as "missing links" between the drafts). The first major development was the May 1973 story treatment already discussed. After that was done, he developed the story even further with the rough draft screenplay, first introducing the concept of the Jedi, here known as Jedi-Bendu as in the *Journal of the Whills*, a powerful group of intergalactic warriors sworn to protect the galaxy, and the Sith,[*] who are

---

[*] The term "Sith" is a tribute to Edgar Rice Burroughs, who first used that word in the first "John Carter of Mars" novel; Burroughs' Sith were fearsome Wasp-like creatures that were few in number but very difficult

*The Star Wars*

portrayed as a sinister warrior sect counteracting the Jedi-Bendu. It was a much different story from his previous synopsis, though he kept much of its characters and basic plot.

According to Lucas, because the elderly General Skywalker left little room for character development he shifted that character into a supporting role and turned the protagonist into an eighteen-year-old named Annikin Starkiller, perhaps someone Lucas could better relate to and whom kids could better identify with.[52] Annikin's brother Biggs is killed by a fearsome Sith knight in the opening scene, and the Sith is in turn killed by their father, Kane. Kane Starkiller and his friend the elderly General Luke Skywalker are the only two surviving Jedi left in the galaxy, having escaped death at the hands of the Sith knights who have hunted down all the other Jedi-Bendu. The two Jedi lead a rebel alliance against the Empire and destroy the "death star" space fortress. The Black Knight of the Sith and commander of the Empire's legions is Prince Valorum, who is assisted by his General, a man named Darth Vader.

Here the story begins to differ drastically from *The Hidden Fortress*. Had Lucas gone and filmed his treatment he would have had on his hands the biggest plagiarism lawsuit in cinematic history—he *had* to change the story. Of course, since August of that year the Lucases had become millionaires due to the success of *American Graffiti*—if Lucas truly wanted to he could have easily purchased *Hidden Fortress*, especially since Fox had agreed to develop his treatment, and so his inaction to do so indicates that he merely felt he could develop the story better if he was not so strict at following Kurosawa's source material.

Instead, Lucas began combing the annals of science fiction literature for inspiration for a more original tale. It seems as though Lucas was not interested in creating something of his own but more in taking from that which he enjoyed—first failing to remake *Flash Gordon* and then failing to remake *The Hidden Fortress*. "If someone tells me an interesting story, I can easily transform it into a screenplay," Lucas once said to Rinzler. "But to be the initiator of the idea, that's very difficult."[53]

The film was ever-present on his mind, obsessing him. "I'll wake up in the middle of the night sometimes, thinking of things, and I'll come up with ideas and write them down," he said at the time. "Even when I'm driving, I come up with ideas. I come up with a lot of ideas when I'm taking a shower in the morning."[54] Lucas explains this further in an interview quoted in *The Unauthorized Star Wars Compendium*:

_____

to kill.

On our first vacation after I'd directed *American Graffiti*, my wife, Marcia, and I went to Hawaii. That was great except that I wrote the whole time I was there. I'd already started thinking about *Star Wars*. A director can leave his work at the studio; a writer can't. There's always a pen and paper available. A writer is thinking about what he's supposed to be doing, whether he's actually doing it or not, every waking hour. He's constantly pondering problems. I always carry a little notebook around and sit and write in it. It's terrible, I can't get away from it.[55]

It is here, when Lucas began to write his own original tale, that the true agony of writing *Star Wars* began. Lucas read science fiction magazines, bought armfuls of pulp fiction and comic books and even looked into fairy tales and children's stories—anything he could get ideas from. It would be a slow and difficult process. Dale Pollock recounted the period:

*Star Wars* ruled Lucas's life. He carried a small notebook in which he jotted down names, ideas, plot angles—anything that popped into his head. On the first page in the notebook was a notation scribbled during the sound mixing of *Graffiti*. Walter Murch had asked him for R2, D2 (Reel 2, Dialog 2) of the film, and Lucas liked the abbreviated sound of R2-D2.

Lucas returned from the local newsstand each weekend with a large collection of science-fiction magazines and comic books. Marcia wondered what was going on, but George told her not to worry, he was making a movie that ten-year-old boys would love...he thoroughly researched the science-fiction field from *Buck Rogers* and *Flash Gordon* to Stanley Kubrick's watershed film *2001: A Space Odyssey*, made in 1968...Lucas also borrowed liberally from the Flash Gordon serials he had watched as a child, transplanting video screens, medieval costumes, art deco sets, and blaster guns to *Star Wars*...Lucas used Ming, the evil ruler of Mongo in the Flash Gordon books, as another model for his emperor. Alex Raymond's *Iron Men of Mongo* describes a five-foot-tall metal man of dusky copper who is trained to speak in polite phrases. From *John Carter on Mars* came banthas, beasts of burden in *Star Wars*; Lucas also incorporated into his early screenplay drafts huge flying birds described by Edgar Rice Burroughs. George watched scores of old films, from *Forbidden Planet* to *The Day the World Ended*, and read contemporary sci-fi novels like *Dune* by Frank Herbert and E.E. "Doc" Smith's *Lensmen* saga.[56]

It is here that the earliest origin of *Star Wars* comes from: not from myth and legend, but from the "schlock" sold on newsstands and played in matinees. Lucas revealed to *Starlog* in 1981: "I have to admit that I read *Starlog*. Starting in 1973 I was very much focused on science fiction—the genre people, the conventions, the magazines, every fantasy thing I could get my hands on—to see where everybody's head was."[57] While the media, in the '80s and '90s, would expound primarily upon the film's ties to King Arthur and The Odyssey, *Star Wars*' origins are rooted in quite the opposite, in comic books and pulp science fiction, the "trash" of literature. Trying to move away from *Hidden Fortress*, he dressed the simplistic plot with an assortment of elements from science fiction, in time culling everything from comic book writers Alex Raymond and Jack Kirby to science fiction sages E.E. Smith and Isaac Asimov, peppered with cinematic influences of everything from John Ford's *The Searchers* to Nazi propaganda milestone *Triumph of the Will* and infused with the constant action and thrill-ride plotting of the 1930s serials.

It was the cumulative influence and absorption of all of this material—including myths and fairy tales, especially in later drafts—that eventually informed the film. Direct elements from a particular film, indirect elements from a genre of novels, iconography from comic books, certain repeated themes from fairy tales, a memorable scene from a movie remade in a different way—many of the influences in *Star Wars* don't come from willful copying or deliberate academic design but rather the unconscious absorption of the whole of these things, of millions of stories, images, scenes, themes and characters that Lucas had been exposed to, from a variety of media. When *Star Wars* was released many critics saw it as a *homage* piece since it was brimming with references to other films, novels and stories, whether directly or indirectly. Although much of it was indeed deliberate mimicry, much of it was also simply due to a sort of unconscious synthesis.

For example, Martin Scorsese would later state that Lucas screened *Adventures of Robin Hood*,[58] and while there are no specific references to that film in *Star Wars*, its style and tone is quite similar, and certain elements such as swashbucklers, sword-duelling and a secret rebellion against a tyrant can be found in common, elements which also are informed by influences taken from other sources (for instance, the swashbucklers in *Star Wars* also are given a spin in the direction of the old west and the superheroics of *Flash Gordon*, while the sword duels fused with the samurai tradition of Japan, and the rebellion plot is common to everything from *Flash Gordon* to *Dune* and hence not owing influence to either of them alone but rather a more indirect amalgamation of all three and more). As Lucas has said, the "research," if one can call it that, gave him feelings for themes and motifs[59] but it was the combined sum of these elements that trickled out of him and into the script, explaining the enormous catalogue of references and influences in the film. "[Analysing it] becomes academic, and when I was doing it it wasn't academic," he said.[60]

At some point, though, Lucas had to finally get to writing the first screenplay of his *Star Wars*. Returning to the more exotic and space opera-like world that his convoluted *Journal of the Whills* had instigated, he prepared himself with the same method he had used at the beginning of that year—by making lists of names. "Kane Highsinger/Jedi friend; Leia Aquilae/Princess; General Vader/Imperial Commander; Han Solo/ friend."[61] He also lists "Seethreepio" and "Artwo Deetwo" as "workmen" in his notes but then later ponders "two workmen as robots? One dwarf/one Metropolis style," the latter in reference to the mechanical woman of Fritz Lang's 1927 film; the idea of robotic workmen characters stuck, as a later note reads "Make film more point-of-view of robots."[62]

Trying to re-develop his story, Lucas expelled his thoughts onto paper by scribbling down notes, some of them specific directions and ideas, some of them vague and ending in question marks, almost stream-of-conscious-like. Jonathan Rinzler transcribed some of these notes as Lucas attempted to develop a new world and set of characters in the latter part of 1973:

> Theme: Aquilae is a small independent country like North Vietnam threatened by a neighbour or provincial rebellion, instigated by gangsters aided by empire. Fight to get rightful planet back. Half of system has been lost to gangsters...The empire is like America ten years from now, after gangsters assassinated the Emperor and were elevated to power in a rigged election...We are at a turning point: fascism or revolution
>
> ...Notes on new beginning...for three main characters—the general, the princess, the boy (Starkiller)—make development chart...Put time-limit in children's packs...every scene must be set up and linked to next...make scene where Starkiller visits with old friend on Alderaan...Han very old (150 years)...Establish impossibility of Death Star...Should threat be bigger, more sinister?...A conflict between freedom and conformity...Tell at least two stories: Starkiller becomes a man (not good enough); Valorum wakes up (morally speaking)...Valorum like Green Beret who realises wrong of Empire...Second thoughts about Plot...Make Owen Lars a geologist or something...The general addresses men...Skywalker leaps across (ramp being pulled away)...thundersaber...[63]

The most significant additions in Lucas' first full-length script were the Sith and Jedi, two rival warrior sects, the latter of which had been peacekeepers of the galaxy until they were wiped out by the former. The concept of the Jedi was created as a basic sci-fi adaptation of the samurai warriors from Kurosawa's films—they are neither superhero-like nor mystical in this version. General Luke Skywalker is still the same character from the synopsis, a port of General Makabe from *The Hidden Fortress*.

The growth that Lucas now gave him was that he is now known as a "Jedi-Bendu," returning to the terminology from the *Journal of the Whills* summary—making the concept of the Jedi from the very beginning synonymous with the military, being the primary forces of the "Imperial Space Force," according to the rough draft. The Force does not exist yet, so naturally they have no super-human powers. Like the samurai, the Jedi-Bendu have been disbanded by the new corrupt Emperor, slowly withering away and being killed off by rivals.

Lucas had transferred General Skywalker to a supporting role and turned the main character into a boy, his apprentice, whom he now named "Starkiller" (to be expanded into "Annikin Starkiller"—his *Journal of the Whills* era writings list a similar name, Anakin Starkiller). Lucas' notes refer to the three characters of the story—like *Hidden Fortress*, there is a princess and a general, but now there is a third character. "Three main characters—the general, the princess, the boy (Starkiller)," Lucas writes. He also developed a comrade of General Skywalker's; Lucas' early notes list "Kane Highsinger" as "Jedi friend." But Lucas soon made a transformation whose repercussions would later echo down to the heart of his future story: it would be General Skywalker who would become the "Jedi friend," while the boy, Annikin Starkiller, would instead be apprentice to Kane—his father. "Kane Highsinger" became "Kane Starkiller," the noble Jedi father of the young hero.[64]

At some point, Lucas also added a younger brother, who would be named Deak—his story was slowly becoming a family affair.

Isaac Asimov's *Foundation* series was incorporated into the setting of Lucas' script, building on the synopsis which had simply adapted Japan's feudal empire which was at war with itself in *Hidden Fortress* into "The Empire." However, while we are now used to the familiar version of *Star Wars* history in which a Republic turns into an Empire after an evil ruler takes over, in Lucas' initial script the history was more like Asimov's *Foundation*, where there was no Republic, only the Empire, a benevolent one of which the Jedi were guardians, until a civil war erupted and a corrupt Emperor took over. The opening text roll-up from the rough draft explains:

> Until the recent GREAT REBELLION, the JEDI BENDU were the most feared warriors in the universe. For one hundred thousand years, generations of JEDI perfected their art as the personal bodyguards of the emperor. They were the chief architects of the invincible IMPERIAL SPACE FORCE which expanded the EMPIRE across the galaxy, from the celestial equator to the farthest reaches of the GREAT RIFT.

Now these legendary warriors are all but extinct. One by one they have been hunted down and destroyed as enemies of the NEW EMPIRE by a ferocious and sinister rival warrior sect, THE KNIGHTS OF SITH.

Lucas also created a number of villain characters, as his initial 1973 outline had no antagonist, plundering General Hyoe Tadokoro from *Hidden Fortress* and splitting him into two personas, calling one Prince Valorum, a Sith Knight who took on Tadokoro's warrior side, and calling the other General Darth Vader, who took on Tadokoro's military side as a villainous henchman.

With all of these elements thrown into the story it now began to resemble a more original creation, however, re-building his treatment from the ground up using a myriad of science fiction pieces made the screenwriting process a long and laborious one. Dale Pollock described the torturous period of creating *Star Wars*:

Lucas confined himself to the writing room he had built in the back of Parkhouse. He spent eight hours a day there, five days a week, writing draft after draft. It was worse than being in school. His smooth features grew haggard, the brown eyes behind the horn-rimmed glasses became bleary, and his scraggly beard went untrimmed. His writing room was tastefully furnished, with a large photograph of pioneer film editor Sergei Eisenstein on one wall and a poster from *THX* facing it from across the room. Lucas's prize 1941 Wurlitzer jukebox, a garish pink-and-purple creation resembling a neon gas pump, dominated the room. George had a self-imposed rule: no music until his daily allotment of script pages was completed. Some days he wrote nothing at all and slammed the door behind him in frustration when it was time for Walter Cronkite and the "CBS Evening News," his traditional quitting time..."You beat your head against the wall and say, 'Why can't I make this work? Why aren't I smarter? Why can't I do what everybody else can do?'" His creative limitations were his own limitations as a person: his inability to express emotions crippled him as a writer...Instead, he suffered stomach and chest pains and headaches until the script was finished.

Lucas tried all kinds of approaches to writing. He organized the screenplay by writing so much description, a short patch of dialog, then more description in the hope that everything would balance.[65]

The agonising scripting turned him into a true obsessive-compulsive. All his *Star Wars* drafts (as well as those for *THX* and *Graffiti*) were written by hand on carefully selected blue-and-green-lined paper, and he used only number two hard lead pencils. If his secretary, Lucy Wilson, didn't buy the right brand he would lecture her on the importance of conforming to his specific instructions (echoes of the L.M. Morris business perhaps). Lucas' weirdest quirk was to cut off his hair with a pair of scissors when he felt frustrated. "I came in one day and his wastebasket had tons of hair in it!" Wilson said to Dale Pollock. "It was driving him that crazy."[66] Lucas made his approach to the writing process explicit in *The Making of Star Wars*:

> I grew up in a middle-class Midwest-style American town with the corresponding work ethic...So I sit at my desk eight hours a day no matter what happens, even if I don't write anything. It's a terrible way to live. But I do it; I sit down and I do it...I put a big calendar on my wall. Tuesday I have to be on page twenty-five, Wednesday on page thirty, and so on. And every day I "X" it off—*I did those five pages*. And if I do my five pages early, I get to quit. Never happens. I've always got about one page done by four o'clock in the afternoon, and during the next hour I usually write the rest. Sometimes I'll get up early and write lots of pages, but that doesn't really happen much.[67]

In early 1974, Marcia joined the production of Martin Scorsese's *Alice Doesn't Live Here Anymore* and was editing on location in Arizona. Lucas didn't like being separated and decided to join her, locking himself in a hotel room and trying to hash out his script as it slowly drove him mad. "I remember George was writing *Star Wars* at the time," Scorsese said to author Jonathan Rinzler. "He had all these books with him, like Isaac Asimov's *Guide to the Bible*, and he was envisioning this fantasy epic. He did explain that he wanted to tap into the collective unconscious of fairy tales. And he screened certain movies, like Howard Hawks' *Air Force* [1943] and Michael Curtiz's *Robin Hood* [1938]."[68]

Finally, an entire year after he finished his first treatment, Lucas emerged with a rough draft screenplay. It was called "The Star Wars" and was dated May 1974. This gruelling time period is indicative of the struggle Lucas was going through in trying to tell his story.

Jan Helander summarized the rough draft:

> Kane Starkiller, a Jedi-Bendu master, is in hiding on the Fourth Moon of Utapau with his two sons Annikin and Deak, when a Sith warrior finds them and Deak is killed. The surviving Starkillers head to the Aquilae system, where they are met by Kane's old Jedi friend, General Luke Skywalker. Kane, whose war-battered body is a concoction of artificial limbs, knows that he is dying, and persuades Luke to become Annikin's Jedi teacher. He then travels to the city of Gordon, leaving his son with Skywalker and the King of Aquilae. Clieg Whitsun, a rebel spy on the emperor's planet of Alderaan, has learned that an Imperial fleet, led by General Darth Vader and Governor Crispin Hoedaack, is about to conquer Aquilae with a "death star" space fortress. Rebel fighters

are sent out to stop the attack, but the Aquilaean king is killed, and instead of Princess Leia (the rightful heir), a corrupt senator takes over, surrendering the planet to the Empire.

Annikin, Luke and Whitsun, joined by Artwo Detwo and See Threepio (two bickering robots who have escaped from the space fortress), bring Leia and her two younger brothers to the spaceport at Gordon, from where they can reach safety. After a fight at a cantina, where Skywalker uses his "lasersword" to kill his antagonists, the group meet up with Kane and his alien friend Han Solo who have arranged transport to a friendly planet. They need a power unit for suspended animation in order to get past Imperial scanners, and Kane heroically rips one from his body, causing his death. After avoiding a trap set by Vader and Prince Valorum (the black Knight of the Sith), the rebels are pursued into space, where the arguing Leia and Annikin realize that they love each other. Their craft is damaged in an asteroid field and Whitsun dies as it explodes, but the others abandon ship in time and land on the jungle planet of Yavin, where Leia is captured by alien trappers. Annikin tries to rescue her, but only succeeds in freeing five "Wookees" (huge, grey and furry beasts), and Leia eventually ends up in the hands of the Empire.

After a tip from two anthropologists, the rebels and the Wookee tribe (including Prince Chewbacca) attack an Imperial outpost, and a forest battle ensues. When he learns that Leia is held captive aboard the space fortress, General Skywalker starts training the Wookees to fly fighter ships in order to conquer the death star. Annikin is sceptical of the plan and gets onto the fortress (together with Artwo) on a mission of his own, dressed as an Imperial "skyraider", but he is soon captured and tortured by General Vader. Valorum sees this and realizes that the Imperials are completely without honour and codes, and that he has more in common with the young Jedi than with the emperor. Turning his back on the Empire, he frees both Annikin and Leia, and they escape down a garbage chute. After almost being crushed in the garbage receptacle, Valorum, Leia, Annikin, and Artwo manage to abandon the station just before the Wookees destroy it, killing both Vader and Governor Hoedaack. Back in her throne room, Queen Leia honours the heroes (including Valorum), and Annikin is appointed new Lord Protector of Aquilae.[69]

This rough draft was a huge step up from the outline previously written. It was also very large, with nearly two hundred scenes, and in the end, would be condensed for the final film, with some of the other scenes recycled in the eventual sequels. When you hear Lucas speak of the script that was too long to be one movie, the one which he supposedly cut into a third and used the other two thirds for *Empire* and *Jedi*, this is the one he is referring to. However, the story bears no resemblance to any of the subsequent films. Concepts are retained, like mechanical limbs, asteroid belt chases and Wookie forest battles (later to become Ewoks), and some names are later recycled throughout the series, but the "epic" story contained in this draft is basically a more elaborate version of a prototype *Star Wars*, loosely based off of *The Hidden Fortress*.

A typical example of Lucas' description of the matter, this one from 2002:

> When I started to write it, it got to be too big, it got to be 250, 300 pages...I said, well, I can't do this. The studio will never allow this. I will take the first half, make a movie out of that, and then I was determined to come back and finish the other three, or other two stories.[70]

Variations on this statement can be found ad nauseam (in some versions with him explicitly describing how his "original script" which he split apart ended with the forest and Death Star battles, indicating that he is indeed referencing the rough draft of 1974[71]).

Aside from the fact that the rough draft was only 132 pages—making it twenty-four pages *shorter* than the final screenplay, and not the exaggerated behemoth he claims—the basic plot is remarkably similar to the final film. The protagonist is introduced on a desolate planet, travels to a spaceport with his mentor, is involved in a cantina brawl, recruits Han Solo and rescues the princess from the space fortress, ending with its destruction by one-man fighter ships, while the mentor is earlier killed and medals are bestowed by the princess in the triumphant ending.

Moreover, when relating this screenplay to the later storyline, Darth Vader as we know him would still not come to be created for many years, and in fact would not be finalized until the 1980s. His character is hardly in this first script, and is nothing more than a minor villain General, nor is he monstrous, memorable or even a Sith Lord; instead he is a slimy Imperial, a spineless General who likes to give orders and collect the spoils of war. A particularly illustrative sense of what this General Darth Vader's characterisation was like can be seen from this excerpt wherein he finally meets Prince Valorum in the first half of the story:

66. LIBRARY - PALACE OF LITE - AQUILAE
The king's old library has been converted into an office for General Vader. He is sitting behind his desk as Prince Valorum, the black knight of Sith, enters and salutes. The black knight is dressed in the fascist black and chrome uniform of the legendary Sith One Hundred. The general returns his salute.

VADER
Welcome, Prince Valorum. Your exploits are legendary. I have long waited to meet a Knight of the Sith. If there is any way I can assist you, my entire command is at your bidding.

VALORUM
I want a tie-in to your computer network, a control center, and communication access.

VADER
Right away! I'll also transfer all information we have on the general. His command post was self-destroyed, but we believe he is still alive. .... Do you really believe he's a Jedi?

VALORUM
If he was not a Jedi, I wouldn't be here.

Lucas admitted in 1983 that no script contained the whole story and that he simply reused deleted concepts in the sequels:

> There are four or five scripts for *Star Wars*, and you can see as you flip through them where certain ideas germinated and how the story developed. There was never a script completed that had the entire story as it exists now...As the stories unfolded, I would take certain ideas and save them; I'd put them aside in notebooks. As I was writing *Star Wars*, I kept taking out all the good parts, and I just kept telling myself I would make other movies someday. It was a mind trip I laid on myself to get me through the script. I just kept taking out stuff, and finally with *Star Wars* I felt I had one little incident that introduced the characters. So for the last six years [1977-1983] I've been trying to get rid of all the ideas I generated and felt so bad about throwing out in the first place.[72]

### Heroes and Villains

The single most important issue introduced here in the first draft is the one which will later become the focus of the "Saga" story: Darth Vader.

Darth Vader was not the mechanical, black-knight "I am your father" super-villain/fallen-hero we know today. Rather, he was simply a man, albeit a "tall grim-looking" one according to the rough draft, but merely a man. And not only that, he is a relatively minor one, acting as more of a bodyguard or muscleman for the Galactic Empire, and he dies along with Governor Hoedaack when the giant "Space Fortress" is blown up by the Wookie attack ships. He doesn't wear his trademark costume or mask—those don't appear until the second draft and wouldn't even become permanent fixtures until the final.

This first draft does however contain a number of separate elements that, in time, would be combined to form the basis of the Vader which we are all familiar with. In simplifying the complicated first draft, Lucas eliminated many characters and elements for the second draft, and instead made the script more focused by combining these, and in the formation of Darth Vader this occurred more than anywhere else.

First, the Imperial bad guy with the name Darth Vader, as discussed above. I must stress that this character bears little relation to the one we are familiar with, and is simply a human General who shares his name (Lucas shuffled names around freely, as will soon become evident). However, he fills the *role* of Darth Vader in the final film—he is the Empire's muscle, a henchman who orders officers and tortures the Rebels.

Second, the idea of a Sith Lord redeeming himself and turning to good. However, it is not Vader, but his boss, Prince Valorum, who, unlike Darth Vader in this draft, is a knight of the Sith. Valorum is also an expert at exterminating Jedi, and along with the other Sith Knights has hunted down and killed all the Jedi-Bendu. When the hero Annikin infiltrates the space fortress Leia has been captured in, he is caught and tortured by General Vader. Valorum sees this and realises that the Imperials are without morals, without any respect for the higher samurai-like code of honour that the Jedi-Bendu and Sith subscribe to. He turns his back on the Empire and helps the heroes escape, and together they free the princess and leave the station just as it is destroyed.

This character, it may be noted, appears to be loosely based off of General Hyoe Tadokoro from *The Hidden Fortress*, continuing Lucas' porting of Kurosawa's film. In that film the heroes are captured and about to be executed when an arch-opponent of General Makabe (Makabe would become the Kenobi character, named Luke Skywalker in this draft) and also a leader in the clan about to execute them comes to pay his last respects. Since he has lost a duel to Makabe earlier in the film his master has punished his defeat by hideously scarring him. The captured princess remarks that General Tadokoro's master must be cruel to punish him so brutally, and Tadokoro realises that the heroes are nobler than his own forces—he turns on his men, freeing the heroes and escaping with them to safety.

Third, the concept of a family of Jedi. Similar to the "Saga" story which tells of a son (Luke), a daughter (Leia), a father (Anakin-Vader) and a mentor (Obi Wan), the dynamic of a family with Jedi ties is introduced here. Annikin is the son of Kane—Kane is one of two surviving Jedi left, and will not be able to train his sons because he is dying. After Annikin's brother Deak is killed in the opening scene, Kane introduces Annikin to his friend Luke Skywalker, the other elder remaining Jedi, and requests that Luke train Annikin in the Jedi ways. The names may be confusing here—they aren't necessarily the same character as in the film. Kane would become Anakin Skywalker, Annikin would become Luke Skywalker, and Luke would become Obi Wan. To get a clearer picture of where the story was headed: Father Skywalker (a.k.a. Anakin), a Jedi who has become half machine in his battles, takes his son Luke to his Jedi friend Obi Wan Kenobi to train him in the Jedi ways.

Fourth is the concept of a man who is becoming a machine, or more specifically a *father* who is becoming a machine. Kane Starkiller is revealed to have all of his limbs replaced with artificial ones, and even parts of his organs, a by-product of years of battle. As a result, he is dying, and requests his friend General Luke Skywalker to train his son Annikin when he dies. He later sacrifices himself by ripping a power unit from his body in order for his son and friends to be able to use it to freeze themselves in suspended animation and avoid Imperial scanners.

So here you have four different aspects, which, when combined together, would form the Darth Vader character presented in the "Saga" version of *Star Wars*. But they are all separate, and will stay that way for many more years, slowly being combined bit by bit in the sequels.

Similarly, although Prince Valorum's renunciation of the Sith/Empire is vaguely reminiscent of the finale of *Return of the Jedi*, the character is wholly and distinctly separate, and bears little resemblance to the Darth Vader of the final storyline; even Valorum's renunciation of the Empire is totally different in nature and style from what appears in *Return of the Jedi*, and is similar only in premise. Additionally, the Sith are less like the evil sorcerer-cult seen in the final films and more like a mercenary band of pirates, thus allegiance is more rough and tumble, rather than the final saga in which one pledges their soul.

### The Force of Others

It is interesting to note that the Force is not existent in this draft—the phrase "may the force of others be with you" is used, but it is merely a generic "good luck" phrase, and is used casually by various people in the script, as are expressions such as "thank god." Most agree that it is a play off of the Christian phrase "May God be with you," intended as a sort of ambiguous science fiction version of a theistic colloquialism. When Lucas began writing the second draft he would transform the samurai-inspired Jedi-Bendu of the rough draft into characters based on E.E. Smith's

Lensmen, making them super-powered warriors. In determining the source of their power, Lucas took his "force of others" reference and turned it into a supernatural power, coupled with a crystal called the Kiber crystal which acts in a similar manner to the Lensmen's lenses, increasing one's natural abilities. The concept behind the eventual "force of others" appears in many science fiction works as a means of giving a general, universal supernatural belief system; for instance, in Jack Kirby's *New Gods* comic books it was called "The Source," and gave the heroes their strength, while in E.E. Smith's Lensmen series it was "The Cosmic All." Lucas himself even admitted this privately to Mark Hamill: "I asked him about the origin of the idea, and he said it's in about 450 old science fiction novels," Hamill told *Preview* magazine in 1983. "He's the first to admit it's not an original concept. It's nice how George presented the idea so everyone can get as much or as little out of it as they want. Some see it as a very religious thing."[73]

The vague notion of some kind of general spiritual belief also has its roots in the New Age spiritualism movement that saturated the hippie-populated San Francisco area in the '60s and '70s, where self-proclaimed gurus indulged in the newly-discovered eastern mysticism. After the Christian stronghold of the 1950s, the aboriginal and eastern spiritualisms were embraced with open arms by counterculturalists looking to experiment and open their minds to alternate systems of belief. They eventually combined all of these beliefs into their own generalised one, calling it a "New Age" religion, a main tenet of which was the belief that all lifeforms emitted some kind of life-energy that flowed throughout the universe. This type of belief was mainly adopted from the east, where it was the Japanese Ki and the Chinese Qi/Chi, but it is found in various aboriginal creeds as well, and is one of the oldest forms of supernatural belief, appearing in ancient Egypt as the Ka. This type of "life-energy" or "life-force" belief was common in the 1970s when New Age spiritualism reached its peak, as were those terms, which also explains its surfacing in science fiction at that time, such as in 1973's *The New Gods*—its appearance in *Star Wars* can be seen as a commentary on the culture of the 1970s.

An oft-reported claim is that Lucas got the term and basic concept of "the force of others" from Carlos Castaneda's book *Tales of Power*, a semi-anthropological account of the author's encounters with a Mexican shaman named Don Juan which talks about warrior mysticism. Castaneda's books had been published since the late '60s, starting with *The Teachings of Don Juan* in 1968, and were very influential in the rising popularity of such mysticism in America.* His early books frequently equate "will" with being a "force" and "force" with "power." In *Tales of Power*, Castaneda also occasionally refers to the soul as the "force of life." This is all a bit of a stretch, however. The error of the *Tales of Power* link is that *Tales of Power* was published in 1975, many months *after* Lucas would have already invented the basic premise of "the force of others" being a supernatural power, in fact many months after Lucas had *completed* the second draft where this is the case. Even Castaneda's seldom and casual reference to "force of life" is a highly unoriginal notion, as the concept of the soul as "a force," "life force," "energy force," "life energy," "force of life," and many similar such terms was common and popular amongst New Age spiritualists by that point. He was, in fact, drawing from the same cultural belief of the 1960s which Lucas himself was reflecting.

Additionally, the strongest supposed influence from Castaneda appears in his book *The Eagle's Gift*, where he describes an energy which defines and shapes the universe and emanates from all living things, finally detailing the vague "force of life" which he earlier spoke of. However, *The Eagle's Gift*, like the frequently cited *Tales of Power*, is published far too late to be an influence—*The Eagle's Gift*, very obviously similar to Lucas' concept of the Force in specific details, was published in 1981. In fact, Castaneda was highly criticised by real anthropologists once his work became known, and many inconsistencies and fabrications have been unearthed—most actual anthropologists believe that Castaneda was making up most of the content, especially since the books have more in common with novels than non-fiction, and he is now regarded as a fraud. Thus, the influence may have been the complete reverse—*Star Wars*' "the Force" may have influenced *Castaneda*, which is why the only explicit link appears well after *Star Wars*, and especially the more spiritual *Empire Strikes Back*, was released. The books were very popular with young people, especially the 1970s New Age spiritualists who dug the similar themes in *Star Wars*—however, most probably didn't realise that there was no relation between the film and Castaneda (at least in this regard—the Don Juan character would have an impact on a certain *Star Wars* character, as we will later see).

---

* Although the Force is absent of any sort of immediate Castaneda influence, Lucas was obviously familiar with Castaneda's work, as it would have been prominent in the Bay area of San Francisco, and Lucas would later make references to it.

Like the film's connection to Joseph Campbell, it was one trumpeted by the intelligentsia after the film became popular in an attempt to explain the success through more scholarly influence. The truth is that "the Force" comes from comic books and science fiction novels if it is to come from any specific source, from Kirby's *New Gods* saga to Smith's Lensmen saga. But it is much more reasonable to observe that this is all a product of the 1970s culture itself, when such notions were "in the air" and especially common amongst young people, artists and those in the area in which Lucas was living. "The 'Force of others' is what all basic religions are based on, especially the Eastern religions," Lucas once said, "which is, essentially, that there is a force, God, whatever you want to call it."[74]

The name and concept behind the Force can also be vaguely traced in influence to experimental Canadian filmmaker Arthur Lipsett's *21-87*, one of the most influential films on Lucas during his years at USC. In one of the film's more memorable moments, the life-energy of the universe or god is referred to as a "force," again showing that the term and concept were common amongst counterculturalists long before Lucas made it famous. The audio clip Lipsett sampled comes from a conversation between artificial intelligence pioneer Warren S. McCulloch and cinematographer Roman Kroitor. McCulloch argues that living beings are simply highly complex machines, but Kroitor replies that there is something more to the universe: "Many people feel that in the contemplation of nature and in communication with other living things, they become aware of some kind of force, or something, behind this apparent mask which we see in front of us, and they call it God."

Steve Silberman brought the similarity to Lucas' attention in a 2005 interview with *Wired* magazine, to which Lucas said that his use of the term was "an echo of that phrase in 21-87."[75]

This specific reference might have influenced this scene from the first draft of *THX 1138*, which contains similar phrasing:

THX
...there must be something independent; a force, reality.

SRT
You mean OMM. [the state-sanctioned deity]

THX
Not like OMM as we know him, but the reality behind the illusion of OMM.[76]

## *The Movie Brats*

Lucas would turn his rough draft *The Star Wars* screenplay into a proper first draft in July of 1974. The only changes made were to names—for instance Kane Starkiller became Akira Valor, Deak Starkiller became Bink Valor, Annikin Starkiller became Justin Valor and Prince Valorum became General Dodona, while the Jedi Bendu became the Dai Noga and the Sith became the Legions of Lettow. The script was exactly the same otherwise. Lucas would revert to the names from the first version—the May 1974 rough draft—rather than the first draft when writing the subsequent scripts; the first draft is also fourteen pages longer than the rough, but no new scenes were added.

It had taken Lucas an entire year to write the rough draft screenplay—and another two months to revise it for the first draft. The creation of the second draft would be nearly just as difficult, finished six months later in January of 1975.

Lucas spoke about his burgeoning *Star Wars* in this rare 1974 interview:

Larry Sturhahn: Would you like to talk about your new film?

George Lucas: Well, it's science fiction—*Flash Gordon* genre; *2001* meets James Bond, outer space and space ships flying in it.

LS: *THX* was a kind of "process" film and *Graffiti* an autobiography—is the new film hooked to you personally?

GL: I'm a real fan of Flash Gordon, and this is a much more plotted, structured film than the other two. *THX* is a milieu film, and *Graffiti* is a character film, but the new one is plot-action-adventure. Since I've never done that before, it's hard to say exactly what it is. Take the first two and combine them with another side of me that hasn't been seen yet and you get this new film. But where it comes from I don't know.

Finally, you know, *American Graffiti* wasn't that hard to write. I did it in 3 weeks, but I've been working on this one for 6 months—it hasn't been easy at all. Maybe that has to do with having to make it up.

I'm doing it myself, like last time, but then I'll look at it and if I'm not entirely satisfied, I'll hire somebody to do a re-write. I discovered something on *Graffiti*, having re-written it twice myself: your mind gets locked into something and it's hard to break loose, to get new ideas, a fresh point of view. It pays to have somebody come in with fresh enthusiasm and a new look.[77]

And yet another early reference from Lucas, in *Film Quarterly* in the spring of '74:

> [*The Star Wars*] is a space opera in the tradition of *Flash Gordon* and *Buck Rogers*. It's James Bond and *2001* combined – super fantasy, capes and swords and laser guns and spaceships shooting each other, and all that sort of stuff. But it's not camp. It's meant to be an exciting action adventure film.[78]

Sometimes George and Marcia would hold barbeques from their San Anselmo "Parkhouse" home (as it was nicknamed); guests often included Gary Kurtz, Matthew Robbins, Hal Barwood, Walter Murch, Michael Ritchie, John Korty and occasionally the Huycks. While the wives cooked, the crowd of bearded men, cokes and beers in their hands, stood around and talked business (a popular topic being Francis Coppola's rising status and corresponding megalomania). Afterwards, Lucas would gather them up and read them his *Star Wars* script and tape record their reactions and criticisms.[79]* Not surprisingly, they understood little. "It was very difficult to tell what the man was talking about," Ritchie remembered.[80]

Francis Coppola saw the first draft as well, and was one of the few who liked it. "You finished the script and then you gave it to me," Coppola recalled in a 1999 conversation with Lucas. "I thought it was terrific. And then you totally changed it! And I kept saying 'Why are you changing it?'"[81] He particularly liked the more outrageous ideas, such as having Princess Leia as a fourteen-year-old girl (an inspiration from *Hidden Fortress*). "George became frightened of some of his own good ideas," Coppola said. "I think he shied away from his innovations somewhat."[82]

Lucas explained the collaborative nature of his circle of friends in *The Making of Star Wars*:

> I run around with a crowd of writers...with the Huycks and with John Milius, and both the Huycks and John Milius are fabulous. John can just sit there and it comes out of him, without even trying. It's just magic. The Huycks are the same way. With the first draft, I showed it to a group of friends who I help; having been an editor for a long time, I usually help them on their editing and they help me on my scriptwriting. They give me all their ideas and comments and whatnot, then I go back and try to deal with it. All of us have crossover

---

* Rinzler states on page 24 of his *Making of* that notes of Lucas' survive indicating he had given his draft to the following eight people: Matthew Robbins, Hal Barwood, Bill Huyck, Gloria Katz, John Milius, Haskell Wexler, Francis Ford Coppola, Phil Kaufman

relationships, and we are constantly showing each other what we are doing and trying to help each other.[83]

Gary Kurtz had an office in a bungalow on the Universal studios lot that Lucas sometimes made use of in order to avoid the Fox executives; Lucas' friend Steven Spielberg also had a bungalow office on the lot and the two would constantly check in on what each other was doing. Spielberg was preparing *Jaws* there at that time. On one occasion, Lucas and John Milius visited the studio space after hours where Spielberg showed them the giant mechanical shark undergoing construction. Spielberg grabbed the controls and began excitedly showing them how the mechanical beast worked, opening the enormous jaws which made a loud grinding noise like an oversized bear trap. Lucas climbed a ladder and poked his head inside the open mouth to see how it worked and Spielberg closed the jaws on him. As they laughed at Lucas' flailing Spielberg realised that the mouth wouldn't open, a troubling premonition of the mechanical failures on the film to come. Finally the mouth was pried apart and Lucas freed himself. The three of them ran back into the car and sped away from the scene of the crime, knowing they had broken an expensive piece of equipment.[84]

The friendship and co-operation within this circle of filmmakers was far-reaching; it was a time when ideas were fluid, collaboration was plentiful and all worked together to support each other. Like any movement in art, it was not one artists would be able to achieve operating independently—its success, both creatively and practically, depended on them remaining inter-connected.

During the troubled early period of scripting *Star Wars* Lucas also drifted to other projects, likely out of the frustrating difficulty he was encountering with his space opera. During the production of *American Graffiti*, Lucas had approached Willard Huyck and Gloria Katz with an idea for a screwball murder-mystery comedy set in the 1930s. "We came up with this idea of doing Ten Little Indians in a radio station," Lucas explained to author Marcus Hearn.[85] Lucas wrote a treatment and held story conferences with the Huycks, who then began work on a screenplay. Shortly after *Graffiti* was completed, Lucas was able to negotiate a deal with Universal to get the film made, and in July of 1974—just as Lucas finished his first draft of *Star Wars*—the Huycks also turned in their first draft, called *The Radioland Murders*. In an interview conducted with *Film Quarterly* in the spring of 1974 Lucas claimed that he would be tackling this film after *Star Wars*, though ultimately it would be plagued by set-backs for many decades.

Shortly later, Lucas developed "The Adventures of Indiana Smith," an action-packed tale about a globe-trotting treasure seeker based on the various jungle and adventure serials of the 1930s that Lucas had been mulling over since the genesis of *Star Wars* back in film school. In 1975 he would meet with Philip Kaufman and flesh out the story, however Kaufman was eventually called away by other filmmaking duties and the project was shelved.[86] The influence of this can be seen in the second draft of *Star Wars* from that same year where Luke is introduced as an aspiring archaeologist.

*Apocalypse Now* was also revived after the success of *Graffiti*, though it would ultimately dissolve into *Star Wars* itself. "We couldn't get any co-operation from any of the studios or the military, but once I had *American Graffiti* behind me I tried again and pretty much got a deal at Columbia. We scouted locations in the Philippines and were ready to go."[87] The *Apocalypse Now* deal would soon implode because Columbia wanted all the rights American Zoetrope controlled and Coppola refused to hand them over. "The deal collapsed," explained Lucas. "And when that deal collapsed, I started working on *Star Wars*."[88] With this, Lucas' *Apocalypse Now* was channelled into *Star Wars*' rough draft, giving the film a strong man versus machine theme and allegorical battles of primitives and rebels against a mechanised empire.

*Star Wars* refused to leave Lucas' mind and he pushed ahead with a second draft.

# Chapter III: Enter Luke Starkiller

"I FIND rewriting no more or less difficult than writing," Lucas once said. "Because when you write, sometimes you rationalise away particular problems. You say, *I'll deal with that later*. So I struggled through the first draft and dealt with some of the problems. But now the next step is even more painful, because I have to confront the problems in a more serious way."[1]

The impending creation of the second draft was a significant development. Building on the first draft, it added a number of expansions, the primary one being the development of "the force of others" into a literal superpower, thus giving the Jedi a more comic-book-like edge. E.E. Smith's *Galactic Patrol* played a prominent role in the plot as well, now featuring the droids jettisoning in a life-boat to bring Luke information about his father and the battle station. The bureaucrats from *Hidden Fortress* that had been downplayed for the rough draft would be re-instated by Lucas as main characters, once again as robots. It has been reported that they are based off Abbot and Costello, Laurel and Hardy, or any other number of comedy duos—they are not. They are merely a straight port of Tahei and Matashichi from *The Hidden Fortress* (who themselves may have been inspired by said comedians), right down to their dialogue. "Having two bureaucrats or peasants is really like having two clowns—it goes back to Shakespeare," Lucas offers, "which is probably where Kurosawa got it."[2]

The Jedi-Bendu and Sith knights of the first draft would be transformed from powerful samurai-like warriors to comic-book like superheroes, mainly due to the massive influence of E.E. "Doc" Smith's Lensmen characters, who first appeared in *Galactic Patrol*.

One of the most influential authors in the genre of science fiction, Edward Elmer Smith is credited with inventing the space opera sub-genre with his 1928 *Skylark of Space* story. Among his most popular works, however, is his Lensmen saga. In 1937, Smith published a novel, first appearing in the pages of *Astounding* Magazine, called *Galactic Patrol* which introduced an elite group of warriors with telepathic abilities known as the Lensmen. Similar to a race of super-police, they were peacekeepers of the galaxy. The Lensmen have said to be inspiration for a number of creations, including the Bene Gesserit super-warriors of *Dune*, which Lucas was also undoubtedly influenced by (the Bene Gesserit practice a technique called "Prana-Bindu," which is probably where Lucas got "bendu" in "Jedi-Bendu" from; hence, the Jedi-Bendu might be seen as an amalgam of the samurai—from "jidai geki"—and the Bene Gesserit and Lensmen—from "Prana-Bindu"). Author Stephen Hart pointed out in 2002:

> Like the Jedi, Lensmen enforce order throughout the galaxy with an arsenal of paranormal powers that render them virtually invincible in combat. Where Jedi pay homage to the Force, Lensmen invoke the "Cosmic All." Lucas' Jedi get their Force quotient boosted by microscopic entities called midichlorians; Smith's heroes are turbocharged by "lenses," collections of crystalline, semi-sentient life forms attuned to their personalities. An early draft of "Star Wars" revolved around...the "Kiber crystal," which sounds an awful lot like one of Smith's lenses. There are even hints that Lucas has worked a Lensman-style breeding program into his saga, judging from the story of Anakin Skywalker's immaculate conception in "The Phantom Menace."
>
> The scale of the action in the Lensman books is broader than anything in the Lucas universe—not content with wiping out whole planets, Smith's Lensmen detonate entire solar systems without breaking a sweat...The series underwent a successful paperback revival in the early 1970s, when Lucas was sweating out the first drafts of "Star Wars." Dale Pollock's biography "Skywalking: The Life and Films of George Lucas" puts the Lensman novels at the top of Lucas' pre-"Star Wars" reading list, though Pollock clearly didn't realize the extent of Smith's influence.[3]

Not only were the Lensmen obvious forerunners to the Jedi, but the plot of *Galactic Patrol* even features many plot elements and devices which would be plugged into *Star Wars*. Kristen Brennan observed:

*Galactic Patrol* tells the story of Kim Kinnison, a Lensman who jettisons in a space lifeboat with a data spool containing the secret of the enemy's ultimate weapon, the Grand Base. He jets around the galaxy in his speeder, gets caught in tractor beams, passes his ship off as a chunk of loose metal, eludes the bad guy's star cruisers by tearing off into the fourth dimension and finally destroys the enemy base in his one-man fighter. During his training he wears a flight helmet with the blast shield down, but he can still "see" what's going on using his special powers. The Lensmen's mystical powers are almost certainly a strong inspiration for The Force: In an early draft of the Star Wars script Lucas calls the good side of the Force "Ashla" and the bad side the "Bogan." In Smith's Lensmen books the benevolent creators of the Lens are the "Arisians," the bad guys the "Boskone."

   Lucas may have absorbed even the language of Smith, who uses the word "coruscant" at least a dozen times (it means "shiny and glittery").[4]

Not surprisingly, *Galactic Patrol* is seen sitting on a shelf in George Lucas' writing room in the first Episode I web documentary. It is clearly one of the primary influences on *Star Wars*.

Lucas' first script had so many action scenes and plot points that he briefly contemplated making two films out of it, with one film comprising the first half up to the triumphant rescue from Alderaan, and the second film beginning with the crash landing on the jungle planet of Yavin and the final attack on the space fortress.[5] However, it was clearly too ambitious a goal, considering that he was already encountering problems getting one film made, let alone stretching the script into two; instead, he made the script less jam-packed by simplifying it, cutting out many of the action sequences and allowing greater breathing room for character and plot.

Discarding much of the first draft, Lucas moved from Kurosawa to Kurosawa's figurative mentor, John Ford, transplanting eighteen-year-old Annikin Starkiller to a desolate farm and renaming him Luke. Lucas' earlier stories (*Journal of the Whills* and rough draft) had attempted to tell the tale of an apprenticeship between an old man and a young boy—but Lucas couldn't help but gravitate towards the youngster, and now the mentor figure disappeared almost entirely. Lucas found a greater identification with the young warrior-in-training, now amalgamating the character with his own adolescence, presenting the young protagonist as a much weaker and intellectual character who must embark on the heroic act of leaving the confines of his isolated home. Without even realising it, Lucas was writing himself into the film, and with this draft he developed the basic story and character that he would later expand into the film we are more familiar with. Appropriately, Lucas changed the name of the character from Annikin to a close approximation of his own, Luke.[*] "I was searching for a story for a long time," Lucas said in *The Making of Star Wars.* "Each story was a totally different story about totally different characters before I finally landed on *the* story."[6] Father Skywalker's physical presence was also made smaller in screentime yet conversely the character's importance grew larger as an emotional weight shadowing his son.

"I wrote from my point of view, as if I were going into that world. It was more fun to write that way and it helped me through the writing process. It's nearly impossible to separate an author from his characters. The hardest thing is to develop characters that aren't a reflection of the mind that creates them."[7]

Once again, Lucas explored character and plot developments through his notes. J.W. Rinzler quoted from some of them:

> Sith knights look like Linda Blair in *Exorcist*...Vader—do something evil in prison to Deak...Luke reluctantly accepts the burden (artist, not warrior, fear); establish Luke as good pilot...farm boy: fulfills the legend of the son of the sons; pulls sword from the stone. All he wants in life is to become a star pilot...Leia: tomboy, bright, tough, really soft and afraid; loves Luke but not admitting to it...Make Han in bar like Bogart—freelance tough guy for hire...whole film must be told from robots' point of view...timelock...the empire has a terrible new weapon, a fortress so powerful it can destroy a planet, possibly even a sun. It must be stopped before it can be put to use.[8]

In January of 1975, Lucas' second draft of *The Star Wars* was finally completed. The script now bore a convoluted title, being called:

ADVENTURES OF THE STARKILLER
(episode one)
'The Star Wars.'

Jan Helander offered the following summary of the second draft:

> Deak and Clieg, sons of the Starkiller, are on their way to their brother Luke on the planet Utapau, sent by their father to retrieve the diamond-like "Kiber Crystal" which a Jedi can use to intensify either side of the force a hundred fold. However, their ship is boarded by Lord Darth Vader (a Black Knight of the Sith) and his stormtroopers, and Clieg is killed. Vader believes that Deak is the last son of the Starkiller, and as Deak wears his father's crest, the Lord takes for granted that the Starkiller is dead, and that he has altered destiny by

---

[*] "I used that [name] because I was identifying with the character," he admits (Baxter, p. 157)

capturing "the son of the suns". Vader orders the attack of the rebel base on Ogana Major, not knowing that Artoo Detoo and See Threepio, two of Deak's robots (or "droids"), have escaped to Utapau in order to bring a message to Luke.

After a run-in with some filthy "Jawa" scavengers, they reach the farm where Luke lives with his two younger brothers Biggs and Windy, his Uncle Owen Lars and Aunt Beru, and their daughter Leia. Luke has never met his legendary father, and when he learns that he must bring the crystal to him he feels intimidated. Owen has taught Luke the ways of a skilled warrior (including the "laser sword"), but the spiritual ways of the Jedi can be taught only by his father. Accepting his destiny, Luke takes the crystal and leaves with the droids for the spaceport at Mos Eisley. There, Luke is forced to use his laser sword against three drunken creatures in a cantina, impressing Han Solo (who claims to be a starpilot) and his companion Chewbacca (a "Wookiee" creature), who offer Luke passage to Ogana Major for a huge sum of money. Han, who is merely a cabin boy, fakes a reactor failure on board his Captain Oxus's ship, tricking Oxus (and the crewman Jabba the Hutt) into evacuating. Han and Chewbacca, together with the ship's science officer Montross Holdaack, then lift off with Luke and the droids.

They reach Ogana Major only to find it completely destroyed. Believing his father is dead, Luke assures Han that his brother Deak will provide payment for the passage - but they will have to rescue him from the Imperial dungeons of Alderaan. Approaching Alderaan, they hide in secret compartments as the ship is towed inside the Imperial city. Their ship is searched without result, as Han and Luke take out two troopers and steal their uniforms. Montross stays behind as Han, Luke, Chewbacca (posing as a prisoner), and the droids leave for the detention area. They find the tortured Deak, and after escaping a horrible dungeon monster, Chewbacca manages to bring him back to the hangar. Luke and Han, however, are cornered by Sith knights and forced to jump down a debris chute, ending up in a garbage room, where they are about to be crushed when the droids rescue them. They reach the ship and blast off into space, defeating their pursuers in a dogfight.

As Luke uses the Kiber Crystal to heal his brother, he receives a mental message from his father, telling him to come to the new rebel base on the fourth moon of Yavin. On the jungle moon, Luke meets his wizened old father for the first time, but the "Death Star" (the battle station which destroyed Ogana Major) is approaching, and Luke's Jedi training will have to wait. An assault on the station is organized, but Han, content with his momentous reward, leaves with Chewbacca and Montross, refusing to help. With Threepio and the ranger Bail Antilles as his gunners, Luke pilots one of the rebel ships attacking the Death Star, while his father uses the crystal to fight the Bogan. Sensing the Ashla, Lord Vader realizes that the Starkiller is alive, and joins the battle in his own fighter. He is just about to destroy Luke's ship, when Han reappears, sending the Sith knight to his doom. In a final attempt, both Threepio and Antilles manage to hit the station's weak point, reducing the mighty fortress to space dust. Back at the base, the heroes are greeted by the Starkiller who praises their victory as the start of the revolution.[9]

Lucas continued to develop his story, with this second draft containing some wildly different ideas, such as Leia as a cameo character with Deak being the one captured, Father Skywalker having over a half dozen sons (the precise number is never specified), and a Kiber crystal which has the power to intensify Force powers. Mysticism also plays a bigger role, recalling *Dune*, with Holy Text-quoting and prophecy. The story was significantly overhauled and rethought, now transforming from an "escape" type of film, as the first draft was for much of it (owing to its *Hidden Fortress* lineage), and instead re-configured as a more fairy-tale-style "quest" type of story, with Luke embarking on a Frodo Baggins-like journey. Lucas shuffled the plot points around and re-organized the set-pieces like a shifting puzzle—the cantina brawl was retained, as was smuggler Han Solo, as an important threshold-crossing; the rescue and escape from the space fortress (now named Alderaan) was moved from the end to the middle of the film and now became a story focus; Yavin was cut out, but to keep the space-dogfight and the Death Star assault set-pieces Lucas facilitated an additional battle after the rescue which combined the two sequences, wherein the protagonist assaults the fortress with a squad of ace fighters. "I sort of tacked the air battle on," Lucas said to author Dale Pollock, "because it was the original impetus of the whole project."[10] Characters, concepts and scenes were transposed and transformed.

In this second draft Darth inherited most of the characteristics of Valorum from the first script, now belonging to the Sith cult, dressing in black and being much more intimidating. He also wears a breath mask in one scene, and serves Prince Espaa Valorum, who is mentioned but never seen. With Valorum of the previous draft eliminated and combined with General Darth Vader, Vader's status was upgraded to be an all-purpose villain. In dealing with villains Lucas had as many as four people—General Vader and Prince Valorum, who were subservient to Governor Hoedaack, who in turn served the Emperor (Hoedaack would be named Tarkin in the final film). The combination of Vader and Valorum gave a less cluttered structure, and the Emperor is now no longer featured in the script, which makes things simpler as well.

However, Vader's presence in the film is surprisingly small: he makes a bold entrance in the opening sequence, wherein the Rebel spaceship is boarded by Imperial troops and a shootout occurs, almost identical to the final film. However, unlike the final film, after Vader enters he engages in a lightsaber match with Deak, defeating him and taking him prisoner. Vader is not seen again until the end, when he pilots a craft to shoot down the attacking Rebel ships before being destroyed himself. It is also noted that the Emperor has many Sith Lords in his service, who all helped hunt down the Jedi in years past and are still functioning to serve him—and in fact we briefly meet some of them.

The father character in the second draft shares more in common with Yoda and Ben Kenobi; known only as "The Starkiller," he is a wrinkled, grey-haired, wise old man said to be hundreds of years old, who, though large, has been shrivelled and bent over with old age, and is the strongest Force user in the universe, the master of all the Jedi. He is spoken of as if a legend, and many doubt if he is still alive—he is revealed in the film's last act.

The main thrust of the plot, the hunt for the stolen Death Star plans, is now in place, taken from E.E. Smith's *Galactic Patrol*, which in turn enlarged the focus of the battle station in the story.

The Death Star/Alderaan plot now includes sequences comparable to *Where Eagles Dare*, with the final attack being harvested out of *The Dam Busters* and *633 Squadron* where a strategic shot will destroy the heavily-armed enemy stronghold. The Death Star assault pieces had originated in the first script (the synopsis had even opened with a similar space battle) but in this draft they become much more involved, with the group sneaking onboard the Alderaan dungeon in a lengthy rescue sequence, and with Luke now piloting a fighter to destroy the Death Star. Although the series of misadventures the heroes encounter on Alderaan (to be transferred to the Death Star for the final film) starting in this draft is somewhat reminiscent of the treacherous journey in *The Hidden Fortress*, the specifics of these sections of the film can also be traced to a handful of wartime adventure B-movies.

Firstly, it can be observed that the 1968 war adventure *Where Eagles Dare* contains a nearly parallel plot to the middle section of *Star Wars*, with Nazis and their secret mountain base substituting for the Empire and its Death Star (here still set on the Alderaan dungeons). This could arguably boil down to coincidence, but the admittedly copy-cat way in which the films are constructed makes one wonder if perhaps *Where Eagles Dare* came back to Lucas' mind and ended up further influencing the plot. In that film, Major Smith (Luke) and Lieutenant Schaffer (Han) have to infiltrate the Castle of Eagles (the Death Star) in order to rescue General Carnaby (Princess Leia), who knows the plans for D-Day (the stolen Death Star plans), from the Nazis (the Empire). On arriving at the town near the mountain (Mos Eisley), they go to a local bar (the cantina) and have to spend most of the time avoiding German soldiers (Sandtroopers). They disguise themselves with Nazi uniforms in order to infiltrate the castle (Luke and Han disguise themselves with stormtroopers uniforms). On their eventual escape, the radio operator sounds the alarm before Schaffer kills him (the cell block control room), which results in a continual gunfight as dozens upon dozens of Nazi Stormtroopers (Imperial Stormtroopers) pour through the door only to be gunned down.

The other sequence owing its lineage to specific war B-movies is the climactic space dogfight. While obviously inspired by *Flash Gordon*, science fiction works in general, and other war films, the specific drama of the Death Star battle can be traced back to films like *633 Squadron* from 1964. That film concerned a squad of ace air fighters who are assigned the mission of destroying a German heavy water plant which is being used to develop the atomic bomb. The factory is in Norway, and considered indestructible since it is shielded by a mountain and guarded by anti-aircraft weaponry (the Death Star is ray-shielded and guarded by turbo lasers). The fighters have to fly down a narrow fiord (the Death Star trench) in order to drop their special "Earthquake" bombs (Proton Torpedoes) at the exact underside of the large overhanging rock (the exhaust port) in order to blow up the factory below, while at the same time dodging the anti-aircraft guns lining the ground and cliff walls. To complicate matters, German fighter planes (TIE fighters) are scrambled to destroy them.

*The Dam Busters*, a 1954 film, was also a large inspiration for the end dogfight and probably *633 Squadron* as well, and is also a tale about Allied fighter pilots who must drop bombs in strategic places in an Axis stronghold. The film even features the line "I'd say about twenty guns, some on the surface, some on the tower." Clips from both of these films were used by Lucas as shot placeholders for the incomplete special effects when editing the rough cut of *Star Wars*.[11]

When Lucas first began scripting he also began making a video compilation of dogfight footage from old war movies.[12] Rinzler wrote that watching television became part of the screenwriting process beginning in the latter part of 1973.[13] "Every time there was a war movie on television, like *Bridges of Toko-Ri*, I would watch it," Lucas said, perhaps explaining how the aforementioned films ended up influencing his script.[14] Rinzler also reported that Lucas took notes on films he watched prior to the second draft, which included *Ben-Hur* and John Ford's *They Were Expendable*.[15]

Seeking to shake off the action overload of the rough draft, Lucas made this script more compact and audience-friendly by using the droids as a narrative compass, telling the story from their point of view and tying the plot together with this more uniform structure.[*] The rough draft has a lengthy beginning section: Kane and his sons are hiding on Utapau from the Sith knights, who have killed all of the Jedi-Bendu; a Sith appears and kills one of Kane's sons, Deak, but Kane finally kills the Sith and takes his remaining son, Annikin, to Alderaan; when they arrive on Alderaan they find the planet under siege, and bureaucrats debate matters in a war room as they struggle to manipulate power from each other (perhaps a nod to *Dr. Strangelove*); Kane leaves Annikin with the only other Jedi left, General Skywalker, and then departs to the spaceport of Gordon to meet his friend Han Solo. Finally, a giant space fortress the size of a moon arrives, and Alderaan scrambles fighters to attack it; inside are the two droids, who jettison to the planet below. The Alderaan fighters are defeated and the planet is invaded, and so General Skywalker and the princess, along with Annikin, make an escape and eventually pick up the arguing droids, much like in the synopsis.

This beginning section was completely cut from the script now, instead simplifying it to a Rebel ship that is quickly invaded, rather than a whole planet, with the droids fleeing in an escape pod to the planet below where they bring Luke the distress message. The two Starkiller brothers are separated instead of together, but Deak is not killed but instead captured, setting up the quest for young Luke (the previous Annikin character), who also now has a "sacred object" to bring his father (the Kiber crystal, much like Tolkien's "One Ring" or the Holy Grail). With the beginning section eliminated, so too was most of the father character's screentime. In simplifying the number of characters and plot points, Lucas also eliminated most of the mentor elements—Father Skywalker is not present until the very end, and there is no General Skywalker to train Luke to be a warrior. Instead Luke is already well-read on the subject of the Force of Others and practices lightsaber fencing in his spare time, and teaches the family heritage to his younger brothers in an early scene. Although presented as more of an intellectual (being a budding archaeologist), Luke has self-trained himself and, though unprepared, must embark on a quest that will test his skills and prove him a hero. However, Lucas would re-instate the essential mentor character in the next draft with the creation of Ben

---

[*] Says Lucas: "The part that was the most interesting in *Hidden Fortress* was that it was told from the point of view of the farmers, and not from the point of view of the princess. I liked that idea. It set me off on a very interesting course because it really did frame the movie in a very interesting way." (*Annotated Screenplays*, p. 10)

Kenobi. In this second draft, Uncle Owen fills in the role to a degree, training Luke on the farm and teaching him about the Force of Others, but once Luke is called on a mission he travels it alone.

The hero's journey of Luke is laid out by his uncle after he receives the challenge to deliver the Kiber crystal to his father:

LUKE
I've never even been past this planet...and I never thought I'd be going alone. [...]

OWEN
How I wish I had the counsel of your father. Ever since your mother died, we have fallen on doubtful times...

LUKE
Deak is in trouble. I should be helping him...

OWEN
If your brother is still alive, they will have taken him to the dungeons of ALDERAAN, at the very heart of the Empire. No one, not even your father in his prime, could help him there...Your father is getting very old. I fear he needs your help more than your brother does, and much more depends on him succeeding. If he at last has asked for the Kiber Crystal, his powers must be very weak. It is a dangerous thing to have loose in the galaxy...and you need him, for you are not yet with the FORCE OF OTHERS. I have taught you the ways of a skilled warrior, but I am not a Jedi Bendu. The ways of the spirit you must learn from your father.

[...]

LUKE
I may be a good pilot, but I'm not a warrior. No matter how hard I try. It's just not in me.

OWEN
I know, you'd rather carve a jud stone, or work on your catalog of the ancients...I've trained seven of your father's sons and it's clear that you are not the most gifted in the disciplines – not in power or speed, at any rate...

[...]

BERU
But you have the way about you...and wisdom far beyond your years...

OWEN
You must learn to use such strength and wits as you have. Your father has need of the Kiber Crystal. The decision is yours. I cannot bear this burden for you, my duty is to the twins. But we must do something soon. The enemy is moving, and we are no longer safe here.

Lucas explained to author Alan Arnold the creation of Luke and Han, both of whom had been created in the rough draft but come to be more like the characters we know in this second draft, with Han a human smuggler and Luke now introduced on his aunt and uncle's farm as a (pudgy,) awkward eighteen-year-old:

I was dealing with two opposites, and these are the two opposites in myself—a naïve, innocent idealism and a view of the world that is cynical, more pessimistic. My starting point was the idea of an innocent who becomes cynical. Should Luke be a brash young kid or an intellectual? Should he be a she? At one point, I was going to have a girl at the center. Luke Skywalker might never have been; he might have been a heroine... [Han] came out of Luke...as the opposite of Luke. Han Solo evolved from my wanting to have a cynical foil for the innocent Luke. A lot of the characters came out of Luke because Luke had many aspects. So I took certain aspects of the composite Luke and put them into other characters.[16]

Here they are still wooden and melodramatic in their characterisation and mannerism. The next draft would solidify these characters as ones more recognizable to us. Han, for example, does not doubt the Force as he will in the next draft, and here even feels it himself. Lucas talked about the evolutionary process of characters in *The Making of Star Wars*:

My original idea was to make the movie about an old man and a kid, who have a teacher-student relationship [treatment, rough, and first drafts]. And I knew I wanted the old man to be a real old man, but also a warrior. In the original script the old man was the hero. I wanted to have a seventy-five-year-old Clint Eastwood. I liked that idea. Then I wrote another script without the old man. I decided that I wanted to do it about kids. I found the kid character more interesting than the old man. I don't know that much about old people and it was very hard for me to cope with it. So I ended up writing the kid better than the old man. Then I had a story about the kid and his brother, where the kid developed—and a pirate character developed out of the brother [second draft]. As I kept writing scripts, more characters evolved...I pulled one character from one script and another character from another script, and pretty soon they got to be the dirty half dozen they are today.[17]

Princess Leia disappears from this draft, with Deak in her place as the hostage. Lucas tried to keep a female character in the story somewhere, and gave the name Leia to a cousin of Luke's who lives on Tatooine and has a crush on him, though she has only a couple scenes. It must be stressed that this character is conceptually different from Princess Leia and should not be confused with her.

Interestingly, this draft introduces the "Episode" concept, labelling "Star Wars" as Episode One in *The Adventures of The Starkiller*. It also has an end title roll-up, providing a teaser for the next chapter in the adventures, indicating Lucas was headed in a totally different direction than what eventually was made, although he had probably not developed this plot in much detail:

> ...And a thousand new systems joined the rebellion, causing a significant crack in the great wall of the powerful Galactic Empire. The Starkiller would once again spark fear in the hearts of the Sith knights, but not before his sons were put to many tests...the most daring of which was the kidnapping of the Lars family, and the perilous search for:
> "The Princess of Ondos."

The absence of Princess Leia thus returns—Lucas was planning on using the idea of a quest for a princess in a never-made sequel.

New to the second draft is the history of the Republic, fleshed out in more detail, providing a significant step to developing the background that would serve as the prequel stories.

In the first draft there was no Republic and Empire, there was only the Empire, a benign one in which the Jedi Bendu served as protectors of the Emperors, of which there was a long line, akin to feudal Japan. One of the Emperors became corrupt and proclaimed a new order of The New Empire, and was aided in his quest to exterminate the Jedi by the Sith knights, a band of mercenary warriors or pirates.

For the second draft, a history was created which was more specific and resembles that of the final film (though containing a number of wildly different elements). The rise of the Emperor in this draft is now based more closely on the dictatorships of Rome, Germany and France, with a strong influence from the recent Nixon scandal. Lucas said to author Jody Duncan:

> The political issues have to deal with democracies that give their countries over to a dictator because of a crisis of some kind...this was a very big issue when

I was writing the first *Star Wars* because it was soon after Nixon's presidency, and there was a point, right before he was thrown out of office, where he suggested that they change a constitutional amendment so that he could run for a third term. Even when he started getting into trouble, he was saying "If the military will back me, I'll stay in office." His idea was: "To hell with Congress and potential impeachment. I'll go directly to the army, and between the army and myself, I'll continue to be president." That is what happens here. An emergency in the Republic leads the Senate to make Palpatine, essentially, "dictator for life."[18]

The Background of the second draft is explained in a scene between Luke and his brothers, the twins Biggs and Windy:

LUKE
In another time, long before the Empire, and before the Republic had been formed, a holy man called the Skywalker became aware of a powerful energy field which he believed influenced the destiny of all living creatures...

BIGGS
The "FORCE OF OTHERS"!

LUKE
Yes, and after much study, he was able to know the force, and it communicated with him. He came to see things in a new way. His "aura" and powers grew very strong. The Skywalker brought a new life to the people of his system, and became one of the founders of the Republic Galactica.

WINDY
The "FORCE OF OTHERS" talked to him!?!

LUKE
In a manner different from the way we talk. As you know, the "FORCE OF OTHERS" has two halves: Ashla, the good, and Bogan, the paraforce or evil part. Fortunately, Skywalker came to know the good half and was able to resist the paraforce; but he realized that if he taught others the way of the Ashla, some, with less strength, might come to know Bogan, the dark side, and bring unthinkable suffering to the Universe.

For this reason, the Skywalker entrusted the secret of THE FORCE only to his twelve children, and they in turn passed on the knowledge only to their children, who became known as the Jedi Bendu of the Ashla: "the servants of the force". For thousands of years, they brought peace and justice to the galaxy. At one time there were several hundred Jedi families, but now there are only two or three.

WINDY
What happened to them?

LUKE
As the Republic spread throughout the galaxy, encompassing over a million worlds, the GREAT SENATE grew to such overwhelming proportions that it no longer responded to the needs of its citizens. After a series of assassinations and elaborately rigged elections, the Great Senate became secretly controlled by the Power and Transport guilds. When the Jedi discovered the conspiracy and attempted to purge the Senate, they were denounced as traitors. Several Jedi allowed themselves to be tried and executed, but most of them fled into the Outland systems and tried to tell people of the conspiracy. But the elders chose to remain behind, and the Great Senate diverted them by creating civil disorder. The Senate secretly instigated race wars, and aided anti-government terrorists. They slowed down the system of justice, which caused the crime rate to rise to the point where a totally controlled and oppressive police state was welcomed by the systems. The Empire was born. The systems were exploited by a new economic policy which raised the cost of power and transport to unbelievable heights.

    Many worlds were destroyed this way. Many people starved...

BIGGS
Why didn't the "FORCE OF OTHERS" help the Jedi to put things right?

LUKE
Because a terrible thing happened. During one of his lessons a young PADAWAN-JEDI, a boy named Darklighter, came to know the evil half of the force, and fell victim to the spell of the dreaded Bogan. He ran away from his instructor and taught the evil ways of the Bogan Force to a clan of Sith pirates, who then spread untold misery throughout the systems. They became the personal bodyguards of the Emperor. The Jedi were hunted down by these deadly Sith knights. With every Jedi death, contact with the Ashla grows weaker, and the force of the Bogan grows more powerful.

WINDY
Where are the Jedi now?

LUKE
They're hidden; but many are still fighting to free the systems from the grip of the Empire. Our father is a Jedi. He is called "The Starkiller" and is said to be a great and wise man, and tomorrow I am on my way to join him and learn the ways of the "FORCE OF OTHERS".

    This is the first mention of the Force, here called the Force of Others—in the rough draft, the phrase "May the force of others be with you" is said, as a generalised form of spirituality, but now in the second draft it becomes an actual power that one can learn to harness and use, with a good and a bad side to it—the concepts of religious supernaturalism and super powers, for all intents and purposes, are not introduced until this second draft.

Here the notion of a Jedi succumbing to the dark side (the Bogan) is introduced. In this case it is part of the distant-past, tracing the beginnings of the Sith, who were formerly a pirate clan but learned to use the Force through the teachings of a renegade Jedi named Darklighter. This history would be transferred over to Darth Vader for the next draft in an effort to simplify the story, marking one of the final transformations into the character we see in the film.

### Visions

Around the time of this second draft, artist Ralph McQuarrie was commissioned by Lucas to produce artwork based on the script, and he appears to have used the second draft as his reference. The first completed colour rendering of Darth Vader is a depiction of the opening sequence, in which he squares off in a lightsaber battle with Deak. This would mold the physical form of Vader, with helmeted breath-mask, flowing robes and black armour.

Lucas explained Vader's appearance in the summer of 1977, this being the very first public reveal:

> It was a whole part of the plot that essentially got cut out... Vader kills Luke's father, then Ben and Vader have a confrontation, just like they have in *Star Wars*, and Ben almost kills Vader. As a matter of fact, he falls into a volcanic pit and gets fried and is one destroyed being. That's why he has to wear the suit with a mask, because it's a breathing mask. It's like a walking iron lung.[19]

By the time August 1977 rolled around, when the above comment was made, Lucas had invented the backstory involving "The Duel" between Obi Wan and Darth Vader, where Obi Wan avenges Father Skywalker's murder by wounding Vader on the site of a volcano and necessitating the costume as a life-support device. However, this story was made to retroactively fit in with Vader's already-invented appearance. At the time Vader was designed, breathing mask and all, Obi Wan didn't exist, and in fact, Vader did not kill Father Skywalker because Father Skywalker—or The Starkiller as he was known in the second draft—was alive and well within the script, and survives to the end (unlike Vader, who perishes). Vader at this point was not a former Jedi, and had no history. The backstory of The Duel apparently did not come about until after the fourth draft was written.

Now that draft two opened with Vader and the troops capturing the Rebel ship and boarding it, Vader required a breath mask like his stormtroopers in order to cross through space to the captured ship, which had been blown open to the vacuum of space; hence, Deak Starkiller has a breathing mask as well. The production painting McQuarrie did can be seen depicting the two masked characters squaring off with lightsabers. What is even more interesting is that this was not Lucas' idea—it was something Ralph McQuarrie added on his own. McQuarrie acknowledged this to authors Mark Cotta Vaz and Shinji Hata, stating:

> Early in the script there was a description of Vader crossing between two ships in space so I created this mask so he could breathe in space, with a suggestion of teeth in the mask's grill work.[20]

McQuarrie's masked drawing inspired Lucas' descriptions, and not the other way around—given that Lucas liked to work this way on the sequels and prequels, this is unsurprising. In fact, McQuarrie began sketching in November 1974[21]—when Lucas was still writing. He elaborates in an interview with *Star Wars Insider*:

> George came along in about a week with a little bundle of stuff he'd gotten out of old science-fiction magazines of the 1930s and material like that. George also supplied some books on Japanese medieval stuff...George had mentioned him having to wear a helmet like a Japanese medieval warrior, one of those big flared-out helmets, and I made it somewhere between that and a German World War II helmet. In probably one day, I made all the drawings that pretty much defined Darth Vader. I was moving very fast and didn't have all week to fool around with Darth Vader—I had lots of other things to work on... [George] was very happy if you came up with some ideas that were completely different. George didn't envision Darth Vader with a mask—he said he might have his face covered with black silk. But I got worried for Vader's health, because he has to transfer to another spacecraft through outer space with stormtroopers who had armored space suits...George said, "Well, all right, give him some kind of breath mask,"—which he wore through all three films.[22]

Darth Vader thus enters the second draft of January 1975:

> For an eerie moment, all is deathly quiet as a huge darker figure appears in the sub-hallway. The remaining stormtroopers bow low toward the doorway. An

awesome, seven-foot BLACK KNIGHT OF THE SITH makes his way into the blinding light of the cockpit area. This is LORD DARTH VADER, right hand to the MASTER OF THE SITH. His sinister face is partially obscured by his flowing black robes and grotesque breath mask, which are in sharp contrast to the fascist white armored suits of the Imperial stormtroopers. The troops instinctively back away from the imposing warrior.

McQuarrie's earliest pencil sketches of Vader, based on the work-in-progress draft two, depict an ordinary man, without a helmet, with average-length hair and a slight build, wearing normal clothes and a face-mask that looks like a kind of futuristic gas mask. He has no electronics, no breathing tubes or any kind of mechanical limbs—nor is he described as having any in the scripts; he is simply a large man. The mask made him seem more threatening and alien and Lucas naturally loved it—the breathing of course was a natural by-product of the character wearing the mask. This appears to be the first drawings that McQuarrie did, which in turn inspired Lucas; Vader appears in the second draft wearing the breath-mask which McQuarrie first sketched. Vader's appearance was subsequently refined at Lucas' request to have a large-brimmed samurai-style helmet and more exaggerated, flowing black robes—the result was what could be called the second, or intermediate, stage of design, where Vader resembles a Bedouin warrior, with a vaguely epee-like sword. The cape was a detail that had existed from the beginning—the characters being based on the medieval designs of *Flash Gordon* and the stylings of the 1930s serials, in which the villain *always* wore a cape. It was also McQuarrie who added armour to the design,[23] toning down the Bedouin-like emphasis on cloth and instead giving a more militant, knight-like appearance, which was given a more futuristic touch for the final design sketches where Vader's appearance was more or less locked.

"The space suits began as being necessary for [Vader and the stormtroopers'] survival in space, but the suits became part of their character," McQuarrie stated in Rinzler's *Making of.*[24]

There has been a lot of speculation about the influence of three pre-existing characters on the Darth Vader design process—two Jack Kirby creations and the villain from the 1939 *Fighting Devil Dogs* serial.

As mentioned earlier, Lucas was no stranger to comic books and not only was he an avid collector, but he bought reams of them looking for inspiration while writing *Star Wars*, and was even the co-owner of a comic book store in New York City. Jack Kirby was one of the most influential comic book artists in the history of the medium and was regarded as a legend by the 1970s, when he was as prolific as ever. It is here, in 1970, that he began his most epic creation, loved by serious collectors but largely ignored by mainstream audiences: his *Fourth World* serial, an epic of interconnected science fiction tales which formed a growing narrative and ran from 1970 to 1973, the year Lucas began writing *Star Wars*. The series would serve not only as an immediate influence on *Star Wars*, but perhaps a later influence, either consciously or residually, on the future shape of the saga in its sequels. For example, in *The New Gods* saga,* a number of obvious influences immediately jump out. For instance, the villain of the series is named Darkseid ("dark side"). The hero (Orion) battles Darkseid, armed with a power which flows throughout the universe and is known as The Source (in other words, The Force) only to discover that Darkseid is in fact his own father.

As for visual inspiration, Darkseid was a hulking, caped, armoured character, adorned in black, with large boots, gauntlets and a helmet-like head.

The second Jack Kirby creation is Doctor Doom, one of the most memorable villains from the popular *Fantastic Four* series. Once a brilliant scientist and friends with the leader of the Fantastic Four, he became bitter with jealousy and was horribly scarred in a laboratory accident. He emerged as Doctor Doom, sworn enemy of the Fantastic Four and forever encased in a large iron suit, complete with a fluttering cape. Not only is his visual design very similar to Darth Vader's but the character's backstory is as well; it may be argued that this is coincidental, as masked characters in literature are often encased in their coverings to hide deformities, reaching back to 1909's *Phantom of the Opera* by Gaston Leroux, but being such an important villain in the comic book world Doctor Doom's influence may very well have been a conscious one. Supposedly Lucas himself has admitted the influence, though I am ignorant to such a reference. Doctor Doom first appeared in 1962, though the character would not gain prominence until the mid '70s.

McQuarrie said in a previous quote that Lucas provided him with 1930s pulp fiction material, which brings us to the last influence, the character of "The Lightning" from *The Fighting Devil Dogs*. *The Fighting Devil Dogs* was a twelve-part serial from 1939, Republic pictures' second lowest-costing serial that was most memorable for its villain, The Lightning, an impressive serial villain by any standard. With a fluttering cape, shiny

---

* As a side bar, it has been said that the 1987 live-action *Masters of the Universe* film is actually a disguised adaptation of *The New Gods*, though it is only a loose one.

black boots and gauntlets, a black helmet that completely covered his face, and dressed from head to toe in black leather, The Lightning was a fearsome sight. Not only was his visual design unforgettable, but his screen presence was truly intimidating: in the first episode the protagonist discovers that his entire platoon has been wiped out by some mysterious force—even flies lay dead on the ground. Entire armies were single-handedly defeated by The Lightning, and he had an assortment of weapons, the main one being the lightning bolts that spewed from his hands, thus giving him his name. When he wasn't killing U.S. marines, he stalked the skies onboard his flying fortress "The Wing." While his henchmen manned the controls in white radiation suits, The Lightning walked the decks with clenched fists.

It may be surmised in counter-point that these three characters were not necessarily *deliberately* copied by Lucas, but rather were swirling around in his subconsciousness as he prodded McQuarrie into the final Vader design, a mental catalog of villains and images that he had absorbed in his thirty years of viewing such material. On the other hand, the fact that Lucas provided McQuarrie with comic books (and showed a very hip awareness to the contemporary comic book scene at the time)[25] and 1930s pulp pages[26] for design references may demonstrate that these similarities are very much intentional.

### Intermediaries

Lucas continued to gather comments and criticisms from his friends as they read the latest drafts, and every few weeks Lucas would fly down to Los Angeles and share the script with the Huycks. "We'd say, 'George, this character doesn't work," Willard Huyck remembers, "and George would go 'Uh-huh' and make a note, and then fly home."[27]

Francis Coppola also read the early drafts and offered his opinions. Lucas said in 1974:

> [Me and Francis] more or less work as collaborators. What we do is look at each other's scripts, look at the casting, then at the dailies, at the rough cut and the fine cut, and make suggestions. We can bounce ideas off each other because we're totally different. I'm more graphic-film-making-editing oriented; and he's more writing and acting oriented. So we complement each other, and we trust each other. Half the time he says I'm full of shit, and half the time I say he's full of shit. It's not like a producer telling you that you *have* to do something. Francis will say, "Cut that scene out, it doesn't work at all." And

I may say, "No, you're crazy. That's my favourite scene. I love it." And he'll say, "Okay, what do I care? You're an idiot anyway." Actually, he calls me a stinky kid. He says, "You're a stinky kid, do what you want." And I say the same thing to him. It works well, because you really need somebody to test ideas on. And you get a piece of expert advice that you value.[28]

With this script, the basic story structure and plot for the final film had been determined but Lucas' characters were stilted, his dialogue poor and melodramatic, and the story was often convoluted and muddied. "My recollection was that George had a whole *Star Wars* script that I thought was fine," Coppola said, "and then he chucked it and started again with these two robots lost in the wilderness."[29]

"It started off in horrible shape," Hal Barwood remembered in *The Making of Star Wars*. "It was difficult to discern there was a movie in there. It did have Artoo and it did have Threepio, but it was very hard for us to wrap our heads around the idea of a golden robot and this little beer can. We just didn't know what that meant. But George never gave up and he worked and worked and worked."[30]

The impending drafts three and four functioned mainly to simplify the elaborate and messy story Lucas had constructed by draft two into more audience-friendly terms. Gary Kurtz has claimed that the more simplified and mystical presentation of the Force beginning with draft three was due to his recommendation. In *Mythmaker* he stated:

> Anybody who read those drafts...said, "What are you doing here? This is absolutely gobbledegook"...Comparative religion is one of the things I studied in university...I also studied the Buddhist and Hindu sects, and studied Zen and Tibetan Buddhism, and also Native American spirituality; shamanistic methods and so on. I got out a lot of my old books, and we talked about it.[31]

It has been said that at this time, before writing the third draft, Lucas re-discovered Joseph Campbell, whose work Lucas had first read in junior college. The repercussions of this can supposedly be seen in the coming draft, where Luke's arc allegedly more closely follows the "hero's journey" monomyth as outlined by the professor, such as the introduction of Ben Kenobi as the mentor to the young hero. Luke starts out as a naïve youth who takes on the call to adventure and becomes an unlikely hero—but it was also an influence culled from folk tales as well as the many John Ford films Lucas admired, and more importantly also a *natural* progression from the second draft where Luke was an awkward farmboy (which in turn was a continuation from the first draft where Luke was an awkward apprentice named Annikin). Princess Leia is now introduced as the damsel in distress that the poor peasant Luke must rescue, bringing the story more in line with traditional fairy tales, while Luke's father would be transformed into wise wizard Ben Kenobi. Campbell's influence on the saga, it must be stressed, has become quite exaggerated over the years, even by Lucas himself; to be sure, Campbell's work had a personal impact on Lucas, but the level of influence beyond that is questionable. The previous drafts contained many of the same arcs and themes, the same ones present in *THX 1138* and *American Graffiti*, and need not invoke the writings of Campbell to explain how they appeared in *Star Wars*. As Lucas has admitted, much of the similarity between the final script and Campbell's structure is due to coincidental alignment.[32] The majority of it was merely "intuitive," as he said, the same storytelling intuition that thousands of writers have instinctively adhered to to produce stories with the same arcs and themes.

"Yes, I've done a fair amount of reading, but a lot of *Star Wars* just came intuitively," Lucas said to author Denise Worrell in 1983. "The reading gave me feelings for motifs and themes, but ultimately most of *Star Wars* is just personal. If I ever consciously used anything that I read, it was to make the story more consistent with traditional fairy tales. For example, if there was a part in which Luke had two trials, I would try to make it three, because three is more consistent with hero myths. But if adding a third trial jeopardized the story, I wouldn't do it. I can't give any specific examples."[33]

Draft two contained the exact same arc for Luke, and in some ways it is even closer to Campbell's structure. Adhering to Campbell's hero characteristics, Luke is a sort of orphan, having been raised by his uncle and not knowing his father, he is the heir to a tradition (the Jedi-Bendu way), learns to use special powers (the Force of Others), and follows a set of moral principles—much like draft one. Draft two also sticks amazingly faithful to many stages of the Campbellian hero pattern:

1) The call to adventure—the droids bring Luke a distress message from Deak, throwing down the gauntlet of embarking on a treacherous quest;

2) The refusal of the call—Luke doubts he can do what is asked of him but his uncle convinces him that he has the strength;

3) Supernatural aid—Luke is armed with the Kiber crystal and the Force of Others;

4) The crossing of the first threshold—Luke travels to Mos Eisley and recruits Han Solo, almost getting killed in the process;

5) Descent into the underworld—Luke finds himself trapped in the Alderaan prison fortress;

6) Initiation—Luke has to battle his way out of the prison and rescue Deak;

7) Atonement with the father—Luke finally meets his father at the end, and after destroying the Death Star his father praises him for having finally become a true warrior. In fact the only major difference in the next draft would be the re-instatement of a mentor figure on the journey.

These stages can be better viewed in the chronological context of script development—most of them are present in draft one, simply in rougher forms, and here in draft two they expand and grow in a way that points to organic story development on the part of Lucas and not epiphany from an outside source, which is consistent with the slight modifications they underwent for the third draft as Lucas' process of cultivating his story finally matured, with finishing touches added in the shooting script.

Lucas is more accurate in this statement from the 1970s: "I spent about a year reading lots of fairy tales—and that's when it starts to move away from Kurosawa and towards Joe Campbell...About the time I was doing the third draft I read *The Hero with a Thousand Faces*, and I started to realise that I was following those rules unconsciously. So I said, *I'll make it fit more into that classic mold.*"[34]

Between the time of the second and third draft Lucas also made a bold experiment in altering the hero to a heroine.[35] "The original treatment was about a princess and an old man," Lucas said in Rinzler's *Making of*, "and then I wrote her out for a while, and the second draft really didn't have any girls in it at all. I was very disturbed about that. I didn't want to make a movie with no women in it. So I struggled with that, and at one point Luke was a girl. I just changed the main character from a guy to a girl."[36] Much production artwork was produced with this conception in mind. However, Lucas eliminated Deak as the captured ally in the next draft, allowing him to be replaced with the princess once again and Luke returned to the male gender. Lucas also stripped away Luke's siblings for the next draft, leaving Luke on his own, an act that would be even more meaningful when Uncle Owen was transformed from gentle father figure to cruel brute. Luke would now be a more downtrodden everyman, who has dreams of greater things but is stuck spiritually suffocating doing chores for his step-parents, much like a character in a fairy tale. Lucas also added scenes where Luke hangs out at a garage in the nearby town of Anchorhead with his friends, who tease him for his grand ambitions, bringing the setting further in line with Lucas' Modesto adolescence.

Before re-structuring the film for draft three, Lucas wrote a new six-page synopsis on May 1st, 1975 before finally tackling the script, called

"*The Adventures of Luke Starkiller. Episode I: The Star Wars.*" The motive for the synopsis is proven to be more business-minded, as Dale Pollock reports that Lucas sent Alan Ladd Jr. a synopsis of his story on that very date, May 1st, in order to update Fox on the state of the story.[37] In it he wrote:

> An engaging human drama set in a fantasy world that paralyses the imagination...A story not only for children but for anyone who likes a grande tale of wonder on an epic scale... filled with marvels and strange terrors, moral warmth, and, most of all, pure excitement.[38]

Pollock stated that it was merely a summation of his previous second draft, and not in preparation for his third, though this is not entirely accurate.[39] We see in this synopsis a few key deviations which would give rise to the third draft—Deak is no longer captured in the beginning, though there is a mention of a Rebel trooper charging Vader with a lasersword. More importantly, the princess from the early drafts has now returned, and Luke must rescue her (with only the droids in this abbreviated version). Pollock also mistakenly claims that it was "Episode four," further imbedding the deceptive notion that Lucas always intended the film to be the fourth chapter of a saga—the synopsis is "Episode I" according to the book *The Annotated Screenplays*, which Rinzler's *Making of Star Wars* corroborates.[40]

However, around the same time Lucas wrote this, he also made a second summary for himself, in which he made a few further key changes in story—in a way, it is a sort of "missing link" between the second and third drafts. "An additional four undated pages, written as notes, supplement the same story, retelling it and adding to it," Rinzler wrote.[41] These typed synopsis notes are the origin of the changes that would occur for the third draft, including a prototype version of Ben Kenobi and a never scripted face-to-face confrontation between Luke and Darth Vader, ending with Vader defeated (and presumably killed as the Death Star explodes). Rinzler summarizes this third draft outline:

> At the moisture farm, Luke talks with the robots about his dreams; at dinner Owen tells him he can't go to the Academy—they argue and Owen strikes the boy, who is protected by Beru. Cleaning the robots later, Luke stumbles on a message from the "Captain" saying the princess has been taken prisoner and sent to Alderaan. Enclosed in R2 is a signal device to locate the princess. Luke rushes outside, then returns to kiss his aunt good night while she's sleeping. He then leaves home with the robots.

On his way to the spaceport, he passes a "poor old man." He picks him up, and the old man talks about his adventures as a Jedi. Luke is "in awe" and wants to become his apprentice; the old man agrees and will train him "for food." When they stop for water, the old man gives Luke a lesson about the "force of others...Old man can do magic, read minds, talk to things like Don Juan."

They arrive the next day at the cantina, and the old man talks to Chewbacca. "Bugs molest Luke, start fight. Old man cuts them down." Chewbacca leads them to Han, who is a captain. They persuade Chewbacca and Han, after negotiating the fee, to take them to Alderaan, where R2's signal device is leading them. There they hide in the ship as TIE fighters escort it into the docking bay. Darth Vader and the other Sith Knights sense the presence of a Jedi, but they find only the robots.

While the old man looks for the Kiber crystal, the others rescue the princess, which doesn't go smoothly. "She's a tough babe; doesn't appreciate their help—a trap? Han punches her in the face and Chewbacca carries her out." They then have to face the Dia Noga and have various adventures, while the old man gets the crystal, at which point the Sith Knights "become ill." They nevertheless confront the old man and wound him, but he's rescued by the others, and they all blast off. Vader "let's them go," but still sends some TIEs after them; these quickly give up. The old man tells them they're being followed, but the princess needs to go to her "hidden fortress anyway."

They crash-land on Yavin, but are located by loyal troops. Han receives his money, after they arrive at the base, and leaves the group, which saddens Luke. In the Control War Room, they "spot something very big." The old man knows it's the Death Star—and the only way to destroy it is by putting a "bomb in its exhaust system."

Most of the rebels are sceptical, but Luke lands on the Death Star with the bomb—"runs into Vader; sword fight—Han to the rescue. Artoo shot...End scene—all come together, cheer. Make Luke a Jedi knight."[42]

Lucas jotted down his thoughts and ideas specifically in some places and loosely in others. The "old man" would grow into Ben Kenobi in the script, though here he is picked up and receives food for instruction, similar to the samurai in *Seven Samurai*. Most interesting is the unique ending for this version of the story, where Luke has to plant the bomb by hand but is confronted by Vader. Once again Lucas made elaborate notes to track his thoughts and changes for the screenplay version. Rinzler lists some of them:

Robots and rebel troops listen as the weird sounds of stormtroopers are heard on top of the ship...Sith rips rebel's arm off at end of battle...only seven Sith—one in each sector...small ships avoid deflector shields/tractor beams...New scenes: Luke sees space battle.[43]

This last note was the response to Matthew Robbins and Hal Barwood, who thought the film would flow easier if Luke was introduced earlier. "Francis had read the script and given me his ideas," Lucas explained in *The Making of Star Wars.* "Steven Spielberg had read the script. All of my friends had read the script. Everybody who had read the script gave their input about what they thought was good, or bad, or indifferent; what worked, what didn't—and what was confusing. Matt and Hal thought the first half hour of the film would be better if Luke was intercut with the robots, so I did that."[44] Another note jotted down speculates "combine Han and Biggs," a concept which never saw fruition (or perhaps, in a way, it did, as the growing comraderie of Luke and Han was more pronounced in the upcoming draft).

The third draft finally turns the "old man" from the outline into a defined character: Ben Kenobi, a legendary Jedi officer now living as a hermit. In this draft, he was Father Skywalker's commanding officer, and Father Skywalker told Luke as a boy to go to him if anything bad ever happened to himself. The next draft would personalise the relationship between Kenobi and Father Skywalker, developing that they were equals who grew up together.

Most of Lucas' notes seem concentrated on expanding Luke's journey and character. One of the more interesting ones is a sort of chart where Luke learns about the Force of Others in specific stages. These stages, and use of the phrase "man of the Force," suggest an influence of Castaneda's Don Juan and his tutelage:

> 1) Luke learns about Force (in desert); 2) Luke tries to experience Force (in ship); 3) Luke becomes a man of the Force (Alderaan); 4) Ben explains Luke's experience (in ship); 5) Luke with crystal struggles with Force (on Yavin)[45]

Below this was a list of key words that Lucas used to inspire his direction—"warrior, power, sorcerer, allies, jedi, the force." Lucas also decided to change the ending from his third draft outline. He explained in Rinzler's *Making of:*

> Between the second and third drafts, Luke stopped on the surface of the Death Star...He and Artoo had to go and take the bomb by hand, open up the little hatch, and drop the bomb in—then they had fifteen seconds or something to get off the surface before the thing blew up—but as they were going back to the ship, Darth Vader arrived. So Luke and Vader had a big swordfight. Luke finally overcame Vader and then jumped in the ship and took off. But in trying to intercut the dogfight with the old-fashioned swordfight, I realised that the film would have stopped dead. It was too risky.[46]

A last-minute temptation would arise around this time, however: *Apocalypse Now* would get a chance to be made at last. With Coppola skyrocketing to fame and becoming the most powerful director on the planet, he finally would make the movie himself. Lucas explained the situation in *The Making of Star Wars*:

> Francis had finished *The Godfather II* and he was saying, "I'm going to finance movies myself—we don't have to worry about anybody, so come and do this movie." I had a choice: I had put four years into *Apocalypse Now*, and two years into *Star Wars*—but something inside said, "Do *Star Wars* and then try to do *Apocalypse Now*." So I said that to Francis, and he said, "We really have to do it right now; I've got the money, and I think this is the time for this film to come out." So I said, "Why don't you do it then?" So he went off and did it...Part of my decision was based on the fan mail I had gotten from *Graffiti*...I seemed to have struck a chord with kids; I had found something they were missing. After the 1960's it was the end of the protest movement and the whole phenomenon. The drugs were really getting bad, kids were dying, and there was nothing left to protest. But *Graffiti* just said, *Get into your car and go chase some girls. That's all you have to do.* A lot of kids didn't even know that, so we kept getting all these letters from all over the country saying, "Wow, this is great, I really found myself!" It seemed to straighten a lot of them out.
>
> I also realized that, whereas *THX* had a very pessimistic point of view, *American Graffiti* said essentially that we were all very good. *Apocalypse Now* was very much like *THX*, and *Star Wars* was very much like *American Graffiti*, so I thought it would be more beneficial for kids...I'd been around kids and they talked about *Kojak* and *The Six Million Dollar Man*, but they didn't have any real vision of all the incredible and crazy and wonderful things that we had when we were young—pirate movies and Westerns and all that. When I mentioned to kids, like Francis' sons who are eleven and eight, that I was doing a space film, they went crazy. In a way I was using Francis's kids as models, because I'm around them the most. They're the ones who I talked to about the story. I know what they like.[47]

### The Story Takes Shape

Finally, we come to the third draft, where the script was once again tightened to a form more resemblant of the final film. The princess was re-instated as the captive rather than Deak and is now a more active character, Ben Kenobi appears for the very first time, and Luke is now the reluctant farmboy we know. The third draft arrived unto the world on August 1st,

1975 and was titled "*The Star Wars*. From the Adventures of Luke Starkiller."
Helander summarised the third draft thusly:

Above the planet of Utapau, stormtroopers led by Darth Vader (a Sith Lord and
right hand of the Emperor) overtake a rebel spaceship, and conduct a search for
the stolen plans to the Empire's "Death Star" battle station. A young rebel
princess called Leia Organa is captured by the Imperials, but she refuses to
reveal the whereabouts of the information. A young farm boy named Luke
Starkiller has seen the space battle from Utapau's wasteland with his
"electrobinoculars", but when he tells his friends at Anchorhead about it, they
dismiss it as a fantasy. Luke is deeply impressed by (and jealous of) his best
friend Biggs Darklighter who has graduated from the academy, becoming a
startrooper cadet.

Before the princess was captured, two robots named See Threepio (a tall
"Human Cyborg relations droid") and Artoo Detoo (a short, beeping triped)
abandoned the rebel ship, crashing in the Utapau desert. Artoo carries the
Death Star plans and a message from Leia in his innards as the two "droids" are
captured by "Jawa" scavengers and taken to the Lars homestead where Luke
lives with his Aunt Beru and Uncle Owen. The Jawas sell the robots to Owen,
and Luke decides to apply to the academy now that they have two extra droids
on the farm. When it turns out that his academy savings were spent on the
robots, Luke wishes his late Jedi father were there. Cleaning Artoo, he stumbles
upon the hologram message, in which Leia wants the droids delivered to
Organa Major and says that she has been taken to Alderaan. Luke runs away
from home with the droids in order to get help from General Ben Kenobi, a
Jedi knight his father had told him about. After being attacked by barbaric
"Tusken Raiders", Luke is found by old Ben who claims he has become too old
for adventures, proving his point by angrily cracking open his artificial arm.
After some thought, Ben changes his mind, but since he has little Force left in
him, he starts teaching Luke about the Force of Others as they leave with the
droids for Mos Eisley spaceport. On Alderaan, Vader and his fellow Sith Lords
feel something old awakening, strengthening the Force.

After using his "laser-sword" to defend Luke against some creatures at a
Mos Eisley cantina, Ben and his friends follow a furry "Wookiee" called
Chewbacca to a nearby docking bay where they are introduced to a cocky
starpilot named Han Solo who agrees to take them to Organa Major for a
considerable amount of money. Han tricks some evil pirates - including Jabba
the Hutt, the financier of his ship - into leaving the docking area, and as the
heroes leave Mos Eisley, a furious Jabba is left behind. Aboard the ship, Ben
feels that something horrible has happened, and when they reach Organa Major
they find the planet destroyed by the Empire. Now they must rescue the
princess from the Imperial city of Alderaan in order to find the rebels. At
Alderaan, their ship is boarded by stormtroopers, but only Threepio is found
since the others are hiding in scan-proof lockers. Luke and Han steal
stormtrooper uniforms, and with Chewbacca posing as their prisoner, they

leave for the detention area, where they wreak havoc and find the tortured Leia. The groggy princess takes command of the situation, and after getting past a "Dia Nogu" monster, they jump down a chute leading to a garbage masher from where they are saved by the droids. Using the Force and his laser-sword, Ben has managed to retrieve one of the Kiber Crystals, but he meets Vader on his way back, and a duel commences. As the others make it to the hangar, Ben slams down a blast door between Vader and himself, and everybody manage to escape in Han's ship.

Four pursuing "tie" fighters are shot down, and the ship reaches the Masassi outpost on the fourth moon of Yavin, where the rebels plan an assault on the approaching Death Star (the plans inside Artoo give a "thermal exhaust port" as the station's weak point). Han leaves after receiving his money, while Luke claims a place in the battle as his reward. The attack has gone poorly for the rebels, when Luke approaches the target with the Kiber Crystal in his hand. Vader feels the Force in Luke and starts chasing him in his fighter, when suddenly, Han's ship turns up firing, causing the Sith Lord to collide with his wing man. As Vader's ship spins out of control, Luke fires a torpedo into the exhaust port and the Death Star explodes. At a ceremony back at the outpost, Luke, Artoo, Threepio, Han and Chewbacca are awarded gold medallions.[48]

The third draft is very close to the final film, though it features some notable departures. The film took on a more explicit fairy tale-like quality, and the grave seriousness of the previous draft was now replaced with an abundance of humour and snappy character interaction—Han became an amusing, cynical foil for the naïve Luke, while Princess Leia's childish arguing with Han provided some needed warmth. The Kiber crystal is still present, which the whimsical Ben Kenobi possesses and which helps Luke destroy the Death Star. Uncle Owen is much crueller to young Luke Starkiller, stealing the boy's savings and spending it on robots. As well, Luke now reveals that his father's name was Annikin (though they are still not Skywalkers but rather Starkillers). Darth Vader also has a larger role—likely due to the fact that the first of his two scenes in the second draft was among the most memorable in the entire film and because McQuarrie had now designed an impressive villain.

Most significantly, Father Skywalker is now dead and gone, and Ben Kenobi is introduced for the very first time. Luke, however, knew his Jedi father before he died—apparently, Luke's Uncle Owen raised him when his father was killed in battle; the history between the Skywalker relatives is developed closer to that of the final film. Father Skywalker told Luke to contact his friend Ben Kenobi, a Jedi, if he was ever in trouble. Luke brings the Princess' distress message to Ben, where for the first time the fallen-student plot point arises. The previous draft contained background about a

Jedi named Darklighter who fell to the dark side (Bogan) and joined the Sith—now Lucas attached this history to Darth Vader as a way of tightening the history, and also made Darth a once-disciple of Ben Kenobi. Ben tells Luke how one of his disciples took a Kiber crystal from him at the battle of Condawn and became a Sith Lord—later this is revealed as Darth Vader. Luke says his father was also killed in the battle of Condawn, but there doesn't seem to be any connection between Ben's disciple and Father Skywalker's death, evidently being a combat fatality; there are many Sith in this version, so if the father was in fact killed by a Sith it potentially could have been any of them. Since the Clone Wars are referenced (for the very first time), it may be read that Father Skywalker was merely a combat casualty, hence the lack of info of any possible murderer—though it is also not clear if the Battle of Condawn is part of the Clone Wars or an unrelated battle.[*]

A crude version of the backstory is now created in this third draft, although it would not fully transform into the one told of in the film until the next, final draft. "It isn't really until it evolved into what is close to what *Star Wars* now is that I began to go back and deal with the stories that evolved to get us to that point," Lucas said.[49] Lucas' notes on the story's pre-history were beginning to amount to a more developed world now that he was introducing specific characters such as Father Skywalker and Ben Kenobi, and it is here that he finally began organizing them into a cohesive pre-history outline, totalling, in Lucas' words, about seven or eight pages by the time the final draft was written the next year.[50] "I just sat down and went through the entire story," he told Laurent Bouzereau. "I think it came around the third or fourth draft. I wrote a treatment or a book of notes…it was reasonably loose, but it laid out the basic story of what happens, who does what to whom, and the various major issues."[51] As he describes, it was not a proper treatment but rather a collection of character descriptions and notes which, taken as a whole, fleshed out the detailed background of the environment:

> When I wrote the…screenplay I had written a backstory for all the characters so I knew where they came from…I had to know kind of where all these characters came from and how they fit together and what the story was. So that

---

[*] In *The Making of Star Wars*, Rinzler reports a private conversation with Lucas in December of 1975 (p. 107) which might reference this version. Lucas describes the backstory but neglects any mention of Vader killing Skywalker, only that Skywalker is killed in a big battle. He may not have integrated the murder-by-Vader plot into the script yet. See Appendix G.

was written up in an outline form with brief descriptions of who everybody was and where they came from. I never really intended it to be turned into a movie…All it really is is just a little backstory of what the Jedi were like, and what the Republic was like, and what the relationship of Obi Wan and Darth Vader was…and the Emperor; "what is the Empire?" The thing about making a movie like this is you have to create a whole world. In this particular case I guess it's a whole universe.[52]

We can see the Father Skywalker character being pushed further and further into obscurity, being a major character in the first draft, a cameo character in the second, and now in the third he has been killed before the story begins—and replaced with Ben Kenobi. In fact, this would become a problem for Lucas when crafting the sequel, when Father Skywalker was re-introduced and the two characters revealed to be essentially one and the same. The next draft would place Father Skywalker's death even further into history.

The seed for this story point can be found in the previous draft—in draft two, Father Skywalker's son Biggs says he believes his father was killed in battle. With the father in that draft not an active participant but rather a presence looming over Luke, eliminating his meagre cameo at the film's conclusion increased the mystery which was already heavily created around him; with him appearing and then merely watching the Death Star battle, he served no purpose, thus he is made to be dead before the film begins.[*]

Ben is created out of a fusion of previous Skywalker ("Starkiller") characters. He shares the warrior history and personality of General Luke Skywalker and Kane Starkiller from the rough draft (the two essentially being the same character) and the wise presence of The Starkiller from the second draft. Ben is essentially a continuation of The Starkiller from draft two—ancient, wise and with a magical aura—but with elements of the previous General Skywalker/Kane Starkiller version also mixed in, being powerful, cunning and fatherly. Since the old and wise Starkiller has evolved into Ben Kenobi, Father Skywalker reverts back to his first incarnation: the powerful warrior from draft one (Kane Starkiller), now re-named Annikin. Ben Kenobi is effectively the uber-father, being made out of the previous three versions, with a slightly more whimsical touch in the vein of wizards Merlin or Gandalf. He is also made to be hiding on Utapau (Tatooine), reminiscent of Kane Starkiller hiding from the Sith on Utapau at the start of the rough draft.

---

[*] Make note of this aspect: Lucas would kill off Ben Kenobi in the third act of draft (revised) four for this same reason

Appropriately, since Father Skywalker is the one who passes on the Kiber crystal to protect Luke in his final battle in draft two, that duty now is transferred to Kenobi.

The Clone Wars are now mentioned for the first time, with Kenobi keeping a "journal of the Clone Wars," which Luke has read. The Clone Wars are not elaborated upon, and as we shall see in the development of *Empire Strikes Back*, it seems Lucas himself had no specific idea of what they were other than a famous long-ago war akin to World War II which involved the Jedi (naturally, since the Jedi are essentially soldiers—Kenobi is said to have once been "The commander of the White Legions"). The "journal of the Clone Wars" reference is reminiscent of the "Journal of the Whills" reference, continuing Lucas' interest in a mythical journal which chronicles legendary events within the story itself.

Ben Kenobi introduces himself in the third draft:

BEN
What brings a young boy like you way out here?

Luke bristles at the use of "boy."

LUKE
I'm Luke Starkiller, guardian of the Bendu.

BEN
Oh, so you're a warrior then?

LUKE
Of course. I'm a Bendu officer.

Ben studies the young farmer through narrowed eyes. He suppresses a smile.

LUKE
Did you take me for a trapper of a farmer? Good! Then my disguise is all right. I was afraid I might not look authentic.

Luke notices the old man is impressed with his story, and begins to feel expansive.

LUKE
You can never be too careful in these times. A Bendu officer never gives himself away. I'm actually on a dangerous mission that's of the gravest importance to the...

Luke suddenly realizes the old man might be an Imperial spy and a worried look crosses his face. Ben laughs heartily.

BEN
You're right! I could be an Imperial spy. For a Bendu officer, you're quite a fool.

Luke is embarrassed and concentrates on making Threepio comfortable.

LUKE
Who are you anyway?

BEN
You might say I'm part of the landscape here. They call me Ben Kenobi.

Luke is dumbstruck. Then with a combination of awe and excitement he finds his voice.

LUKE
You're General Kenobi?!? The Jedi knight! The commander of the White Legions?

BEN
I'm afraid it's been a long time since the White Legions roamed the stars. But I have the memories.

With Kenobi, the backstory now evolved further and there appears to be a subtle influence from the subtext of John Ford's *The Searchers*, an influence which first began to seep in with the frontier setting introduced in the second draft—its influence here may even be not a deliberate one but an unconscious one from absorption of the film. The strongest similarities are present in Kenobi, who is comparable in some ways to John Wayne's character of Ethan Edwards. In *The Searchers*, Ethan is an old, hardened veteran of a legendary war: the American Civil War. He fought on the side of the Confederacy, and so ultimately lost, but, much like the Jedi who eventually lost the Old Republic, Ethan has not given up his oath of allegiance, nor has he given up his sabre. Ethan eventually passes on the sabre to his brother's son, Ben, as a gift. The film begins with him returning home to the desolate homestead of his brother, Aaron, who has a wife and four children. The film follows the relationship of ex-Confederate Ethan and his brother's eldest son, Martin, as they embark on a rescue mission together. Martin, we later learn, was actually adopted—Ethan himself rescued him as a baby when his real parents were killed and took him to live with his brother on their farm (we will later see this brother plot point incorporated in *Revenge of the Jedi*).*

Also notable is that the family's neighbour is a man named Lars—"Lars" being one of the first names Lucas jotted down in 1973, again perhaps indicating a more subversive, unconscious influence. As the frontier setting of the moisture farm became more important in the script, Lucas continued to pluck similar elements from *The Searchers*—for instance, though Kenobi is mostly comprised of the former father characters as well as the Mifune-derived General Skywalker from previous drafts and embellished with wizard and shaman-like touches, the multi-faceted Kenobi also shares some qualities with Ethan Edwards in his history and relationships with other characters. Lucas would finally place in the fourth draft an explicit mimicry of *The Searchers* when Luke returns to the ravaged moisture farm.

The Force of Others has been somewhat simplified in this third draft, though it is still explained in detail, but here it begins to take on a more mystical form. Ben Kenobi explains the Force to Luke:

LUKE
My father used to talk about the Force of Others. But he never told me what it was...

BEN
Let's just say the Force is something a Jedi Warrior deals with. It is an energy field in oneself, a power that controls ones acts, yet obeys ones commands. It is nothing, yet it makes marvels appear before your very eyes. All living things generate this Force field, even you.

LUKE
(amazed)
You mean I generate an energy field?

---

* In a remarkable coincidence, Martin and Ethan are searching for Martin's adopted sister Debbie—Leia, whom Kenobi and Luke must rescue, would also be made into Luke's sister in 1981 as we will later learn. They eventually discover that she is being held captive by an imposing, grim-looking Comanche named Scar—it is later revealed that Scar was the one who in fact massacred Martin's family. This parallels *Star Wars*, where Luke resuces the princess from the man who killed his father (and the Lars).

BEN
It surrounds you and radiates from you. A Jedi can feel it flowing from him...
(patting his stomach)
... from here!

## In the next scene it is elaborated upon:

BEN
A Jedi's power is measured by the amount of the Force that is stored within him, and I have little of the Force left in me.

LUKE
How can you store an energy field within you?

BEN
When a creature dies, the force it generated remains. The Force is all around us. It can be collected and transmitted through the use of a Kiber crystal. It's the only way to amplify the power of the Force within you.
[...]
I had one, but it was taken at the battle of Condawn...

LUKE
That's where my father was killed.

BEN
Yes. It was a black day. One of my disciple's [sic] took the crystal and became a Sith Lord. It was a black day. The few crystals that remain are in the possession of the Sith Lords on Alderaan. That's how they've become so powerful.

LUKE
Do the Sith know the ways of the Force?

BEN
They use the Bogan Force.

LUKE
Like Bogan weather, or bogan times. I thought that was just a saying.

BEN
There are two halves of the Force of Others. One is positive and will help you if you learn how to use it. But the other half will kill you if you aren't careful. This negative side of the Force is called the Bogan, which is where the expression came from, and it is the part that is used by the Dark Lords to destroy their opponents. Both halves are always present. The Force is on your

right, the Bogan is on your left. The Kiber Crystal can amplify either one. The Crystal Darth stole was the last one in the possession of the Jedi. When he joined the Sith, the power of the Dark Lords was completed.

Of note is Kenobi's above reference to "Darth," illuminating the forgotten aspect of the film that Darth was Vader's literal first name and not a title or rank.

The theme of artificial limbs reoccurs in the third draft, this time in Ben Kenobi. The previous draft had a character named Montross Holdaack with artificial parts as well. Lucas was very much interested in incorporating this into the film.

Vader still wears his breath mask in the opening scene. He is also much crueller and sinister in this draft, and is even seen drinking from a flask—this curious incident indicates that, once again, he only wears his mask for the opening sequence, or at least has removed it for this particular scene. He also faces Kenobi in a lightsaber match but Kenobi escapes and is not killed, and Vader finally survives the final attack on the Death Star, his ship limping off into space to fight another day.

The next version of the script would be the final draft.

A major new plot point introduced in the third draft is that of Ben Kenobi and his fallen student, Darth Vader. The backstory begins to be shaped closer to that of the final film, with Luke claiming that his father was killed in the same battle in which Vader betrayed the Jedi. Darth was a student of Kenobi's when he betrayed the Jedi, while Father Skywalker was an elder Knight of close age and status to Kenobi. It is said in the third draft that Kenobi fought in the Clone Wars, and it is presumed that Father Skywalker did as well, perhaps chalking his death up to simply being killed in battle. Alternatively, since the Sith were exterminating all the Jedi, it also makes logical sense that a Sith Lord killed him. Whether that was Vader is never mentioned, though it is a strange coincidence that Vader was also at the battle of Condawn, but we must assume that a point of such significance would be made clear.[*]

More likely the close connection inspired Lucas to make Vader outright kill him in the next draft since Father Skywalker was already killed in the same battle—it was a way of tightening the story, of connecting characters and relationships, which is the main thing Lucas was doing in the third and fourth drafts, such as the connecting character of Ben Kenobi. In draft two, this history was attached to the Jedi Darklighter, who abandoned his

---

[*] Appendix G contains a discussion of one possible exception to this

training and joined the Sith; Lucas tightened the script by attaching this history to Vader in draft three. In draft four, taking this history further by having Vader be the killer of Luke's father gives the hero extra incentive to fight the Empire as well as giving Vader an extra menace and interconnecting all the major characters of the story.

The name of the battle, Condawn, is also curious. It is well known that Lucas eventually centred the death of Father Skywalker and the subsequent duel between Kenobi and Vader around some kind of volcanic setting, a "volcano," or fiery "pit," or "crater," as is most often described. The name itself, Condawn, with "dawn" being the root word, connotes imagery of flames. Lucas may have had in mind the volcanic setting in this draft, or, more likely in my opinion, his own naming of the battle inspired him to set the eventual incident on a fiery landscape, a highly evocative image.

The concept of a character falling or being thrown into a fiery pit of some kind can even be traced back to the first synopsis of 1973, where General Skywalker is thrown off a thousand-foot cliff and into a boiling lake—luckily for him he is able to grab a vine and survive. When the issue of wounding Vader in a fiery setting came about, Lucas may have consciously or unconsciously recycled this idea.

So, with the third draft, we finally start seeing personal backstories being developed. Though there is a history to the galaxy in the previous drafts, personal histories do not emerge until the third draft, where characters begin to have rich and dynamic pasts and become interconnected to each other. The fundamental chassis for the final story is also laid in this draft, and it is here that the first hints of a larger series begin to manifest—Luke poised to be developed as a Jedi by his newfound mentor Ben Kenobi, Darth Vader limping off into space to fight another day and other plot threads left open-ended. The film was structured as a self-contained tale but, as Lucas would stipulate in the contracts he would fight for shortly after the creation of this draft,[53] there was the distinct possibility to progress the series in continuing adventures, much like the serials the film was supposed to emulate. Lucas, however, wasn't sure if these would ever be made, so he hired author Alan Dean Foster to write them first as a duo of sequel novels.

## *Home Stretch*

Lucas' notes reveal possibilities for the next draft: "Change Death Star name...Luke doesn't know father Jedi; Ben tells Luke about father."[54] In a December 29th, 1975 conversation with author Alan Dean Foster, Lucas expressed additional thoughts on his in-progress fourth draft:

> I'm thinking I'm taking the Kiber Crystal out. I thought it really distracted from Luke and Vader; it made them seem too much like supermen, and it's hard to root for supermen...I'm dealing with the Force a little more subtly now. It's a force field that has a good side and a bad side, and every person has this force field around them; and when you die, your aura doesn't die with you, it joins the rest of the life force. It's a big idea—I could write a whole movie just about the Force of Others. Now it really comes down to that scene in the movie where Ben tries to get Luke to swordfight with the chrome baseball when he's blindfolded. He has to trust his feelings rather than his senses and logic—that's essentially what the Force of Others comes down to...Vader runs off in the end, shaking his fist: "I'll get you yet!" In a one-to-one fight Vader could probably destroy Luke...I'm going to have [Luke's] father leave him his laser sword. I have to have a scene where Luke pulls out the laser sword and turns it on, to give the audience a sense of what laser swords are all about. Otherwise there is no way in the world to explain what happens in the cantina. It happens so quickly that unless you know that it's a laser sword, you'll be lost...[Luke's] uncle isn't a son of a bitch anymore; because he gets killed, I have to make him more sympathetic, so you'll hate the Empire.[55]

After exploring nearly a half dozen different stories and scripts, Lucas had finally found the film in the fairy tale adventure of young farmboy Luke Starkiller becoming an unlikely galactic hero and discovering the ancient ways of the Jedi. After a struggle of almost three years, Lucas' story had evolved to its finishing state. On December 17th, 1975, Lucas spoke to Charles Lippincott about the ongoing writing process as his fourth draft neared completion, just days after the film was finally green-lit by the Fox board of directors:

> The problem is what happens in a lot of movies. It started as a concept. So I wanted to make a movie in outer space, let's say an action-adventure movie just like Flash Gordon used to be. People running around in spaceships, shooting each other, and exotic people and exotic locations, and an Empire. I knew I wanted to have a big battle in outer space, a dogfight, so that's what I started with. Then I asked myself, *What story can I tell?* So I was searching for a story for a long time. I went through several stories, trying to find the one that was right, that would have enough personality, tell the story I wanted to tell, be

entertaining, and, at the same time, include all the action-adventure aspects that I wanted. That's really where the evolution came from: Each story was a totally different story about totally different characters before I finally landed on *the* story. A lot of the scripts have the same scenes in them. On the second script I pilfered some of the scenes from the first script, and I kept doing it until I finally got the final script—which is the one I am working on now—which has everything from all the other scripts I wanted. Now what I'm doing in this rewrite is I'm slowly shaving down the plot so it seems to work within the context of everything I wanted to include. After that, I'll go through and do another rewrite, which will develop characters and dialog.[56]

Which finally brings us to the fourth draft, and, basically, the movie itself. The fourth draft was titled *"The Adventures of Luke Starkiller* as taken from the Journal of the Whills. Saga I: *Star Wars,"* and is dated as January 1st, 1976. The characters underwent minor changes, the additional Sith Lords were cut out of the film with Vader now as their single representative, the Kiber crystal was no more, and all the scenes on the Alderaan dungeon were transferred to the Death Star, making it the all-purpose threat.[*] Luke now *discovers* that his father was once a Jedi—but there is still no mention of Vader killing him. The sixteen-year-old Princess Leia had also now become the centre of a mild love triangle between Luke and Han. In this draft, the more basic story of the third draft was simplified even more—Ben is now wiser and more magical in his presence, while the Force of Others is now known only as the Force, and is talked about only in the most general and mystical of terms. The specific, science-fiction aspects of the earlier drafts have now become generalised "archetypes."

Recognizing this, Lucas opened his script with the familiar storybook tagline. He said in late December, 1975 of the upcoming fourth draft: "I put this little thing on it: 'A long time ago in a galaxy far, far away, an incredible adventure took place.' Basically, it's a fairy tale now."[57]

A frantic period of pre-production followed in early 1976, as Lucas moved to England and the production began gearing up for shooting in Tunisia in March. Costumes, casting, sets and designs were finalized and completed, but Lucas still managed to find time to improve his script.

---

[*] Rinzler says this came down to budget cuts, in his *Making of Star Wars*, p. 106. He also provides a transcription of a meeting between Lucas and Kurtz on January 10th, 1976 where Lucas describes an alternate version of the Death Star escape involving the group being captured and Kenobi ambushing their captors as they are arrested (pp. 114-115).

Just as he promised, Lucas followed up the fourth draft with a revision that focused on character and dialogue, and smoothing out scenes. This was accomplished mainly by his friends: Gloria Katz and Willard Huyck came to England and polished up the fourth draft, adding humour, rewriting dialogue and humanising the characters, amounting to about thirty percent of the dialogue by Lucas' estimate.[58] "Just before I started to shoot I asked them to help me rework some of the dialog," he said in *The Making of Star Wars*. "When I'd finally finished the screenplay, I looked at it and wasn't happy with the dialog I had written. Some of it was all right, but I felt it could be improved, so I had Bill and Gloria help me come up with some snappy one-liners."[59]

Further changes gave scenes more convincing life, including a sassier Princess Leia, and a scene where Han Solo blows away an alien bounty hunter sent to kill him. Ben Kenobi is also now formerly-known as "Obi Wan," creating a more interesting dynamic where Luke doesn't realise that Leia's "Obi Wan" is the same person as "old Ben."

Among other scene changes Lucas made in this revision was a crucial extension of the scene between Luke and Ben in his hut: not only does Kenobi reveal to Luke that his father was really a Jedi, but now he gives him a further revelation about how he died: "He was betrayed and murdered...by a young Jedi, Darth Vader."[60]

A month into shooting, Lucas then made the decision to change "Starkiller" to "Skywalker."[61] "When Charles Manson was in the news," Lucas explained in *Mythmaker*, "people who knew about the name Starkiller started asking, 'Are you making a movie about mass murderers or something?' I said 'Okay, I won't use that name.'"[62] During production, Lucas also decided to have Darth Vader kill Kenobi in their duel, resulting in his disembodied voice aiding Luke in the Death Star attack. "I started writing the revised fourth draft while we were in London doing preproduction," Lucas said in *The Making of Star Wars*. "I continued it when I was in Tunisia and didn't finish it till we were back in England."[63] With these final additions, *Star Wars* as we know it had come into existence.

Let's examine it a bit.

### Subtext

The character of Obi Wan was relatively new to the story, having only appeared for the first time in the previous draft. Similar to the way the final version of Darth Vader was created, Kenobi is a combination of previous characters and elements, fitting since the two are in many ways opposite forces, and though Kenobi first appears in the third draft his presence has been in the script since the beginning in various disjointed forms, specifically as Kane Starkiller, General Skywalker and The Starkiller. With Ben Kenobi the story of *Star Wars* took on a new dynamic, and the character centred the plot much more than the previous drafts Lucas struggled through. Kenobi also gave the story a firmer sense of history and depth, and with him came a fascinating backstory which linked all of the central players of the film together—Father Skywalker, Leia, Luke and Darth Vader. The creation of Ben changed the story of *Star Wars* more than anything else, and suddenly all of the story threads and vague histories came into sharp focus. Luke's mysterious Jedi father, the newly-invented Clone Wars, the rise of the Empire, Darth Vader's past, Uncle Owen's antagonism of Luke, the introduction of Han Solo, and Luke's connection to the droids and Princess Leia are all linked up with Kenobi, who also fills the audience in on the history of the Jedi and the Republic, while acting as a mentor and father figure to Luke. Kenobi ties the story together and without him, it would fall apart. Lucas finally found the story he was searching for for three years.

With Ben Kenobi and the fourth draft, Lucas had now created a rich backstory to both the environment and the characters. Father Skywalker lived on Tatooine with his friend, Ben Kenobi. When the Clone Wars began, Kenobi convinced him to go off and fight, but Owen, Father Skywalker's brother, thought that he should stay on Tatooine and remain as a farmer. Father Skywalker was already a great pilot and naturally became a great warrior in the war, with Kenobi becoming a General. Together, the two became Jedi knights of the Republic, and fought side by side. Kenobi began training others to be Jedi, but one of them, a man named Darth Vader, fell to the dark side of the Force. When the Emperor maneuvered his way into dictatorship, Darth Vader joined him. The Jedi opposed the new dictatorship, and thus became enemies, and Vader hunted down the Jedi, murdering Father Skywalker. Kenobi was able to escape the genocide by returning to Tatooine as a hermit, and Father Skywalker's only son, Luke, was adopted by Owen, who resented Ben for the burden of Luke and for the death of Luke's father.

Re-constructing the initial history of Father Skywalker must be done by the clues contained in the film, some of them explicit, many of them implied. One of the keys to this re-construction is the compelling character of Owen Lars, Luke's uncle. His cautious and grumpy demeanor and restrictive attitude towards Luke reveals a bitter resentment of the adventurous lifestyle of his brother, Father Skywalker, a lifestyle which drove Father Skywalker away from the Tatooine farm and into a life of heroism that left him dead. As Ben says to Luke of the fundamental split between the two Skywalker siblings, Owen "didn't hold with your father's ideals, thought he should have stayed here and not gotten involved."

Owen represented the traditional man, the unchanging man, the man who lives a content and uninteresting life, doing what he is told and keeping the family tradition. Perhaps above all else, *Star Wars* is about change—about Luke growing up, leaving his farm and becoming an adult. Owen represents the antithesis to this theme; he is everything that Father Skywalker and Luke are not. He is unadventurous, uninquistive, unchanging and afraid of the world outside his sphere of existence. He probably came from a long line of farmers—he is a farmer because his father was a farmer, and his father before that, and so on, all afraid to break out of the mold and become something more, to defy what is expected of them. Father Skywalker, on the other hand, was the black sheep, the one who was not afraid to break tradition and leave home. Owen, of course, disagreed with this lifestyle and tried to convince him to stay on Tatooine when Father Skywalker went off with Ben Kenobi to get involved with the Clone Wars. Owen stayed on the farm, doing what he always did, and of course his brother ended up dead, re-enforcing his fearful view of change. His murdered brother's only son was thrust upon him, and Owen blamed Obi Wan for all the misfortune that had occurred, forbidding Luke from ever talking to Obi Wan when he returned to hide from the Sith Lords who sought to kill him. He tells Luke that Kenobi is senile, and keeps the truth about his father's heroic past a secret. "[Owen] was afraid you'd follow old Obi Wan on some damned fool idealistic crusade like your father," Kenobi admits as he passes on the lightsaber that represents the fundamental difference between Owen and his brother. "Your father wanted you to have this when you were old enough, but your uncle wouldn't allow it."

Owen, of course, fears that Luke could become like his father, could become seduced by the ideal of adventure, and so he tells Luke that his father was a boring old navigator on a spice freighter and tries to keep Luke on the farm as long as possible, discouraging him from any kind of grand ambition. Luke mustn't dream, mustn't leave Tatooine. Owen is hard on Luke because he believes it is for Luke's own good—those who venture off the farm end up victims of the outside world. But Luke naturally takes after his father, being an instinctive pilot and dreaming of joining the Imperial space academy, clashing with his strict uncle on this. "Luke's just not a farmer, Owen, he has too much of his father in him," Beru says with empathy, to which Owen tersely confesses, "That's what I'm afraid of." The third draft communicates this original intent more explicitly, as Luke runs away from the farm to embark on his quest, to which Owen observes "That boy's going to get himself killed; he's just like his father." But all of Owen's efforts cannot stop Luke, and as he takes on the lightsaber from Obi Wan that represents the adventurous spirit of his father, Owen's fears of the boy following in his father's footsteps are realised—he has, as Obi Wan says, taken his first step into a much larger world. Luke's destiny is inevitable, and the lesson is that you must take risks and leave the security of the traditional life if you want to achieve greatness. In this, we see a direct port of Lucas' own life, leaving the confines of Modesto at the protest of his fearful father, who was sure Lucas would be corrupted by the "cesspool" of L.A.

One conclusion from a consideration of all the data thus far that runs contrary, perhaps shockingly so, to common knowledge is the realisation that at this time Darth Vader was not yet written as the father of Luke. Nor was Princess Leia written as Luke's sister. Not only were these concepts absent from the earliest written material, they are absent from the finished film itself. The irony is quite staggering considering that these relations are now the core of the storyline. Vader was always meant to be a simple villain, and Father Skywalker a separate character. Lucas' personal notes expelled his every thought on the film, often in a stream-of-conscious matter, and contain all sorts of alternate possibilities and tentative ideas that are suffixed with question marks—if such a major idea had entered his head he would have surely made a note of it and given it some exploration. Even more significantly, in Lucas' private conversations and in his own personal notes the characters are still conceived as separate, even in 1975 and 1976, where the concept of Father Skywalker being murdered (by Vader starting in 1976) frequently is referenced, and this story perspective privately continues well into 1977.

Not only is the concept of Vader being Father Skywalker *absent* from any and all drafts and writings, but the idea is contradicted at every turn. The father is alive and well until the third draft, and by that point it is clear that he and Darth Vader are still continuing as the characters they were in the previous drafts—noble Jedi and evil henchman respectively. In fact, even in the third draft Luke knew his father as a boy, making the notion impossible still; it isn't until the final draft that the character became a true part of history. Reading the scripts in the order in which they were written, there is a very clear linear progression of creative ideas. If Lucas had at one time speculated creatively about such a concept as a "Father Vader," he very clearly had dismissed it and *instead* pursued the orthodox storyline where Skywalker and Vader are separate; Lucas' own notes and private discussions indicate that there are no "red herrings" in the film—the orthodox backstory was a sincere and concrete commitment and was an integral part of the film. As an example further bringing all of these arguments together, Lucas spells out the Vader backstory in a private conversation with Carol Titelman in 1977, not only showing him as a separate character from Father Skywalker (now named Annikin) but also laying out exactly how Vader was to hunt down the Jedi until only Kenobi and Luke's father remained:

> When the Jedi tried to restore order, Darth Vader was still one of the Jedi. What he would do is catch the Jedi off-guard and, using his knowledge of the Force, he would kill the Jedi without them realizing what was happening. They trusted him and they didn't realize he was the murderer who was decimating their ranks. At the height of the Jedi, there were several hundred thousand. At the time of the Rebellion, most of them were killed. The Emperor had some strong forces rally behind him, as well, in terms of the army and the Imperial forces that he'd been building up secretly. The Jedi were so outnumbered that they fled and were tracked down. They tried to regroup, but they were eventually massacred by one of the special elite forces led by Darth Vader. Eventually, only a few, including Ben and Luke's father, were left. Luke's father is named Annikin.[64]

Later on, as more and more sequels were made, new meaning was retroactively inserted into existing scenes. When Vader was revealed as Luke's father in *Empire Strikes Back*, it raised a lot of question, namely who was lying—Vader or Kenobi? It turns out the bad guys tell the truth, and now when looking at the scene where Luke asks Ben of his father the scene plays totally different—the pause Alec Guinness took to deliver Luke the heartbreaking news that his father was murdered by Vader, Kenobi's own student, now reads as him pausing to make up a lie. The change comes not in alteration to the content itself, but in the mental perception of the audience caused by subsequent revelations. But make no mistake about it: although the retroactive changes to old scenes like this still work in the dramatic sense, it was never the original intention. Kenobi paused because it was hard news to tell his young friend, who had been deceived by his uncle; as the novelisation described the scene, although Uncle Owen could lie to Luke, it was something the noble and truthful Ben could not bring himself to do.[65]

Similarly in Luke and Ben's first meeting: Father Skywalker obviously knew he had a son and wished that he would one day be able to pass on to him his lightsaber, however, with his death at Vader's hands, it is Obi Wan's duty to honour his friend's wish. Owen didn't want Luke to learn of the Force or to talk to Ben not because Ben let his father become evil but because Ben's persuasion to become a Jedi ended up causing Father Skywalker's death. This is the reason Luke's aunt and uncle are wary of Ben, despite the fact that the exchange "He's got too much of his father in him," "That's what I'm afraid of," pays off better with the retroactive change.

These types of retroactive changes are common in complex and long-running series such as what *Star Wars* would eventually become, where the interpretation of previous tales is altered by information revealed in subsequent entries, and are known in fan communities as "retcon," or "retroactive continuity" alterations. Often, retcons are simply the result of ongoing writing that is primarily made up on the go, desire on the part of the writer to keep things fresh for his or herself, and the demands of keeping an enraptured audience surprised with a previous continuity already established. Perhaps the best example of this method of ongoing writing is the most popular form of serial in the modern world: daytime soap operas. "I wasn't dead, it was really my twin brother!", "I'm really the baby's father!", "I shot J.R.!" etc., where unexpected twists leave the audience tuning in next episode and keep the story fresh by constantly reinventing what had already preceded.

The retroactive changes also make Kenobi into a lying manipulator, instead of the truthful father-figure he was supposed to be, while Vader becomes more humanised and less of a villain—an ongoing transformation that would occur in the following films.

Similarly, the fact that Darth Vader's name is in fact Darth Vader—and not a rank, title or alias—is reinforced when Kenobi finally meets him and calls him "Darth," rather than "Vader."

> BEN
> Only a master of evil, Darth.

And again:

> BEN
> You can't win, Darth. If you
> strike me down, I shall become more
> powerful than you can possibly
> imagine.

This is consistent with the earlier scene wherein Kenobi says "a young Jedi named Darth Vader." Back in the days of the film's release, everyone referred to him as Darth, such as Carrie Fisher in *The Making of Star Wars* 1977 television special, as it was obviously his first name. For a much more thorough examination of this point, see Appendix C. Lucas himself treated the character rather flippantly behind-the-scenes, referring to the above scene merely as "the final battle between Ben and the warlord" in one production meeting with cameraman Gil Taylor,[66] a perspective that is consistent with the lack of importance beyond the role of serial-henchman Lucas grants the character in his private notes and conversations. In fact, in Rinzler's authoritative *Making of Star Wars*, Lucas barely even mentions the character, fitting since Vader has only a few scenes in the film.

In addition, in the above-quoted scene, Vader says "When I left you, I was but the learner. Now, I am the master." This of course is perfectly in keeping with what Obi Wan tells Luke earlier—Darth was a student of his, who turned evil. However, Obi Wan also says, "I was a Jedi knight, the same as your father." Vader was only a student when he left Obi Wan, "a young Jedi," while Father Skywalker was close to Obi Wan's age and was a full, experienced knight. If they are to be the same person, then there is direct contradiction here—was he a young student or was he an older Jedi knight? As it stands, the viewers can now, in the "Saga" viewpoint, contrive an explanation by reasoning that Vader was hyperbolizing his inexperience as a Jedi and meaning to say that he is now wise and fully trained through the dark side, and that Kenobi was talking in general terms.

It would now be pertinent to discuss the matter of whether or not Vader and Obi Wan have met since Vader left him, as we will uncover that this is a pivotal plot point—but one that is actually nowhere hinted at or implied in the film itself. By the time *Return of the Jedi* was released it was revealed that Ben fought Vader on a volcano and wounded him to such an extent that he required the mechanical suit to survive, having fallen into a fiery pit; so-dubbed "The Duel." Since *Star Wars* was written under a different context, with Vader and Father Skywalker separate characters, it is at first not clear if Lucas had the duel in mind, and if he did, what was the form in which it occurred? Did Vader simply abandon Obi Wan and begin hunting down the Jedi knights, or was there a conflict between them? The volcano duel is still viable, even with the original context of the characters in mind—Obi Wan was not battling Father Skywalker because he turned to the dark side, he was battling Vader to *avenge* Father Skywalker's death. This is the story that would eventually be decided upon, to be explored shortly. Another possibility is that Vader came for Obi Wan when the Jedi purge began but Obi Wan fought him off and escaped; Lucas' comments in 1977 may point to this.[67]

Certainly it appears the scene between them on the Death Star can be read either way. Vader says "We meet again, at last"—does this imply "finally we meet since I left you" or "finally we will have a re-match"? Vader follows it up with "When I left you I was but the learner. Now, I am the master." However, this "re-match" interpretation is itself a giant leap that overlooks a simple but often-ignored piece of investigative logic—why are we even looking for hints of a previous encounter? What suggestion or evidence is there in the film itself to propose that such a history even exists?

Without knowledge of the backstory to bias one's perspective of the scene, any reference to a prior conflict vanishes. There is nothing to imply they have fought before; Kenobi says Vader simply abandoned his Jedi training, and when they meet again twenty years later Vader says that the last time they were together he was a mere student and that he left him. Looking at the dialogue and attitudes of the characters, there doesn't seem to be any indication at all of a prior battle between them, and most significantly Kenobi is silent to Luke about any sort of volcano duel between himself and Vader, which surely would have been relevant to Luke. The Death Star confrontation plays out as if it is the first time they have faced each other since Vader joined the dark side.

The issue of Vader leaving Kenobi is a continuing development from draft three, where Vader takes Ben's Kiber crystal. In that version there wasn't any conflict indicated—Kenobi states that Darth merely took the crystal and joined the Sith. No former confrontation is ever implied between them, and perhaps a likely scenario is that Vader took the crystal behind Kenobi's back and never even had to face him, which seems to be a bit more in keeping with the character's backhanded treachery. This whole issue of leaving the Jedi was in turn a continuing development from draft two, where the history played out in a manner similar to this, and was attached to former-Jedi Darklighter—whom Lucas explicitly states did not battle his mentor but that he simply "ran away from his instructor and taught the evil ways of the Bogan Force to a clan of Sith pirates." Lucas simply attached this to Vader for draft three, and it doesn't appear to have changed, nor in draft four.

As well, in draft three when this history is first attached to him, Vader's mask is not yet a permanent fixture—as mentioned before, in one scene it is removed and Vader is drinking from a flask. Vader's armoured space suit might have only been worn for the opening boarding sequence and perhaps the end space battle, with the rest of the film depicting him in some kind of Imperial uniform and of course his face uncovered and portrayed by whatever actor was cast in the role. Thus, he would not have been hideously scarred and certainly not to the extent of having to be encased in a suit to hide his deformities (although, being a hardened war-lord, it would be a reasonable act to give him a face blemished with some of the scars of battle—Lucas' notes for the second draft state that the Sith Knights have gruesome faces to symbolize their evil, "like Linda Blair from *The Exorcist*,"[68] though Lucas may have relented on this with the more humanised Vader in draft three). It is not hard to picture all of Vader's scenes onboard the Death Star, attending conferences and duelling Ben, as being visualised with a "tall, grim" Imperial General much like he is described in the first draft. However, with the fourth draft, Lucas simply decided to use McQuarrie's effectively frightening mask—a skull crossed with a wolf—as the physical personification of him, and, as will be examined shortly, this inadvertently ended up giving Vader a somewhat robotic aura. The fact that the final script and film never show Vader without the mask is purely coincidental in the sense that it is not prompted by anything specific (for the sake of logic, it can be plausibly argued that Darth donned the fearsome suit and helmet upon his turn to the dark side and alliance with the Empire as a symbol of fear and intimidation, much like how stormtroopers adopt their suits as a permanent public image for these reasons. Lucas would implement a similar concept to this orthodox Vader in *Willow*, in the character of General Kael, a tall, grim-looking war-lord who wears a skull mask for most—but not all—of the film).

However, by the time Lucas got to actually shooting the film he had in mind the concept of "The Duel," as he revealed to Mark Hamill on the set in 1976. However, it wasn't the immobilizing, near-fatal duel that would later be decided on, nor anything requiring medical encasement in an iron lung. Rather, Obi Wan and Vader were to fight, and Vader loses the battle when he falls into some kind of volcanic pit. Vader emerges from the pit intact and alive, but he has been hideously scarred, so much so that he must wear a mask and full-body suit to cover his disfiguring injuries, much like Doctor Doom. This was the initial significance of the The Duel.

It would appear that The Duel was invented *after* the fourth draft, after Darth had been written to kill Father Skywalker, as a means of both providing some resolution to that story thread by Kenobi's vengeance as well as explaining why Vader wears the suit, which, because it is worn in every single scene, now came off as being a permanent encasement.* This

---

* Perhaps the second-draft era concept of the Sith having gruesome faces mixed with the permanently-suited Vader to naturally create the story that the encasement was a deliberate cover for a deformity.

indicates The Duel's genesis as probably being somewhere between January, when the initial fourth draft was written, and March, when filming commenced, whereupon the tale was related to Mark Hamill (though filming main unit did not end until July, and the revised fourth draft was being re-written with major story revisions as late as the halfway point of production, so this time period is conservative as Hamill does not specify a date). The revised fourth draft where the plot point of Vader killing Father Skywalker first appears was itself written during this period.

Mark Hamill recalled Lucas telling him the story of The Duel—Hamill's version is somewhat unique, as it includes Obi Wan and Father Skywalker battling Vader *together*, rather than Obi Wan avenging Skywalker's murder afterwards, with Vader and Skywalker both falling into the volcanic pit simultaneously, as well as including additional details about the Emperor scaring Obi Wan "into the forest." Lucas would later tell that after the initial Jedi purge, Obi Wan and Father Skywalker were the last Jedi left alive, with Vader personally hunting down the survivors[69]—perhaps he confronted them both on the site of a volcano, managing to kill Father Skywalker but then was struck down by Kenobi. Other likely explanations are that Lucas told variations on the story since it was not yet set in stone, or simply that Hamill's memory is a bit foggy. Hamill said in 1980:

> I remember very early on asking who my parents were and being told that my father and Obi-Wan met Vader on the edge of a volcano and they had a duel. My father and Darth Vader fell into the crater and my father was instantly killed. Vader crawled out horribly scarred, and at that point the Emperor landed and Obi-Wan ran into the forest, never to be seen again.[70]

This disfiguration encasement would soon become a life-support necessity. In his August 25th, 1977 interview with *Rolling Stone*, George Lucas told this fascinating story, the first public reveal of the newly-created backstory:

*Why does Darth Vader breathe so heavily?*

I had wanted to do that and tie it in with the dialogue…Ben [Burtt] had a lot of work in that too. He did about eighteen different kinds of breathing, through aqualungs and through tubes, trying to find the one that had the right sort of mechanical sound, and then decide whether it would be totally rhythmical and like an iron lung. That's the idea. It was a whole part of the plot that essentially got cut out. It may be in one of the sequels…It's about Ben and Luke's father and Vader when they are young Jedi knights. But Vader kills Luke's father, then Ben and Vader have a confrontation, just like they have in *Star Wars*, and Ben almost kills Vader. As a matter of fact, he falls into a volcanic pit and gets fried and is one destroyed being. That's why he has to wear the suit with a mask, because it's a breathing mask. It's like a walking iron lung. His face is all horrible inside. I was going to shoot a close-up of Vader where you could see the inside of his face, but then we said, no, no, it would destroy the mystique of the whole thing.[71]

In the interview with *Rolling Stone*, Lucas says he initially wanted breathing only over Vader's dialogue, as if his speech was merely filtered through the mask. But when Ben Burtt did the sound design he came up with a constant rhythm, a cold mechanical sound, like an iron lung. It was an aspect Ben Burtt added in post-production.[72]

When Lucas saw how robotic Vader looked in the suit with the rhythmic, cold mechanical breathing Burtt had created, he might have decided that perhaps Vader wore the suit as a form of life-support and that he was partially re-assembled as a cyborg, which fit in perfectly with the continuity, since Lucas had already come up with the idea that Vader was hideously scarred by Kenobi. Thus, Vader might not have truly become mechanical until the final film, until the sound mix. Lucas had always been fond of the idea of someone having their battle-related injuries re-habilitated with mechanical parts—it appears in every draft *except* the final one. Now he had a chance to finally use it. In fact, after Lucas became excited by the idea, the "walking iron lung" concept was overzealously emphasized, as Burtt tells, and was then reverted back to a simpler and less distracting breathing. Ben Burtt explained in a 1993 interview:

> The original concept I had of Darth Vader was a very noise-producing individual. He came into the scene, he was breathing like some queezing windmill, you could hear his heart beating, he moved his head [and] you heard motors turning, and he was almost like some kind of a robot in some sense. And he made so much noise that we sort of had to cut back on that concept. In the first experimental mixes we did in *Star Wars*, he sounded like an operating room, you know, an emergency room, you know, moving around.[73]

The first *official* mention of The Duel in a Lucasfilm publication does not occur until late 1977, in the magazine *Star Wars Poster Monthly*:

> What is less well-known is that Vader himself was then almost killed by Ben Kenobi, who was understandably enraged at his disciple's fall from grace. Vader's life might have ended then and there with a quick stab of a lightsaber; instead, during the fight, Vader stumbled backwards and fell into a volcanic pit

where he was nearly fried alive. What remained of his human body was dragged out and preserved by encasing it in an outsize black metal suit— virtually a walking iron lung. His face, now too horrible to behold, remains permanently hidden behind the sinister metal breath screen from which his red eyes glint unmercifully. Only his heavy, rasping breath reveals the suit's true function.[74]

Now that the iron lung version had been settled on, the above quote in turn *emphasises* how badly Vader was hurt, seeing as his remains had to be dragged out and resuscitated (presumably by the Emperor, as Hamill implies in his less severe version of the tale).

### End Point

With the completion of the revised fourth draft screenplay, the final script was tightly paced— "always on the move," as Obi Wan would put it—but now had the strength of strong characters to support the outlandish plot and design. From clever ironies like the "damsel in distress" grabbing the gun from her rescuers and shouting orders at them ("I mean they can't even rescue her!" Lucas once said of his lovably clumsy characters[75]), to outright comedy like Han's failed attempt at explaining the prison shootout to a radio dispatcher, to the touching sentimentality of Obi Wan's self-sacrifice, the script had finally arrived as an engaging adventure film that would become a cinema classic. Remember, back in 1977, a simple thing such as the cantina sequence was astonishingly original—in fact, people were blown away by Greedo's appearance, with his bizarre language and subtitled dialogue. Outrageous aliens drinking ale, getting into bar brawls and listening to swing music—nothing so imaginative and unique had ever been attempted in a film before. Today it seems almost a pedestrian concept but back then it was absolute genius, something never before put on a movie screen, and the scene finishes as if it were written by Sergio Leone. "Cowboys in space," Lucas had once said. He gave us so much more.

Lucas recollected writing the film in a candid 1977 interview with French magazine *Ecran*, revealing how fluid and collaborative the undertaking truly was:

It took me about three years to write the screenplay. I wrote four versions, meaning four completely different plots, before finding the one that satisfied me. It was really difficult because I didn't want [*Star Wars*] to be a typical science-fiction…I wanted it to be a truly imaginative film. I had some good ideas in the first version, but no solid storyline, which is a challenge for me because I hate 'plots'. The difficulty was managing to find an overarching theme.

*You wrote the screenplay all by yourself?*

Yeah, it's terrible. It's painful, atrocious.

*You didn't work with screenwriters?*

At the end I had some friends come to England to do some last-minute rewriting when we were just about to shoot.

*But before that you didn't discuss it with anyone?*

Well, yeah! We're all one group of friends here: Francis Coppola, Matt Robbins, Bill Heiken, Gloria Katz, and a friend I went to school with who works in my production office here; we're all screenwriters. We read each other's scripts and comment on them. I think this is the only way for us to keep from writing in a total void. I respect the opinions of these friends; their comments are intelligent because they're into the same thing as me.

There are also those who, in addition to being screenwriters, are directors and friends of mine: Coppola, whom I've already mentioned; Phil Kaufman; Martin Scorsese; and Brian de Palma. I show them all of my footage, and they give me precious opinions that I count on. When you don't know people well, they either give you dishonest compliments or tell you how they would shoot it. And that's not what I'm asking them for.

We serve as sounding boards to help at two crucial times in film creation: the first version of the script and the film editing. That's when you need a friend whom you have total confidence in, to tell you: here, you have to cut; there, you have to do this. Often, these are obvious things, but often, too, they're sections that you've spent months on, that you've worked on so long you can't see them objectively anymore.

*Tell me a bit about how these discussions worked...*

I wrote the first version of *Star Wars*, we discussed it, and I realised I hated the script. I chucked it and started a new one, which I also threw in the trash. That happened four times with four radically different versions. After each version I had a discussion with those friends. If there was a good scene in the first version, I included it in the second. And so on... the script was constructed this way, scene by scene.

According to the case, I had this person or that person read it. Coppola read three versions, while the friends I invited to England to polish up the dialog saw only the final version. Let's say it was the directors from San

Francisco in particular—Coppola and Phil Kaufman—who followed everything, the ones I went to school with.[76]

Here, the writing method Lucas had slowly cultivated is made explicit. He had previously expressed that his attempts at getting others to write the scripts for his films were so laborious that he finally "gave up" and just did it himself for *Star Wars*[77]—but this is a gross simplification. As the above interview sums up clearly, the process maintained a highly collaborative nature. Lucas would act as the overseer, bouncing the script around to a myriad of editors and co-writers to help steer and shape it, with Lucas himself acting as a filter to take these suggestions and then put them down on the page in a manner which suited his own tastes. On top of that, these efforts still did not render characters as fully as was needed, so the Huycks re-wrote his final draft to give more convincing dialogue and characterisation. The earliest treatments and screenplays were practically all George Lucas, and unsurprisingly they are stilted, confusing and not as convincing or emotionally moving—as the drafts went on, his friends and colleagues had more of an influence, steering characters and dialogue and giving input as to what was working and what wasn't, and in the final draft the script finally emerges as a dramatic and emotional thrillride, given even fuller life by the cast and focus by the picture editing. The cover may have stated "written by George Lucas" but like any competent writer he knew how to overcome the limitations of his own talent.

"This film has been murder," Lucas groaned in *The Making of Star Wars*.[78] "*Graffiti*, I wrote in three weeks. This one took me three years. *Graffiti* was just my life, and I wrote it down. But this, I didn't know anything about. I had a lot of vague concepts, but I didn't really know where to go with it, and I've never fully resolved it. It's very hard stumbling across the desert, picking up rocks, not knowing what I'm looking for, and knowing the rock that I've got is not the rock I'm looking for. I kept simplifying it, and I kept having people read it, and I kept trying to get a more cohesive story." He then adds: "But I'm still not happy with the script. I never have been."[79]

Nonetheless, production was beginning, and whatever it is he had, it was the film. *Star Wars* had been born.

# Chapter IV: Purgatory and Beyond

THOUGH Lucas initially began the project with the thought of doing a mere singular film as a homage to *Flash Gordon*, as he slowly carved out his own unique storyline and universe the notion of sequels began to appear. The second draft from early 1975 is the first sign of potential evidence—it is labelled as "Episode I," and ends with a teaser text roll-up for another adventure. Though it can be argued that this was primarily a narrative device to evoke the serials and not necessarily evidence of a genuine plan to sequelise, Lucas had in fact taken this device into the realm of reality and begun to impose the idea that he could explore more stories in the galaxy he had created. This was not just idle daydreaming: when contracts were first negotiated for the film just prior to this draft,[1] Lucas insisted on sequel rights for himself and later made agreements with the actors as well, in this case the two leads of Mark Hamill and Carrie Fisher. In total, he had three contractual films.

Like the *Flash Gordon* series that endured for chapter after chapter, Lucas had in mind the possibility of continuing adventures in his galaxy, but it seems as though he didn't have many specifics, but rather the *concept itself* of continuing the adventure. With his first stipulations for sequels occurring so far back, they are effectively divorced from the storyline of the final film, thus revealing the primary attraction being the idea itself. But by 1976, certainly there were many specific avenues now available to Lucas—the love triangle between Han, Luke and Leia, Luke's continuing

Jedi training (initially by Ben, but since he had re-written him to die he needed to invent a new teacher), the Rebels' continued battle against the Imperials, Darth Vader's revenge, Father Skywalker and Kenobi's past, the mysterious Emperor...and those were just existing story threads. The possibilities were potentially endless.

Although Lucas states that he only thought about doing sequels after the film became a hit,[2] he also mentions that he had sketched out a vague arc for Luke to go through in sequels, as Luke is trained and becomes a Jedi master.[3] Lucas couldn't help but project where the story might progress, even if there was a good chance that none of this would ever see the light of day. "By the time I finished the first *Star Wars*, the basic ideas and plots for *Empire* and *Jedi* were also done."[4] Lucas said around the same time that he had collected his background notes into a pre-history outline, circa draft three and four, that he had also begun thinking about these very sequel threads mentioned previously, and had developed a very vague arc for Luke through the contractual duo of sequels[5]—the Rebels have established a new base to continue their fight against the Empire, while Luke begins training as a Jedi and falls in love with Leia, finally culminating in the epic clash between hero and villain and the Rebels and Empire. This plan, though thin, is given credence by Lucas' admission that he had to invent Yoda unexpectedly since that role was originally intended for Kenobi, but Kenobi had been killed off in the first film when it was thought that Lucas might never get a chance to make subsequent entries.[6] With an actor's contract that stipulated two more films for Luke and Leia and the rights for those films obtained at the expense of a pay cut, it is unsurprising that Lucas had at least pondered where he would ultimately take the story.

Having sequels meant needing conflict, and though the Empire could still be around it needed specific personalities. Darth Vader's survival of *Star Wars* emulated the serial episodes where the villain always escapes at the end to fight another day (Lucas described this draft three development in 1975 as: "Vader runs off in the end shaking his fist: 'I'll get you yet!'"[7]) but it also served the practical purpose of providing the threat for the next film. In the third draft outline Luke confronts Vader face-to-face in a lightsaber duel and kills him—but when Lucas cut this scene out (due to pacing reasons, he states[8]), he had Vader survive the space battle so this scene could be used in the sequel (*Splinter of the Mind's Eye*, which did indeed reprise this).

With Luke's arc complete by the picture's end, Lucas would essentially re-configure the original film into a trilogy, remaking the arc of that film as a three-part series wherein each act of *Star Wars* can be seen as extended as its own film—*Star Wars*, being the first film in the trilogy, would represent act one, showing Luke's initiation into the larger galaxy and introducing all the characters (essentially the Tatooine section of the film); the second film would represent the second act of the original film, developing the content further, having Kenobi train Luke in the Jedi ways (here taking Luke's training onboard the Millennium Falcon and remaking it as its own dedicated arc) and culminating with Luke facing his first trials—in *Star Wars*, it had been the Death Star rescue, but for the sequel it would build on the development of the first film's ending: Luke would have to confront his nemesis, Darth Vader, face to face. The outcome of this confrontation would be a draw, but Luke would come out of the experience now as a full adult and Jedi Knight. The third film would be the resolution and triumph—in *Star Wars*, Luke was put through trials onboard the Death Star, transforming him into a hero, but he then had to take his newfound skills and return to the enemy to destroy it, in that case obliterating the Death Star, which the original film had implied would lead to the fall of the Empire itself. This third act would then be remade as its own film—after his first trial and confrontation with the black knight, Luke had to return, now a full Jedi, and finally slay Darth Vader, which would parallel the final fall of the Empire. Of course, working within the same budgetary confines of the first film—or perhaps less—these films would not contain the scope and scale that the mega-budget sequels of *Empire* and *Jedi* would contain; *Splinter of the Mind's Eye* provides us with a more modest, medium-scale sequel, which we will explore in a few moments.

"I know I've got a better one in me, one that is more refined" Lucas said of sequels in late 1976. "Gene Roddenberry wrote about his *Star Trek* series, and pointed out that it wasn't really until about the tenth or fifteenth episode that they finally got things pulled together. You have to walk around the world you've created a little bit before you can begin to know what to do in it."[9]

These sequels, however, were not yet concrete commitments—*Star Wars* was designed to be a single film, and though he had ideas for additional stories, these were, at this time, to be done only as novels, as he outlined to Alan Dean Foster in a late 1975 meeting, describing the two sequel books the author was to write.[10] However, as we will later learn, he kept the option of making them into films, though he would not make such a decision until after *Star Wars* was a hit.

Thus, the *Adventures of Luke Skywalker* trilogy remained only as an interesting possibility, and that is an important factor to recognize. In 1974 and 1975 Lucas had taken steps to enable the possibility of sequels, but by the time the film was actually shot in 1976 many of these dreams had begun to fade: the 1976 fourth draft, in contrast to the second and third drafts from

1975, is notable for undergoing changes that make the film more satisfying as a stand-alone adventure.

The main change is that, unlike the previous draft, the revised fourth draft sets up that destroying the Death Star will topple the Empire. A new scene appears on the Death Star where Tarkin announces that the senate has been dissolved—an officer protests that without the public illusion of bureaucracy the Empire will not be able to maintain control. Tarkin replies that the senate is no longer needed now that the Death Star is around; if a system were to misbehave, it would simply be obliterated. "Fear will keep the local systems in line—fear of this battle station." Thus, when the Death Star was destroyed, the infrastructure of the Empire collapsed and freedom was restored to the galaxy. The film had also slowly drifted away from sci-fi serialism and more into the realm of a fable—as the "A long time ago" tagline now opens the film, giving it a more self-contained vibe. Luke also completed his arc—he left home, stepped into a larger world, became a hero, and at the end of the fourth draft Ben Kenobi announces to Luke that he is now a Jedi Knight; "You have stepped into your father's shoes," he says when Luke returns from the triumphant Death Star assault.[11] The film now ends on a note that everyone lives happily ever after and that the story is finished. Taking this further, Lucas then killed Kenobi off in the fourth draft revision, believing it would work best for the dramatic arc of the film as a standalone tale.

These changes were probably the response to the enormous difficulties Lucas was encountering with the film at that time, including aggravation in getting a green-light (which did not occur until December 1975), the threat of Fox pulling the plug on the entire production, logistical trouble in the impending production, budget issues, further tensions with Fox, and the realisation that *Star Wars* had little support and would probably not be very successful. As Rinzler describes, Lucas was forced to re-think the script for the fourth draft in more practical terms related to the production, which was not going very smoothly.[12*] Though Lucas still retained tentative measures for an *Adventures of Luke Skywalker* trilogy, and would at the very least make them as novels, he protected himself by approaching *Star Wars* with the pragmatic understanding that it might be all that moviegoers ever

---

* In fact, as Rinzler shows, the contract which would stipulate said sequels still had not been drawn up as Lucas was writing the fourth draft—legally speaking, he only had the single film (though it was probably seen as a likely possibility that he would eventually be granted such rights due to the unimportance generally regarded of them).

saw—and there was always the possibility that he simply wouldn't feel like making sequels, preferring to move on to other projects. If he was unable or decided not to pursue any other material in the *Star Wars* galaxy, the film was a self-contained fable that didn't need any elaboration.

### Numbers and Letters

It may be appropriate now to discuss a final, related issue, which is the whole "Episode" dilemma. Lucas claims that he always wanted to have the "episode" subtitle, but that the studio thought better of it because it would be too confusing—after the sequel came out, the episode subtitle suddenly made more sense and it was reinstated. This story seems believable, although Rinzler's exhaustive *Making of Star Wars* conspicuously has no documentation that this occurred, and no early draft title crawl ever carried an episode listing. But, after all, Lucas clearly had the concept of more chapters in mind, and the whole episode structure is straight out of the serial films. The question then is this: what episode was *Star Wars* originally supposed to be?

At the time it was made, Lucas had spent all of his time developing the world of the Rebels and the Empire. The backstory enriched the current one, but it was still very vague, a set of mere notes. As Lucas has said on more than one occasion, "The backstory wasn't meant to be a movie."[13] All of this information existed, pretty much in similar form, in the previous drafts. Draft two had a similar backstory, minus Father Skywalker's murder, and the basic plot was the same—yet, it was titled as Episode I. Further re-enforcing this, when Lucas finally began work on the sequel in 1977, he initially titled it as "Chapter II,"[14] and the draft which he himself wrote was titled "Episode II,"as we will later see.

Indeed, the shooting script was titled:

The Adventures of Luke Starkiller
as taken from the 'Journal of the Whills'
by
George Lucas

(Saga I)
STAR WARS

Revised Fourth Draft
March 15, 1976

Lucasfilm Ltd.
20th Century Fox

A previous draft of the script was labelled as "Episode I." Now it changed in the fourth draft to "Saga I." *Star Wars* was to be the first film in the series—the series of Luke, as it was called *The Adventures of Luke Starkiller*, which was then changed to *The Adventures of Luke Skywalker* after Lucas altered the protagonist's name during shooting. The backstory was in place at this point, but like any well-developed story it was not part of the actual plot, it was simply what it was—backstory. Like the serials that inspired it, *Star Wars* would begin in the thick of the action, with all sorts of events already having transpired that would never be seen and that the viewers would fill in with their imagination; in fact this was part of the intrigue and allure of the film. This literary device is known as *in media res*—"in the middle of things." It increases audience interest by not revealing how things got to be where they are at the outset of the story or bogging the film down in exposition. Like *THX*, it was also an inspiration taken from a westerner's perspective of Japanese films. Lucas explained to Charlie Rose in a 2004 interview:

> I'd like to use, as a vehicle [for *Star Wars*], Saturday matinee serials, which were these really high-powered action adventures that existed for 15 minutes, each Saturday they'd show a different one, and if you missed one you just sort of picked it up. So you never really saw, unless you were a really avid moviegoer, you never saw the whole thing. You only saw parts of it. And so it was designed to be like that... You know, you're in the middle of the thing and that would be the end of it. It was one movie, it just grew to be three movies, unfortunately, because I wrote more than I expected.[15]

While on the topic of titles, it is also interesting to note that the immortal title itself, "The Star Wars," or simply "*Star Wars*" as it eventually became, at one time stood poised to be changed. Lucas said in 1980 that he actually came up with the title before any plot was developed;[16] "When I made the deal I had to give it a name," he said of the 1971 United Artists development agreement.[17] Lucas commented further in 1979's *The Movie Brats*:

> The title *Star Wars* was an insurance policy. The studio didn't see it that way; they thought science fiction was a very bad genre, that women didn't like it, although they did no market research on that until after the film was finished. But we calculated that there are something like $8 million worth of science

fiction freaks in the U.S.A. and they will go see absolutely anything with a title like *Star Wars*.[18]

Mark Hamill also remembered an amusing anecdote in an interview from 2004:

[Fox] didn't want to have "wars" in the title… [Executives said their research] shows that women between the ages of 18 and 36 do not like films with the word "wars" in the title. I'm not making this up. This was a real memo. So we had a contest–"Naming the Movie"–and we put it up on the call sheet: Anybody that can come up with a better title than *Star Wars*, if their title was selected, they'd win something–I forget [what it was]. And nobody came up with anything any better.[19]

### *The Aftermath*

By late 1975, with the completion of the third draft, Fox still hadn't officially green-lit *Star Wars*, but Lucas had learned a good lesson from Coppola: if the studio didn't commit, then force them to. Lucas began storyboards, hired art department crew, secured his entire cast as well as soundstages in England and founded Industrial Light and Magic, all with his own money. *American Graffiti* had given him enough profit to push on without Fox's approval, even when the studio threatened to stop pre-production in light of re-negotiating the budget (which was on its way to becoming one of the more expensive pictures of its day). "We decided to go ahead with the picture whether they financed it or not," Kurtz said. "It forced them to make some quick decisions."[20] Were it not for Lucas' personal investment, the film would have undoubtedly stalled out before Fox greenlit it.

On March 22nd, 1976, cameras rolled in Tunisia, as *Star Wars* began production.[21] The shoot is legendary for its difficulty, and has been documented in a plethora of other sources. Lucas reflected on the root of the difficulty in a 1977 interview with *Rolling Stone*:

I struggled through this movie. I had a terrible time; it was very unpleasant. *American Graffiti* was unpleasant because of the fact that there was no money, no time and I was compromising myself to death. But I could rationalize it because of the fact that, well, it is just a $700,000 picture–it's Roger Corman –and what do you expect, you can't expect everything to be right for making a little cheesy, low-budget movie. But this was a big expensive movie and the money was getting wasted and things weren't coming out right. I was running the corporation. I wasn't making movies like I'm used to doing. *American Graffiti* had like forty people on the payroll, that counts everybody but the cast. I think *THX* had about the same. You can control a situation like that. On *Star Wars* we had over 950 people working for us and I would tell a department head and he would tell another assistant department head, he'd tell some guy, and by the time it got down the line it was not there. I spent all my time yelling and screaming at people, and I have never had to do that before.[22]

With the film finally completed, Lucas was sure it would be a disaster. In his mind, it already was. Robots that never worked, sets that were too small, rubber masks that were laughable, his inability to emotionally connect to strangers or properly articulate his vision, a foreign crew that was at times hostile to him, homesickness, and special effects that were too limited, coupled with a hard time in the editing room, convinced Lucas that the film was a strange and bizarre failure. "I [also] wasn't happy with the lighting on the picture," Lucas said in a *Rolling Stone* interview. Lucas had chosen the elderly Gil Taylor to shoot the film, whom had also shot *Dr. Strangelove* and *Hard Day's Night*, two of Lucas' favourite films.[23] "I'm a cameraman, and I like a slightly more extreme, eccentric style than I got in the movie. It was all right, it was a very difficult movie, there were big sets to light, it was a very big problem. The robots never worked. We faked the whole thing and a lot of it was done editorially."[24]

The rough cut of the film was also a disaster, as scenes dragged on endlessly and a more traditional approach to cutting robbed the film of its kinetic energy. Editor John Jympson was fired and Marcia took over, starting over from scratch and salvaging the film as best she could, shaping it into a more exciting and emotional experience. By Christmas, Marcia was still re-cutting the picture, and as she was re-working the Death Star trench run Martin Scorsese called her up—his editor of *New York, New York* had died and he desperately needed her help. She departed for L.A., tired of *Star Wars* and eager to work on something more artistic and that wasn't being made by her husband. "For George the whole thing was that Marcia was going off to this den of iniquity," Willard Huyck explained to author Peter Biskind. "Marty was wild and he took a lot of drugs and he stayed up all night, had lots of girlfriends. George was a family homebody. He couldn't believe the stories that Marcia told him. George would fume because Marcia was running with these people. She loved being with Marty."[25]

In late spring, *Star Wars* was screened for studio executives and Lucas' friends. When the house lights came up there was no applause, and Marcia burst into tears. "It's the *At Long Last Love* of science fiction,"* she cried. "It's awful!" Gloria Katz took her aside. "Shhh! Laddie's watching," she hushed. "Marcia, just look cheery."[26] Among those in attendance that night were Steven Spielberg and Brian DePalma, the latter of whom viciously criticised and mocked Lucas when the group went out for dinner afterwards to discuss the picture. Spielberg, however, reassured Lucas that he had made a modern classic, which Lucas of course refused to believe. Paul Hirsch and Richard Chew had been brought in to finish the edit after Marcia left but she returned for a week as the release date bore down upon George. As they scrambled finish the picture, Lucas was sure he had produced a uniquely-strange flop.

Realistically speaking, *Star Wars* would likely make back its budget—science fiction films at least had some kind of pre-existing fan base—but it didn't seem poised for any huge success. Dreaming of sequels, Lucas had Lucasfilm hold on to most of the props, costumes, sets and models from *Star Wars* so that they could be re-used for inexpensive follow-ups and costs cut down. If he fought hard, Lucas might be lucky enough to get a green-light on his sequels, but with budgets of the same size or smaller. It would be nice if he could have the budget to do some of the grander things he had envisioned in some of the earlier drafts—Wookie forest battles, for instance—but crafting a medium-budget space adventure seemed to be the only option.

Fortunately, he already had another adventure to send Luke and company on. With so many ideas left over from the previous drafts, he had a wealth of ready-made concepts. One of them, which had survived all the drafts but the final, was the Kiber crystal. Perhaps a good adventure would be one involving that. Lucas began developing a new and exciting story, using his *Raiders of the Lost Ark* plot as the base—Luke is on an adventurous treasure hunt through an alien jungle world for the Kiber crystal, racing against Darth Vader for possession of the artifact, and battling with the evil Imperial forces. Lucas had been developing this kind of adventure for some time by 1977, having already outlined *Raiders* two years earlier,[27] with Nazis in place of the Imperials and the Ark of the Covenant in place of the Kiber crystal. The adventure would have Luke and Leia crash landing on a mysterious jungle world and discovering stormtroopers and Imperials carrying out a secret mining operation. There

---

* *At Long Last Love* was a then-recent homage to 1930s musicals that Peter Bogdonavich had directed in 1975, which was regarded as notorious awful.

is a mix up with the miners, a sneaky Imperial, capture, imprisonment, a rescue, and a wild adventure ride through the jungles in search of the elusive crystal—the story climaxes when Luke and Leia encounter Darth Vader himself just as they find the crystal; Luke is injured by falling stones, but Leia battles Vader in a lightsaber match, being badly injured and leaving Luke to finally duel him and send Darth falling down a bottomless well while the heroes escape with the artifact.

Alan Dean Foster had been hired to write the novelisation of *Star Wars* (though the book gave credit to Lucas himself) and was in the process of developing this low-budget sequel into a novel as well, with the option of adapting it into a screenplay somewhere down the road. It would be titled *Splinter of the Mind's Eye*, and notated as being "From the further adventures of Luke Skywalker," the second story in the *Adventures of Luke Skywalker* trilogy. Whether or not Lucas himself would direct it if it was ever made is up for debate; perhaps he would act as executive producer, as he was on the eventual sequel, *Empire Strikes Back*. If Lucas decided not to make sequels and concentrate on other films then *Splinter* would at least make for a marketable book tie-in, leading into the third and final chapter that Lucas planned on having Foster write.[28] Foster recalled the process in a 2002 interview with Lou Tambone:

> When George commissioned *Splinter*, he wanted me to write a story that could be filmed on a low budget. That's why, for example, everything takes place on a fog-shrouded planet. His idea was that if *Star Wars* didn't flop, wasn't a huge success, but maybe made a few bucks, he would have a story in hand that could be done using many of the props, costumes, etc., from the first film. It's the approach of a good engineer, who always includes a backup system in his design.
>
> The book was written and completed before *Star Wars* was released, hence it was always intended to appear as a book. Also, proceeding on the assumption that the film was a success, George didn't want any fans to have to sit around and wait for the next film...he wanted them to have additional *Star Wars* material available...[ Lucas] did request a couple of changes to *Splinter of the Mind's Eye*...The main change involved the opening of the book. I had started out with an elaborate space battle...Bearing in mind his intention to keep open the option of filming *Splinter* on a low budget, George asked me to delete the sequence... As to other changes, they were all minor, and few, and I can't recall them.[29]

Although in recent interviews, Foster has said that the majority of the story was actually invented by himself,[30] the similarities to *Raiders of the Lost Ark*, which Lucas had been developing with Philip Kaufman since

1975, and especially other elements such as the Kiber crystal, very obviously a Lucas creation, suggest that Lucas may have had more influence than Foster remembers. A Foster interview from decades prior reveals that this in indeed the case, as he indicates that he and Lucas *together* hashed out the plot. "We sat down to consciously design a book which could be filmable on a low budget," Foster said of his and Lucas' efforts.[31]

An even closer inspection of the plot is more revealing: it also contains many elements that Lucas would later put to use in the filmed sequel, *Empire Strikes Back*, and uses elements that were cut out of the previous *Star Wars* drafts, much like the sequels would. Like *Empire Strikes Back*, Darth Vader is given more power and action, and he kills a commanding Imperial officer for his failures. The story takes place on a swamp-planet which Luke crash-lands and is stranded on, much like Dagobah, filled with lizards, overgrown vines, giant trees with twisting roots, thick fog and a gloomy, foreboding ambiance, and at one point Luke is attacked by a swamp creature. A particular sequence recalls Luke's experience in "the cave" in *Empire Strikes Back*, where Luke wanders into a dark tunnel that turns out to be a partially man-made entranceway (much like the cave in *Empire* appears to be); inside lurks a phosphorous, ethereal creature, described as a "spirit," that Luke must finally confront and slay with his lightsaber (similar to the film in which the Vader-apparition symbolised Luke facing his fear). One character has his arm destroyed but it is medically re-constructed in a scene which has overtones of Luke's re-construction at the end of *Empire*. Luke and Vader finally meet in a lightsaber duel at the climax as well, and Vader uses the Force to throw objects (large stones) at Luke, who bats them off with his saber but is slowly overwhelmed. Vader also faces Leia at first, using one hand as he does against Luke in *Empire*, and taunts her, trying to provoke her anger. Vader also throws an energy bolt from his hands, much like The Lightning from *Fighting Devil Dogs* and the Emperor in *Return of the Jedi*.

Finally, the story contains explicit, undeniable references to the 1973 synopsis and the 1974 rough draft. In those stories, General Skywalker (in the synopsis) and Annkin Starkiller (in the rough draft) find themselves on a jungle world and are captured by giant furry native-aliens (Wookies). The leader challenges him to a spear fight and Skywalker/Starkiller is able to prevail over the warrior, impressing the natives, and they accept him into their society and help him fight back against the Imperial outposts on their world; Skywalker/Starkiller begins training them and they are ultimately victorious. In *Splinter*, an identical sequence takes place: Imperials are carrying out operations in an outpost on planet Mimban, and Luke is captured by a group of native aliens. The leader challenges Luke to a fight but Luke is able to beat him, and the natives accept him into their society. They agree to help him fight back against the Imperial outpost, and with Luke's training they are able to prevail, much to the bafflement of the Imperials. Lucas would eventually put this concept to use in *Return of the Jedi*.

The story of *Splinter of the Mind's Eye* was very much in the same vein as *Star Wars*, with humour, adventure and a quick-moving, action-packed plot with many throwbacks to the adventure serials which the original film was based off. Harrison Ford had not signed a contract for any sequels, which is why Han Solo is mysteriously absent from the story, nor had Alec Guinness. Luke and Leia are obviously in love with each other, and their sexual tension is a major part of their adventure together. Darth Vader perhaps was now decided to be cybernetic, and so Lucas had a chance to imply as much with a scene where Vader's arm is cut off and Luke is surprised that hardly any blood comes out; Vader simply pries his saber from his severed arm and begins attacking with his remaining one. Although it is still kept ambiguous, it strongly implies that Vader is not completely natural. The book was eventually released in February of 1978.[32]

An early meeting between Lucas and Foster in late December 1975 revealed Lucas' first thoughts on the sequels and the contractual trilogy, at this time conceived only as novels:

> I want to have Luke kiss the princess in the second book. The second book will be *Gone With the Wind in Outer Space*. She likes Luke, but Han is Clarke Gable. Well, she may appear to get Luke, because in the end I want Han to leave. Han splits at the end of the second book and we learn who Darth Vader is[*]...In the third book, I want the story to be just the soap opera of the Skywalker family, which ends with the destruction of the Empire.
>
> Then someday I want to do the backstory of Kenobi as a young man—a story of the Jedi and how the Emperor eventually takes over and turns the whole thing from a Republic into an Empire, and tricks all the Jedi and kills them. The whole battle where Luke's father gets killed. That would be impossible to do, but it's great to dream about.[33]

Of course, much had changed by 1977. Harrison Ford was not prepared to appear in sequels, so Han was written out of book two, with Luke and Leia having more of a straightforward romance. Vader's past, hinted at

---

[*] If this strikes you as suspiciously prophetic Appendix G has an elaboration of the above explanation

being explored in book two, was then moved into *Star Wars* itself—in December 1975, when Lucas made the above statement, we do not find out in the film that he was in fact the murderer of Luke's father. Lucas had planned for Luke and Darth to face each other with lightsabers in *Star Wars*—in the third draft outline—but when he couldn't fit this into the film he saved it for the sequel. Three months after this conversation with Foster, however, sensing the precariousness with which the film hung, Lucas moved the background information about Vader into the film itself, as Kenobi finally reveals to Luke in the March, 1976 revised fourth draft that not only was his father a Jedi but that he was killed by Vader.[34]

At the same time that *Splinter of the Mind's Eye* was being written, Lucas was touring science fiction and comic book conventions to raise awareness of *Star Wars*. Lucas insisted on developing a novel and comic adaptation, which were both released well before May 1977. As Lucas scrambled to finish the post-production and Alan Dean Foster wrote the sequel novel, a small but steady buzz began to build about the film.

### Dreamland

Before *Splinter of the Mind's Eye* was ready to be released, however, the unthinkable happened—May 25th turned over on the calendar, and a science fiction film that had developed quite a bit of word of mouth about it was debuting that night in the few select theatres in which it had been booked. On that auspicious date, *Star Wars* was released—and to the surprise of everyone involved, became a hit! And not just a hit, a *smash* hit! Taking fifty-four million dollars in just the first eight weeks, even the soundtrack was certified gold. Audiences around the world fell in love with Lucas' simple yet magical fairy tale of a youth becoming a hero amidst an operatic fantasy backdrop. Children, adults—people of every age, gender and ethnic background all found a common love of Lucas' unlikely film.

Lucas remembered his experience of May 25th, 1977 in an article from *Starlog*:

> I was mixing sound on foreign versions of the film the day it opened here. I had been working so hard that, truthfully, I forgot the film was being released that day. My wife was mixing *New York, New York* at night at the same place we were mixing during the day, so at 6:00 she came in for the night shift just as I was leaving on the day shift. So we ran off across the street from the Chinese Theatre—and there was a huge line around the block. I said, "What's that?" I had forgotten completely, and I really couldn't believe it. But I had planned a

vacation as soon as I finished, and I'm glad I did because I really didn't want to be around for all the craziness that happened after that.[35]

Soon after the film opened, Jay Cocks was at director Jeremy Kagen's house; an exasperated Harrison Ford arrived, completely dishevelled, his shirt half ripped off.

"Jesus, Harrison, what happened?" Cocks asked.

"I went into Tower Records to buy an album and these people jumped on me."[36]

Word of mouth spread like wildfire and its box office numbers climbed quicker than Fox executives could keep track of. Show after show was selling out, and there were permanent line-ups around city blocks. Thousands of miles from the chaos of movie theatres, Lucas lay on a beach in Hawaii with Marcia, a well-earned break from the stress of their work. Alan Ladd Jr. would call up every night and report the climbing box office figures to Lucas, who could only listen in stunned silence. Steven Spielberg and his wife Amy joined George and Marcia, bringing news that *Star Wars* was in all the papers and on television shows. Building a sand castle on the beach together, Spielberg remarked that he'd like to do a James Bond film one day, a real action-packed thrillride; Lucas offered him an even better idea—his *Raiders of the Lost Ark* project that was in temporary hibernation. As George and Marcia spent the rest of their vacation on the island of Maui they started wondering how they would spend the millions of dollars that would be coming their way, but all Lucas could find was a frozen yogurt stand. "You know, these yogurt things are really going to take off, maybe I'll buy a yogurt franchise," he said.[37] Perhaps it is here, as Lucas started thinking of ways to spend his wealth, that an ambition began forming which would later consume his life. "Before *Star Wars* I was going to restore the building we're in—which was sort of run down," Lucas remembered. "Then when the film was such a success I realized we could do this the way the original dream was, which was the dream for American Zoetrope."[38]

By the first week of June, *Star Wars* had practically made back its budget. When George and Marcia returned to San Francisco a few days later they were returning to a world that would never be the same for them again.

As its popularity gained momentum like a cinematic avalanche, the film became the event of the summer and *Star Wars* was a success beyond anyone's wildest dreams and expectations. Audiences were thrilled and touched by the warm characters and unprecedented kinetic graphics. "A grand and glorious film that may well be the smash hit of 1977, and certainly is the best movie of the year so far," wrote *Time* Magazine. "Star Wars is a combination of Flash Gordon, The Wizard of Oz, the Errol Flynn swashbucklers of the '30s and '40s and almost every western ever screened...The result is a remarkable confection: a subliminal history of the movies, wrapped in a riveting tale of suspense and adventure, ornamented with some of the most ingenious special effects ever contrived for film. It has no message, no sex and only the merest dollop of blood shed here and there. It's aimed at kids—the kid in everybody."

Roger Ebert praised: "Every once in a while I have what I think of as an out-of-the-body experience at a movie," and went to on state, "the characters in 'Star Wars' are so strongly and simply drawn and have so many small foibles and large, futile hopes for us to identify with...the movie's heart is in its endearingly human (and non-human) people." The *L.A. Times* raved, "'Star Wars' is Buck Rogers with a doctoral degree but not a trace of neuroticism or cynicism, a slam-bang, rip-roaring gallop through a distantly future world full of exotic vocabularies, creatures and customs, existing cheek by cowl with the boy and girl next door." *Variety* claimed it "a magnificent film," stating, "Like a breath or fresh air, 'Star Wars' sweeps away the cynicism that has in recent years obscured the concepts of valor, dedication and honor. Make no mistake–this is by no means a 'children's film,' with all the derogatory overtones that go with that description. This is instead a superior example of what only the screen can achieve."

"When I saw *Star Wars* in its finished form," Francis Coppola remembers, "and saw the complete tapestry George had done, it was very compelling and it was really a thrill for the audience."[39] Tom Pollock, "the prototype of the cynical Hollywood attorney,"[40] remembered with an amazement that still seems vivid his first viewing of the film: "The experience is not like any experience I have had since I was a child. It's reliving the first time you see a certain kind of movie when you're eight or nine years old. You feel you can never get it back again but seeing *Star Wars* is getting it back."[41] Saul Zaentz, producer of *One Flew Over the Cuckoo's Nest*, took out a page in *Variety* with an open letter to "George Lucas and all who participated in the creation of *Star Wars*: You have given birth to a perfect film and the whole world will rejoice with you." Lucy Wilson, Lucas' assistant, remembers, "You'd go to restaurants and people were sitting around you talking about the person you work for and the movie you were working on—and it's on the cover of magazines."[42] Most amusingly, Harrison Ford retracted his infamous statement on the script after seeing the wonderful heart the completed picture exuberated with: "I told George: 'You can't say that stuff. You can only type it.' But I was wrong. It worked."[43]

The film was an out of control phenomenon, like a cinema version of Beatle Mania. Everyone involved in the film became celebrities, and kids would ask ILM modelmakers for autographs, while the stars of the film could hardly venture outdoors without being mobbed in the streets. At work, adults excitedly talked about the film around the water cooler, while at the playground kids excitedly talked about the film around the jungle gym. It was an unprecedented feat in the entertainment business.

Lucas' plans were thrown for an unexpected loop. Already fans and the press were beginning to ask about a sequel—it was obvious from the film's ending that there could be one. What happens next? That was the million dollar question that only Lucas could answer.

"At first I was contemplating selling the whole thing to Fox to do whatever they wanted with it," Lucas told Alan Arnold in 1979. "I'd just take my percentage and go home and never think about *Star Wars* again. But the truth of it is I got captivated by the thing. It's in me now."[44]

"George and I didn't actually make the decision to go ahead with the second movie until a month after *Star Wars* was released," Gary Kurtz remembered in a *Starlog* interview. "Neither of us was positive about how people would react to the first film but, after a month, we knew that interest was high enough to go with a sequel."[45]

With the success of *Star Wars*, Lucas no longer had to restrain himself with budgetary demands. His low-budget sequel was shelved, book three was cancelled, and he began thinking of new, more extravagant stories, the kinds he wanted to put in the film in the first place. He also saw a means to an ends: with personal ownership of sequels to what was on its way to becoming one of the biggest hits of the decade, Lucas could turn his trilogy into a franchise that he could use to fund a dream of his—a private retreat where filmmakers could come to research and develop movies together. His Parkhouse office was one thing—but this would be something far bigger.

Taking inspiration from Coppola's decisions, Lucas would finance *Star Wars II* himself and maintain complete control over the film (and greater financial profit points). His rights to any *Star Wars* sequels would expire if he didn't start making one of them within two years, and so work would begin on the film just over six months after the release of *Star Wars*.[46]

Producer Gary Kurtz remembered some sequel plans immediately following *Star Wars* in this 1999 interview with IGN *Film Force*:

> At the very tail-end of the shooting of *Star Wars*, when Laddy had seen more of the footage, they started to come back with saying–'Well, how much would

it be to just to maybe save these sets or shoot part of another movie and make a sequel which could be done kind of on the cheap.' And we said there was no way we could do that, because we didn't have a script, and there was no time to write a script, and anyway it would probably be quite different, and if they wanted a sequel we had to do it properly. The idea kind of faded away at that time, because we were just interested in getting the film made.

When it opened, and it was quite popular, the idea of doing a sequel came back. So immediately, the idea was—all right, let's sit down, find a writer, and do a proper job on this treatment material and odd notes and things that we already had extracted from the first time around. Because George originally wrote a lot of different—well, you've probably read some of the different versions of the screenplay. The story shifted back and forth a great deal...So doing a sequel was fairly easy to structure out, and then it became clear that Fox wanted it right away...But we kept a lot of props, some set pieces and things–design things–around the idea of being able to use them for two films.[47]

As Lucas was contemplating *Star Wars II*, *Star Wars* was the most popular event of the summer and no character was more loved than Darth Vader. He was the first instance of such an iconic villain, personifying evil and villainy in a universal way while also providing crowd-pleasing scenes—he was the villain the world loved to hate. Although Lucas recognized that Darth was a strong character, having grown much since the first and second drafts and now surviving the end battle, even Lucas did not intend for the character to be so popular. Audiences loved Darth Vader, and his mysterious nature made him all the more intriguing—who was he? What did he look like underneath? Was he a human or an alien?

"Darth Vader became such an icon in the first film," Lucas said. "That icon of evil sort of took over everything, much more than I intended."[48] The popularity of the character suddenly thrust him into a completely unintended status of celebrity, and therefore it became paramount to not only give him more screen time for the next film, but to expand on his mythos. This is why Darth is merely a rather minor henchman in *Star Wars* but becomes an all-powerful central character for the sequel, one who seemingly controls the Empire and is feared by all (as opposed to *Star Wars*, where he is talked down to by everyone from Princess Leia to Imperial officers and has only nine minutes of combined screentime). One thing was clear: Darth Vader had to be a major part of *Star Wars II*.

But what was *Star Wars II*? Lucas had a wealth of material on the events which occur before the first film—he had notes on the structure of the Old Republic, the Jedi order, the Emperor's rise to power, the downfall of the galaxy and the beginning of the civil war, with Darth Vader's betrayal of Obi Wan Kenobi and Father Skywalker occurring at the history's climax. A storyline detailing Obi Wan's adventures with Father Skywalker would make an interesting film, and now that he was the most successful director of all time, Lucas entertained the possibility of one day portraying this in a sequel.

Contrary to popular belief, *Star Wars* was not designed with these prequels in mind, but rather they were added as afterthoughts, as can be clearly seen. Lucas admitted in a 1997 interview:

> After the first film came out, and suddenly it was a giant hit, I said, "Oh, I get to do these two movies." Everyone said, "What [else] are you going to do?" I said, "Gee, I could do these back stories too. That would be interesting." That's where the [eventual idea of] starting in episode four came [from], because I said, "Well, maybe I could make three out of this back story." That evolved right around the time the film was released, after I knew it was a success.[49]

Lucas first publically considered making a sequel about the young Ben Kenobi in the late summer of 1977. He told *Rolling Stone* in August:

> [I have sequel agreements with] All the actors except Alec Guinness. We may use his voice as The Force–I don't know. One of the sequels we are thinking of is the young days of Ben Kenobi. It would probably be all different actors.[50]

Unfortunately, making a "young days of Ben Kenobi" film would require completely new casting as well as building an entirely new world, one which was much grander and special-effects driven than the more small-scale one he was currently engrossed in. Perhaps he could do this story some time later, but for now he needed an immediate sequel to *Star Wars*.

Making a follow-up to *Star Wars* left Lucas with a lot of possible routes to travel. Conveniently, because the story was an ensemble cast, if one of the actors refused a sequel they could be easily written out. Although Luke was clearly the main character in the film, with the series known as "The Adventures of Luke Skywalker," a spin-off or sequel had the potential to follow Han, Leia, or new characters on the Rebel Alliance, and Lucas was smart enough to have the villain escape at the end. Lucas said in 1977:

> It was one of the original ideas of doing a sequel that if I put enough people in it and it was designed carefully enough I could make a sequel about anything. Or if any of the actors gave me lot of trouble or didn't want to do it, or didn't want to be in the sequel, I could always make a sequel without one.[51]

*Star Wars* was a hit but to Lucas it was still a frustration. It didn't turn out the way he had envisioned it—"*Star Wars* is about 25% of what I wanted it to be. It's really still a good movie, but it fell short of what I wanted it to be," he told *Rolling Stone* in 1977.[52][*] The process of making the film wore him out—he admitted himself to the hospital on one occasion, fearing a heart attack, and was diagnosed with hyper-tension and exhaustion. Directing the next ones no longer enticed him—he directed *Star Wars* mostly because he had to, because no one else would have wanted to. "I hate directing," he told *Rolling Stone* in 1980. "It's like fighting a fifteen-round heavyweight bout with a new opponent every day. You go to work knowing just how you want a scene to be, but by the end of the day, you're usually depressed because you didn't do a good enough job."[53] Now, however, he could have others do the dirty work for him—Lucas could write the scripts, finance the film and supervise the project, while someone else could do the more tedious work, in Lucas' mind, of actually being on set and filming the material.

With an unlimited number of possible adventures, he could turn it into a bona fide franchise, having new directors have their go in the *Star Wars* galaxy, each making their own version of it, like a space opera version of James Bond. The adventures could be more stand-alone types like the first film, or could also slowly develop themes and storylines throughout the series, and end in cliffhangers, like the serial episodes the movies were inspired by, or perhaps even follow side-characters and different time periods. His contract only stipulated a trio of films but with *Star Wars* quickly becoming the most popular film ever made, his plans for it were growing as well.

In the 1977 television special, *The Making of Star Wars as Told by C-3P0 and R2-D2*, producer Gary Kurtz stated the following:

> We've had a lot of speculation about sequels to *Star Wars*, and we are working on story material that will develop into potentially one or more motion pictures that will use the same characters. I like to consider them different adventures rather than direct sequels.[54]

Mark Hamill echoed that sentiment in a June 1978 article in *Science Fiction Magazine*:

---

[*] "In fact, it was probably 75% of what I wanted it to be, but to me it *felt* emotionally like it was 25%," he admitted of these statements on the Charlie Rose show in 2004

They always wanted to set up their own little James Bond series–taking the environment George has set up but keeping it limitless in terms of what the characters can do. For the sequel, he's going to add new characters. It won't be a direct sequel to the first story; it'll be a series of adventures, you know, in that galaxy...If the *Star Wars* series runs as long as I think they're going to run, I will be Ben Kenobi's age when I do the last one![55]

Unlike the contemporary view of *Star Wars*, the series was not planned as an elaborate, self-contained story divided in six chapters—it was to be in the vein of *Adventure Theater*, with different "adventure of the week" type of films, and even the time periods of the films could differ and be presented in a non-linear fashion. As Alan Arnold wrote in 1979:

[Gary Kurtz] described [*Star Wars II*] as "a new chapter in the *Star Wars* saga," because the intention is never to refer to it as a sequel for the simple reason that future George Lucas stories do not have chronological sequence.[56]

Now armed with a bigger budget and more resources at his disposal, Lucas could let his friends have their chance to play in the world and make something out of it, and the series could endure for as long as Lucas wanted it to. He said in a 1977 conversation with Paul Scanlon:

I think the sequels will be much, much better. What I want to do is direct the last sequel. I could do the first one and the last one and let everyone else do the ones in between.

*It wouldn't bother you to have someone else do the ones in between?*

No, it would be interesting. I would want to try and get some good directors, and see what their interpretation of the theme is. I think it will be interesting, it is like taking a theme in film school, say, okay, everybody do their interpretation of this theme. It's an interesting idea to see how people interpret the genre. It is a fun genre to play with. All the prototype stuff is done now. Nobody has to worry about what a Wookie is and what it does and how it reacts. Wookies are there, the people are there, the environment is there, the empire is there...I've put up the concrete slab of the walls and now everybody can have fun drawing the pictures and putting on the little gargoyles and doing all the really fun stuff. And it's a competition. I'm hoping if I get friends of mine they will want to do a much better film, like, "I'll show George that I can do a film twice that good," and I think they can, but then I want to do the last one, so I can do one twice as good as everybody else. [Laughs][57]

Mark Hamill was gladly aboard for more than his contract, as he told a 1978 issue of *Gossip Magazine*:

> I am definitely going to do two more and they have asked me to do a fourth one and at this point, I can't see any reason why I wouldn't. I haven't signed for it, yet, but it is a really exciting thing for me and I think for everybody involved.[58]

In the excitement of the film's enormous success, Lucas had let his *Adventures of Luke Skywalker* trilogy dissolve into a massive franchise to explore the galaxy he had created. The film had become the biggest hit of all time and Lucas was going to take advantage of it—his idea for a filmmaker's centre needed the funding of more than just the profits of one or two hit movies. It needed the strength and stability of a mega-hit franchise behind it in order to pay for its annual million-dollar overhead, and Lucas found himself in the position to provide that.

The initial plan was that the series was infinite, but by 1978, after actual development on the future storylines was done, a numerical figure was attached, as we shall examine in the next chapter. Most fans will tell you Lucas had six episodes planned, and the most astute ones will correct you that it was nine episodes, with the fabled Sequel Trilogy that never was following the original three. But Lucas initially envisioned *twelve* films. *Time* magazine reported in 1978:

> Lucas has set up four corporations: Star Wars Corp. will make STAR WARS II, and then, count them, ten other planned sequels.[59]

In the same article Lucas says that because of the eleven sequels it will take twenty-three years of constant filming to produce them all, with 2001 as the projected date of completion.

Lucas' comments on the sequels are wildly contradictory at times, with his plans changing drastically as actually story development was made, as we shall examine in the next chapter; to sum up the problem, it boils down to Lucas simply being excited by the recent success of *Star Wars* and talking about huge numbers of sequels without any concrete plans or ideas. Why twelve episodes, one might ask? *Star Wars* was to be an adventure serial, which traditionally lasted for twelve episodes or chapters. It is no surprise that all of the 1930s serials Lucas loved, like *Flash Gordon*, *Buck Rogers*, *The Fighting Devil Dogs* and *The Phantom Empire*, were all twelve episodes long—the twelve-parter was a staple of the serial formula and in trying to emulate those films as closely as possible Lucas naturally decided that *The Adventures of Luke Skywalker* would also have to run for twelve episodes. "This was done in the style of a 1930s Saturday matinee serial, which were usually in twelve episodes," Lucas has said.[60] Seeking a franchise to fund Lucasfilm for many years to come, twelve films also happened to fit the requirements. The twelve episode plan was totted over and over again—many times in Lucasfilm's own official newsletter, *Bantha Tracks*. In issue two:

> Based on the second of twelve stories in George Lucas' Adventures of Luke Skywalker series, the first draft of the screenplay [of *Empire Strikes Back*] was written by Leigh Brackett.[61]

And again in issue three:

> The sequel will be based directly on the second of twelve stories George Lucas wrote in the Adventures of Luke Skywalker.[62]

We see an early example of the sort of misconception about the story which the public was being influenced by—rather than claiming to have stories for all six episodes, as most are used to hearing, here it is claimed that Lucas has already written stories for *twelve*. This form of exaggeration was perhaps used a hype ploy, to stimulate interest in what appeared to be an already-written epic that was slowly being revealed. These quotes also demonstrate the significant period in the franchise's early public life before it had officially become known as *Star Wars*. The change may have been fostered by marketing forces; before the sequel gained its official title, it was known as simply *Star Wars II* and the series commonly referred to as "the *Star Wars* series," leaving *The Adventures of Luke Skywalker* to gradually fade away.

The last official mention of the twelve-part saga is in the sixth issue of *Bantha Tracks*, in autumn of 1979:

> Overseeing it all are Director Irvin Kershner... and Executive Producer George Lucas, making sure that every phase of production keeps to his vision for the entire twelve part saga.[63]

The next time a numeric figure is officially attached to the films is the eighth issue of *Bantha Tracks*, from spring 1980. George Lucas addressed the issue personally:

> SW: At one point there were going to be twelve *Star Wars* films.

GL: I cut that number down to nine because the other three were tangential to the saga. *Star Wars* was the fourth story in the saga... after the third film, we'll go back and make the first trilogy, which deals with the young Ben Kenobi and the young Darth Vader.[64]

In reality, Lucas never had a real story arc until he fused the characters of Darth Vader and Father Skywalker, thus creating the prequel trilogy and setting *Star Wars* up as the fourth film in a nine-film series. This will be the focus of the next chapter.

Regardless, Lucas had to get to work on the sequels and figure out just how many he would actually be making. He didn't start working on the story to *Star Wars II* until the end of 1977, being preoccupied with the success of his film and trying to get a firm grasp on his two new companies, Lucasfilm and ILM, moving them from Van Nuys to Marin County, California. He had also followed through on the agreement he made with Spielberg in Hawaii earlier that year for *Raiders of the Lost Ark*; Spielberg had been impressed with a screenplay he read by a young Chicago copywriter named Lawrence Kasdan and in late 1977 hired him to script the project.[65] Lucas also began dreaming up Skywalker Ranch at this time, a concept which had grown out of the elaborate Lucasfilm headquarters developed at Lucas' Parkhouse home as a sort of filmmakers paradise that was to be a communal resource centre and think-tank. The means of creating this compound required huge sums of money, far more than *Star Wars* had afforded him.

"He took me into a workroom," Irvin Kershner remembers in *Mythmaker*, "and on the wall were plans for Skywalker Ranch. He said, 'This is why we're making the second [*Star Wars* film]. If it works, I'll build this. If it works, we'll not only build it, we'll make more *Star Wars*! If it doesn't work, it's over.'"[66]

The *Star Wars* franchise was built as a means to fund more personal, uncommercial projects, similar to his student films, which he would make with the aid of his "research center," eventually dubbed Skywalker Ranch. "When I was in film school, I was into a very abstract kind of filmmaking. I want to get back to it," he told Alan Arnold in 1979. "Which brings me again to the research center. That is really the core of my drive to make this work. Movies cost a lot of money. You can't just go out and make them, no matter how rich you are. You have to devise a mechanism, a funding machine that will allow you to make movies...Now I want to use it to make the kind of films I'm interested in, regardless of their commerciality."[67]

He began thinking about ideas for the new *Star Wars* film.

As fall of 1977 approached, *Star Wars* mania began to subside as kids went back to school and Lucas' corporate restructuring began to take shape—it was time to finally tackle the writing of the *Star Wars* sequel.

Lucas had a lot of story points to address and develop. One of them was an expansion on the Force itself, and with it both Obi Wan and the Jedi. Unlike *Empire Strikes Back* and *Return of the Jedi*, Obi Wan's "spirit" was a much more ethereal and subtle addition to the first film—in fact, it was mostly unplanned, as Obi Wan's death was written into the original film while shooting. Lucas told *Rolling Stone* in 1977:

> I was struggling with the problem that I had this sort of dramatic scene that had no climax about two-thirds of the way through the film. I had another problem in the fact that there was no real threat in the Death Star. The villains were like tenpins; you get into a gunfight with them and they just get knocked over. As I originally wrote it, Ben Kenobi and Vader had a sword fight and Ben hits a door and the door slams closed and they all run away and Vader is left standing there with egg on his face. This was dumb; they run into the Death Star and they sort of take over everything and they run back. It totally diminished any impact the Death Star had... Anyway, I was rewriting, I was struggling with that plot problem when my wife suggested that I kill off Ben, which she thought was a pretty outrageous idea, and I said, "Well, that is an interesting idea, and I had been thinking about it." Her first idea was to have Threepio get shot, and I said impossible because I wanted to start and end the film with the robots, I wanted the film to really be about the robots and have the theme be the framework for the rest of the movie. But then the more I thought about Ben getting killed the more I liked the idea because, one, it made the threat of Vader greater and that tied in with The Force and the fact that he could use the dark side. Both Alec Guinness and I came up with the thing of having Ben go on afterward as part of The Force.[68]

In *Star Wars*, Obi Wan is represented by a voice which only Luke can hear—in fact, he himself is not even sure if he is hearing it. The use of the voice is a way to cinematically represent that Obi Wan will always be with Luke, that his mentor will always be with him in spirit.* *Empire Strikes Back* and *Return of the Jedi* obviously took a different route, as Obi Wan actually materializes and has conversations, but the whole story point surrounding his death and the Force itself was never supposed to be so

---

* It was also a cliché of mentor-student pictures of the 1970s, which inevitably were of the kung-fu genre, where the student hears the recently-killed mentor's advice in his head during a pivotal moment in the climax, allowing him to triumph. See *Enter the Dragon*, for example.

literal. As Lucas said in the 1977 interview with *Rolling Stone*: "We may use his voice as the Force—I don't know."

Although the second draft of *Star Wars* portrayed it as a more comic-book-like superpower, the simplified third and especially fourth draft would present the Force in a very ambiguous way, essentially being a metaphor for believing in yourself—Luke succeeds because he believes he can; he uses the Force because he simply believes and it gives him the strength to triumph. It was in this way, this intangible, metaphorical way, that the film addressed issues of god and the supernatural, by refuting cynics through the notion that seeing comes from believing.* The sequels would basically do away with this more mysterious, unprovable view of the Force in favor of the original literal superpowers; Han would hardly be able to doubt the Force as he did in *Star Wars* if the ghost of Ben Kenobi materialized and levitated him off the ground. When Luke reached out his hand in the opening sequence of *Star Wars II*, suspended upside down in the wampa lair, and his lightsaber began to quiver before it leapt into his grasp, a new threshold had been crossed in which the Force became a material superpower.

Lucas dreaded returning to the writing process, which he has described as painful and tedious. For *Star Wars II*, he turned to Leigh Brackett. Brackett was a legendary writer of pulp science fiction in the 1940s and '50s, a writer of crime novels, and screenwriter for Howard Hawks—their pairing seemed like a natural formula for success. In fact, her husband was Edmond Hamilton, also a noted science fiction author, whose story "*Kaldar, Planet of Antares*," published in *Weird Tales* magazine in 1933 and reprinted in paperback in 1965, has been thought to have been an influence in the development of the lightsaber since it featured one—Hamilton's version was called a "lightsword." Brackett was brought to Lucas' attention by a friend, who handed him an old science fiction

---

* In opposition to the sequels, there is no physical dimension to the Force in *Star Wars*—it exists only in the mind, as a mental state. The only uses of it as a "power" are mental ones: the mind trick on the stormtroopers, while Vader's strangulation is conveyed by a visual—the pinching of his thumb and index finger, that almost suggests that he is making the officer *believe* he is being choked and thus reacting due to the power of Vader's mental projection; in *Empire* Vader would simply look at a person and they would keel over unexpectedly, implying a direct physical connection, much different in style from *Star Wars*

novel and said, "Here is someone who wrote the cantina scene in *Star Wars* better than you did."[69]

He contacted the elderly Brackett, who was living in Los Angeles at that time, and asked her to write *Star Wars II*. "Have you ever written for the movies?" Lucas asked her.

"Yes, I have," Brackett replied simply—she began recounting her credits, which included *Rio Bravo*, *El Dorado* and *The Big Sleep*, co-written with William Faulkner, the Nobel-prize-winning novelist.

An awkward silence followed. "Are you *that* Leigh Brackett?" Lucas gasped.

"Yes," she replied. "Isn't that why you called me in?"

"No," Lucas said, "I called you in because you were a pulp science fiction writer."[70]

On November 28th, 1977, Lucas hand-wrote the *Star Wars II* story treatment. The film was titled *The Empire Strikes Back*.

# Chapter V: Revelations

UNLIKE *Star Wars*, the early drafts of *The Empire Strikes Back* were largely similar in construction. The film starts off on the ice planet, the Rebel base is invaded and the group of heroes splits into two; Luke trains with Jedi master Yoda, while Han and Leia are pursued and captured, and eventually they all meet back on Bespin where Luke faces Darth Vader.

Lucas wanted to retain the serial feel of *Star Wars*, with constant peril for the heroes. Luke is attacked by a beast in the film's opening and escapes from the creature's lair only to be stranded in a snowstorm. After being rescued by Han, the Rebel base comes under attack by Imperial Forces and the Rebels flee, with Luke traveling off to train as a Jedi and Han and Leia being pursued by Darth Vader and his minions. It was a tight script.

On the same date as Lucas' November 28th story treatment, he and Leigh Brackett began having story meetings until December 2nd, where many ideas for the film were developed.

The timeline of the early development of *Empire Strikes Back* is a somewhat tricky subject. According to personal correspondences, the *Magic of Myth* Smithsonian exhibit presented the treatment as being a result of the story conferences, and not the other way around (for example, as is the case with *Return of the Jedi*):

"The treatment is actually a culmination of the story conferences. This is the way it was presented in the Smithsonian exhibit (it served as kind of a roadmap for other parts of the exhibit). Even though the treatment I saw was typed up, it actually started out as Lucas's own hand-written notes from the conferences. The reason why it has the same date as the start date of the conferences is the same reason why a student's Calculus notes might have a date attributed to them—to document the day that person took those notes. November 28, 1977 was the first day Lucas started taking notes. As a result, this is the date that gets attached to his treatment."[1]

This is given credence by the development of Yoda: Laurent Bouzereau in *The Annotated Screenplays* states that the creature's existance was first proposed in story conferences and was known only as "the critter"; in the treatment, Lucas finally names him "Minch Yoda." This is the main piece of evidence: if Yoda was already in the November 28th treatment, then how could he have been developed in the supposedly-subsequent conferences? Thus, the treatment came second.

The reason for the treatment bearing the same date as the first day of the conferences might be extrapolated from *The Annotated Screenplays*:

> The opening scene was discussed at length by Lucas and Brackett; a helicopter shot would reveal two men riding the snow dunes on some kind of giant snow lizard. One guy calls the other on his walkie-talkie but can't reach him; he hears all kinds of weird sounds. His friend eventually replies and says he's okay, but suddenly a beast attacks and kills him. The other man gets back to the base and reports that his friend has disappeared.[2]

Lucas, having the opening sequence vividly in his mind, must have put it to paper directly after the very first story conference of November 28th, upon which he annotated it with that date, turning the two anonymous characters into Luke and Han, but then withheld writing the rest of the treatment until later in the conferences or after they were complete, by which point more elements of the storyline had been decided upon.

This is similar to the way the conferencing and treatment of *Raiders* occurred only a few months later, in early 1978: Lucas met with writer Lawrence Kasdan and director Steven Spielberg beginning on January 23rd, 1978, which lasted until January 27th, but the *Raiders of the Lost Ark* treatment bears a date of January 25th, right in the midst of the conferencing.[3]

According to Laurent Bouzereau, during story meetings, Brackett and Lucas decided that the Emperor and the Force had to be the two opposing issues in the film. The Emperor was virtually non-existent in *Star Wars* and now he would be dealt with in person—however, he was still a Nixonian bureaucrat at this point, described as a "Wizard of Oz-type person," a master manipulator.[4] In story meetings it was decided that Vader would also be shown in a black castle surrounded by lava, with gargoyles and gremlins.[5] This frighteningly powerful imagery is indicative of the transformation Darth Vader had undergone since *Star Wars* was released, a far cry from the petty bickering with Tarkin in the first film. Later, the Emperor has a discussion with Vader on a communication screen—the Emperor is described as "caped and hooded in a cloth of gold"—and says that he has felt a disturbance in the Force, due to Luke's Jedi training. Joe Johnston did sketches of Vader's castle but before he got too far Lucas said that he would be saving this for future episodes.[6]

The development of Yoda was a major addition to the series—Obi Wan wasn't the last of the Jedi after all, and in fact his former master is still in hiding. Laurent Bouzereau wrote in *The Annotated Screenplays*:

> The idea of using another person, perhaps an alien, for Luke to play off of came up during story meetings. George Lucas and Leigh Brackett thought that the alien could be an Indian desert type, very childlike even though he's an old man. He at first should be repulsive and slimy but then should become kind and wise. He appears as a crazy little nitwit that goes around scurrying like a rat but ultimately teaches Luke a great deal about the Force.[7]

This description sounds similar to the original conception of Ben Kenobi from the third draft of *Star Wars* where he is portrayed as crazed and child-like until Luke realises that he is the great Jedi Master he is looking for. But with Ben dead and gone, Lucas had to introduce a substitute. Minch Yoda, as he was later called, says that he knew Obi Wan and Father Skywalker, and that they used to train on the bog planet.

In the story conferences the frog-like appearance was decided upon: "It was suggested that he should be very small, about twenty-eight inches high," Bouzereau reported. "He should be slightly froglike, with slick skin, a wide mouth, no nose, bulbous eyes, thin spidery arms...he should have a rounded body with short legs but very large, floppy webbed feet...basically he would have the personality of a Muppet, only with almost human and realistic behavior...at that point Yoda did not have a name and was referred to as 'The Critter'."[8]

Bouzereau also reported that "Lucas and Leigh Brackett had lengthy discussions about Luke's training with Yoda and decided to turn the lessons into proverbs or commandments. Through the lessons, Luke should learn to respect Yoda and Yoda should realise that the boy is a great warrior."[9] There was also more elaboration on what the Force was and how it functioned:

It was decided that learning the ways of the Force had to be a constant struggle for Luke and that he would always have to prove himself. In regard to the dark side of the Force, the story meeting transcripts suggest that although one can't see it, it should be the real villain of the story. In his training Luke discovers the roots of the evil Force. The danger, the jeopardy is that Luke will become Vader, will become taken over. He has to fight the bad side and learn to work with the good side. Lucas felt that at one point during the training Ben should explain to Luke that he should use his powers with moderation. If he uses too much of the Force, it will start using him. For example, to lift objects Luke has to use the bad side of the Force, so if he overuses this power, the dark side will start taking him over as it did with Vader. When Luke fights, he has to use the dark side, but he is also using the good side for protection. In this episode Luke should embody the classic tale of the ugly duckling who becomes a hero, and by the end of the film Luke should have become Ben.[10]

In addition to the ice planet Hoth, many more planets were brainstormed in story conferences, including a water planet with an underwater city, a fairy-tale-like garden planet, and a "city planet" that might be the home of the Empire.[11]

Bouzereau described new developments for Han Solo:

Many changes in Han's character were discussed during story meetings. In coming up with a possible mission for Han, George Lucas fleshed out the character's backstory.* Han is an orphan and was raised by Wookies on their planet. He left, flunked out of the Space Academy, and then met some kind of Ernest Hemingway character, a very powerful trader in the galaxy who took Han under his wing until they had a falling out. Han swore he'd never talk to him again.

When the story begins, the Rebel Alliance needs this man, this powerful trader, on its side; by now he controls all nonmilitary transports in the galaxy and is the head of some sort of transport guild. Leia tells Han that they've made contact with him and that he'll talk only to him. Another plot line suggests that Han is the only one who knows where this man is hiding and that the Rebellion wants Han to contact him. In either case the future of the Rebellion is in Han's hands. At first Han refuses to go, but eventually he agrees to take on the mission, although it is aborted once the Empire attacks the Rebel base.[12]

This sub-plot would be left out of Lucas' treatment, but Brackett would incorporate it into her first draft. Lando was also first discussed in story

---

* The backstory of Han being raised by Wookies had existed since the first film (see Rinzler's *Making of Star Wars*, for example), but this trader figure is new to it

meetings, as "a new Han Solo character."[13] Bouzereau describes the many ideas bandied about for Lando:

> He is described as a slick, riverboat gambler dude. Unlike Han Solo, this guy should be elegant, sort of like James Bond. There were discussions about getting this new character a sidekick, a girl or female alien or a matched set of girls... another permutation had Lando be a gambler who runs a general store on the Wookie planet or a trader, some sort of businessman who works with smugglers.[14]

A bit of development on the mysterious Clone Wars was then done: a final idea proposed was that Lando was a clone. Laurent Bouzereau reported in *The Annotated Screenplays*:

> Leia doesn't trust him because of the war that practically wiped out his species. He could be one of the last clones, and in another episode he could run across a clan of clones who are all exactly like him. He came from a planet of clones; the planet had maybe seven hundred different countries, and each country was composed of a clone clan and he was the ruler of one of the clans.[15]

This would be incorporated into the treatment and first draft but then dropped from the story.

Ideas for the climactic fight between Vader and Luke were developed in the story meetings as well. Luke had to be trained as a good swordsman so that it would payoff in his fight with Vader. Bouzereau described the challenge as playing the fight "like a seduction, a temptation; the audience knows that Luke is not going to die, so the ultimate hook is the fear that Luke might turn to the dark side."[16] Bouzereau also reported:

> The idea of Vader using telekinetic powers during his fight with Luke was created during story meetings. There was concern, however, that the audience might think back to the first film and wonder why Vader didn't use all his powers on Ben; this was easily explained by the fact that Ben was probably stronger than Vader. George Lucas and Leigh Brackett also discussed the different levels of the Force; maybe Ben was a six, Vader was a four, and Luke is now at level two.
>
> Another idea that came out of story meetings was to have Luke wedged up against a wall; there's a pipe next to him, and Vader and Luke duel, trying to bend it until it buckles and ties itself up.[17]

With the basic backbone of the movie now developed, Lucas fleshed out a treatment. Written by hand, the nineteen-page treatment[18] is crude and briskly developed (with many spelling and grammar mistakes), representing Lucas' first thoughts on the story.

The story treatment for *Empire Strikes Back* began as the film does, with Luke being attacked by the wampa. This has been theorized to have been written due to the fact that Mark Hamill was in a rather serious car accident in 1977, which resulted in some plastic surgery to correct his facial structure, thus the scarring Luke endured was used to explain his subtly altered appearance (though the fact that Lucas had this scene in mind before it was attached to Luke seems to put this theory in doubt). Lucas' treatment begins thusly:

> Open on the bleak white planet of Hoth. Luke is riding across the windswept ice slopes on a large snow lizard (taun taun) He reins up on the shaggy two legged creature when he spots something on the horizon; a strange ice formation, or meatorite hit. Luke talks into his walkie-talkie which is on his helmet. He lifts his snow goggles as he says "Han, ol buddy everythings OK here, but I saw a glint on the next ridge, and I want to check it out." Over the com link we hear Han say "OK but don't take too long kid, nite storms comming up." Luke says a few kind words to his lizzard, sinks his spurrs in, and the beast leaps forward. He rides over the ridge when suddenly, out of nowhere, a giant snow creature jumps up in front of him, causing the lizzard to rear back and throw Luke to the icy ground. the monster grabs the taun taun by its neck, killing the poor lizzard, then bashes Luke in the face. Unconscious, covered with blood the young warrior from tatooine is dragged across the snow by the horrible snow monster.[19]

Meanwhile, Han has made it back to the Rebel base, and announces to Leia that he must be leaving:

> The princess and the Pirate meet in one of the ice corridors outside the control room. Han Explains the reason he has to go, important. He has no choice. It's a mission that he must go off and complete at the end of the film. Han comes on to Leia, but she won't have much to do with it. She stays aloof of the whole situation and doesn't have time to fall in love. She rejects Han as a rogue, and puts him in his place, but she gets a sparkle in her eye, and is slightly attracted to Han.

The undeveloped and creatively vague motivation of Han here might reveal that this early section (page two, in fact) was written before the story conferences developed that Han would embark on a quest to contact his estranged mentor-figure on behalf of the Rebellion; Lucas knew he wanted Han to leave on a mission, but had not yet come up with a reason. The first draft would then adhere to the mentor-figure sub-plot developed in the conferences.

Luke, meanwhile, is in the "ice monster's" lair:

> He regains consciousness and uses the Force for escape. He's fumbling with the use of the force. it's not very strong with him... the ice monster is always vague, and mysterious. Luke fingers a talsman around his neck, and talks about Ben to himself. He feels he must go to the planet described on Ben's talisman. Luke finally shows up at the base and explains the monsters, and danger.

Here, Ben does not appear and instruct Luke to go to Dagobah; instead, Lucas came up with the idea of Luke wearing a talisman that used to belong to Ben with markings that give the name and location of a planet, and by instinct Luke would go there.

The blossoming romance between Luke and Leia was much more pronounced in the early material—further reinforcing the notion that they were obviously not supposed to be related. In the treatment, Luke outright proclaims his love for her but Leia explains that a relationship would be impossible because of her duties (Lucas would write a similar scene years later for *Attack of the Clones*). Later, Vader uses Leia as bait for Luke, telling her that he knows Luke is in love with her.

> In the recovery room Leia takes care of Luke. he is obviously in love with her, and he tries to Express this to her. Leia says she can't love him, job etc, but gives him a sentimental kiss.

The "snow monsters" begin to break into the Rebel base and cause havoc, and soon Vader, who is described as "waiting at the center of the Imperial stronghold," is revealed to somehow know where the Rebels are. The Rebel base is attacked by the Empire and everyone disperses, with Luke and R2 venturing off in search of the bog planet and Leia, Han, Chewie and 3P0 meeting the rest of the fleet in the Millennium Falcon. Leia gives Han the co-ordinates for the Rebel rendezvous but when they come out of hyperspace they are met with an Imperial ambush, are pursued into an asteroid belt and hide in an asteroid cave (where they have their first kiss).

Meanwhile Luke and R2 arrive on the remote bog planet and meet Jedi master Minch Yoda. Minch Yoda "tells Luke that Ben gave him the talisman he wears around his neck so that he could find him," according to Bouzereau. "Luke is starving, and Yoda says he has food but won't give him any until Luke starts learning about the Force."[20]

The scene discussed in story conferences where Vader is in a castle on a hell-like world does not appear in the treatment, but it is present in the first draft; possibly, this idea was developed at the end of the conference sessions, while Lucas had already written past that point in the story treatment at the time it was developed. Bouzereau describes it as:

> In the first draft the scene with Vader in his castle is intercut with Luke beginning his training. Vader lives in what's described as a grim castle of black iron that squats on a rock in the midst of a crimson sea. He is feeding gargoyles from a golden bowl, and he suddenly stiffens, frightening even the creatures; he has felt a disturbance in the Force.[21]

As Luke trains as a Jedi, Han Solo remembers his friend, Lando Kadar, who lives on a gas planet. They go there, but Leia says she doesn't trust him (it is later learned that he is a clone).

Luke meanwhile dreams of Vader and takes off to face him, a Jedi knight by now, using the Force to locate Leia, who has been captured with Han, Chewie and 3PO as in the final film. Vader uses them as bait for Luke, who arrives and duels Vader. Han, Leia, Chewie and 3PO escape and make it back to the Millennium Falcon while Lando eludes the stormtroopers. Luke is tempted by Vader to join the dark side but refuses and jumps off a ledge and into a debris chute, where he dangles above the city before being rescued by the Falcon.

They land on a beautiful jungle garden planet at the end, where the heroes say goodbye to each other before the Falcon takes off into the sunset. Bouzereau describes it as:

> Han, Chewie, and Lando are getting ready to leave; the Wookie hugs everyone, even Threepio, who thanks him for putting him back together. Han gives Leia a long kiss. The *Falcon* takes off at sunset: "Twin suns low on the horizon as the *Falcon* becomes a tiny speck, then disappears behind the silhouettes of Luke, Leia, and the robots."[22]

The adventure would continue in the next chapter...

The basic story of the treatment is fairly similar to what ended up on the screen; only the details changed, and until the last quarter the plot is exactly alike. You will notice that there is no "I am your father revelation" in Lucas' outline. Nor would there be in the first draft screenplay. This is the most crucial development in all of *Star Wars'* story history, and we will soon get to it.

The style and tone of the story is also more like *Star Wars* rather than the sepulchral undertones that *Empire* would eventually be known for—the action is constant, the plot moves quickly, there is a much less pronounced darkness compared to the final film, and the story ends on a resolved and relatively light note, and could be said to be a self-contained adventure film like *Star Wars*. However, a maturity had been introduced into the story, leaving behind the naiveté and innocence of the original, and a foreboding atmosphere of danger hung over the characters.

In coming up with an actual story for *Empire Strikes Back*, Lucas turned to a film of Akira Kurosawa's called *Dersu Uzala* and filled in the rest using elements from the other *Star Wars* tales—Luke's confrontation with Vader from *Splinter of the Mind's Eye* was reprised, and an exciting chase through an asteroid belt from *Star Wars'* 1974 rough draft was re-used as well; a city in the clouds also appeared in the earlier drafts of the first film as the prison complex of Alderaan, which was now re-integrated as Lando's "Cloud City." Together, *Dersu Uzala* and the recycled strands and set pieces from the previous unmade stories, eventually with a romance inspired by *Gone With the Wind* (and even containing identical dialogue from Margaret Mitchell's novel;[23] see end note) would form the skeletal foundation of *The Empire Strikes Back*.

The development of Yoda and most of the Dagobah and Hoth plots stem from Kurosawa's film *Dersu Uzala*, which had just been released two years earlier, in 1975, and marked the beginning of Kurosawa's return to popularity, winning the Oscar for Best Foreign Language Film. Based off the famous Russian memoir of the same name written in 1923, it tells a tale of survival in the Siberian wilderness where a Russian explorer encounters a tiny Asiatic hermit named Dersu who lives amongst the woods, has a simple child-like charm to him, and speaks in a broken backwards language. Dersu teaches the explorer about the spirituality of nature and how man can live in harmony amongst it and ultimately becomes a sort of spiritual guide to him. The film was photographed in panoramic 70mm widescreen and provides the visual and tonal blueprint for the Hoth[*] and Dagobah sequences, as well as a prototype for Yoda and his tutelage of Luke, even down to dialogue in some instances. The film's most memorable scene is a gripping snowstorm sequence where Dersu rescues

---

[*] The snow planet concept might have also been influenced by *Flash Gordon Conquers the Universe*, the third Flash Gordon serial from 1941, which featured a lengthy section on a frozen snow-planet. An ice-planet also was one of the first concepts Lucas wrote down in 1973, where it was known as Norton III.

the unconscious explorer from a blizzard in the Siberian plains and keeps him alive by stuffing his body in a pile of grass.

The poignant and touching film was partially a response of Kurosawa to his depression and suicide attempt only a few years prior, reflecting the director's realisation that he had outlived his career and grown frail, manifesting itself in this unique and hauntingly beautiful entry in Kurosawa's diverse repertoire. *Dersu Uzala* would prove to be an international hit and give way to Kurosawa's renewal in the 1980s; his next film would be the acclaimed *Kagemusha*, partly financed by Lucas himself.

One of the primary themes of the developing *Star Wars* series was the impending clash between hero and villain—Luke and Darth. The Black Knight had become the central antagonist of *Empire Strikes Back*, and his inevitable confrontation with the hero was its natural climax. Although here Luke loses his first duel with Vader he is triumphant in the spiritual sense for refusing Darth's offer of power; as the series developed, the two rivals could grow in strength before finally facing each again. The confrontation of Luke against the black-hatted monster of the series represented Luke facing his destiny, and the ultimate conquering and slaying of Vader would represent his final triumph as a Jedi and the just retribution of his father's murder.

Their connection could become more complicated as the series went on, with a very personal relationship naturally growing in the series. Luke represents the last of the Jedi, and with him the ultimate hope of the Rebel Alliance for victory, for the Force is with Luke—only Vader could realise this, and it would build into his obsession to complete his mission and finally exterminate the last bastion of the Jedi knights; Luke's death would mean the death of the Rebel Alliance, just as the destruction of Vader would symbolise the fall of the Empire. It was the personification of the main theme of the series, the elemental struggle between the forces of good and evil. In Lucas' treatment Vader has become obsessed with destroying the young Jedi and in a very chilling scene reaches into the Force to find Luke and choke him as he flees the Hoth base; Luke frantically jumps to hyperspace, escaping the mental grip of the Dark Lord.

In the development of *The Empire Strikes Back*, the ambiguous Clone War was finally fleshed out in some detail, first attached to Lando, but then dropped and an alternate storyline was settled on revolving around an army from a remote part of the galaxy that attacked the Republic. This storyline was also tied to bounty hunter Boba Fett, a concept which would be hinted at in the Expanded Universe material but ultimately dropped from Episode II in its original form.

This information is first revealed in the summer 1979 issue of *Bantha Tracks*:

> Not much is known about Boba Fett. He wears part of the uniform of the Imperial Shocktroopers, warriors from the olden time. Shocktroopers came from the far side of the galaxy and there aren't many of them left. They were wiped out by the Jedi knights during the Clone Wars.[24]

The newer Boba Fett angle seems to be where Lucas settled regarding the Clone Wars. This background also found its way into *Empire*'s novelisation: "[Fett] was dressed in a weapon-covered, armored spacesuit, the kind worn by a group of evil warriors defeated by the Jedi Knights during the Clone Wars," author Donald F. Glut wrote.[25]

On a related note, the stormtroopers would be revealed by Lucasfilm a few years later to be made up of cloned soldiers, in the 1981 publication *The World of Star Wars: A Compendium of Fact and Fantasy From Star Wars and The Empire Strikes Back*:

> The creation of an Imperial Stormtrooper. A cloned man is one of a group of genetically identical humans, an assembly-line product. He is a thinking man, but he serves a specific purpose and no other. A clone has no mother; only his trainers, and he accepts his fate because he believes it is inevitable. A clone is, physically and emotionally, a normal man. He simply has no human rights and no name. He is the property of the Emperor.[26]

This seems to be much different from the original film, where they were implied to be simply recruits from an Imperial space academy; in fact, Lucas in 1977 even says, "Some of the stormtroopers are women, but there weren't that many women assigned to the Death Star."[27]

The developments of Boba Fett as a prominent player in the Clone Wars and then the stormtroopers as clones is a curious one, though it does not appear that there is any relationship between the two that implies them to be of the same source as it is *Attack of the Clones*. Perhaps we see here a reconstruction of what the Clone Wars may have been settled as, circa 1979: Imperial Shocktroopers, including Boba Fett, came from a distant part of the galaxy and waged war against the Republic, who in turn created their own clone army of stormtroopers which were led by the Jedi and defeated the invaders; the few Shocktrooper survivors dispersed themselves amongst the galaxy, including Boba Fett, who became a bounty hunter.

Though the information supporting this reconstruction is slightly sketchy, it may prove to be the first indication that Lucas may have been moving the timeline up, in this case moving the Clone Wars closer to the birth of the Empire (instead of thirty years prior) in order to allow both Boba Fett and the recently-revised Darth Vader to participate in it (Darth Vader would be decided in 1981 as being roughly 65 at the time of *Return of the Jedi*, which is still too young for the original timeline which places the Clone Wars as roughly fifty years prior to *Star Wars*; this will be explored in detail in chapter VIII, and later in this chapter).

Similarly, although Fett's costume is vaguely reminiscent of a sort of prototype stormtrooper outfit, there is no relation other than they were both designed by Joe Johnston and thus reflect his aesthetics. In Episode II, both (Jango) Fett and the clone troopers would be linked through conscious design choices but this is not based upon the initial developments from the '70s. It is reported in *The Art of Attack of the Clones* that "[Concept artist] Chiang and Lucas simultaneously recalled old mythology implying that Boba Fett might have been a stormtrooper. That fusion of ideas resulted in the final approved sketch [for the clone trooper where the designs merge]."[28]

This, however, is an oversight; the background that *Attack of the Clones* concept artist Doug Chiang and Lucas recall is from the comics and novels, which revealed that Boba Fett is really a man named Jaster Mereel, who was once a stormtrooper but defected after murdering his superior officer and became a bounty hunter. All indication is that the original concept was that Fett was a "shocktrooper," who were the enemies of the Republic in the Clone War and were all but destroyed by the Jedi.

### The Great Divide

After story conferences ended on December 2nd, 1977, Lucas finished his *Empire Strikes Back* treatment and then Leigh Brackett began writing the first draft screenplay. Finally, on February 23rd, 1978, Brackett finished her first draft of the script, which is essentially identical to the treatment with a few notable elaborations. Tragically, she died from cancer on March 18th.

The first item of note at this point is that *Star Wars* was not the fourth entry but the first, as discussed earlier, with *Empire Strikes Back* following as the second chapter. During story meetings between Brackett and Lucas, the film was identified as "Chapter II, The Empire Strikes Back,"[29] and by the time the second draft was finished, the familiar episode listing was in place.* However, it was not Episode V, as we now know the film to be—the opening crawl read "Episode II The Empire Strikes Back."[30]

However, after the second draft, the film would be known as Episode V. So, what was it that happened? What occurred that suddenly made Lucas take a major step and add another *three* episodes to the *Star Wars* story? Obi Wan Kenobi's tales were already in place, but they were not to be a "prequel" trilogy—they would either continue in the episode listing, which was not necessarily progressing in chronological sequence at the time of the first draft as Gary Kurtz explained,[31] or they would simply be a spin-off. From what Lucas says of it, "One of the sequels," it appears to be a single, standalone movie, tangential to the main Rebel versus Empire plot. The actual prequel *story*—the prequel *trilogy*—would not take shape until after the second draft of *Empire Strikes Back.*

It is abundantly clear that at this time Darth Vader was still not Father Skywalker. All Lucasfilm publications are consistent with what Obi Wan says in the film (naturally), for example, the first Marvel comic annual references an adventure participated by Obi Wan, Darth Vader and Father Skywalker together as a threesome. Furthermore, they remain separate in Lucas' *Empire Strikes Back* treatment, in the story meetings with Leigh Brackett, and even in the first draft of the screenplay.

Some have tried to claim that Lucas came up with the idea of converting Father Skywalker into Darth Vader in 1977, between the release of *Star Wars* and the start of story development of *Star Wars II*, but there is no indication that such a process occurred, and in fact this argument is easily refuted (see Appendix C for more detail). In fact, we can pinpoint the exact month when the milestone event occurred—which would have been after Lucas read Brackett's first draft, completed at the very end of February, but before he finished his own second draft in April, placing the genesis of this idea around March (Brackett herself died on March 18th and was in the hospital some time before that).

Most surprising of all is that in the first draft of *Empire Strikes Back*, Father Skywalker's ghost appears to Luke while he is training on Dagobah and gives Luke advice. Naturally, when Luke finally faces Darth there is no "father revelation"—he beckons Luke to join the dark side, Luke refuses, Vader attacks Luke and Luke jumps off the ledge; the point of Luke's confrontation with Darth is that he refuses the dark side. Father Skywalker

---

* Many note the change from "Chapter II" to "Episode II"—Neil Simon was working on a film adaptation of his famous play, *Chapter II*, which was released in 1979; Lucas may not have wanted the two films to have such similar titles

is described as "a tall, fine looking man," and is referred to only as "Skywalker." Luke takes the oath of the Jedi from his father.

Leigh Brackett died only a few weeks after she completed her first draft of *Empire Strikes Back*, which bears a February 23rd, 1978 date. Lucas was not happy with the script. Similar incidents had happened when Lucas hired writers to script *THX 1138* and then *American Graffiti*—the vision in his head was so specific and particular that no one else could write it quite the way he wanted. "During story conferences with Leigh, my thoughts weren't fully formed and I felt that her script went in a completely different direction," he explained to Laurent Bouzereau.[32]* When Lucas called Brackett in early March to discuss the script, someone else answered—she was in the hospital. A few days later she succumbed to her cancer.[33] Lucas said in *Annotated Screenplays*:

> Writing has never been something I have enjoyed, and so, ultimately, on the second film I hired Leigh Brackett. Unfortunately, it didn't work out; she turned in the first draft, and then passed away. I didn't like the first draft script, but I gave Leigh credit because I liked her a lot. She was sick at the time she wrote the script, and she really tried her best.[34]

Lucas' dissatisfaction with the first draft of *Empire Strikes Back* forced him to think of new ways to approach the story, new ways of building the plot and characters. George and Marcia had planned to vacation in Mexico over Easter (which fell on March 26th that year) with their friends Michael Ritchie and his wife—while everyone else sunned themselves on a beach, Lucas was holed up in his hotel room with a pen and paper, more worrisome matters to deal with.[35]

"No matter how much I wanted to get out of writing, I was somehow always forced to sit down and work on the script," he confessed to Laurent Bourzereau.[36] With the release date of May 1980 already announced and drawing ever nearer and no replacement available, Lucas had to write a second draft himself, by hand. But as he sat in the confines of that hotel room somewhere in Mexico, the story strangely came out of him in an unusually compelling manner. Lucas explained to Alan Arnold in 1979:

---

* "It was sort of old-fashioned," Lawrence Kasdan recollects of her draft. "The character's all had the right names, but the story's spirit was different." (Baxter, p. 271) Kurtz reports that Lucas' changes from her draft were rather minor, stating that Lucas basically fleshed out her draft because she never had the chance: "She was going to do two drafts and a polish," Kurtz says (*Starlog*, July 1987, p. 52).

I hired Leigh Brackett to write the screenplay, but tragically she died right after completing the first draft. Faced with the situation that somebody had to step in and do a rewrite, I was forced to write the second draft of this screenplay. But I found it much easier than I'd expected, almost enjoyable.[37]

In this draft, Father Skywalker's ghost does not appear. In this draft, Darth Vader reveals that he is Father Skywalker.

The moment comes during the climactic lightsaber fight on the 128th page of Lucas' hand-written second draft:

Luke
Enough! He said you killed him.

Vader
I am your father.

The two have been battling all through this dialog. Luke pulls away at this revelation. The two warriors stand staring at one another; father and son.

Luke
That's impossible. It's not true.

Vader
Search your feelings you already know it to be true. Join me.[38]

This is the first time that this shocking notion appears. What happened? What made Lucas change gears considerably and make such a *major* change to the story? The answer, simply put, is that it was the easiest story solution. It was a way of tying up multiple story threads which became redundant and all converged. The development of Father Skywalker into Darth Vader is based more on convenience, and was in many ways a *natural* progression of the two characters, given the trajectory left off in *Star Wars*. During the development of *Empire Strikes Back*, Lucas had to flesh out the backstory and the character histories in much more detail than the vague notes he already had—most of which he had already given to the audience in the first film. When he looked at the history he had created, he obviously realised that the characters of Father Skywalker, Darth Vader and Obi Wan Kenobi were redundant in many ways, and that a more interesting past could potentially be created.

Lucas has said he was unhappy with Brackett's draft, and it was obviously hampered by this redundancy issue, made material by the introduction of Ben Kenobi and Father Skywalker together as ghosts—Lucas quickly changed it once he realised what the problem was, and it is one of the few story changes Lucas made from Brackett's draft. In the history of Darth Vader and Father Skywalker there are enormous parallels. Both were friends with Ben Kenobi, both were Jedi, both have a mysterious past and one kills the other. Their histories converge at a critical point and where one history ends, the other begins. Similarly, both Ben Kenobi and Father Skywalker were Jedi, both are father figures to Luke, both want to mentor him, both were friends with each other and both were killed by Darth Vader. This is no surprise: as covered earlier, in draft three of *Star Wars* Obi Wan was created to *replace* Father Skywalker, who had since been re-written to die in the past (at the hands of Darth Vader himself in the revised fourth draft). But once Father Skywalker was brought back into the story—in ghost form, no less—the fact that he and Obi Wan were the same character became painfully clear. How do you solve these story-similarities? The answer for a better storyline thus leapt out at him: make Father Skywalker and Darth Vader the same person! It was a great twist, and it was so obvious, just sitting there waiting to happen.*

No wonder Lucas enjoyed writing this draft so much—and he was able to hammer it out in under a month. In fact, so satisfying and successful was this new story that he not only wrote the second draft, but he wrote the revised second draft *and* the third draft all in April of 1978—compare that with the year-long struggles he endured for *Star Wars*. This story was a success from the minute Lucas thought it up.

Now a much simpler and more dynamic history was written. Obi Wan and Father Skywalker were master-student, Skywalker fell to the dark side, battled his former master and was horribly wounded before being resurrected as Darth Vader. This seemingly simple change would have enormous consequences for the rest of the series. With this change in character and story, the *Star Wars* series would irrevocably shift from the *Flash Gordon*-type "Serial" style to a more epic *Dune*-type "Saga," from a storybook-like tale of good versus evil to a complicated chronicle of temptation and redemption. With the second draft of *Empire Strikes Back*, George Lucas created the basis for the *Star Wars Saga*. "When you're

---

* Lucas has admitted this to a degree on one rare occasion on the 2004 DVD featurette "The Characters of Star Wars," although he implies that this occurred in early drafts for the first film. Here he says that Father Skywalker and Vader merged. "The good father was Annikin Starkiller and the bad villain was Darth Vader," he says. "Ultimately they merged into being one character."

creating something like that the story itself takes over and the characters take over and they begin to tell the story apart from what you're doing," Lucas once explained. "And you kind of go with it, and you have to go with it, and it sends you down some very funny paths. And then you have to figure out how to break that apart and put the puzzle back together so it makes sense and is cohesive. But that's the adventure of writing—it's the fact that you're not sure where it's going to go."[39]

Lucas was obviously keen on exploring the issue of Luke's father, especially since it was such a significant story point for Luke's character in the first film, but having already introduced Obi Wan it was difficult to explore Father Skywalker in any significant way without bumping against the fact that his character had become somewhat irrelevant, especially now that Yoda was in the story. Once Lucas brought Father Skywalker back into the series, he and Obi Wan became redundant, as Obi Wan was essentially a copy of him (a noble elderly Jedi who is a father-figure to Luke and is betrayed by Vader), and suddenly Dagobah is full of old, noble Jedi ghosts who are basically the same character. To make matters worse, Yoda was created to replace *Obi Wan*—he was even based off an early version of him. So really, *he too* is born out of Father Skywalker in a way—Father Skywalker is killed off and then turns into Obi Wan and Obi Wan is killed off and then turns into Yoda. You can see Lucas writing himself into corners and having to invent new story directions. But once the characters were all brought together, the story did not work dramatically—perhaps the idea of a "Jedi Trinity" worked better in concept, but once actually implemented in script form it revealed itself to not be the success Lucas envisioned.

Luckily, hardly anything was known about Father Skywalker and Darth Vader, other than they were both Jedi friends of Obi Wan and that Skywalker was killed by Vader. With the two characters already connected in a way which defined both of their identities, with both already sharing many similarities, and with both presented in a mysterious light, it was perhaps inevitable that Lucas would hit upon such a transformation, recognising the enormous power and resonance of such a development, which was also allowed by the deeper mythological probing that Lucas was exploring in *Empire*.* The vagueness and mysteriousness of Darth Vader and Father Skywalker allowed Lucas to merge the two characters and create

---

* Recalling Greek myths like the legend of Perseus, who battles and slays his evil grandfather, King Acrisius, or the myths of Oedipus and Cronus.

a more interesting story dynamic, especially for Luke's arc.

This is when the prequel trilogy was formed. It is this monumental event, the merging of Father Skywalker and Darth Vader in the April 1978 second draft of *Empire Strikes Back*, which prompted Lucas to change *Empire Strikes Back* from Episode II to Episode V. Now Lucas had more than simply a backstory to his current films—he had a tale of adventure, betrayal and tragedy of galactic proportions, a tale which could be a series unto itself. Father Skywalker and Obi Wan become master-student and fight in the Clone Wars, while in the meantime the Republic falls and the Emperor rises to dictatorship; Skywalker succumbs to the dark side, betrays his master, is wounded and resurrected as Darth Vader and then begins to exterminate the Jedi. Meanwhile, Obi Wan hides Skywalker's son away, and he and Yoda escape into exile as the Empire takes over, the Rebellion is formed and the galaxy is plunged into civil war. It was now a tale as rich and dramatic as the current one, perhaps more so—it was one much more operatic and epic in scope.

### Re-Writing History

The Emperor would also be a prominent figure in the reconfigured back story, and with the merging of Father Skywalker and Darth Vader, the character of the Emperor was irrevocably changed, intertwined in it all.

In the original film, the Emperor was a Nixon-like politician, a corrupt ruler who had turned a democracy into a dictatorship, one who had manipulated his way into office, bribing senators and rigging elections. Darth Vader joined him as a minion along with the rest of the Sith knights when Palpatine ascended to office, helping the Empire hunt down the Jedi. The 1976 novelisation even implied that the weasely despot was no longer in control, and that the Empire was instead being manipulated behind the scenes by the Emperor's own advisors. Some have written this off as an addition of Foster's, but the fact that we witness a remnant of this plot point in *The Phantom Menace* suggests that it was indeed based off of Lucas' then-current notes (ref: Supreme Chancellor Valorum—in place of the Emperor in this version—is controlled by the bureaucrats, his advisors; as Palpatine observes, "Enter the bureaucrats, the true rulers of the Republic.").

The novelisation also contains a mention that there have been *multiple* Emperors. Kenobi explains:

Vader used the training I gave him and the force within him for evil, to help the later corrupt Emperors.[40]

This is an interesting statement for many reasons. For starters, it implies that there have always been Emperors, even good ones. This has its roots in the first draft of *Star Wars*, where the Empire was a benign one in which the Jedi served as protectors. In this version one of the Emperors became corrupted and brought fascism to the galaxy; the Sith Knights, basically a mercenary band of warriors and sworn enemies of the Jedi, joined this Emperor as enforcers and hunted down their nemeses, who opposed the new tyrannical rule. In this draft, the current Emperor is seen giving an impassioned Hitler-esque speech to a rally of troops and is described as "a thin, grey looking man, with an evil moustache which hangs limply over his insipid lip." Humorously, his name is Cos Dashit, appropriate for someone who has caused so much trouble.

In the second draft there was now once a Republic which *turned into* an Empire through the corrupt senate, with the citizens welcoming a police state due to war and terrorism. The Sith Knights then joined the Emperor, later revealed as a senator who was elected as supreme ruler. This seems to have been carried over into the third draft, even though the background information was cut out of the script itself in an effort to streamline the pacing. In the fourth draft, the additional Sith were cut out of the film altogether (though not necessarily the story) and Vader is their all-purpose representative. It is interesting to imagine that in the original *Star Wars* there are many other Sith servants of the Empire, as there were in the previous drafts, whom we merely aren't yet introduced to.* With the neglect to show them in *Empire Strikes Back* as well, it seems Lucas decided that Vader was indeed the last of them.

But, getting back to the initial point, the first instance of multiple Emperors comes from the first draft of *Star Wars* where the Empire was once good until later corrupted. What makes the line in the novel interesting is that it of course is not based off the first draft, but the final draft. So, in light of the fact that this script (and the novel) also explicitly state that the Republic turned into the Empire, it must mean that the elected ruler of the Republic must have *also* have been referred to as the Emperor. As it says, the *later* Emperors were corrupt. Although it may seem strange that an elected official is named the Emperor, let us not forget that Lucas

---

* One of Lucas' notes from the third draft states that there is one Sith for "each sector" of the Empire, indicating that they each are responsible for assigned territories, perhaps with Darth Vader appointed to service on the Death Star

would reuse this concept in *Phantom Menace*, with the elected ruler of Naboo being *Queen* Amidala. This, however, is all a bit confusing, as the novel prologue also says that Palpatine was elected as President of the Republic, not Emperor, though the Kenobi line seems to provide an alternate viewpoint, and in the actual prequel films he is titled as neither of these two options. Perhaps Lucas used both at different times, hence they both ended up in the novel when the editor failed to notice the mistake (Lucas, by mid-1977, had privately begun to call the Republic's ruler a "chancellor"[41]).

This line tells us another thing—that there have been multiple Emperors since the Republic became the Empire. The line is not "the later corrupt Emperor"—it is "Emperors," plural. The initial Emperor who declared himself dictator was replaced, perhaps due to assassination or power struggling, by more Emperors in the twenty-year period since the Empire's formation. In this light, Emperor Palpatine no longer reigns and was likely *killed* nearly two decades earlier. The subsequent Emperors themselves are then implied to have no real power, instead being figurehead puppets for the bureaucracy.

Once again, some have written these off as additions by Alan Dean Foster, but there is very good reason to believe they are based off of Lucas then-current notes. The fact that Lucas' original conception was that there was a long line of Emperors, and that only recently had one of them become evil, is a telling sign, as is the statement that the current Emperor was being manipulated by his advisors. As each draft got more and more streamlined, less and less background information was given, and as can be seen by the information in the novel on Senator Palpatine becoming Emperor, its exclusion from the final script does not at all imply its elimination from the story. Lucas simply included in the novel some of his ideas that he didn't have room to make explicit in the script. With Lucas being notorious for moving the story along as quickly as possible, it is fitting that the only place he found room for this type of material was in a book.

The prologue explains in more detail the galaxy's history; further backing up the hypothesis that all of this information was coming from Lucas, much of it is identical to the prequels, even naming the Emperor as Palpatine, the first time this name ever appeared in print. The prologue states:

> Once, under the wise rule of the Senate and the protection of the Jedi Knights, the Republic throve and grew. But...Like the greatest of trees, able to withstand any external attack, the Republic was rotted from within though the danger was

not visible from outside.

Aided and abetted by restless, power-hungry individuals within the government, and the massive organs of commerce, the ambitious Senator Palpatine caused himself to be elected President of the Republic. He promised to unite the disaffected among the people and to restore the remembered glory of the Republic.

Once secure in office he declared himself Emperor, shutting himself away from the populace. Soon he was controlled by the very assistants and boot-lickers he had appointed to high office, and the cries of the people for justice did not reach his ears.

Having exterminated through treachery and deception the Jedi Knights, guardians of justice in the galaxy, the Imperial governors and bureaucrats prepared to institute a reign of terror among the disheartened worlds of the galaxy. Many used the imperial forces and the name of the increasingly isolated Emperor to further their own personal ambitions.

But a small number of systems rebelled at these new outrages. Declaring themselves opposed to the New Order they began the great battle to restore the Republic...

From the First Saga
*Journal of the Whills*[42]

The end note "From the First Saga, Journal of the Whills" is yet another use of the storytelling device to imply that the tale is taken from a larger chronicle. See Appendix A for more information.

Ben explains how Father Skywalker grew up on Tatooine as a farmer and ran off with him to fight in the Clone Wars, an "idealistic crusade."

"Owen Lars didn't agree with your father's ideas, opinions or philosophy of life. He believed that your father should have stayed here on Tatooine and not gotten involved in..." Again the seemingly indifferent shrug. "Well, he though thought he should have remained here and minded his farming...Owen was always afraid that your father's adventurous life might influence you, might pull you away from Anchorhead." He shook his head slowly, regretful at the remembrance. "I'm afraid there wasn't much of a farmer in your father."

..."I tried to give [this lightsaber] to you once before, but your uncle wouldn't allow it. He believed you might get some crazy ideas from it and end up following old Obi-Wan on some idealistic crusade.

"You see Luke, that's where your father and your uncle Owen disagreed. Lars is not a man to let idealism interfere with business, whereas your father didn't think the question even worth discussing.

...at one time [lightsabers] were widely used. Still are, in certain galactic quarters."[43]

More interesting information is peppered throughout the book, which reveals a quite different conception of *Star Wars* than exists today. It also better illustrates how different the Empire and the Rebellion and their relation to the galaxy were in the first film. Geoffrey McKinney examined it best:

> The soldiers on board Leia's starship attacked by Vader and the stormtroopers were Imperial troops on board an Imperial vessel guarding an Imperial senator. The Empire had to be careful about what the Senate heard: "Holding her is dangerous. If word of this gets out, it could generate sympathy for the Rebellion in the senate."
>
> The discussion by the Imperial officers on the Death Star makes it clear that the Rebel fleet was powerful enough to pose a threat to the Imperial fleet. Sympathy for the Rebel Alliance in the Imperial Senate was another problem for the Imperial officers, but they needed the bureaucracy of the Senate to maintain control.
>
> After the Emperor dissolved the Senate, control was maintained by fear of the Death Star. If a system were to step out of line, it would risk getting destroyed. It did not matter what anyone thought of the Empire any more so long as the threat of the Death Star existed.
>
> When the Death Star was destroyed (the Empire having put all its eggs in one basket, so to speak), the infrastructure of the Empire would have been dealt a crippling blow. Otherwise everything that the Imperial officers said about the Senate would be rendered meaningless. "Pursued by the Empire's sinister agents, Princess Leia races home aboard her starship, custodian of the stolen plans that can save her people and restore freedom to the galaxy..."
>
> Obviously, these plans restored freedom to the galaxy by leading to the destruction of the Death Star. When Luke destroyed the Death Star, the infrastructure of the Empire was annihilated, leading to the fall of the Empire and to the restoration of freedom in the galaxy.[44]

Getting back to the topic of the Emperor, some have put forth the theory that Lucas had turned the Emperor into a Sith as far back as the second draft of *Star Wars*. The proof asserted is that in the second draft, Vader is said to have a Sith Master named Valorum (based off the Prince Valorum character in the first draft), who is mentioned but never seen; he is also portrayed as a separate character from the Emperor, who is also mentioned but never seen. The logic behind this theory is that since neither of them are seen, and since virtually no information is given, there exists the possibility that they were really meant to be the same person, but that Lucas simply didn't make this obvious, instead planning to reveal it in a sequel as he did with *Empire Strikes Back*.

However, this theory holds little weight; we must apply Occam's Razor here. Valorum is clearly based off the character from the previous draft, as is the Emperor, and furthermore while the Emperor is meant to reside somewhere on the Imperial capital, Prince Valorum, the "master of the Bogan," is said to live in the inner dungeon area of the Alderaan fortress.

The notion that "The Emperor was a corrupt politician" is not made explicit anywhere in the final film of *Star Wars*—it stems from early drafts and background material. It is the second draft of 1975 that best details this history, only here there appears to be no central figure in the Republic's demise, instead it is the corrupted senate itself—the bureaucracy—who does the manipulating, who make deals and bribes with corporations and various guilds and causes social instability such that a police state is formed to maintain order; an Emperor is mentioned as the head of this Empire, whom has the Sith knights as his personal protectors. This second draft begins with: "Ruthless trader barons, driven by greed and the lust for power, have replaced enlightenment with oppression, and 'rule by the people' with the FIRST GALACTIC EMPIRE."

Here we see that the takeover of the Republic wasn't necessarily a planned takeover. Instead it is the gradual result that is caused by the corruption of the senate, who allow the public to be exploited by traders and corporations in order for the senators to gain personally through bribes. Their greed results in social negligence, with crime rates and terrorism soaring as the senate collects pay-offs from these criminals; in order to maintain social order a police state is formed—the Empire—which the public willingly accepts due to the crumbling social order. A great number of the populace, however, refuses to accept any more and this is how the rebellion is formed; as we enter the film, the Empire/former Republic has corroded even more, and the rebellion has resulted in further unrest, as the second draft opening scroll states: "It is a period of civil wars. The EMPIRE is crumbling into lawless barbarism throughout the million worlds of the galaxy."

It isn't until the novelisation of 1976 that a detailed history of the Emperor is fleshed out, as excerpted previously, though just how old Lucas' notes were on this aspect is unknown. But, like the second draft, it is the corruption of the senate that collectively forms the Empire, though here a central public figure emerges in Senator Palpatine, who is elected the leader of the Republic under the guise of attempting to undo the damage the Republic had inflicted upon itself. Once in office, however, Palpatine proclaimed himself Emperor, became isolated, and the bureaucracy which he was part of took over and used the Empire to further their own agenda, while the Emperor was content to live in his own world apart from the populace.

The Black Knights of the Sith, essentially a band of pirates and sworn enemies of the Jedi Bendu, joined the Emperor as minions and hunted down the Jedi, who had tried to rebel against the Empire. The fact that the Sith Knights are a group of individuals completely separate from the Emperor and operating on their own is key—they only link to him once he gains power, and since the Jedi had attempted to dethrone the Emperor when he first took power (it is referred to as the Great Jedi Rebellion in the rough draft and the Holy Rebellion of '06 in the second draft), the Emperor uses the Sith warriors to destroy them and maintain order since they now shared a mutual enemy. In the third draft the history of the Jedi, the Sith, and the Empire are pretty much continuing as they were from the second draft, and in the fourth draft (in other words, the final film) they are basically continuing as they were in the third draft. This is then reinforced by the novelisation, which contains information obviously based off Lucas' notes and consistent with the previous drafts.

Lucas himself reinforces this, though he soon altered the Emperor's character to be in league with and cleverly manipulating the bureaucracy, rather than being a somewhat powerless figurehead for them (or, rather, was content with using his place of power to live in isolation while the bureaucracy takes advantage and assumes true control). This change began formulating around the release of *Star Wars*—in private, Lucas lays out the Emperor's history in great detail, relating how he was simply a devious politician that was brilliantly skilled in the art of machiavellian politics, but in this version he eventually figures out a way to manipulate the bureaucracy into serving him, instead of the earlier version related in the novel, and also developed Darth Vader as a more personal servant. This last point was likely an evolution born out of the fact that Lucas decided around this time that Vader was the sole Sith and thus given more stature. When the Sith collectively joined the Empire as a group in the original, earlier version, they hence had a more impersonal, administrative function, much the same as the SS had to Hitler—however when the collective group was eliminated and only Vader remained, it necessitated some kind of personal relationship between the two, hence the re-development that Vader joined the Emperor's side as his personal commander ("Lord Vader worked directly for the Emperor and was the Emperor's emissary," Lucas commented in 1977[45]); at the same time, however, this is not *wildly* different from the original storyline, where it is stated in the second draft of *Star Wars* "[the Sith knights] became the personal bodyguards of the Emperor." Lucas explained to Lucasfilm's Carol Titelman in August of 1977:

In the Old Republic, all the systems sent their representatives to the Senate. It wasn't an Imperial Senate; it was a Republican Senate, which made the decisions that controlled the Republic. There were 24, 372 systems in the Galactic Senate. The Senate would vote in a Chancellor or an overseer who would work for four years as the leader of the executive branch of the Republic. You were only supposed to be able to run for one four-year term—you were only eligible for one term.

What happened was one of the Chancellors began subverting the Senate and buying off the Senators with the help of some of the large intergalactic trade companies and mining companies. Through their power and money, he bought off enough of the senate to get himself elected to a second term, because of a crisis. By the time the third term came along, he had corrupted so much of the Senate that they made him Emperor for the rest of his life.

Giving the Emperor that title for life and doing away with the elective processs was all done with a lot of rationalizing. Many in the Senate felt that having elections and changing leaders in the time of an emergency disrupted the bureaucratic system. And the bureaucracy was getting to be so big that changing leaders made it impossible to have any effect on the system and make it work—moreover, the bureaucracy was running amok and not paying attention to the rulers. So they reasoned that the Emperor could bring the bureaucracy back into line. So the Emperor took control of the bureaucracy. The Galactic Senate would meet for a period that was similar to a year, but after it became the Imperial Senate, the meetings were less and less frequent until finally the meetings were only once a year, and they were very short.

With the bureaucracy behind the Emperor, it was impossible and too late for the Senate to do anything. He had slowly manipulated things; in fact, it was he who let the bureaucracy run amok and therefore had blackmailed the Senate into doing things because he was the only one who really had any power over the bureaucracy. It was so large there was no way to get things done, but he knew the right people; the key people in the bureaucracy were working for him and were paid by the companies.

When he became Emperor, a little over half the Senate as it turned out was not involved, was not corrupted—and they reacted strongly against the whole thing. There was a rebellion in terms of the Senate against the Emperor; they tried to oust him legally and have him impeached. But many of the Senators who were fighting the Emperor at that time mysteriously died. The Jedi Knights were alerted immediately and they rallied to the Senate's side. But there was a plot afoot and when the Jedi finally rallied and tried to restore order, they were betrayed and eventually killed by Darth Vader.[46]

This is all further backed up by the first draft of *Empire Strikes Back*, where the Emperor is seen communicating to Vader via hologram, similar to the final film—but he is not portrayed as the decrepit, evil sorcerer. Instead, he wears a cloak of gold, evidently symbolic of his corruption and vanity. *The Annotated Screenplays* states that at the time of the first draft he was still "envisioned as a bureaucrat, Nixonian in his outlook and sort of a Wizard of Oz-type person."[47] In this version he is more mysterious, being a "Wizard of Oz" type of manipulator, but still basically just a tyrannical ruler, although he appears to be in genuine control of his dictatorship rather than the bureaucracy ruling as per the first film. However, most curious is that he can feel a disturbance in the Force—to feel the Force, one need not be a Jedi or Sith, but the inclusion of this element is meant to suggest that the Emperor is more mysterious and clever than first anticipated.

Even after this first transformation from puppet to puppet master, he doesn't become the shadowy, black-hooded sorcerer until the second draft of *Empire Strikes Back*—when Father Skywalker was merged with Darth Vader.

Once the story was changed to Father Skywalker falling to the dark side and becoming the Sith Lord Darth Vader, Lucas had to explore just *why* Father Skywalker had turned, even if just in general terms. In the first version of the saga, Darth Vader's betrayal was always one-dimensional—he seems to have simply had a lust for power, as Kenobi explains in the third draft of *Star Wars* when he relates how Vader stole the Kiber crystal and sided with the Emperor. The young Vader was simply a bit of a bad seed from the beginning—in this first version the Sith come to the Emperor and not the other way around so there is no seduction involved. One of the draws of the story of *Star Wars* was its black and white morality; characters were either good or evil. Now that Father Skywalker's turn to the dark side was a major story point, both because Vader was now a central character and because Luke's temptation was now a story focus as well, that black and white morality was beginning to erode to shades of grey, and Lucas had to psychologically explore why Father Skywalker, a heroic good guy and much-admired hero, succumbed to the dark side. The previous one-dimensional villain angle *couldn't* work.

The story he came up with was that the Emperor *lured* him to the dark side. Now that Lucas had made the good-natured Father Skywalker into an evil character, he softened his turn, victimising him by having the Emperor manipulate him—this then necessitated that the Emperor himself was a Sith Lord. Lucas brought back the Sith Master character of Valorum from drafts one and two of *Star Wars*, combining him with the Emperor and giving Vader an all-purpose master (This would create a bit of a problem for Lucas when crafting the prequels; the Emperor was originally supposed to be merely a corrupt politician, but now he had also made him into a decrepit Sith Lord—so how does a Sith Lord get into politics? This would create the inevitable dual persona of Sidious/Palpatine). Once again, old characters are combined into new ones, and this would not be the last time this process occurred.

Lucas gives us a brief history, as described in a 1980 issue of *Time*:

> For years the universe was governed by a Republic, which was regulated by the order of Jedi Knight who bore a vague resemblance to Japanese Samurai warriors. But eventually the citizens of the republic "didn't care enough to elect competent officials," says Lucas the historian, and so their government collapsed. A sorcerer, a bad counterpart of Yoda, blocked all opposition and declared himself Emperor. He was not seen in Star Wars: Episode IV, but he makes a brief appearance in The Empire Strikes Back.
>
> The Emperor subverts Darth Vader to his side, and together he and Vader betray the other Knights, nearly all of whom are killed in their trap. Ben Kenobi escapes, and after a fierce struggle he does such injury to Vader that forever after Vader must wear a mask and that noisy life-support system. The fall of the republic and the rise of the empire will form the first of Lucas' three trilogies.[48]

Now the Emperor is "a sorcerer, a bad counterpart to Yoda"—while Yoda is the master of the light side of the Force, the Emperor is the master of the dark side. Father Skywalker's fall is given an extra layer of complexity, with implications that the Emperor helped lure him; his choice is not an all-together evil act. The Emperor was made into a sorcerer, a Sith Lord, once Lucas merged Father Skywalker and Darth Vader in order to set up being able to manipulate Skywalker to the dark side.

Additionally, the purge of the Jedi is more explicitly laid out, some kind of trap which results in nearly all of them being killed. This raises a number of issues—for starters, how many Jedi are there supposed to be in the universe? A thousand? A hundred thousand? This is the number Lucas gives in a 1977 conversation: "at the height of the Jedi, there were several hundred thousand"[49] The "trap" might indicate that some kind of mass execution is arranged; perhaps they are all assembled somewhere and the Emperor's stormtroopers ambush them. Given the clone trooper betrayal in the eventual Episode III, this is not too far off the mark; Lucas would, in 1977, tell how the Jedi were outlawed and hunted down but then tried to re-group and were massacred by Vader and an elite team of special forces.[50] This story point stems from draft two of *Star Wars* which described a similar "betrayal," and may have been inspired by the betrayal and execution of the Atreides House by the Emperor in *Dune*. The second draft also stated that they were publically outlawed after they rebelled against the new Empire, and that most were arrested and executed, with the survivors then fleeing and being hunted down. The Knights Templar underwent a betrayal similar to this by King Philip in 1307, who framed the knights in order to finance a war and turned the public against them, arresting and executing nearly the entire order, with the survivors dispersing. In any case, the point is that Father Skywalker's doom now had been given another emotional element to it, set against a tragic backdrop of betrayal.

### Commitment

With this, Lucas had created an intricate story which spanned generations, and with the further complexities and depth of *Empire Strikes Back*, the series was headed far, far away from the simple, *Adventure Theater* style of *Star Wars*—it was growing into a decade-spanning epic, a grand saga of tragedy and heroism. *Empire Strikes Back* now contained intellectual philosophy on the nature of the Force, on the nature of good and evil, and was much darker and serious in tone, even if Lucas' drafts were rather briskly developed—it took the charmingly simple mythology of *Star Wars* and broadened it to much further horizons. Moral grey area was introduced, with the black and white view of *Star Wars* slowly eroding.

Luke's temptation to the dark side now had even greater meaning—the danger was not just that Luke would follow in Vader's footsteps, but that he would follow in his *father's* footsteps. Luke's greatest desire is to be a Jedi, to become his father, but now it was his greatest danger. It could also be used as a ploy by Vader to beckon Luke to join him. All in all, the new story change seemed to benefit the series in every way.

With the entire arc of the saga now altered, Lucas had to basically re-write all of its history to accommodate his story changes, especially where the Skywalker family was concerned. How does Luke fit into the story? Is Owen really his uncle? How did Obi Wan end up on the same planet as Luke? What of Luke's mother? Does Vader even know he has a son? There were many more issues created that needed some exploration.

The new revelation also had to be able to fit into the pre-existing information in *Star Wars*, despite the fact that the audience had been explicitly informed that Father Skywalker and Darth Vader were two separate people, with one murdering the other. Lucas was in luck—an exchange between Owen and Beru concerning Luke's father worked even better when viewed in the new character context; they were no longer wary of Luke being killed in adventures like his father, they were wary of Luke turning to evil like his father, and despised Obi Wan not because he led

Father Skywalker to his death, but because he failed as a teacher. Less graceful was Ben's tale of Father Skywalker and Darth Vader; however, Lucas decided that he could make it seem as though Ben was lying to protect Luke, and that in a sense, Father Skywalker metaphorically "died" when he became Darth Vader. The confusion due to the contradicting stories could also create suspense before the third film confirmed that Vader was indeed the father of Luke. It also gave Lucas the option of backing out if he changed his mind after completing the film.

Lucas speaks about the prequels in a 1981 interview conducted for *Starlog*:

> Well, the next trilogy—the first one—since it's about Ben Kenobi as a young man, is the same character, just a different actor. And it's the same thing with all the characters. Luke ends up in the third film of the first trilogy just three-and-a-half years old. There is continuity with the characters, in other words, but not with the actors—and the look of the films will be different.
>
> The first trilogy will not be as much of an action adventure kind of thing. Maybe we'll make it have some humor, but right now it's much more humorless than this one. This one is where all the excitement is, which is why I started with it. The other ones are a little more Machiavellian—it's all plotting—more of a mystery. I think we'll try, on the next one, to write all three scripts at once. Then they can come out every year instead of every three years.[51]

### Mark Hamill remembered in a 1983 *Prevue* article:

> I did ask what happened to my parents during *Star Wars*. If I remember, he gave me a really detailed answer which turned out to be completely different when I got the *Empire* script... He told there was a great duel between Vader and Obi-Wan, and that Vader had fallen into a volcanic pit and was hideously burned beyond recognition...But, I always wondered if it was true that he really had all nine parts written out, whether it was sketchy or well-developed. Supposedly, he has an outline of them all.[52]

Another significant note from the second draft of *Empire Strikes Back* is that, according to *The Annotated Screenplays*, Vader's scarring transformation was altered to be that Obi Wan cut his arm off and pushed him down a nuclear reactor, twisting him into a grotesque mutant. Laurent Bouzereau wrote:

> The notion of Vader being Luke's father first appeared in the second draft. Vader became attracted to the dark side while he was training to become a Jedi. He became a Jedi and killed most of the Jedi Knights; very few escaped. Ben

fought Vader and pushed him down a nuclear reactor shaft. One of his arms was severed, and Ben believed he had killed Vader; in fact, Vader survived and became a mutant.[53]

While this alternate version was toyed with briefly it seems the familiar volcano duel was eventually reinstated, as this is the version described in *Return of the Jedi* (though it was ultimately cut out of the final film).

Lucas was concerned that the shocking news that the series' villain was the father of the series' hero could be traumatic to kids. He consulted psychologists, who advised him that those who couldn't accept it would believe that Vader is lying. "In fact, I'll tell you an interesting thing," director Irvin Kershner related in an interview with *Comingsoon.net*. "As I traveled around the world and people came to me and talked about *Empire*, whenever I talked to little kids, like six and seven, eight even, they say, 'Darth Vader's not really his father, is he.' When they get to be about nine, ten and on, they accept it."[54] With that, Lucas set the new story in stone.

Lucas made this second draft even *more* interesting by now having Han frozen in carbonite—in the previous draft he had escaped with Leia and Lando and rescued Luke; the script ended with him leaving in search of his adoptive stepfather. Lucas took this rather dull last act and made it bleak and dangerous—Han is frozen and doomed, while Luke has been defeated and learned the horrible truth that Vader is his father. These two story points all led into the next film, which would continue the story and conclude it.

With all of these transformations, the film was becoming a totally different animal, offering a story that was very much opposed to the original film; the wise-cracking ensemble cast was split apart and separated, the lovable duo of R2-D2 and C-3P0 were broken up, Han got the girl instead of Luke, bouncy humour was replaced with troubled brooding, the Emperor became a Force-using sorcerer, Obi Wan became a questionable liar, Darth Vader seemingly controlled the universe and was revealed to be Luke's father, morality and ethical philosophy were explored, and the film ended on a downer.* Such unconventional deviations cumulatively had built a series that was drifting apart from the intentions

---

* Dale Pollock makes note of other significant additions in Lucas' draft in *Skywalking*, p. 210, such as the editorial cross-cutting of scenes, physical humour, the malfunctioning Millennium Falcon hyperdrive and the bickering Han and Leia.

of *Star Wars* and with these new elements re-writing the storyline, the *Star Wars* series as we know it had begun to take shape.

Lucas' drafts were hastily written, and resembled something of a cross between a rough draft and a treatment, having the barest of dialogue, the thinnest of characters and advancing the story as quickly as possible—but now that story, those characters and their dialogue needed to be developed. "I don't know what of Leigh's draft survived into the draft George wrote," Lawrence Kasdan said to *Cinefantastique*. "[His] was a very rough first draft, really somewhere between an outline and a first draft. The structure of the story was all there—it was the skeleton for a movie. What was needed was the flesh and the muscle."[55]

### Flesh and Muscle

With a solid story now written, the pressure of the time-crunch was felt even more as the production raced to its imminent start; Gary Kurtz had drawn up a list of potential directors for the picture in late 1977 and Lucas had selected Irvin Kershner, an old acquaintance from USC who used to teach there between gigs. "It'll be your film," Lucas had promised Kershner, who was adamant that he have creative freedom.[56] Kershner would spend most of 1978 meticulously storyboarding every single shot of the film. With all of his producing chores to attend to, Lucas felt that he could use help to further develop the script. Lawrence Kasdan had just turned in the first draft of *Raiders of the Lost Ark*, and even though Lucas had not yet read it, he decided to hire Kasdan to co-write the subsequent drafts of *Empire Strikes Back*. "I was desperate," Lucas confessed. "I didn't have anybody else."[57]

Lucas was in tremendous luck—Kasdan loved genre movies and Kurosawa films, but he was equally at home with snappy banter that recalled screen greats like Howard Hawks. He could do broad humour and playful romance, but was even more adept at personal intimacies and infusing characters with a thoroughly human emotional subtext. He was exactly what the film needed.

Kasdan recollected the experience in an interview with *Star Wars Insider* on the film's twentieth anniversary:

> When I finished *Raiders*, I took the script up to George to give to him. I was very ceremonial back then. He said "Look, Leigh Brackett has died, and I want you to write *Empire*." I said, "Well, don't you think you ought to read *Raiders*

first?" And he said, "Well, if I read it tonight and I hate it, I'll withdraw the offer."

But he didn't—he really liked it, and I started working on *Empire* immediately. They were under the gun, because they were in pre-production already, and they had no script...They were already building the monsters and stuff...With *Raiders*...I was on my own for six months and really had just an outline from George and Steven, and had to go off and write this whole thing by myself.

But with *Empire*, George had the whole story in his head. It was really a question of getting the script done, and getting Kersh in agreement. So there were very intense, highly adrenalized, fun sessions with George and Kersh, and then I would go away and write, and in two weeks we'd come back and look at the new draft. I wrote it really fast.[58]

Dale Pollock described this second series of story conferences, almost a year after the initial ones with Leigh Brackett:

It was November of 1978 and filming was to begin in five months. Lucas gathered Kershner, Kasdan and Kurtz in his Parkhouse office, turned on a tape recorder, and set to work. Over the next two weeks each page of Lucas's script was dissected; George explained the purpose of each scene, what he wanted to achieve dramatically, and how Kasdan could improve it.

*Empire* had three acts, each about thirty-five minutes long by Lucas's estimate. The script was to be no more than 105 pages: "short and tight," he told Kasdan. All of them agreed *Empire* had to grapple with the philosophical issues raised by *Star Wars*, but Lucas wanted them disposed of quickly. *Empire* had to be fast-moving, not complex. Lucas emphasized his two rules over and over: speed and clarity. "The trick is to know what you can leave to the audience's imagination," he said. "If they start getting lost, you're in trouble. Sometimes you have to be crude and just say what's going on, because if you don't people get puzzled."[59]

However, with the shaping of Kershner, Kasdan and Kurtz, the film became slower and more interior, and the characters began to emerge as more complex beings. "Kasdan's main criticism was that Lucas glossed over the emotional content of a scene in his hurry to get to the next one," Pollock wrote, and Gary Kurtz had similar concerns.[60] Lucas' response to these criticisms was characteristic of his storytelling philosophy: "Well, if we have enough action, nobody will notice."[61]

"He's afraid of going too slow," Kurtz remarked.[62] Pollock reported that Lucas' script was also plagued by poor dialogue and thin characterisation,[63]* and in *Mythmaker* Kasdan said of Lucas' drafts, "There were sections of the script, which, when I read them, made me say to myself, 'I can't believe George wrote this scene. It's terrible.'"[64] Kasdan took notes at the story conferences, went back to Los Angeles, and according to Pollock "returned with his first twenty-five pages of *Empire*, which Lucas and Kershner promptly tore apart."[65]

Slowly, the script was built, developing characters, adding nuances, heightening tension, emphasizing themes, slowing the pace and distilling the story. Kershner immersed himself in mythology and embraced the darkness of *Empire Strikes Back*, seeing it as a gloomy fairy tale that could reach the subconscious fantasy life of children, much like the dark tales of the Brothers Grimm. "I wanted them to see the expression of a lot of their anxieties, fears, and nightmares and offer a way to deal with them," Kershner said to Dale Pollock.[66] The splintering cracks of style and tone that had first emerged in Lucas' drafts finally split open, breaking off and growing into a separate beast that gave birth to the *Star Wars* Saga.

Kasdan related to the *Baltimore Sun* how his and Lucas' styles complemented one another:

> [George] doesn't care about the relationships between people beyond the broad strokes; he's not interested in the humor that can be wrung from understanding the characters' eccentricities. If the humor isn't there in the simple version of a scene he has to do, he's not interested in it. What he's interested in is moving the plot forward. He doesn't want a three-minute scene about character. So he's the opposite of me that way.
>
> I'm not interested in plot, I'm interested in characters surprising you—scenes when you discover something new about them or they change their relationships to each other. I like fast-moving narrative too, so it was easy for me to get on George's train. I just wanted to mix it up. That's not to say he isn't interested in larger matters. He's always filling out some large scheme, and the people are there in his movies to represent different philosophical [constructs].[67]

Director Irvin Kershner recalled to *Star Wars Insider* the story meetings he partook in:

---

* On page 210 Pollock gives an example of some not-so-snappy dialogue between Han Solo and Princess Leia: "Don't worry, I'm not going to kiss you here. You see, I'm quite selfish about my pleasure, and it wouldn't be much fun for me now." Shades of *Attack of the Clones*, indeed.

> I went up and met with George at his house, and he introduced me to a lot of
> the people working on it. Then, when the initial draft came in, we weren't
> happy with it, but there was no chance to rewrite it, because the writer died. So
> we started meeting with Larry [Kasdan] and re-working the script, and we all
> threw in ideas. I kept thinking in terms of character, George was thinking more
> in terms of the actual story, and then Larry was thinking of dialog, which ties
> in with character and story. So it was a very good moment there. We worked
> for many weeks, and finally got the script.[68]

Amazingly, it appears draft one and two were both leaked, as this quote
from a 1978 issue of *Future Magazine* testified, though it seems that
without the internet or any major newspapers picking up the news it did not
spread:

> Author Leigh Brackett has been approached with the task of writing the
> screenplay for the big-budgeted sequel. One of the key elements in the second
> script may be the origin of the Dark Lord, Darth Vader. One version of his life
> being considered for the forthcoming production will reveal a young,
> handsome Darth turning rogue Jedi, killing Luke Skywalker's father and being
> pushed into a pool of molten lava by avenging angel Ben Kenobi. Darth is so
> badly scarred that he dons his black armor forever. It serves as a combination
> exoskeleton and walking iron lung. The second version portrays Darth as
> being, in reality, Luke Skywalker's father. After a psychological trauma,
> Luke's father succumbs to the darker nature of The Force and allows all that
> is good within him to die. And rising from the ashes of his soul is Darth, the
> arch-foe of all that is righteous. Whatever Vader's fate in the as-yet-embryonic
> script, the film began pre-production in London in January."[69]

### *Another Hope*

The first draft of *Empire Strikes Back* contained another significant
revelation that I have omitted thus far, one which has sparked speculation
regarding the sequels. When Father Skywalker's ghost appears to Luke in
draft one, he also tells Luke that he has a twin sister, but won't reveal
where she is for fear that Darth Vader would then be able to find her. In
story meetings it was developed that Father Skywalker had twin children,
and took one to an uncle and the other to a remote place on the other side
of the universe, so that if one was killed, the other would live.[70] It was
suggested that Luke's sister was going through Jedi training as
well—eventually, in another episode, the two of them would fight side by
side as Jedi knights, perhaps avenging their slain father by defeating Vader
and the Emperor. The notion of twin children was an echo from the first

drafts of *Star Wars*, where the father had many children, over seven in draft two, and Lucas had considered a female Jedi briefly when he toyed with the idea of making Luke a girl in the early drafts.

Now that the story had been changed so drastically with the second draft, was it possible for this story thread to continue? Evidently, Lucas thought better of it—in the infamous second draft there is no mention of a sister or even a mysterious "Other," as Yoda says in the final film. "Now we must find another," Yoda says in the revised second draft, to which Obi Wan replies, "He is our only hope."

It is likely that Lucas thought the idea of Darth Vader having not one but two children was a bit unbelievable, even if they were twins. The issue of twins and the "Other" leads us to sequel discussion. It has been erroneously reported that the original story for the *Star Wars* series, between 1977 and 1980, was that Luke's twin sister would appear from across the galaxy but that this story point was scrapped and Leia hastily written in as a substitute for Episode VI. This is not true—the sister subplot was attached to draft one of *Empire Strikes Back* only, and when the nature of Father Skywalker was changed in draft two this story point was naturally thrown out—but, as you well know, a line about a mysterious "Other" later ended up in the final film. The series at the time of the first draft was a twelve-episode serial. Now the sequel plans were radically re-structured with the massive story change in the second draft. So, why was an "Other" line instated in later drafts, in an almost off-handed way? Lucas gave his explanation in *The Annotated Screenplays*:

> I was trying to set up subliminally in the audience's mind that something is going on here, that [Luke] could fail. And if he does fail, "there is another hope." So the audience is saying, "don't go, finish your training."[71]

The throw-away reference to "another hope" was not done for any larger story arc in mind, according to Lucas—it was used as a plot device to make the audience think that Luke might fail, that he is not necessarily the main character in the saga and that the story can continue without him. "It sets up the fact that, in this series, Luke could be expendable at this point," Lucas elaborated on the 2004 DVD commentary track. "We don't need Luke to tell this story. We could get somebody else to do it... 'He's not the important one—there is another.' It's a cheap trick but it works."

Though Lucas now claims that the line was merely a suspense device, an examination of the evidence suggests that indeed the line had to have been meant for a sequel set-up, especially when compiled with his plans for a third trilogy; Lucas' silence on this aspect of it is undoubtedly due to the fact that he now contends that this Sequel Trilogy never even existed and was a media invention, thus it follows that he would deny that the "Other" line was connected to any sequel plot.

The infamous "Other" line is not even present in the second draft, and its earlier version first appears in the revised second draft—"Now we must find another," Yoda muses as Luke flies away in his X-Wing, to which Obi Wan replies, "He is our only hope." Similarly in Lucas' third draft: "That boy is our only hope," Obi Wan says, to which Yoda replies "No…We must search for another." These all are consistent with Lucas' explanation and accomplish his motive for the line. However, the line underwent a subtle yet significant metamorphosis for the fourth draft: "No, there *is* another" (emphasis mine). Lucas deliberately changed the line to imply that there is someone already *out there*, available and ready to substitute for Luke.

So, how might we explain this? The explanation is that Lucas was simply covering his bases for the Sequel Trilogy, giving himself a set-up for the protagonist of those films. As we will learn in a moment, around the time when this line first appears the series was changed to a nine-episode saga made up of three trilogies. Trilogy one would follow Obi Wan in his younger days as he trains and ultimately fails Father Skywalker, trilogy two would follow Luke and trilogy three, we might then conclude, would follow this Other. Lucas appears to have not yet concretely developed who this character would be, being deliberately vague in order to allow himself creative freedom when the time came to write those future episodes. Given that Obi Wan believes that Luke is the last hope but Yoda says there is someone else, the most logical conclusion to be made is that it would be another Force-user that only Yoda knew of, perhaps hidden from birth like Luke, who could become the central character in the Sequel Trilogy, perhaps even a youngster at the time of the middle trilogy.

But just what was this infamous Sequel Trilogy exactly and what were Lucas' plans for the saga at the completion of the *Empire Strikes Back* script? We now come to a maze of story points and half-truths so tangled that no one has ever truly re-constructed them; what follows is the timeline of the shifting *Star Wars* series in its pivotal first three years of release.

### *A Labyrinth of Plots*

With the new 1978 storyline involving "Father Vader," Lucas' story was fundamentally changing, and the *Star Wars* series was taking its first steps in a very different direction than what had been indicated in 1977, not even a year earlier. This point in the history of *Star Wars* is one fraught with the most vagaries, inconsistencies and contradictions—the point where Lucas made his first sequel revisions and prequel creations. Trying to establish just what Lucas had in mind at what point in time is a very tricky subject, especially between 1978 and 1980. Publically, Lucas was assuring audiences that all was proceeding according to his long-laid plans, but behind closed doors the story was undergoing fundamental changes with a rapid pace. It seems that it was very clear when Lucas first began work on *Empire Strikes Back* in late 1977 that he intended the films to be a non-connected franchise which could continue indefinitely, but as the first story work was done it was eventually settled on being twelve episodes long, the common amount in a serial. With the second draft of *Empire Strikes Back*, however, the story underwent fundamental alterations, and the sequel planning reflected this—by the time *Empire Strikes Back* was in production Lucas had revealed that the series was now to be a nine-episode "trilogy of trilogies" with twenty-year gaps between each set.[72]

It is unknown just when this changeover actually happened; the closest we can come to pinpointing it is that it had occurred by July of 1979, when *Empire Strikes Back* was in production, which was when the nine-film plan was first mentioned in any record.[73] For the second draft of *Empire Strikes Back* it is possible that the series was still to be twelve episodes, but I think it is likely that at this point or shortly thereafter Lucas realised that twelve would be too much for where the series was headed. Far from being episodic adventures, the series was quickly becoming an inter-connected narrative, outgrowing its serial roots and its "adventure of the week" style plotting.

Much of this was likely encouraged by the practical matter that the characters were played by human actors. After all, Carrie Fisher and Mark Hamill only signed a three-film contract, and Harrison Ford and Alec Guinness were employed on a movie-by-movie basis—nothing was guaranteed. Even though in the twelve-film configuration the series might follow side-characters and establish new ones, the core group that was introduced in *Star Wars* was clearly driving the story, which especially became clear as *Empire Strikes Back* was written.

Therefore, all that Lucas had guaranteed for him at the moment was the trilogy; other trilogies or films detailing other eras of the galaxy remained possible to be made at later dates, however, with different actors. But Lucas probably realised that if he left the immediate story incomplete at the end of the third film—and so incomplete that the story was only one quarter of the way finished—and he suddenly lost all his actors, he would be faced with a monumental disaster that would be impossible to write around. The story which was introduced in *Star Wars* had to resolve itself by the third film.

It might also be difficult to sustain "episode of the week" type of plots for twenty years, and making twelve, nine or even six episodes of a continuous narrative was even more dangerous because of actor availability. His original plan was simply too ambitious for a single storyline. Therefore, the three films he had contractually guaranteed by both Twentieth Century Fox and the actors would constitute the immediate series—the first film was the introduction, the second presented a new level and this led continuously into the third film which resolved everything, similar to the Alan Dean Foster three-book structure of 1975. It was a continuous-narrative trilogy, which would be the structural basis for any other trilogies Lucas would make. He eventually settled on three trilogies, one taking place before which followed Obi Wan, and another taking place afterwards. With the franchise designed as the main source of income for Lucasfilm, Lucas still needed the series to be kept around for at least another decade.

The common story of the "secret history" of *Star Wars* is that Luke's tale would be a hexology, that is, a continuous tale which spans six episodes, IV to IX, with his sister, the "Other," showing up in Episode VII or VIII and the Emperor being battled in the final Episode IX, while the first three episodes would be about the young Obi Wan and Father Skywalker. This information mainly comes courtesy of Gary Kurtz, who in recent years has "revealed" the *Star Wars* series that once-was. A logical mapping of *Star Wars* history then went something like this:

> *In April of 1978, Lucas writes draft two of* Empire Strikes Back *and revises* Star Wars *history, making Darth Vader Father Skywalker. The script essentially remains the same, and in the final drafts Yoda mentions an "Other" ["that boy is our last hope," "No, there is another"] who is Luke's twin sister. The series is to be nine episodes, with Luke's story comprising a hexology; Darth Vader would die in Episode VI, Luke's twin Jedi sister would show up in Episode VII or so and the Emperor finally revealed in Episode IX where the story finally ends. Then,* Empire Strikes Back *goes into production, is a major disaster and with Lucas' personal life in shards he decides to end the series with Episode VI—doing four more sequels does not entice him and even the actors are weary. He hastily crams the sequel plots into a final film, writes in Leia as the Other and ends the series.*

There is certainly much truth in that hypothesis, and it is not *totally* off the mark, but unfortunately it is indeed inaccurate. It is based on Kurtz' statements, which in turn are a tangled combination of Lucas' statements, and does not make logical sense when subjected to scrutiny—Kurtz' version of the sequels are instead a confused recollection of disparate and separate concepts. See Appendix E for an examination of this.

This is all blown apart by the fact that while *Empire Strikes Back* was *still filming* Lucas mentions that the *Star Wars* series is three trilogies, with twenty years between each one, making the series nine episodes, and that the Rebels versus Empire story would end with the middle trilogy at Episode VI—thus shattering the theory that the remaining three episodes, VII-IX, were crammed into Episode VI because of Lucas' personal troubles following *Empire Strikes Back*. This appears in Alan Arnold's monumental diary on the production of *Empire Strikes Back*, recorded on July 19th, 1979. Lucas said:

> The first script was one of six original stories I had written in the form of two trilogies.
> After the success of *Star Wars* I added another trilogy. So now there are nine stories. The original two trilogies were conceived of as six films of which the first film was number four.[74]

Although the information is mixed amongst falsehoods about having pre-written the entire story and that *Star Wars* was always to be Episode IV, it does establish the basis for the three-trilogy version of the saga existing early in *Empire*'s production. A short while later he would elaborate, with this quote occurring on October 29th:

> There are essentially nine films in a series of three trilogies. The first trilogy is about the young Ben Kenobi and the early life of Luke's father when Luke was a little boy. This trilogy takes place some twenty years before the second trilogy which includes *Star Wars* and *Empire*. About a year or two passes between each story of the trilogy and about twenty years pass between the trilogies. The entire saga spans about fifty-five years... After the success of *Star Wars* I added another trilogy but stopped there, primarily because reality took over. After all, it takes three years to prepare and make a Star Wars picture. How many years are left? So I'm still left with three trilogies of nine films... The next chapter is called '*Revenge of the Jedi*.' It's the end of this particular trilogy, the conclusion of the conflict begun in *Star Wars* between Luke and Darth Vader. It resolves the situation once and for all. I won't say who survives and who doesn't, but if we are ever able to link together all three you'd find the story progresses in a very logical fashion.[75]

As Lucas mentions, his initial story material only composed of the story for the first two trilogies, even though the prequels were never to be filmed. But the third trilogy, the so-called Sequel Trilogy, was an entirely new creation that was mainly a response to the success of the first film. Because of this, it would inevitably be abandoned, as Lucas had little emotional investment in it.

But, the Sequel Trilogy did exist, for certain in 1979 and 1980, and likely in 1978 as well. But what was the story? This is probably the least-known story point in *Star Wars'* history, and as far as actual plot we know very little—it is likely that Lucas himself only had vague ideas; as he would later admit, he never developed the plot, at least beyond the broad strokes.[76] Based on the few comments he gave between 1979 and 1983, it appeared to revolve around "the re-building of the Republic," and was to be a more introspective series of films about "the necessity for moral choices."[77] His set-up for the "Other" offered the main character of this third trilogy. Contrary to popular belief, the Sequel Trilogy was *not* supposed to follow a grey-haired Luke and company with the aged original cast portraying their elderly selves—this was a later addition used as an alternative once the original Sequel Trilogy was cancelled. All that can best be speculated is that the trilogy would likely follow this "Other," likely a protégé of Luke (Lucas said in 1983 that the sequels will be about "passing on what you have learned,"[78] very similar to Yoda's final command in *Jedi*). For a more in-depth exploration of this Sequel Trilogy, consult Appendix D.

As you can see, the future films changed shape rapidly and radically in those seminal years between *Star Wars* and *Empire Strikes Back*: So convoluted is Lucas' constantly-changing plans on the story that at the same time Lucas was making those comments to Alan Arnold about a three-trilogy saga *Bantha Tracks* was still publishing that Lucas' series was to be comprised of twelve films.

To alleviate this contradictory chronology and make things a bit easier, here is a general timeline of the major story revisions:

**Pre-1977:** *Star Wars* is a stand-alone film, but due to the fact that it is in the serial tradition, it is constructed in such a way that sequels can potentially be made if so desired. The second draft from 1975 ends with a teaser for "the search for the Princess of Ondos." In late 1975, Alan Dean Foster is hired to write a novel to be used as the basis for a lower-budget sequel Lucas might attempt to make, which becomes *Splinter of the Mind's Eye*, eventually published in 1978. Lucas negotiates with Fox a contract for rights to sequels, two of which Carrie Fisher and Mark Hamill sign for; Lucas plans with Foster to write a third book as well, which would be adapted for the screen following *Splinter*, that is if Lucas decided to pursue cinema possibilities at all, which he had not concretely decided at that point. The *Adventures of Luke Skywalker* trilogy hangs over the creative precipice.

**Summer 1977:** *Star Wars* is a hit and with unlimited resources at his disposal Lucas decides he will turn it into a franchise. The films are not connected in a single narrative, although one might presume that the Rebel versus Empire battle will progress through the series, along with Luke's Jedi training, culminating in victory in the final episode. Hamill compares it to James Bond and says that by the end of filming he will be becoming like Obi Wan Kenobi. Lucas also mentions wanting to do a "young days of Ben Kenobi" sequel. The episodic adventures will have a new director for each film, offering a slightly different take on each entry, and Lucas says he will likely direct the last film, and that the films will follow new characters and time periods, implying a truly episodic, non-linear series.

**November 1977:** Lucas begins conferencing with Leigh Brackett on November 28th and writes the treatment for *Star Wars II*. It is designated as Chapter II and is titled *The Empire Strikes Back*, and is similar in most respects to the final film except Vader is not Luke's father, Han is alive and well, and the twin Jedi sister subplot is referenced. Lucas reveals some months later in *Time* magazine that the series will be twelve episodes long—this might have been decided in later parts of the development, perhaps not until after the Christmas break.

**February 1978**: Leigh Brackett completes the first draft of *Empire Strikes Back* on February 23rd.

**March 1978:** The March 6th edition of *Time* magazine runs a story on *Star Wars II*, wherein Lucas states the series will be twelve episodes long and take until 2001 to film. On March 18th, Leigh Brackett dies.

**April 1978:** Lucas completes the second draft screenplay where he completely alters *Star Wars* history by merging Father Skywalker and Darth Vader. He revises all story points, eliminating the Jedi sister subplot; Leia is not the sister, and in fact there is no sister. No "Other" is mentioned either. It is not known how long the series is to last at this point, but the storyline is very much becoming inter-connected in one large narrative. The film would later be changed to Episode V, with the first three films now being "prequels," that is, films set before the first one. However, *The Annotated Screenplays* indicates that draft two was designated as Episode II—likely it wasn't until six months later, when the next batch of drafts was written, that Lucas had concretely committed to integrating the three prequels into the storyline and episode listing. *The Annotated Screenplays* omits any title information from drafts revised-two and three in its list of sources, and perhaps in their rushed nature Lucas didn't assign them any episode designation. Pre-production artwork continues to carry an "Episode II" stamp until after the fourth draft a few months later, perhaps implying no definitive decision until that time.[79]

A revised second and third draft were also completed in April. The absence of any "Other" mentioned may indicate that the Sequel Trilogy was not yet in place, although it may be surmised that Lucas simply hadn't decided to set up such hints in film two yet.

Pinning down the exact plan at this stage is difficult. Lucas may have never even considered such things as the number of episodes—he was under the gun and writing at an incredibly rapid rate, penning three drafts in a single month. He may have simply wrote the scripts and said "I'll deal with the episode number later." The nine-film three-trilogy plan to be revealed the next year could have been in place for all we know, with Lucas later thinking it best to set up the future protagonist by writing him/her into the script through the later mention of an "Other," but it is important to keep in mind that virtually nothing can be stated with any degree of certainty—my personal opinion is that such things were never even considered by Lucas whilst writing these drafts.

**October 1978/ February 1979:** The fourth and fifth drafts are written. The fifth draft is the first confirmed appearance of "Episode V."[80] Yoda's line is now the familiar "No, there is another." This is the first notion of someone being out there, already ready. By this time, Lucas must have been thinking about the later episodes, which he was obviously afforded by the large space of time between the writing of the third and fourth/ fifth drafts (six months), which also explains his commitment to the prequels.

**July 1979:** On the set of *Empire Strikes Back*, on July 19th, Lucas reveals to Alan Arnold that the series is nine episodes long and contains three trilogies, later elaborating (in October) that the first trilogy is the prequels, the second the current trilogy with the Empire defeated in Episode VI and a Sequel Trilogy will follow, with twenty years between each trilogy and the entire saga spanning roughly fifty-five years.

**November 1979:** The script for the first *Star Wars* film is printed in a published version in *The Art of Star Wars*, identifying it as Episode IV and subtitled *A New Hope* in accordance with changes Lucas had made following draft two of *Empire Strikes Back*. This would eventually be incorporated into the film itself in 1981 (not 1978 as some have incorrectly reported).

With all of Lucas' radical changes, he now was faced with formulating some kind of story resolution for the third film, *Revenge of the Jedi* (as he tells Alan Arnold in 1979 that it will have this title[81]). The goals of this resolution were fairly obvious—Luke faces Vader once again and defeats him; the Emperor is finally revealed and dealt with; the Rebels are victorious. "Dagobah does appear in the next film," Lucas told Alan Arnold in 1979,[82] implying he had plans for Luke to resolve his vow to return to finish his training—although Lucas' initial draft of the film did not feature this. The love triangle between Han, Leia and Luke would also effectively be resolved, even though Han and Leia admitted their love for each other in Lucas' *Empire Strikes Back* drafts, leaving much less room for any kind of romance for Luke; if Han Solo survived his carbonite imprisonment in the next film then Han and Leia would resume their romance.

A more complicated matter would result if Harrison Ford did not participate in the final film and Solo had to be terminated. Would Luke finally get Leia? Gary Kurtz has recently suggested an unaccounted for storyline where Han dies and Leia becomes the "Queen of her people" (presumably meaning the refugees from Alderaan), leaving her isolated from Luke and the others.[83] This story point would certainly fit into this version of the third film, although like all of Gary Kurtz' recent "reveals," this is not to be taken as gospel on the matter.

Han's fate at the end of *Empire Strikes Back* was ambiguous, so if Ford turned down the third film he could be killed off—the final scene of *Empire Strikes Back* is set up so that Lando could take over the Han Solo role, with him not only piloting the Millennium Falcon but wearing Solo's trademark costume. And if Ford accepted, Han could be saved in a daring rescue sequence. "Look at what's happening to Harrison," Hamill said to Alan Arnold in 1979. "He wasn't sure if he wanted to repeat his role as Solo, and he's not at all committed to do a third one. So George has left him in limbo in this one. As Lando Calrissian says after Han is hauled up from the carbon-freezing chamber: 'He's in a state of perfect hibernation.' So George has given himself an option."[84]

The resolution of the infamous "Other" is another highly contested topic. The notion that the Other was intended mainly for the third film is illogical for a number of reasons, not the least in that it begs the question "Why would Lucas write himself into such an obvious corner?" With enough characters in the third film as it was, this arbitrary "Other" would have little effect on the plot and crowd an already-full story, especially when this character is so important that Yoda considers him or her to be "another hope" for the galaxy. Another Jedi, or at the very least another Force-user, which is what Yoda seemed to be implying this person was, would nullify Luke's significance as well. The most logical answer thus must be that the set-up was intended primarily for the Sequel Trilogy and not for a part in the third film, perhaps beyond some hinting, foreshadowing or a final set-up (i.e. Yoda reveals to Luke that another hope exists elsewhere, perhaps as a viable apprentice to continue the Jedi way—maybe an echo of this in the final film is Yoda's dying wish for Luke to "pass on what he has learned").

In Lucas' trilogy-of-trilogies nine-episode structure, each trilogy would hence follow a different protagonist, with only the droids being in all three sets as Lucas would later state.[85] The first trilogy would follow Obi Wan; the second trilogy would follow Luke, with Obi Wan in a cameo role; the third trilogy could therefore follow this Other, perhaps with an elderly Luke in a smaller Obi Wan-like role.

This seemingly insignificant line about an "Other" turns out to be a major clue to Lucas' story. When Lucas eventually eliminated the Sequel Trilogy this reference hence became a lingering plot point that was unresolved and hence forced to be included in the plot for the third film. The "Other" line was simply a throw-away reference to a yet-to-be-decided character, but as we shall see in chapter VII, Lucas simply plugged Leia into the role because there wasn't anyone else. The "Other" comment was deliberately vague so that when and if Lucas had to confront it, he could have the potential to turn it into anything he wanted—including making the "Other" Luke's sister, who is also Leia. It paid off as a lucky escape hatch.

But there is even more to Lucas' original plan: despite the fact that Darth Vader was now revealed to be Luke's father, it appears he was not to be redeemed. Vader was to be destroyed, along with the Empire; as the original title implied, *Revenge of the Jedi*, Luke would have his vengeance. Vader's eventual redemption would stem from a by-product of the resolution of his paternity, which placed more emphasis on him and introduced the first notions of him returning to good, which eventually and naturally developed into him being redeemed as more drafts were written, as we will later see.

With Han's fate unknown, Vader's parentage unresolved and the "Other" left deliberately vague, the story was completely open-ended to develop in any number of directions. Once again, Lucas had covered all his bases…just in case.

The last article in need of mentioning is the fate of the characters following the wrapping of this middle trilogy. Lucas had his "Other" set up to provide the main character for the Sequel Trilogy, but Luke certainly seemed to be favoured by fans and would surely need to be at least mentioned in the third trilogy—as the series was, at least initially, known as *The Adventures of Luke Skywalker*. Mark Hamill of course was contracted to only do the third film, and although Lucas had apparently approached him years earlier about doing more, which Hamill informally agreed to,[86] this was for the much different conception of the series, and he was not approached for any contract renewal after the wrapping of *Empire Strikes Back*'s production. Harrison Ford did not even want to do a third film, let alone an additional trilogy, and it is likely that Carrie Fisher would be hesitant as well. This, of course, does not imply their absence from the story in the third trilogy: Lucas would comment in 1983 that Mark Hamill could play an elderly version of himself *if* he looked old enough[87]—implying that Lucas was comfortable and willing to simply recast the characters with older actors, which it appears was his plan and which he implied in additional interviews.[88] It is unlikely that the characters of the middle-trilogy would be tossed aside. What role they would play in the story and how they would function is a matter of speculation; see Appendix D.

### Public Relations

But regardless of where the story was headed, with his new story arc surrounding Father Vader, Lucas now had a terrific set-up to his current series, a melodramatic and dark tale about a fallen hero and a galaxy plunged into tragedy and war. This was more than just backstory—this had enough depth and intrigue to be an entire series in itself. Not sequels, for the episodes would occur before the original *Star Wars*—they would be "prequels," occupying the first trilogy of the three-trilogy structure. Interviews from around this time also indicate that Luke would be seen as a three-year-old toddler in the third film,[89] perhaps implying a slightly different timeline than the one eventually decided on a few years later; in this version, Darth Vader may have known he had a son from the very beginning and had raised him for a few years before his turn to evil, but Luke was then hidden away from him and could not be located until Luke came out of hiding in *Star Wars*.

When Lucas stumbled upon the plot twist which merged Vader and Father Skywalker he began immediately instituting changes in the current films. *Empire Strikes Back* was changed from Episode II to Episode V, which had occurred at least by February of 1979 with the fifth draft. This meant that *Star Wars* was also in need of altering. In 1979 the subtitle *A New Hope* was created, with the film now denoted as Episode IV. This altered the title to the overall series—no longer was it *The Adventures of Luke Skywalker*; now the series itself would be called *Star Wars*. The first time the public was introduced to the film's new identity was November 1979, when the *Art of Star Wars* book was released with the very first published version of the script. It should be noted that the new changes to the script were not stated—rather, they were passed off as if always existing as such, bearing a 1976 date.

Unlike as stated on page 139, the 1979 script was titled as follows:

Star Wars
Episode IV
A New Hope

from the
Journal of the Whills

by George Lucas

revised fourth draft
January 15th, 1976

Not only that, the *Art of Star Wars* script wasn't even the authentic revised fourth draft but more like a transcription of the final film, edited and combined with the real fourth draft.

Here, a new threshold in *Star Wars* history was crossed, where material was altered to coincide with a new version written over top of the old one. To make matters worse, not only were these reflections of the original story covered up, but Lucas would claim that it was as it had always been, obfuscating the truth that any changes had even occurred—for example, this 1979 "public" script which falsely indicated a 1976 date of creation.

The results of such seemingly-trivial embellishments have cumulatively written a sort of alternate history for the franchise. Actions such as these may finally bring us to addressing the tales of the story's origins, and in particular the controversial ones which reinforce the current story at the expense of accuracy, as suggested in the introduction. With the series and story literally changing in their entirety, a coherent and consistent new story paradigm must be created and maintained by those presenting the material. By this I mean that all the information and material floating around in the public concerning the *Star Wars* story was made to be compatible with the latest version of the story being presented in the films. In other words, Lucas offered only the version of the story that he wanted presented to the public, and thus the fact that the series previously had existed as a totally different—and often contradictory—entity was suppressed. Admitting to these changes and over-writings, it may be hypothesized, might encourage audiences to reject the new story or to continue to view it from the previous perspective, or may even provoke outrage that such a popular storyline was being altered post-release after being cherished by so many. Maintaining that such changes were always part of the story is in many ways a security measure.

With the series now a nine-part saga wherein the original film was "Episode IV" and Darth Vader was the same character as Luke's father, all material had to be made to be in accordance with this change, and thus all the earlier material which still contained explicit elements of the initial, orthodox storyline was either altered to match the changes or else suppressed and destroyed. When viewed in this light, what we witness here is not spectacularly unique—Lucas created a story, changed where the story was headed and where it had come from, and then revised the earlier material to be consistent with these new changes. This is common in long-running series and has even developed a term, "retcon." In the early 21st century, when Lucas would make even greater fundamental story changes with his three prequels, this process would occur once more, as the original non-Special Edition versions of the films would be suppressed, much to the outrage of loyal fans (not to mention film buffs), and Lucas began to assert that his original *Star Wars* concept was really *The Tragedy of Darth Vader*—this is merely an extension of the actions which we witness here, after the solidification of the new storyline with *Empire Strikes Back*.

However, unlike the "retcons" in most other film, television or literary series, what marks *Star Wars'* in particular as worthy of discussion is the fact that Lucas would deny that many of the most important changes had occurred in the first place, instead insisting that they had been in place all along, presumably in order to encourage audiences to accept and view the material from this redacted perspective. Today, this deliberate "spin" on the story material has truly resulted in a re-writing of history—few journalists, press agents, film scholars, and even most viewers and fans of the series doubt that the entire storyline was established before the first film was released, at least in broader terms. This misconception has become a part of film history, unfortunately, and is an ever-present part of the legendary record of the *Star Wars* series. Lucas' current statements are that the series could be referred to as *The Tragedy of Darth Vader*, and that this was what his early material was actually about. Few would care or be compelled to investigate beyond Lucas' apparently-authoritative statements on the matter.

With the unspoken elimination of the original *Star Wars* script and the instatement of the updated one, Lucas was now actively engaging in re-shaping the public perception of where the story had come from—this occurred shortly after *Star Wars* became a mega-hit, with Lucas and his company claiming he had written twelve stories which were to be made into films. From here on, the "Official" story would change depending on where Lucas was in inventing the saga. Lucas put forth the image that all had been elaborately planned by him, a years-old preparation that was finally seeing its satisfactory realisation. He began to boast about how he had "detailed histories," "voluminous notes" and "treatments on all the films"—although based somewhat on truth (he did indeed have notes on character backgrounds, as all writers do), they were also quite misleading.

A typical example comes in an interview in Alan Arnold's book on the making of *The Empire Strikes Back*:

> Alan Arnold: Tell me more about the overall concept of the *Star Wars* saga.
>
> George Lucas: There are essentially nine films in a series of three trilogies...
>
> AA: How much is written?
>
> GL: I have story treatments on all nine...Originally, when I wrote *Star Wars*, it developed into an epic on the scale of War and Peace, so big I couldn't possibly make it into a movie. So I cut it in half, but it was still too big, so I cut each half into three parts. I then had material for six movies. After the success of *Star Wars* I added another trilogy...So I'm still left with three trilogies of nine films. At two hours each, that's about eighteen hours of film![90]

In another part of this interview, he also goes on to state that his original script was a prequel one:

> The first [script] was about Luke's father, and the second one took place at a later time and was mainly about Luke.[91]

But in fact, that script—the rough draft—was merely an early version of the final film; it has the same protagonist (a young man, here named Annikin but later renamed Luke and placed on a moisture farm), the same basic plot and is set in the exact same time period (a time when the Jedi have been wiped out, the Empire has taken over the galaxy and a group of rebels fight back).

Lucasfilm press material would later state that the series was planned as a nine film saga, and that Lucas chose to "start in the middle story," or "start with his favourite story," as were the most popular reasons cited. For example, in the June 1980 issue of *American Cinematographer*, it is reported:

> Lucas [designed] a nine-part saga...an epic adventure spanning forty years. The whole trilogy is divided into three trilogies, with STAR WARS and THE

EMPIRE STRIKES BACK as the first two parts of the middle trilogy. "In choosing the first chapter to be filmed," Lucas says, "I chose the chapter I felt most secure with and which I liked the most."[92]

His statements here and elsewhere suggest he had all nine episodes written out and that he merely picked the fourth entry, or at the very least that he had sketched out a detailed epic but chose to begin filming from the middle section; this was related by Lucas and his company's press materials many times over the decades in their repeated explanation of the saga's origins. But the only script Lucas had was *Star Wars*, a single, stand-alone film, with various early drafts that did *not* contain the plots for the additional episodes; although a few scenes and characters would be lifted, borrowed and transformed into the future episodes, this hardly counts as having pre-written episodes in the series, and is simply a matter of re-using old ideas, as is to be expected. Lucas indeed had come up with notes on events and plot points which took place before the first film (and even a few for after) but again, these are merely the basic background development that occurs for any creation as grand as *Star Wars*, and were not written with filming in mind, instead being a necessity of the story development to establish where characters had come from and what the history of the environment was; strangely, Lucas even admits to this.

With *Star Wars* heralded as the most popular work of pop art ever made, public expectation was naturally very high—and perhaps we should be unsurprised that the humble creator of it, whom it seems had succeeded in his career mainly through incredibly lucky timing, assured the public that their story was in confident hands, while unbeknownst to them it was being re-written regularly.


### Dark Father

Before leaving this section we should perhaps turn our attention to a subject that is at the heart of the revision *Empire Strikes Back* brought to the series—the "I am your father" subject. There is no doubt that Father Skywalker and Darth Vader were always two distinct characters; this of course changed when Lucas was forced to write the second draft of *Empire Strikes Back* himself, following Leigh Brackett's death, and stumbled upon a brilliant storyline which could be built around the pre-existing one. While at the very least we can say that this is the first time Lucas pursued the idea on paper, it is quite possible that this is the first time Lucas had even conceived of the very concept of a Father Vader. Like many tales surrounding his creation, Lucas himself offers a version of events which insists that Father Vader was always part of his storyline; as he says in *Annotated Screenplays*:

> I didn't discuss the notion of Vader being Luke's father with Leigh Brackett. At that point I wasn't sure if I was going to include it in that script or reveal it in the third episode. I was going back and forth, and rather than confuse things for Leigh, I decided to keep the whole issue out of the mix. I figured I would add it later on.[93]

This, however, seems to fly in the face of every available piece of evidence. Why would Lucas not reveal a *major* plot point, perhaps the most important story point in the entire series, to the author of the film? Lucas had no problem discussing every other piece of future plot development. During story conferences, Lucas discussed in detail how Luke had a twin Jedi sister who was training across the galaxy, and how in a future episode she would be revealed, or how Lando was a survivor from the Clone Wars, and that in the days of the Old Republic the war tore apart the galaxy. Lucas also had no problem discussing in detail the Emperor, and how he was like a Nixonian bureaucrat and that in a sequel he would be dealt with more concretely. From the current film to future plot points, no stone was seemingly left unturned.

It is very unusual that Lucas would not inform Brackett of the pertinent little detail that Vader was Luke's father. As far as confusing her, with all the complex historical detail necessary to bring the rich galaxy to life, this one simple plot point would hardly have befuddled Lucas' collaborator and detracted from the script. Perhaps Lucas would have a somewhat legitimate excuse if he said he kept it from her because he was afraid the secret would be leaked to the public if he told everyone—but Lucas has never made this claim, and certainly someone as respectable as Brackett would not have leaked Hollywood's biggest secret; the secrecy surrounding the film would obviously not extend to the person writing it.

But this is besides the point, because Father Skywalker himself appears in the first draft—how can Lucas be "saving it for later" if the ghost of Father Skywalker is training Luke? It may then be posited that perhaps the ghost of Father Skywalker was Brackett's idea or that Lucas was unaware that this plot point was being written—but since Lucas himself used Obi Wan's ghost in his own drafts and even more prominently in his *Return of the Jedi* drafts this is not totally convincing. Additionally, the issue was indirectly discussed in story conferences, where the twin sister plotline which Father Skywalker reveals was developed, indicating that Lucas should have been aware of the idea, if not the originator, though this is not totally conclusive.

More importantly though, the twin sister plotline rules out such a Father Vader concept at that time—since, as we have seen, such a concept as Darth Vader having not one but two children was considered unbelievable, and was written out in the second draft when Lucas integrated the Father Vader plot point. That Lucas discussed and assuredly was the originator of the twin sister point in the story conferences indicates that Lucas regarded the film as operating under the orthodox history where the characters were separate. If Brackett's use of Father Skywalker's ghost was an invention of her own, it was still consistent with the plotline Lucas had developed at that point.

Lucas' explanation also does not imply any kind of "experimentation"—that Lucas came up with the notion of a Father Vader earlier but withheld it and experimented with the orthodox Father Skywalker storyline for draft one before going ahead and instigating his controversial Father Vader plot point for draft two. Had this been the case, Lucas would have surely spoken of it to explain the startling first draft. Instead, he maintains that it was always in place.

It seems abundantly clear that the *Star Wars* histories were continuing right along where they left off in the first film, that is until the second draft in April 1978. While it is not unreasonable to speculate that perhaps Lucas had indeed come up with the Father Vader concept earlier but then dismissed it initially, such presupposition is not indicated by any evidence. Evidence, on the other hand, seems to suggest that it was a 1978 concept. April 1978 was a 180-degree turn from everything else before it. Lucas wrote of and explicitly talked of Father Skywalker as a separate character until 1978, even in private conversations and his own story notes; invoking any kind of pre-existing Father Vader plan on the part of Lucas requires huge leaps of logic and many convoluted and improbable explanations. Rather, the more realistic assessment is that Lucas simply changed his mind about a story point in early 1978, and that this caused an observable chain reaction in the story construction.

This issue is more complicated than can be summed up here; see Appendix C: The Dark Father for a lengthier examination of the issue of Father Vader.

The suspicion that Lucas was obfuscating the story changes was further reinforced the more he talked about the issue. Lucas now makes the statement that the story was always meant to be about Darth Vader[94]—that, from the very beginning, he set out to tell the tale of Anakin Skywalker and his redemption from evil, even that his first script from 1973 was titled *The*

*Tragedy of Darth Vader.*

When statements such as these are coupled with Lucas' previous statements about not telling Brackett, it is clear that something else is going on. This is not a question of "a certain point of view," as Ben Kenobi would later say—as if speaking as Lucas himself in an attempt to explain the contradiction to viewers. In fact, this ham-fisted explanation by Kenobi is still is a bit difficult for many fans to swallow.

Observe, for a moment, what Lucas has been saying as of late, about the story of *Star Wars*, and in particular, Darth Vader, as quoted in Germany's *Berliner Zeitung* in 2005:

> What I had in mind in the first time was filming these three movies...no, actually I wanted to film one movie: the tragic story of Darth Vader. In the beginning he should have appeared as a monster; in the middle part the monster should reveal itself as the father of the hero—and at the end of the movie as the true hero himself.[95]

Lucas' recent statements such as this are the most extreme ones yet, so far removed from what the truth actually is that one has to wonder how he could think that no one would notice. From the very start, Lucas set about to tell the story of Luke Skywalker, not Anakin—the first treatment had the protagonist as an elderly General but he was soon demoted to a naïve youth, being caught in the middle of a civil war between the Galactic Empire and the Rebel Alliance. It was to be a light adventure of the Errol Flynn, Ray Harryhausen and Flash Gordon vein, as Lucas often described it as himself, a superficial swashbuckler about a young man's adventure. Nowhere in the story did Darth Vader or Father Skywalker figure prominently except in relation to supporting Luke's tale, and in fact they were two separate and minor characters up until *The Empire Strikes Back*. After struggling through many different drafts of *Star Wars*, Lucas' creation of Ben Kenobi finally centred the story and gave it a history, and when faced with tying up a number of unresolved and redundant story threads for the sequel as a result of this history, the transformation of Father Skywalker into Darth Vader gave him the answer he needed, simultaneously leaping out as a more interesting story direction.

This, in turn, set off a chain reaction—the prequel trilogy was formed, changing *Star Wars* from Saga I to Episode IV, the original script was rewritten, the series was turned into a nine-film saga and Lucas began telling the world that it was as he had always intended. It is perhaps precisely because the series now is so different that, for example, Lucas asserts that Darth Vader's fall and redemption by his son was always the heart of his original story: it makes the audience view the original trilogy, and specifically *Star Wars*, under the perspective and story configuration that Lucas now wishes audiences to view it with. This, however, does not fully account for the true extent of the exaggerations that began as far back as 1980. Why Lucas feels the need to present himself as an all-knowing, master-planning genius appears to be born out of his insecurities as *Star Wars'* popularity grew larger than his grasp could hold.

### A Cultural Phenomenon

After the enormous success of *Star Wars*, the over-hyping press placed an inordinate amount of pressure on him. In its first few months the film was viewed as a fun and exciting adventure film, with a positive and spiritual message—but not anything particularly deep and history-making beyond being a current hit. Critics were thankful for such a refreshing and entertaining film in an age of pessimism, but neither critics nor Lucas himself could have anticipated the progression it would quickly take that year. The film refused to disappear from screens, and as the summer went on it became the event of the season, an absolute smash that every single moviegoer had seen and loved, and worked its way so far into the fabric of the culture that embraced it that it appeared in variety show skits and talk shows, on the cover page of *Time* Magazine, the footprints of Darth Vader and C-3P0 were preserved in concrete outside Mann's Chinese Theater, and a disco re-mix of *Star Wars* was heard playing in clubs around cities. Fans dressed up in costume, and some proclaimed it a religious experience—it was on its way to becoming a phenomenon. It was the first film to become an *event*, something that impacted every aspect of culture in an immediate way, and people were excited by it.

Lucas could no longer venture outdoors, for *Star Wars* fans would mob him in the street, and by the end of the year the film was approaching the $200 million mark, an unprecedented box office feat at the time. A knife-wielding maniac barged into Lucas' office claiming that he wrote *Star Wars* and that he had parked the Millennium Falcon outside, while fans would pilgrimage to Lucas' parents' house claiming to be sent by god.[96] Religious-minded viewers began reading into the film whatever belief they subscribed to—Christians thought it was in support of Christianity, Buddhists (especially those in the west coast) found it to be in support of Buddhism, and New Age spiritualists of every type loved the film's supposed support of their niche faith. Word of Lucas' interest in fairy tales and mythology got out and soon the film's perception began to change.

It is around here that the intelligentsia, some of whom had dismissed the film as "cotton candy"-like summertime fluff (albeit one that was well-crafted), after it became popular began taking a closer look at the film, dissecting all sorts of comparisons to Ulysses and The Odyssey. This is around the time Lucas began claiming he had twelve and later nine stories written, derived from a long-existing plan. *Time* magazine began labelling the film as "mythic," as something akin to the Greatest Story Ever Told, making it appear as though Lucas was some Harvard educated anthropologist who poured through endless texts of all the world's myths and religions and studied them until he could distil their very essence into one universal film. Right around here, at the height of all this craziness, Lucas began covering up history, such as the retroactive rewriting of the *Star Wars* script. In fact, in a weird case of Orwellian backwardness, Lucas seems to now be imitating the very journalists who initially held him captive by mimicking their claims. The truth is much simpler—Lucas liked a bunch of cheesy sci-fi serials and comic books and was blessed with an innate sense of storytelling that, like all great natural storytellers, tapped into the same collective unconsciousness that all of mankind's greatest myths do.

When Lucas began looking for inspiration for *Star Wars* in books and films, he also began looking at scholastic analysis of fantasy material, partly out of his own personal interest, as he always was fond of anthropology—in this he (supposedly) came across Bettelheim, who dissected common psychological subtext in children's fairy tales, and Campbell, who dissected common subtext in world mythology, but this was merely research into the genres and not anything that resulted in a specific influence on the script per se.

In fact, though Lucas makes the claim in Rinzler's *Making of Star Wars* book that he read Bettelheim,[97] Bettelheim's book on fairy tales was not published until after *Star Wars* was filmed, thus Lucas was probably not being accurate about this; Rinzler attempts to defend in that he must have read an advance copy but this seems contrived and unrealistic, especially when considering impact on the screenplay. Bettelheim's 1976 book received much attention in the late '70s, which is where Lucas probably came across it, but it is impossible to have influenced the script. Again, this shows Lucas' interest in this type of scholastic analysis as more of a personal curiosity.

As mentioned before, Lucas' pre-*Star Wars* stories contain the same structural elements as *Star Wars*. What many don't realise is that pretty much every well-told story follows the Campbellian Hero's Journey pattern, and you don't have to be aware of it to write something that way—it is the natural way of telling a story, especially one in which a character embarks on a quest or a personal journey, which is precisely what Campbell was trying to show in his book; even *Rocky* adheres very closely to the formula. In fact, in this BBC interview Lucas admits to this coincidental alignment with the "Hero's Journey" pattern when he later reviewed his early drafts against Campbell's model:

> I was going along on my own story, I was trying to write whatever I felt. And then I would go back once I'd written a script, I would go back and check it against the classic models of the hero's journey and that sort of thing to see if I had gone off the deep end, and simply by following my own inspiration, the thing that intrigued me the most is that it was very close to the model.[98]

As Lucas also admits, he didn't even meet Campbell or hear one of his lectures until after the original trilogy was finished, despite being called Campbell's "greatest student." Judging by his comments made in the *Empire of Dreams* documentary and elsewhere, Bill Moyers, who interviewed Campbell for the famous *Power of Myth* series and also talked to Lucas in the *Mythology of Star Wars* PBS documentary, seems to believe that Campbell acted as a sort of consultant on *Star Wars*, mentoring young Lucas in a literal manner, further imbedding this misconception. Lucas was only casually familiar with Joseph Campbell's work, and *Hero With A Thousand Faces'* influence on *Star Wars* is minimal, if anything at all. During the 1980s however, Lucas would become more immersed in proper mythological analysis and Campbellian study, which are more clearly influential in the prequel films. Lucas said in a recent web interview:

> I studied anthropology in college and took a class in mythology; I read some of [Campbell's] stuff there. When I started *Star Wars*, I did more research before I wrote the screenplay. I reread *A Thousand Faces* and a few other things he did, and that was the influence he had on me. Later, after I did *Jedi*, somebody gave me a tape with one of his lectures and I was just blown away. He was much more powerful as a speaker than as a writer. Shortly thereafter, we became friends, and we were friends up to his death.[99]

After meeting, the two used each other's status and exaggerated connection to sell themselves: for Lucas, it gave him proper scholastic backing for his "mythic" B-movie, and for Campbell, it finally gave him worldwide recognition due to the association with George Lucas. Luke Skywalker posed alongside Greek gods on a new edition of *Hero With A Thousand Faces*, while Campbell's most famous work, the *Power of Myth* television series produced by PBS and conducted by Bill Moyers, was filmed at Skywalker Ranch and featured clips from the *Star Wars* trilogy. More importantly, the connection presented a good opportunity to educate young people who might not have an interest in the subject otherwise, and so both men went along with it. Ancillary items such as the Smithsonian "Power of Myth" *Star Wars* exhibit and companion best-selling book are more the result of an acquiescence of inaccuracies of the series' origins for the sake of educational purposes of a field of study close to Lucas' heart.

*Star Wars* was praised for its light-hearted thrills upon its release, and critics did not expect much from it aside from revitalising the fantasy and adventure genres. It quickly skyrocketed to popularity, and in 1977 it was *the* thing of the summer, a pop fad as intense as disco or the hoola hoop; Donny and Marie Osmond made a *Star Wars* musical out of one of their shows, magazine pages were covered in *Star Wars* images and Darth Vader and the droids appeared in press and publicity events around the world, and even on cereal boxes (who can forget General Mills' "C-3P0's" cereal?). It was a film everyone *had* to go see, back in a day when there was no such concept as a "blockbuster."

The revolutionary launch of Kenner's toy line later that year (albeit the infamous "empty box" early-bird Christmas sets) kept the *Star Wars* flame burning and helped maintain interest long after kids had left the cinema. As 1977 turned over to the new year its popularity was still as strong as ever, and when audiences kept going back to the film, critics began to take a second look at it, and all sorts of analysis of its subtext was made. In the ensuing years since *Star Wars'* release, the film took on a genuinely religious-like status, perhaps the only instance of a known fictional creation achieving this status in human history. As such, the fact that it was intended to be nothing more than a B-movie adventure film was severely downplayed, and the more fairy-tale-like aspect—the mythological aspect, the *scholarly* aspect—was pushed to the forefront. After all, it would not look good for this developing new-age entertainment-religion to be revealed to be of such lowly origins as comic books, pulp fiction and B-movies, what the intelligentsia would consider juvenile schlock—Lucas' insecurities about his story were well justified.

Author Steven Hart made the following observation:

> *The Empire Strikes Back*...marks the beginning of Lucas' unheroic journey from honest entertainer to galactic gasbag. The first recorded blats are to be found in Time magazine's May 1980 cover story. Associate editor Gerald Clarke, who had praised the original flick for its lighthearted refusal to offer anything like a serious message, now finds "a moral dimension that touches us

much more deeply than one-dimensional action adventures can." A sidebar, ponderously headlined "In the Footsteps of Ulysses," cites everything from "The Odyssey" to "Pilgrim's Progress" before concluding that the "Star Wars" films "draw from the same deep wells of mythology, the unconscious themes that have always dominated history on the planet."[100]

As well as the following:

> Better still, "the epics" make for an infinitely classier set of influences than stories rooted in what remains one of the most stubbornly down-market literary genres America has produced. Would an eminence grise like Bill Moyers want to be seen trifling with spaceships and ray guns? Would film buffs who pride themselves on knowing every nuance of a silly Western like "The Searchers" stoop to analyze a lowly science fiction movie? Certainly the New Yorker would not have sent John Seabrook to profile Lucas for its January 1997 issue if people thought there were nothing more than sci-fi thrills going on.[101]

Hart's comments may be vitriolic, but they do illustrate a forgotten aspect of the original film and shed light on Lucas' exaggerations. Intended only as a thrilling adventure to stimulate the imagination of young people, the movie had become a living myth in itself, and Lucas a prophet. Michael Pye and Lynda Myles give a similar assessment to Hart in their 1979 article, reacting to the growing status of the film and providing more realistic theories as to *Star Wars'* popularity. Here, Pye and Myles identify that much of the film's power comes not from the content itself but by the emotion projected onto it by the audience due to the film's construction and use of "archetypes." The film "lacks true narrative drive and force," they argue. "It is a void, into which any mystic idea can be projected." They go on to state:

> The true curiosity of *Star Wars*, beyond its clever artifice, is the ways in which public response was molded and stimulated. Publicity discussed the sources on which Lucas drew to construct his story. Indirectly that is a key point in the film. It does use the film language that derives from the strengths of certain genres—the films about the Knights of the Round Table, the old moralistic Westerns, and the cheap serials that poured from Poverty Row, in which Buster Crabbe was always a hero whether he appeared as Buck Rogers, Flash Gordon or Tarzan. The story advances, not by orthodox storytelling, but by telling the audience what to expect. It depends on their cine-literacy...Luke Skywalker pleads with his homesteading relatives to be allowed to be released from the harvest to join the space academy; it is the repeated theme of the films by John Ford...The only direct quotation from Ford in the film, and that a tenuous one, is the fact that the relatives die and their ranch is burned, as in Ford's *The*

*Searchers*. But our experience of Ford's films, and others that use the convention, allows us to read the scene between Luke and his aunt and uncle in more depth than the scene itself would permit. The same mechanism works for the character of Han Solo, a cowboy braggart who blends cynicism with potential heroism... and it works when a monster tells Luke that it does not like his face. We can immediately read the start of a saloon brawl. Duly, that is what happens.[102]

Myles and Pye go on to analyse some of the individual elements, which don't necessarily cohere with each other and in some cases are even contradictory—Darth Vader, the evil villain, is dressed in black, but his forces are stromtroopers, dressed contradictingly in white. The evil Grand Moff Tarkin lives in a cold grey world, with grey uniforms that clearly are supposed to denote comparison to the Nazis, yet when our heroes receive their reward at the end of the film the sequence recalls Leni Riefenstahl's *Triumph of the Will* Nazi propaganda film. "Critical confusion is not surprising when there are allusion to Nazism as both good and bad," Myles and Pye remark. "French leftist critics thought the film was Fascist-oriented; Italian rightists thought it was clearly Communist-oriented."[103]

The film plundered themes and images with enough specificity to arouse nostalgia and stimulate response but enough vagueness to maintain its own power and identity. The Force does not fair any more exceptional: "*Star Wars* talks much of the Force, a field of energy that permeates the universe and can be used for both good and evil," they continue. "But when the Force is used by Luke Skywalker to help him destroy the monstrous Death Star, he is urged only to relax, to obey instincts, to close his eyes and fight by feeling. The Force amounts to building a theology out of staying cool."[104] They remind readers of a more basic explanation as to the films success with audiences:

Star Wars has been taken with enormous seriousness. It should not be. The single strongest impression it leaves is of another great American tradition that involves lights, bells, obstacles, menace, action, technology, and thrills. It is pinball, on a cosmic scale.

...The cheap serials that poured from Gower Gulch used similar devices [of archetypes and audience expectation]. There were conventions for how a proper villain and a proper hero would look. In Ben Kenobi, the hermit knight, we have a perfect equivalent of a Merlin...But what [Lucas] takes from the serials is their morality. They always pitted good against evil, without equivocation. They used romantic dress, predictable stories; and "most of the stories," according to Gene Fernett, a historian of Poverty Row, "were glorified morality plays, much more acceptable to audiences as Westerns than were the old morality plays." Now that serials are dead, and Westerns have absorbed ethical relativism, *Star Wars* is left to inherit that tradition of moral certainty. It is no accident that it should also have the romantic dress and the distant setting that absolute moral values now require: "A long time ago in a galaxy far, far away." It offers the ultimate escape, withdrawal from complex questions of morality, and a display of magnificent fireworks as a bonus. It is a holiday from thought.[105]

Mark Hamill gave perhaps the most down-to-earth assessment of the film in 1980:

In the States the film was like a Hula-Hoop or a Frisbee, a summertime fun thing. It coincided with people getting out of school, taking their holidays. They were ready to laugh, to be thrilled. *Star Wars* was a celebration.[106]

Even Lucas realised this, as he attested in a 1977 interview:

I think one of the key factors in the success is that it's a positive film, and it has heroes and villains and that it essentially is a fun movie to watch. Its been a long time since people have been able to go to the movies and see a sort of straightforward, wholesome, fun adventure.[107]

His tune would change, come 2004:

I did research [on world mythology] to try to distil everything down to motifs that would be universal. I attribute most of the success to the psychological underpinnings which had been around for thousands of years, and people still react the same way to the same stories as they always have.[108]

The truth is that the crowds came for the excitement, the explosions and the inspiring story of the little guy triumphing, the you-can-do-it-if-you-believe-in-yourself philosophy, but came to delve into the mythic subtext more and more on repeat viewings once the initial superficial thrill had worn off. Lucas says way back in 1974:

Some of my friends are more concerned about art and being considered a Fellini or an Orson Wells, but I've never really had that problem. I just like making movies...I'm more drawn to Flash Gordon. I like action adventure, chases, things blowing up, and I have strong feelings about science fiction and comic books and that sort of world.[109]

This illuminates the true purpose of *Star Wars*—it was nothing more than an exciting action picture, with whiz-bang graphics and lots of excitement, meant to harken back to the adventure films of yesteryear. Disco nightclubs had recently risen, with their pounding bass, strobing lights and perpetual flash, as had laser light shows, and pin-ball arcade games also had returned to popularity at that time, with their loud noises and buzzers, flashing lights and constant action, and here was a cinematic equivalent, a natural extension of the type of excitement audiences were inundated with. In designing this type of film as best as possible, Lucas inevitably gave it a depth that made it survive longer than other action pictures, with an uplifting message and memorable characters. It was a film that was designed to blow its audience away with its sights and sounds, a superficial roller-coaster thrill ride with a visual-graphic sense far beyond anything seen before, but the talent of Lucas naturally led to the characters and subtext being highly developed.

It was also the exact type of film that audiences would be craving by the time of its release, and this is the precise reason why the film became such a hit.

Just as Lucas' success with securing funding for *THX 1138* and the box office profit of *American Graffiti* coincided with the rise of the "personal" films of the American New Wave, *Star Wars* also happened to luckily come out just as America was ready to embrace such material.

The American New Wave was characterised by its grittiness and downbeatness, the countercultural response to the glossy, false, optimistic films of the 1950s and '60s. Even the more traditional, studio-controlled Hollywood pictures started reflecting this pessimistic mindset, giving audiences *Dirty Harry*, *Airport*, *Earthquake*, and *The Towering Inferno*—Hollywood became infamous in the 1970s for churning out big-budget "disaster" films and low-budget "revenge" flicks, though the popularity of these paled in comparison to the material being produced by the "New Hollywood," the American New Wave. But after *French Connection*, *Straw Dogs*, *Godfather*, *Dog Day Afternoon* and *Taxi Driver*, audiences were growing tired of the negative onslaught of the cinema of the early and mid '70s; they wanted to get past Vietnam and Watergate, to forget the grim reality that had gripped the country for the past decade and escape to a world were things were good, where serious or challenging messages were absent and where superficial thrills took precedence over all else. The public consciousness was changing.

*Jaws* was the first of these in 1975, arguably the world's first blockbuster. The year after *Jaws* and only one year before *Star Wars*, *Rocky* won the Oscar for Best Picture in 1976 with an uplifting tale nearly identical to *Star Wars*' of the little guy "going the distance," and the year following *Star Wars* would see Richard Donner's *Superman* electrify audiences, an indestructible man of steel to save humanity from the grim and alienating Watergate era; that same year would also debut *Halloween*, giving the blueprint for the endless "slasher" knock-offs throughout the coming decade, *Rocky II*, introducing the first significant entry in the sequel-happy '80s, as well as *The Rescuers*, returning animated films to popularity after having been totally absent from the New Wave domination of the first half of the '70s. It was a return of light and optimistic fare, where audiences could be thrilled and stimulated, where they could turn their brains off and be swept away by sights and sounds. With good and evil clearly drawn in *Star Wars* and audiences able to cheer the heroes on, it was a welcome relief from the challenge of morality that had characterised the decade.

After *Star Wars*, America rejected the American New Wave full-heartedly, resulting in the box-office failure of films such as *New York, New York*, *Heaven's Gate*, *Raging Bull* and *Days of Heaven*, and ushering in the era of blockbusters, where studios regained their dominance, producers replaced directors as creative heads of films and the American New Wave collapsed—only Scorsese managed to escape the extinction, although seriously wounded, while Spielberg and Lucas transformed into blockbuster moguls.

Lucas was blessed with the gift of impeccable timing. "I mean, there's a reason this film is so popular. It's not that I'm giving out propaganda nobody wants to hear," he said.[110] "No one's been able to read the audience, ever, so you have to kind of rely on your own instincts," Gary Kurtz explained.[111] Lucas himself credits his ordinariness with allowing him to be so in sync with audiences. "I'm so ordinary that a lot of people can relate to me, because it's the same kind of ordinary that they are," Lucas maintains. "I think it gives me an insight into the mass audience. I know what I liked as a kid and I still like it."[112]

*Star Wars* was successful because Lucas allowed himself to think like an audience member, recognizing the noticeable void of uplifting adventure spectacles. He gave the public exactly what they needed and wanted, capitalising on the growing wave of *Jaws* and *Rocky*—it was a film his more serious-minded peers like Scorsese and Coppola could never have accomplished, for they lacked Lucas' naiveté and genuine love of the schlocky material which inspired the film.

*Star Wars* was exciting and funny, and this made the unconventional subject matter accessible to audiences who would otherwise not have an interest in science fiction or fantasy, which only made the freshness of the content even more impactful. This was the true secret to the film's success, while many other films of the same genre failed.

In addition to providing a "warm and fuzzy" style of optimism that audiences were eager for once the Vietnam war and Watergate scandal ended, *Star Wars* also capitalised on the underground growth of science fiction and fantasy; the once-obscure genres were experiencing a resurgence, and their imminent break into the mainstream coincided with *Star Wars*.

The *Dungeons and Dragons* roleplaying game had been released in 1974 and was growing in popularity, while a renewed interest in Tolkien followed in the wake of the author's 1973 death (with a *Lord of the Rings* feature film already planned and being made before *Star Wars* was out, hitting theatres in 1978), and with novels being released which drew heavy inspiration from his work (such as Terry Brooks' landmark 1977 novel, *The Sword of Shannara*, the first fantasy novel to appear on the *New York Times* bestsellers list). Robert E. Howard's *Conan* was undergoing a large re-discovery due to the popular Marvel comic series, which first started in 1970 and had amassed a substantial following by the mid 70's and had a feature film in development by 1977, and comic books in general were undergoing a maturation of sorts, with France's 1974 *Metal Hurlant*—imported to the US in early 1977 as *Heavy Metal*—offering the medium a promising new horizon. Sci-fi, fantasy and comic book fan "conventions" had also begun to become popular with their devotees. Science fiction, such as *Star Trek* and *Flash Gordon*, was undergoing a massive re-emergence as well, with respective feature films of each of those franchises already in production before *Star Wars* was released, and in 1974 Paul McCartney approached Isaac Asimov about writing a science fiction rock musical together. In 1975 producer Hampton Fancher began to develop and write *Blade Runner*, and recalled, "There was this smell of science fiction in Hollywood, and I had the gut feeling that science fiction was going to happen in a big way, just like cowboy movies had happened."[113]

The influence of this underground re-popularity had begun to creep into the mainstream public by 1977—medieval fantasy imagery was popular in posters and artwork, with fantasy illustrator Frank Frazetta's paintings becoming hugely popular. Subtler imagery was made known by the rising prominence of New Age spiritualists, who emphasised supernatural mysticism and space-related matters such as astrology, and were particularly fond of surrealistic images depicting these aspects of their faith. Science fiction and fantasy artwork became popular on record album covers as well, and in music many bands and artists wrote songs and even entire albums around fantasy and sci-fi themes: David Bowie's 1973 *Ziggy Stardust And The Spiders From Mars* concept-album concerned an intergalactic rock star, while Led Zeppelin adapted *Lord of the Rings* into songs such as Ramble On, and by the late '70s album art frequently was of the science fiction and fantasy variety, if only in non-pop categories (such as Alan Parson Project's *I Robot*, Hawkwind's *Warrior on the Edge of Time*, Queen's *News of the World*, Electric Light Orchestra's *Out of the Blue*, Yes' *Relayer*, Uriah Heep's *Demons and Wizards*, Rush's *Caress of Steel* and Kiss' *Destroyer*, most of which contained songs of the same fantasy-based nature).

*Star Wars* was the catalyst for finally breaking this growing subculture into the mainstream, partially coinciding with its rising popularity but, even more significantly, helping audiences become more familiar with the subject matter through *Star Wars'* mainstream accessibly. In the aftermath of *Star Wars*, virtually every record album cover featured fantasy and sci-fi art (even disco funk group Earth Wind and Fire's 1977 *All 'N All* album), and the mass of sci-fi/fantasy material that had been brewing before *Star Wars'* release finally came out, such as the feature film adaptations of *Superman*, *Star Trek The Motion Picture*, *Lord of the Rings* and *Flash Gordon*.

The material became one of the trends of the late '70s, and an uncountable slew of sci-fantasy films, novels and comics were churned out due to the massive audience demand, most of which were largely unsuccessful with general audiences (with some notable exceptions, such as Steven Spielberg's *E.T.*, John Milius' *Conan the Barbarian*, Ridley Scott's *Alien* and Richard Donner's *Superman*)—while the imitators thought *Star Wars* was so massively popular because of its otherworldly and fantastic setting, which is what many viewers were so impressed with and raved about, those viewers were, in fact, hooked by the characters and the touching emotion invested in the film, an elusive quality that most of its successors and imitators could not match. Dale Pollock asserted that "*Star Wars* was effective because, for all its fantastic elements, it had the ring of truth. George Lucas was the farm kid on Tatooine, hungering to escape a safe existence. He was the young initiate confronted with a difficult calling and finding the strength within himself to meet it."[114]

By the early '80s, as the initial thrill of the newly discovered genres wore off and less-engrossing films pushed audiences away, the material was abandoned by the general public and was once again seen as "nerdy," retreating back to non-mainstream status, though its devotion by fans and especially youngsters was now considerable and so it remained as a profitable niche genre, mostly for kids. This is what led to the massive outpour of adolescent science fiction and fantasy in the 1980s.

*Star Wars* was made and released at the best possible time, being at once both a reflection of audience tastes and a landmark innovation that captured their attention—it gave them exactly what everyone wanted and needed, even if they hadn't realised this gaping void existed. It revitalised the science fiction and fantasy genres while also capitalising on their growing underground popularity, provided a story that was fresh and unique while also being archetypal and universally familiar, depicted a world that was strange and captivatingly exotic but that was also nostalgic and vaguely recognizable, was emotional and touchingly human while still being thrilling and startlingly alien, and it blew away the audience with revolutionary sound, music, editing and visual effects, while also giving them a spiritual sense of optimism and most importantly an overriding sense of joyous fun. If the film had been released in 1973 or 1983 it would not have been nearly as effective or successful, but in May of 1977 it was like a divine revelation from the gods of cinema, impressing critics and audiences equally with its cinematic innovation and warm heart.

Lucas provided a humble assessment of his own film in 1981:

> The underrating and the overrating are the same kind of reactions. The people who are saying "It's nothing; it's junk food for the mind," are reacting against the people who are saying "This is the greatest thing since popcorn!" Both of them are wrong. It's just a movie. You watch it and you enjoy it...It's just that people tend to take those things so seriously and get carried away when they should realise that it's just something you enjoy—like a sunset. You don't have to worry about the significance of it. You just say, "Hey, that was great."[115]

*Star Wars* began to be showered with praise of the highest sorts, put on a pedestal that would be difficult for it's creator to maintain. Its status as a summertime event slowly changed into that of a new mythology, and its reputation was growing beyond the control of any one individual. Lucas mentioned early on that he had notes on the background history, and as the status of *Star Wars* grew from blockbuster film to modern myth, so too did Lucas' statements on his own pre-planning—soon the public was led to believe that Lucas basically had designed an elaborate, multi-film saga of Biblical proportions. "Most directors are insecure, and I'm no exception to that," he admitted in 1983.[116]

Lucas clearly lacked confidence in his writing skills, previously confessing many times that he is "a terrible writer" and always seeking help from his friends to write scripts for him. *Star Wars* had taken on a quasi-religious status with many fans, and rather than admit that he was stumbling in the dark and yet somehow continually finding his way, he put forth the image of some long-ago devised "master plan." There is no master plan—and there never was. It was all made up as he went, and any plans laid would prove only temporary.

The fact is that no writer will immaculately come up with a story as rich and great as that of the *Star Wars* saga. It takes many agonizing drafts, many bad ideas, and many transformations before the final story is made clear. The best of ideas are stumbled upon by accident, inspired by outside sources and made in a continuing evolution, as a story like the *Star Wars* series was written over many decades, from 1973 to 2005 (and beyond). Whether it is written by a Sarah Lawrence anthropologists like Joseph Campbell or a small-town north Californian who happened to like poorly-written sci-fi serials, it is what it is.

The excuse "that is the way it always was" became Lucas' security blanket, his shield, with which he can safely hide behind. It renders him invulnerable to criticism. When Mark Hamill was filming *Empire Strikes Back*, he protested to Lucas about the mention of the "Other." As he recollected in the November 1980 issue of *Starlog*:

> It didn't sit so well with me at first...I told George that people would think I was pulling a $5 million holdout on something that made it necessary, but he said if anyone suggested that, he would tell them it wasn't so...I thought it made me look bad. But George insisted it had always been part of the storyline.[117]

Hamill was suddenly forced to accept the story change when George defended that it had "always been part of the storyline"—despite the fact that the line about the "Other" was placed in the script on a whim and reflected a last-minute story change. When making any major story changes, rather than look as if he was making it up, Lucas often claimed that that was the way it always was—as if to therefore absolve himself of responsibility.

An example, after deciding to portray the unmasking of Darth Vader as a sad old man, instead of the hideous monster he had previously been, Lucas said in the 1983 documentary *From Star Wars to Jedi*:

> After Darth Vader has been...thrust into this huge persona that I never expected to have happened, do I still take the mask off and have him be this funny little man? Well, again, I sort of came to the decision that that was the original story, that's the way it should be, and if the public can't deal with it then what can I do about it?[118]

In the years of the prequel trilogy, he would cement this reputation—and after the vicious criticism which followed in the wake of Episode I, Lucas needed this crutch more than ever. If people criticised the film, it was unfortunate. "That's the way the story was always written," Lucas could say, as if he was a prisoner to it and thus granted critical immunity. Lucas is a person especially sensitive to criticism, as his wife once told Dale Pollock—when it came to the ever-changing story of *Star Wars*, taking unexpected turns and frequently worrying him, the ability to say "that's the way the story always was" was a convenient escape:

> Right or wrong this is my movie, this is my decision, and this is my creative vision, and if people don't like it, they don't have to see it.[119]

# Chapter VI: The Wreckage

FILMING on *The Empire Strikes Back* began in Norway on March 5th, 1979. The process of filming this installment would be more important than the production of any of the other films, for the troubles and tribulations that resulted since that March 5th would have large consequences on the future of the series. A disastrous endurance test, it was the *Apocalypse Now* of fantasy films.

In 1976, Francis Coppola had finally decided to film Lucas and Milius' *Apocalypse Now* script, fashioning it to his own liking. With the *Godfather* films thrusting him to fame, he became the world's first superstar director and finally had the professional muscle to make the picture, which studios had previously rejected because of its subject matter; American Zoetrope, nearly destroyed by *THX 1138*, was reborn. Lucas and Kurtz gave him all of their pre-production scouting, which had determined the Philippines as the ideal shooting location, and with his army of cast and crew—and a fleet of helicopters provided by the Philippine military—Coppola set out to make his most epic creation yet.

The film was budgeted at $13 million, and in order to ensure creative control he had raised the money himself—which also made him financially responsible for the film's budget. All of his personal assets were put up as collateral, including his San Francisco home. The project was more complicated than anyone anticipated, and as the schedule and budget ballooned, Coppola began investing all of his personal funds into the picture to save it, eventually putting up millions, all of his savings. His entire livelihood was tied up in the troubled picture and if it failed he would be obliterated. Typhoons destroyed sets, actors showed up drunk and high, Philippine guerrillas struck nearby, and leading man Harvey Keitel was fired after the first week of production only to have his replacement, Martin Sheen, suffer a heart attack, all the while Coppola wrestled with the elements of location shooting, the ego of Marlon Brando and a script which was being re-written and improvised live. The 16 week shooting schedule eventually became a marathon of madness—286 days and a final budget of $31 million. Coppola lost nearly a hundred pounds of weight and threatened suicide multiple times. "My film is not a movie," Coppola explained when it finally debuted at Cannes three years after it began production. "My film is not about Vietnam. It *is* Vietnam. It's what it was really like. It was crazy. And the way we made it was very much like the way the Americans were in Vietnam. We were in the jungle, there were too many of us, we had access to too much money, too much equipment, and little by little we went insane."[1]

Though Lucas would not be beset by problems of the magnitude that his mentor was, it would be enough to personally change him, even when he was not directing the picture and hardly on set.

Director Irvin Kershner, known for more character-oriented films, was chosen by Lucas to helm *Star Wars II* at the suggestion of Gary Kurtz, and gave the film a sophisticated depth and an emphasis on characters and emotion, rather than action and special effects—a stylistic departure from Lucas and *Star Wars* which sometimes led to resentment from the all-powerful executive producer. Lucas gritted his teeth as the director allowed actors to improvise and change lines to allow for a more believable performance,[2] such as the carbon freezing scene which Alan Arnold's book reveals was mostly improvised,[3] and Kershner often butted heads with Lucas on his policy on moving the film along as quickly as possible (Kershner still thinks *Empire Strikes Back* moves too fast[4]).

Kershner explained his involvement to *Sound and Vision* magazine:

[Why did Lucas choose me to direct?] That's what 20th Century Fox wanted to know, because they thought I was too old. I was over 55. They said, "Get a young man. Get someone in their 30s, somebody who will understand the kids." But George said, "No," he wanted me. George had been in my classes, my seminars at USC. I was teaching there, on and off, and we became friends. Later, we would meet every once in a while, and he would talk about some of the films I'd done—*Eyes of Laura Mars*, *The Return of a Man Called Horse*, and *The Flim-Flam Man*. He loved them. "I want you to do the film," he said, "because you know everything a Hollywood director's supposed to know, but you're not Hollywood."

I turned it down. I told him, "I don't know anything about special effects." But he said, "You don't have to. You think up anything you want and it's up to Industrial Light and Magic to make it work." Now, I don't know of anyone else who could have said that, but he owns the company. So I'd ask for the most impossible shots, and they would do it.[5]

Like his mentor Francis Coppola did for *Apocalypse Now*, Lucas had decided to finance the film himself to ensure personal profit and creative control, but even all the riches that *Star Wars* brought him were not enough to pay for the film. Lucas had quickly become a businessman and an entrepreneur, setting up multiple corporations to help him make his films. ILM had just moved out of its original building in Van Nuys into a more impressive lot in Marin County, a chaotic and expensive undertaking, and Lucasfilm and Star Wars Corporation were still being consolidated and managed by Lucas and his partners. He also began making plans for Skywalker Ranch, a filmmaking nexus where he could centralize all his resources, and so his lawyers began purchasing land in Marin County. A dream of his for years, it was his personal version of Coppola's American Zoetrope, where filmmakers could share resources outside the Hollywood system. The ranch would eventually cost nearly $20 million. Re-investing all of his earnings from *Star Wars* back into his companies, Lucas was forced to secure a bank loan in order to complete the financial backing for *Star Wars II*. However, the production was plagued by many problems, which eventually led to the skyrocketing of its original budget. Lucas' fiscal problems only added to the pressures of making the second *Star Wars* film, and he was worried that the over-budget, behind-schedule movie—being directed overseas in England, away from his watchful eye—would ruin him. All of his personal assets were tied to the production and invested in it—if the film was a flop, Lucas would be ruined.

On one of his set visits, Lucas related to Alan Arnold the financial pressure he was under:

I'm faced with a situation where everything I own, everything I ever earned, is wrapped up in this picture. If it isn't a success not only could I lose everything, but I could also be millions of dollars in debt which would be very difficult to get out from under. It would probably take me the rest of my life just to get back even again. That worries me. Everybody says "Oh, don't worry, the film will be a huge success" and I'm sure it will be, but if it is just one of those mildly successful film sequels, I'd lose everything. It has to be the biggest grossing sequel of all time just for me to break even.[6]

Coppola was about to find out whether *Apocalypse Now*, debuting later that year, would sink or sail, and with it his career—Lucas suddenly saw himself being reeled into the same filmmaking nightmare Coppola had been caught in for three years. The American New Wave had been steadily declining since *Star Wars*—due to big-budget flops, such as William Friedkin's *Sorcerer* and Martin Scorsese's *New York, New York*. *Star Trek: The Motion Picture* and *The Black Hole* had also recently been over-budgeted science fiction films with poor box-office reception, and Lucas had just produced *More American Graffiti* which was released later that year—and was not the success many had hoped. The footage Lucas saw in dailies and on his few set visits did not instil him with much confidence. Just as on the original film, Lucas suffered from anxiety because of the high-risk filmmaking. But it wasn't just Lucas who was affected by the production—the film took its toll on everyone. "It was the most wearing film I've ever done," associate producer Robert Watts once remembered.[7]

Filming would be delayed when Stanley Kubrick's *The Shining* accidentally burned down an entire stage, leaving sixty-four sets to be divided into seven stages; In Norway, huge storms left the crew trapped in their hotel; production designer and second-unit director John Berry would unexpectedly die during production; Carrie Fisher would battle a heavy drug addiction; and every conceivable mechanical failure would occur. The film was more logistically complicated than anyone had anticipated, and a string of bad fortune, combined with Kershner's desire to shoot the material slowly and methodically, resulted in massive management breakdowns.

Kershner remembered the troubled production in a *Sound and Vision* interview:

> When you're working on a film for almost six months . . . It was so difficult—every shot was like pulling a donkey out of a hat. Because things didn't work, you had to *make* them work and improvise every time. [Director François] Truffaut said it better than I could—something like, "You start a film and you want to make the greatest one ever made. Halfway through, you just want to finish the damned thing." That's the way I felt. Halfway through, my crew was falling apart. Many of the people left; they were ill. So, no, I never stopped and said, "Boy, oh boy, have we made a terrific film."[8]

The production may have been more complicated than Lucas originally anticipated; Kershner explained the madness of *Empire Strikes Back* to *Star Wars Insider*:

George also came over once when I was shooting the X-wing being pulled out of the water and moving across the swamp, based on the magic power of our little man. It had taken some time to set up, a few hours actually, and now we did the shot, and the haze was right—because we had the set closed off so that you actually had clouds hanging—and then the ship came out of the water. It looked beautiful, and there was moss and seaweed, and the water is dripping off, and suddenly the two wings just collapsed.

I felt so badly for George, because I knew it was his money. I said, "What happened?" And they said, "Well, we didn't realize it wasn't waterproof, and all the wings are wood, and they couldn't take all the weight." I said, "Now you tell me." It took hours to rebuild it—they put in structural things and a little steel. Ten hours to do the shot, and it was maybe six seconds...But you know, when I came to the swamp set, it wasn't ready, so while they were working on one part of it, I'd start shooting another part...While we were lighting, they were banging away with hammers and pulling things in place. Also, people were sliding and slipping into the water, and we had a couple of broken arms...Sometimes I had to wear a gas mask, because we had so much smoke pumped into the set, and I stood there for twelve hours a day...so I started getting ill, and they gave me a gas mask with a microphone inside, so I could talk to everybody.

...It sounds like fun, but it wasn't. It was a hell of an experience—and it went on a long time, unfortunately. I once called George and said, "George, it's taking a little longer than we thought. Do you want me to take some pages out of the script or, you know, what the hell can we do?" And he said, "Don't do anything, just keep shooting." Those were his words. And that's, of course, the one thing you want to hear.[9]

Mark Hamill recalled the pressure of making the film in a 1983 *Starlog* article:

On the other hand, *Empire* seemed like nine months of torture to me. I really got the stuffing kicked out of me in that movie. I'm supposed to be an actor, not a stuntman. And, because of the mechanical problems with Yoda, I was the only human being listed on the call sheet for months. Everything else was puppets, props and special effects...Overall, I probably had more differences of opinion with Kersh...I liked his work, but he was an eccentric guy. I didn't find that to be a problem, but sometimes it was more difficult to get across what I was trying to say. He was very preoccupied, so I had to grab him by his collar and look him in the eyes to get his attention.

Kersh also changed his mind frequently, particularly with camera set-ups. For example, we would rehearse a set-up for the next morning, but the odds were by that time, the shot would change. Usually, it would be a better shot, but if they had let him, he would have changed it again.[10]

Tension also began to build between Lucas and producer Gary Kurtz. Lucas was irritated with Kurtz for not restraining Kershner. "The director needs to do what he needs to do, that's all," Kurtz says simply.[11] But Lucas saw it differently: "Gary never said no to anything."[12] In their daily telephone calls he urged Kershner and Kurtz to "scale down and speed up."[13]

"George wasn't *here*," Kurtz noted in *Mythmaker*. "*I* was here. He was back there, working with ILM, getting the visual parts together…I kept telling George, 'Look, you've got to let me do this my way, because if you push him too hard, it'll just make things worse, not better. I've seen it. I've experienced it myself. What we're getting is very good. Don't make it worse than it is.'"[14] Kershner related his side of the balancing act between quality and quantity in this *Star Wars Insider* interview:

> In terms of just the logistics, George would've been much happier had I been able to shoot it faster. But frankly, to get what I was trying to get, I couldn't. I couldn't get the performances as well. I'll give you an example:
>
> We were shooting a very difficult scene with Harrison, and there were some special effects in the scene. We shot it in one take, and I said, "That's it, we move on." Harrison said, "Wait, hold it—tell me something: was *I* good, or did the special effects work and therefore you don't want to shoot again?" I said, "Harrison, by now you gotta trust me. You were great. The special effects happened to work, but you were great." And he looked at me with that wonderful look of his. "Uh-huh, okay," he said, and he pointed his finger at me, wagging it, and said, "Now you better watch yourself."
>
> Because the temptation, if the special effects work, is to say, "OK, the performance is good enough." Well, I couldn't get away with that with Harrison, and I didn't want to get away with anything with Mark, because I knew that it was important for him, and for Carrie. So I'd have one eye on the special effects and one eye on my characters—and boy, they better come together, or else it didn't work.[15]

The production, however, fell more and more behind schedule, while the budget escalated with each week. Eventually, disagreements between Lucas and Kurtz would lead to the two parting ways for the third instalment after being partners since *American Graffiti*.

Lucas had been apprehensive about hiring Kurtz for *Empire* in the first place, feeling that Kurtz had aggravated the tensions on set during *Star Wars*, particularly with cameraman Gil Taylor, but at Kurtz' persuasion he gave him a second chance.[16] "I suspected there would be problems and I knew I was asking for trouble," Lucas later would say.[17] Kurtz was supposed to be Lucas' representative on the set, but, in a sense, Kurtz betrayed him—he saw the film from Kershner's point of view, agreeing that the film should be serious and slower, and was impressed with what they were able to achieve, allowing the schedule and budget to swell. Although some critics of Lucas have accused him of firing those who encouraged and challenged him creatively and seeking more slavish "Yes Men" producers for the rest of his career, Lucas' actions here were not wildly unreasonable—Kurtz let the production run massively over budget and weeks over schedule, which was all the more horrifying when one realises that all of Lucas' future was tied up in the production. With Lucas' production responsibilities more as a manager, his department was an expensive failure.

Kurtz however looked at it in a different light, confident that the film would return its monetary investment regardless of its increased expenditure, and felt that the quality of material was ultimately worth the budget crisis. Interviewed by *IGN Film Force*, Kurtz said:

> One of the arguments that I had with George about *Empire* was the fact that he felt in the end, he said, we could have made just as much money if the film hadn't been quite so good, and you hadn't spent so much time. And I said, "But it was worth it!"[18]

Perhaps there is a dichotomy here—Lucas would thankfully never run into the production, budget or schedule problems of *Empire*, and yet he would never achieve the same level of critical and artistic success as he would eventually have with that film. Perhaps the reason that the film's producer and director were more concerned with its artistic quality than its mogul executive producer was because, as Lucas stated many times during the era, the *Star Wars* sequels' primary purpose was to provide him with funding for Skywalker Ranch, an investment Kershner or Kurtz had little concern for.[19]

"The ranch is the only thing that counts," Lucas told Lucasfilm president Charles Weber in 1980. "That's what everybody is working for."[20] With his hand in so many different ventures, Lucas only had so much attention to go around—he was managing his many companies and launching more, such as Pixar and the computer division, supervising the production of *Empire*, dealing with its troubled financing, building Skywalker Ranch, as well as planning other projects such as *Raiders of the Lost Ark*. *Star Wars* was not his number one priority, and he didn't mind if it was merely "good enough" instead of the more idealic aspirations that Kershner and Kurtz were striving for. "It looks pretty because Kersh took a lot of time to do it," Lucas stated of *Empire* to Dale Pollock. "It's a great luxury that we really couldn't afford. And ultimately it doesn't make that much difference…It was just a lot better than I wanted to make it."[21]

Meanwhile, once filming finished, the editing began another series of disasters. A rough cut had been assembled in 1979 and when Lucas screened it he felt the same sense of panic and disappointment as he had at the disastrous rough cut screening of *Star Wars*. "I was extremely upset, because I felt it wasn't working at all," he told Dale Pollock. "Here I was, way over budget, running out of money, and I had a movie I thought was no good."[22]

Pollock provided an account of how tense the situation got, as Lucas scrambled to "save" the movie by re-cutting it himself:

> Lucas' revised version was heavily criticized by Kershner, [Editor Paul] Hirsh, and Kurtz. "A lot of it didn't work and some of it was cut too fast," Kershner says. Lucas finally lost his temper. Duwayne Dunham, who accompanied George, sat in amazement as his boss exploded: "You guys are ruining my picture! You are here messing around and we're trying to save this thing!" Kersh calmly pointed out what he thought Lucas had done wrong, but George became even more upset. "It's my money, it's my film, and I'm going to do it the way I want to do it," he declared.[23]

Lucas soon reconsidered once he had calmed himself—the stress of the film had taken its toll, and now finally it ruptured out. "I never got on Kersh about the fact that he was over schedule and putting a great burden on me and my life," Lucas admits. "Everything I owned was wrapped up in that damn movie. If he blew it, I lost everything."[24]

"But they were right," he told Dale Pollock. "It didn't really work very well. *That* was what made me angry—I couldn't make it work."[25] Kershner suggested some changes and Lucas recut the film following his advice. "It came together beautifully," he says.[26]

However, even as personal differences began to subside, the budget continued to escalate and required a second bank loan, which also went over-budget, requiring a *third* loan, which would only be given if Twentieth Century Fox would step in to guarantee it—leading to an improved distribution deal on their part ("we're still suffering from it," Lucas lamented in 1983[27]). What had started as a $15 million budget had more than doubled to $33 million when all was said and done.[28]

Coppola's *Apocalypse Now* had been released the year before—the film was a critical hit and managed to take in over $100 million, Cannes' Palm d'Or and two Oscars. His younger protégé awaited to see if he would have as much luck. But for all of Lucas' worries and troubles, *Empire Strikes*

*Back* was an enormous hit when it was released to much fanfare on May 21st, 1980. A decidedly darker and more sophisticated continuation of the story, it was the complete opposite of what everyone expected from a *Star Wars* sequel, and ended on a cliffhanger that guaranteed more films to resolve all of the shocking plot developments that had been left open. The budget and schedule problems turned out to give the film the care and attention to subtleties that make it considered the best of the series, and the emotional depth and deliberate pacing that Lucas loathed about Kershner's style would become the fan-favourite film's most enduring strength. "It has to be slower and more lyrical," Kershner explained of his method. "The themes have to be more interior, and you don't have a grand climax."[29]

But Lucas still seemed to harbor some resentment for all the grief he went through: "I appreciated what Kersh was trying to do and I sympathized with his problems. The film was well directed, it was just differently directed."[30] But even Lawrence Kasdan, who objected like Lucas to the on-set improvisations,[31] admitted that the film's unique style stems from the perfectionist director:

> It has a quality I think Kersh gave it... It's just not like any of the others. I really loved Richard Marquand. But he didn't put as distinctive a stamp... But I think Kersh just directed *Empire* great. He loosened up George in a lot of ways. George wanted the movie to be his, the way he wanted, but he knew how to use Kersh and trust him—even though it scared George at times.[32]

*The Washington Post* raved: "'Empire' turns out to be a stunning successor, a tense and pictorially dazzling science-fiction chase melodrama that sustains two hours of elaborate adventure while sneaking up on you emotionally."[33] There were, however, some who criticised the film, and it inevitably had a divided release—many felt the film lacked the warmth and heart of the original film, and were put off by the lack of a proper introduction or resolution to the story. In spite of some criticism, however, the film was an all out success, taking in a massive $209 million at the box office.

### *In the Wake of Empire*

But by 1980, Lucas had been irrevocably changed. He was literally working himself to death, trying to control not only a disastrous major motion picture in which was wrapped his personal fortune, but also a growing corporation with many subsidiaries. "I don't know how one person has that much energy," production co-ordinator Miki Herman once observed of Lucas' exhausting efforts.[34] His marriage was beginning to grow strained, his company was developing out of control (leading to massive layoffs as he downsized), and he suffered from chronic headaches and bouts of dizziness, eventually being diagnosed with an ulcer that year. Only seven more *Star Wars* films to go! The behind the scenes workings of those eventful years changed the *Star Wars* story more than anyone realises.

Even before the troubled second film was released, Lucas had begun to reconsider his elaborate plans for the series as the realities of shooting set in. If he was to go along with his epic of nine films, he still had roughly twenty more years of straight filming ahead of him. After all that he had gone through, first on *Star Wars* and then again on *Empire Strikes Back*, it is unlikely that he was looking forward to seven more of those experiences—making *Star Wars II* was not the fun romp he had envisioned in 1977, and in fact the third installment would be done under mostly obligatory conditions. "I was ready to quit [after *Star Wars*]," Lucas reflected in an interview with Denise Worrell. "I wanted to quit then. But I kidded myself into thinking that if I stopped directing, it would be like quitting. I thought I could just oversee it. But it didn't work that way."[35]

The decision Lucas began considering was a fairly obvious consequence of such strife: was it really necessary to extend the series beyond *Star Wars III*? A vague series of sequels which Lucas only added to the story because he could suddenly began to look like an unnecessary chore, and starting over from scratch on a series of "prequels" was no less difficult. Before *Empire Strikes Back* was finished, Gary Kurtz even claimed that Lucas' plan for the third film was shifting:

> At that time [during the making of *Empire Strikes Back*] we were still talking about what was happening with *Jedi* and it already was apparent that he was changing his mind with what he wanted to do with *Jedi*.[36]

Not only were Lucas' plans for the story changed by *Empire*'s making, but also his plans for its execution: *Star Wars* was supposed to be a collaborative series, one in which Lucas himself had only a delicate influence, where he would step away and a new director would steer the story and style of each film. Every few years a new director would make a *Star Wars* film, putting a slightly different spin on each movie.[37] In this, Irvin Kershner was the only one who was allowed the privilege of playing in Lucas' world, of making it and adapting it into his own. After the personal disaster that was *The Empire Strikes Back*, Lucas withdrew this plan and spun 180 degrees for the final sequel: he would choose a director more in line with his own style, be on set every single day, film much of the material himself, and for all intents and purposes become a co-director; this shift was encouraged by the fact that the series had strayed from the disconnected adventure-of-the-week style of 1977 which Kershner had been hired under to a more epic, connected "Saga," with a pre-planned story arc and stylistic continuity.

By the time of *Empire*'s release, Lucas had become somewhat disillusioned with the series, and his personal life also was feeling the consequences of such laborious work—George and Marcia's already-strained marriage was in worse shape than ever, and Marcia wanted to start a family, as did George, but as long as he was working on *Star Wars* he knew he would never have enough time to properly raise a child. Their marriage would sadly not last the release of the final *Star Wars* film three years later.

Another separation would occur with Lucas, immediately following *Empire*'s wrap—this one with Gary Kurtz. With irreconcilable differences over what had happened during *Empire* and over where the series was headed, the two parted ways. Kurtz reflects on the split in an interview twenty years later with *Film Threat*:

Film Threat: So when did you and George Lucas start to not see things the same way? What was the beginning of it?

Kurtz: I think that was during the making of *Empire*. George got really concerned about how long we were taking, we didn't go over budget and he banged me for the cost overruns on *Empire*.

FT: And taking Irvin Kershner's side...

Kurtz: And taking Irv's side, yeah...it was kind of a mutual parting. It wasn't acrimonious, it was just that he felt he would probably be more comfortable with someone else to handle the production chores on *Jedi* and I felt that I would prefer a different kind of challenge, that wasn't kind of repeating something I had already done. Jim Henson had asked me to produce *The Dark Crystal*, something he had been working on for about ten years.[38]

Kurtz also began to loathe the growing Lucasfilm empire. What was once a modest company run by Lucas, Kurtz, Marcia, a book-keeper (Lucy Wilson) and a secretary (Kurtz' sister-in-law, Bunny Alsup) had since grown into a sprawling empire, symbolized by "Fortress Lucas," the under-construction Skywalker Ranch, perhaps the inspiration for the under-construction Death Star that Lucas would write a few months later. Lucas himself was becoming more and more isolated from the real world, with fame catapulting him into such stratospheres of celebrity that he no longer could live and work like a normal human being. "People can be pests," Lucas commented at the time. "Everyone wants to be my friend now…and they all want something. I don't want any more friends."[39] Looking back, Kurtz mused to John Baxter:

> The saddest thing about watching that process was the slow takeover by the bureaucracy…With that slowly came this thing about dress code, company policy, and nobody talking to press, and a firm of PR people, and it was quite frustrating really. I was there longer than anybody, and had been with him for the longest period of time, and I just felt that I didn't like it…The bureaucracy grew and grew. You couldn't talk to George. You had to talk to his assistant. It became more Howard Hughes, in a way. I decided I was more interested in working on interesting films than in being tied to a machine like that.[40]

Lucas had blamed Kurtz for the cost overruns on *Empire* but by 1983 accepted responsibility. "Gary did the best job he could, he made enormous contributions, but he was in over his head," Lucas told Dale Pollock. "If anybody is to blame, it's me. Because I was the one who knew and stayed over here [in California] until it was too late."[41]

Lucas would turn to Howard Kazanjian, a friend from his days at USC who had produced the flop sequel *More American Graffiti* in 1979, and who was also currently producing *Raiders of the Lost Ark*, to manage the third *Star Wars* film.

While *Raiders of the Lost Ark* was being filmed in July 1980, Lucas was readying to work on *Star Wars III*. During this time, Lucas undoubtedly was weighing the future of the saga. The truth was that everyone was beginning to tire of the films—in fact, Harrison Ford fought hard to see to it that his character not return for the third instalment and instead be killed off. Mark Hamill and Carrie Fisher had since been typecast in their respective roles, with their likeness emblazoned on everything from t-shirts to coffee mugs to action figures. Rabid *Star Wars* fans would swarm them in the streets, and the only way many of the actors could find work was when it was reprising their *Star Wars* characters—such as on *The Muppet Show*, or the *Star Wars Holiday Special*. The actors were under contract for only one more film, and though Lucas had at one time hoped to include them in additional films, he may have realised that not even *he* would be up to the task of doing more than three. Meanwhile, Marcia hounded George to step back and settle down for a while before their relationship crumbled any more—he had been working round-the-clock since 1976. It appears Lucas took his wife's advice—although he had previously refused to start a family because his *Star Wars* trilogy was all-consuming in his life,[42] he and Marcia would soon adopt a baby girl, Amanda, in 1981, after Lucas decided to give up his space opera.

With *Revenge of the Jedi* poised to end the conflict begun in the first film—the Empire defeated, Darth Vader dead, Luke a Jedi and the heroes victorious—there was little need to extend the story beyond this. Of course one vestige of the Sequel Trilogy remained in the form of the "Other" that was mentioned and now needed to be addressed, but with some clever writing it could be resolved and the series finished.

It seems Lucas' generation-spanning, nine-film epic was dead before it ever got off the ground. Just two short years after he mapped out a nine-film structure, he was ending it.

The public world was still waiting on the edge of their seats to find out what happens to the heroes and villains of *Star Wars*. Was Vader lying to Luke? Was *Obi Wan* lying to Luke? Could Luke go to the dark side? Would Han be saved? Was Luke still in love with Leia? And just who was the "Other" that Yoda refers to? Lucas may have been wondering some of the same things since so much of his story was up in the air.

Speculation was abound by the public and the press. Mark Hamill offered some amusing speculation in a 1980 *Starlog* article. David Packer wrote:

"George insisted [the "Other"] had always been part of the storyline, though he never told me who it might be. Somebody suggested it might be the Princess, but I think that would be a letdown."…Judging from Hamill's remarks here and other things he has said, it seems likely that the story has a life of its own, anyway, and not even George Lucas knows for sure how it will emerge until it is down on paper and then on film… "I remember very early on asking who my parents were and being told that my father and Obi-Wan met Vader on the edge of a volcano and they had a duel…Now I wonder if it's true? I mean, there are so many things. For example, remember the Clone Wars? They could have cloned my father."

…"But changes are inevitable," he continues, "and Darth Vader is a good example of changing a character to please the people. I think, originally, if you follow classic drama, I would have to kill him in the third episode. But now he's a cult figure and, in a way, George may not want to do away with him," Hamill confides. "Ultimately, the Emperor should be the main bad guy— someone you try to get through nine movies, and in the ninth one you succeed...There has got to be something to the fact that he looks and sounds a bit like Obi Wan."[43]

There were many possibilities to where the story could be headed.

One last fact of significance from *Empire Strikes Back* is the premiere of the Episode listing. When *Empire Strikes Back* was released, the opening titles proclaimed, to the confusion of most audience members, *Star Wars Episode V The Empire Strikes Back*. Following on the change that appeared in the "public version" (as it was officially designated) of the script which appeared in *The Art of Star Wars*, an alternate title card was filmed for *Star Wars*. When *Star Wars* was re-released the following year in 1981, the updated titles now read: *Star Wars Episode IV A New Hope*. *The Washington Post* reported in 1980:

> The first indication of unexpected developments comes almost immediately. It is the appearance of the heading "Episode V" at the top of a prologue that crawls from the bottom to the top of the screen. Could one "Star Wars" plus one "Empire Strikes Back" equal five?...When "Star Wars" is reissued, probably next summer, the prints will include the subtitle, Episode IV: A New Hope. This adjustment may already be seen in the published screenplay, which came out last winter in an attractive book called "The Art of Star Wars."[44]

The missing three episodes that begin the saga of course came into existence once Lucas developed the backstory to Obi Wan and Father Skywalker, in which the latter falls to the dark side and becomes Darth Vader, back in 1978, as already covered. This began the first of two main events that would lead to the formation of the prequel trilogy. It provided the basis for the creation of the story, but another event would shape and mould the focus of that story—but its effect would not come to pass for over an entire decade. That event is what we now come to, when George Lucas altered his plans for the saga and ended the series on Episode VI.

This is, of course, the humanisation and redemption of Darth Vader, and the creation of Anakin Skywalker, the fallen hero.

# Chapter VII: Demons and Angels

WITH the final chapter of the story looming, Lucas now had to bring the series to a satisfactory close while resolving all the subplots set up in the previous film. The main one, the one which everyone who had seen *Empire* was looking forward to with anticipation, was the resolution to Vader's shocking line: "I am your father." Because of this the story would ultimately shift to one in which a son must confront his father—a plot point which had not necessarily been planned upon as being so significant but was now thrust into Lucas' writing out of necessity. This unexpected turn would become one of the most important events in the creation of the Saga. Because the shocker of "I am your father" was so momentous, Lucas had no room to develop the series beyond this plot point, and instead, *Star Wars III* would become about Darth Vader and his relationship with his son. It would become, inevitably, about Vader's redemption, and thus forever change the series.

As noted before, all indication is that Vader was *not* initially supposed to be redeemed, at least not in the manner in which the eventual film played out—his return to the light side and the emphasis placed on him would be natural developments that came out of the story as it was written draft by draft, although the notion of him confronting his Jedi past was likely in place as a possible story thread ever since Lucas began thinking about future episodes after writing draft two of *Empire Strikes Back*. Lucas said in a 1980 *Rolling Stone* interview:

> In the next film, everything gets resolved one way or the other. Luke won the
> first battle in the first film. Vader won the second battle in the second film, and
> in the third film, only one of them walks away. We have to go back to the
> beginning to find out the real problem.[1]

The exploration of Vader's humanity is first hinted at, as Lucas seems
to be implying that going back "to the beginning," in other words to
Vader's fall from grace, is where the real heart of the conflict lies. Prior,
even in the nine-film version of the story, Vader's humanity would have
likely been explored—making him into Luke's father had humanised him
enough, and with issues of temptation and betrayal at hand and the notion
that Vader was once a hero, it would be natural to bring forth these issues
at some point. However, it seems that as the newly-created story point
surrounding Father Vader soaked into his mind, he began to develop the
idea of Vader and Luke confronting each other as father and son and not
enemies, a story point which can be seen in its early stages with Vader's
invitation to Luke to join him and overthrow the Emperor at the end of
*Empire Strikes Back.*

The rough draft of *Revenge of the Jedi* resumed this thread, but with a
more humanised and personalised version of Vader—it was this seed that
would soon grow into the "redemptive savior" version that we are familiar
with, the tragic hero of the final draft. Gary Kurtz told *Film Threat* of
similar story development that never came to complete fruition but rather
transformed:

> The one story thread that got totally tossed out the window [for *Jedi*], which
> was really pretty important I think, was the one of Vader trying to convince
> Luke to join him to overthrow the Emperor. That together they had enough
> power that they could do that, and it wasn't him saying I want to take over the
> world and be the evil leader, it was that transition. It was Vader saying, "I'm
> looking again at what I've done and where my life has gone and who I've
> served and, very much in the Samurai tradition, and saying if I can join forces
> with my son, who is just as strong as I am, that maybe we can make some
> amends." So there was all of that going on in *Jedi* as well, that was supposed
> to go on.[2]

Vader's "redemption" was not the compassionate one of salvation seen
in the final film, but rather a redemption based on loyalty and honour. It
was, as Kurtz points out, very much a samurai tradition, and this precise
point stems from the character of Prince Valorum in the 1974 rough draft
of *Star Wars*, who was an adaptation of a samurai character from *The
Hidden Fortress*, General Tadokoro.

Lucas first mentioned the film's title in a conversation with Alan Arnold in 1979,[3] and in May 1980, just as *The Empire Strikes Back* was hitting theatres, the third film was officially announced: *Star Wars III* would be known as *Revenge of the Jedi*. Reports *Bantha Tracks*:

> Now that *The Empire Strikes Back* has been completed, Lucasfilm, Ltd. is preparing work on the third film in the *Star Wars* saga, to be called *Revenge of the Jedi*. Preproduction will begin in January of 1981, and the film is tentatively scheduled for release during the spring of 1983.[4]

However, when Lucas began to actually flesh out the story it ended up subtly changing. In its initial conception it was about the heroes fighting back after their defeat and Luke's ultimate triumph as a Jedi, the triumph of good over evil in the destruction of Vader and the Empire—but when Vader and his redemption became the eventual focus of the film, the story ceased to be centred on vengeance and instead revolved around deliverance, leading to a controversial last-minute title change, to be discussed later.

In July of 1981, just after the revised rough draft was written, Kerry O' Quinn asked Lucas if he had the nine-film series already plotted, to which Lucas replied: "Yeah, but it's a long way from the plot to the script. I've just gone through that with *Revenge of the Jedi*, and what seems like a great idea when it's described in three sentences suddenly doesn't hold together when you try to make five or six scenes out of it. So plots change a lot when they start getting into script form."[5]

### Reaching for the Future

Before Lucas sat down in his writing office, *Raiders of the Lost Ark* had to be filmed. "I probably had more fun on that picture than any other," Lucas said to Dale Pollock. "I didn't have to do anything but hang out. I had all the confidence in the world in Steve [Spielberg] and I was not at risk financially."[6]

With *Raiders of the Lost Ark* Lucas finally had a chance to institute the James Bond-style adventures that he had dropped during the development of *Empire Strikes Back*. Not surprisingly, he only had the concept itself of doing sequels and not actual stories. In fact, as Spielberg recounted the making of the *Raiders* sequels in a 2003 interview, it is remarkably similar to the process of scripting the *Star Wars* sequels:

When George and I were in Hawaii and I agreed to direct *Raiders*, George said that if I did wind up directing the first one that I would need to direct three of them. He said he had three stories in mind—it turned out George did *not* have three stories in mind, we had to make up all the subsequent stories... *Raiders of the Lost Ark* was too super-packed with gags, and stunts and set-pieces—no movie could hold that much. So certain things carried over, and I always remember the river rafting scene which we had written for *Raiders*, which I saved and kind of bookmarked for another *Raiders* movie. That went into *Temple of Doom*. And then we had an entire mine-cart chase, like a roller coaster ride. That was originally written for *Raiders*. And so I basically just took it out of *Raiders* and kept it in a drawer and then when it came time to figure out set pieces for *Temple of Doom* we dusted it off and stuck in the end.[7]

*Raiders of the Lost Ark* was a massive hit, and Lucas already had sequels planned before the film was even released. As *Star Wars* was ending, another franchise was beginning.

The smashing success of *Raiders* has been said to have changed much of the direction of the future *Star Wars* films. "This idea that the roller-coaster ride was all the audience was interested in," said Kurtz, "and the story doesn't have to be very adult or interesting, seemed to come up because of what happened with *Raiders of the Lost Ark* and the Indiana Jones films—and the fact that that seemed to make a lot of money."[8] *Star Wars*, by the end of its first theatrical run, had domestically grossed $307 million. Rejecting the conventional approach to sequels, Lucas ultimately made a follow-up that wasn't at all like the original, being darker, more adult and introspective. Kids understandably were not as enamoured by it as they were with *Star Wars*, nor were critics, and *Empire Strikes Back* domestically grossed $209 million—a full $100 million less than the original. Lucas returned to the light-hearted, more accessible, action-packed roots with *Raiders*. *Raiders* would become a bigger hit than *Empire* ever was, with audiences and critics alike, especially those youngsters who had first experienced *Star Wars*, and without any built-in audience managed to inch past the $200 million mark. There was a clear message that the younger audiences had been alienated by the darker themes of *Empire*—indeed, *Empire* is often the least favoured of children but most favoured of adults, while *Jedi* would inevitably be the most favoured of children but least favoured of adults. Perhaps this explains the more kid-friendly turn in the third film; while the only puppet in *Empire* had been a grumpy Buddhist philosopher, *Jedi* would give kids an entire palace full of zany muppets, including a brief musical number, and a whole planet full of teddy bears.* Lucas' instincts paid off—the film would prove to be a whopping $50 million more successful than its predecessor.

Lucas had made bold choices to ignore conventional sequel rules, but *Empire*'s stunning disengagement in style from the original film was almost entirely due to Irvin Kershner and Lawrence Kasdan, who shaped the material to be a serious adult fantasy film with an emphasis on character. Lucas argued in story conferences that the film had to be faster, less developed, more focused on action—more like an adventure serial—but, ultimately, Kershner took the film away from Lucas, and Kasdan was on the same page as Kershner. "[I] thought the movies could hold more character and more complexity," Kasdan said in *Mythmaker*. "George thought they should be simpler in another way. It was a serious philosophical difference."[9] In script form it was not quite the way Lucas wanted it but once filming commenced Kershner put even more emphasis on the interior, on character motivation and introspective visual lyricism, and it horrified Lucas—for someone as powerful as Lucas, he *should* have been able to put his foot down and stop this, and that's why he had Gary Kurtz on set. But Kurtz was on the same side as *Kershner*, and fought Lucas about the same issues as he did, feeling that the film should be slower and more serious, and that the extra money being spent was ultimately worth it. Lucas of course did not agree, and with only a limited emotional investment in the franchise he became infamous for saying "it's good enough." Kurtz explained to *IGN Film Force*:

> I think that he did chafe a bit under the idea of someone saying "that's not a good idea," some of the time. At the very end of *Empire*...we decided that there had to an extra shot at the very end, to identify this rebel fleet.
>
> If you remember how the end works, it's before you go into the medical department, who are working on Mark's hand. It's the establishing shot of the fleet...They weren't very difficult to do, and all the ships were there...just pile up the composites, and they were rushed through, just to get it done. Very last minute. One of them wasn't particularly good, and George said, "Oh well, maybe we should just let it go."
>
> I said, "It's worth at least one more go through. One bad shot can ruin the whole movie, basically."[10]

Lucas tried to take back the film once filming was over, re-editing it to be fast and action-oriented like he envisioned, but it was a complete disaster because it simply wasn't the way the material was shot.[11] Although

---

* This shift to more children-friendly fare might also be seen as a reflection of the fact that Lucas now had an infant daughter

many find the film to be a superior artistic endeavour, Lucas admits that he wasn't concerned with making it as such—he was more interested in producing a product that would appeal to kids and finance his other ventures. It is important to understand that he truly *did* care about the sequels, and was very protective of the galaxy he had created—but it wasn't the be-all end-all creation that some may see it as today. It was a product that Lucas intended to use to finance the projects that he *truly* had his heart set on, namely Skywalker Ranch and the personal films that he would develop out of the facility—*that* was his goal, to make an independent filmmaking empire, not to make *Star Wars* sequels. The "filmmaker's community center," as he described it at the time, cost more money than he had, which is why he intended to use the *Star Wars* sequels to make him box-office green—commercialism took precedence over the actual content, though he very much was still concerned about that as well, just in a more casual producer-like manner.

"The idea for [the Ranch] came out of film school," Lucas explained to *Rolling Stone* in 1980. "It was a great environment; a lot of people exchanging ideas, watching movies, helping each other out. I wondered why we couldn't have a professional environment like that."[12] He had made a small-scale version of this with his Parkhouse office in the 1970s, where he rented rooms out to other filmmakers and they all shared ideas and worked together—now he was attempting to construct this in much grander proportions, the ones originally envisioned for Zoetrope. "I figure it will take between five and six years and cost in excess of $20 million," he continued. "That's way beyond my personal resources."[13] Indeed it was, as Lucas estimated at that time that his personal net worth was somewhere around $20 million,[14] much of which he had invested into purchasing the real estate for the Ranch—which was why he couldn't personally finance *Empire Strikes Back* himself but had to instead go through bank loans. Realising such an elaborate facility was something only oil tycoons could do, and though Lucas was rich, he wasn't rich enough, so he had to devise an investment scheme—while dumping his personal fortune into the real estate, the sure-to-be-lucrative *Star Wars* sequel would be financed by a bank, and then the huge box-office return would both pay off the bank's initial investment as well as provide Lucas with the additional funds required to build the Ranch, with additional sequels and merchandising keeping the facility in business.

If, however, *Empire* failed to cover its overhead, which was much more than $30 million when you account for advertising, distribution and other costs, then the bank would own the film, Lucas would be millions of dollars in personal debt, and the dream of running an independent filmmaking empire would be impossible, with him instead forced to sell the $30 million Lucasfilm corporation[15] and indebted to make more commercial projects to keep himself afloat. Perhaps now the financial tunnel-vision that Lucas expressed in 1979 is made clearer—*Empire* had to be hugely successful for him not only to repay the bank, give Fox their share of gross, finance the many companies and subsidiaries and make some personal profit, but it also had to bring him an *additional* $20 million personally if he were to pay for the research-facility—which was his chief goal. Although the film probably would have done this regardless of how good or bad it was, Lucas' obsession with making it commercial and low-cost is not hard to understand, nor is his paranoia of failure, especially when the sequel to *Graffiti*, presumed to be a guaranteed hit, performed poorly at the box-office, warning Lucas that nothing was guaranteed.

Lucasfilm, ILM, and the Ranch would also need a steady supply of funds once they were set-up to pay for the enormous overhead that they would generate every year. At the time of *Empire*, Lucas envisioned a steady stream of *Star Wars* sequels to keep him in business. He said on an *Empire Strikes Back* set visit in 1979:

> Most of this filmmaking effort is so I can create a dream, a dream I've had for a long time, which is to build a research retreat for film. The amount of money needed to develop a facility like that is so enormous that the money I have doesn't amount to anything. You need millions and millions of dollars to build such an operation. The only way I can do it is to create a company that will generate profits...[The *Star Wars* films] are the core [of Lucasfilm], which is why I have to concentrate on them. I don't want to spend the rest of my life making *Star Wars* pictures, but I do want to get them set up so that they'll operate properly without my having to get completely involved in all of them. They've got to be self-generating to support the facility.[16]

But by the completion of that film, forces in his personal life had compelled him to diminish his reach. His marriage was on the rocks, and the Lucases had decided they would say goodbye to *Star Wars* and adopt a child, which they did in 1981. Ridding himself of his burdensome aspirations of imperialism, *Revenge of the Jedi* nonetheless remained as a final attempt at creating his facility—with the land already purchased and the buildings under construction in anticipation of the returns of *Empire Strikes Back*, *Jedi* was his ace-in-the-hole that could potentially pay it all off. Lucas talked about his plan in a 1980 interview:

Lucas: We are taking the profits from *The Empire Strikes Back* and the next film, *Revenge of the Jedi*, and investing them in outside companies, then using those profits to build the ranch and maintain the overhead.

Jean Vallely: *What happens if* The Empire *doesn't make enough money for your ranch?*

Lucas: Well, if it doesn't happen with this one and the next, then that's the end. I'm not going to spend the next fifteen years of my life trying to make hit movies to get the ranch.[17]

Thus, it was highly important that *Revenge of the Jedi* be made his way and that the struggles with the director not re-occur, that *Jedi* be constructed as a "hit movie" so that Lucas could finally "get the ranch," as he explained above. And Lucas got his wish—*Empire* was a huge success, to his relief, and it helped make the first payment for the construction of the high-tech facility itself, which was helped along the way by additional income from *Star Wars* merchandising, *Raiders of the Lost Ark* and finally *Return of the Jedi* when it was released. Unexpectedly, however, the dream would crumble before Lucas' eyes—but we will come to that in the next chapter.

Thanks to the profit from *Empire*, Skywalker Ranch was beginning construction just as Lucas was readying to work on the third *Star Wars* film. Dale Pollock described it in 1983 as it was undergoing its final phases of development:

Skywalker Ranch promised to fulfill many of Lucas' long-standing goals: it would give him a headquarters unlike that of any other movie company. It would be a motion picture think tank, where movies would be conceptualized, rather than physically made. It would be neither a film studio nor a film campus but something in between.[18]

Eventually, it would become home to Lucas' many future companies: Lucasfilm, Industrial Light and Magic, Skywalker Sound and more.

A complete re-organization of Lucasfilm was needed in order to both secure the impending move to the Ranch and to regain control of the company into Lucas' hands; under the successful leadership of president Charles Weber, the company had grown out of control and threatened to become the very corporate entity Lucas despised. In the end, Weber was fired, and in the move to Skywalker Ranch nearly half of Lucasfilm's employees were laid off—Lucas gave them all six months to find new jobs and vocational counsellors to help them, as well as generous cash settlements.

With all of this business drama occurring, it was clear that *Star Wars* was no longer Lucas' number one priority. He had since moved on to other things, and saw his primary responsibility as the head of his enterprises and as a founding father in a new independent filmmaking horizon.

### A Return to Writing

Perhaps because of all of this, it wasn't until February 20th, 1981 that Lucas finally completed the handwritten rough draft of *Revenge of the Jedi*. The story had to be epic in scope, yet personal in its conflicts—a grandiose, spectacular climax had to occur against the personal relationships of the characters. There were a lot of loose ends that needed to be quickly tied up, and the public expected a spectacular ending to the trilogy. "[The series] started out as a simple fairy tale, and that's all it really is," Lucas said in 1981. "It's really a little bit more controlled than you might think. When [*Revenge*] comes out, people will say, 'Oh, my god. How obvious! Why couldn't they think of something more interesting than that?'"[19]

Lucas had brainstormed a vague arc for the two sequels around the time he had written the third or fourth draft of *Star Wars*, but this brief outline—Luke begins training as a Jedi under Obi Wan's tutelage, the Rebels re-locate to a new base and continue their battle, and Luke confronts Darth Vader—had basically been funnelled into *Empire Strikes Back*, leaving very little story for the third film other than a concluding, grand climax that finally resolved the conflicts. As such, the story was "stretched thin," as Lucas admitted—all that was actually needed was a final confrontation between Luke and Darth and the concluding battle between Rebels and Empire, with Leia and Han's romance finally culminating and the Emperor destroyed. Because of this, the majority of the actual plot had to be recycled; Lucas turned the capture of Han Solo into a lengthy action sequence that returned to Tatooine and one-upped the creatures seen in the cantina, re-used the Wookie subplot from the 1974 rough draft as a race of primitive forest creatures called Ewoks that battle the Empire, and recycled the Death Star attack in a sequence with more advanced special effects (and with not one but two Death Stars in the initial drafts).

"There were a lot of things that were added into this one because of the fact that by the time I got down this far from the original [outline] the story had become pretty thin and I had to fill in a lot of blanks," Lucas admitted in 2004's DVD commentary. "This whole sequence with Jabba the Hutt was more an afterthought than anything else...because Han Solo had become such a popular character."[20]

Gary Kurtz argued that these newly added elements cumulatively diluted the power of what he maintains was originally to be a more mature and sophisticated plot that was not as convoluted as these additions made it, especially once Leia was also written in as Luke's sister. "The idea of another attack on another Death Star wasn't there at all," Kurtz says. "It was a rehash of *Star Wars*, with better visual effects. And there were no Ewoks...it was just entirely different. It was much more adult and straightforward, the story."[21]

Denise Worrell described Lucas' writing environment as he sat down with a pencil and stack of paper in early 1981:

> Lucas's writing room is what Marcia calls a "tree-house environment," which used to serve as their mansion's carriage house. Marcia decorated the suite of rooms—a writing nook and desk built into a windowed wall a few steps up from a large living room, a bathroom and a tiny kitchen—with redwood paneling and forest-green fabrics. As you enter, there is a green couch in front of a fireplace and a stack of wood. There are bookshelves around the room and a TV and stereo system on one wall. The carpet is beige. Lucas's desk is stained redwood, and on it are a Mickey Mouse phone, a Wookie pencil holder, a telescope, and several books: Joseph Campbell's *Hero With A Thousand Faces*, Bartlett's *Familiar Quotations*, Webster's Dictionary, Harper's Bible Dictionary, *The Foundations of Screenwriting* by Syd Field, and *Roget's Thesaurus*, opened to a page that has the word *imagination* at the top. There is a little Sony television to the right of the desk, and five three-ring notebooks containing Lucas's notes and sketches for the entire *Star Wars* epic, past, present and future. There is also a picture of Marcia and the baby. When he is writing, Lucas spends about eight hours a day in his "tree house," with a short break for lunch. "If I spend eight hours 'writing,'" he says, "I probably spend three hours writing and the rest of the time thinking."[22]

Lucas' rough draft had the most important parts of the story occur on Had Abbadon, capital of the Galactic Empire—a planet covered in cities and enshrouded in smog. This is the planet that would eventually become Coruscant in the prequel trilogy. There are also two Death Stars under construction instead of merely one, orbiting Had Abbadon's Green Moon, which is being harvested as a sanctuary for the overpopulated metropolis. In the opening scene, Leia and a platoon of Rebels troops, under the guise of Imperial soldiers, sneak into the orbiting Green Moon—where they plan to then assault the Imperial capital in a final battle to destroy the Empire.

Meanwhile, Darth Vader and Moff Jerjerrod, similar to the Imperial bureaucrat Moff Tarkin in the original film, land on Had Abbadon and meet with the Emperor, who is finally revealed—in order to reach him, they must first go to his grand palace and then travel many miles underground. The Emperor dwells in the very bowels of the planet, so deep underground that his throne sits atop a lake of lava, a truly satanic image.

Vader and Jerjerrod kneel before the Emperor, who tells Vader that his powers have gotten weak and that Luke has grown in power and must be destroyed. Vader tries to disagree, but is choked through the Force. Luke is the Emperor's to destroy, and he orders Vader away. Once gone, the Emperor tells Jerjerrod to watch Vader and that Luke will not be destroyed but instead turned into his new apprentice.

This then becomes the crux of the film. Jerjerrod and the Emperor compete with Vader for Luke—the Emperor wants Luke to kill Vader and rule with him, while Vader wants Luke to kill the Emperor and rule with him. Unlike what is seen in *Empire Strikes Back*, where Vader was still portrayed as a two-dimensional evildoer, he is now implied to have some feelings for his son, and expresses concern that Luke may be in danger from the Emperor. The start of Vader's humanisation thus begins and the true villain of the film becomes the Emperor.

On Tatooine, Luke is dreaming of Vader and the dark side. Yoda and Ben are also in the dream, and Luke criticises Ben for not telling him the truth about Vader. Yoda explains that soon he will join Ben in the Netherworld, and will therefore be stronger and able to help Luke in his destiny with the Emperor. Luke and Lando then free Han Solo from Jabba's palace in a sequence similar to that of the finished film. They all leave onboard the Falcon where Luke has another dream: Yoda tells Luke that he must destroy Vader, but Luke doesn't think he can do it; Obi Wan then appears, and reveals that Luke has a sister—Luke searches his feelings and knows that it is Leia. The Falcon then travels to the Rebel base, where the attack is planned; meanwhile on the Green Moon, Leia meets the "Ewaks," short furry creatures with big yellow eyes, in a sequence similar to the final film.

Luke has a vision that Leia will be in danger and that the Rebel attack on Had Abbadon will fail—Luke decides to help her, and so now he must face Vader, whether he is ready or not. Luke travels with the Millennium Falcon to the Green Moon, but they are met with an ambush. Han, Chewie and the robots escape, but Luke climbs a tree and hides; after convincing from the spirit of Ben Kenobi, he surrenders to the Imperials with the intention of finally confronting Vader.

Luke is to be taken to the Emperor on Had Abbadon but Vader instead wants Luke to be brought to him. General Veers, loyal to Vader, delivers Luke to Vader's Star Destroyer, where Vader tempts Luke to join the dark side. Luke refuses, and Vader tells him that he is not strong enough to destroy the Emperor. Moff Jerjerrod suddenly enters, enraged that Vader has taken Luke for himself. Vader grabs him by the throat and kills him, and then takes Luke to see the Emperor.

The Ewaks help the Rebels fight on the Green Moon, using gun emplacements to blow up the communications disk on Had Abbadon. The Rebel fleet then comes out of hyperspace, and the space battle occurs.

As Vader is escorting Luke to the Emperor's throne room on Had Abbadon, Obi Wan's ghost appears. He tells Vader he is there to save him, that the Emperor wants to destroy him. He tells Vader that if he turns to the good side he will pass through the Netherworld when he dies and Obi Wan will rescue him before he becomes one with the Force, so that he will retain his identity. Vader refuses and brings Luke to the Emperor's lava lair. Once there, Luke refuses to kneel before him, and the Emperor says that he will not be destroyed by Luke. Obi Wan suddenly appears, defying the Emperor, followed by Yoda, and the Emperor begins to panic. He orders Vader to destroy Luke, and father and son begin to fight, jumping from rock to rock over a river of lava.

Luke eventually cuts off Vader's arm, and the Emperor orders Luke to finish him off. Vader begs Luke to kill him but Luke refuses, and tosses aside his lightsaber. The Emperor begins to shoot lightning bolts at Luke, but he is protected by an invisible shield—wherever the lightning strikes him, the images of Obi Wan and Yoda appear, but Luke soon collapses under the strain. Suddenly, Vader charges the Emperor, grabbing him, and they both fall into the lake of lava.

As the Rebels celebrate their victory, Luke tells Leia that she is his sister. Obi Wan then appears in flesh and blood, followed by Yoda and, finally, the elderly Annikin Skywalker.

The script has the same basic plot as the actual movie but a number of significant variances are obvious. The driving force of the script, however, is Vader and his relationship to Luke. Perhaps more so than even the final film, Vader is presented as a character with his own struggles—just as Luke struggles with Vader and the Emperor, a parallel subplot is created in which Vader struggles with Luke and the Emperor; we view Luke's temptation from both sides. Vader himself experiences a temptation, this time in the form of Luke and Obi Wan, who beckon him to become good again. However, he nonetheless remains somewhat unemotional about the matter—his mission to save Luke is not done out of overridingly compassionate means, but rather more for practical means to keep Luke as his own apprentice and rule together, not wildly different from the finale of *Empire Strikes Back*. His ultimate sacrifice in killing the Emperor comes across as being done to prevent his prize from falling into his rival's hands, and he ends up, unintentionally it seems, tumbling into the lava with him.

Nevertheless, the first steps towards humanising Vader had occurred, and as the audience views his struggle to claim Luke while competing with the Emperor, he becomes a somewhat sympathetic character, despite the fact that his intentions are at odds with our hero, Luke. His character had taken strides in development compared to what was seen in any of the previous films, where he was still in the role of "menacing villain."

This first rough draft depicted him as trying to save Luke to overthrow the Emperor, but the first hints of a more humanised Vader emerged, with a moment where he is offered a chance of redemption in returning to the light side—with each subsequent draft, this seed would be magnified, and more depth given to Vader and Luke's relationship until we arrive at the final draft where Vader saves his son out of pure compassion and finally makes amends.

### A Family Affair

Lucas had a lot of issues to deal with in crafting *Revenge of the Jedi*. The "Other" he had made mention of in the second film is the most notorious of the loose ends he had to tie up. Lucas would have probably liked to not deal with the issue at all, but viewers eagerly looked forward to the reveal of whom this person could be. However, with the Sequel Trilogy abandoned, Lucas was now forced to address this issue and resolve who this person was. The most obvious solution was to make the character another Jedi whom had survived the great Jedi purge, similar to Yoda and Obi Wan. However, arbitrarily introducing another character to satisfy this plot point was not very practical from a storytelling point of view, and with another Jedi on the side of the Rebels, Luke's character would be significantly diminished. With no room to satisfyingly introduce a plausible new character, Lucas felt it best to make this character into one of the pre-existing ones. But who would it be? Han, perhaps? He was a character who acted on instinct, a trait Kenobi described Force-users as possessing, and we had seen him use a lightsaber in the previous film—but having Han as the Force-using last hope of the galaxy did not seem like a very good idea.

Lucas had written himself into a corner and there weren't very many places for him to go.

One of the abandoned concepts from the first draft of *Empire Strikes Back* was to make Luke have a twin sister that was also skilled in the Force. Of all the pre-existing characters, making Leia both the "Other" as well as Luke's sister was the best option available. For one, Lucas could bring back the twin-sister subplot from draft one of *Empire Strikes Back*—minus her being a Jedi, of course. It would also finally put a definitive end to the Han-Leia-Luke love triangle, even though that had pretty much been resolved in *Empire Strikes Back* when Leia said she loved Han; here at least it would give Luke a good reason to resolve his attraction. Mark Hamill also agreed, Luke's story was not one that needed to involve a romance: "Luke's got a mission, and a romance would dilute his forward line through the story," he told *Prevue* Magazine in 1983.[23]

Making Leia not only the "Other" but Luke's *sister* had another logical reason to it—it was perhaps the only way to satisfy the notion that she was the galaxy's "last hope," as Yoda implied, if Luke failed. Leia obviously did not have any serious Force-potential, although she resists the mind probe in *Star Wars*—a remnant from the third draft, in which she knew "the art of mind control." However, if Yoda said she was the last hope, what was his basis for believing such? Certainly she is a prominent leader in the Rebellion, but not to the extent that would warrant such a status. The only way she could be seen as "another hope" is if she was biologically related to the most powerful Force-using family in the universe—just as Luke was strong in the Force because he was the son of Annikin, so Leia was strong in the Force because she was his daughter. "The Force is strong in my family," Luke would later explain in the final film. "My father has it. I have it. And my sister has it. Yes, it's you, Leia." This is the first introduction in the films of some kind of biological link to the Force; in the first film, Luke wanted to be a Jedi simply because his father was one, and was able to use the Force simply because he believed in himself. Now, the linking together of a family in order to satisfy story threads was introducing genetic aspects.

The creation of Leia as Sister Skywalker then necessitated alteration to the Darth Vader backstory once more. Instead of simply having one son hidden from him, he now had a daughter as well. This then raised some major plot issues. For one, how and why does Vader not know about her? It seemed very obvious that Vader knew he had a son; it seemed implied that Annikin turned to the dark side when Luke was just a baby, and therefore had full knowledge that he had a son out there somewhere, hidden away from him—what happened to Luke's mother was never even mentioned or explored (assumedly she was also dead). When Lucas turned Vader into Father Skywalker in 1978 he eliminated the sister plot because it seemed contrived and unrealistic—but now he was forced to somehow justify it.

Skywalker history had already been re-written in the previous film. Instead of Luke simply living on Tatooine with the rest of his family, along with his father's friend Ben Kenobi who also grew up there with him and later returned in isolation, Luke was now *hidden* there. A contradiction would thus loom for the eventual prequels, as Tatooine was supposed to be Father Skywalker's place of birth—hiding his son from him on his home planet made little sense. Also, if Owen or Beru were Annikin's siblings, that would also mean they had Force-potential as well, as "the Force runs strong in [the Skywalker] family." What was Owen and Beru's backstory now? Were they genuine relatives or more like godparents or guardians? Why is their surname Lars and not Skywalker, and is Owen really to be Vader's brother? Now that the backstory was beginning to grow seriously contrived, they needed to be re-explained in some manner. Lucas came up with the story that after Kenobi wounded Annikin in his duel on the volcano, he brought the infant Luke to Tatooine, an isolated back-water planet where Vader would never find him, to live with *Kenobi's brother* Owen. The original film was hence altered even more, now making Owen and Beru impostors. This plot point was cut out of the final film however, but was well-known in the fan community as it was included in the *Return of the Jedi* novelisation. *The Annotated Screenplays* indicates that this plot point was first thought up in story meetings for *Jedi*.[24]

Because Annikin had turned to the dark side when Luke was just a baby, Leia had to have been a twin birth, since there was no more time for Annikin to conceive. If Annikin then had twins but did not know of one of them, it seemed to indicate that he did not witness or know of their birth, now implying they were born *after* he turned to the dark side. This then seemed at odds with what is seen in the films—if Vader had never met his children, how did he know of Luke? Did he even know he had children? For such a major plot point, it was a bit odd that it was left so confusing, and with all the plot trappings Lucas had created for himself the story was becoming a patchy mess. The most logical explanation one can gather is that Annikin left his wife while she was pregnant, making him aware of having an offspring somewhere in the galaxy but not knowing that it was a twin birth. However, this would be refuted in later drafts of *Return of the Jedi*, where it is revealed that Annikin never even knew his wife was pregnant at all, leaving one to assume he discovered Luke's existence off-screen between *Star Wars* and *Empire Strikes Back*.

So what happened to baby Leia then? Lucas came up with the idea of Kenobi taking Leia to live with his friend, Bail Organa, the governor of Alderaan, where she would grow up with a different name and hence not be found. The character of Bail Organa had supposedly first been developed when Lucas was writing *Star Wars*, being the father of Leia and a senator and early opposer of the Empire in the last days of the Old Republic, though he was never seen or mentioned in any of the scripts. In order to now justify how Leia could be Luke's sister yet also the daughter of the royal Organa family of Alderaan, Lucas decided that she was adopted, the only logical solution to the amalgamation of the concepts of Leia *Organa* and Leia *Skywalker*. The original character of Leia was the genuine daughter of the Organa household, as can be seen from the fact that Lucas' private and public material treats her as such; there are no such references to her being adopted before 1981, and as *Annotated Screenplays* implies, the first time it was brought up was in 1981 where the new backstory of the twins was revealed in order to justify how Leia could be the "Other."[25] In continuing the parallel of Lucas' personal life finding its way into the story, it is an interesting link that Lucas himself had just adopted a baby girl at this time in 1981.

The move of making Leia Luke's sister was not a very graceful one—it is one that put many holes in the story, holes it would take Lucas over twenty years to fill, and it still does not sit as completely believable. However, Lucas wanted to be done with *Star Wars*, and based on what was available to him, it was the best option.

Mark Hamill scoffed at this plot development when he first read the script. "In fact, I tried to get George to admit, I said, come on you made that up on the plane ride over here. He said, no, I had the whole thing written."[26]

Another issue Lucas had to own up to was Obi Wan's contradictory story of Father Skywalker's history. The only way around it was to simply state what the truth of the situation now was—that Obi Wan lied to Luke in order to protect him from the painful truth. This however, turned the previously saintly Obi Wan into a liar. In later drafts, Lucas would come up with Kenobi's infamous "certain point of view" explanation to try and dampen this character change, but also accepted the somewhat soiled view of the seemingly-flawless Obi Wan and turned him from "noble Jedi master" to "tragic failure," which I'll elaborate on later in this chapter.

*Revenge of the Jedi* was much more plot heavy than the previous film, but for this third instalment Lucas dusted off the original script for *Star Wars*—included in *Revenge of the Jedi* is a variation on the battle of primitives and Imperials, which was a major part of the plot to the first draft of *Star Wars*. In that draft, Wookies helped the rebels fight the

Empire, first in a ground battle on their jungle home world—and then in attack ships, for it was Wookie-piloted ships who assaulted the Death Star. Lucas told Laurent Bouzereau:

> The Wookie planet that I created for *Star Wars* was eventually turned into the Ewok planet in *Jedi*. I basically cut the Wookies in half and called them Ewoks! I didn't make Endor a Wookie planet because Chewbacca was sophisticated technologically and I wanted the characters involved in the battle to be primitive. That's why I used Ewoks instead.[27]

The recycling of old ideas would become quite common among all of the *Star Wars* sequels:

> Usually, if I like something and I have to drop it, I put it on the shelves and very often end up using it somewhere else later on. The thing about writing is that ideas aren't precious...when you think of something, you have to be willing to throw it away.[28]

### A Human Being After All

Lucas would next revise the rough draft of *Revenge of the Jedi* and alter it considerably. In this revision, he would give Vader even more character, and add more emotional depth to his intentions, with his struggle to secure Luke for himself becoming an even greater focal point. It is in this *revised rough draft* that the true nature of Anakin Skywalker finally emerged.

He would now be regarded as a fallen hero, one who lost his way and turned to the dark side—and was serving the Emperor seemingly against his will, a tragic victim himself. This was all building towards his redemption at the film's conclusion. It was in this revised rough draft that the six-part saga of *Star Wars* would be truly solidified.

Vader's encounter with the Emperor does not occur in the film's opening scenes. Instead, Vader's screen introduction comes in a scene with Jerjerrod. In this version, Jerjerrod is given even more power—so much, in fact, that he is Vader's superior. However, whereas Tarkin was Vader's superior for the simple reason that Vader was meant as a more minor henchman, here Jerjerrod's contempt for Vader serves the specific purpose of making the audience identify and sympathize with Vader. Jerjerrod talks down to Vader, orders him around and is closer to the Emperor than he is.

Jerjerrod is also portrayed as someone to be feared, as even Vader is cautious around him. As Admiral Piett and Vader walk to meet Jerjerrod's arrival in the film's opening sequence, they discuss him: "Never before have I heard of the Grand Moff leaving the planet to greet someone," Piett observes. "You are greatly respected, my Lord."

"Or greatly feared," Vader grumbles. "The disgusting little bureaucrat is attempting to lay a trap for me."

"He's a fool to think that you would not know," Piett reassures him.

"The Emperor's counsel is no fool. He is very clever and quite dangerous."

In the opening scene onboard the Star Destroyer, Moff Jerjerrod arrives with his dignitaries, and a welcoming party of officers and stormtroopers honour his visit:

VADER
You honor me with your presence, My Lord.

JERJERROD
Yes, I know. (looking around) You may rise. All this fuss just for me, an impressive display I must say. (sniffs the air) Yes, well the Emperor sends you his blessing....

VADER
But he still refuses to answer my transmissions.

JERJERROD
I'm afraid he's quite too busy.

VADER
Then why was I ordered to return?

JERJERROD
He feels your prolonged stay in the outer systems has not agreed with you.

Vader is very angry and it takes all the control he can muster to contain himself. Jerjerrod starts for the hanger entrance. Vader follows.

VADER
Don't you toy with me.

JERJERROD
All right then.... the Emperor is disturbed with your failure to deal with young Skywalker and he has decided to handle the matter personally. You will supervise the construction of the Battle Stations; a task he feels will be much less demanding.

VADER
But, I have all but turned him to the dark side of the force.

JERJERROD
The Emperor does not share your optimistic appraisal of the situation. Skywalker is more powerful now, than before your feeble attempts to convert him.

12. INT. BRIDGE STAR DESTROYER
Vader, Jerjerrod and company walk onto the vast Star Destroyer bridge.

VADER
He can't do this. The boy is mine!

JERJERROD
That seems to be part of the problem. It would appear that you still have some feelings for your troublesome offspring...
 The Emperor will succeed, where you have failed. You are weak Lord Vader, more machine than man. The Emperor's plan has already been put into motion. The entire rebel force is on its way to us, for one last, hopeless confrontation, so I suggest you prepare your fleet.

VADER
My son would not be so foolish as to fall into such a trap.

JERJERROD
Ahh but, he is not with them. Your son is on his home planet of Tatooine. He will soon be in our hands, and the Emperor will have his way with him.

VADER
Get off my bridge!

JERJERROD
As you wish...

The Grand Moff turns and walks off the bridge followed by the dignitaries. The Admiral and his Captains go back to their duties. Vader stand alone on the bridge looking out across the vast sea of stars.

VADER (to himself)
Luke, beware, you are the Emperor's prey now.

It is quite a startling scene of character depth for Vader. He is shown to have feelings for Luke for the first time, and is genuinely concerned that his son will be in danger. Clearly, Lucas was shifting the focus towards Vader and his redemption—from the opening of the film, this is a very different character than the one we were introduced to in 1977.

It is interesting to also note that much of the exchange in the above scenes would be transplanted to the Emperor's arrival in the final film, and other sections would be reused in Jerjerrod's arrival in the opening scene—but with the roles reversed.

Vader's paranoia of the Emperor is also much more developed, but he has good reason to believe as such, for Jerjerrod is in league with the sinister tyrant. Vader learns that Jerjerrod is in a private communication chamber talking to the Emperor, but Piett informs him that all surveillance in the room has been cut off and a special coded transmission is being used that is undecipherable. It is soon revealed that Vader's fears are correct:

49. INT. VADER'S STAR DESTROYER - COMMUNICATION CHAMBER
The Grand Moff Jerjerrod kneels before a huge holographic image of the Emperor.

THE EMPEROR
Take extra precautions. He is far stronger than his father.

JERJERROD
Yes, Master. We will have the boy quite soon.

THE EMPEROR
Vader is to know nothing of this. Young Skywalker must be brought directly to me. Do you understand?

JERJERROD
Yes Master.

THE EMPEROR
....and watch Lord Vader closely. He is powerful and not to be underestimated.

JERJERROD
Yes Master. He will be quite distracted. The Rebel attack is proceeding as you planned, and Lord Vader already suspects their presence. He has sent several units to the sanctuary moon.

THE EMPEROR
Good. Everything is falling into place.

JERJERROD
It is as you have foreseen, my Master.

The Grand Moff bows low, and [the] supreme Emperor passes a hand over the crouched Jerjerrod and fades away.

(The above scene also bears a striking similarity to one between General Grievous and Darth Sidious in *Revenge of the Sith*.)

After rescuing Han from Jabba the Hutt, Luke, Han, Lando and the droids travel to a spaceport to leave onboard the Falcon, a great sandstorm raging. In the confusion of the storm, Luke is ambushed and kidnapped. He awakens in a metallic cell onboard an Imperial transport, being brought to the Emperor. He begs out loud for Ben to help him but Yoda appears and reveals that Ben's power is drained and that he will soon become one with the Force. Luke says he cannot kill his father, and Yoda reveals that if Luke fails, his twin sister will be the only hope—Leia!

Luke is brought to Had Abbadon—however, Imperial officers loyal to Vader see Luke and realise that their Lord is being deceived. Luke meets the Emperor, who says Luke will soon turn to the dark side, but Luke defies him:

LUKE
You cannot turn me to the Dark Side as you did my father...

EMPEROR
I did not turn him to the Dark Side. That is something he did for himself...as you will do for yourself.

LUKE
Never!

EMPEROR
We will see. Take him to the tombs.

Meanwhile, Vader finds out that the Emperor has Luke. He becomes consumed with rage and confronts Jerjerrod. "What is the Emperor doing with my son?" he demands, but Jerjerrod instead states that Vader should stay away. Vader finally lifts Jerjerrod up by the throat and breaks his neck. He then storms towards the Imperial Palace to rescue Luke from the Emperor's clutches:

84. VADER'S PRIVATE CHAMBER - STAR DESTROYER

The door to the private chamber slides open, and the Dark Lord of the Sith storms into the room. His voice echoes through the chamber.

VADER
Jerjerrod!

JERJERROD
(V.O.)
It is not necessary to shout, my old friend.

VADER
What is the Emperor doing with my son...

JERJERROD
My Lord Vader, the Emperor does not have to answer to you... besides, I don't believe he has your son. Where did you come by this piece of erroneous information?

VADER
He's been seen at the palace...and that's where I'm going!

JERJERROD
The Emperor would prefer you didn't...you would go against his wishes. The Rebel attack is about to begin. You are truly fearless, my old friend.

Vader lifts the Grand Moff by the neck and begins to lift him off the ground with one hand; Jerjerrod gasps for air and struggles to free himself from the Dark Lord's iron grip.

VADER
You are not my friend, bureaucrat. I will go to the palace, but you will not live to see it. I no longer wish to be annoyed by your simpering ways.

JERJERROD
The Emperor will destroy you for this.

Vader snaps the man's neck, and he drops to the floor in a heap.

VADER
I think not...your importance has been greatly exaggerated.

As before, this is a revolutionary turn for Vader's character. As the film progresses, he becomes a character of equal importance to Luke, and one much more interesting. In fact, in this scene, he becomes a bizarre sort of hero, killing the Emperor's minions to save his son.

Luke meanwhile is in the tombs. Here, the underground lava setting from the rough draft is reprised—Luke awakens on a small island on a lake of lava. Luke turns around to see Obi Wan—in the flesh! He says that he and Yoda will help him defeat the Emperor and Vader, but Luke protests that he still cannot kill his own father.

Meanwhile, Vader marches on the Emperor's palace to save Luke. He storms the fortress, killing Imperial guards who stand in his way and forces his way into the throne room, finally confronting the Emperor about his betrayal—but the Emperor begins choking Vader with the Force until he finally submits to him:

97. INT. THRONE ROOM - HAD ABBADON
Vader storms into the throne room and marches right up to where the Emperor is sitting. The Emperor slowly raises his head to stare at the Dark Lord.

VADER
Where is he?

EMPEROR
Safe...There is no need for you to worry. I will take good care of him...

VADER
It is for me to train my son...you must...

The Emperor raises his hand, and Vader's breathing suddenly stops. The Dark Lord struggles at his controls, attempting to regain his air supply. He chokes.

EMPEROR
You forget yourself...Lord Vader. I will tolerate no more discussion on the subject. The boy is mine to train. Your place is with the fleet.

Vader collapses on the floor and the Emperor lowers his hand. Vader starts breathing again and rises to a kneeling position.

VADER
Forgive me, master.

EMPEROR
The Rebels will soon begin their attack. You must be ready for them. For now that I have all of them in one place, they will be crushed once and for all.

VADER
Yes, my master.

EMPEROR
Now take your leave, for I have your son to attend to.

Vader rises and exits the throne room, and the giant door slides closed behind him.

This scene is pivotal in Vader's character development. We finally see the power of control the Emperor has over Vader—Vader's servitude to him is revealed as not a partnership of evil, as the previous films had portrayed it as, but a rather tragic one of unwilling obedience.

Soon after this scene, the Emperor travels down the elevator to confront Luke in the tombs. Vader watches from the shadows, secretly following him down there. The Emperor arrives and sees Obi Wan with Luke. Yoda appears as a ghost, and the Emperor has a very curious reaction to him—"You!" he says in shock upon seeing the Jedi master. Lucas may have indeed have had in mind a previous confrontation between them, perhaps when the Emperor first seized power and destroyed the Jedi knights—a fact which we would not find out until 2005 (although Lucas would also later imply that the Emperor never even knew of Yoda's existence[29] and the novelisation implies that the Emperor only vaguely remembers him; apparently Lucas never really delved into Yoda's history when writing the films. Frank Oz recalled in *Starlog*, "I went through the scripts of *Star Wars* and *Empire*, writing down all the things that Yoda knew about Luke, what Luke knew about Yoda, what Yoda knew about Darth Vader, the Force and Obi Wan. I asked George Lucas at lunch one day for his thoughts on Yoda, and he said, 'Just make it wonderful.'"[30]).

Vader steps out of the shadows as the confrontation starts and joins his master. After the Emperor's treatment of him previously, we now view his siding with him as a much more pitiful action. Vader must obey his master, though he remains torn between the loyalties to him and his son. The Emperor orders Vader to kill Luke and gives him a lightsaber, and the battle ensues. As father and son duel, the Emperor tells Obi Wan that the boy will soon fall to the dark side; Obi Wan says he has foreseen the Emperor's death but the Emperor refuses to believe it. Luke fights his father across the lava rocks with all his strength and gives into his anger, finally forcing Vader to fall, his arm slipping into the lava. The Emperor goads Luke to finish him off, telling him it is the power of the dark side that he feels, but Luke refuses, tossing away his lightsaber and saying "if he is to be destroyed, you must do it."

The Emperor turns and fires lightning at Obi Wan but Luke jumps in front of him, and Yoda shields Luke as in the previous draft. Luke soon begins to tire under the strain of the Emperor's power, but as his strength is about to disappear Vader runs at the Emperor to save Luke, and both Vader and the Emperor tumble into the lava and are destroyed:

EMPEROR
This is the power of the Dark Side that you deny. Your strength will never match it.

Luke struggles to remain conscious against the superior power of the Emperor.

LUKE
Yoda...

EMPEROR
Obi-Wan foresaw my destruction at your hands, young Skywalker, but it seems his vision was clouded...Perhaps there is still another Skywalker. Why can I not see, could the netherworld have influenced my perception? Another Skywalker...your father!

The Emperor turns around to see Lord Vader flying at him. The lightning bolts around Luke disappear as Vader hits the Emperor, knocking them both into the fiery lake of lava. The hideous screams of the Emperor are soon muted. Luke struggles to his feet and stares at the spot where his enemy and his father disappeared into the cauldron of molten rock.

Ben puts his hand on the young Jedi's shoulder.

BEN
It is in Yoda's hands now.

LUKE
He turned back to the good side.

BEN
Yes, he did.

Vader finally chooses to turn on his master once and for all when he sees his son in danger, and dies killing the Emperor. Once again, as in the rough draft, his final sacrifice is rather glazed over and not as poignant as in the final film, but his motivation leading up to it is developed enough that his action is still quite powerful.

As the Rebels celebrate, Luke talks to Ben, and Yoda appears as flesh and blood. His stay in the Netherworld has ended since Vader has turned to the good side and he has been able to save Vader's spirit and allow him to retain his identity. Annikin appears, and they all join the celebration, except for Yoda, who watches them all from the side:

> Quietly watching the festivities from the side is Yoda, the Jedi Master. He scans the crowd picking out Artoo, Threepio, Lando and Chewie, Han and Leia, and finally Ben, Luke and his father. He lets out a great sigh.

END CREDITS

The script is perhaps the most important piece in the development of Anakin Skywalker and the prequel trilogy. Darth Vader's characterisation is turned on its head, and he finally becomes the tragic figure he would later be known as.

The rough draft introduced the first instances of the humanised Vader, but he was not yet a truly sympathetic character, and still retained his villain-like personality for much of the film. This time, in the *revised* rough draft, he was brought to the foreground and turned into a tragic hero. However, it seems Lucas thought this revised rough draft humanised him too much. The next draft—which would be called the second draft—would downplay Vader and his role as a sympathetic character.

### Gatherings

With the revised rough draft completed on June 12th, 1981, Lawrence Kasdan stepped in to finish what Lucas started. Kasdan had since become a regular Lucas collaborator, first on *Raiders of the Lost Ark* and then on *Empire Strikes Back*, and was hired to co-write the subsequent drafts in preparation for the film's shooting. Kasdan was ready to retire from screenwriting and concentrate on directing, but with the release date drawing near and much work to do, Lucas was in need of a writer again and Kasdan was willing to help out the man who gave him his career.

Design work was already underway, with the art department commencing work on locations, vehicles and creatures for the film. Lucas wouldn't have as much time to dedicate to the writing, as production on the film was beginning, and so he relied on the creative crew to do the actual work while he supervised and guided the overall shape of the film.

When the revised rough draft was completed, before he had even hired his co-writer, Lucas needed to find a director for the film. At first he considered directing the picture himself. "I took one look at the amount of work and thought, 'Oh my god, my life is complicated enough.'"[31]

Perhaps not surprisingly, Irvin Kershner was not asked to return. Kershner speaks in a 2004 interview:

*Why didn't Lucas have you direct Return of the Jedi?*

Kershner: For two reasons: One, I didn't want to. Two, I was asked halfway through shooting *Empire*, and by that time I knew that *Jedi* would be a three-year project. It took two years and nine months for me to do *Empire*, and I didn't want to go through that again. Also, I didn't think it was good to do two for George. I didn't want to be a Lucas employee. And I'd read the script of *Jedi*—not the whole script, but a scaled-down version—and I didn't believe it.[32]

It has been said that Lucas' first choice was Steven Spielberg, but since Lucas was operating independently and had quit the Hollywood unions after *Empire* it was impossible for Spielberg to helm the film since he was a union member. David Lynch was approached, but the young visionary turned it down, essentially due to authorial issues—"Obviously, *Star Wars* is totally George's thing,"[33] Lynch stated, and he instead went on to make the more personalised *Dune*. Lucas then turned to Welsh director Richard Marquand, best known for the tense war drama *Eye of the Needle*. Following the large control issues on *Empire*, Lucas wanted a team that he knew could give him what he wanted, and wouldn't want to impose their own "vision" on the film—the movie would be Lucas'. "You're working for George—it's his story, his baby," *Jedi* producer Howard Kazanjian said. "It's his child, so you're representing his wishes."[34] *American Cinematographer* reported in 1983:

Since Lucas chose not to direct *Return of the Jedi* himself, there was an extensive search conducted for a director who would mesh well with Lucas and his approach to the film...[Says producer Kazanjian:] "We were looking for a director that was rather young, that was flexible, that had not established himself as a great independent filmmaker, that would follow the tradition of *Star Wars*, that would let George be as closely attached as he likes to be on these projects."[35]

Someone easy to keep a finger on in other words. But Marquand saw it another way, comparing his relationship to Lucas to that of an orchestra conductor to a composer.[36] He admitted though, "It is rather like trying to direct *King Lear*—with Shakespeare in the next room."[37] Gary Kurtz believes that Lucas' failure with *Empire Strikes Back*'s production led him to ultimately select a more controllable director, as he tells *IGN Film Force*:

> George, I think, had in the back of his mind that the director was a sort of stand-in–that he could phone him up every night and tell him what to do and kind of direct vicariously over the telephone. That never happened [on *Empire Strikes Back*]. Kershner's not that kind of director, and even when George showed up a couple of times on the set, he found that it wasn't easy to manoeuvre Kershner into doing what he would have done. So, on *Jedi*, he was determined to find a director who was easy to control, basically, and he did. And that was the result, basically–the film was sort of one that George might have directed if he had directed it himself.[38]

Director Richard Marquand also had aesthetic ideas that were different from the beautiful cinematic storytelling of Kershner's film. Marquand explained in 1983:

> I like the way George has made the three movies that he's actually directed. He's a very deceptively simple stylist...That's part of what makes *Star Wars* so available to children, and I wanted to go back to that sort of presentation on *Jedi* rather than the highly sophisticated, sexy way in which Kershner made *Empire*, which I enjoyed—I thought it looked like an incredible, glossy, glorious sort of machine—but I prefer the other way.[39]

Mark Hamill concurred that same year:

> We went back to that smash-and-grab technique, which was also used for *Raiders*. The energy generated when you get that kind of rhythm going is terrific. They say, "Okay, we can't spend all day on this! Do another take, and if we can't get it, let's move on!" Rather than slapdash, the technique creates its own momentum. That kinetic energy made *Star Wars*. The pace on *Empire* was more leisurely. Also, Yoda and the technical problems slowed it down. We were over-schedule almost six weeks, which added a lot to the budget. George was very unhappy. With *Jedi*, he felt we should return to the *Star Wars* style. Just go, go, go![40]

Lucas planned to be on set nearly every day to personally supervise the filming, and would direct second-unit material and even portions of the main unit material. In fact, one urban legend states that on the set of *Jedi* some of the crew were initially confused as to who was really the director. Carrie Fisher once related a story where Marquand gave her one direction and then Lucas came up and gave her contradicting direction, and in a visit to the set Dale Pollock related how Lucas checked through the lens to approve most shots and was observed moving cameras around and selecting angles.[41] To this day there is long-standing controversy over whose film it really is. Lucas was also determined not to repeat the same cost overruns that had occurred on *Empire Strikes Back*; with a projected budget of $32 million—all of it fronted by Lucas himself—the film had no major schedule or budgetary issues, largely due to the meticulous planning of producer Kazanjian. The release date was set before a script was ever written—in a race against the clock to get the film finished on time, careful planning was essential.

With a solid script ready in rough draft form, Lucas began having story meetings with Kasdan, Marquand and producer Howard Kazanjian, from July 13th to July 17th, 1981.[42] Kasdan recollected the experience to *Star Wars Insider*:

> I had already directed *Body Heat*, I was about to direct *The Big Chill*, and I wasn't writing for anyone else anymore. But George had been really helpful to me, and he said, "Will you do me this one favour? I really need your help." Richard Marquand was already involved, and we had a very similar situation [to *Empire*]—very intense. George had written the previous draft, and we did it really quick, with Richard, and nailed it down.[43]

During these story meetings, Lucas' draft was hammered out until it resembled what appears in the final film. A number of ideas were dropped, expanded or altered, and each of the participants brought ideas and suggestions to the script. The conferences were taped, and when it was all over Kasdan was left with a voluminous transcript containing all the rejected ideas and agreed-upon decisions about how the script should be structured.[44]

Many minor yet still important details were added to the script. The obvious thought of having Leia rescue Han was added, instead of having her uncharacteristically wait on the Green Moon (to be renamed Endor) as had been the case with Lucas' drafts, with Leia now infiltrating Jabba's palace in the disguise of a bounty hunter.

Much of the character relationships with Luke were expanded in the second draft. One of the most significant of these was Yoda and Obi Wan's. Firstly, Marquand felt that Yoda's absence from the film was a let-down, since he dies off-screen and only appears briefly as a ghost, and

Luke's vow to return to his training was set-up so strongly in *Empire Strikes Back*.[45] Lucas agreed with this inclusion—it also made the exposition less awkward, since Yoda does not simply appear and give Luke information.

Obi Wan also needed a more graceful resolution, and a scene was written in which he appears to Luke after Yoda dies and fills in the missing pieces of information. "During story conferences George Lucas suggested that Lawrence Kasdan write a great scene for Alec Guinness with powerful Shakespearian dialog," Laurent Bouzereau reported in *The Annotated Screenplays*.[46] In this scene, Obi Wan could quickly do away with the expository information needed to tie up the loose ends. However, Kasdan gave the scene a more satisfying emotional payoff. Perhaps more significant was the extensive dialogue that was excised from the final film, in which Obi Wan talks much about Anakin Skywalker and his relationship to him.

Ben says that when he first met Luke's father he was already a great pilot, and was amazed at his connection to the Force. Ben reveals he was arrogant and thought he could train the young man as well as Yoda. Kenobi failed, as Anakin turned to the dark side. He battled Anakin on the edge of a volcano and thought he had killed Anakin, but Anakin survived and when he was healed he became Darth Vader. Ben is filled with regret and sadness over his actions—now the entire galaxy is suffering for his arrogance, and his foolishness has cost many billions of people their lives. This would be emphasized even more in the third draft.[47]

Obi Wan Kenobi, the noble Jedi presented as a clear-cut good guy, the saintly Holy One in contrast to the villainous Dark Invader, is revealed to be a tragic figure as well, a man who is suffering with the guilt of his failure. His one hope at redemption thus becomes the training of Luke to destroy Vader and the Emperor and undo the damage he has inflicted upon the galaxy. The character took on a new dimension, a much deeper and complex one in which he is a troubled soul—once again, the saga had taken another step away from its simple fairy tale roots to a more serious, complex narrative in which all the characters are tragic figures with grave secrets and painful flaws.

This notion of Obi Wan having trained Anakin was a major change from the original pre-1978 conception, where they both embarked on their adventure together and were simultaneously trained.*

---

* In the second draft of *Empire Strikes Back* Yoda reveals that he trained both Obi Wan *and* Father Skywalker; however, the *revised* second draft altered the history considerably: it was

Lucas had since come up with a new history for Luke's father, which Ben briefly outlines to Luke, detailing how as the Emperor rose to power he sensed Anakin's potential and gradually lured him to the dark side. That name is also significant—the name Anakin, as opposed to Annikin, is used. Some say Lucas developed the name in tribute to Ken Annakin, a director and supposed-friend of his; another origin may be the Scandinavian language, where the name "Annikin" or "Anniken" means "favour" or "grace" and is not uncommon as a (female) first name; a third speculative origin is the Biblical "Anakim," who were a feared race of giants descendant from Anak.

Information on Luke's mother also surfaces for the first time. Lucas finally decided on a timeline to the discrepancy of Vader's knowledge of his children—he never knew his wife was pregnant, and she and Obi Wan worked together to hide them from him. This leads one to then assume that Vader learns of Luke's existence off-screen, logically between the time of *Star Wars* and *Empire Strikes Back*.

Obi Wan also reveals that uncle Owen was really his brother. It was decided during story meetings that they were related, and that Owen always resented Ben for imposing Luke on him.[48] This fascinating scene revealed much of the saga's history which would be explored in the prequels. It is unknown if the extended version of this scene was ever filmed:

BEN
Luke, you're going to find that many
of the truths we cling to depend greatly
on our own point of view.

*Luke is unresponsive. Ben studies him in silence for a moment.*

BEN
I don't blame you for being angry.
If I was wrong in what I did, it
certainly wouldn't have been for the first time.
You see, what happened to your
father was my fault.

---

revealed that Yoda trained Obi Wan, who then trained Father Skywalker. This was presumably done because the initial second draft forgot to account for the fact that since Father Skywalker was now also Darth Vader he would also have been Obi Wan's student.

*Ben pauses sadly.*

BEN
Anakin was a good friend.

*Luke turns with interest at this. As Ben speaks, Luke settles on a stump, mesmerized. Artoo comes over to offer his comforting presence.*

BEN
When I first knew him, your father
was already a great pilot. But I was
amazed how strongly the Force was with him.
I took it upon myself to train him as a Jedi.
I thought that I could instruct him just
as well as Yoda. I was wrong.
My pride has had terrible
consequences for the galaxy.

*Luke is entranced.*

LUKE
There's still good in him.

BEN
I also thought he could be turned
back to the good side. It couldn't be done.
He is more machine now than man.
Twisted and evil.

LUKE
I can't do it, Ben.

BEN
You cannot escape
your destiny.
[...]
Vader humbled you when first you
met him, Luke...but that experience was
part of your training. It taught you,
among other things, the value of
patience. Had you not been so impatient
to defeat Vader then, you could have
finished your training here with Yoda.
You would have been prepared.
[...]

To be a Jedi, Luke, you must confront
and then go beyond the dark side -
the side your father couldn't get past.
Impatience is the easiest door - for you,
like your father. Only, your father was seduced
by what he found on the other side of
the door, and you have held firm.
You're no longer so reckless now, Luke.
You are strong and patient. And now,
you must face Darth Vader again!

Luke then asks about the "Other" that Yoda spoke of, which results in
a much more detailed history of Leia to be given:

LUKE
Leia! Leia's my sister.

BEN
Your insight serves you well.
Bury your feelings deep down, Luke.
They do you credit. But they
could be made to serve the Emperor.

*Luke looks into the distance, trying to comprehend all this.*

BEN
(continuing his narrative)
When your father left, he didn't know
your mother was pregnant. Your mother
and I knew he would find out eventually,
but we wanted to keep you both as safe
as possible, for as long as possible.
So I took you to live with my brother
Owen on Tatooine... and your mother took
Leia to live as the daughter of
Senator Organa, on Alderaan.

*Luke turns, and settles near Ben to hear the tale.*

BEN
(attempting to give solace with his words)
The Organa household was high-born
and politically quite powerful in that system.
Leia became a princess by virtue of lineage...

no one knew she'd been adopted, of course.
But it was a title without real power,
since Alderaan had long been a democracy.
Even so, the family continued to be politically
powerful, and Leia, following in her foster
father's path, became a senator as well.
That's not all she became, of course...
she became the leader of her cell in the
Alliance against the corrupt Empire.
And because she had diplomatic immunity,
she was a vital link for getting information to
the Rebel cause. That's what she was doing
when her path crossed yours...for her foster
parents had always told her to contact
me on Tatooine, if her
troubles became desperate.

*Luke is overwhelmed by the truth, and is suddenly protective of his sister.*

LUKE
But you can't let her get involved
now, Ben. Vader will destroy her.

BEN
She hasn't been trained in the ways
of the Jedi the way you have, Luke...
but the Force is strong with her,
as it is with all of your family.
There is no avoiding the battle.
You must face and destroy Vader!

Obi Wan's line "So what I have told you is true...from a certain point of view" was the best Lucas could do to excuse the obvious contradictions in the films, despite the fact that it was somewhat clumsy and unconvincing. But with all of the plot trappings Lucas had ensnared himself in, it really was the best he could do.

Luke's revelation to Leia about their relationship was also given much more dramatic impact. Instead of revealing it to her at the very end of the film, an entire scene was written around it, where Luke tells her everything and says he will be surrendering to Darth Vader. During story meetings Leia was judged as being too hard, and it was suggested that she become emotional when Luke reveals that she's his sister—perhaps she could start crying and tell him that they should run away and hide from everything. In the second draft the scene was played more dramatic, with Luke leaving Leia in tears. In the revised second draft, Han Solo consoles her afterwards.[49] Lucas admitted: "It's one thing for Darth Vader to tell Luke that he's his father, and it's another thing to have Luke tell Leia that he is her sister and that Darth Vader's his father. That really gets hard to swallow."[50]

There was also a brief mention of Mother Skywalker. In this scene, Luke asks Leia about their mother, for he has no memory of her—she describes her fleeting recollections of her as "very beautiful. Kind, but sad." It seems Lucas had decided that Mother Skywalker accompanied Leia to Alderaan, but soon passed away, whereupon Bail Organa raised her—as Kenobi explains to Luke on Dagobah, "Your mother took Leia to live as the daughter of Senator Organa, on Alderaan." *The Annotated Screenplays* states:

> Ben reveals to Luke that he has a twin sister and that they were separated; Luke was sent to stay with Ben's brother, Owen, on Tatooine, while his sister and mother were sent to the protection of friends in a distant system. The mother died shortly thereafter, and Luke's sister was adopted by Ben's friends, the governor of Alderaan and his wife.[51]

In this version, Obi Wan sent Leia and Mother Skywalker to a group of friends in a distant system *and then* the governor of Alderaan adopted Leia once Mother Skywalker died; in this early version, attributed to draft two, a second group of protectors is in the mix. The details on Mother Skywalker were never full developed by Lucas; he stated in *The Annotated Screenplays*:

> The part I never really developed was the death of Luke and Leia's mother. I had a backstory for her in earlier drafts, but it basically didn't survive. When I got to *Jedi*, I wanted one of the kids to have some kind of memory of her because she will be a key figure in the new episodes I'm writing. But I really debated on whether or not Leia should remember her.[52]

The earliest drafts of *Star Wars* briefly mentioned her but not much was divulged other than she was dead. In the second draft Luke fondly remembers his mother, who has long since died, and dearly misses her—her body is buried on a hill on the moisture farm, marked by a headstone, which Luke visits in one scene and speaks aloud to (later to be incorporated into *Attack of the Clones*). As Lucas says, the earlier backstory of her didn't survive to the *Return of the Jedi* era—because Lucas had completely altered Skywalker family history with his fusion of Father Skywalker and

Darth Vader in 1978.

One of the big issues was whether or not the heroes should escape the series unscathed. Lawrence Kasdan felt that the film lacked any real gravity, and that one of the main characters should be killed off, perhaps in the beginning of the final act in order to put doubt in the audience's mind that there will be a happy ending. "I also felt someone had to go. Someone had to die," Kasdan related. "And I thought it should happen very early in the last act so that you would begin to worry about everybody."[53] Kasdan also made the suggestion that perhaps Luke could die and his sister take over, but Lucas protested, arguing how upset he was as a child when a hero was killed.[54] Harrison Ford thought it would be best if Han Solo was killed off. Ford explained in the documentary *Empire of Dreams*:

> I thought Han Solo should die. I thought he ought to sacrifice himself for the other two characters...I said "he's got no mama, he's got no papa, he's got no future, he has no story responsibilities at this point, so let's allow him to commit self-sacrifice."[55]

It would have been the natural culmination of his character's arc—a selfish loner who learns the value of friendship and finally makes the ultimate act of giving his own life to save another's. But Lucas disagreed—he wanted a fairy tale happy ending:

> It would really have put an unfortunate twist on everything if we had killed off one of the main characters. Luke needed to live, and we needed to have Han and Leia together at the end. The fact that the boy gets the girl—or the girl gets the boy—in the end was a key factor and was as important as Luke overcoming his demons.[56]

Kasdan had another suggestion where Luke pretends to join the Emperor. According to *The Annotated Screenplays*, Luke could pretend to join the dark side and put on Vader's mask; the Emperor would then take him to the Death Star controls and tell him to destroy the fleet but instead Luke aims it at Had Abbadon and fires.[57] Obviously, this strange twist didn't make it far.

During the story conference sessions, the movie was also scaled down significantly. In an effort to one-up the original film, Lucas had initially written two Death Stars into the film—Kasdan suggested they be combined into a single threat.[58] Had Abbadon was also dropped entirely. Instead, all of the action was moved onto the Death Star, with the Emperor arriving to supervise its construction and direct the attack on the Rebels. Rather than spread the action out over three separate threats (Had Abbadon and the two Death Stars), they were combined into one single element.

"In the end it didn't seem necessary to show the home planet of the Empire," Lucas said to Bouzereau. "It seemed more important that we focus on the major target of what we were going after in the movie. So to show Vader and the Emperor in an area that didn't relate to the story didn't seem necessary."[59] Budgetary issues may have also been motivating the elimination of this location, as the script was written to be made on a budget of $25-30 million.[60]

### *The Resolution of Darth Vader*

Lucas at this point was still undecided about how Vader's persona should be portrayed—he would write many variations on him, trying to peg down just how to characterise him. The rough draft had him as a humanised villain, while in the revised rough draft he would be a tragic figure; the second draft *unmasks* him, and does not have him appearing in spirit or flesh form post-death, while the third draft would reveal him to be a hideous mutant, as he had been since *Star Wars*. There is some interesting discussion to be had regarding the age of Darth Vader. Due to the fact that his character literally became different people as the series progressed, Vader's age, as well as that of Obi Wan, changed drastically. This is explored in detail in chapter X. Suffice it to say, although Darth began as roughly forty years old in *Star Wars*, after he was turned into Father Skywalker, he became an old man of nearly Obi Wan's age—and when finally unmasked, portrayed by seventy-seven year-old Sebastian Shaw

There was one last plot point that needed to be worked out—the resolution of Darth Vader and his son. In Lucas' scripts, Vader saves Luke by sacrificing himself in a kamikaze assault on the Emperor, but there was little development on Luke's end and the entire father-son dynamic never had a real resolution ("He turned good," Luke says. "Yes," Ben replies, "he did." That was it). Kazanjian said in 1983:

> George Lucas did a first draft screen play—one he sort of doesn't admit doing—which laid down the plots, story, and characters. It wasn't quite resolved in the last fifth of the movie, but we all knew what was happening.[61]

For the second draft, the redemption of Vader was to be seen mostly from Luke's perspective, instead of Vader's as it had been in the rough drafts; the script was edited so that it focused more on Luke and his quest to bring his father back into the light instead of Vader trying to save his son. This better re-aligned the film into the overall series—Vader's redemption was merely a sub-plot, and it existed not as an issue unto itself but as a personal goal of Luke's, the finale of his journey as a Jedi as he finally makes peace with his father. The plot surrounding Jerjerrod and the Emperor scheming against Vader was also eliminated from the film, taking away much of Vader's sympathy and character—he became much more ambiguous in terms of loyalties, and was hence more threatening. The Emperor was given more scenes, and the focus was shifted towards Luke being tempted to the dark side—for instance, the scene in which Luke gives in to his anger and defeats Vader was given more importance and gravity, putting emphasis on Luke's subsequent emotional triumph as he succeeds where his father failed and refuses the Emperor.

With the newly written scene involving Obi Wan on Dagobah, Luke was armed with intimate information on Vader's past, which he could in turn use against him to lure him back to the light side of the Force. In the first rough draft Luke surrenders to the Imperials on the Green Moon and is taken to Vader onboard his Star Destroyer, where Vader tries to tempt Luke to join the dark side. The scene was reprised onboard an Imperial landing platform on Endor for the second draft, but with Luke now possessing the knowledge that Vader was once the noble Jedi Anakin Skywalker, creating a new dynamic in which Vader must confront the knowledge that he was once good—planting the first seeds towards his eventual turn.

Luke was now given a fundamental change of character related to this arc; he enters the film believing that Vader still has good in him. While Obi Wan's spirit had tried to bargain with Vader to turn away from the dark side in Lucas' revised rough draft, Luke would now take up this thread, with a more emotional motivation in which he believes he can save his father (though for such an about-face in character from *Empire*, it is rather odd that Luke's epiphany is left entirely between the films).

Vader had become more villainized than the previous draft, in which it was probably felt that he was too soft, but once he had turned a final scene of resolution had to address the fact that Vader had become good again. With the action occurring on the Death Star and not the lava pits of Had Abbadon, Vader disposes of the Emperor by tossing him down a nearby reactor core—but instead of tumbling down with him, Vader survives. He would at last say a final goodbye to his son, now turned away from the dark side. After much deliberation, Lucas decided to finally unmask Darth Vader and reveal the man inside, the ultimate act in exploring the character. Lucas explained to Laurent Bouzereau:

I didn't have a very specific idea about what Vader might look like underneath the mask. I knew that he had been in a lot of battles, and at one point I thought that he had had a confrontation with Ben and Ben had sent him into a volcano. But he was all but dead, and basically he was manufactured back together even though there was very little left of him. So he is kind of this three-quarter mechanical man and one-quarter human, and the suit he wears is like a walking iron lung. By the time we got to the third film, we were able to articulate what Vader looked like underneath the mask, but until then I just knew that he was pretty messed up simply because he could barely breathe or speak.[62]

Previously, he had been thought of as a hideous monster, and Lucas claimed in 1977 that he even considered filming a shot of Vader's deformed face for the first film.[63] Irvin Kershner of course had a similar vision of Vader, especially since it had been discussed in story meetings that Darth Vader was a horrible mutant.[64] He even gave the world the first glimpse of Vader's true figure in a memorable moment in *Empire Strikes Back*. Kershner stated in *The Annotated Screenplays*:

I shot this scene very carefully. When the captain comes in and Vader is sitting in his capsule with his back towards us, all you see are scars on the back of his neck for a second. I didn't want the audience to see anything else. I imagined that beneath the mask Vader was hideous; his mouth was cut away, and he had one eye hanging low. I was very surprised to see that he was an ordinary man in the third film.[65]

But with the plot of *Revenge of the Jedi* now revolving around Vader being redeemed and humanised, the former monstrous depiction of him was no longer viable. There would be many variations experimented with, as *The Annotated Screenplays* describes:

Luke taking off his father's helmet became a real issue during story meetings. One problem was that by taking the helmet off, Luke might seem to be killing his father, who can't breathe without the helmet. It was suggested Luke take the helmet off after his father dies. At the same time George Lucas explained that Vader wants to see his son in a human way, without any machinery, and also suggested that Vader's voice should change once the helmet has been taken off to a much weaker version of the same thing, something much older-sounding. Luke's father should be in his sixties, about ten years younger than Ben. He should be a continuation of what we saw of him in the *Empire Strikes Back*. He should be sad-looking, not repulsive. Maybe one of his eyes could be completely white with no pupil and the other could be sort of clouded over. Lawrence Kasdan suggested that he might have a light grey beard to give him a little normality.

In the second draft Anakin is described as an elderly man with a scarred face and a white beard. In the third draft the description is a bit more gruesome, suggesting that Vader is a horrible mutant, hardly recognizable as human.[66]

Finally, he would be revealed as a sad old man—bald and scarred from his injuries, and pale from having not seen natural light in decades. He weakly smiles at Luke before saying "you were right about me"…and then gracefully dies. The revised rough draft had first introduced Vader as tragic hero, and now starting with the second draft he is explicitly redeemed.

A schedule devised in early 1981 proposed that the final script should be delivered by September of that year,[67] though *Jedi*'s would in fact arrive late. "The screenplay is the blueprint for everything, and without it you tend to flounder a bit," producer Robert Watts said in *The Making of Return of the Jedi*. "We'd had indications, we'd had discussions, we'd had drafts, but the final script did come very, very late."[68] Though Kasdan's second draft was on time for September of 1981, revisions on it continued until November, and a third draft was written for December.

While filming began in January of 1982, the scene where Luke gives in to his anger and strikes down Vader still had not been written with clear motivation on Luke's part, but Lucas suggested a change that would more smoothly integrate the Leia-as-sister plot point into the storyline. He remembered in a 1983 interview:

Richard [Marquand] was trying to block out the fight between Luke and Vader, and we got down to that point underneath the throne room there, and he said the script sort of said "Vader says something that upsets Luke" or something vague like that…and I had never really come up with a satisfactory answer to that, of what he could possibly say that would set Luke off. And in the process of evolving the script and evolving the importance of Leia as the sister—you know, it was sitting right there in front of my face. And it became obvious that turning her to the dark side would be the thing that would set Luke off again.[69]

A scene would then be added in pick-up shooting in which Luke burns his father's body, adding both resolution and a poignant, sacrificial touch to the Vader subplot. "It gave more closure in terms of Luke's relationship to his father and letting go of his father," Lucas said.[70] Editor Duwayne Dunham said, "I remember that we said, 'what happened to Vader? Did Luke leave him on the Death Star?' So the scene was shot up at Skywalker Ranch."[71]

The *Return of the Jedi* novelisation contained numerous references to Anakin's past that did not appear in any of the scripts. Obi Wan tells of The

Duel:

> You should not think of that machine as your father...When I saw what had become of him, I tried to dissuade him, to draw him back from the dark side. We fought...your father fell into a molten pit. When your father clawed his way out of that fiery pool, the change had been burned into him forever—he was Darth Vader, without a trace of Anakin Skywalker. Irredeemably dark. Scarred. Kept alive only by machinery and his own black will.[72]

Finally, Vader's last thoughts as he lays dying make another reference to being burned by lava:

> These were memories he wanted none of, not now. Memories of molten lava, crawling up his back...no.
>     This boy had pulled him from that pit—here, now, with this act. This boy was good.[73]

With that, Darth Vader's character had been finally written and sealed, and *Star Wars* was over. What began as a modest and light-hearted adventure film, made as a homage to the science fiction fantasy serials of the 1930s and told as a witty coming-of-age odyssey, had since progressed to a much grander narrative of failure and redemption—and a character who had started out as nothing more than a black-hatted villain, an inconsequential henchman, had since grown into a fallen angel, one who finally finds redemption in the love of his son. Finally, with *Return of the Jedi*, as the film's title would be changed to, Anakin Skywalker and Darth Vader had become the character we know today.

### Getting It Done

Lucas had also grown—he had grown from an eager wannabe-mogul, ready to helm a twelve-part serial based on his original story, to a man tired by the troubles and turmoil of the success of *Star Wars*. He had since abandoned his master scheme for a dozen films and ended it after only two subsequent episodes, too worn out to continue.

He wanted to wrap up the series as quickly, easily and cheaply as possible. With a director he could control, there would be no "artistic differences"—similar to the old Hollywood system, the money-controlling producer was calling the shots and directing the picture from a distance, although the "dirty work" of actually shooting the film and working the actors would be done by the official director, Richard Marquand. Lucas admits on the documentary *Empire of Dreams*:

> I hadn't realized that ultimately it's probably easier for me to do these things
> than to farm them out. Because [*Return of the Jedi*] was even more complex
> than the last one, I really did have to end up being there every day on the set,
> and working very closely with Richard, and shooting second unit, and there
> was really more work than I thought it was going to be.[74]

Lucas had a hectic shoot to supervise, with simultaneous shooting
around the world in order to ensure the pre-decided release date was met.
"We were constructing really in two places in California, shooting at
ILM—that's three—and of course working and shooting in London at the
same time," Kazanjian noted in *Empire of Dreams*.[75]

The *Star Wars* series had become an uncontrollable phenomenon by
then, and in order to avoid media attention when the movie came to the
United States for location shooting, it was filmed under the false title "Blue
Harvest," with the tagline "Horror Beyond Imagination."

But another title soon came about. With the release date looming, and
only a few weeks to go, the film was re-named.[76] No more was it *Revenge
of the Jedi*—it was now known as *Return of the Jedi*. Controversy
surrounds the motives behind this decision. Kazanjian offered his version
of the story in *Empire of Dreams*:

> George came to me and he said the title of Episode VI is *Return of the Jedi*.
> And I said, "I think it's a weak title." And he came one or two days later and
> he says "we're calling it *Revenge of the Jedi*."…Just before it got to the
> theatres, George came back and he said, "I want to go back to *Return of the
> Jedi*." Now, the logic behind that was a Jedi does not take revenge.[77]

*Time* Magazine critic Jay Cocks offers a similar tale in the 1997
television special *Star Wars: The Magic and Mystery*:

> We got some t-shirts from George in the mail, from the set, that said *Revenge
> of the Jedi* on them…After I started wearing these shirts around I saw George
> a couple months later and he said "Well you know, we're not doing that
> anymore," and I said "Why is that? What's the title?" and he said "*Return of
> the Jedi*." I said "What's the difference?" He said "Revenge isn't a Jedi
> concept."[78]

Lucas offers a curiously different version of the story in *Annotated
Screenplays*:

By the time we got down to doing the third film, we'd had so many difficulties with people trying to report stuff with the media and the press and everything that we called the film *Revenge of the Jedi* to throw people off. The title was always intended to be *Return of the Jedi*, but we made the film under the code name *Revenge of the Jedi*. Unfortunately, what happened is Fox started promoting the film before we could tell them not to use the title. We were lucky that they didn't start promoting the film under the title *Blue Harvest*, because we were also using that as a bogus title.[79]

This doesn't seem to make any sense though. The film was already operating under the code name *Blue Harvest*—why would it have two different code names? More importantly, it makes even less sense to call it *Revenge of the Jedi* to deceive the media; no one would doubt that a film called "Revenge of the *Jedi*" was the next *Star Wars* film. In fact, Lucasfilm itself had been promoting the film as such since May 1980. Lucas had been referring to it in private as *Revenge* ever since 1979,[80] and his own script drafts bore this name, as did call-sheets and other internal Lucasfilm documents. Everyone knew that it was the next *Star Wars* picture—which was why *Blue Harvest* was created. Production supervisor Jim Bloom explains that it was he who suggested they change the title to *Blue Harvest*, due to issues related to being overcharged on equipment fees.[81]

Just as well, a one word difference was hardly anything exciting, and all it did was confuse fans and retailers. Paramount Studios certainly must have been—their latest *Star Trek* picture was to be called *The Vengeance of Khan* but when it was announced in 1980 that *Star Wars III* would be called *Revenge of the Jedi*, the film was re-named *The Wrath of Khan* to avoid confusion.

Dale Pollock reported a similarly weird explanation, this one dating back to the time of the film's release in 1983:

Although *Revenge of the Jedi* was the first title announced, Lucas always intended for the film to be called *Return of the Jedi*. He just didn't want to give away the plot. The switch came no less than six months before *Jedi*'s release and cost several thousand dollars.[82]

What seems to have happened is that Lucas did indeed suggest *Return* as a possible title but at Kazanjian's recommendation changed it to *Revenge*. It wasn't intended as a "fake" or temporary title—it was Lucas' genuine choice. This was in 1979, when the focus of *Star Wars III* was to be Luke and Rebels fighting back after their defeat in *Empire Strikes Back*. However, as the actual script to *Revenge of the Jedi* began to be written, it eventually evolved to being about Luke redeeming Darth Vader—and thus the vengeance angle of the script was no longer present, and made Lucas realise that an aggressive motive like revenge would not even be a Jedi trait in the first place. Later drafts experimented with the original "Return" variation but Lucas didn't commit to it, as *Revenge* continued to be used in official documents and private conversations.

As the release date began drawing nearer, however, Lucas began to have second thoughts. Steve Sansweet noted this in Lucasfilm's *The Vault*: "It's clear there had been an internal debate raging, with producer Howard Kazanjian favoring what he felt was the stronger *Revenge*, and George Lucas slowly coming to the conclusion that the word just didn't fit the movie."[83] Viewers realised this long before the film was released, as when Howard Kazanjian gave a *Revenge of the Jedi* presentation at Ireland's Octocon in 1982 fans apparently criticised him that Jedi don't take revenge.[84] In November 1982 Lucasfilm formally launched a market-research report on whether audiences would respond better to "Return" or "Revenge" of the Jedi. The report concluded that:

> While younger respondants are somewhat excited by the term revenge, many movie goers over 30 are turned off by its violent connotations. The implications of the term revenge do not fit the good guy/Jedi image as portrayed in the first two installments of the Star Wars saga. In conclusion, if the saga is to continue with the good versus evil theme it has delivered to date, return, rather than revenge might be more effective in communicating this message.[85]

The film was rushed to completion, ending up on time and on budget—in fact its release date was bumped ahead by two days to make it coincide with the release date of the original film. It had been six years since *Star Wars* was introduced to the world and cinema was in the midst of a reversal of the upheaval that had occurred in 1969, as executives began to take back film as a broad form of commercialism. Don Simpson and Jerry Bruckheimer were starting their careers, while Arnold Schwarzenegger, Sylvester Stallone and Eddie Murphy were breaking out into superstardom and the box office was being dominated by films such as *Friday the 13th Part 3*, *Flashdance*, *Superman III* and *Staying Alive,* a far cry from the days of *American Graffiti*, *Mean Streets* and *The Conversation*. The next year would bring hits such as *Beverly Hills Cop*, *Karate Kid*, *Police Academy*, *Purple Rain* and *Terminator*—as *Star Wars* bowed out, the '80s arrived in all its glory. Finally, on May 25th, 1983, the *Star Wars* trilogy came to an end.

# Chapter VIII: Endings

THERE was an air of relief as the film neared completion—the tiring saga was finally coming to a close. As Lucas reflected on what was to come next in his life, he knew one thing was for sure—it would not be more *Star Wars* films. Dale Pollock reported in early 1983:

> The most logical thing for George Lucas to do is direct more *Star Wars* movies, which is precisely what he won't do. He only completed the first trilogy, he says, because "I had a slight compulsion to finish the story." *Jedi* may be the last film George Lucas really cares about. He has little emotional investment in future Indiana Jones movies, or even in the next *Star Wars* trilogy, should it ever be made. Nothing will match the all-consuming sense of mission that he brought to the first three films.[1]

Lucas himself had finally had enough of the series—its hectic schedule had been all-consuming and taken over his entire life for the past six years. Dale Pollock reported on Lucas' frustrations:

> There are times when Lucas is ready to chuck the whole thing. Walking across Elstree Studios during the filming of *Jedi*, he fantasizes selling *Star Wars*—the concepts, the characters, and the plots for all six films.
>
> What if the inheritor of the *Star Wars* legacy screwed up and made a lousy movie? Wouldn't that be painful? Not at all, Lucas says. "I've always thought I did a bad job. This might make me feel better."...Later he admits that the

fantasy of dumping *Star Wars* is an escape valve, giving him the illusion he can always back out. "Emotionally, it would be very hard to do," he admits.[2]

Comments like these reflect Lucas' bitterness at the time. He had gone through much personal grief in the course of making the films; the small-town experimental filmmaker had grown into the biggest movie mogul on the planet and the Lucasfilm kingdom consumed his every waking hour. "I see [my daughter] a couple hours a night and maybe on Sundays if I'm lucky," he said at the time, "and I'm always real tired and cranky and feeling like, 'Gee, I should be doing something else.' I sort of speed through everything…It's been very hard on Marcia, living with someone who constantly is in agony; uptight and worried, off in never-never land."[3]

As Lucas admitted to *Time* in May 1983, just as *Return of the Jedi* achieved completion, the hectic and stressful making of the *Star Wars* trilogy had taken a personal toll on him:

> The sacrifice I've made for *Star Wars* may have been greater than I wanted…After *Graffiti*, *Star Wars* could have gone in the toilet and it wouldn't have mattered financially. It's an interesting choice I made, and now I'm burned out. In fact, I was burned out a couple of years ago, and I've been going on momentum ever since. *Star Wars* has grabbed my life and taken it over against my will. Now I've got to get my life back again—before it's too late![4]

The price of success could be seen in his personal life as well. As filmmakers will often bemoan, balancing a professional and personal life is a very difficult task. Lucas had been working around the clock since getting married in 1969, and becoming the head of an empire did not make things easier. He told *Starlog* in 1981:

> When I was in film school, it was 24-hours a day, seven days a week—that was all I thought about and did. I didn't do *anything* else! Then when I started working professionally and got married, I *had* to work all the time in order just to get anywhere. And I didn't have a vacation until I finished my first film and went to Europe. I had a couple of bucks in the bank, and I said, "It's now or never." My wife had been bugging me. I'd been at it for four or five years straight, and she said, "You can't go on like this." That was in 1973. I didn't have another vacation until 1977—when I went to Hawaii, after *Star Wars*.
>
> My wife likes to have vacations. She doesn't like not to be able to go anywhere, year in and year out. She'd like to be able to say, "Look, let's take off for two or three weeks and just cool out." So I *promised her* that after *Star Wars* every year we'd take two vacations—two to three weeks each year. That lasted for one year. Now, I try to get in one vacation a year, for a week or so, it always comes down to saying, "Next week. Just let me get past this thing…"

By the time you get past this thing, there's always something else, and you can't leave. Now, 1983 is my goal; I intend to take off for a year, if I can, and just not do anything. And that is why I'm not planning any other projects.[5]

By May 1983, on the eve of the release of *Return of the Jedi*, he seemed more miserable than ever, as he told Denise Worrell:

It is hard to describe the amount of detail, the amount of work involved [in making a film]. It's a three-year deadline with two years of really concentrated, serious work, ten to twelve hours a day, six days a week. There are periods of four or five months in those years [during shooting] when the work is sixteen to eighteen hours a day. You get not much more than five hours of sleep a night. And that's hard. On Sunday you're wiped out and you're still thinking about the movie. People usually don't understand the implications of what I'm saying, living this way, day after day, but it's awesome. You can do it for a couple of months, but year after year its gets to be grim. I've been doing it for god knows how long. It's more and more pressure and I'm more and more unhappy, and tired and exhausted and dragging home endless problems at the end of the day. I'm not having much fun. It's all work. It's very anxiety-ridden, very hard, very frustrating and relentless. The extent to which one's personal life is usurped cannot be overestimated. It has made me less of a happy person than I think I could be. It has disrupted my family life. I have a wife and a two-year-old daughter, and they are the most important things in my life. My family is it for me. Amanda is two years old now, and she's magic. She's this little girl and she ain't going to wait for me. She's going, she's growing. The last thing in the world I want is to turn around and have her be eighteen and say, "Hi, dad, where have you been all my life?"[6]

Dale Pollock's book, published in early 1983, offers some sad clues to the unhappy state of Lucas' marriage. In many instances, Marcia complains that George is always so busy that their personal life has become a struggle, and in a particularly sad moment she reflects on how unhappy their wealth has ultimately made her—an unpretentious woman used to living in small homes, she now was faced with a mansion so big that she had to depend on maids to clean it. She used to resent her rich friends when she was young but now she wears a large diamond ring and does her errands in a Mercedes Benz—for such a humble couple, coping with their fame was equally difficult for both of them. "I think some of the striving has been taken out of my life," she said quietly. "I was a great achiever, a self-made girl who started from nothing and worked hard and got rewarded. In a way, I regret having all those obstacles removed."[7] Perhaps the most telling sign of the state of their marriage comes from Marcia's observation of their current life: "Getting here was a lot more fun than being here."[8]

George and Marcia had just adopted a baby girl, Amanda, in 1981—adoption was a necessity due to the fact that George himself was diagnosed with infertility. Having been married since 1969, Marcia had wanted to slow down and start a family ever since then.[9] Their life had begun to grow out of control with the mega-success bestowed upon them in the last half-decade, and with Lucas sworn to have dictatorial control over his expanding empire and its films, there was little time left to enjoy real life. "For me, the bottom line was just that he was all work and no play," Marcia told Peter Biskind in 1997.[10] Their relationship had become strained, but, it seemed, they had made it through the worst of it and could finally resume their lives. But sadly, shortly after Pollock's book was published, and only weeks after the final *Star Wars* film opened, with Lucas hoping to finally be able to give his family more attention now that his saga was finished, the Lucases took a turn for the worst. George and Marcia got divorced.

As Lucas recalled with regret on the 2004 documentary, *Empire of Dreams*:

> The challenge is always trying to do something that is all-consuming with having a private life. And I had made the decision after *Star Wars* that I had certain goals in my private life. One was to be independent of Hollywood. The other one ultimately was to have a family. I finished *Return of the Jedi*; I figured that was the end of it for me. I figured that "Well I've done it, I've finished my trilogy." This is what I started out to do, this is what I was determined to get finished, and it was overwhelming and difficult but fate has a way of stepping in. I ended up getting divorced right as the film, *Jedi*, was finished, and I was left to raise my daughter.[11]

Early in June, 1983, Lucas called his staff into his office and as he and Marcia held hands, he informed them that they were divorcing after fifteen years of marriage.[12] His staff stared back in shock. The news was made public shortly after.

Just as it seemed that a new horizon was looming, Lucas' life suddenly came crashing down, his marriage unable to sustain itself to the completion of the film, and the icy tension that had existed beneath the quaint exterior of their relationship finally bubbled up in all its ugliness. Richard Walter saw the Lucases at a party at Randal Kleiser's house just before the divorce and recalled to John Baxter:

> I ended up in the corner with Marcia, chatting with her, and what she told me underscored a sense I'd always had that [intimacy] was not a gigantic part of

George's life… She just sort of blurted it out that it was extremely isolating; it was like Fortress Lucas. I'd heard this from people who worked with him at that time. They would say, "I can't stand it. He's brilliant, but it's so cold. I feel like I'm suffocating. I've got to get out of here." Marcia told me she "just couldn't stand the darkness any longer."[13]

Although he planned on semi-retiring to be with his wife and daughter it was too little too late—the emotional distance between them had been festering for some time, and in George's absence Marcia had already fallen in love with another man. With George off shooting *Return of the Jedi*, Lucas turned supervising the still-under-construction Skywalker Ranch to Marcia; the beautiful library was garnished with a stunning stained-glass domed roof, which was designed by an artist named Tom Rodriguez. Marcia began seeing him.[14]

Marcia's subsequent disappearance from Hollywood has left the event shrouded in much mystery but she revealed her side of the story in a rare interview for Peter Biskind's book *Easy Riders, Raging Bulls*:

I felt that we had paid our dues, fought our battles, worked eight days a week, twenty-five hours a day. I wanted to stop and smell the flowers. I wanted joy in my life. And George just didn't. He was very emotionally blocked, incapable of sharing feelings. He wanted to stay on that workaholic track. The empire builder, the dynamo. And I couldn't see myself living that way for the rest of my life.

I felt we were partners, partners in the ranch, partners in our home, and we did these films together. I wasn't a fifty percent partner, but I felt I had something to bring to the table. I was the more emotional person who came from the heart, and George was the more intellectual and visual, and I thought that provided a nice balance. But George would never acknowledge that to me. I think he resented my criticisms, felt that all I ever did was put him down. In his mind, I always stayed the stupid Valley girl. He never felt I had any talent, he never felt I was very smart and he never gave me much credit. When we were finishing *Jedi*, George told me he thought I was a pretty good editor. In the sixteen years of our being together I think that was the only time he complimented me.[15]

The divorce was significant not just for Lucas but for his films. Marcia had long been regarded as George's "secret weapon." Throughout the writing, shooting and editing of all his films, she would be there with him, giving him advice and keeping him down to earth when no one else would (or could). George Lucas met Marcia Griffin while on his first real job, working for legendary film editor Verna Fields; with an overflow of footage coming in, Fields needed a professional editor to help in the workload, and hired Marcia—because she was already a professional, Fields paired her up with the just-graduated film student Lucas.

The two were somewhat a pair of opposites, he calm and introverted while she feisty and social. Lucas' friends recall meeting her: "She was a knock-out," John Milius told Dale Pollock. "We all wondered how little George got this great looking girl. And smart too, obsessed with films. And she was a better editor than he was."[16] John Plummer couldn't quite figure out how someone as reserved as George was doing with such a strong-willed dynamo. Marcia said, "He's got a very childish, silly, fun side, but he doesn't even like me to talk about that because he is so intensely private."[17]

As a woman working in the film industry in the 1960s, she had to be strong-willed; having come from a poor family, she was a self-made woman. "'Marcia and I got along real well," Lucas noted to Pollock. "We were both feisty and neither one of us would take any shit from the other. I sort of liked that. I didn't like someone who could be run over."[18]

Marcia was a constant source of strength and encouragement for Lucas, and one of his strongest assets, though she was critical of both *THX 1138* and *Star Wars*, illustrating the fundamental aesthetic differences between herself and her husband. During the making of *Star Wars*, when many others dismissed the bizarre and hard-to-understand film, Marcia was one of the few who offered him useful criticism. Pollock reported:

> Marcia's faith never waivered—she was at once George's most severe critic and most ardent supporter. She wasn't afraid to say she didn't understand something in *Star Wars* or to point out the sections that bored her. Lucas got angry, but he knew Marcia was articulating his own suspicions. "I'm real hard," Marcia says, "but I only tell him what he already knows."
>
> She was also the only person to whom Lucas could vent his frustration. "A marriage where both people are in the same business and both are very strong is a challenge. You've got to go through a lot of changes," says George. Marcia's suggestions were among the few Lucas took seriously.[19]

Pollock described how Marcia's contributions complemented Lucas' weaknesses:

> George had a secret weapon in Marcia. Like every director who has worked with her, Spielberg thinks she has an excellent eye. Marcia is indispensable to Lucas because she compensates for his deficiencies. Where George is not unduly concerned with character and lacks faith in an audience's patience, Marcia figures out how a movie can be made warmer, how the characters can be given depth and resonance.[20]

George's mother Dorothy remembered with fondness, "Marcia spoiled George terribly when he was making films. She'd bring him breakfast in bed after the nights he worked late."[21] "I have an innate ability to take good material and make it better, and to take fair material and make it good," Marcia said in *Skywalking*. "I think I'm even an editor in real life." [22] On the business front, she was pivotal in the creation of Lucasfilm and Skywalker Ranch, which she also managed while Lucas was shooting *Return of the Jedi*. Pollock also made note of an amusing incident involving the ending of *Raiders of the Lost Ark*:

[Marcia] was instrumental in changing the ending of *Raiders*, in which Indiana delivers the ark to Washington. Marion is nowhere to be seen, presumably stranded on an island with a submarine and a lot of melted Nazis. Marcia watched the rough cut in silence and then levelled the boom. She said there was no emotional resolution to the ending, because the girl disappears. "Everyone was feeling really good until she said that," Dunham recalls. "It was one of those, 'Oh no we lost sight of that.'" Spielberg reshot the scene in downtown San Francisco, having Marion wait for Indiana on the steps on the government building. Marcia, once again, had come to the rescue.[23]

Mark Hamill remembered her being a severely underestimated influence in her husband's films and whom was responsible for providing their warmth and emotion:

You can see a huge difference in the films that he does now and the films that he did when he was married. I know for a fact that Marcia Lucas was responsible for convincing him to keep that little "kiss for luck" before Carrie [Fisher] and I swing across the chasm in the first film: "Oh, I don't like it, people laugh in the previews," and she said, "George, they're laughing because it's so sweet and unexpected"—and her influence was such that if she wanted to keep it, it was in. When the little mouse robot comes up when Harrison and I are delivering Chewbacca to the prison and he roars at it and it screams, sort of, and runs away, George wanted to cut that and Marcia insisted that he keep it. She was really the warmth and the heart of those films, a good person he could talk to, bounce ideas off of.[24]

Clearly, Marcia was a pivotal player, not only in Lucas' life, but in his films. Her departure from him would be felt in the cinema that followed.

Perhaps just as sadly for her, *Return of the Jedi* would be her last credit as editor.*

The split was heartbreaking for Lucas—and probably for Marcia too. In the ten years since *American Graffiti* catapulted her husband to success, their marriage had slowly but surely eroded, especially in the last seven years in which Lucasfilm ruled George's life. Some of their friends were unsurprised by the split, such as Ronda Gomez and Howard Zieff. "He just didn't want to have fun," Gomez said to author Peter Biskind. "Marcia wanted to go to Europe and see things. George wanted to stay in the hotel room and have his TV dinners."[25] In interviews Lucas would tell how his wife wanted to be able to go to restaurants and be like normal couples but the onslaught of success threw a roadblock of work in front of him and left the empire of Lucasfilm forever separating the two. Marcia had wanted to have children since the 1970s, and after *Star Wars* was filmed they tried to conceive but were unable to because of George's infertility—however, after *Star Wars* was released they did not immediately adopt. With the success of *Star Wars* bringing him so many opportunities, George knew his work would keep him so busy that he would not be able to make the films and raise a family at the same time—he had to choose between *Star Wars* and family, and he chose *Star Wars*.[26] His window of opportunity to make these blockbusters may have been finite and celebrities come and go with the regularity of tide changes—the amount of profit the films would bring him would set him up for life and Lucas could settle down then instead.

"I was desperate to have a family," he recalled in 1983, just before the divorce would hit. "Yet I knew when I had a family I couldn't devote ninety-eight percent of my time to the company. Since my daughter, the focus has changed."[27] Marcia pressured him into eventually settling for a compromise—they finally adopted in 1981, after Lucas decided to be done with the saga.

"I love *Star Wars*," he said in 1983. "I think it's great, but I just don't want to sacrifice my entire life for it. I don't want to be an all-consumed workaholic. I want to enjoy the better things in life like a normal person—just, say, go out and stand on a hill and enjoy life."[28]

For two brief years Lucas had this one and only window into a normal life that could have been. He had a beautiful, brilliant wife and a wonderful

---

* Denise Worrell reported, "her husband says she is 'great with emotions and characters, the dying and crying scenes.' She cut Yoda's and Vader's deaths in *Jedi*. But she also cuts the space battles. George listens to her very carefully." (*Icons: Intimate Portraits*, p. 191)

daughter, and for once was doing his best to enjoy such happiness. "I make everyone leave at six o'clock so that when George comes home, it's just the two of us and Amanda," Marcia said at the time. "Now that we have Amanda we actually have dinner at the table. I cook, I do the dishes, and we give Amanda a bath together. George sometimes feeds her a bottle in the TV room. We just decided to try to keep our lives as normal as possible."[29] But it was not to last. The three were seldom together and although they tried to mend things at the very end it was not enough to close the wounds in their relationship that were already opened.

Towards the end of their marriage Marcia suggested they see a marriage counsellor but George refused the idea, an attitude Peter Biskind surmises was likely picked up from his small-town father.[30] She later suggested a trial separation but he rejected that as well and begged her to wait until the last *Star Wars* film was done.[31]

"I know he wanted me to stay, but it was just too little too late," Marcia said.[32] Walter Murch offered his view of the collapse to Biskind, saying, "I think what Marcia saw was that his success was winding him tighter and tighter into a workaholic control-driven person, and she thought that this was destructive, which it probably is in the long run."[33] Lucas' obsession with Skywalker Ranch turned him into a distant workaholic, as he channelled all his time and energy into the *Star Wars* series in order to realise the facility, gambling away all of their fortune, but Lucas knew that with *Return of the Jedi* the dream would finally be complete. But Marcia could care less about Skywalker Ranch. She was happy with just being a regular union editor, and George was maintaining that all he wanted to do was make experimental films; *THX 1138* was made on a shoe-string budget and edited in the attic of their home, and nothing was stopping him from doing this again. She wanted to enjoy life, and being millionaires they had the unimaginable chance to do so in luxury, to not have to worry about the future after having lived on the edge of poverty for so many years. Lucas was simply too wrapped up in his own empire-building to see his private life disintegrating around him.

"Marcia complains that I either live in the past or in the future, but never in the present," Lucas once remarked to Dale Pollock after a days work filming *Return of the Jedi*. "In a way, she's right. I'm always thinking about what's going to happen or what has happened. I think when I finish this film I'll be able to live in the present—maybe."[34]

The release of *Return of the Jedi* would be bittersweet for Lucas.

## The Worst of Times

Anticipation for the film was incredible, and the film broke all opening records at theatres. But nevertheless, the film was met with some harsh criticism. Whereas *Star Wars* had been showered in praise, *Empire Strikes Back* had its share of detractors—but none were as bad as the backlash *Return of the Jedi* endured. For the first time, one of Lucas' films was regarded as a disappointment.

Gene Siskel complained it lacked "the humanity and richly drawn characters that brighten *Star Wars*," while *Newsweek* proclaimed "*Jedi* is downright repetitive!" and *The New York Times* wrote "the old 'Star Wars' gang are back doing what they've done before, but this time with a certain evident boredom." The use of cute and cuddly Ewoks was heavily criticized as being an obvious merchandising ploy, while many also noted that the characters and dialogue lacked the sharp wit or compelling depth of the previous two films.

Nonetheless, the film was still received well by many, even if it had unfavourable reviews. "*Return of the Jedi* is fun, magnificent fun," Roger Ebert wrote in the *Chicago Sun-Times*. "The movie is a complete entertainment, a feast for the eyes and a delight for the fancy. It's a little amazing how Lucas and his associates keep topping themselves." The film would go on to gross over $260 million dollars domestically.

For Lucas, things were not so celebratory. His separation and impending divorce left him shattered and in a state of emotional depression, and with a bitter ending to his space saga. And although the divorce left a hole in Lucas' heart, it left a bigger one in his wallet. As Lucasfilm president Bob Greber noted to Dale Pollock in 1983, "People sometimes forget that Marcia Lucas owns half of this company and is a very important part of it."[35]

In the divorce settlement, Lucas lost much of his fortune— as much as $50 million according to Peter Biskind's reports.[36]* His riches from the success of the *Star Wars* films were suddenly taken from him—with Marcia playing such a prominent role in both Lucasfilm and the three *Star Wars* films, she was entitled to her share of it. Custody of their daughter was split between them,[37] but it was decided that George would care for her; Marcia was said to visit occasionally but this quickly tapered off to the point where they hardly saw each other. Marcia and Tom Rodriguez had already bought

---

* More conservative estimates place it closer to $35 million.
(Baxter, p. 335)

a house in the San Francisco suburb of Belvedere, and she quickly became pregnant with her first natural daughter, Amy.[38]

Emotionally, Lucas was a wreck, and financially he was in an equally ruinous position. After all the struggles Lucas had made to film the *Star Wars* trilogy, the sacrifice that was supposed to grant him his personal and financial freedom, his reward for it was heartbreak, plunder and desertion. His position as "Empire-Builder" had not only pushed away his wife but his friends as well. He had an infamous falling out with Francis Coppola at the start of the decade due to many things, such as Coppola having abandoned San Francisco and moved Zoetrope back to Los Angeles; Coppola on the other hand, descending into personal ruin, resented Lucas for not saving him from bankruptcy after Lucas refused to loan him a few million dollars to pay off his debts (Lucas replies his money was tied up with *Empire Strikes Back*). "When he got divorced, George came to me and wanted to be my friend," Coppola recalled to Peter Biskind. "He apologized."[39] Many of his film school friends were seldom seen anymore as well. After all was said and done, Lucas was left only with his crumbling Empire from which to rule from his lonely throne. And it wasn't just him—all the major players of the American New Wave were falling simultaneously. Coppola was bankrupt and ruined and Scorsese had made a series of disasters; even Spielberg's marriage was about to implode, leading to an infamous $100 million settlement, and the careers and personal lives of major players like Peter Bogdonavich, Paul Schrader and William Friedkin went into nosedives. Independent and personal films were failing at the box office, which was again being dominated by studio-controlled pictures. By 1983, the glory days of the '70s would be dead and buried. Lucas' destruction was a representation of his entire era.

Lucas looked back on the tragedy sixteen years later in an interview with Lesley Stahl for *60 Minutes*:

Lucas: It was very hard. The divorce kind of destroyed me. It did take me a couple of years to sort of unwind myself and come out of it.

Lesley Stahl: You didn't see it coming?

Lucas: Oh, no, I didn't.

Lesley Stahl: You were happy, everything was fine and—there was another man. And you didn't know.

Lucas: Ten years younger than I was. It was one of those classic divorce situations.[40]

Lucas' close friend Steven Spielberg, whom Lucas would be working with on the *Raiders* sequel as the divorce was occurring, remembered the time in an interview with *60 Minutes*:

> [The divorce] pulverized him. George and Marcia, for me, were the reason you got married, because it was insurance policy that marriages do work. And it working together and living together. And having understandings on many, many different planes—"[it] does work." And when it didn't work, and when that marriage didn't work, I lost my faith in marriage for a long time.[41]

Marcia took her half of the companies and left—she had no interest in a corporate empire and gladly took her financial share in cash so that she could settle down with her new family. But Lucas remained with the corporation, determined to rebuild himself. Just as he had finally earned his freedom from Hollywood—to be financially secure enough to never have to be involved with a movie studio again—the dream unexpectedly crumbled; it would be over two decades before he would be able to climb back to this position.

His dream of Skywalker Ranch also collapsed—at first thought to be a communal filmmaking Xanadu, its unusual location far, far away from Hollywood led to it essentially being forgotten and deserted. Its facilities were so state-of-the-art and expensive that none but the biggest Hollywood blockbusters could use it—exactly the type of productions that Lucas claimed the facility was built to dethrone. Its lavish library, the one garnished with that infamous domed stained-glass roof, went virtually unused and no indie filmmaking paradise ever sprouted. In the end, Skywalker Ranch turned into the $20 million Lucasfilm office, and from it ruled George Lucas, alone and without purpose.

### Treading Water

Lucas may not have had the lucrative riches that he once did—but he did have a ready source of income at his disposal.

ILM had grown to become the leading special effects house in the world, achieving Academy Award winning work on *Poltergeist*, *Star Trek II* and *ET: The Extra-Terrestrial*, and had become a significant financial asset for Lucas, all the while leading the forefront in technological development. Lucasfilm meanwhile had a source of income far greater than the *Star Wars* films themselves: the merchandising based on them. *Star*

*Wars* had revolutionized the marketing of movies—Lucas promoted the films with toys, action figures, books, clothing and any sort of product imaginable, from Pez dispensers to Underoos to colouring books. At the time Lucas had negotiated his contract with Fox, merchandising in movies was not seen as profitable—*Star Wars* would change this forever; Lucas was able to retain merchandising rights in exchange for a pay cut, and as a result received the main source of funding for his empire.

Action figures continued to sell—though with the series over, not nearly as well—and with the explosion of video games in the mid-'80s, LucasArts would be created to cater to this market with interactive software for home computers and video game systems. Television would also prove a valuable asset in the continuing expansion of Lucasfilm. First, there would be a made-for-television movie called *The Ewok Adventure,* a live-action spinoff designed for children (Lucas once described it as a "gift" for his daughter); the plot concerned Wicket and his Ewok friends helping two children find their parents after their ship crash-lands on Endor. The film featured the first appearance of the name Mace, a name from Lucas' early *Star Wars* notes and which would be later used in the prequels. After the first Ewok movie in 1984 there would be another made-for-television film in 1986, this one concerning a tyrant and a witch trying to attack the Ewok villages—the film was titled *Ewoks: The Battle for Endor.* In a familiar move, the previous film was retitled to match it, now known as *Ewoks: The Caravan of Courage.* Not one but two animated *Star Wars* spinoffs would be created for Saturday morning programming in 1985. The first was *Ewoks,* hot on the trails of the TV movie, featuring Wicket and the Ewoks in episodes set before *Return of the Jedi.* The second was *Droids,* featuring the adventures of R2-D2 and C-3P0 before they joined Luke. Merchandise was of course produced for all of these spinoffs. More ambitiously, Lucasfilm teamed up with Disney, first in 1986 to produce a Michael Jackson 3-D sci-fi film called *Captain EO* for Disneyland (directed by Francis Coppola), and then a *Star Wars* theme-park ride which opened to much success in 1987 as Disneyland's *Star Tours.*

The Lucasfilm products and corporate diversification would become the key to rebuilding the empire; Lucas no longer had enough money to self-finance another film, as he had done in the past. Just as well, he no longer had the desire to—when *Return of the Jedi* was nearing completion, Lucas remarked how he would like to return to making the abstract "art house" type films he had dreamed of in his youth when he first moved to San Francisco with Marcia, as Dale Pollock reported in 1983:

> Lucas wants to rediscover the virtues of being an amateur. He has wanted to make esoteric movies like *THX* since he left USC; now he has the time and money to do it...He's determined to make films that are abstract and emotional, without plot or characters. He won't talk about specific ideas—he seems unsure exactly what he wants to do—but it's clear that these impressionistic works are the complete opposite of his professional films...Whatever Lucas find with his experimental films he'll probably keep to himself: "If they don't work, I'm certainly not going to show them to anybody. If they do work, they'll probably get a very limited release."[42]

Lucas had been talking about making these "experimental" personal films since the 1970s, as far back as a 1974 interview with *Film Quarterly* magazine following the release of the commercial *American Graffiti*, and well after the millennium he would still be talking about "one day soon" making these films. As of 2008 he has not yet. Like his infamous "that's the way it always was" statements, these may be observed as more examples of his security blanket; after *American Graffiti* and *Star Wars* became huge mainstream blockbusters associated with Hollywood, the success of which is credited with killing off the personal films of the American New Wave, Lucas would be quick to remind listeners that he was really an experimental art-house type and that the whole mainstream thing was accidental. As if uncomfortable with being such a mainstream blockbuster-maker, declaring that he will be making experimental personal films that are destined to fail may be his way of coping with such fame. In 1974, he vowed to make such films after *Star Wars*; in 1978 he vowed to make such films after the *Star Wars* trilogy; in 1983 he vowed to make such things in the near future; in 2005 he vowed to make such things now that he was done with *Star Wars* (again); now in 2008 he has vowed to make such things after the *Star Wars* television series is complete (sometime close to 2010). Coppola is famous for once having remarked "*Star Wars* robbed America of one of its most challenging filmmakers,"[43] but it was a choice Lucas made on his own. In fact, Marcia Lucas seems perplexed by Lucas' inability to return to the field, as she told Peter Biskind:

> By the time George could afford to have a film facility he no longer wanted to direct...After *Star Wars*, he insisted, "I'm never going to direct another establishment-type movie again." I used to say, "For someone who wants to be an experimental filmmaker, why are you spending this fortune on a facility to make Hollywood movies? We edited *THX* in our attic, we edited *American Graffiti* over Francis' garage, I just don't get it, George." The Lucasfilm empire—the computer division, ILM, the licensing and lawyers—seemed to me to be this inverted triangle sitting on a pea, which was the *Star Wars* trilogy.

But he wasn't going to make any more *Star Wars*, and the pea was going to dry up and crumble, and then he was going to be left with this huge facility with its enormous overhead. And why did he want to do that if he wasn't going to make movies? I still don't get it.[44]

Indeed, such actions seem to fly in the face of the philosophy he espouses. Nonetheless, by the mid-'80s, it seems Lucas had resigned to the life of a businessman. "One of the great losses is that Marcia never became a filmmaker and continued as an editor," John Milius mused in *Mythmaker*. "But one of the other great losses is that George stopped making movies, and got interested in the sort of stuff that Lucasfilm puts out. Because he was a really dynamic filmmaker."[45]

In the aftermath of his divorce, Lucas was left with nothing but his companies—and his daughter, Amanda. She was the only remnant from his happier life, and Lucas focused all of his attention on raising her as a single father, one who was as devoted as a parent could be.

Trying to rebound from his divorce, Lucas was in a relationship with singer Linda Rondstat starting in 1984, which apparently went as serious as an engagement ring[46]—but, somehow, their relationship would fizzle out. Afterwards, Lucas apparently decided he didn't need a wife to have a family—he would adopt another daughter, Katie, and finally a son, Jett. He has never re-married, and would remain dedicated solely to his kids and his companies. Lucas speaks with *60 Minutes* in 1999:

Lesley Stahl: Did the divorce hurt you so badly that that's gonna be it [for marriage], you think?

Lucas: Well, I dunno, I fell in love a couple of years later after that. I felt in love with another woman...

Stahl: Linda Rondstat?

Lucas: Yeah... But she was somebody who just didn't want to get married. And eventually I wanted to get married. And I think as you get older and as you get burned a few times you either get wearier or wiser, I don't know which. I guess I'm wearier and wiser and older. And I have a big life. And I have three kids.[47]

Lucasfilm was since making a slow but consistent recovery from Lucas' divorce. It had since spawned many smaller sub-companies, and its computer division, headed by Pixar, had become a pioneer in the digital arts. Editdroid became the first non-linear editing system, eventually becoming the industry-standard AVID, while ILM continued to grow exponentially, being the first company to fully-integrate CGI into a film (i.e. *Young Sherlock Holmes*). In 1986, Lucas would sell Pixar to Apple Computer co-founder Steve Jobs for $10 million, giving Lucasfilm a needed shot of capital.

Marcia, meanwhile, was slowly fading from the film community and from Lucas' life. "He was very bitter and vindictive about the divorce," Marcia remembered in Peter Biskind's book. "Francis and Ellie [Coppola] used to have an Easter party out in Napa, and the first couple of years after the divorce, I used to get to see everyone, the Barwoods, the Robbinses, and then I stopped being invited. Years later I ran into Ellie down in L.A., and she said, 'I always wanted to call you to explain that when Francis and George were working on *Tucker*, George asked him not to invite you, because he was very uncomfortable around you.' That really hurt. It's not enough that I'm erased from his life, he wants to blackball me too, with people who were my friends. It's like I never existed."[48]

In the meantime, Lucas was enjoying a casual life of executive overseer, easily managing his companies while caring for his children. Since his divorce, the sequel to *Raiders of the Lost Ark—Indiana Jones and the Temple of Doom*—was the only major film involvement he had; in fact, the story was written by him in the bitter shadow of his divorce trial, lending the film a dark and violent tone that led to the creation of the PG-13 rating in the United States. The film was popular among audiences but heavily criticised by critics (and parents!). His only other efforts in cinema came when he occasionally helped his friends by executive producing their films—Walter Murch's *Return to Oz* (which Lucas bailed out of serious debt at the hands of producer Gary Kurtz), which would prove to be an interesting but expensive bomb, Willard Huyck's *Howard the Duck* (based off the popular comic book), an embarrassing disaster that would be virtually disowned by all (though Lucas' creative involvement is often exaggerated), Francis Ford Coppola's *Tucker: The Man and his Dreams*, which would also have a disappointing release, Jim Henson's *Labyrinth*, another bomb, and Steven Spielberg's animated hit *The Land Before Time*, among others. *Willow* marked Lucas' return to the industry in a more active role in 1988, when he conceived and produced the Ron Howard film with a story that combined equal parts of *Lord of the Rings* and *Star Wars*. It too had a disappointing release, though it has since become an '80s favourite. A third Indiana Jones film would be made shortly after, which he again produced with Spielberg at the helm, and was one of 1989's biggest hits, perhaps making up for some of the financially unsuccessful cinema ventures Lucas had taken that decade. Lucas explained to *The Hollywood Reporter*:

> I had the 20-year gap because I finished (1983's) 'Return of the Jedi' and I had a daughter. I had just gotten divorced, (and) I was raising my daughter and felt that was the most important thing—and I was going to spend my time raising her. Then I adopted other children and spent 15 years raising them. At the same time, there was another aspect to it: Because of the divorce, (Lucasfilm) was in difficult financial straits. To straighten out the company and get it solid without "Star Wars," without me producing product for them, I basically ended up getting a job where I could go to work at 10 or 11 (a.m.) and come home at 4 or 5 (p.m.).[49]

But what was happening with *Star Wars* while all of this was occurring? Lucas had lapsed into semi-retirement, and it did not seem as if *Star Wars* was on the radar at all. In 1983, he had claimed to want to never make another *Star Wars* film again. "I am afraid that if I did another *Star Wars* movie now, I'd be straying from my path," Lucas said in May 1983. "To me that would be like being seduced by the dark side, but more than anything else, I think I'd be unhappy."[50]

Fans patiently waited, fed on Lucas' claims that after *Return of the Jedi* there would be a prequel trilogy, followed by a Sequel Trilogy. Since he had made those claims, much in his life had changed. The Sequel Trilogy had all but evaporated; Lucas publicly speculated that perhaps a trilogy detailing post-*Return of the Jedi* stories could be written later, with the aged cast of the originals returning, but this did not seem very likely at all, although Lucas would not admit this for over a decade.

The prequel trilogy remained in Lucas' mind as a possible storyline however, though at that time he had no desire to make them. But he genuinely liked the story and had sketched out a fairly elaborate plot over the years, refining the details and characters as they changed throughout the process of writing the original trilogy. The prequels would also be much more complex than the second trilogy, and of a more sophisticated nature, with heavy political plotting and tragic betrayal afoot. As was described by *Time* Magazine in 1983:

> The films that record what went on in the beginning—if they are ever made—will be altogether different in look and tone from the existing trilogy, says Lucas. They will be more melodramatic, showing the political intrigue and machiavellian plotting that led to the downfall of the once noble Republic. They will have only enough outward action to keep the plot moving. Obi-Wan Kenobi, the elderly Jedi played by Alec Guinness in the Star Wars series, and

Darth Vader will be seen as younger men, while Luke Skywalker will make a brief appearance as a baby in Episode III.[51]

The outline he had developed since 1977 was vague, giving only the major plot revelations, and was under a dozen pages long, according to Lucas. The story would be about Obi Wan Kenobi, a Jedi in the final days of the Old Republic, who recruits and trains a brilliant prodigy named Anakin Skywalker. At the same time, a devious politician and secret Dark Lord named Palpatine schemes his way into office, manipulating the people and proclaiming himself Emperor. He lures young Skywalker to the dark side, and turns him against his fellow Jedi knights, laying a trap where the Jedi are all but wiped out. Obi Wan confronts his student to turn him away from the dark side but a battle ensues on the edge of a volcano and Obi Wan defeats Skywalker, horribly burning him. The Emperor is able to salvage his dark apprentice before the boy is completely dead and resurrects him as the bionic Darth Vader; meanwhile, Obi Wan aids Skywalker's wife in escaping with her secret children. Luke is taken to Tatooine, to live with Obi Wan's brother, where Obi Wan also remains in exile, while Leia is taken to Alderaan to live with senator Bail Organa. Darth Vader meanwhile, has become the right hand of the Emperor, hunting down the remaining Jedi, as the Empire engulfs the galaxy. During the course of the story, the Clone Wars would occur, which Kenobi and Anakin would fight in and become galactic heroes; C-3P0 and R2-D2 would also be in the story somewhere, the only common elements throughout the entire saga.

But with his children still young and his empire still expanding, Lucas lacked any desire to immediately return to either *Star Wars* or directing, as he told *Rolling Stone* in 1987:

> I'll do more [*Star Wars* films] eventually; I just don't know when. I've done a lot of research, but my heart is in other areas right now. I can make more *Star Wars* and make zillions of dollars, but I don't need to do that, and I really don't have the interest right now. There is a story there I would like to tell. It's just that it isn't beating in my head hard enough to say, 'I have to get this out of here.' I'm more interested in other things.[52]

"*Star Wars* is sitting on the shelf—and I'm not under *any* pressure to do anything with it," he remarked during this period.[53] However, with more and more time passing since his last venture behind the camera, Lucas was beginning to get the itch to return to moviemaking.

"It will be unbelievably expensive," Lucas said of the new *Star Wars* trilogy at the 1989 opening of Disney-MGM Studios. "And that's one of the things holding it up. If there was a way of doing them less expensively, it could make it easier to go ahead and do more. But there are just huge, huge amounts of money involved."[54] Lucas didn't have a bottomless pit of money, especially after his divorce, which he had only begun to recover from at that point, which is another prime reason for the wait—it wouldn't be until the 1990s that Lucas had regained enough wealth to personally fund a blockbuster film, and he wasn't interested in placing the franchise in the hands of a studio.

As the 1990s came about, Lucas continued to sit on his prequel story, but realised that if he were to make it at all, it would have to be soon. Huge strides were being made by ILM in computer graphics technology—James Cameron's *The Abyss* and *Terminator 2* made great leaps in the field, offering photo-realistic creatures integrated into live action, although they were simple and crude: a water tentacle and a similar-looking liquid metal shape-shifter. Still, Lucas knew that the complex prequel trilogy would require more advancements than that for the fantastic vision he was interested in portraying, but it was clear that the technology was rapidly approaching that would allow him to make truly imaginative films, no longer bound by simple puppets, models and matte paintings. That day would come sooner than anyone realised.

Around the same time, *Star Wars* was about to undergo a sort of renaissance.

The trilogy had since slumped into decline, with no new toys having been manufactured since the mid-'80s, and with the advent of home video, no theatrical re-releases (save for a very limited and seldom-remembered 1985 triple-bill). A new generation had since been born, one that had never experienced the original releases first hand but grew up weaned on television and home video incarnations of the saga—in fact, *Star Wars* was the first video cassette to make a million dollars in rentals. The films had been parodied in the 1987 film *Spaceballs* but as reviewers of the time pointed out, by then even a satire of the trilogy was out of date. The mass-produced toys and merchandise soon became unpopular and found their way into second-hand stores and garage sales as kids embraced the latest trends such as the new *Transformers* and *My Little Pony* toy lines, each with their own popular television cartoons. West End Games had produced *Star Wars* role playing games, but those catered to a very small, hardcore sci-fi fanbase. In winter 1987, *Bantha Tracks* and the Official Star Wars Fan Club closed down, with a written promise from George Lucas in one of the final issues that the club would be reactivated once more *Star Wars* films were made. However, even as *Star Wars* slowly began to disappear from contemporary culture and move into the realm of "classic"—the original film was inaugurated into the Library of Congress' National Film Registry in 1989—a loyal yet invisible following, spanning all ages, quietly lay in wait for the coming years when *Star Wars* would return. *Star Wars* was thought to be dead, but in reality it was only in hibernation.

# Chapter IX: The Beginning…Again

IN 1989, Bantam publishing proposed to Lucasfilm that a new *Star Wars* book be commissioned.[1] Novels which went beyond the films had been experimented with in the days of the original trilogy—*Splinter of the Mind's Eye* in 1978, a trilogy of *Han Solo Adventure* novels from 1979 to 1980 and a *Lando* trilogy in 1983—but no new developments had been made in the *Star Wars* universe since then, aside from the once-popular Marvel comic series which had been put to rest in 1986.

It took Lucasfilm over a year to reply to Bantam's proposal, when it was finally decided to make another *Star Wars* novel. Award winning science fiction author Timothy Zahn was contacted. Zahn recalled in 1992:

> Well, I understand that Lou Aronica, the publisher of Bantam Spectra, contacted Lucasfilm about three years ago to suggest a new *Star Wars* book. He didn't hear back from them for about a year. Then they said, "Yes, this sounds interesting; let's talk." Aronica and his editors assembled a list of potential writers and I guess I was the first one they asked. I took the job.[2]

It seems, in that waiting period, Lucas had finally decided that the Sequel Trilogy was a no-go—the closest he could ever come was to continue the saga as novels, a concept he himself had first implemented with Alan Dean Foster in 1975, and here awaited the perfect opportunity. He told *Wired*:

The sequels were never really going to get made anyway, unlike 1, 2, and 3, where the stories have existed for 20 years. The idea of 7, 8, and 9 actually came from people asking me about sequels, and I said, "I don't know. Maybe someday." Then when the licensing people came and asked, "Can we do novels?" I said do sequels, because I'll probably never do sequels."[3]

Timothy Zahn would eventually compose a trilogy, and it seems as if it was the Sequel Trilogy that never was. The story would feature a character similar to the abandoned Jedi-sister concept from the *original* sequel plots of 1977, Mara Jade, as well as ample substitutes for Vader and the Emperor in "dark Jedi" Joruus C'Boath and Grand Admiral Thrawn. Had Abbadon, the planet-wide metropolis from the early drafts of *Return of the Jedi*, would be resurrected as well, now renamed Coruscant,[4] and the story would revolve around the rebuilding of the Republic as Lucas had stated for his own Sequel Trilogy. Although Zahn was given ample freedom to construct the story as he wished, Lucas himself would be more involved in the writing than any of the subsequent novels, the volume of which would later grow far beyond his control—for Zahn's sequel trilogy, Lucas would personally read and approve the treatments, and have veto power in story development. His first rule: the story is set shortly after the events of *Return of the Jedi*. Zahn said in 1991:

My original instructions from LucasArts consisted of exactly two rules: the books were to start 3-5 years after *Return of the Jedi*, and I couldn't use anyone who'd been explicitly killed off in the movies. Aside from that, I was given essentially a blank check to do what I wanted. A couple of other rules came in later after I'd submitted my outline, but they required only minor changes in the story itself. LucasArts has complete veto power over everything I do, of course, but so far they've allowed me pretty much a free hand. Which is not to say they're not keeping close watch on what I'm doing. They are... [George] Lucas did read the original outline.[5]

Zahn talked about the process of negotiating the plot with Lucasfilm in this early interview:

They looked at the outline and told me a couple of things I couldn't do. They cut out my favorite character. And originally, Joruus C'baoth was going to be a clone of Obi-wan Kenobi, but they said no. They didn't want me to refer in detail to the clone wars which took place before the movies began. I guess by that time Lucas had decided he was going to go back and make the prequel movies, and they didn't want me treading on his turf.

But I got my way on most of it and conceded on the things they simply didn't want me to do. So, aside from relatively minor things, I had pretty much of a free hand...I was a couple of months into writing when they suddenly decided they wanted me to coordinate with the West End Games role-playing materials, too. They filled in a bunch of the gaps that I hadn't gotten around to filling in.[6]

The fact that the trilogy would have the *Star Wars* brand name on it guaranteed it some success, but the *Star Wars* series had disappeared from the limelight and was only popular with its devout fans. Zahn reminisced about the issue in an interview with *Echostation.com*:

*Back when you were writing the first novel, did you ever question what you were doing? Did you ever stop and say to yourself "Why am I doing this? No one likes Star Wars anymore, who is going to read this book?"*

Zahn: You bet I wondered about the project at times. No one had any idea how well this was going to do out in the marketplace; certainly the initial book stores' reaction and orders indicated it would be only a mild success."[7]

By the time the first book was complete it was 1991. The Gulf War was ending, kids were enamored with *Teenage Mutant Ninja Turtles*, while MC Hammer and Salt-N-Pepa ruled MTV and Nirvana stood poised to unleash grunge rock upon the world. Moviegoers eagerly looked forward to the impending release of *Terminator 2* while *Silence of the Lambs* and *Thelma and Louise* continued to draw Oscar buzz. *Star Wars* was thoroughly dead and buried. The first book of Timothy Zahn's trilogy was titled *Heir to the Empire* and was released on June 4th, 1991—to success that was as shocking as Lucas' was in 1977. The first printing of 60,000 sold out in its first week in stores, and the novel immediately became a national best-seller. It won rave-reviews from critics and fans alike and stayed on the *New York Times* bestsellers list for 29 weeks.[8] The message was clear: *Star Wars* was as popular as it ever was.

This unexpected turn set in motion a new phase in Lucasfilm. The two sequels were released each subsequent year, with *Dark Force Rising* in 1992 and *The Last Command* in 1993. Before even the second book was released, plans were underway to totally revamp *Star Wars* into the new decade. More novels were quickly planned, and emerging comic book company Dark Horse launched many new series, all of which did outstanding sales. *Dark Empire* was the first, hot on the trails of *Heir to the Empire* in 1991, and told the stunning tale of Luke's fall to the dark side and subsequent redemption in a story meant to parallel his father's, which Lucas also had some level of involvement with.[9] *

Within a few years, there would be over a dozen *Star Wars* novels, expanding the story beyond the films in works such as *The Jedi Academy Trilogy* and *The Truce at Bakura*, and comic lines would spring up with equal frequency, from the ancient pre-history of *Tales of the Jedi* to the dogfights of *Rogue Squadron*. Merchandising would slowly return to production: as the books and comics continued to be popular, new lines of Micro Machines playsets were launched, and reprintings of posters, the original novelisations and the *Art of Star Wars* books became hot selling items. *Splinter of the Mind's Eye* and the *Han Solo Adventures* were republished, and Dark Horse re-released the original Marvel comic line. *Lucasfilm Magazine* was revamped in 1995 to deal with the huge resurgence of *Star Wars* activity and the once-struggling fanclub magazine became a hot newsstand item as *The Star Wars Insider*. Topps launched a slew of trading card lines, as well as its own *Star Wars Galaxy Magazine*. *Star Wars Galaxy Collector* was later launched as a dedicated collector's magazine—there was so much merchandise produced that it needed an entire bi-monthly magazine to keep track of it all! LucasArts, the software division, surged in size as it developed hugely successful video games, such as its acclaimed *Super Star Wars* series for the Super Nintendo, as well as its popular *X-Wing* flight simulator for the computer; the 1995 CD-ROM game *Rebel Assault II* featured live-action segments featuring David Prowse as Darth Vader as well as original props and costumes, and was photographed by Gil Taylor, the director of photography of the original *Star Wars*. Art work, posters, collectable mugs, models, t-shirts and Pez dispensers were all sold once again, and Galoob was making $120 million a year from *Star Wars* toys[10]—perhaps most significant of all, Kenner re-launched its *Star Wars* action figure line in a revamped 90's version in 1995. Darth Vader was even seen battling the Energizer Bunny in a humorous 1995 commercial.

*Star Wars* was back. Big time.

---

* *Dark Empire* had actually been in development since 1989 as a one-off with Marvel, whom had given up the *Star Wars* licence a few years prior. Management changes left the unfinished project in limbo, but Dark Horse, having had success with *Alien*, *Predator* and *Terminator* comic lines, eagerly picked it up—just in time for the *Star Wars* renaissance that began that year. They have held the licence ever since.

Perhaps because of all this, Lucas decided that he would make his prequel trilogy sooner rather than later.

"When I went and decided that I would tell the backstory, it was a very difficult decision at the time," Lucas later recalled. "I figured I was done with *Star Wars*. I didn't want to do *Star Wars* any more."[11] But with the discovery of such a large audience and the emerging digital technologies of ILM, Lucas now had incentive—and, with the added wealth this *Star Wars* renaissance had brought, the financial ability to independently make the films. "It technically became possible to do it and I had this backstory. The backstory intrigued me because it kind of turns the whole series on its head."[12]

Throughout the '80s, Lucas had given vague promises that he would "one day" make the prequel trilogy, but these seemed somewhat empty, and by the 1990s the three films had grown to the status of legend. Lucas' decision to take time to raise his children paid off, and he maintained a happy family; he adopted his first son and third child, Jett, around this same time. "They wanted a brother," he said of his two daughters in his *A&E Biography*. "I wanted another daughter because the girls were so wonderful...but it's great to have someone that understands explosions."[13] Now that the '90s were on their way, things were beginning to change in his life.

In 1992, Lucasfilm premiered *The Young Indiana Jones Chronicles*, a television series inspired by the opening sequence from *Indiana Jones and the Last Crusade* portraying the title character as a boy. The series utilised all of Lucas' resources, providing ILM with a fertile testing ground for emerging digital techniques. Crowd replication, set extension, wire removal, digital matte painting and digital compositing techniques were developed and refined—and most importantly, at an inexpensive cost. It was here that Lucas proposed that the future of filmmaking would be a digital one, as he told *American Cinematographer*:

> On the TV series, I was able to work in a much lower-res medium; we were able to move things around much more quickly and cheaply, so I could use [digital technology] more often. I said "I want to be able to do a couple hundred shots in every hour-long episode and still have a budget that's under $50,000." I wanted to be able to play with this stuff and see how it worked. In the end, we made 22 "feature films" in the space of five years, and we experimented with all kinds of things. Some things worked, some didn't. We learned a lot in the process, and that's what I'm using now.[14]

The series was also significant because of those involved in its making, for it was here that the future of *Star Wars* would be found.

The original trilogy was crewed with people from Lucas' youth, many of them friends from film school, but with many either drifted away, retired, or moved on to larger things, Lucas needed a newer, younger crew. *Young Indy* marks the beginning of the second stage of Lucas' career, when he would find a new entourage and a new way of producing films; he would even find himself back behind the camera directing segments of the series—in effect, it was a rebirth of sorts. Gary Kurtz would morph into Rick McCallum, Willard Huyck and Gloria Katz into Frank Darabont and Jonathan Hales, Haskell Wexler into David Tattersal and Walter Murch into Ben Burtt. To manage the *Young Indy* series, Lucas would recruit Rick McCallum as producer. This would be the start of a collaboration that would span decades—McCallum easily filled the role as producer and so impressed Lucas that he stayed onboard for every subsequent Lucasfilm production: *Young Indy*, *Radioland Murders*, *Star Wars* trilogy Special Edition, the *Star Wars* prequel trilogy and the two subsequent *Star Wars* TV series. Costume designer Trisha Biggar, production designer Gavin Bocquet and more minor players such as set decorator Peter Walpole and editor Ben Burtt (famous for being the sound designer on the *Star Wars* trilogy, now trying his hand at picture cutting) would also find their start on the series. The creative core of the trilogy would be forged during the *Young Indy* run, nearly all of them getting their first big break with the series.

"We all had enormous fun doing *The Young Indiana Jones Chronicles* and I think that re-energized George to a degree," writer Jonathan Hales recalled fondly in *The Cinema of George Lucas*. "I remember Rick [McCallum] saying excitedly, 'We could go anywhere with this, do anything!' and that enthusiasm was certainly infectious. It was a unique working situation, and the Ranch was a fascinating working environment. I spent many years working on that series and it was a great experience. It was the best job I've ever had."[15]

The series was envisioned by Lucas as being a vehicle to educate young people through entertainment; Lucas would come up with the stories himself, researching each episode's historic background, and work with a team of writers to develop the ideas into screenplays. "They would come to the office every day and George would tell them these stories," assistant Jane Bay explained to author Marcus Hearn. "They were based on historical information, most of which he knew but some of which came from research provided by the library. It was the first time he had collaborated with a group of people in this way, and I have never seen him happier in a creative environment."[16]

The series would last from 1992 to 1993 and go on to win ten Emmy awards. It was critically acclaimed, especially with its big-budget look, but a changing timeslot on ABC eventually led to low ratings and the series was cancelled. The remaining episodes were later strung together to form made-for-television movies.

The personal success of the show was enough to make Lucas seriously consider the prequels—not only were they fiscally tempting because of the *Star Wars* re-popularisation occurring, but now it was becoming technologically possibly to make them the way Lucas imagined, without having to spend $200 million. "I didn't take seriously the idea of doing prequels to *Star Wars* until I had the digital technology to do it," Lucas said.[17]

By the time the *Young Indy* series had finished it was 1993. That was a significant year for many reasons. The first was *Jurassic Park*. Lucas remembers the early CG tests ILM created in 1992, as he told *The Wall Street Journal*:

> We did a test for Steven Spielberg; and when we put them up on the screen I had tears in my eyes. It was like one of those moments in history, like the invention of the lightbulb or the first telephone call. A major gap had been crossed and things were never going to be the same.[18]

*Jurassic Park* would hit the world of cinema like a battering ram, bringing with it a new revolution—a digital revolution. No longer confined to metallic objects and inorganic robots, *Jurassic Park* showed that computers were capable of creating life-like, living, breathing animals, as authentic as anything in reality. It was an unexpected leap in technology that was even more thrilling to filmmakers than it was to audiences. For Lucas, it was a revelation. He told *Wired*:

> We had made such advances at Industrial Light & Magic, especially with *Jurassic Park*. That was the watershed of being able to create realistic characters using digital technology. So I thought about it again. I could do cities like Coruscant, I could do a pod race, I could do other things that up to that point had been impossible.[19]

Lucas had always yearned to make abstract experimental films, and with the new digital advancements he could have more creative freedom than ever—and yet, the prequel trilogy continued to pull at him. With his children growing older, Lucas finally had the chance to go back to directing as the '90s were being ushered in—but directing what? He looked back on that pivotal period in a 2004 interview with Charlie Rose:

> At the same time, my kids are getting older now. That's why I got to go back and do more *Star Wars*. And when I went back to do more *Star Wars* I had a very soul-searching discussion with myself about "should I go off and do these three *Star Wars* or should I go off and do these other movies that I want to do?" And now my kids are old enough that I can go back and direct movies—which is what I wanted to do. And I opted for the *Star Wars* thing because again it was one of these "well, the opportunity is there and I think I'd be foolish not to do it."[20]

With the *Star Wars* series at an all-time high, there wasn't a better time to finally make the prequels; it was a lucky coinciding of elements. "[I realised the] *Star Wars* audience was still alive—it hadn't completely disappeared after fifteen years," Lucas said to *Wired*. "I decided that if I didn't do the backstory then, I never would. So I committed to it."[21] He also dryly remarked, "Part of the reason for doing it is that it's the first question I get asked. Not 'This is who I am' or anything, but 'When are you going to do the next *Star Wars*?' So if I do the next ones hopefully people will introduce themselves first."[22]

Moreover, the profits from the sure-to-be-lucrative trilogy would re-establish Lucas' independence after his 1983 divorce had snatched that dream away. "I got a divorce and that sort of set me back quite a ways," Lucas said to Charlie Rose in 2004. "And then I decided one of the reasons to go back to *Star Wars* was that it would hopefully make me financially secure enough to where I wouldn't have to go to a studio and beg for money."[23]

Readying the second season of the *Young Indy* series, Lucas remarked in the *Lucasfilm Fan Club Magazine* in 1992:

> I've said that I would always try to at least do the next trilogy, which is the first trilogy...I have said that I would start working on the next trilogy in the mid-nineties, which is coming up pretty quickly, and that it would come out a year or two after we started...I'll probably start writing it in the next couple of years. Somewhere between 1995 and the year 2000 there should be three more *Star Wars* movies that will come out.[24]

In the fall of 1993, Lucas formally announced, in *Variety* among other sources, that he would be finally making the *Star Wars* prequel trilogy.

The announcement was a breath of fresh air for many fans. Although Lucas had been talking about making "the young days of Ben Kenobi" films since 1977—and technically officially announced them in May 1980 in *Bantha Tracks*—this was the first time it was actually confirmed: the films were going into production.

### First Steps

There were more *Star Wars* goings-on than simply the prequels that year. The twentieth anniversary of *Star Wars* would soon be arriving in 1997—and Lucas had plans to re-release the movie. "One of the reasons I chose to reissue the films rather than do a convention or one of the other things that was suggested for the twentieth anniversary was at the time we thought about all of this I had a two-year-old son," Lucas would later explain. "And I thought, 'I'm not going to show him the film on video, I'm going to wait and let him see it on the big screen the way it was meant to be, and let him really be overwhelmed by the whole thing.'"[25] The re-release also presented a chance to touch up the film. Lucas recalled in a 2000 interview:

> The opportunity [to fix the film] came along with the twentieth-anniversary celebration. There were a lot of ideas bandied about what we were going to do. Everybody both at Fox and Lucasfilm said, "We've got to do something. This is an important thing to us, it's an important thing to a lot of our fans, we should celebrate the fact that we've been here for twenty years." I said, "If you're going to put that much money into reissuing the movie, I want to get it right this time."[26]

The opportunity allowed Lucas to finally fix the technical limitations he had been lamenting about for nearly two decades, such as an underpopulated Mos Eisley and unconvincing creature effects. As Mark Cotta Vaz reported in *ILM: Into the Digital Realm*, in late 1993 Special Edition work commenced with a brainstorming session between Dennis Muren and art director TyRuben Ellingston, with Lucas' major interests being expanding Mos Eisley and adding the discarded Jabba the Hutt scene; "The initial scope of it involved just two dozen shots," Tom Kennedy said to *American Cinematographer*.[27] Muren then suggested that the release offered the opportunity to correct a list of fifteen to twenty shots that had always bothered him. "I suggested to George that we expand the vision and he was open to it," Muren later said. "Motion issues, particularly in the space battle scenes, were my concerns. Then Tom Kennedy and the others contributed their own ideas for redoing shots."[28]

What was more, the advanced digital techniques that would be put to use in the Special Edition would serve as an extensive test run for the prequels.[29] "We called it an experiment in learning new technology," Lucas said, "and hoped that the theatrical release would pay for the work we had done."[30] Lucas' enthusiasm for the project was starting to bring much more ambitious revisions.

Lucas' main priority was the prequels though, which he slowly but surely began to work on. His first task to complete was the writing. This was not an easy one—Lucas had to sketch out an outline not just for the first film in the series but for all three, expanding his original material with details, specifics and characters. One of the benefits of designing the entire story before a single script was completed was that the trilogy would have a purposeful arc and a logical continuity—although the original trilogy had a unifying arc to it, it was still hampered by the fact that it was mostly a patchwork of improvisations. Now Lucas would finally have the chance to design a true "master plan" from the beginning—and stick with it. With the story's ending already revealed in Episode IV, he had a clear finishing line in the plot progression. But, perhaps a testament to the fragility of creative planning, even this would be upheaved, as we will see throughout the coming chapters.

Lucas dusted off his old binder and poured through his notes, many of them written down nearly twenty years earlier. Some were still valid, some had been written out of history by subsequent changes he had made while making *Empire* and *Jedi*. For much of it, he had yet to write anything, and for others there were multiple alternatives. Who was Mother Skywalker? What were the Clone Wars about? Where did Boba Fett fit into it, if at all? What were Obi Wan and Yoda's origins? In other areas, Lucas would change his mind from his original ideas.

The actual original pre-1983 "outline" itself was only brief in length and vague in content—Lucas' description of it wavers from seven pages to twelve pages. The actual length of it is almost certainly the lower estimate, roughly seven pages, and that also appears to include the background information, miscellaneous notes and character sketches. Lucas basically lumps these all together into one description, which he terms "the outline." For example, when describing it on the *Star Wars* 2004 DVD commentary track, he says it has plot point description, character background and general information on the environment—a loose and vague collection of miscellaneous notes that, taken together, provide a sort of backstory. It seems as though it is not an actual seven-page narrative summary of the prequel story the way many might assume, but rather it is merely seven pages of notes, perhaps many of the very ones excerpted in chapters II and III of this book.

"It's mostly historical background that's not pinned to any particular story," he says of the outline.[31] "I have a little story treatment, a little outline that says this happened here, this happened here," he continued. "Where the characters came from and what they did. It's only about seven or eight pages."[32]

His task was not as easy as it seemed.

At first progress was slow, with Lucas casually juggling many different jobs—he continued to run his companies and raise his three children; he continued to produce other projects, such as the remainder of the *Young Indy* series and the feature film *Radioland Murders*, a project he had been planning with Willard Huyck and Gloria Katz since the days of *American Graffiti*, and which would be another testing ground for digital technology; he continued to work on the upcoming *Star Wars* Special Edition; and finally, he continued to work on the writing of the prequel trilogy. Quotes from McCallum and Lucas suggest that the first planning stages occurred as early as 1992, but mostly in 1993.[33]

That year, Rick McCallum began recruiting a writing partner, as Lucas had initially planned on handing his eventual first draft over to an additional writer as he had for the previous two *Star Wars* films. He turned to *Young Indy* alumnus Frank Darabont, who would soon be enjoying success for the critically-hailed *Shawshank Redemption*. Darabont remembers in an interview with *Creative Screenwriting*:

> I was approached very early on in the process. In fact, I was in the cutting room with *Shawshank*—late '93, I guess that would be. Rick McCallum called me and said, "Hey, we're starting to take the preliminary steps to do the next *Star Wars*, and George would like to know if you're interested in performing screenwriting services for him down the road." I said, "Sure—what are you—kidding?" Pin me to the wall; twist my arm. "Be happy to. Give me a call when you guys are ready."[34]

Pondering how to tackle the series, the promise of constructing films that would alter the original trilogy appealed to Lucas' experimental sensibilities. "I became fascinated by the idea of making a new trilogy that would forever change the way we see the original movies."[35] Obi Wan Kenobi had long been envisioned to be the protagonist of the prequel trilogy—the films would not follow Anakin but Obi Wan, with Anakin

Skywalker's fall seen through his eyes; the true pathos of the trilogy would hence be the failure of Kenobi and the betrayal of their friendship. As Lucas had said years earlier, they were "the young days of Ben Kenobi," and every description of them before the early to mid '90s described them as such. However, as Lucas set out to write the trilogy, reflecting on the story and speculating on its execution, a realisation obviously dawned on him.

Far more tragic and powerful than Obi Wan's story was the story of Anakin himself—the story of a brilliant prodigy, corrupted by greed, manipulated by an evil ruler and cast into darkness. As Lucas began to come up with a more detailed outline, the story of Anakin gradually—and naturally—wound its way into the forefront and overpowered Kenobi's, being intrinsically more interesting and offering more opportunity to develop a character and add dramatic interest.

It was an obvious story point; with *Return of the Jedi* placing so much emphasis on Anakin/Vader, the original trilogy was unexpectedly shifted in favour of him, so much in fact that the final moments of *Return of the Jedi*, when the true meaning of the saga comes to crystallization, are revealed to be between Anakin and Luke, father and son. The original trilogy could hence be viewed as largely the saga of a son battling his father and finally redeeming him to goodness. With Anakin being an important player in the films, with the story of Episodes I-III mainly revolving around him and his fall from grace, it became clear that the *Star Wars* saga could be told as the story of Anakin Skywalker—beginning with his discovery and ending with his death, broken into six chapters and two trilogies. Although Lucas had often described the original three films as "chapters of a book," the book itself was the original trilogy, and the prequel trilogy was still described as "another book," such as in Denise Worrel's 1983 article.[36] Now those two books were being combined into one.*

This joining of the six episodes into one epic film surrounding the character of Anakin Skywalker, however, introduced its own problems. The

---

*Though tangential here, it is interesting to ponder the influence *Godfather II* might have had on Lucas; did seeing Coppola turn the backstory of Michael Corleone's father into an interesting "origins" film influence Lucas' eventual decision in the 1970s to do the same? We can only speculate. The shifting form of the *Godfather Saga* has enormous parallels as well: originally a single movie about Michael Corleone, Coppola soon filmed a prequel and sequel meant to parallel father and son, and finally edited them together chronologically.

original concept of the prequel trilogy came about from the 1979 three-trilogy plan—each trilogy would have different characters and a different style, and the nine films would *not* form one large tale but three separate ones which were chronologically connected. The subsequent prequel story was proposed with this in mind. However, the series was now becoming a six-chapter narrative which told a single tale—yet the stylistic disconnectedness from the initial plan remained. The prequels were melodramatic and tragic costume dramas about a hero's fall from grace while the original films were light-hearted adventures about believing in yourself and the value of friendship. This posed no issue under the original structure but now that the two trilogies were being merged into one "Saga," an inevitable disconnectedness would result between the two sets of films (which explains why many viewers still have difficulty seeing the six films as one saga and not two separate trilogies).

This was a major milestone—prior to this, the prequels were more of a tangent, a "filling-in" of backstory, fleshing out the history of events and characters from the three *Star Wars* films as a separate series unto itself.

As the prequel trilogy began to be written, the roles of the main characters thus switched—Obi Wan's failure was now seen through the eyes of Anakin, with Obi Wan now being the secondary protagonist and Anakin the primary. When exactly this occurred is up for debate. Although it seems Lucas still favoured Obi Wan as late as the early '90s, likely it occurred when reviewing his notes and sketching out the prequel outline around 1993 or so (although Lucas' comments in 1992 *may* perhaps indicate it had occurred around this time, though his description is inconclusive[37]). While here we have the primary transformation of the narrative framework, this framework was still not as acute as it would be in the trilogy's final form —as will be examined in chapter XIII, the Anakin-centric story would continue to swell in each coming sequel, while at the time of Episode I it was comparatively understated.

Lucas had a chance to explore a truly complex character in Anakin, one who begins the story noble and heroic but undergoes a horrible transformation into a twisted figure of evil. Lucas' original outline had only detailed the character's final hours as a Jedi, when he fell to the dark side as an adult; even his initial discovery by Obi Wan seemed to have occurred when Anakin was a young man. Lucas, however, wanted to use the character to explore deeper issues about the roots of evil. Rather than present the character of Anakin as a demon-seed, a dark character whom always had a murderous streak in him, Lucas opted to present the character as a good-natured human being, a person full of compassion and enthusiasm. He stated on the Episode I DVD commentary track:

> One of the key elements...in the introduction of Anakin and the development of Anakin in [Episode I] was that I wanted him to be a very earnest, very honest, very good-natured person; just the opposite of the way you think of Darth Vader. Because the larger story is really "How does a sweet kid like this turn into something as evil as Darth Vader?"...Part of the story is how does he become bad, what choices does he make to become bad? Not, "Well he was bad to begin with so it's obvious that that's where it was going to go."[38]

Lucas decided to explore this concept to its full potential; as a result, he set the story much earlier than he anticipated. In order to fully explore the innocence and subsequent fall of Anakin, and in order to give motivation for Anakin's eventual turn, he went back to the character's childhood.*

This was a significant deviation from his original plan. Lucas' first story had been that Anakin and Obi Wan grew up together on Tatooine, together becoming war heroes and Jedi knights until one of Obi Wan's students, Darth Vader, slew Anakin. When *Empire Strikes Back* turned Anakin *into* Darth Vader, he ceased to be Obi Wan's equal and thus became his student, and therefore the original storyline no longer made sense. With *Return of the Jedi*, Lucas provided an alternate, as Obi Wan explains: it seems Obi Wan, already a Jedi knight, "discovered" Anakin, recognizing that the young man was strong in the Force and would make an exceptional Jedi prodigy, and took it upon himself to train him. This "discovery" was carried over to the prequels, and the original plot point that Anakin grew up on Tatooine residually remained—with the events now occurring in his childhood. You can see the different accounts being mixed into a new version that adds unique elements of its own.

While Lucas had to create a whole new set of worlds and develop the basic characters and plot for all three films, he also had to balance them against the original trilogy to make sure the series was consistent. This last point seemed especially troublesome, as Lucas' changing storyline had brought unexpected inconsistencies, a problem he had struggled to overcome in the previous two films as well. He told Laurent Bouzereau in *The Making of Episode I*:

> "In writing Episode I, I spent a lot of the time doing research. I had to develop an entire world. I had to make a lot of decisions about things that would affect

---

\* Lucas had already become enchanted by the idea of portraying his characters as kids, as his *Young Indy* series followed a ten-year-old Indiana Jones for much of its first season.

the next two movies, as well as this movie. Everything had to be laid out in this script so that the next two scripts would follow as they should. I also had to play this script against the three movies that had already been made, making sure that everything was consistent and that I hadn't forgotten anything. There was a tremendous amount of minutiae in these movies that I had to consider."[39]

### *Elements of a Story*

Perhaps the most complex plot point to write was the one that would nonetheless become the crux of the trilogy, that of Palpatine's rise. When Lucas originally wrote the storyline in the '70s, Palpatine was merely an unscrupulous politician who seized power through bribery and manipulation, taking advantage of a government that had lapsed into corruption, declaring himself Emperor. It also appears, hinted at in the *Star Wars* novelization, that there were actually a long line of Emperors that were really just puppets of the bureaucracy, who were the real menace. However, starting with *Empire Strikes Back*, the character was made more evil and sinister, a supreme ruler that even Vader bowed down to, and in *Return of the Jedi* was revealed to be a satanic sorcerer. Lucas now decided that Palpatine was a Sith, a fact that had never been officially confirmed—the Emperor was a master of the dark side in the original films, but not necessarily part of any official order, and the term Sith had never even been used in the films. However, Lucas now was faced with a slight dilemma: how does an evil Sith Lord get into politics? It was plausible for Palpatine to manipulate himself into office when he was merely a corrupt politician, but he was now presented as a black robed, lightning-spewing Dark Lord. To solve this, Lucas came up with the dual persona of Palpatine/ Sidious. Palpatine's manipulation into office was now much more complicated than before, and must have cost Lucas many hours to flesh out the complex subplot, the majority of which was so subtle and intricate that it went over the heads of most viewers.

Rather than seizing power in a coup, Lucas had always envisioned Palpatine manipulating the state and the people into handing over power to him. Lucas tells *USA Today*: "This was written during the Vietnam War and Nixon era, when the issue was how a democracy turns itself over to a dictator—not how a dictator takes over a democracy."[40]

Palpatine's rise to power would coincide with the Clone Wars, a subject of much mystery, and though Lucas had toyed with many different concepts back in the days of the original trilogy, the vagueness of the war allowed him free reign to make up whatever he wanted. The Expanded

Universe, a term given to the comics, books, games and other forms of media which expanded the franchise beyond the films, had since touched upon the Clone Wars, implying that an army of Mandalorian Warriors, of which Boba Fett was a member, fought a vicious battle against the Jedi knights—this was of course based off a small blurb that appeared in the Summer 1979 issue of *Bantha Tracks* (where they were not called Mandalorians but Shocktroopers) as well as the *Empire Strikes Back* novelisation. However, Lucas decided to disregard all the Expanded Universe material and instead linked the Clone Wars directly to Palpatine's manipulation of the galaxy.

In the second draft of *Star Wars* it was stated that the Republic grew corrupt from within, and war and terrorism persuaded people to accept a police state—now this notion was realised as the Separatists, a group of dissenters who cause a civil war and launch terrorist strikes upon the Republic, eventually becoming the enemies of the Clone War. It also seems that the Clone Wars, in Lucas' original conception (vague as it was), occurred much earlier than what we would be shown in the films.

The macro event of the Clone War was thus now shifted to a micro event, an event personally connected to Palpatine—this type of alteration would be a continuing trend in the writing of the prequels, as the epic plot was condensed into a personal tale which closely linked together events and characters; the scope of the *Star Wars* galaxy was becoming considerably smaller.

Palpatine's manipulations begin even before the events which open Episode I. Secretly a Sith Lord, Darth Sidious, with an apprentice, Darth Maul, the time has finally come for the Sith to return from secrecy after being wiped out by the Jedi a millennia earlier. Although Lucas had created the Sith as far back as 1974, their order would undergo as drastic a change as the Jedi had. In addition to re-writing Palpatine as a character named Darth Sidious, Lucas also had to re-develop who the Sith were, how they came to be and why they went away. He explained to Bill Moyers in a 1999 *Time* article:

> One of the themes throughout the films is that the Sith Lords, when they started out thousands of years ago, embraced the dark side. They were greedy and self-centered and they all wanted to take over, so they killed each other. Eventually, there was only one left, and that one took on an apprentice. And for thousands of years, the master would teach the apprentice, the master would die, the apprentice would then teach another apprentice, become the master, and so on. But there could never be any more than two of them, because if there were, they would try to get rid of the leader, which is exactly what Vader was trying

to do, and that's exactly what the Emperor was trying to do. The Emperor was trying to get rid of Vader, and Vader was trying to get rid of the Emperor. And that is the antithesis of a symbiotic relationship, in which if you do that, you become cancer, and you eventually kill the host, and everything dies.[41]

Thus was born the so-called "Rule of Two," a complete turnaround from the previous incarnation in which they were a warrior clan with many members. A more detailed history between the Sith and Jedi was fleshed out in Terry Brooks' *Phantom Menace* novelisation. The name "Darth" also underwent a transformation, initially being Vader's first name, then in 1978 the alias "Darth Vader" became Anakin's Sith identity—now the word "Darth" became a Sith designation (see Appendix C "Dark Father" for more information).

The "greedy trade barons" mentioned in the second draft of *Star Wars* as being prominent in the galaxy's fall became the Trade Federation of the film, showing Lucas' distrust in the political entanglements of corporations. Palpatine is a man with two identities: his true self, the twisted Darth Sidious, and his unassuming alter-ego, Palpatine, a gentle senator from the quiet and peaceful planet of Naboo (or Utapau in the initial draft). He contacts the Trade Federation and sets up a clever ploy whereby the planet is blockaded due to a dispute over trade routes. Finally, an invasion occurs after Palpatine is able to exploit a loophole in the law, with the people enslaved in camps, and the Queen on the run for her life. On Coruscant, the galactic capital, Senator Palpatine is able to use the victimisation of the peaceful Naboo to expose the corruption and uselessness of the current Supreme Chancellor, and a vote of "no confidence" is enacted. The dire situation creates a sympathy vote, and Senator Palpatine is ushered in as the new elected ruler of the galaxy.

His apprentice, Darth Maul, is slain by Obi Wan Kenobi, and so Palpatine searches for a new apprentice as he begins to enact phase two of his plan. He secretly commissions a clone army to be created, based off bounty hunter Jango Fett (father of Boba), to be used ten years later. The corruption in the Republic has led to civil unrest, and Palpatine uses his persona of Darth Sidious to create and foster a Separatist movement, threatening to bring civil war to the Republic. After being in office for ten years, the clone army is ready, Palpatine has found a new apprentice, and the Separatist army—secretly controlled by Palpatine himself—declares war on the galaxy, beginning the fabled Clone War. The Jedi, sworn to protect the Republic, reluctantly become soldiers in the war, decimating their numbers, while Palpatine uses the situation to manipulate the people into giving him "emergency powers," slowly turning the democracy into a dictatorship. As the war wages on, the Jedi begin to suspect Palpatine and turn on him, but Palpatine is able to manipulate Anakin into siding with him. Finally realising that Palpatine is a Sith Lord, the Jedi attempt to assassinate him. They fail, and Palpatine uses the incident to frame the Jedi as traitors. The Clone Army turns on the Jedi, and Anakin falls to the dark side and begins hunting down the survivors. Meanwhile, Palpatine declares himself Emperor and turns the Republic into the First Galactic Empire as a means of guaranteeing security as the Clone War transforms into a new civil war. Anakin is near-fatally wounded in a duel with Obi Wan on the site of a volcano, but Palpatine rescues his apprentice, resurrecting him as Darth Vader as the dictator consolidates his rule of the galaxy.

Palpatine's schemes however, are plagued with set-backs and defeats, and as a result, he must re-evaluate his plan; initially, it seems the Trade Federation was contracted to supply the army for the Clone War, with the Queen of Naboo to be captured and executed, leaving Palpatine, able to avoid the invasion due to his senatorial duties on Coruscant, to use the tragic death of her as a springboard to vote out the Supreme Chancellor and elect himself in place out of sympathy, with his apprentice Maul filling in the enforcer role Vader would eventually inherit. However, the Jedi's interference leaves the Queen safe, the Trade Federation defeated and Maul slain—but Palpatine is able to improvise and better his own situation, such as using the Queen herself to vote the Chancellor out of office, and noticing young Anakin, whom he begins grooming for future Sith-hood. With a plot as elaborate as that, it is no wonder that it took Lucas so long to write the scripts—and this was merely the outline.

During the writing of the prequels, the Jedi order itself underwent a fundamental change. The Jedi first were conceived in *Journal of the Whills* as intergalactic super-police, having their own army, requiring training at an academy, and providing military services such as escorting cargo through hostile territory. They re-appeared in the rough draft of *Star Wars* and were now more closely based on the samurai warriors Lucas came to be familiar with through Akira Kurosawa's films. As the drafts went on, sci-fi mysticism and E.E. Smith's Lensmen mixed in with the samurai aspect to create more superhero-like characters partly reminiscent of the original *Journal of the Whills* presentation, and a wizard-like spin provided by Alec Guinness and the character of Ben Kenobi gave them a quasi-magical quality that emphasized their spiritual aspect.

The final product introduced to audiences in *Star Wars* was that they were a mystical police force, a mysterious group of warriors which anyone could be recruited for and who called upon the powers of the Force, a power which anyone could learn to harness if only they believed in themselves.* Even in the sequels the Force was usually seen in a mystic, spiritual light, but Lucas brought back the "superpowers" he may have originally envisioned, such as acrobatics, telekinesis and levitation. For the prequels, Lucas decided to make the Jedi into outright religious monks, a route that the comics and novels had been heading along as well. This of course was born out of the strong Zen Buddhist overtones of Yoda in *Empire Strikes Back*—appropriately, Lawrence Kasdan and Irvin Kershner are both Buddhist, and although Lucas was raised Methodist, he has not surprisingly professed heavy Buddhist leanings in the years since: "I was raised Methodist. Now let's say I'm spiritual. It's Marin County. We're all Buddhists up here."[42]

During the initial period of pre-production for Episode I, Lucas had toyed with his original concept of a more police-like Jedi, similar to the Templar Knights of myth, the Lensmen, or the samurai warriors, as can be seen in Episode I production artwork where Obi Wan is portrayed in black body armor (Episode I's rough draft explicitly describes him as being dressed in black[43]). In the 1983 *Return of the Jedi* documentary *Classic Creatures*, Lucas remarked to Mark Hamill during a costume fitting that his new, militaristic black costume was "Jedi-like." However, in re-developing the Jedi order as a dogmatic monk-like organisation for the prequels, their visual look shifted accordingly, presenting them clad in priestly robes. "At one point during the Episode I design, we were thinking of the Jedi as lone samurai, then as teams of samurai," concept designer Ian McCaig said in *The Art of Episode II*. "They were going to be like a police force, dressed in black and a lot more militaristic. But they evolved into the peacekeeping force they are in the current film."[44] The designing of the prequel costumes was described by Laurent Bouzereau:

> Everything from full body armor to long, flowing capes were considered for the Jedi's costumes—although Lucas eventually went back to the designs from the first trilogy. "George wanted to make sure that when the audience saw these characters for the first time, it would immediately register that these were Jedi knights," McCaig explained. "For these characters and for Yoda, we had to establish some familiarity in the costumes with those existing films. I looked at the original *Star Wars* costumes to understand the style and influence, and I realized that those designers were very medieval, so we kept to that."[45]

---

* "Anyone who studied and worked hard could learn [the Force]," Lucas said in 1977 (Rinzler, p. 353)

However, this decision was based on a major oversight—the "Jedi garb" of the original trilogy was not Jedi garb at all. Obi Wan wore the standard desert robes of an inhabitant of Tatooine, modelled after middle-eastern dress—in fact, Uncle Owen is dressed in almost the exact same costume. Yoda as well is not wearing Jedi robes but merely hand-crafted rags. This problem may have been fostered due to a misinterpretation in *Return of the Jedi*—when Anakin appears in spirit in the final scene, rather than coming up with a proper Jedi costume, he was simply dressed identically to Obi Wan, perhaps creating the confusion that his clothing, identical to Obi Wan's and similar to Yoda's, the only Jedi ever seen in the films, was the traditional Jedi garb. There is at least an in-universe answer—since Anakin is from Tatooine, his traditional clothing might be the same desert garb that Uncle Owen and Obi Wan wear. In any case, this decision is a minor but often forgotten evolution (and certainly it may confuse future viewers who may be wondering why everyone on Tatooine, especially Uncle Owen, is dressed as a Jedi).

The Jedi were also now made to indoctrinate potential members from infanthood, and forbade any attachment to loved ones, like Buddhist monks—this was presumably done to tie into Anakin's tragic flaw, and thus serve as his main motivation for turning to the dark side. In this light, the Jedi were more like a dogmatic religious institution, with strict codes, organised councils and their own private society, the complete opposite of the swashbuckling para-military warriors of the original film. Here their heroism was also re-interpreted, portraying them as sowing the seeds of their own demise with their arrogance, complete with an "ivory tower" temple where they reside.

Lucas also chose to include Yoda in the films. While in *Empire Strikes Back* he was simply a wiseman, a shaman on a holy mountain or a zen master isolated on a monastery, designed and written as if a part of Dagobah itself with its primordial swamps teeming with life, Lucas was now faced with a dilemma—if the Jedi were an organized religious society, with councils and a bureaucracy, then he had to decide if Yoda, whom the original films had portrayed as the wisest and most powerful Jedi of all, would partake in the galactic intrigue. Lucas engineered a new interpretation of the character, placing him in an urban metropolis as part of the political scene. Lucas had not come up with a personal history to Yoda in the original films,[46] and while his role in the backstory could simply be ignored back then, fitting him in, in tangible terms, would now drift Yoda into a much different character than his former depiction. Slowly, as each element in the prequel trilogy underwent subtle but significant changes, a new storyline was seeping out.

In developing Anakin's character, Lucas realised that, like all tragic heroes, he had to have a tragic flaw, or "hamartia" as it was known to the classic Greeks. The most common flaw amongst the classic tragic heroes was "hubris"—arrogance or pride. This was the flaw that Obi Wan Kenobi had, the tragic quality that led to his failure to train Anakin and his subsequent guilt over the consequences. In time, this quality would shift from Obi Wan into Anakin, as he would become overconfident in his own abilities. But perhaps the main tragic flaw that Lucas would create for Anakin would stem from his attachment to loved ones, his possessiveness and his fear of loss, an influence Lucas obviously took from his Buddhist beliefs (main tenets of which are these exact issues).

The main plot device for this was the separation between Anakin and his mother, the primary reason Lucas set the first act of the trilogy to occur during Anakin's childhood.[47] With the Jedi's outlaw of attachment, Anakin is wrenched away from the only person who ever loved him, his mother, a point made all the more severe when Lucas decided to make him born into slavery; eventually, he is to be reunited with her as she lay dying, a event that traumatises him so much that Anakin takes his first step towards the dark side by slaughtering her captors and vowing that he will never again allow a loved one to die. This vow is complicated by his love for his wife, whom he quickly begins to have dark premonitions about, just as he had of his mother before she died. Fearing that he will lose the love of his life, Anakin is offered the dark side by Palpatine as the ultimate power. As Palpatine's years-old plot to turn Anakin and the galaxy against the Jedi finally comes to fruition, Anakin's vow to save his wife from death tragically leads him on a quest for control and ultimately to the dark side as he is slowly consumed by its tempting power.

This seems to be the basic skeletal plan that Lucas drew up when crafting the journey of Anakin; the details in between would be mostly invented on the fly as he wrote the actual scripts, but he had a clear plan for the character's arc. Episode I would pose the question, "how does a good person become evil?"; Episode III's answer is summed up by Lucas during a press interview at Cannes as the film was released: "On the personal level it was how does a good person turn into a bad person, and part of the observation of that is that most bad people think they are good people, they are doing it for the right reasons."[48]

Anakin's acceptance of the dark side as a means to grant him the knowledge and power to save his loved ones is also reminiscent of the tragedy of *Faust*. *Faust* is a medieval legend, whose precise origin is still unknown, which concerns a man named Faust who, in his quest for greater knowledge or wealth, makes a pact with the devil (named Mephistopheles or Mephisto) which ends up costing him his soul. This legend was most famously portrayed in a play by Christopher Marlowe, first published in 1604 (but performed at least a decade earlier). In continuing the thread of storytelling borrowing, the late-16th century Faust legend which Marlowe based his play on is actually taken from an earlier legend concerning Theophilus of Adana who makes a pact with Satan in order to make himself elected Bishop in the 6th century.

Luke and Leia's mother, a character shrouded in much mystery, would figure strongly into Anakin's turn, and now her character had to be developed. Lucas decided to make her into a person of politics, similar to Leia's role in the first *Star Wars*, in order to include her in the galactic intrigue and keep her involved in the story. Lucas set her up as the Queen of Naboo, an elected teenage ruler, in order to involve her prominently in the events of Episode I, which Lucas had now unexpectedly set in the days of Anakin's childhood. Anakin develops an innocent crush on her, and in the second Episode, the two of them now full adults, they would fall in love and secretly get married. Setting her age as a fourteen-year-old Queen allowed her to realistically have a relationship with Anakin some years later, and was also an idea from the 1974 rough draft of *Star Wars* in which Princess Leia was fourteen (being based on Princess Yuki from *The Hidden Fortress*, who was the same age). Episode I's rough draft, however, would state only that her age is "hard to determine, but she is a young woman."[49]

### Without Borders

As Lucas explained to Leonard Maltin in 2005, Episode I was most troublesome because he had to devise a plot from scratch: "The one we worried about the most was 'Episode I.' The backstory wasn't meant to be a movie."[50]

Lucas' decision to set the events of Episode I during Anakin's childhood had drastic effects on the rest of the story, however. For one, the original storyline had been conceived as occuring across a time span of only a few years. Now it spanned well over a decade. As a result, the first Episode contained very little of the original plot, while the second and especially the third episode had to be condensed—instead of the events occurring across three films, they were now compressed into two. "[Episodes I and II] were character pieces with lots of exposition," he said to the *Seattle Post-Intelligencer*. "Episode I was a film about a kid, the young Anakin Skywalker, and Episode II was his (coming-of-age). The problem is that 60 percent—maybe 80 percent of the backstory—is contained in Episode III."[51]

The story would hence be spread much thinner than Lucas originally had intended, as *Empire* Magazine reported in 2005:

> Only last month, Lucas, now 61, told an audience of fans what has been increasingly obvious since 1999. *The Phantom Menace* contained just 20 percent of this original outline's first three episodes, ditto *Clones*; the picnics and pod races, George confessed, were "padding." Lucas may have numerically bound himself to three full prequels long ago but for fans the truly essential material amounted to one story, an origin story that still has a [60-80] percent remainder: [Episode III].[52]

"I did run into the reality of the first film," Lucas admitted to *Static Multimedia* in 2005. "Basically, he is a slave kid. He gets found by the Jedi and he becomes part of the Jedi order and that he loves his mother. You know, that's maybe a half hour movie. And so I did a kind of jazz riff on the rest of it and I said, 'Well, I'm just going to enjoy myself. I have this giant world to play in and I'm going to just move around and have fun with this.'"[53]

The lack of original story material would actually become one of the prime draws to making the film—it would give Lucas the chance to essentially start over from scratch, to construct a truly limitless children's fantasy adventure film, without thought or worry about its connection to any sort of pre-set history or storyline. In 1976, after the disappointing reality of the compromising production of *Star Wars*, Lucas remarked: "Someday I'll do another movie like this, maybe, which will be much closer to my original plan. I didn't get the illusion that I'd seen in my mind. I got something else, which is all right, but it wasn't what I started out with."[54] Now, he would finally realise that far-out vision.

As Lucas was developing the overall story for the prequel trilogy, he was also organising its production with Rick McCallum. The plan was to follow the production guideline of the successful *Young Indy* shoot, where the episodes were filmed back to back in one long production period—the first film was expected to be released in 1997, with Episode II following in 1998 and Episode III in 1999. Lucas said in a 1992 interview with *Lucasfilm Fan Club Magazine*:

> Shooting the new *Star Wars* films back to back has always been the plan. What we're doing is planning it out very carefully, like the *Young Indy* TV series. The production technique we're using in the TV show are going to be the kind of technique that we use for the *Star Wars* feature films.[55]

This also meant that Lucas would have to write all three scripts at once. The workload was quite daunting. As Rick McCallum and production designer Gavin Bocquet embarked on a series of recces—reconnaissance missions to search for possible filming locations—in the summer of 1994,[56] Lucas finally began preparing to write Episode I's screenplay.

It had been eleven years since a *Star Wars* film had played on silver screens, and much in the world had changed—was Lucas ready to go back?

# Chapter X: Returning Home

IN 1983, staring down the final curtain of his trilogy, Lucas reflected on what he was sure was going to be "goodbye" to *Star Wars*. "I think what happens in a project," he said, "is you fall in love with the characters, and you fall in love with the environment. It's like a home. You feel very comfortable making up things that happen there; it becomes your own little fantasy land. The reality is that I love that world. I mean, there are friends there. It's like a home. I have a home there. And so there's always going to be a desire on my part to go home again, or to be with my friends again."[1] Espousing the message of the original film, however, he would add: "As attractive as the *Star Wars* world is, sooner or later you have to leave home and go on to some other place."[2]

Over a decade later, Lucas finally touched his number two pencil to a blue-lined yellow pad of paper, held in the same binder in which he had written the original *Star Wars*. As important as it was to "go on to some other place," he somehow found himself back where he started.

On the morning of November 1st, 1994, after taking his children to school, Lucas began writing Episode I. That eventful day was covered by a documentary crew, hired to record the process of making the trilogy. In the first segment of a twelve-part series, initially released on the internet website *Starwars.com*, Lucas prepares for writing:

This is the first of November, 1994. Today is my first day of writing the new *Star Wars* series. Took my kids to school this morning. My oldest daughter was sick all night. I got no sleep whatsoever.[3]

He takes the camera on a tour of his writing office. "I have beautiful, pristine yellow tablets ready to go," he comments, holding up the yellow pads of paper he traditionally hand-writes the first drafts of his scripts on. "A nice fresh box of pencils," he continues, pulling out a rattling box of number two pencils from his desk drawer. "I'm all set," he says, and then slumps into his chair. "Now all I need is an idea."

His famous *Star Wars* binder is shown, containing all the notes on the history of the galaxy which he had accumulated and organized over the twenty year period and which he meticulously expanded in preparation for the prequel scripts. The red two-inch binder is full of tabs, with headings such as "character," "plot," "outline," "jedi" and "empire."

Undated notes are shown, such as one detailing Anakin, which appears to be a recent creation. "Ages 9-20" is written next to his name, the timespan of his life which the prequels would occupy. The description is thus:

A boy who builds droids and races powerpods
Ernest and hardworking
who dreams of becoming a starpilot and a jedi
good at heart
Blue eyes
Whenever he gets near a machine he gets an intuition and knows what makes it work
Is he a mutation? Who was his father? Why was his mother outcast

Lucas reflects on the writing process: "It's great to be able to sit by myself and just be able do this. It's like a real luxury, actually. And, you know, I don't feel a lot of pressure, it's kind of fun. I'm getting to do a lot of research, which I love to do, and I'm getting a chance to think."[4]

On Lucas' bookshelves are shown dozens of hardcover volumes on mythology and anthropology, as well as paperback sci-fi novels by Edgar Rice Burroughs, Leigh Brackett and E.E. Smith.

"I think about scenes all the time," he continues. "And they come in a mosaic, and eventually all the pieces come together. And then there'll be some missing ones and then I have to sort of sit down and really work hard to get from point A to point B."[5]

Presumably, after the four-minute documentary piece was completed, Lucas began writing the script.

"The story for the three new films was meant to be the backstory of the other films," he later explained to Laurent Bouzereau. "That backstory was sketched out in a rudimentary fashion when I wrote the first trilogy, and there were certain things I knew even then. I knew, for example, that there was a character named Anakin Skywalker who grew up on a small planet, had special skills, and was found by the Jedi. I knew where everybody came from, who they were, and how they got to be what they were. A lot of the story points were there. But the actual scenes and many of the characters were not."[6]

As *The Making of Episode I* noted, "Quietly, secretly, Lucas devoted five days each week to writing, while Rick McCallum travelled the world in search of locations."[7] As of November 1st, 1994, George Lucas was officially writing another *Star Wars* picture.

The traditional opening scroll read:

It is a time of decay in the Republic. The taxation of trade routes to the tiny planet of Utapau is in dispute.

Hoping to force a resolution with a blockade of deadly Star Destroyers, the greedy Federation of Galactic Traders has cut off all shipping and supplies to the small, peaceful planet.

While the Congress of the Republic endlessly debates the alarming chain of events, the Supreme Chancellor has secretly dispatched a young Jedi Knight to settle the conflict... [8]

The script told the story of Obi Wan Kenobi, a Jedi knight, and Anakin Skywalker, a gifted slave-child. The peaceful planet of Utapau is invaded by the nefarious Federation of Galactic Traders, but Obi Wan Kenobi, after uncovering the invasion plot, intercepts the captured Queen Amidala and flees the planet with her retainers, including the bumbling Gungan Jar Jar Binks, whom Obi Wan saves in the swamps of Utapau while en route to secure the Queen. Their ship is damaged and forced to land on the desert planet of Tatooine.

In the first draft of the script it is Obi Wan who uncovers the invasion, meets Jar Jar (who speaks normal English), saves the Queen, ventures into the city of Mos Espa and discovers Anakin—Qui Gon does not appear until the Coruscant section, and Obi Wan's characterisation is essentially that of Qui Gon in the final film, having many of the same lines and mannerisms as well as being an older, full Jedi knight in his '30s. Obi Wan discovers the gifted slave-child Anakin Skywalker on Tatooine, and through a reckless but ultimately triumphant wager with Anakin's owner, Watto, the boy's freedom and the hyperdrive part the Queen's ship requires is won in a spectacular pod race.

Before Anakin enters the race, as they sit in Anakin and his mother Shmi's hovel, Obi Wan asks him if he fears or hates his rival, Sebulba, to which Anakin replies no. "He doesn't know he's bad," Anakin says, "He is full of pain, and I think he is afraid of me." Obi-Wan says that fear is the root of all evil and the path to the dark side. He tells Anakin that "The greatest challenge a Jedi must face is to resist the temptation of fear. The fear of letting go of things: possessions, friends, yourself...accepting change." Just before they depart for the podrace, Padme notices Obi-Wan staring out a window of the hovel. "You look like you're trying to solve the problems of the universe," Padme says. "Only our own," Obi Wan replies, "but maybe they will become the problems of the universe. I don't know..." It appears that Obi-Wan senses that this seemingly small-scale struggle will have larger, darker ramifications for the galaxy as a whole. After Anakin has won his freedom, Obi Wan makes him an offer. Obi Wan has recognized that Anakin is strong with the Force, and wants him to come with him to the Jedi Temple on Coruscant to be trained as a Jedi. Anakin agrees, but is forced to leave his mother. As they depart, they are attacked by Darth Maul, a Sith Lord, and Kenobi fights him; the two combatants are shown "levitating objects, moving extremely fast, and vibrating to the point of becoming almost invisible." They also leap "over one another in an incredible display of acrobatics."

Obi Wan fends him off and they escape to Coruscant. There, the Queen meets with Senator Palpatine, where they plan to bring their case before the Senate. Obi Wan meets up with his former master, Quigon Jinn, whom he introduces as "my mentor and good friend," and they bring the boy before the Jedi Council for evaluation, where they inform the council of the new Sith menace.

The Jedi Council, which consists of three Jedi Elders—Mace Windu, Yoda and Ki-Adi-Mundi—agrees to test Anakin, but Yoda warns Obi-Wan that, while the boy's existence was foreseen, he is too old and his future is "blank" and dangerous. Quigon takes Anakin to "the tower" for testing, while Obi-Wan remains with the Elders. Mace tells him, "Anakin will be returned to you after the test. He is your ward now, Kenobi. You realize there is little chance he will be accepted. You must decide what is to be done with him."

Later, Anakin tells Obi Wan that he didn't understand the Jedi tests, to which Quigon replies "You were not meant to." Obi Wan says the Council will make a decision after reviewing the results.

Valorum is not removed from office in these scenes, and instead the senate proves useless to resolve the Queen's dilemma. She decides to return to Utapau to take back her planet from the Federation army. Valorum protests, and vows to force the senate to deal with the matter before the Queen gets herself killed. Quigon accompanies Obi Wan back to Utapau with the Queen's entourage, with Anakin in tow. In order to bypass Utapau's blockade of battleships, Kenobi comes up with a plan of coming out of hyperspace right in orbit. The ship's captain protests that no computer is capable of that, but Obi Wan has a plan. He brings Anakin to the co-pilot's chair and says to him "Think of yourself racing...take the controls. We're heading towards a planet...Concentrate. Stop right before the surface." Anakin closes his eyes, and as everyone waits tensely he brings the ship out of lightspeed right in front of the planet.

The Utapau freedom fighters then make a plan to siege the capital. Setting aside their differences, the Gungans help them with their army, 10,000 strong, and Jar Jar courageously becomes a war hero, while Anakin and Padme take part in the battle and together they pilot a two-man starship and destroy the droid control-ship.

Quigon and Obi Wan battle Darth Maul, but eventually Quigon is struck down. Battle droids attempt to enter into the facility and aid Maul, but Kenobi uses the Force to "slam the door shut, crushing several droids in the process." Throughout the battle, the two warriors use the Force to hurl objects at one another. Soon afterwards, Padme and Anakin destroy the droid control ship, and the battle droids in the generator area begin running into the walls. Maul wades through the droids, cutting them down to get to Kenobi, and finally, they stand face-to-face. "Your style of fighting is old, but I understand it now," Obi Wan says.

"You learn fast," Maul replies.

"You don't bother to learn."

"I don't have to."

Before Maul can act, Kenobi lashes out and cuts the Sith warrior in half. He studies his fallen enemy and says: "Learn not...live not, my master always says."

The Federation of Galactic Traders is defeated and Utapau is saved.

Palpatine reveals he has become Supreme Chancellor and the Jedi Council agrees to train Anakin. After Quigon's funeral, Yoda calls the boy forward; Anakin kneels, and each Jedi comes forward to touch the boy's forehead. A final victory parade on Utapau ends the film.

On January 13th, 1995, the first draft of Episode I had been completed.[9] The script was titled *The Beginning*. "Writing the script was much more enjoyable this time around," Lucas said to Laurent Bouzereau, "because I wasn't constrained by anything. I didn't have to say to myself, 'Well I can't have one of these creatures, because there's no way to do it with a guy in a suit.' You can't write one of these movies without knowing how you're going to accomplish it. With CG at my disposal, I knew I could do whatever I wanted."[10]

Lucas had finally taken all of his newly created and organized notes and made his first attempt at writing. Much of it was new to Lucas himself. In an interview with Johnny Vaughan on *The Big Breakfast* television show in 1999, Lucas dispelled some public preconceptions:

> Johnny Vaughan: The way I imagine it is that George has this great big leather book, covered in dust, it's the Chronicles of Space and you've written the whole thing already and it's complete in your own mind. Is that right?

> George Lucas: No, that's wrong.

> JV: You don't have the complete story, mapped out from the start, all those years ago?

> GL: No.

> JV: Okay, nice one, so you're winging it.

> GL: No, I have a little story treatment, a little outline that says this happened here, this happened here, and in the first one I had all the scripts, but I had to rewrite the scripts so they went along because since they became three movies they had to have different structures and things, but the ones I'm working on now was the backstory which I'd written out, which was this was where he comes from, this was were he comes from, this is what the Clone Wars were about; it's just a little outline that goes right through the plot of the movie and where the characters came from and what they did. It's only about seven or eight pages.

> JV: Oh, that's brilliant, all those people that think you've schemed the whole thing up, but in fact, George Lucas, he makes it up as he goes along.[11]

Because Lucas had to think up almost the whole film—only ten to twenty percent of Episode I was taken from his original material[12]—progress was unexpectedly slow. The plot for the next two films was largely pre-existent, however Episode I was uncharted territory, with the only pre-meditated plot points being that Obi Wan discovers Anakin (which did not even survive in the final film) and that Palpatine ascends to Supreme Chancellor (occupying one scene in the finished piece, and absent from this first draft). Lucas had to come up with a totally new and original story.

Or perhaps not as new and original as it first seemed. In his struggle to devise an actual plot for Episode I, Lucas went back to the same source which he had borrowed from when plotting *Star Wars* in 1973: Akira Kurosawa's *The Hidden Fortress*. The film told the adventurous story of a General/samurai who attempts to escort a royal princess to safety across enemy territory and along the way picks up two bumbling peasants who add comic relief as they are pursued; the princess switches place with her bodyguard in order to avoid assassination, donning the disguise of a peasant, and they eventually find themselves in a small local town where they must barter for additional transportation, and end up buying a slave-girl's freedom, who then joins them on their adventure. In *Star Wars*, the samurai had been Obi Wan, the princess had been Leia, and the peasants had been the droids. For Episode I, the samurai was once again Obi Wan, the princess was Queen Amidala, and the peasant was Jar Jar. Instead of delivering Princess Leia from her captors to the safety of the Rebel stronghold on Yavin, Queen Amidala is delivered from her captors to the safety of Coruscant; and instead of Princess Leia deciding to take a stand and fight back against the Death Star to save her people, Queen Amidala decides to take a stand and fight back against the Trade Federation to save her people. *Phantom Menace* even sticks to some specific plot points of *Hidden Fortress* more closely than the final version of *Star Wars*—the Japanese town the group stops at while disguised as farmers becomes Mos Espa, which Qui Gon and Amidala also venture into dressed as farmers. They end up bartering for transportation, just as in *Hidden Fortress*, and buy a slave's freedom, just as in *Hidden Fortress*, who accompanies them despite the protests of others.

The plot points of trade routes and war treaties echoed down from the rough draft of *Star Wars*, which had minor appearances of such things. Other elements, from handmaidens to a master-padawan duo protecting young royalty to a peaceful planet being invaded and occupied, can also be found in the rough draft of *Star Wars*.

The pod race set-piece also has its roots in early *Star Wars* lore—the wonderful 1981 *Star Wars* radio drama was a thirteen-part adaptation which expanded upon the unseen moments in the film, and among its most memorable was the introduction of Luke (voiced by Mark Hamill himself) in a thrilling T-16 Skyhopper race with his Anchorhead friend Fixer, as they precariously swoop through Beggars Canyon at breakneck speeds.

The concept of Naboo (or Utapau in this draft) and Theed City as a Romanesque garden city perched on the top of a beautiful waterfall can be traced to James Gurney's famous children's book *Dinotopia*. The first in the *Dinotopa* series, *Dinotopia: A Land Apart From Time*, was released in 1992 and became an award-winning *New York Times* bestseller. The story revolves around a nineteenth-century scientist and his son, who are shipwrecked and discover the magical city of Dinotopia where humans and dinosaurs live together. The books were renowned for their stunning artwork which depicted this lush world. A comparison of Theed city to the Dinotopia city reveals a nearly identical copy, and the film's parade finale is a direct port of the finale of the book. Lucas came to be exposed to the *Dinotopia* books in 1994; Columbia Pictures optioned a movie adaptation the year before, and the producers came to Lucas to discuss ILM creating the special effects, since they had just finished *Jurassic Park*. Supposedly, Lucas showed the book to his children, and it became his son's favourite storybook. A few months later, Lucas began working on the Episode I screenplay. The connections go even deeper, however. The original Columbia deal fell apart, and *Dinotopia* was eventually released as a television mini-series in 2002. However, the original feature film had gone far enough to have pre-production artwork produced for it—one of the storyboard artists, Ian McCaig, eventually joined the Episode I art department as a concept artist when the *Dinotopia* project was cancelled, creating costume, set and character designs as well as storyboards for Episode I. Set decorator Peter Walpole would also later end up set-decorating the *Dinotopia* mini-series.

"I nearly dropped my popcorn, because I thought it looked so much like Dinotopia," says *Dinotopia* author James Gurney about *Phantom Menace*.[13] James Gurney even issued a statement on his website after Episode I was released to address the issue:

> From the moment the movie came out, I have been amazed at the reaction. One little girl stopped me in the lobby of the movie theater and said, "Why did George Lucas put Dinotopia into his *Star Wars* movie?" Parents and kids told me they watched the credits and didn't see my name. Dozens of fellow artists and writers, including many who worked in the *Star Wars* universe, called to express their astonishment at the parallels...The strangest thing was that George Lucas himself called me the day after the movie came out. He said that he was concerned that I might be concerned.
>
> My only concern was that once *Dinotopia* comes out as a film, people might think we got the idea for a waterfall city or a saurian parade from *Star Wars*. But I'm not too worried about that. All the *Dinotopia* fans noticed. And a lot of people who had never heard of *Dinotopia* before came to check out the *Dinotopia* website.

I've tried to look at the situation as a Dinotopian would. It's a great compliment that someone as masterful as George Lucas might be studying *Dinotopia* for inspiration. It's an honor to learn that *Dinotopia* is a book that he reads to his own kids...Even if Mr. Lucas is not comfortable with publicly acknowledging any inspiration from *Dinotopia*, I am happy to admit my admiration for *Star Wars*, which captured my imagination when I was in art school.[14]

### Shifting Pieces

As the developing script finally started to take shape, Lucas began organizing the art department to begin designs based off of his first draft. By January of 1995, Doug Chiang was selected to head the newly formed department, and as soon as Lucas' draft was completed that month, conceptual work began.

However, even by that point, major shifts were occurring in the production schedule. For one, the release date was being pushed back by at least a year. The development and writing of Episode I had taken Lucas much longer than anticipated, and with none of Episodes II or III written by spring, the release date was moved at least until 1998, with principle photography to occur in 1997. Rick McCallum reported to *Star Wars Insider* in 1995:

Until the scripts are complete, I can't give you a definite timeline [as to when filming will begin]. I'd like to start shooting major second unit action sequences summer of next year, do some blue screen work in the fall, and then principle photography in 1997, but again, this is dependent on when I receive the scripts.[15]

As Rick McCallum attested in the same interview, the plan was still to shoot all three films back to back. "Although until we get closer to the actual start date, I can't say for sure," he also added.[16] This of course meant that Lucas would have to finish the final drafts of Episode I, complete the designs, write Episode II and III, do all the conceptual work for those two films, cast the trilogy and hire the rest of the crew, all to be ready for filming of all *three* films in 1997, just two years away.

With Lucas' plate clearly full, it comes as no surprise that he planned on having others write and direct the material. Lucas would pen the first drafts, pass on the scripts to another writer and hire a director to film the material, with Lucas acting as executive overseer. Rick McCallum said in the summer of 1995:

[Frank Darabont] is definitely being considered [as a writer]. He's worked with us for a long time on *The Young Indiana Jones Chronicles* as has Jonathan Hales. We think they are both terrific. We're not, however, going to make any final decisions until George completes the storylines.[17]

Lucas was eager to direct and surmised that he could possibly helm the first of the films, perhaps to set the stage as he had done on the first trilogy, logical since he was already doing conceptual work on the first film at the time. Lucas related in a question and answer session at the Second Star Wars Summit, held on April 20th 1995 at Skywalker Ranch, as quoted in *Star Wars Insider*:

There's a possibility that I might direct one of them, but I haven't really decided yet. I'm writing them, at least writing the first drafts myself, then I'll probably bring other writers in to do second and third drafts, but there's a possibility that I'll direct the first one.[18]

Lucas' comments reveal that by the end of April he hadn't yet started the second draft of Episode I and was instead concentrating on other things while he searched for another writer (with Darabont and Hales considered as likely candidates). McCallum's previous comment also reveal that Lucas hadn't yet finalized the storylines for the trilogy, and, following the first draft, was reworking them as late as summer of 1995.[19] This was likely due to the fact that he was re-developing the character of Quigon Jinn, seen in a smaller role in the first draft, which would lead to the creation of the Prophecy, as well as the midichlorians, three factors which would figure prominently into the final trilogy and have a large effect on the storyline. These elements would be seen in Lucas' major re-write in the second draft.

There were other happenings at Lucasfilm, this time related to the original trilogy. With the twentieth anniversary of *Star Wars* approaching and the original 35mm negative now restored, Lucas was hard at work on the *Star Wars* Special Edition. Lucas also began considering restoring and revising the two sequels:

I'm looking at those films now, but they don't have the same restriction that the first film had with scenes having to be taken out because we were rushed. The first *Star Wars* film just barely made it into theaters. I'm looking at them to see if there are things that need to be cleaned up that would make me happy but I'm just starting that process now, so I don't really know.[20]

That year, a highly-successful home video release of the original trilogy hit stores. With the Special Edition finally "completing" the films, Lucas hoped to say goodbye to the "rougher" original versions, and so they were remastered to THX standards for optimal sound and picture quality and re-released, offering fans their last chance to own the original versions of the films. The videos were released in August of 1995, and were produced in a limited run until January of 1996. This event signified the then-current height of the *Star Wars* renaissance, with Kenner relaunching its long-cherished action figure line just months prior. A worldwide marketing blitz was enacted, with commercials, billboards and cereal tie-ins; nine full-sized X-wings toured internationally, and in Spain a 150 foot replica of the Millennium Falcon and a twenty-story billboard were used to promote the films.[21] The videos sold nine million units in the first week,[22] and helped initiate a new generation into the *Star Wars* mythos, an act which would be completed with the theatrical re-release two years later.

At Skywalker Ranch, Lucas continued to indulge in conceptual art work as he refined the prequel storylines. McCallum's comments in the summer of 1995 would be the last time the back to back shooting plan was spoken of. With principle photography fast approaching and much work to be done on Episode I alone, it seems that it finally dawned on them that the plan to shoot the entire trilogy at once was not feasible; the only solution would be to delay the shoot, and perhaps it was thought the trilogy would be easiest shot in regular intervals instead of one lengthy period.

Perhaps because of this decision, Lucas wrote the subsequent drafts himself. As he continued writing, the need for an additional writer gradually faded away. Frank Darabont explained in a 2000 interview:

> The very simple truth is that George, in sitting down and starting to write it himself, fleshing out the treatments and working out the broad storylines of the three films—he just kept going. He didn't stop one day and say, "Okay, bring in the writer." He was the writer. He brought himself in. People were wondering why the movie was delayed two years from its original announcement. Well, the reason was that George—and very appropriately so—chose to fashion the script himself. So, yes, there was some preliminary interest, but then the need for me never arose, because George was doing it. More power to him. I certainly thought that it was appropriate that George do that. That is the thing that I believe is dearest to him. That's his world; he invented it.[23]

This was a significant departure from his previous methods. While writing *Star Wars* he had plenty of help; Marcia provided valuable criticism, and his close circle of friends—Coppola, Barwood, Ritchie, DePalma, Spielberg, Kaufman and others—all read each draft and offered comments and suggestions. Gloria Katz and Willard Huyck also rewrote much of the dialogue for the final draft, and the edit was salvaged by a team of experts, including Marcia Lucas herself. The sequels of course all had input from Marcia (who continued to work as editor of the films) as well as story conferencing and co-writing from Leigh Brackett, Irvin Kershner, Lawrence Kasdan, Richard Marquand and Gary Kurtz. But now Lucas chose to do it all on his own. Kerry O' Quinn asked in his 1981 *Starlog* interview if Lucas would ever turn the scripting of the prequels over to someone else. "I don't know," Lucas replied. "I'd love to. But I don't think its going to be possible."[24] It seems that in his mind the amount of minutiae and careful balance of story and character would be impossible for anyone but himself—the elements had been in his head for so long that he felt that only he could get them on paper.

### *Qui Gon and Anakin*

With the subsequent drafts of Episode I, Lucas would re-introduce the character of Qui Gon Jinn; although he appeared in the first draft, his appearance henceforth was, plot-wise, a new element to the story, and replaced Obi Wan as the primary Jedi protagonist. Surrounding this newly created central character were a number of significant additions as well—those of the Prophecy and midichlorians. All three new factors had a common connection with Anakin, and were created to support his character.

The promotion of Qui Gon Jinn to the status of central character had a number of advantages for Lucas' writing. It better established the proper master-padawan relationship, perhaps in order to contrast the tension of Obi Wan and Anakin's in the next films, and it gave the central Jedi character someone to play off of; in the first draft, since Obi Wan is solo for the first quarter of the film, he cannot express or relate information to the audience until he meets Jar Jar. Having two Jedi instead of one provided practical writing support and added a good dynamic. With this, Obi Wan was demoted to padawan learner, dropped in age and given only a supporting role.

There is the question of "why Qui Gon?" He diminished Obi Wan's character and central role, and also impeded the all-important relationship between Kenobi and Anakin since there would be less time to establish this in the next film. There is no clever answer to be given—the character wasn't a storytelling necessity, since Obi Wan filled the same purpose in draft one, and it could even be said that the character introduced some inconsistencies in the original trilogy. It may be that Lucas simply wanted to try something different, and he was always interested in portraying a true master-padawan duo (reaching all the way back to the 1973's *Journal of the Whills*) and with Episode II splitting Anakin and Kenobi up for much of the film and portraying them bickering whenever together, perhaps Lucas felt that this would be his only opportunity to portray such a concept. Qui Gon's death also would later reveal the secret of immortality, although this was possible with the earlier Obi Wan-centric story of the first draft where Quigon is also a significant character and is killed by Maul (the character's name, "Jinn," is Arabic for "spirit," indicating that Lucas might have had this device in mind). In short, Lucas probably felt that this was simply a more interesting direction to take the story.

The biggest influence of Qui Gon would be felt in the second act of the film. Once the characters land on Tatooine, Obi Wan now remains with the Queen and is rarely seen. Qui Gon meets Anakin, is impressed with his connection to the Force, and decides to barter for his freedom, hoping to train him as a Jedi. In this light, one of the only story points in Episode I from the original outline was done away with.

Evidently, Lucas also thought the Jedi Council and Qui Gon/Obi Wan needed more incentive to suddenly begin training a ten-year-old slave-boy with a clouded future. Although it is clear that the boy is gifted, there needed to be more than just Qui Gon/Obi Wan's high opinion of him to result in such a highly unorthodox event. In this, the Prophecy, Chosen One and the midichlorians have been created.

The midichlorians and the Prophecy were controversial upon the film's release, although the two concepts exist for very specific story support. The midichlorians allow for an objective "rating" of Anakin's ability, to show that he is truly special and important beyond Obi Wan or Qui Gon's opinion that "he is gifted." The initial concept of the Jedi was that anyone could be picked up and trained by a Jedi master, and so Obi Wan began training Anakin simply because he believed the boy had potential; this posed no problem under the original samurai-like conception of the Jedi, but now that they were essentially an organized religion, with dogmatic codes and councils and with initiates indoctrinated from birth, there needed to be a very important and *objective* reason to train him. This necessitated the creation of the midichlorians—microscopic lifeforms which act as conductors of the Force, loosely based off real-life mitochondria.[25] The more midichlorians a person has, the greater their connection to the Force. This had its roots in the early drafts of *Star Wars*, such as in the third draft where Obi Wan says that he is old and has little of the Force left in him, implying some kind of physical link, as well as the Kiber crystal which intensified one's Force powers; Lucas also makes reference to them behind the scenes in 1977.[26] Anakin is now revealed to have the highest midichlorian count ever seen—higher than even Yoda. This is objective evidence that cannot be debated. He is now revealed to be so powerful that it is possible that he was even conceived by the midichlorians themselves—as he is now revealed to be the product of a virgin birth[27] (what info Lucas developed about Anakin's father before this draft is a mystery—even the pages seen in Lucas' binder in the web doc state that it was unknown and that he may be a mutation, though these are obviously notes from the 1990s. This also may indicate that *Revenge of the Sith*'s "revelation" about Anakin's origin was invented for that film. Cryptically, in Episode I's rough draft Shmi's last name is not Skywalker but Warka[28]).

The midichlorian plot point is then reinforced with the Chosen One prophecy, that Anakin is actually some sort of foretold savior. This makes Qui Gon convinced that the boy *must* be trained, with or without the council's approval, and places even more significance on Anakin's abilities. Because of this, the Council, whom under other circumstances would dismiss the boy instantly, must now seriously consider his tutelage.

Because it is no longer Kenobi's decision to train Anakin, the problem of somehow getting him to mentor Anakin by the film's end was resolved in Qui Gon's death, where Qui Gon's dying wish is for Obi Wan to take Anakin as his apprentice.

With his new status as "Chosen One," the prophesized savior of the galaxy, Anakin's importance was increased yet again. This is a telling sign in how the overall story of the saga was shifting: in the second draft of *Star Wars*, the "son of the suns" heralded in the opening "Journal of the Whills" verse is actually revealed to be Luke—though this aspect was excised from the actual film itself, it shows how the focus of the story had changed. When Lucas began *Star Wars*, Luke was the prophesied messiah of the galaxy; by the time of the prequels, it is Anakin.

The greatest effect of the "new" Qui Gon Jinn was that of Obi Wan's character. First, Anakin was made into the protagonist of the trilogy, and now Obi Wan was being pushed into the background even more, and the film could be designated as more of an "old Qui Gon" film rather than a "young Ben Kenobi" film. In fact, Qui Gon not only replaced Obi Wan, but he more or less *became* him. The "arrogant" and "reckless" Obi Wan described in the original trilogy and present in the first draft was now meek and obedient, with much of his dialogue relegated to "yes, master." It was now Qui Gon who became the reckless one as he absorbed Obi Wan's character—betting the Queen's ship on Anakin, bringing slave boys to be trained as Jedi and arguing against the Council. He retained the same basic dialogue and actions of Obi Wan from draft one.

The character swap would be reconciled by having Obi Wan vow to train Anakin at the film's conclusion and clashing with the Jedi Council on the matter. Lucas explained in *The Making of Episode I*: "In the beginning, Obi Wan is at odds with Qui-Gon, who rebels against the Jedi rules. But by the end of the film, he has *become* Qui-Gon by taking on his rebellious personality and his responsibilities."[29]

The next films would portray Obi Wan as more of a swashbuckler, but the character described in the Dagobah scene in *Return of the Jedi* no longer existed. Obi Wan was no longer reckless and no longer took upon training Anakin out of arrogance because he thought he could be "as good a teacher as Yoda." The character was less of a tragic figure—no longer would his pride "have terrible consequences for the galaxy," as he relates in *Return of the Jedi*, haunted by his failure. He essentially returned to his original image from *Star Wars*, a valiant role model that was good to the core.

This may have been due to the fact that Anakin was to be portrayed as a rash and reckless padawan in the next films, as opposed to the original conception where he was a noble and stoic Jedi knight. Having a master that was as arrogant as his student would have been less interesting than if Kenobi was constantly trying to reel Anakin back, much to Anakin's frustration.

This was a significant turn for Anakin's character. Although the immediate film Lucas was working on, Episode I, featured the character only as an innocent child, Lucas was obviously making decisions for future episodes, where the plot thickens.

While it is true that in *Empire Strikes Back* Yoda says of Luke, "Much anger in him—like his father," this must be taken in the proper context. Yoda's description not only applies to Luke but Obi Wan as well, as Obi Wan replies "Was I any different when you taught me?", and is not of an angst-ridden delinquent, but of a person who suffers from frustration and impatience as any human. Although this is assuredly true of Anakin in the prequel films, the comparison Yoda was using implied that Anakin was as "angry" as Luke (or a "good" Jedi like Obi Wan), and discounting Yoda's Jedi master standards, Luke was not an angry young man. The point being made here is that the "impatient" and "angry" Anakin of the prequel trilogy largely did not exist prior to the mid-'90s. The change came about now that he was being combined with Darth Vader, who *was* written as an impatient and frustrated young adult. Vader obviously fell to the dark side because of his quest for greater power, as is revealed in the third draft of the *Star*

*Wars* script; it was a personality flaw, and Vader left Obi Wan after only a brief training time. He was fairly two-dimensional, labelled as "bad." On the other hand, Father Skywalker was an admired example of a Jedi, one who was an elderly veteran of the Clone Wars and a galactic hero—lusting for power was not in the nature of his personality. He was also fairly two-dimensional, labelled as "good." Now, however, the angry and impatient young student, Darth Vader, and the valiant and heroic Jedi master, Father Skywalker (Anakin Skywalker), had to be combined—the contradicting images could be ignored in the original trilogy but now they had to be addressed in specific and tangible ways. In deciding which presentation to go with, Lucas had to choose Vader's.

Again we see an unfortunate obstacle due to the improvised nature of the original trilogy. This will not be the last time the issue of conflicting personalities will arise.

Much of the new Anakin seems derived from the lead character of Hiroshi Inagaki's *Samurai* trilogy—*Samurai I: Miyamoto Musashi*, *Samurai II: Duel at Ichijoji Temple* and *Samurai III: Duel at Ganryu Island*. Inagaki was considered Kurosawa's rival, and the first instalment of the trilogy beat *Seven Samurai* for the Oscar for Best Foreign Language Film in 1954. Given the enormous influence of Kurosawa and samurai films, and the fact that Inagaki's films are fashioned as a serial-esque trilogy which charts the development of a powerful warrior, it is probable that Lucas would have seen and enjoyed this sweeping epic, which is based off of Eiji Yoshikawa's novel, *Musashi*, chronicling the mythic history of the real-life legendary swordsman. The trilogy has been described as "Japan's *Gone With the Wind*."

The story tells the tale of an orphan, a wild young man named Takezo, who leaves his town with his friend Matahatchi to join the army and fight in the war. After a complicated romance with a peasant girl, Takezo is rescued from death by a monk, who sentences him to the study of the samurai code. After years of training, Takezo emerges as Musashi, a reformed man, now a great warrior and noble samurai. He becomes Japan's greatest swordsman, but he still must contend with rival fencers who challenge his status, as well as a tumultuous romance. Musashi is seen as prideful and arrogant due to his high status, but in time he becomes wise and learns control, finally settling down on a farm with his future-wife after vanquishing a vengeful nemesis, who issues an operatic duel on the beach at sunrise in the series' flame-tinted finale. The similarities with Anakin's story are clear—Lucas may have even had these Musashi films in mind when he came up with the original backstory in the '70s, where Father Skywalker leaves his Tatooine farm with Ben Kenobi to fight in the Clone

Wars and become a Jedi. The "new" Anakin would derive much more of the arrogant and prideful side of Musashi, as the Chosen One who seeks to control everything but himself.

One particularly interesting exchange comes early in the second instalment in Inagaki's trilogy, where Musashi meets an old monk after killing an opponent in a duel. The monk says that Musashi is still a poor fencer. "But I won the duel!" Musashi protests.

"Of course you won the fight," the monk agrees, "but you lost as a samurai."

"I won there, too" Musashi objects, "I'm not even scratched. Look, I'll show you."

The monk laughs softly to himself in amusement. "You seem to trust your skill very much," he says. "You are really strong. But you're not mentally relaxed." Musashi listens to the monk's words with a frustrated sense of awakening. "That means you may win in a match," the monk continues, "but you are not yet a true samurai. You'll always remain just a tough man." With that, the monk picks up his walking stick and continues down the road. Musashi remains where he is, his head hanging low, and finally races to meet up with the monk, kneeling in front of him and pleading, "Teach me further!"

"All I can tell you is just this," the monk replies, "You are too strong. Understand, Musashi?" Musashi listens attentively. "Swordsmanship means chivalry," the monk continues. "Remember: a man cannot forever remain physically strong. You are too strong," he repeats again. "Decidedly too strong." With that, the old man leaves, and Musashi realises that he himself is still only a student, despite his reputation.

The structure of Inagaki's trilogy is similar as well—the first film ends with Musashi being initiated as a samurai, while in film two he struggles with his power and impatience, finally becoming a master in film three. The Anakin of the prequel trilogy would play out in a similar manner, only without the humble awakening to the monk's wisdom. Instead, Anakin would reject the advice of his Jedi mentors and follow the path of the dark side, the ultimate realisation in his quest for greater power.

Some of Anakin's characterisation would also show inspiration from the character of Katsushiro from Kurosawa's *Seven Samurai*. In that film, Katsushiro is a young man who meets a wise samurai and becomes his apprentice. He yearns for experience and a forum to prove himself but is disappointed at being held back by his master, and during the long battle to defend a village from bandits, he has a secret relationship with a young woman (the specific imagery of which Lucas would carry into Anakin's courtship of Padme in Episode II[30]). As an aside, *Seven Samurai* would also give Lucas the direct inspiration for Jar Jar in the bumbling character of Kikuchiyo, played with explosive energy by Toshiro Mifune, a vulgar peasant who tries to be a samurai and provides juvenile comic relief but ultimately becomes a heroic warrior.

## *A New Chronology*

Finally, we should examine the topic of age. This would be a major yet seemingly-unimportant part of the prequels which may in later years be overlooked and forgotten. There has been a lot of confusion on this complicated and convoluted matter, and I hope I can once and for all clear this up.

The prequel trilogy pushed the original timeline forward by about a decade, sometimes two or three decades, depending on which character or event in question. This results in events and characters from the original trilogy becoming at least ten years younger than previously indicated. Much of this results from the fact that *Star Wars* was originally written under the orthodox Father Skywalker viewpoint, where Anakin and Obi Wan were friends of roughly the same age and not master and student, with Darth Vader a separate person.

Luke appears to be roughly twenty years of age in *Star Wars*—his actual cited age is inconsistent, as initially some sources claimed 18, some 19, some even 20 (this is actually what the script states); the "Official" age has now been settled at 19. Similarly, Leia's age was originally much younger, specifically described as 16 years old in the fourth draft screenplay, but has accordingly been "Officially" raised to match Luke's. So it is obvious that all the drama of the prequel trilogy—i.e. the death of Anakin, the Jedi purge, the Empire's rise—could only have happened roughly twenty years prior to *Star Wars*, since it would coincide roughly around the time of Luke's conception; his mother was obviously impregnated by Father Skywalker/Anakin before he died, and all the other events revolve around his death, so 20 is the maximum. This is unalterably established in the first film, and so the timeline of these events remains constant throughout the changes. But what Lucas did play around with was the ages of the characters themselves and all of the preceding occurrences.

Obi Wan appears to us to be roughly 70 years of age—Lucas decided when writing *Return of the Jedi* that he would be "in his seventies," as per *Annotated Screenplays*,[31] so let's say 75, which is also consistent with the second edition of *The Guide to the Star Wars Universe*; the third draft of *Star Wars* also describes Ben as in his 70s. This would mean he was roughly 55 years old when Father Skywalker died and the Empire took over (remember this is the original pre-1978 version). Darth Vader, of course, was his student—pegging Vader to be roughly 40 years old at the time of *Star Wars*. This is concluded by reasoning that, given Darth was a student, he would have been a young man, of similar age to someone enlisting in military service—that is, roughly 18-25, with 20 being a good estimation. This is augmented by the fact that in *Star Wars* Obi Wan remembers him as "a young Jedi." Also, given that he left Obi Wan while still a student, we can conclude that he was Obi Wan's pupil for only a brief period, certainly no more than a few years, and more likely a single year. Therefore, if, for instance, he began training under Kenobi at 20 he would have joined the Empire by 21.

Anakin (Father Skywalker), on the other hand, was Obi Wan's equal, a Jedi knight himself. It seemed implied that the two grew up together as friends on Tatooine, and therefore would be close in age—certainly not much more than five years apart. It is probable that Obi Wan was a few years older than Anakin—after all, it is Obi Wan who dragged Anakin on a "damned fool idealistic crusade" to become a Jedi, an action that seems to suggest that Obi Wan was perhaps a sort of bigger brother to Anakin, much the same way Biggs tries to bring Luke with him to join the Rebellion (Biggs is described as "a few years older" in the script).

The Clone Wars, as described in *Star Wars*, also were not implied to be so recent. It seemed that Anakin and Obi Wan went off together to become Jedi Knights and fight in the war—akin to adventure-seeking young men enlisting in the armed service to fight for a cause (ie. WWI/WWII); this is what prompts their adventure, and it isn't until much later that Darth Vader and the Empire come around. This then places the Clone Wars much farther back—back to when Obi Wan and Anakin were young men of 18-25 years old. In other words, if Father Skywalker enlisted at the youngest possible age, 18, the oldest age plausible for Obi Wan would be 28; any gap greater than that between the two and it begins to loose plausibility (a teenager running off for military service with a thirty year old?). Likely they were very close in age, probably both around 20, the same as Luke and Biggs in *Star Wars*. After training to become Jedi they become war heroes, with Obi Wan ascending to the rank of General after many years of combat and Father Skywalker becoming a legendary pilot.

Obi Wan eventually begins mentoring at least one student—in fact, this may have occurred with Anakin as well. Consider: the only reason Obi Wan's General rank and student are mentioned is because they are incidental. Princess Leia mentions that Obi Wan was a General in the Clone Wars, and his student Darth Vader is only brought up because Luke asks how his father died. Obi Wan himself never goes out of his way to divulge these facts; it is part of the charm and mystery that such interesting things are part of a Jedi's everyday life.

Therefore, as Obi Wan and Anakin were meant to be best friends of equal status who embarked on their adventure together, it is probable that Anakin had at least one student as well.[*] It is also likely that Anakin was a high-ranking military man, especially being "a cunning warrior" and "the best starpilot in the galaxy." Being a Jedi is synonymous with being in the military; as mentioned earlier, the Jedi were initially conceived as a mystical force of soldiers, and not the more Buddhist-oriented monks that they became after Yoda's introduction in *Empire Strikes Back*. In fact, in the third draft, Ben Kenobi claims to be a "Bendu *Officer*"—a Jedi *Officer*, in other words, a war hero who was part of the "Imperial Space Force" and "commander of the White Legions," reinforcing this original militaristic view of the Jedi. As Luke says in this draft, "I am going to become a startrooper and fight in the wars. My father was a Jedi!"

So here we have extrapolated many things in terms of establishing a chronology. Going backwards from most recent to most distant:

> (-20 years) Luke is born. The Jedi are exterminated and the Empire created. Obi Wan fights and wounds Vader. Vader kills Anakin. Vader leaves Obi Wan. (-21 years) Obi Wan mentors Vader. (-40 years) Vader is born. (-55 years) Anakin and Obi Wan become Jedi knights and fight in the Clone War. Obi Wan and Anakin leave Tatooine to enlist. The Clone Wars begins. (-70-75 years) Anakin and Obi Wan are born on Tatooine.

If Anakin was alive at the time of *Star Wars* he would have been anywhere between 70-75 years old, assuming Obi Wan is 75 and that Anakin was the same age or no more than five years younger. This, however, raises one unusual issue, that being the fact that he would have been 50-55 years old when he conceived Luke, a little on the old side. It is also possible that the Clone *Wars*, as Leia calls it,[**] were a series of wars spread out over many decades, leaving Anakin unable to start a family until after the war ended, explaining why Obi Wan appears to have never had children, since the Jedi purge would have occurred so soon, and explaining

---

[*] In 2008's *Clone Wars* series, Lucas would follow through with this as Anakin trains a padawan named Ahsoka.

[**] In both the third and fourth drafts it is only ever written as Clone Wars. Mark Hamill, however, calls it Clone War in the film

how Obi Wan was able to become a General in the Clone Wars if he was only recruited at its start. On the other hand, Kenobi might not have been a General *during* the Clone Wars, as this is never specifically stated, but rather that he eventually achieved this rank through his thirty years of service to the Republic, as the Jedi were a galactic military power—a far more likely possibility in my opinion.

All of this is speculation, of course, since the facts are vague. Some may theorise that the Clone Wars represents the perfect opportunity for Obi Wan and/or Anakin to begin training more Jedi since new soldiers would be needed, and this may have very well been the case, as it remains a very strong possibility that not only did Anakin have an apprentice of his own, but that Obi Wan and Anakin may have had multiple students, perhaps both at the same time and perhaps both having whole *groups* of students. In the original *Star Wars* synopsis from 1973, this happens—General Skywalker trains a group of boys he meets to help attack the Imperials and save the princess. Obi Wan implies as much in the third draft: when recounting the tale of Vader's betrayal he says, "One of my disciple's (sic) took the crystal"—plural, meaning that he indeed had more than just one. Darth was the last in a long line of protégés to Kenobi.

Darth, however, could not have become Obi Wan's student until *after* the war, since the Clone Wars appears to have ended before the Empire's rise, during which Vader had already joined the dark side, and he was only with Obi Wan for a brief period (given that Vader never even completed his training, he wouldn't have known Obi Wan very long).

So, to summarise the original ages at the time of *Star Wars*, as they appear in the film:

Vader is approx. 40
Obi Wan is approx. 75
Father Skywalker/ Anakin is approx. 75 (perhaps slightly younger)

Once again we see a problem here. There is a contradiction between the two characters Lucas had created—Father Skywalker (later officially named Anakin) and Darth Vader. Anakin was written to be a fully trained Jedi knight, a hero of the great Clone Wars and almost certainly a highly decorated pilot, so well known and liked that even random pilots Luke encounters in the Rebellion such as Red Leader remember him (in a scene cut out of *Star Wars*, but partially restored for the Special Edition) and would have been roughly 50 years old at the time of the prequels. Darth Vader, on the other hand, was a student of Obi Wan's, a young man who became seduced by the dark side and betrayed the Jedi, killing Anakin and joining the Empire, and would have been roughly 20 years old at the time of the prequels, and was too young to see the Clone Wars.

How can a thirty year contradiction be somehow written around? Lucas took certain things from *Darth Vader* and certain things from *Father Skywalker* and came up with the new *Anakin*. He also had to somehow incorporate the timeline he created post-1977, such as Anakin being "discovered" by Obi Wan and trained by him.

As a result, the characters' ages differed from their original depiction in *Star Wars*. Anakin obviously had to be Obi Wan's student since Darth Vader was. Therefore, Lucas had to go with Vader's age and not Father Skywalker's, making Anakin 20-23 in the last two prequel films, instead of 50. This drastically changed the rest of the chronology, with Anakin now conceiving his children in his early 20s. In the original chronology, Vader would have been too young to fight in the Clone Wars, which began as late as fifty years before *Star Wars* and thirty years before Vader's fall to the dark side. The dating of the Clone Wars remains a tricky subject—it is still possible that Father Skywalker and Obi Wan's initial adventure-seeking was not prompted by the war itself but merely by the idea of becoming a Jedi, with their successful initiation drawing them into the war later on. However, considering that Obi Wan says in *Star Wars* that Anakin followed him off on an "idealistic crusade," the Clone War theory seems to fit much better.

Obi Wan's age could have remained roughly the same, however, much like in the first draft of Episode I, with him being a full Jedi knight when Vader/Anakin was a boy, allowing him to still be (roughly) in his 70's in *Star Wars*. However, with his replacement by Qui Gon Jinn in draft two, Lucas had now written that in Episode I Obi Wan was still a student. Lucas placed him at the oldest possible age a Jedi padawan realistically could be—25. When dealing with Obi Wan's old age in *Star Wars*, every year added or subtracted was substantial. Now, instead of being roughly 75, Obi Wan is a scant 57—not even a legal senior citizen.

Additionally, Vader, originally a man of healthy middle age, being roughly 40 at the time of *Star Wars*, previously, during the making of *Empire Strikes Back* and *Return of the Jedi*, was to have been an old man only ten years younger than Obi Wan. Hence, we see that the new prequel timeline was in actuality the third timeline created! The first was the original one revealed in 1977 for *Star Wars*, as described previously. The second one existed between the time when Father Skywalker was made into Darth Vader in 1978 and revealed in 1980, and the formation of the prequels, around 1993 or 1994. This one again cobbled together elements of Darth Vader and Father Skywalker to create a unified character, but retained Obi Wan's original age. This was decided upon when revealing Anakin at the end of *Return of the Jedi*—Lucas decided Vader was ten years younger than Obi Wan, pegging him at 65,[32] and, when unmasked at the film's conclusion, portrayed by 77-year-old Sebastian Shaw. This timeline introduces a curious anomaly—accounting for the roughly three years that pass between *Star Wars* and *Empire/Jedi*, Vader would have been 62 at the time of *Star Wars*. This meant that he fell to the dark side at 42, indicating that Darth Vader began his Jedi training in his forties—and Yoda thought *Luke* was too old! Likely, Lucas never even considered this aspect.

The third timeline written for the prequels revised this by lowering everyone's age by two decades. Anakin joins the Jedi when he is nine years old now and Obi Wan is no longer 55 when he discovers Anakin, rather he is less than half of that, 25, and it is no longer he who discovers him—although initially in the first draft Obi Wan's character was more consistent with the first and second timelines. Because Obi Wan also now discovered Anakin as a *child* and not a young man, the entire chronology now was pushed back another whole decade.

The final timeline settled on after the second draft of Episode I is that Anakin was 9 and Obi Wan 25, making Anakin/Vader 41 and Obi Wan 57 at the time of *Star Wars*, since it is officially 32 years after Episode I:

| Timeline one (1977) | Timeline two (1980) | Timeline three (1999) |
|---|---|---|
| *Star Wars*: | *Star Wars*: | *Star Wars*: |
| Vader: approx. 40 | Vader: approx. 62 | Vader: 41 |
| Obi Wan: approx. 75 | Obi Wan: approx. 75 | Obi Wan: 57 |
| Anakin: approx. 70-75 | | |

That is quite the variation. Vader ages over twenty years older on the second timeline, and poor Obi Wan drops almost twenty years younger due to the prequels' final revision.

The notion of the Clone Wars occurring much earlier is reflected in the second edition of *The Guide to the Star Wars Universe* from 1994, which states that the war occurred roughly thirty-five years prior to *Star Wars*. This date, being thirty-five rather than roughly fifty years earlier, is likely the result of the revised storyline from timeline two, where Anakin/Vader was discovered by Kenobi and the Clone Wars brought closer to the creation of the Empire, also allowing Boba Fett, at the time conceived of as being part of the enemy forces of the Clone Wars,[33] to have participated in it. The second edition of *The Guide to the Star Wars Universe* states:

The Clone Wars was a terrible conflict that erupted during the time of the Old Republic (some thirty-five years prior to the start of *Star Wars IV: A New Hope*). The conflict produced such heroes as Bail Organa, Anakin Skywalker, and Obi-Wan Kenobi, who served as a general. Few details about the period have been revealed, but we know that the Jedi Knights and their allies battled to defend the Old Republic against its enemies.[34]

Anakin's depiction in Episode I was a point of debate with Lucas. Lucas had decided to set the film in the character's childhood, but initially he had conceived the character as twelve years old, explaining a few of the extraordinary events which seem incredible even for a nine-year-old Chosen One. However, many key story points necessitated the trauma of a boy leaving his mother, something Lucas felt was not as acute had the character been on the brink of his teens. Lucas explained in *The Making of Episode I*:

There were a lot of things that would have been easier if Anakin had been twelve...The casting would have been easier, for one thing; and it would have been easier to justify things like the podrace or the way he is able to fly a starfighter at the end of the movie. But the problem was that a twelve-year-old leaving his mother—as Anakin does—is not nearly as traumatic as a nine-year-old leaving his mother. And there is a key story point that revolves around the fact that he was separated from his mother at an early age, and how that has affected him. So I slid the age down as far as I could—but then I had the problem of him being able to race a pod and fly the starfighter. Ultimately, it wasn't that hard to justify the podrace. I set it up that he had done this kind of thing before; and there *are* nine-year-old kids who race go-carts, fly planes, and ride motorcycles—so it wasn't too farfetched. Having him pilot a starship was my main worry, and that was the thing I struggled with to make believable. I set it up that he is very bright, that he learns quickly, that he is already a pilot. I put in these little scenes in which he is learning about the ship—and a lot of that was interwoven throughout to make the ending work. I also had Artoo-Detoo in there with him, helping to fly the ship. All of these things helped; but making that ending credible was definitely one of the tougher issues.[35]

### Almost There

Lucas continued to write the script after overhauling the prequel storyline in draft two. Considering the amount of broad revision done for the second draft, it is no surprise that 1996 rolled on by in the time it took to write it. The writing had taken much longer than originally anticipated—so much, in fact, that the release date was eventually pushed back to 1999. The initial projected budget of roughly $60 million was also revised to roughly $100 million, as it was realised that with so much computer generated imagery, and with the rising cost of production, this figure was not realistic. Fronting the money from his own pockets, the financial issues of the prequels had risen sharply for Lucas. "When you're making a $100 million movie and it's your own money—pretty much all the money you've got—there's a huge risk," Lucas explained to author Marcus Hearn. "If I didn't get my money back on Episode I, I wouldn't have been able to make Episode II."[36]

Lucas had also finally committed to directing the film, which he announced on September 25th, 1996.[37] Reflecting on how much work the first two sequels were with other directors at the helm, he said to Hearn, "[the] reason I wanted to direct Episode I was that we were going to be attempting new things; and, in truth, I didn't quite know how we were going to do them—nobody did. So I figured I needed to be there at all times."[38]

With the all-important second draft complete, the script remained more or less set in stone, and as the scheduled production year of 1997 approached, the crucial matter of casting became apparent. For this, Lucas turned to Robin Gurland, who had been scouting potential actors since 1995. Casting the prequels would not be easy. Not only were the roles crucial for the immediate film, but many of the cast would be signed to a three-film contract, and in some cases also had to physically resemble cast members from the original *Star Wars* trilogy.

Qui Gon Jinn would be played by Liam Neeson, who won an Academy Award for playing the title character in *Schindler's List*. Although younger than initially anticipated, Gurland felt "he had that strong mythic hero quality and a strong physical and spiritual presence."[39] The actor prepared for the part by watching the original trilogy as well as *Seven Samurai*; "I wanted to get a feel for the depiction of characters with great dignity and courage," he remarked to Laurent Bouzereau.[40]

Playing Queen Padme Amidala was Natalie Portman, the child prodigy who had electrified audiences with her mature performance in the risqué *Leon* (known as *The Professional* in a watered-down U.S. version). Portman had the challenging task of playing the role in all three films—being a teenager, only sixteen at the time, it was no easy feat to convincingly portray both a fourteen-year-old queen in Episode I and a twenty-four-year-old senator in Episode II all within three years. Being mature far beyond her years, much like Carrie Fisher, she managed both.

A stroke of luck was stumbled upon in the key role of Palpatine. Ian McDiarmid, who had played the Emperor in *Return of the Jedi*, just happened to be the right age to play his "younger" self (he was actually only thirty-eight years old when first portraying the character in 1982). Being an accomplished stage actor, he gave the role regality and legitimacy, and balanced both subtlety as Palpatine and caricature as Sidious.

Samuel L. Jackson, considered one of the world's most prolific actors and already an established star, began a campaign to appear in the films in any capacity[41]—he was granted the prestigious role of Jedi master Mace Windu.

That left Obi Wan Kenobi and Anakin. The role of Obi Wan was small in Episode I, but would become prominent in the next two films. Perhaps the most challenging role in terms of physicality, casting director Robin Gurland compared actor headshots to photos of Alec Guinness as young man; one of the best candidates was Ewan McGregor. Lucas was impressed with the young Scotsman upon meeting him, and also discovered that his uncle was Denis Lawson, who had played Rebel pilot Wedge in all three original films (the character had since become a fan-favourite). McGregor was best known for his role in the dark comedy *Trainspotting*, and had the right amount of "enthusiasm" and "grace" to play both the young padawan and the wise mentor across the span of the three films. One of the unique challenges to his role was matching the accent of Alec Guinness. "There was something very paternal and calming about his voice," McGregor told Laurent Bourzereau. "I had to undergo a lot of dialog coaching to get a younger-sounding version of that voice. It was quite tricky."[42]

Casting a child to convincingly play Anakin was a more difficult matter; Gurland would end up seeing over three thousand children in person, one by one. After much deliberation, Lucas chose seven-year-old Jake Lloyd, who had appeared alongside Arnold Schwarzenegger in *Jingle All the Way* and Marisa Tomei in *Unhook the Stars*.

In the months leading up to the casting announcements, all sorts of wild rumours abounded, and the internet, just beginning to rise in popularity, was rife with speculation and gossip. Kenneth Branaugh was long rumoured to play a significant role, as was Charlton Heston. There was even a bizarre rumour that Lando's father, named Grando, would be in the film and played by Gregory Hines. The June 13th, 1997 issue of *Entertainment Weekly* reported that Harry Connick Jr. would play a Jedi, Claudia Ramirez would play "Lady Kenobi" and that Alec Guinness would narrate Episode III. Most of these were put to rest once the actual casting was announced, and yet as we can see in the case of the *Entertainment Weekly* report from June, rumours of "cameos" and "bit parts" continued to persist, even during and after filming.

Lucas also came into contact with Lawrence Kasdan around this time. With Episode I nearing production, Lucas asked Kasdan if he would like to take a pass at the script. Kasdan declined. He told the *Baltimore Sun*:

> I saw him a couple of weeks before he left to shoot *Phantom Menace*–and we did a speaking thing at USC–and the first remark he made to me was, "Hey, do you want to write *Phantom Menace*?" I asked, "Aren't you starting to shoot it?" "Yeah," he said, "but it would be great if you took a second pass at it."[43]

He elaborated to *Eon* magazine:

> I said "no" for various reasons. Basically I thought he should do it. Because what happened on *Empire* and *Jedi* was that between me and Irvin Kershner who directed *Empire* and Richard Marquand who directed *Jedi*, George's relationship to the movies had gotten one step back. I thought he should take responsibility and make exactly the movie he wanted to make, and that's exactly what he did.[44]

Many have observed that this likely was Kasdan's diplomatic way of saying he simply wasn't interested; as he himself once said, he only wrote *Return of the Jedi* to repay Lucas for starting his career, and since then had not written a single screenplay for anyone else. He had retired and was instead enjoying life as a successful director.*

### *A Hint of Things to Come*

However, as 1997 came around, a *Star Wars* milestone occurred—the twentieth anniversary of the series and the theatrical release of the Special Editions.

The Special Edition of *Star Wars* had come a long way since George Lucas proposed adding a few enhancements to Tatooine for the film's twentieth anniversary back in 1993. Aside from an extensive restoration process, as well as a new Dolby Digital sound mix, the film now sported dozens of newly created additions and enhancements to both sound and

---

* As well, he says that Lucas simply asked him, spontaneously, to go over his final draft in 1997 after bumping into him, much like a college student asking his roommate to proof-read his term paper on the night it is due (unlike Darabont, who was actively sought out before scripting began but then passed over).

picture, from obvious touch-ups such as a completely revised Battle of Yavin, to more subtle fixes such as altered colour grading and the deletion of a few frames of violence. The Special Edition had become increasingly elaborate in its alterations.

The hype leading up to the release was enormous—and largely unexpected. A trailer for the remastered trilogy started showing in theatres in November of 1996; it was so impressive that there were rumours that some were paying full ticket prices just to see the preview. Fans had taken notice of the impending release. "Originally, we were only going to do a limited release—twenty-five to fifty prints, tops," Rick McCallum stated in a *Dallas Morning News* article. "Then the trailer drew applause from the fans and their kids. We said, 'Let's do it for them.'"[45] The *Star Wars* renaissance had been steadily rising since the 1995 THX video sale, and soon it would become full-on mania. As the trailer stated, an entire generation had grown up watching the films only on home video; with a fanbase which was growing by the day, the re-release was not going to be a minor event. As the premiere date grew nearer even the press began to take notice of the excitement surrounding the films. After a long break period, *Star Wars* once again began to triumphantly adorn the covers of *Entertainment Weekly* and *Rolling Stone*. Perhaps most impressive was the February 10th cover of *Time*, which was once again covered in *Star Wars* characters along with the title "The Return of Star Wars." The phenomena was back. For the first time since the early '80s, there were *Star Wars* television specials, such as *Star Wars: The Magic and Mystery*, and all of January television specials and news segments featured *Star Wars*, from the E! Channel to VH1 to *Entertainment Tonight*, with commercials for Pepsi promoting the upcoming release with Darth Vader battling an elderly theatre usher.

In their January 10th cover story, *Entertainment Weekly* called the re-release of the decades-old films, which Fox had purportedly spent over $20 million restoring and enhancing, one of the biggest gambles of the year.

Finally, on January 31st, 1997, the *Star Wars* Special Edition opened in theatres.

The twenty-year-old film opened at number one at the box office, with $35 million, the biggest January opening ever, even to this day; the number two film was Tom Cruise' *Jerry McGuire* with a scant $5 million. The film stayed at number one for four weeks in a row—before being dethroned by *Empire Strikes Back*! It was unprecedented. This was not a simple re-release of a classic film. This was something far greater. For many, it was the first time seeing the films in theatres, and for others it was a return to their adolescence. This was truly the first time in history a phenomenon of this nature occurred on such a scale—parents were taking their children to see a movie they themselves had seen as youths, a movie which was as popular now as it was then, a movie which was somehow still more popular than any contemporary film being released at the time. "The fun part of this has been taking [my son] to the theatre and watching it through his eyes," Lucas proudly stated, who says that he was motivated for an anniversary theatrical release for this very opportunity, "because I've never really seen it through a four-year-old's eyes before and it's pretty amazing."[46]

*Empire Strikes Back* opened on February 21ˢᵗ, and *Return of the Jedi* followed on March 14ᵗʰ (scheduled for March 7ᵗʰ but delayed a week).

Astoundingly, the Special Edition of *Star Wars* earned over $138 million—when added to the original box office gross, this placed it once again as the most successful film of all time at $460 million, inching past *E.T.*, which had dethroned it in 1982. *Star Wars* was king once again.

Lucas had to have known that the re-release would be popular, but the staggering level of excitement surrounding it was unexpected to all. "This was supposed to be a nice little twentieth anniversary for the fans and it's turned into the same event [as 1977] all over again," Lucas said in amazement in early February. "It's like being in the twilight zone. It's like it's not just the re-issue, it's like a revisiting of the entire event! I certainly didn't expect this to happen."[47] The spirit of 1977 had returned in all of its excitement and chaos, and also confirmed that the prequels were not going to be minor releases by any stretch. With the casting announcements made only weeks later, and the actual filming to commence only a few months afterwards, the public prequel anticipation had begun years in advance.

The stars of the impending trilogy must have been watching this unfold with a certain sense of dread—they certainly had a legacy to live up to.

Finally, on June 26ᵗʰ, 1997, cameras rolled on another *Star Wars* picture—and for the first time in over twenty years, Lucas himself was officially behind the camera.

## Chapter XI: The Madness

FILMING commenced in Leavesden Studios, England, before moving to location work. Once again, filming was done in Tunisia, as it had been in 1976—and once again, a bizarre sandstorm destroyed the sets. Production moved on to Italy and then wrapped after only nine weeks. Digital effects had a large impact on how the film was made. Much more than any other movie at the time, many of the sets contained more bluescreen than actual constructed façade; some of them—such as the senate set—were nearly *all* bluescreen, and most of those which did contain practical set pieces were only built to the top of the actors heads, with the rest being extended digitally. In fact, as producer McCallum once pointed out, Liam Neeson's imposing 6' 4" figure cost the production many thousands of dollars, as all sets had to be built to his height.

Security around the sets were tight, and journalists and civilians alike went to great pains to find out the inside scoop on the film. Grainy photos leaked from the studio were published and posted on the internet, and all sorts of wild rumours festered when bits and pieces of information were obtained. For months, many were convinced that Liam Neeson was playing the part of Anakin's father, and much controversy was made over inaccurate reports that footage was discovered to be out of focus (which must have caused focus-puller Graham Hall many sleepless nights).

Finally, in November of 1998 the first footage of the film was released: the teaser trailer. In a darkened theatre, the familiar Twentieth Century Fox fanfare slowly faded away to reveal the shimmering image of the Lucasfilm insignia. Earlier that summer, *Austin Powers 2* had spoofed the prequel anticipation by disguising its trailer as the next *Star Wars* picture, driving fans wild before revealing that it was in fact the next *Austin Powers* film. But now this was the real deal. The Lucasfilm logo faded away into blackness. For a tense second there was silence. Then John Williams' music slowly crept in. "Every generation has a legend..." the titles quietly proclaimed. A mysterious image faded from black, showing obscured creatures advancing through a shroud of mist. "Every journey has a first step..." stated the next, as breathtaking images of Theed City played against the near-silent soundtrack. As they faded to nothingness, the iconic breathing of Darth Vader was heard before retreating to silence. The theatre remained dark. Then, an explosion. The *Star Wars* theme blared through the speakers amidst a flurry of images. Landscapes raced by in the pod race, lightsabers blazed across the screen, Jedi knights engaged in battle and starships blasted each other out of the air. Hints of a plot were revealed—Anakin being discovered by the Jedi, believed to be some sort of chosen one foretold by a prophecy. The final bombardment of images showed armies of thousands advancing on each other while a demonic Sith Lord revealed a double-bladed lightsaber and battled two Jedi knights at once, as John William's score climaxed to reveal the title—*Episode I: The Phantom Menace.*

For fans around the world, this was the first tease of something many had waited twenty years for, and for everyone else it was a preview to what was sure to be an exciting and important entry into filmdom. Theatres reported as much as half of movie audiences leaving after the trailer had been played—fans had payed full ticket prices just to see the two-minute teaser. It was downloaded from the internet over a million times, an astounding feat in 1998, and the *Star Wars* website became the most viewed site on the web. Toy stores even opened at midnight to accommodate the mobs of fans who eagerly snatched up the pre-release Episode I toys like drug addicts hungry for their fix. Around the world fans began waiting in line as far back as April; a bizarre new social event was created, with many *Star Wars* line-ups linking via the internet and creating genuine community as hundreds camped out in front of theatres for the months. In the weeks leading up to the premiere, *Star Wars* was literally everywhere. On the news, in the papers, in every magazine and conceivable form of media. CNN even reported that the national cost due to people skipping work to see the film would be $293 million.[1]

It was a level of hype and full-on mania that had never been seen before, and has not been repeated since. The film's reputation had grown to an uncontrollable level and George Lucas was regarded as a living legend, himself as much a myth as his films, treated with the highest of reverence that only John Lennon and Stanley Kubrick at their peak received.

Despite the wave of venomous disappointment that washed over the film's reputation, though critics had both negative and positive things to say about it, audience reception was warm, and the first posted reviews from viewers of the pre-release screenings were optimistic.[2]

Richard Corliss wrote in *Time* Magazine in late April:

> Based on reading the script (hasn't everybody?) and seeing scraps of the film, we get intimations of something fresh, handsome, grand. Naboo's golden underwater city glows like an Art Nouveau chandelier, while the Jedi knights' home base, Coruscant, could come from a spiffier Blade Runner. The new sidekick, a computer-birthed frog boy named Jar Jar Binks, is a vexing, endearing mix of Kipling's Gunga Din and Tolkien's Gollum, and speaks in a pidgin English ("Yousa Jedi not all yousa cracked up to be!") that will be every kid's secret language this summer. Even on paper, the film's set pieces—a 10-min. Podrace and the climactic battle between the ragged forces of good and the minions of the dark side—have power and razzmatazz.
>
> The human characters are briskly developed in the script. And the cast is certainly tony: Neeson; art-house sex pistol Ewan McGregor as young Obi-Wan; Ingmar Bergman favorite Pernilla August as Anakin's mother; Natalie Portman (Broadway's Anne Frank) as the young Queen; and, brooding on the Jedi Council, Samuel L. Jackson. The completed film will offer definitive evidence, but for now there is reason to give Episode 1 the subtitle of the original Star Wars movie: A New Hope.[3]

Roger Ebert correctly stated in his review of the film, "If it were the first 'Star Wars' movie, 'The Phantom Menace' would be hailed as a visionary breakthrough," and concluded that "What [Lucas] does have, in abundance, is exhilaration. There is a sense of discovery in scene after scene of 'The Phantom Menace'…We are standing at the threshold of a new age of epic cinema…As surely as Anakin Skywalker points the way into the future of 'Star Wars,' so does 'The Phantom Menace' raise the curtain on this new freedom for filmmakers. And it's a lot of fun."

Ebert also wrote an appraisal of Jar Jar Binks, which some critics had shown distaste for at that point (which would soon bloom to full out hate), in a May 16th article:

> I was intrigued by Jar Jar's oddness, as I was by such earlier "Star Wars" inhabitants as Yoda, Jabba the Hutt, Chewbacca or the regulars in the bar on

the planet Tatooine. Too many science fiction movies give us aliens who look like humans with funny heads. When Spielberg gave us spindly child-creatures in "Close Encounters of the Third Kind," I found that fascinating. And when Lucas gives us Jar Jar, with his eyes perched on stalks growing atop his kangaroo/rabbit/donkey head, with his weirdly backward speech, with his body language that seems generated by second thoughts, I am delighted. If it takes animation to make a creature like that–well, I'm glad they can do it.[4]

However, as the first sneak previews gave way to the press screenings and then the wide release, and critics and audiences saw the film, reaction slowly began to turn more and more sour. Well before the May 19th release most critics found the film rather uninspiring, and in fact its worst reviews were among the earliest.[5] Richard Corliss, who had surmised that the characters might be well-developed and whom had shown fascination with Jar Jar and the film's plot, now, after actually seeing the film, complained how dull and lifeless the story was. Much of the reaction from the older *Star Wars* fans was lackluster, and as the fans who had camped out for weeks outside theatres finally saw the film, many were unsurprisingly disappointed. Far from any work of genius, the film was remarkably average, and the world had not waited for a film that was ultimately deemed "so-so."[6] As the uncontrollable hype and mountainous expectations all converged into the film's release date, it was perhaps inevitable that critics would react against these things. Criticising the film soon became a trend and Lucas himself became the target of much abuse, being labelled a bloated, soulless technocrat without any sense of emotional storytelling; the internet in particular was an outlet of bitter despondency.

Many ethnic minority groups voiced efforts to boycott the film, alleging everything from the Neimodians being Asian stereotypes to Watto being an Arab stereotype to Jar Jar being a Rastafarian stereotype. Even homosexual groups went after Jar Jar.[7] This infamous character took the brunt of the abuse, upheld as an effigy for all that was wrong with the film, as older fans saw his comedic antics and low-brow humour as utterly disgraceful, with entire anti-Jar Jar web groups springing up, such as the now-defunct Jarjarbinksmustdie.com. Meanwhile, in the fan community a bitter civil war was being waged online, with the camps split into *Phantom Menace* "bashers" and "gushers" who expressed brazen hatred and love for the film respectively.

However, regardless of this over-the-top harshness from certain groups of people, the film was an all-out box office success. Children loved the film, as did many fans and casual moviegoers, and the movie went on to gross well over $400 million domestically. But nevertheless, it was

ultimately regarded as a critical failure, a visually impressive film fraught
with many fundamental flaws, and after a sixteen-year wait many felt let
down. Although the film was the single highest-grossing release in the
entire *Star Wars* series and broke practically every box office record in
history except for *Titanic*'s, much of this was due to the fact that every fan
of the original trilogy showed up, expecting it to recapture the magic of
those films—utterly perplexed by the averageness of the film, many did not
return for the sequel (or at least did not see it more than once), as did many
non-fans who saw Episode I out of curiosity, hence leading to Episode II's
box office gross to be massively smaller than that of its predecessor (a great
many still hoped that the two remainders would improve and hence saw the
films *despite* their disappointment).

Even Walter Murch felt Lucas had lost his touch. "For me, those films
pummel you into submission," he told *Wired* in 2005. "You say, OK, OK,
there are 20,000 robots walking across the field. If you told me a 14-year-
old had done them on his home computer, I would get very excited, but if
you tell me it's George Lucas—with all of the resources available to
him—I know it's amazing, but I don't *feel* it's amazing. I think if George
were here and we could wrestle him onto the carpet, he'd say, 'Yeah, I've
gotten into that box, and now I want to get out of that box.'"[8]

"The thing about *Star Wars* for me," Ewan McGregor remarked in
2006, "is that I'll always hold the first three in the '70s with just huge
regard, and the ones I did—as the ones I did."[9]

In retrospect, many who had hated the film upon initial viewing have
since softened up on their criticism. Frank Darabont gives an honest if
defensive assessment of the out-of-control criticism the film endured in a
2000 interview:

> Creative Screenwriting: You're quoted as telling George Lucas, "I wouldn't
> change a single damn word, and I hope he didn't." Is the script you read what
> everyone else saw on screen?
>
> Darabont: It is very much the movie that hit the screen. I still like it very much.
> I find the backlash perplexing and a little disheartening. To hear some people
> tell it, it's like crapping on the Mona Lisa. But this has more to do with
> people's expectations, which were so very high, more than it has to do with the
> quality of the resulting film. No film could possibly have pleased them. It's
> hard to have perspective when you're in the heat of the moment. I think
> *Phantom Menace* will be assessed some years down the road more fairly than
> it is now. I thought it was a very smart film. I thought it worked. And what is
> this "Oh, it's just for kids" comment? What is that about? Who the hell do you
> think any of the *Star Wars* films were for? They were very much in that milieu

of mythology for children. What's the problem? The problem is that everybody who saw those movies has grown up, and their memory of the impact of those films has been diluted through the years. [The films have] become so iconic that disappointment was inevitable. George Lucas is capable of many, many things. But making you feel like that wonder-struck eight-year-old again isn't one of them. It can't be done. You're not eight years old; you can't be wonder struck in the same way. Sorry. In terms of its intelligence and its approach, I'd put *Menace* up there with *Empire Strikes Back*, which was the darkest and most adult of the original trilogy.[10]

Typically, whether valid or not, every popular film inevitably becomes victimised with unfair criticism, simply out of the fact that it is a popular film. *The Matrix* and *Lord of the Rings* endured similar accusations of racism shortly after, as did the original *Star Wars* (with nary a coloured person to be seen onscreen). *American Graffiti* was accused of being chauvinistic. In fact, modern audiences may forget that in 1977 there eventually arose some critical recoil as well. *Star Wars* came out of nowhere and while critics loved the film as a moving (if brainless) adventure flick, it was the audiences that went ballistic over it. It opened humbly in some thirty-two theatres, without any major stars—its popularity grew through word of mouth and the film became an instant hit. However, as it grew in popularity, backlash rose up against it, if only in small pockets. It was criticised for its lack of roles by women and visible minorities, and for supposed racial portrayals of everyone from Arabs to the English. Some critics bashed its wooden dialogue, cardboard acting and simple story. As the film became known as a science fiction movie, some hardcore sci-fi fans began to attack the movie, claiming it was an insult to realistic science fiction.

Of course, those critics in 1977 were a small minority, and so their efforts gradually faded away. *Phantom Menace*, on the other hand, was faced with a bevy of attacks, tempered only by fact that the film had nonetheless become a box office hit. The criticism that Jar Jar Binks represented a stereotypical and racist depiction of Rastafarians as funny-talking, funny-walking, slow-witted, inept comedians was a constant accusation levelled at Lucas and the film. Much evidence was brought forward in favour of the accusations, from comparisons of Jar Jar's floppy ears to dreadlocks, to parallels of his speech ("yousa", "messa"), to his name ("Jah" is the Rastafarian god), to the fact that the actor who played him was black.

George Lucas, of course, is an avid fan of silent film, especially the slapstick genre of the 1920s (and 1930s), and came to be exposed to the material through film school. Regardless of Jar Jar's racial origins, the character is very clearly based off the physical comedians of that era, such as Buster Keaton, as Lucas readily admits. Charlie Chaplin, Harold Lloyd, Laurel and Hardy and the Marx Brothers all grew out of this time period, later followed by the more juvenile hijinks of the Three Stooges and Tex Avery's cartoon embodiments such as *Looney Tunes*. In the first installment of the Episode I web documentaries, on the first day of writing Episode I, Lucas pops a VHS tape into his VCR and watches an old silent-era comedy—two frantic actors race along the top of a train, desperately trying to avoid being driven into the archway of a tunnel, eventually tumbling off. "How?" Lucas says incredulously at the hilariously impressive display of physicality. "How do they do that?" It is easy to see a direct connection to Jar Jar, haphazardly juggling items in Watto's shop and outrunning rampaging tanks in the film's climax. "The major influence for Jar Jar was a lot of Buster Keaton," actor Ahmed Best explained to *Starwars.com*. "But as far as comedy and timing, for me it was Bugs Bunny... And there were a couple of Buster Keaton movies that we were inspired by for some of the scenes, especially in the army scene in Episode I."[11]

Beyond the usual suspects of Buster Keaton and Tex Avery, there is another comedian of this period that is often deliberately overlooked because of modern political correctness, but is nonetheless a significant part of film history. That man is Lincoln Theodore Monroe Andrew Perry—commonly known under his stage name, Stepin Fetchit, the first black actor to become a millionaire. Stepin Fetchit was a legendary black comedian known for his slapstick humour in the 1920s and 1930s, in which he played inept, slow-witted servants who always seemed to get in the way of things; his popularity rode on the wave of the then-popular "Blackface" style of comedy, which had just given way to black comedians such as Fetchit.

Though it's unlikely that Lucas would deliberately design Jar Jar to emulate a racial stereotype, there are some observers, such as Columbia University's Professor of African-American studies, Michael Dyson, that argue that in borrowing from the adventure and comedy films of the 1930s, Lucas unwittingly also borrowed their cultural steretypes on some level.[12] While Jar Jar's brand of humour, unintelligent construction and the casting of a black actor in the part can be overlooked as coincidence, it is strange that in this context Lucas made the decision to give Jar Jar speech-patterns that distinctly recall Caribbean and African stereotypes of America's past—terms like "mesa", "yousa", "mui mui", and "Jah" are strongly related to said stereotypes, and even invented words such as "bombad" share a level of etymological similarity, which implements some degree of design on the part of Lucas. With the character introducing himself "mesa your humble servant" in a manner which would be at home with any of the minority roles in some of the Three Stooges shorts, Lucas might have been subconsciously shaping the character to emulate those roles, which are transmitted to us mainly through the film material of the '20s and '30s—even the beloved serial films themselves are guilty of perpetuating these types of characters.

Whatever the case, one can see that Jar Jar's racial origins become evident in his character alone—other Gungans in the film, such as Captain Tarpals and Boss Nass, have some of the same mannerisms, physical details and speech patterns, yet do not evoke as strong racial comparisons, nor were they accused of any. The point is still very subjective—millions saw the film without any thought of racial overtones. Lucas himself was incredulous to the accusations—in a July 14th, 1999 interview on BBC's *Newsnite* program he exclaimed "How in the world you could take an orange amphibian and say that he's a Jamaican? It's completely absurd." He went on to defend that the accusations "started out as a way of selling newspapers"[13] and decried:

> What happened was, now with the internet, the American press uses the internet as their source for everything, so when people were creating websites saying "Lets get rid of Jar Jar Binks, he's terrible" and everything and some of the critics would described him as a kind of comic sidekick Stepin Fetchit character [and then] they say "Oh, its racist." So they come in and they start calling the film racist. Its very ironic that you have, in this particular film, the head Jedi is an African-American. Nobody even mentions that. And you have an orange alien character that speaks...[in] a foreign language. Its like Yoda. He speaks more like Yoda than anything else.[14]

Nevertheless, the backlash that *Phantom Menace* endured seems to have affected Lucas, and perhaps the following two screenplays. Jar Jar, a vital character who had more screen time than Obi Wan Kenobi in *Phantom Menace*, was reduced to an ancillary character in Episode II, and was practically absent from the third film, nor were the equally-hated Gungans ever heard from again. Had the character been a hit, he would have surely found a significant place in the following films. Additionally, the midichlorians, a key story aspect of Episode I, were not to be made mention of again, except in passing in Episode III, after fans bitterly complained that they reduced the spiritual aspect of the Force to science. One has to wonder if Lucas bowed down—ever so slightly—to the pressure placed on him by the onslaught of attacks. Episode II would be distinguished by containing a number of elements which cater specifically to fans, foregoing Gungans and Jar Jar in favour of Boba Fett, the Tatooine homestead and Jedi battles. When designing the Episode II Yoda, Lucas is heard remarking during a design meeting: "The secret is making [the new CG Yoda] look like a rubber puppet. The problem we got to last time [on *Phantom Menace*] was that when they made the upgrade it didn't look like the [original trilogy] rubber puppet anymore. So then everybody complained that he didn't look real. But they were saying 'Well he looks better than he did before.' Yeah, they made him better but people don't like that, they want him look like he did in the first film."[15]

The critical reaction to Episode I proved an interesting example of how the contemporary world had shifted in its media and communication. With such a large emphasis placed on the mass media which permeates our culture—often entertainment-obsessed—as well as the massive shift in public opinion due to the voice provided by the newly-emerged internet, the criticism of *Phantom Menace* was heard loud and clear, especially with so many millions of fans of the series.

A consistent defence of the film, and the prequels in general, remains in the fact that a close inspection of the actual reaction and reviews indicates *Phantom Menace* was better received than any of the original *Star Wars* sequels. In the fact, the prequel trilogy as a whole was better reviewed than the original trilogy.

This infamous notion comes courtesy of *Rotten Tomatoes*, a portal site that collects movie reviews and averages their ratings, which conducted an interesting experiment following the release of *Revenge of the Sith*—they compared the reviews of all six films. The problem when comparing reviews is that most available today are written retrospectively; with the original trilogy regarded as magical classics, many of those reviewing the films today were kids themselves when they first saw them. Predictably, you will find nary a negative review of any of the original films. To solve this roadblock in assessing true measures of the films' critical success, *Rotten Tomatoes* ignored all praise-laden contemporary reviews of the original trilogy and instead dug up as many reviews from their original release as could be found. Because most of the original reviews—and in particular the negative ones—were not available online, library archives served as the reservoir for dozens of vintage reviews of the original films during their initial releases. The website then took an average of each film's total ratings (gauged with a device affectionately termed the "Tomatometer") to arrive at a true critical measure of each film. Their results were surprising:

Tomatometer Scores for Original Trilogy During Original Release Dates:
31% - Return of the Jedi
52% - The Empire Strikes Back
79% - Star Wars
Average Tomatometer: 54%

As one can see, only "Star Wars" managed to be Fresh, with a respectable 79% on the Tomatometer, while the other two sequels got successively worse. Most of the critics thought the first film was an inventive, fun, and entertaining summer popcorn movie. It's interesting that they complain about the dialogue back then too. "Empire," which is regarded as the best of the series nowadays, only managed to score a mixed 52%. It received great technical grades, but critics had problems with the plot, one way or other, and thought it was just "minor entertainment." It got worse with "Jedi"—uneven pacing, no character development, tired acting, and hollow and junky filmmaking. It scored a moldy 30% on the Tomatometer. Prequels were probably the last thing critics wanted back then after the thrashing of the last film.

Ironically, if you compare the average Tomatometer of the prequels and the original trilogies during the time of their respective original release dates, the Prequels are actually better reviewed by 16%—70% to 54%, respectively.

Tomatometer Ranking of Star Wars Series Based on Critical Reaction During Original Release Dates:
83% - Star Wars Episode III: Revenge of the Sith
79% - Star Wars
65% - Star Wars Episode II: Attack of the Clones
62% - Star wars Episode I: The Phantom Menace
52% - The Empire Strikes Back
31% - Return of the Jedi[16]

This would seem to reveal a very interesting facet of the contemporary world. Although the films were allegedly better received by the media, the public opinion is that they were—save perhaps for Episode III—failures and bitter disappointments. What is the cause of this massive contradiction? One explanation states that the prequels were the first time *Star Wars* sequels had premiered in a globalised web-connected online world, and more importantly with a well-established fan-base. Indeed, had the original sequels been released during the era of the internet, their status as treasured classics might be tarnished by bashing and complaints from the more jaded online viewers. But what was forgotten was that while many adults enjoyed the original films as well, the films had endured largely through the legacy of children. Adults had always criticised the films, but the real audience the movies were intended for—kids—loved them. And now, in the online world, while adults were given a loud and clear voice to spread their criticism and disappointment with, the real audience of the films remained silent—the children. *The Phantom Menace* was a sleeper hit with kids, and you'd be hard pressed to find anyone under twelve who didn't enjoy the film, which is unsurprising given that *Phantom Menace* is the most child-targeted film of the series. Lucas himself realised this age divide, as he attested in an interview at Cannes in 2005:

> We've discovered that we have two fan bases. One is over 25 and one is under 25. The over 25 fan base is loyal to the first three films and they are actually in their 30s and 40s now, so that they're in control of the media, they're in control of the web, they're in control of everything basically. The films, which those people don't like, which are the [prequels], actually are fanatically bored by the other two. And if you get on the web and you listen to these conversations, they are always at each other's throats and the devotion for each group is pretty equal.[17]

However, this issue is not so cut-and-dried as it may seem. For starters, *Star Wars* swept the awards in 1977—it was not children who nominated the film for Best Picture at the Oscars; it was as much a hit to adults. What is not apparent is that *Rotten Tomatoes'* study is fraught with fundamental inaccuracies—the prequels' rating comes from a majority of website sources rather than legitimate publications, such as *Ain't It Cool News*, *Dark Horizons* and *CHUD*, while the original trilogy rating sources *Newsweek*, *The New Yorker* and *Chicago Sun-Times*, very different sets of viewers. *Rotten Tomatoes* is aware of the slant that their web-based majority causes, and offers a feature to counter-act this: a "top critics" selection that discounts sources such as websites and takes its rating from the more legitimate sources such as *Variety*, *Rolling Stone* and major newspapers. Since their rating for the original trilogy is *only* based off these types of sources, this is the only fair comparison to make. When we make this adjustment, *Revenge of the Sith*'s proud 83% drops to a less-impressive 68%, and the other films change accordingly.

Phantom Menace: 40%
Attack of the Clones: 37%
Revenge of the Sith: 68%
(Trilogy average: 48%)

This, not surprisingly, better reflects the public's collective memory of the films' reception and the media artifacts from 1999-2005, which held that *Phantom Menace* was a great disappointment, *Attack of the Clones* had embarrassing acting and writing, but that *Revenge of the Sith* was surprisingly watchable. On the other hand, the original trilogy is nonetheless revealed to have been not as treasured as it is regarded today.*

*Star Wars* was an instant critical hit when it was released (scoring an impressive 79% on the tomatometer) but its reputation grew rapidly thereafter; following in the release pattern of its era, it premiered on a small number of screens, which then expanded exponentially as word of mouth helped generate the overhead needed for the increased number of theatre bookings. After a month, it was generating much more than an 80% critical approval rating, and was being labelled in *Time* as "The Year's Best Movie!", and quickly proceeded to become the most successful film in box office history, garnering seven Oscars that year (including nominations for Best Picture, Best Director, Best Screenplay and Best Supporting Actor—highly prestigious nominations, on par with *Godfather* or *One Flew Over the Cuckoo's Nest*, in addition to all the technical nominations it also earned). Adults were equally fond of the film as their younger counterparts. *Star Wars* was not a children's film, though its subject matter was appealing to them, similar in this respect to *Lord of the Rings*. It was a film that was accessible to everyone, that was universal in a way that anyone could relate to, regardless of whether or not spaceships and doomsday devices were your cup of tea.

Its sequels, however, were not—they were accessible mostly to fans of the first film, and to those of the science fiction and fantasy fan base, delving deeper into the film's own universe and mythology and with characters no longer in need of introduction. Moviegoers who otherwise would never have an interest in a science fiction or fantasy film but had nonetheless enjoyed *Star Wars* ventured back to see if its sequel tickled them in the same way—unsurprisingly, many were turned off, mostly due to the nature of the material itself. This is why *Empire* had such a divided "love it or hate it" initial reaction—most devoted *fans* of *Star Wars*, which included adults and newspaper critics, liked the film, but many moviegoers who didn't necessarily consider themselves "fans" of the series did not. This then results in its corresponding 52% tomatometer rating. *Star Wars* appealed to the same people who voted *Annie Hall* Best Picture at the 1978 Oscars, it functioned as contemporary art by being culturally relevant and culturally ironic. By contrast, *Empire Strikes Back* is more of a traditional or normal sci-fantasy film, just told with A-list credentials; it was not as fresh and surprising in the same manner that *Star Wars* was and didn't have

---

* Though my own study of reviews from original release rates them higher than *Rotten Tomatoes*', especially the two sequels, so this should also be kept in mind.

as much broad appeal. Released today, it might be hailed as a minor masterpiece, but in 1980 critics reserved that label only for traditional dramas with important messages like *The Deer Hunter* or *Taxi Driver*—many people were turned off by a sci-fantasy drama that took itself as seriously as *Empire* did (which reminds us how much things have changed in the modern world, where the practically melodramatic *Return of the King* swept almost every Oscar award in 2004).

But it was *Return of the Jedi* that truly disappointed—no longer were there divides between moviegoers who had loved *Star Wars* and "fans" of the series, but now the fans themselves split. *Return of the Jedi* was a film made exclusively for fans of the first two films; it was the second part of *Empire Strikes Back*, with characters and plot points that the film assumes the audience is already familiar with, and with in-jokes and references to the previous entries. This of course meant that many casual moviegoers, the same ones who were enraptured by the universality of the original film, would be instantly turned off—but even worse, many fans, who had liked *Empire*, were disappointed by the film, feeling it dull and contrived, and this continues even to this day. This is reflected in its lowly 31% rating.

In fact, it might not be accurate to say that the two *Star Wars* sequels were originally received poorly but then became known as classics—rather, it was only *Empire* that underwent a significant re-appraisal. Kids historically have preferred *Return of the Jedi* to *Empire Strikes Back*, which is no surprise given the content of the two films; but as the eight-year-olds who first saw *Jedi* in 1983 grew up, they realised that *Empire* was in fact a much more sophisticated and mature film, and critics too began to understand that there was much more to the film than they first judged—which is why in the 1990s *Empire* suddenly became known as one of the great sequels of all time and a film that was equal or superior to its predecessor.[18] *Return of the Jedi* continued to be criticised as a much weaker film, though not with the harshness of its original release.

Over time, of course, the *fans* of the series made their way online—casual moviegoers had no more to say about the series: they had paid a combined $300 million to see *Star Wars* in 1977, watched it, loved it, and moved on. Those who were fans of all three films, however, grouped together and shared their views—this continues to provide a slanted world view in the fan community, where most of their points of reference come from themselves and not the general public. It was here that *Empire Strikes Back* became known as the best of the series; for many fans of the original, it expanded on the mythology and provided a mature exploration and a dark sophistication that only appreciates as one ages. *Return of the Jedi* was still criticised as the weakest of the three, but as the concluding entry, the second half of fan-favourite *Empire*, it was tolerated.[19]

By this point, however, the films were being regarded as magical classics, modern masterpieces, especially since the generation who were youngsters at the time of original release were now adults (and also now in control of much of the media). Yet when the series was re-released in 1997, it was not *Empire* that rocked the box-office, it was, as always, the public's favourite, the movie everybody loved: *Star Wars*. The *Star Wars* Special Edition made an astounding $138 million in theatres; it was and is arguably the most popular film ever made. *Empire Strikes Back*, the film that most fans of the series even to this day say is the best, made less than half of that, $67 million, though still impressive. *Return of the Jedi*, the film which fans consider not as good as *Empire* or *Star Wars*, made a corresponding third of the original, a scant $45 million, being attended to exclusively by devotees (the still-impressive amount is a good indication of the vast amount of followers the franchise had amassed by this point, the height of the *Star Wars* renaissance). Even in 1997 the two sequels combined couldn't equal what *Star Wars* still managed. The sequels, and hence the overall series, endured mostly due to the hordes of fans who regarded the films and cemented their reputation into cinema history but it was truly only the original film that was ever considered a masterpiece by critics and the general public.

Lucas gave the fans their own masterpiece with *Empire Strikes Back*—it is a rare example of a sequel not only considered "good" by most public opinion, but better than the original by many fans. Sequels typically are not well regarded, even by followers of the respective series—*Ghostbusters 2* and *Die Hard 2* have their devotees, but even they regard the originals as much superior. *Empire* accomplished that rare feat of not only matching the original, but for many surpassing it—the *Star Wars* series was now at consistent level of high craftsmanship and artistic brilliance, and many expected Lucas to deliver again, especially since the story was not wrapped at the end of the second film. Unsurprisingly, the rest of the entries were closer to the level of quality normally attained in franchise sequels: average overall, but regarded to varying degrees by devotees of the series. *Empire* set up the expectation that every episode would be brilliant. *Return of the Jedi* was included in the pantheon of *Star Wars* and *Empire* because it was the conclusion to them, the second half of a sequel considered better than the original and the climax of those two fantastic films; it was a film viewed as flawed and uneven, but it was tolerated because it rode on the coattails of the first two films.

*Phantom Menace*, of course, had no coattails to ride on, except for fan nostalgia of the originals—it had to start the story over, introduce a new cast and survive on its own, and the same flaws seen in lesser degrees in *Return of the Jedi* suddenly were exposed without any sort of crutch.

*Phantom Menace* was, of course, unfairly reviled, and many moviegoers truly were unprepared for a film that was predominantly meant for children (rather than *everyone*), blindsided by the pre-release marketing that focused on the tragic and mature nature of the prequel trilogy and did not correctly set up expectation that the movie would be so light and juvenile.

"I gave [the fans] as much as I could—I gave them a 110 percent," Lucas insisted in a *Cinescape* interview.[20] "George worked very hard on it," Coppola defended him in a *CNN* report. "I know he's gotten some bad reviews, but he didn't slough it off or anything."[21] In the aftermath of the criticism, Lucas would report a number of justifications to explain the criticism: people weren't interested in a film revolving around a child, people wanted to see Darth Vader killing everyone, people wanted to see more serious subject matter and not Saturday matinee material. In truth, the juggernaut hype machine, blood-thirsty media, nostalgic fan memories, and more colourful plotting indeed helped bring down the film's reception, but with all the criticism the film continues to receive from fans and non-fans alike it would be ignorant to say that the movie simply was misunderstood. Had the material been presented in a more dramatically engaging manner, audiences would have fallen in love with the light-hearted adventure fantasy that Episode I's story presents, as they would with such similarly styled films that came out shortly after, such as *Harry Potter*, *Chronicles of Narnia* and *Fellowship of the Ring*.[22] Could it be that Lucas simply reached his peak in 1977? It is not an unfamiliar occurrence—few directors have the consistent longevity of, for example, Steven Spielberg or Martin Scorsese. Even Coppola could not even come close to his achievements of the '70s, despite a few notable, if overlooked, feats such as *Rumble Fish* and *Tucker*. Irvin Kershner, the supposed genius responsible for the majesty of *Empire Strikes Back*, could only follow that film up with such deplorable efforts as *Never Say Never Again* and *Robocop 2*.

"Even without the pre-release hoopla, *The Phantom Menace* would be a considerable letdown," the *Los Angeles Times* reported in 1999. "While the new film is certainly serviceable, it's noticeably lacking in warmth and humor, and though its visual strengths are real and considerable, from a dramatic point of view it's ponderous and plodding."[23]

Behind the scenes even Lucas secretly suspected that the film had problems. "It's a little disjointed," he mused in the silent aftermath of the rough cut screening. "It's bold, in terms of jerking people around, but…" He paused and shook his head: "I may have gone too far in a few places." Afterwards, Rick McCallum assured him the film was fine but Lucas discussed ways to alleviate the problems. "It's a very hard movie to follow and at the same time I've done it a little more extremely than I ever have in the past. It's stylistically designed to be that way and you can't undo that. But we can diminish the effects of it. We can slow it down a little bit. If it's intense for us, a regular person is going to go nuts."[24]

Even the actors of the film were put off by the impersonal experience of making it. Just days before the film premiered, a disgruntled Liam Neeson announced he was retiring from the tedious and superficial world of movie-making. "Honest to god, I don't want to do it anymore," he said. "I don't think I can live with the inauthenticity of movies anymore. I don't like watching them, especially my own stuff."[25] Terence Stamp also lamented the disappointing experience of filming *Phantom Menace*. "When I walked onto the set, no Natalie [Portman]. 'We've given Natalie the day off,' they said. 'That bit of paper on the post? That's Natalie. Deliver your lines to the paper'… The movie was a bit disappointing. But then it's not possible to feel empathy when you're watching something done digitally: You're not responding to a human."[26]

"As a film-maker and a person I can say I always had problems with Jar Jar as he started to develop in the screenplay," Rick McCallum admitted to *Starbust* in 1999. "I loved him on paper, actually, more than I did when I saw the animation starting to come out. There was a point where I said, 'George, is this working? Is this really…' and George said, 'Remember, just remember. Try to find that moment. What did you love to do with your parents? Bug them. Annoy them.' We will only know if George was right after the film opens."[27]

### Getting Personal

Lucas was doing his best to keep his head up, but the maliciousness with which the film was attacked took a toll on the filmmaker. He spoke with Lesley Stahl a few years later:

Lesley Stahl: When [the critics] go after your writing, your directing—it has to hurt.

Lucas: Oh, it always hurts. It hurts a great deal. But part of making movies is you get attacked, and sometimes in very personal ways… The point is, it's like if you paint your house white and somebody comes over, "Well that should be a green house." Well, fine, but I wanted to paint it white. I don't think there was anything wrong with painting it white. I don't think there's anything wrong with me for painting it white. Maybe it should be a green house, but I didn't want it to be a green house. I wanted it to be a white house.[28]

The backlash must have been especially disheartening since Episode I was such a labour of love for Lucas. Rather than simply adapt his prequel notes, he created a mostly-original story from scratch, an entirely new world with original characters that took over five years to create, filled with his signature eccentricities and quirky humour. Especially since it was his long-awaited return to directing, the relentless criticism must have been heartbreaking:

Everything I write is my life. I'm not writing some sort of hypothetical thesis on something, I'm writing a story that I have to get extremely emotionally involved in because its going to take two or three years of my life to do it. So I can't just sort of say "Well, this will be fun," and knock it off in a week. This is like a marriage. You have to be in love with this thing for at least four or five years and probably for the rest of your life.[29]

Although one could easily presume that the fantastic and impossible world of *Star Wars* has little personal connection to George Lucas' private life, there may indeed be more of him in *Star Wars* than he realises. Lucas' escape from Modesto, the act of leaving the safety of the small town in which he was raised, seems to find its way into virtually every film he has made. In *Star Wars*, the most identifying theme was naïve Luke wanting to leave the mundane confines of his farm and explore the galaxy—it was Modesto transposed to the space fantasy vernacular, with the isolated walnut ranch turned into a desolate moisture farm, irritable George Lucas Sr. turned into grumpy Uncle Owen, sympathetic Dorothy Lucas turned into kind-hearted Aunt Beru, and young Lucas turned into young Luke, who "wastes time with [his] friends," as his uncle scoffs, and races T-16s for fun but dreams of bigger things. "The auteur theory of film actually is very true if you know directors," Lucas once said. "Because they *are* very much like their movies. And in the case of somebody who writes *and* directs—it *is* my life."[30]

Luke's battling of his father is also a theme which stems from Lucas' tumultuous relationship with his own dad. Vader's offer of the Empire to Luke parallels Lucas Sr.'s offer of his Modesto business to his son—"Join me, and we can rule the galaxy as father and son." But, like Lucas, Luke refuses, vowing to never be like him. Luke's horrific realisation that his worst enemy is his father—and that he could *become like him*, perhaps the most significant thematic point for Luke—also parallels Lucas' gradual progression to the businessman he swore he would never be; exactly like his father. "I've become the very thing I swore to destroy," Lucas admitted in 2004,[31] as he has now transformed into the type of studio executive he once loathed. Lucas clashed with his father throughout his childhood, culminating in the moment when he refused his father's offer to take over the L.M. Morris stationery business—the event created a rift between them for years. His father was sure his son would never amount to anything and hated the idea of him getting into the film industry. When his son became the most successful filmmaker of all time and millionaire to boot, George's father changed his mind; he raved about his son to everyone, telling them what a success his young George was. Their relationship was finally resolved. In this can also be seen the redemption of Darth Vader, as Luke finally reconciles with his father—Lucas' own reconciliation had occurred only a few years prior to the writing of *Return of the Jedi*.

"There is a lot more of me in *Star Wars* than I care to admit, for better or worse," he said to Denise Worrell. "A lot of it is very unconscious, very personal. You can't get away from that. It comes out of you. It's not something that is done by the numbers, it's very personal. Luke more or less is my alter ego. He can't not be."[32] In 1977 Lucas said: "I wasted four years of my life cruising like the kids in *American Graffiti* and now I'm on an intergalactic dream of heroism. In *Star Wars*, I'm telling the story of me."[33]*

"One cynic, in advance of its completion, has called it *American Graffiti* in outer space," Stephen Zitto wrote about *Star Wars* in 1977, with all the autobiographical implications that comment suggests.[34] Mark Hamill finally understood his character once he got to know Lucas personally. "George is Luke," Hamill said in *The Making of Star Wars*. "He is. I always felt that way. We were in the desert one time—it was the scene where I had just found Artoo after he ran away—so I ran up and said, 'Hey, where do

---

*    Perhaps unsurprisingly, Lucas today rejects any parallel between Luke and Vader and himself and his father. "Well, a lot of people assume that, because they say, oh, he must take it from his own father. But my father wasn't at all like Darth Vader," he told CNN on May 7th, 2002. Obviously the personal details of a robotic super-villain don't directly translate to a 1950s small town American stationery store owner, but the overall themes and arcs are designed at perhaps such an unconscious level that Lucas himself is unaware of the parallels.

you think you're going?!' And to Threepio, 'Do you think I should replace the restraining bolt?!?' But George came up to me and said, 'It's not a big deal.' He acted it out, just walking up and saying, 'Noo, I don't think he's going to try anything.' At that point, I was thinking, *Well, he's doing it so small, so I'll do it just like him—and he'll see how wrong he is.* So I did it like that—and he said, 'Cut. Print it. Perfect.' So I though, *Oh…I see.* After that I often felt like I was playing George."[35]

If Lucas' personal history is charted through Luke in the original trilogy, the events since then are charted through Anakin in the prequel trilogy. Lucas was hailed as the greatest storyteller who ever lived, the savior of cinema, put on a pedestal so high that he was threatened with losing touch with reality. His status as "mythmaker" was so disproportionate to the humble realities he suspected about himself that he knew he could never satisfy everyone. He proved this with the release of Episode I—he was destined to fail. It is no surprise then that the protagonist of the prequel trilogy is introduced in a similar manner: a humble slave boy who is snatched up and proclaimed as the greatest Jedi to ever live, the Chosen One, whom all are disappointed with when it is revealed he is not performing to their expectations.

The issue of conception is also a very significant factor, as Lucas himself is cursed with sterility. When he learned the news it was difficult for him to accept at first, but he soon learned to overcome this barrier with an "unnatural" way of bearing children—adoption. Small wonder then that Anakin is also surrounded with "unnatural" conception, first in his fatherless virginal birth and then when Palpatine reveals that Darth Plagueis created life purely through the Force.

Anakin's circular fate in Episode III also draws a parallel to Lucas'; Anakin swears to destroy the Sith but ends up becoming one, and Anakin's attempts to save his wife only end up killing her. "I'm not happy that corporations have taken over the film industry, but now I find myself being the head of a corporation, so there's a certain irony there," Lucas admitted to *Wired* magazine in 2005. "I have become the very thing that I was trying to avoid. That is Darth Vader—he becomes the very thing he was trying to protect himself against."[36] His attempt to break free of Hollywood only resulted in him becoming a prime representative of the mogul-like billionaire atmosphere so associated with Tinsel Town, and his determination to funnel the profits of *Star Wars* into securing personal and financial freedom for himself and his wife only resulted in their divorce. Like Anakin, it was at first a means to an ends, to living comfortably and having personal and financial freedom, but soon it became an ends to itself, as his Empire ballooned to grand heights. He told Marcia that he was doing it for her, to secure their future and make sure that they would hold the key to their own destiny, but in a very real sense he was justifying his own power aspirations, having been the powerless underdog his whole life—Marcia didn't care about Skywalker Ranch, she didn't need or want it; they were already millionaires and had the power to simply enjoy living, and she begged Lucas to let go and just get on with his life. Perhaps it is appropriate that the final scene between Anakin and Padme plays out in a mirror scenario, with all the disastrous repercussions that Lucas endured.

"Everybody thought of Darth Vader as this big evil guy that had no heart and that he was just evil," Lucas said in 2005, "But in the end it's not that at all. I mean, here is a guy who has lost everything."[37] Including his wife, his status as Chosen One, his friendships and his former power, now regarded as an isolated technological monster.

"You can't write a main character and not have him be a part of you and not be able to identify with him," Lucas once said to Denise Worrell.[38]

Although some of these themes are obviously inspired by other sources—virginal conception for example being a common mythological motif in savior legends—and come from other storytelling necessities, Lucas' draw to them might be traced through identification with his own life.

Following *Phantom Menace*'s release, Lucas took a much-needed vacation, while the film went on to gross hundreds of millions of dollars and create uproar, both positive and negative, all summer long. Lucas, who had been away from the spotlight for well over a decade and had become regarded as a recluse, was now a media focus, giving interviews on a daily basis and even appearing on talk shows like *Rosie O' Donnel*. Times had certainly changed.

# Chapter XII: Stitches

IT is no surprise then, after the harsh treatment of Episode I, that Lucas would have returned to writing with some trepidation. Perhaps as a direct result of the backlash *Phantom Menace* received, Lucas mulled over Episode II for quite some time, and didn't start writing until the fall, despite the fact that filming would commence in June. Author Jody Duncan reported that Lucas took a family vacation to Europe just after *Phantom Menace*'s release, "but the movie that would become *Star Wars* Episode II *Attack of the Clones* was never far from his thoughts," she wrote. "Even while vacationing, Lucas took note of possible locations; in quiet moments, he scribbled down ideas for the as-yet-unwritten screenplay."[1] In fact, he would discover Lake Como while in Italy, which he would later write much of Episode II's romance around. As Episode I faded from theatres as the summer weaned and Lucas' kids went back to school, he had to finally begin tangible work on the second film in his trilogy.

With the script and designs targeted for completion in May 2000, that left only a nine-month pre-production period from the September start[2]—contrasted with the three years it took to write and design *Phantom Menace*.

It is unknown how much of Episode II was planned beforehand by Lucas when plotting out the trajectory of the prequel trilogy in the early-mid '90s. We can be certain that the first three *Star Wars* sequels—that is, *Empire Strikes Back*, *Return of the Jedi* and *Phantom Menace*—were original creations predominantly made up on the fly, and Episode III, the film containing most of Lucas' initial prequel ideas, was largely already known by the time he started scripting. However the gap between Episode I and Episode III is still largely mysterious in its formation. The broad strokes were known—Anakin and Padme fall in love, the Clone War begins and the Republic gets its army, Anakin's mother dies and Palpatine continues his ascent to dictator—but the specifics of the plot still remain somewhat ambiguous in their formative stages. No early drafts are available, save for a shooting script, and Lucas himself has been somewhat tight-lipped about the process in order to preserve the myth that all was worked out decades prior, and so is not a source of much information on the episode's creative origination.

However, it seems that Lucas had enough broad plot strokes to keep himself busy, with his task in crafting Episode II mainly being to fill in the specifics. Whereas Episode I was likely a more enjoyable process of creating a new story and Episode III a more satisfying process of finally crafting the galaxy's doom, Episode II seemed to serve more as a link in the series, filling in the little blanks between the two films.

At a glance, examination would seem to indicate that most of the main plot pieces were present, presumably including the Separatists plot, but only in the vaguest of detail. Tatooine's reappearance was in place from the start, as producer Rick McCallum and production designer Gavin Bocquet scouted Tunisia in the summer of 1999.[3] During that same series of recces, they also visited "several lakeside locations in northern Italy, searching for a Naboo summer retreat that would be a pivotal setting in Episode II," in addition to revisiting Caserta palace which had stood in for Theed palace in the prior film, indicating the related scenes Lucas already had in mind going into the scripting process.[4]

The nature of Anakin and Padme's courtship appears to have been created when crafting the arc of the prequels in the '90s. When Episode I was released, many fans noticed a shot which placed emphasis on a character watching the pod race, showing a bald, white-skinned alien standing on the edge of a balcony as Anakin zips by in a canyon below. The Expanded Universe material revealed her to be a character known as bounty hunter Aurra Sing, and, intrigued, many fans wanted to know more about her. It was soon leaked that she might play a role in Episode II.

Her character became a huge hit with fans, even going as far as getting her own comic series. However, viewers will note that this once-obscure character obviously does not appear in Episode II. Could this character have become Zam Wessel, the female bounty hunter that works with Jango Fett to assassinate Padme? Certainly that fits into the picture. Perhaps because of Aura Sing's popularity Lucas opted to redesign the female bounty hunter for Episode II; the fact that she would be killed in the film may have also been a factor, as Aurra Sing enjoys a healthy living in her many Expanded Universe stories. This then would indicate the assassination plot surrounding Padme existed beforehand, which would presumably extended to include Anakin's involvement in her protection and their subsequent falling in love (as the assassination subplot is a device to get the two of them together).

In describing Episode II beforehand, Lucas frequently called Episode II a "romance" or "love story." The wedding of Anakin and Padme was originally to be a bigger focal point and occurred earlier in the initial draft, according to author Marcus Hearn, but Lucas decided that their romance needed to be gradual rather than abrupt, even if the final script itself is rather rapid in the growth of their relationship.[5] Ian McCaig recalled in *The Art of Attack of the Clones*, "At one point, George said the wedding might be at the center of the conflict, rather than an idyllic moment [as in the final film]."[6]

In addition to returning to Naboo and Coruscant, Episode II would feature a significant appearance of Tatooine, and in particular the Lars homestead seen in *Star Wars*, marking a significant transition in linking the two trilogies together. Tatooine's return would serve as a major turning point for Anakin's character and would lead to the discovery of many revelations. For starters, his mother has married her new slave owner, Clieg Lars, leaving Anakin with a step-brother, Owen Lars. This dashed the previous notion that Owen was in fact Obi Wan's brother, developed during *Return of the Jedi* and even present in that film's novelisation, and restored Owen and Beru's status as legitimate relatives of Luke. We also discover that C-3PO was bought by the Lars' and works on the farm, further bringing together the characters in the saga. It is also learned that Anakin's mother has been kidnapped by Tusken Raiders, and in a sequence derived from John Ford's *The Searchers*, Anakin ventures out into the Tatooine wilderness to rescue her, only to have her die in his arms as he at last tracks her down.

One of the most important story points to finally address was the Clone War. The details of Episode II's clone subplot were probably invented in mid-'90s, but likely only in broad strokes. Kamino and the Geonosis subplot may have well been creations devised after Episode I, simply due to the large number of original elements involved.* Many feel Lucas' inclusion of Jango and Boba Fett to be an attempt at appeasing fans since the character had become the most popular individual in the series, citing his seemingly-unnecessary insertion into the Special Edition. In reality, Boba Fett was always tied to the Clone Wars, as was revealed in a *Bantha Tracks* issue from 1979, and his insertion into the Special Edition might have been made with his upcoming prequel role in mind. Playing on his popularity, of course, Lucas enlarged his role as a central figure at the heart of the Clone War's origins, instead of the former conception where he was an anonymous participant.

As early as 1998 Lucas confirmed Boba Fett would feature prominently in the second film. "He's definitely going to play a part in Episode II," Rick McCallum said in the August 1998 issue of *Star Wars Insider*. "There's a real story point for Boba Fett."[7]

On the other hand, the character of Jango Fett, his father, is an entirely new character. Although it is at this time unconfirmed, it seems fairly apparent that Jango wasn't merely added to Episode II—he replaced Boba. Instead, Boba would be his cloned son, who would grow up to fill his father's shoes. The original conception of Boba Fett was that at the time of the original trilogy he was somewhat aged, being a veteran combatant of the Clone War era—which would follow if he was in the role that Jango filled. Creating Jango gave Lucas an opportunity to create a new character, and the only villain who could be killed in the film's climax, while bringing an interesting twist to Fett's character and the ongoing father-son theme of the series. Boba Fett's central role clearly foreshadowed an important place in the next film, although, as we will see in the next chapter, Lucas then eliminated him from the story, leaving his prominent appearance in Episode II somewhat unresolved considering his meagre screen time at the end of *Empire* and beginning of *Jedi*.

The introduction of the clones not only served to lead into the impending-Empire's stormtroopers, but also to provide the linchpin in the Jedi's destruction—as Lucas had described way back in 1980, the Jedi were "betrayed" with some kind of "trap" set up by the Emperor,[8] a plot point first hinted at in the second draft of *Star Wars*. Such vague statements are short on details of any kind; arguably some kind of ambush or execution seemed implied, which is exactly what would happen when Anakin and the

---

* The gladiatorial arena in Episode II seems to be very conveniently timed in that Ridley Scott's Oscar-winning *Gladiator* would be debuting just a few months after Lucas wrote the script and was drawing heavy interest

clones march on the Jedi temple in Episode III. In 1977 Lucas revealed similar details, stating that Vader first began secretly assassinating them and that after the Jedi initially rebelled and had been decimated "they tried to regroup, but they were eventually massacred by one of the special elite forces led by Darth Vader."[9]

However, as many fans were surprised to find, the clones of the infamous Clone Wars were not an outside enemy attacking the Republic—an implication made all the more misleading by the film's eventual title, *Attack of the Clones*—but the Republic army itself, and the actual Clone Wars to be a battle fought from *within*. This seems to be a complete 180 from Lucas' original plan, which went through many permutations from what we know but always involved some kind of external threat. The first recorded speculation by Lucas occurred when Lando was introduced in *Empire Strikes Back*—he came from a planet of clones, and it seems either a planetary civil war or the planet's assault on outlying worlds resulted in the galaxy being ravaged. This was dropped and replaced with Boba Fett and the "Imperial Shocktroopers," warriors who came from across the galaxy but were wiped out by the Jedi.

That they are known as *Imperial* Shocktroopers may be misunderstood as implying that they were part of the Galactic Empire, but the fact that it is stated in *Bantha Tracks* that they had a distant origin and were defeated by the Jedi seems to contradict this (aside from the fact that the Empire would not be in place yet); likely they belonged to another empire on the other side of the galaxy that tried to invade the Republic. A subsequent Lucasfilm publication from 1981, *The World of Star Wars*, revealed that the stormtroopers were actually cloned human beings. This then presents an interesting possibility: perhaps the later Boba Fett/Shocktrooper concept was taken even further, with the Jedi now leading the Republic's own clone army against the invading Shocktroopers. In this later version, circa 1979, the Clone Wars also occurred closer to the Empire's birth (rather than some decades prior), a chronology change that is reinforced by the fact that Boba Fett was implied to have participated in the war, allowing Palpatine to have a ready-made army which eventually became the Imperial stormtroopers.[*]

---

[*] Of interest is that in the third draft of *Star Wars* Kenobi was said to be the commander of the "white legions", though this is very ambiguous. However, it would still be allowed in this original chronology that the army of the Republic, which the Jedi led during the Clone Wars, were the same soldier design as the later stormtroopers, and that the Empire simply inherited the Republic army as the Imperial army. On the other hand, Kenobi says that it's been "a long time since the white legions

In any case, Lucas chose to start over almost from scratch on the issue, linking the Clone Wars much closer to Palpatine, the Jedi and the fall of the Republic, now being an artificial manipulation orchestrated by Palpatine in order to dominate the galaxy. This reveals an interesting example of how the original storylines were being re-shaped to reflect the new, personalised conception of the saga. The original Clone Wars, a macro event which was merely a heroic war that Ben Kenobi and Father Skywalker fought in, was now turned into a micro event which was a personalised plot point surrounding the new storyline involving Darth Sidious and the Sith's dominance, drawing in all the characters of the story.

A clever plot had been engineered by Lucas—Palpatine creates and fosters a civil war in order to manipulate the people into giving him more power in the name of security, all the while controlling and orchestrating both sides. The enemies of this war would be members of a rebellion within the Republic, an alliance of systems that would include the Trade Federation from Episode I. The clone army then would be the Army of the Republic, led by the Jedi Generals. The second twist came when their true purpose would be revealed in Episode III—not only would they give Palpatine a ready-made personal army, but they could be "programmed" to turn on their former comrades. Lucas explained in a 2005 interview:

> I was always worried in Episode II that I was giving away too much in terms of people asking questions about "Where did the clones really come from?" Because if you go back, they mention the fact that Lord Tyranus and Count Dooku are the same person. You know, Darth Tyranus. And that Darth Tyranus is the one who started the clones. So if you are paying attention it is very easy to figure out what's going to happen to the clones, I mean that they're going to be the ones that betray everybody. Tough to put in things like that without giving everything away.[10]

Another major shock to fans was the inclusion of a lightsaber duel by Yoda. To many viewers this seemed silly, as did Palpatine's duels in the following film—the characters were thought to be "above" such physical feats, instead relying on their minds and the Force as their source of power. However, these were, in fact, faithful to Lucas' first conceptions. In the first draft of *Empire Strikes Back*, Yoda reveals his true nature by fencing in a lightsaber match with the ghost of Ben Kenobi, and in the rough draft of *Revenge of the Jedi*, the Emperor is revealed to have a lightsaber. The characters' subsequent transformation from those early drafts, however, provides merit to the criticisms.

---

roamed the stars."

A major event in the screenwriting of Episode II was the creation of the new Sith apprentice, Count Dooku, also known as Darth Tyranus. For such a major player in the last two episodes, Dooku was invented considerably late in the game, during the pre-production period of Episode II. Lucas' outline for Episode II must have been merely that Sidious somehow fosters a Separatist movement, possibly by manipulating a powerful politician to lead the faction; at the same time, Sidious has found a new Sith apprentice, who duels Yoda and Anakin at the end of the movie, and in the subsequent film Anakin could finally slay the apprentice and take his place as his final act towards the dark side (though this would inevitably be re-structured). The new Sith apprentice was at first thought to be similar to Darth Maul in the previous film, powerful and menacing, but whom served little plot use other than providing a threat and duelling the heroes at the film's conclusion. Likely, the new apprentice was to oversee the Separatist leader, similar to the way Maul protected and kept an eye on Nute Gunray and the Neimoidians in Episode I. The art department went back to some unused designs from Episode I, namely the popular "Sith Witch" design, which would eventually find its way into the *Clone War* cartoon series as Asajj Ventress.[11] At one point Lucas suggested a robot-cyborg, indicating he was interested in the concept that would eventually become General Grievous in the following film.[12]

However, Lucas soon drastically changed his plan, offering concept artists the idea that the new Sith would be a completely different character played by Christopher Lee[13]—the apprentice could be the opposite of the fearsome and acrobatic Maul, instead a thinking man, older and with a sense of elegance and regality. Whether before or after this happened, it seems Lucas struck upon a much more interesting direction to take things—the Separatist leader and the Sith apprentice would be the same person. Thus was born Count Dooku, also known as Darth Tyranus. Once again we see a similar situation and process which led to the merging of Father Skywalker and Darth Vader in 1978, or to the merging of General Darth Vader and Prince Valorum in 1974, as character and story redundancies are simplified. In Dooku, Lucas created one of the prequels' most fascinating characters. An elderly Jedi knight who left the order after becoming disillusioned with the Republic, he is picked up by Sidious, who tells him of his plans to create a New Order and thus rid the Republic of its corruption. Dooku secretly joins the Sith, becoming Darth Tyranus, and creates the Separatist movement. Later, during pick-up shooting, Lucas would write that he was also Qui Gon's master (probably an inspiration taken from a scene in which Jocasta Nu compares the two), adding further complexity and perhaps linking Qui Gon's outsider tendencies as a trait picked up from Dooku, creating an interesting relationship between Dooku and Obi Wan and Anakin.

In effect, Lucas combined Palpatine and Anakin into a new character—a Jedi who becomes a Sith while also being a political figure and master manipulator with a secret identity. Lucas also developed an interesting history that would be cut out of the final film, that of the "Lost Twenty." The scene is portrayed in the shooting script:

INT. JEDI TEMPLE, ARCHIVES LIBRARY - DAY

A bronze bust of Count Dooku, stands among a line of other busts of Jedi in the Archive Room. [...] OBI-WAN studies the bust for a few moments before MADAME JOCASTA NU, the Jedi Archivist is standing next to him. She is an elderly, frail-looking human Jedi. Tough as old boots and smart as a whip.

JOCASTA NU
Did you call for assistance?

OBI-WAN
(distracted in thought)
Yes... yes, I did...

JOCASTA NU
He has a powerful face, doesn't he? He was one of the most
brilliant Jedi I have had the privilege of knowing.

OBI-WAN
I never understood why he quit. Only twenty Jedi have ever left
the Order.

JOCASTA NU
(sighs)
The Lost Twenty... and Count Dooku was the most recent and the most
painful. No one likes to talk about it. His leaving was a great loss
to the Order.

OBI-WAN
What happened?

JOCASTA NU
Well, one might say, he was always a bit out of step with the
decisions of the Council... much like your old Master, Qui-Gon Jinn.

OBI-WAN

(surprised)
Really?

JOCASTA NU
Oh, yes. They were alike in many ways. Very individual thinkers...

JOCASTA NU stares at the bust

JOCASTA NU
(continuing)
He was always striving to become a more powerful Jedi. He wanted
to be the best. With a lightsaber, in the old style of fencing, he
had no match. His knowledge of the Force was... unique. In the
end, I think he left because he lost faith in the Republic. He
believed that politics were corrupt, and he felt the Jedi
betrayed themselves by serving the politicians. He always had very
high expectations of government. He disappeared for nine or ten
years, then he just showed up recently as the head of the
separatist movement.

The development of Count Dooku was an organic and unplanned
process, and his central role and highly developed characterisation were
entirely serendipitous. As quickly as Dooku was developed, however, he
would also be eliminated. After a crucial role as the chief villain in Episode
II he would practically disappear from Episode III—for reasons which we
will examine as we cross that point in the next chapter.

Lucas also returned to abandoned ideas from the *Empire Strikes Back*
story conferences with Leigh Brackett, which he had also utilised in
*Phantom Menace. The Annotated Screenplays* described that, in addition
to brainstorming an "ice planet" which became Hoth and a "gas planet"
which became Bespin, they also developed the concepts for the following
environments:

"The Water Planet": an underwater city
"Ttaz: The Rock/Desert Planet": gray, colourless with a civilisation living in
caves.
"The Garden Planet": Slightly fairy-tale-like; very lush environment with
gardens rather than forests...
"Ton-mummd: The Grass Planet": with tall wheat fields, grass, and giant
rolling hills as far as one can see.
"The City Planet": sort of like the Death Star, a completely built-over planet
and possibly home of the Empire.[14]

The "water planet" may have given birth to both Kamino and Otoh Gunga, the Gungan city, while Ttaz—the rock planet with civilisations living in caves—seems to have grown into Geonosis, with its rock-covered surface and cave-dwelling insects. Naboo seems to have also previously stemmed from a combination of garden and grass-based planets, while "the city planet" Lucas had devised in 1978 as possibly being home to the Empire became 1981's Had Abbadon, later named Coruscant by Timothy Zahn and adopted by Lucas.[15]

Lucas also implemented an early design from *Empire* for the Kamino aliens: Lucas' 1977 notes for *Empire Strikes Back* describe aliens on Bespin called "Whatnots" that are "semistoic creatures, sort of tall, thin, white, maybe similar to the aliens in Steven Spielberg's *Close Encounters of the Third Kind.*"[16]

Writing Episode II gave Lucas a chance to shape the characters into more defined personas than the ones introduced in Episode I. Padme's backstory was greatly fleshed out, and we are introduced to her family and told much of her childhood in a sequence that was eventually cut out of the final film. As previously noted, Kenobi's brash persona was done away and transferred to Anakin, making Kenobi more of the straight-arrow type, but given that Kenobi spoke of his non-existent "arrogance" in the original films, Lucas seemingly split the difference and gave him a wise-cracking, swashbuckling edge. Anakin also was remade. Gone was the rosy-cheeked, optimistic boy from *Phantom Menace*, replaced with a brooding and disobedient teenager-on-the-verge-of-adulthood that talked back to his mentor and complained about the Jedi code.

This re-introduction was a curious one. As Lucas has noted, one of the prime fascinations with the prequel trilogy was the exploration of how a good person becomes bad, the exploration of the choices and psychological processes which turn a person to evil. But, curiously, this essential linchpin of Anakin's character is absent from the film—the transformation is an offscreen one, and we are re-introduced to him, essentially, as a new character. In a way, Lucas reverted back to the initial characterisation of the impatient student Darth Vader from 1977.

Much of the Episode II script was fashioned after the "film noir" movies of the 1940s. Anakin and Palpatine's arcs in the film seem to comprise the majority of Lucas' outline for the episode, based on what he says[17]—which meant he would have to think up a story for Obi Wan. In this, Lucas sourced the film noir genre to come up with a detective subplot wherein Kenobi uncovers the clone conspiracy—investigating murder, dealing with hitmen, discovering forgeries, getting hot tips from underground friends, and uncovering a disturbing scheme on Kamino.

Film noir is an elusively-defined genre of movies that is considered to have sprung up in the early 1940s, though its appearance and disappearance are somewhat blurred. The plots and content of this genre usually involve a cynical protagonist with a dangerous past who gets mixed up in a fatal conspiracy involving murder and corruption. Content-wise, the films were often detective and crime based, and were precursed by the gangster films and "hardboiled" crime novels of the 1930s. Film noir is much better known for its visuals and stylistic devices—rain-soaked streets, dark alleyways, extremely contrasty lighting, heavy shadows, venetian blinds, subjective and stylised composition, urban settings and the use of voice-over. The films' distinct visuals were primarily born out of the German Expressionists, who had just immigrated to Hollywood after the Nazi takeover of Germany.[18]

1940's *Stranger on the Third Floor* is often cited as the earliest film noir, with the genre perhaps culminating with 1944's *Double Indemnity*; other notable mentions include *Out of the Past* (1947) and *The Asphalt Jungle* (1950). Orson Wells' *Touch of Evil* (1958) is said to be the last of the "classic" film noirs. The genre resurfaced in 1973 with "neo-noir" *Chinatown*, later followed by *Body Heat* (1981) and *Blade Runner* (1982), and in the '90s a healthy renewal was led by virtually all of the Coen brothers' films, as well as films such as *Gattaca* and *Dark City*. The frequent synthesis of film noir and science fiction has often been noted; one argument states that nearly all science fiction stories are really either disguised detective or western tales. In fact, the entire "Cyberpunk" genre is essentially born out of the film noir genre. Amusingly, Lucas staged one of the primary scenes in Kenobi's subplot in a 1950s diner, modelled after the very same one seen in *American Graffiti*.

This may bring us to a particular subject of observation. Though the prequels were designed to flow and fit together in a continuous fashion, they all have their own identity and disconnected personality that at times is quite startlingly dissonant: *Phantom Menace* is a whimsical children's fantasy, *Revenge of the Sith* an operatic character-based tragedy and *Attack of the Clones* a direct emulation of pulp science fiction and matinee B-movies, referencing everything from *Mysterious Island* to *War of the Worlds* to *Flash Gordon*.[19] Much more than any other film in the series, Episode II owes direct inspiration to 1930s and '40s pulp fiction and B-movies, containing many retro designs and serialesque cliffhangers, as well as a contrived love-story with its excessively-flowery language and formalized pre-Method acting. Lucas commented to author Jody Duncan on the writing of the romance:

It wasn't that the writing of it was so difficult...I'd done a bit of writing a love story in *American Graffiti*, so writing wasn't the challenge. The challenge was that I wanted to tell the love story in a style that was extremely old-fashioned, and, frankly, I didn't know if I was going to be able to pull it off. In many ways, this was much more like a movie from the nineteen thirties than any of the others had been, with a slightly over-the-top poetic style—and they just don't do that in movies anymore. I was very happy with it the way it turned out in the script and in the performances, but I knew a lot of people might not buy it. A lot of guys were going to see this movie, and most guys think that kind of flowery, poetic talk is stupid—"Come on, give me a break." More sophisticated, cynical types also don't buy that stuff. So I don't know if people would laugh at it and throw things at the screen, or if they would accept it.[20]

This highlights an aspect of the changing *Star Wars* universe, one that had apparently escaped even Lucas himself. *Star Wars* did indeed draw inspiration from the matinee adventure films of Hollywood's bygone era, but it was still quite contemporary in its drama and developed in its content;* it referenced certain elements of the serial films but it was, overall, simply a moving fantasy epic about a young man becoming a hero. When Lucas first wrote its sequel, *Empire Strikes Back*, his drafts were faster and less developed than the final film, foregoing more complex character development in favor of action and excitement—Irvin Kershner, however, allowed the story to breathe naturally, and with him and Lawrence Kasdan it became a serious drama, a sophisticated adult fantasy film that was also accessible to kids. It was not a serial and not reminiscent of Saturday matinee material in any way other than the fact that it contained spectacular action scenes. *Return of the Jedi* saw Lucas return to more prominent involvement, and the film does indeed have more action and less seriousness than its predecessor, but it was still, by and large, a character-centric drama (the only exception perhaps is the Errol Flynn-like sail barge battle, which is mostly unrelated to the rest of the plot). It was these last two films that solidified the "Saga" and laid the groundwork for the style and content of future films.

However, this subtle but significant transformation seems to have escaped Lucas. He approached the original two sequels with the mindset of *Star Wars*' lighter frivolity but the films ultimately did not reflect this

---

* Harrison Ford related that while "it was a bizarre situation—outer space and everything—the film was very contemporary. The characters were very contemporary as well...I just went ahead and did it." (*Starburst* Vol. 1 No. 3, 1978, p. 20)

perspective; perhaps he couldn't see how much they had actually deviated from his initial "vision" from the early 1970s. This is reflected in his more recent comments, where he explains that the saga was meant to emulate the serial films of the 1930s—but with the exception of *Star Wars*, they clearly are not. Even that film is only *vaguely* serial-like, utilising those genre conventions in a melting pot of adventure nostalgia that included John Ford and Errol Flynn more prominently than anything.

This transformation was not carried into the prequels, however. Despite the fact that the material was far more serious, and a natural continuation from the more solemn developments of *Empire* and *Jedi*, Lucas inevitably reverted to his default perspective of *Star Wars*—1930s serial material. As such, the content was dark and far more dramatic than anything seen in *Empire* or *Jedi*, but presented with the lightest and quickest of developments. The story was being pulled in two different directions. A parallel event might be seen in Lucas' initial re-cut of *Empire Strikes Back*; the material was serious and adult, but Lucas tried to fashion it to be quick and light, eliminating subtleties in favor of action and a fast pace. The cut was a unanimously-decreed disaster that only came together when Kershner re-fashioned it to reflect the character of the actual material.

### Struggle

Pre-production on Episode II was difficult, and the leisurely pace with which Episode I was written and designed under was replaced with an air that resembled that of a race.

Lucas had previously said that he would direct only the first instalment, and, like on the original trilogy, hire others to direct the final two episodes. The prime candidate was Spielberg in the eyes of many speculators, although Frank Darabont was also rumoured after word got out that he had been considered for involvement in Episode I. However, Lucas would eventually direct the films himself, something he decided as far back as the production of Episode I. Following Episode I's 1999 media premiere in New York, Lucas sat down with *The Star Wars Insider*:

> I'm back as a director now, and I will be directing II and III. I found going back to directing just like I hadn't stopped. And in some ways I *hadn't* stopped, because I had been directing second unit, and I've been very involved in the creative process in everything I've done since I stopped directing.[21]

The writing was another matter. Given that Lucas wrote *Empire* and

*Jedi* in collaboration with others, many expected him to do the same, and with the criticism Episode I's script received, rumours were abound that Lucas would hand over the writing to someone else after penning the first draft, as he had planned to do for Episode I.

As can be seen in the first half of this book, the writing of the original trilogy was a fairly collaborative undertaking—though *Star Wars* bore only Lucas' name on the script cover, it had still seen the influence of his many close friends, whom all collaborated on each others projects. In the 1970s, this circle of filmmakers included Francis Ford Coppola, Walter Murch, Matthew Robbins, Hal Barwood, Steven Spielberg, Marcia Lucas, Brian DePalma, Martin Scorsese, John Milius, Gloria Katz, Willard Huyck and more, and they all acted as a sort of filmmaking dream team—every project one of them did was supported by others, and all of the above were also writers who at some point had all worked on one anothers scripts. When Lucas was writing *Star Wars* all of these people saw the drafts and gave criticism, and most gave input in the edit stage; the community of San Francisco filmmakers such as Philip Kaufman and Michael Ritchie were all involved in each others work as well.

"You ask why there are movements in movie history," Coppola said in *Cinema by the Bay*. "Why all of a sudden there are great Japanese films, or great Italian films, or great Australian films, or whatever. And it's usually because there are a number of people that cross-pollinated each other."[22]

But since Lucas had found fame and fortune in the late '70s and most of this circle of players had encountered similar success, their collaborative efforts had since nearly ceased, and creatively they had all drifted apart from each others work. Not surprisingly, most of those filmmakers' heyday existed in the 1970s, when they worked as a group. "It started out that everybody worked together, helped everyone else," Milius said of the implosion of the American New Wave in the early '80s. "But as soon as they got money, everyone turned on each other...Steven and George had tremendous power, and they never asked me to do anything for them."[23] With financial independence they all went their separate ways, though a few relationships would survive, such as Spielberg and Lucas, or mended, such as Lucas and Coppola. Nonetheless, the absence of this group of active collaboration, and especially Marcia's presence, is felt in the post-'70s period. While perhaps not as terrible as Lucas' more vicious critics would have you believe, the new scripts were unsurprisingly weaker than their predecessors. Even Lucas realised that he was in trouble once he finished Episode II and had Jonathan Hales do a polish.

Lucas also consciously altered his method in another way, chosing to shape the story from the art department, giving concept artists plot details, seeing their visual interpretations and revising his script material from there. While this had also occurred on the original films, the importance placed on this process for the prequels gave them a significant emphasis on visuals but without a counterbalance of input with regards to character, story or dialogue. Lucas regarded these elements as being weak in the original films and so perhaps he was not very concerned—although this was arguably a severe underestimation on his part.

Perhaps it is unsurprising that Lucas tackled his craft with a different mindset; he had become a very different person from the one who wrote *Star Wars* in 1976, arguably more detached from the world due to his legendary celebrity status, divorced and having run and lived in a business empire for the previous twenty-five years. "He's in his own world," Mark Hamill observed in 2005. "He's like William Randolph Hearst or Howard Hughes, he's created his own world and he can live in it all the time. You really see that in his films, he's completely cut off from the rest of world. You can see a huge difference in the films that he does now and the films that he did when he was married... [Marcia] would tell him when he was wrong. Now he's so exalted that no one tells him anything."[24] Even back in 1983, seeing the Lucasfilm kingdom ever-consuming him, Willard Huyck cautioned Lucas, "When you're that successful and you've been proven right too many times, you don't give people an opportunity to argue with you because they can't argue with success."[25]

The longer Lucas remained with the "vision" of *Star Wars* in his head, the more stubborn he was to not "compromise" it by having others shape the material, despite his initial hopes in 1977 for other filmmakers to carry on the *Star Wars* story in a sort of "film school competition."[26] This changing mindset can be seen in a 1981 interview where he expressed doubts that anyone but he could ever be able to script the prequels,[27] and this conviction only festered in the twenty-year period since then. As the final weeks of Episode II's pre-production ticked by and the stress of the approaching shoot bore down, however, Lucas would finally ask for a script polish—though the aims and results of this are somewhat controversial, to be discussed shortly.

The writing of Episode II was a slow, and, it seems, a somewhat difficult process.

Given the time crunch, there was an extraordinary amount of work to be done on the film. Sony and Panavision were commissioned to build a new high definition digital camera to shoot Episode II with—the first major motion picture shot without a foot of film.* As well, the entire production was moving across the world to Sydney, Australia, the first *Star Wars* film not shot in England. Aside from these monumental tasks, there was the still the actual burden of designing and prepping the film. With only a nine-month pre-production period, swift action was a necessity.

However, Lucas was slow at turning over a screenplay. Months went by, and still no first draft was in sight, even as the millennium passed. "I would write three days a week and do design work two days a week," Lucas told Jody Duncan. "Later, when the crunch came, I worked on Saturdays as well, writing four days a week. But even so, I had to work awfully hard and fast to get all the drafts finished in the amount of time I had."[28] Without an actual script, the art department began designing based off Lucas' descriptions and supervision, and known locations—Tatooine, Geonosis, Naboo—were scouted during the summer of 1999 (Geonosis was eventually realised without location work). However, there were many crucial tasks to do, such as the construction of sets and the all-important casting of Anakin.

This last point was one which had been rife with rumours. Leonardo Dicaprio was a media favourite, as was Joshua Jackson and Paul Walker. However, many were surprised when a virtually unknown Canadian actor named Hayden Christensen was announced on May 12th, 2000, just weeks before the start of photography.

With the production gearing up, nobody had seen a draft of the script yet. Rick McCallum told *Star Wars Insider* in its February 2000 issue:

McCallum: George is in the midst of writing as we speak. This is his primary task while continuing to oversee the entire production. We're not putting any pressure on him. As he comes up with a scene, he tells us the basic backbone of what it is and what takes place there, and we start to design the sets. But right now we don't need a script—we just need the locations and the actual places where everything takes place. It's better for him to concentrate on the

---

\* Ironic that Lucas' decision to shoot HD to save costs and improve post-production workflow backfired as well—the prototype Sony HD camera's primitive sensors ended up creating more work for compositing and bluescreen extractions. "Trying to get fine extractions for hair and thin, wispy objects without getting a bit of a line was tricky," John Knoll said. "We got good results, but it was more work than with a film scan." See "Jedi HD Tricks" by Barbara Robertson in Studio Daily's Film & Video, May 1st, 2005 http://www.studiodaily.com/filmandvideo/searchlist/4413.html

dialog and themes as he goes along, while we're working on the look.

Insider: When will the script be completed?

McCallum: I don't know—whenever George hands it to me! It's like *Citizen Kane*—the script was finished two days before the film started shooting. This is about serendipity, alchemy—it comes together when it does.[29]

However, even Rick McCallum probably didn't expect that the script would not be finished until the day before Lucas left for Sydney. "My assistant handed me that draft to proofread as I was getting on the airplane," Lucas said to Jody Duncan, "just one week before I started shooting. Nobody on the crew had received a script yet. I had given them a rather detailed outline of what the scenes were so they'd know what sets and props we needed—but that was it."[30]

For Episode II, Lucas had recruited a co-writer for his final draft of the screenplay—*Young Indy* alumnus Jonathan Hales.* Though this elicited much delight from critics, who held that Lucas' dialogue was flat and his pacing uneven, one has to wonder just how much of a contribution Hales could make to the script. With Hales brought in as shooting was about to commence, the scenes were already written and locked, with the sets and shooting schedule completed and production imminent—Hales' main duties then would have been mainly to clean up the dialogue as best as possible within the confines of the scenes already written, and therefore his influence on the script not as drastic as many hoped; he simply came on board far too late to have significant impact.

The actors themselves were unenthusiastic to the dialogue. "[I was] definitely worried when I read the script for the first time," Hayden Christensen admitted to the *Denver Post*. "The dialogue was, well... I didn't know how I could make it convincing."[31]

The highly compressed time period of pre-production brought unexpected rushes. Previously, the film had been targeted to be written

---

* For those curious about Hales, he was actually in his early 60s at the time of writing Episode II. Before *Young Indy* his background was in UK television, including some forgettable Agatha Christie series but also the popular (locally) *Dempsey & Makepeace* and the long-running *Van der Valk*. His most significant feature-film contribution was an unsuccessful caper from 1981 called *Loophole*; regrettably, he is also credited with the story for 2002's *Scorpion King*, starring WWF wrestler The Rock.

along with Episode III back in the 1994-1997 period of pre-production of *Phantom Menace*; however, with that plan of attack abandoned when Lucas decided to concentrate solely on Episode I, perhaps Lucas estimated that he had more of Episode II thought out than was that case, anticipating that the script would "write itself." Rick McCallum seemed to believe so: he claimed during *Phantom Menace*'s premiere in early May of 1999 that Lucas had already written a quarter of Episode II's script and would have it finished by September of that year.[32] Factually, this was untrue, and may merely be the sort of reassuring publicity one might expect from a producer and one of the prequels' prime individuals in public relations—Lucas in fact did not *begin* scripting until September of that year, according to his interviews.[33] Nonetheless, the statement that it would be finished well before year's end probably reflects the ease with which it was anticipated the two sequels could be prepped; an anticipation that turned out to be not the case. Indeed, one gets the impression that Lucas didn't quite know what to make of Episode II, perhaps a result of its rushed nature which continuously pushed him forward before he was completely ready—the script never even received an official title.

Set construction had begun as late as February, perhaps in the hopes that Lucas would have a draft of the script completed by then so that decisions could finally be committed to (even though rough drafts are a tentative view of the film, at best), but it would be another month before the official rough draft would be typed up. "We really should have started building in mid-January," McCallum related to Jody Duncan, "but we pushed it to the second week of February—and at that point we were really up against it. In order to make our schedule, we had to build a complete set every other week until March, and then, from March on, we had to build *a set a week.*"[34] Crews worked seven days a week, fourteen hours a day to finish in time.[35] "George had always told us that Episode II was going to be a much smaller, more intimate film than Episode I," designer Gavin Bocquet said, "with, presumably, fewer sets. But it didn't turn out that way."[36] In *Mythmaking*, McCallum described the process as "backwards," comparing it to designing a skyscraper without building a foundation first.[37] "Do you know what it's like to budget a film without a script?" he asked.[38] Sony and Panavision meanwhile were still working on their prototype digital camera, which meant the crucial tests for the problematic hardware would have to be rapidly crammed into the final months of pre-production. An enormous amount of activity was overlapping as the crew scrambled to get the film ready, while Lucas himself was forced away to his writing room, struggling to pull a first draft out of himself.

Lucas' rough draft is dated March 13th, 2000[39]—filming would begin just two months after the *rough* draft was complete, let alone a proper first draft, in contrast to the comparatively-lengthy period of development that the other entries received. For instance, the time period between Lucas' rough draft of *Revenge of the Jedi* and Kasdan's second draft is six months, and the period of development between that second draft and the third draft is another three, with filming still another month away while the final shooting script was cultivated, altogether amounting to a total of nearly twelve months from the completion of Lucas' initial screenplay; the other films had development periods two to three times longer.

In defence of the fleeting scripting period, Lucas argues that he actually had hammered out a few completed goes at the script before March 13th. Doug Chiang remembers that Lucas finally had a draft in January, perhaps giving us a timeline for what can only be called a rough-draft of a rough-draft.[40] "I sat down to write the screenplay in September," Lucas said to Jody Duncan, "starting on page one and working my way through a first draft as quickly as possible. As soon as that initial draft was done, I started right away on a second draft. I do lots of drafts, rather than continually reworking the first twenty to thirty pages. I've found that if you keep trying to fix things, you rewrite the first thirty pages a hundred times, and you never get to the end. I called the first one typed up by my assistant my 'rough draft,' but I'd done fourteen or fifteen drafts *before* that one, and I did another two or three before I had it typed up again."[41]*

Some weeks later, Lucas had completed a third draft and handed it over to Hales while he left for Sydney to prepare shooting.[42] This was basically a necessity rather than design: Lucas had dragged out the scripting process as far as he could, working four days a week on it,[43] but he was also the director and executive producer of the blockbuster film and he could no longer neglect the many other duties that required his attention as the mammoth picture headed to its start.

"Our first story conference lasted a day and a half, and I mainly listened," Hales said to author Marcus Hearn. "Then I went back to London and wrote the first draft. After George read it, he called me from the set in Australia and said, 'Some of this is brilliant, some of it is not so brilliant—we'll talk about what's not so brilliant.' We went from there and I wrote another draft."[44] Lucas then re-wrote Hales' version into the final

---

* It seems Coppola's advice to Lucas made an impression: this method is the very same one Coppola told him to use when he first forced him to write a screenplay in the late '60s. See page 26.

script as shooting commenced.[45] The script was delivered to crew just three days before principle photography.[46]

Production began on June 26th, 2000 at the newly-erected Fox Studios Australia, before moving to location work in Italy and then Tunisia, where the original Lars homestead was re-created in its original location, making the filming particularly poignant. Lucas also filmed a scene for Episode III in which Obi Wan delivers the infant Luke to Owen Lars so that he would not have to return for the single shot years later—although the scene would be redone on a soundstage when it came time to actually make Episode III.

In post-production Lucas continued using his method of shoot-edit-shoot-edit, wherein multiple periods of pick-up filming are scheduled to provide pieces needed for the evolving edit of the film. For instance, the entire droid factory fight involving Padme and Anakin was created entirely in pick-ups since Lucas felt that section of the movie needed more action; it is worth noting that Spielberg was finalising *Minority Report* at this time, which features an identical sequence through a car factory.

With so much of Episode II having been rushed ahead, post-production was in some sense a period where the filmmakers could finally catch up with the movie. Concept artist Ryan Church noted in *The Art of Attack of the Clones*:

> Some of the things that are normally figured out during preproduction were actually being done *during* production...It allowed George, while he was cutting and editing, to bounce off our artwork and ask for new stuff. It's kind of backward, but a lot more fluid too. This is more typical of an [animated] feature than a typical live-action show.[47]

When Lucas finally went back to film new scenes, he also created, somewhat unexpectedly, an elaborate mystery angle to the film that remains conspicuously unresolved: Sifo-Dyas and the creation of the Clone Army. In the final film, we discover that the clones were ordered on behalf of the Republic by a well-known Jedi, Sifo-Dyas, who very ambiguously, as far as the film explains it, died ten years earlier. Sifo-Dyas, Obi Wan recalls, died before the order was even placed, and therefore it was not actually he who made the order but someone using his identity, as Mace Windu later implies. This is actually a red-herring, though it raises a number of issues that are never fully explained or explored in the trilogy. It follows that Dooku himself erased the Jedi archives, possibly even killed Sifo-Dyas, and ordered the clones in conjunction with his master Sidious, after joining the dark side ten years before the film begins, recruiting Jango Fett as the template, who continues to work for the Seperatists as an assassin once

Dooku instigates the Seperatist group. While this seems somewhat easy to figure out, it is indeed unusual that the protagonists do not seem cognisant of it, nor of any of the suspicious issues resultant from this plot.

In the original version of the film, however, things are much simpler: there is no Sifo-Dyas. Rather, Sidious himself orders the clones using an alias; there are no ties to a former Jedi who actually existed, and no mystery about how a Jedi could have placed an order. The shooting script introduces the issue:

> LAMA SU
> And now to business. You will be delighted to hear we are on schedule. Two hundred thousand units are ready, with another million well on the way.
>
> OBI-WAN
> (improvising)
> That is... good news.
>
> LAMA SU
> Please tell your Master Sido-Dyas that we have every confidence his order will be met on time and in full. He is well, I hope?
>
> OBI-WAN
> I'm sorry Master - ?
>
> LAMA SU
> Jedi Master Sido-Dyas. He's still
> a leading member of the Jedi Council, is he not?
>
> OBI-WAN
> Oh, yes. Sido-Dyas.
>
> LAMA SU
> (rising)
> You must be anxious to inspect the units for yourself.
>
> OBI-WAN
> That's why I'm here.

Here, in this shooting script, the mystery man is named Sido-Dyas. While claiming to be a Jedi, there is in fact no such person:

> OBI-WAN (V.O.)
> ...I've never heard of a Jedi

called Sido-Dyas, have you, Master?

MACE WINDU
No. Whoever placed that order was not a Jedi, I can assure you.

OBI-WAN (V.O.)
I have a strong feeling that this bounty hunter is the assassin
we're looking for.

YODA
Who he is working for... discover
that, you must.

OBI-WAN (V.O.)
I will, Master, and I will also find out more about this clone
army... May The Force...

The hologram switches off, and OBI-WAN fades away.

WINDU
A clone army! Ordered by someone
in the Senate perhaps... Someone's out to start a war.

YODA
Inform the chancellor of this, we must.

WINDU
Who do you think this impostor Sido-Dyas, could be?

In this version of the film, the Jedi are shown to suspect and acknowledge that the creation of the army may be a ploy to foster the impending war. Unlike the final film, which points to Dooku as the culprit and thus should evoke strong suspicions about the war's motivation (i.e. that is a ruse where both sides are manipulated by the Sith), here the Jedi's motivation is explained clearer: they believe that it is a member of the Republic senate who is in favor of propagating the war who ordered the clones (remember, the senate is equally split in its pro-war and anti-war supporters, so this is logical), but that he used an alias and claimed to be a Jedi in order to protect his identity.

In another scene it is explained that Sido-Dyas requested the Kaminoans keep the clone army a secret, explaining how the Kaminoans developed an army on behalf of the Republic for an entire decade without any communication through official lines. The motivation of why Sidious or Dooku would go through the trouble of framing the Republic and the Jedi as the progenitors of the clone order, rather than just ordering it on behalf of the Seperatists and letting the Republic discover and seize it, is explained—the Kamino cloners would never have created an army if they knew it was for the Seperatists.

The name Sido-Dyas was too obvious, at least for the audience's sake—Lucas wanted the identity to be kept a mystery, but you wouldn't need a Ph.D to realise that Sido-Dyas is just a variation on Sidious. Instead, Lucas re-wrote dialog in pick-up scenes to not only drift the name further away from the Sidious origin, but to throw audiences off the trail by asserting that this character actually existed and was personally known to the protagonists of the film. It seems, however, that Lucas was not quite prepared to deal with all the issues he raised in making this last-minute change, as the central mystery of *Attack of Clones* basically remains unacknowledged.

Episode II had been untitled during production (jokingly named in the script as "Jar Jars Great Adventure"[48]), unlike Episode I which was originally called *The Beginning*. Episode II's title was announced on August 6th, 2001 on the *Starwars.com* website. *Attack of the Clones*, the website said, "harks back to the sense of pure fun, imagination and excitement that characterized the classic movie serials and pulp space fantasy adventures that inspired the *Star Wars* saga."[49] This announcement came just as the world was thrown into a flurry of debate after US and European researches announced their plans to clone the first human being. Fan reaction to the title was generally negative, despite being similar in prose to the beloved "*Empire Strikes Back*"; Ewan McGregor, informed of the title on-camera during a press event, remarked "Is that it? That's a terrible, terrible title." (He later admitted: "When I initially heard about it I was doing a press line up in America and somebody went, 'What do you think of *Attack of the Clones*?,' and I said, 'I didn't see it'! So they said 'No, what do you think of that?' And [Lucasfilm] hadn't even told me! So I said, 'I think it sounds terrible,' because it does sound like a sort of 'Flash Gordon in A-t-t-a-c-k-O-f-T-h-e-C- l-o-n-e-s!' But I suppose in a way it is a kind of serialized science fiction thing so maybe that's just the way it should be."[50])

When it came to releasing the film, Lucas exercised caution. Burned from the uncontrollable hype and overexposure the first episode suffered from, Episode II arrived in theatres amidst a much calmer air, with virtually no fast-food tie-ins, less merchandising and an altogether more adult-aimed marketing plan which emphasized the romance and war aspect of the film.

The film opened to slightly better reviews than *Phantom Menace* had, but critics were still quick to trash Lucas' dialogue and stilted directing. Roger Ebert, longtime defender of the franchise, disappointedly remarked, "It is not what's there on the screen that disappoints me, but what's not there." The *Los Angeles Times* observed, "only a teenage boy would not notice the flimsy emotions and underdeveloped acting," while *Washington Post* critic Stephen Hunter concluded "it's too long, it's too dull, it's too lame." However, the backlash that *Phantom Menace* generated was not repeated (if only because expectations were not analogous), and Mike Clark in *USA Today* stated "No screen fantasy-adventure in recent memory has the showmanship of *Clones'* last 45 minutes," while *Time* magazine raved "when the now computerized Yoda finally reveals his martial artistry, the film ascends to a kinetic life so teeming that even cranky adults may discover the quivering kid inside." *Newsweek* perhaps summed up the general reaction when it said the film was "A decidedly mixed bag."

However, it was considered an improvement over *Phantom Menace*, even if just barely.[51] The movement from the more kid-friendly fare of *Phantom Menace* to the dark overtones of *Attack of the Clones* received much praise, as did the jaw-dropping finale wherein the massive Clone War occurred, the largest battle scene ever accomplished in a film at the time (to be quickly topped in grandeur by the *Lord of the Rings* sequels debuting shortly after). The film did not perform financially as well as *Phantom Menace*, as expected, but still managed the impressive feat of surpassing the $300 million mark. Audience response to the infamous Yoda finale resulted in much of the film's post-release ads focusing on this aspect of the film, and the movie was eventually released in the large-format IMAX process, albeit in a truncated form to accommodate the two-hour limit IMAX films could run for.

Still, a *Simpsons* episode from the time featured characters Lenny and Carl fighting each other with fluorescent tubes, arguing "I say *Phantom Menace* sucked more," "No, I say *Attack of the Clones* sucked more!" Publically, Lucas and the franchise had been greatly tarnished, though the next instalment would offer some redemption.

As he had done following the release of Episode I, Lucas took a family vacation, this time to Canada, before sitting down to finally tackle the big episode...Episode III.

Although Episode I received more attention than any film in history, Episode III was the real film that everyone had waited for—including Lucas himself. The height of the Clone War, Anakin and Obi Wan fighting side by side in full Jedi bloom, Darth Vader, the Emperor and the end of the Republic. Lucas remarked: "Act III is when everything comes together.

That's going to be the most fun to do."[52]

# Chapter XIII: The Circle is Complete

MAKING Episode III would be both satisfying and challenging for Lucas, for it was the story of this film that gave rise to the trilogy itself, and after more than twenty years of talk Lucas now had to construct this story in literal terms. McCallum commented on the difficulties of the prequel trilogy in this 2005 interview with *Science Fiction Weekly*:

> There's no question we knew way back in 1990 that *Episode I* and *II* were going to be very tough, especially with anyone over probably 18 years old or anyone who had had any relationship with the original trilogy...But we also knew that [*Episode III*] was the film that everybody who was older wanted *Episode I* to be. We never knew if it was going to be enough to try and tie everything together, or if it was going to be too quick, it wasn't going to go deep enough, or that things were going to be missing...but we knew that, in some kind of collective déjà vu sentiment, [*Episode III*] would definitely have enormous impact with all of our hard-core fans—both young and old. I think we finally delivered some peace and safety to everybody.[1]

Lucas had been dropping hints about Episode III for some years by the time 2002 rolled around. "The third film is very, very, very dark. It's not a happy movie by any stretch of the imagination. It's a tragedy," Lucas told *Empire* magazine in 1999. "Ultimately the final story is between Yoda, Obi-Wan, Anakin and the Queen. It's really their story. Those four characters."[2] The appearance of the bionic Darth Vader in the last minutes of the film was also revealed some time beforehand. "I saw George Lucas in Idaho and asked, 'Do I work again?'" James Earl Jones revealed in 2001, "and he said, 'Well, at some point in the third episode, Darth will become bionic and he should sound like you then.' He said there might be no more than five minutes at the end."[3] In fact, Lucas had told him this as far back as the 1990s.[4]

Eager to start, Lucas began work on Episode III even before *Attack of the Clones* was released, with the crucial first art department meeting occurring on April 25th, 2002, as reported thusly in Jonathan Rinzler's *The Making of Revenge of the Sith*:

> Lucas' first story fragments are both embryonic and epic: Episode III will take place approximately three years after Episode II. At that time, the Clone Wars will be wrapping up, with seven battles raging on seven new planets...Jedi Masters Kenobi, Windu and Yoda are on different planets fighting for the Republic. We may see bounty hunter Boba Fett as a fourteen- or fifteen-year old. We will visit Princess Leia's home planet of Alderaan; we may visit the Wookie planet Kashyyyk... By meeting's end, Lucas has divulged just enough to provide the artists material to work on until the next gathering, and, for the next nine months, this will be the pattern. Indeed, for most of preproduction, the concept art department will be working blind—without a script—because there is no script, no treatment, no outline. "We never truly know what George is doing," explains McCallum, "but it's no different than Episode II, because we didn't know what he was doing on that one, either."[5]

"The first ten minutes are going to be a huge spectacle," Lucas said later in June. "You're not going to know what is going on, other than it's the Clone Wars."[6]

One of the first things to be developed was the volcanic world "Mufasta" (later changed to Mustafar) where Anakin and Obi Wan would have their final confrontation. This hell-like imagery was a recurring one for Lucas, who first tried to use it in *Empire Strikes Back* for Darth Vader's castle. Lucas would finally portray this pivotal scene that had been stuck in his mind for so long. "These are old, old, old. Mufasta's been around a long time," Lucas said while overlooking concept art. "I've always had this set piece: the end between Obi-Wan and Anakin. I knew that's where this movie was going to end up. It's all volcanic land, with lava shooting up, so it's almost monochromatic in its red and blackness. I've had that image with me for a long time."[7] The transformation of Anakin into Vader would be handled in a very nostalgic way, evidently something Lucas had envisioned for some time before 2005. Much of the imagery surrounding Sidious and Vader is born out of the earliest films of the horror genre. The frightening appearance of Sidious' true form, though similar to that which is seen in *Return of the Jedi*, would be given a much more monstrous look, now being reminiscent of the horrid creature makeup of Lon Chaney. Lon Chaney was known as "the man of a thousand faces," and is perhaps best known for his performance as the title character in 1925's *Phantom of the Opera*, notable for the fantastic and hideous makeup worn by him; his son, Lon Chaney Jr., would go on to play the Wolf Man, Dracula, the Mummy and Frankenstein's monster in many Universal films of the 1940s.

Darth Vader himself would be re-assembled and revived in a sequence referencing *Frankenstein*. The classic 1931 film was directed by James Wale and took heavy visual inspiration from German Expressionism, and was responsible, along with *Dracula* that very same year, for popularising the "gothic horror" genre in film, which arguably had its basis provided by *Nosferatu* (1912) and *Phantom of the Opera* (1925), and was characterised by heavily stylised visuals, dramatic and shadowy lighting, castles, dungeons, laboratories and an otherwise grim ambiance. *Frankenstein*'s most famous scene is, of course, the one where the monster is brought to life. Assembled and stitched together out of grave-robbed corpses, the monster is laid on an operating table in Dr. Frankenstein's laboratory, located in his towering castle. As rain crashes down through the dark and stormy night, lighting strikes ominously, providing the electricity needed to re-animate the dead matter. The creature lurches off the operating table as the mad doctor exclaims "It's alive! It's alive!" *Frankenstein* would spawn many silly sequels in the '30s and '40s.

"The scene where Anakin does actually become Vader is pretty good," Lucas told *Starlog* in July, 2002. "I mean, I like it. It's a little in the vocabulary of...I don't know how much I want to give away...but it's in the vocabulary of a time—of the 1930s and 1940s. It's a pretty neat little thing, I think, and hopefully it's going to work."[8]

### Early Transformations

After the preliminary art department meeting in April for the opening montage of the Clone Wars on seven planets, Lucas returned in June to begin refining designs now that *Attack of the Clones* was released. Environments, aliens, vehicles and weapons were conceptualised and evolved. "Basically, I would tell them about a scene, an animal or a character," Lucas said to author Jonathan Rinzler, "and they would do a bunch of designs. I would okay some or modify or change them, and we build."[9] Alexander Jager told Rinzler, "For the first part of the design process, it seemed like George was going from what we were drawing, rather than telling us what to do."[10]

As Rinzler documents, on Friday, August 2nd, Lucas had his last art meeting before leaving for a family vacation, his last time off before three years straight on Episode III.[11] He had returned by August 23rd, but the script was as ethereal as ever—costume designer Trisha Biggar attempted a preliminary meeting to get her up to speed on the movie, but Lucas reminded her, "Well, we can talk about the costumes, but it's hard to discuss the script. I know the story, but..."[12] By November Lucas had decided on the planets and major sets that would be seen in the film,[13] and a few specific story details, drastically changing the first act of the film,[14] but still had yet to tackle the writing—the story was undergoing fundamental changes at this point.

On a November 1st, 2002, design meeting, Lucas said he will have to begin writing soon—"You said you've *been* writing," Rick McCallum protested. "I've been *thinking* about it," Lucas replied.[15] His story was still too embryonic to put down on paper with the changes Lucas was internally mulling over. Some days later Lucas approached the artists with the idea of creating a droid General for the Separatists, whom he says will then be one of the main villains of the film.[16]

Although work on the script would not start until much later, Lucas explained that as he started working on the outline in August of 2002, laying out the plot in more tangible ways than the evanescent vision floating in his mind, he encountered problems he hadn't anticipated. His story would require re-structuring if it were to work. He told Jonathan Rinzler:

> Back in August, I started writing this thing...But the script starts to have its own life. Characters start to tell you what to do—and you end up with problems. By the third film, you have a lot of characters left over from before, and they're all running around yipping and yelling and saying "what about me?" And you have to solve these problems, because what you thought was going to happen isn't happening. I got far enough with the outline to realise that the bridge between Episode III and Episode IV still had about fifty feet apart. So I had to disassemble Episode III and rethink it, to make it line up with Episode IV. When you actually put it down on paper and start doing it scene by scene—when you really start pulling it apart—you say "Well, I have to have a through-line. And I have to stick with it."[17]

This is a very interesting admission by Lucas, and one wonders just how the details of the script changed, especially since so much of the script was pre-determined. In fact, this may have been a contributing factor—there was so much that *had* to happen in this film that there was little room for manoeuverability. This may have been due in part to Lucas' plan to abandon a proper continuous trilogy and set Episode I back in the days of Anakin's childhood, leaving a three-film story to be mostly carried into two films, and leaving less time to bridge smoothly into Episode IV since the timeframe of Anakin's adulthood would be compressed.

But what were these extra characters and elements which went by the wayside? What didn't work and had to be rethought? Was Anakin's arc not believable? Was Boba Fett, whom Lucas at one time earlier confirmed was going to be in the film, to get his revenge and hunt down the Jedi?[18] Did Nute Gunray or Bail Organa have more screentime? Was the mystery of Sifo-Dyas to be addressed and resolved?* It seems that, because Lucas had taken so much time setting up the story in the first two films, he underestimated the quality and quantity of material needed to conclude the story and bring Episode III into properly transitioning into the originals.

Whatever tangential plot elements this story revision eliminated, however, the more important aspect to keep in mind is that this revision was primarily a re-*structure*, as Lucas and Rinzler report,[19] re-thinking the manner in which the story unfolded, how it did so, and how it involved the characters. Though the details of how the film was originally to be structured are sketchy at best, it is my belief that these changes were likely enacted to re-adjust the arc of Anakin's turn to the dark side, which then necessitated a change in structure for most of the plot; for reasons to be discussed shortly, in the original version, Anakin's turn might have involved him killing Dooku much later in the film as a direct transition point to the dark side. However, due to issues of believability in Anakin's arc, Dooku's execution was instead moved from the middle to the beginning of the film, thus necessitating the creation of General Grievous as the Seperatist leader to inherit the role in the film Dooku was originally supposed to fill, and with Samuel L. Jackson's repeated request for a grandiose demise[20] giving Lucas an opportunity to make Mace Windu Anakin's sacrificial victim. "You're pretty much the only important character that I can actually kill off, so it has to be a pretty spectacular

---

* On the 2002 *Attack of the Clones* DVD commentary, Lucas states that the mystery behind the erasure of the Jedi archive files and the corresponding Kamino conspiracy will be answered in Episode III, which obviously did not come to pass. This is consistent with my hypothesis regarding Dooku's re-configured role in Episode III, for the associated plot threads would have been tossed out with him.

death," Lucas told Jackson that summer.[21]

While the plot would hence be re-configured, the essential *nature* of Anakin's turn remained as it was originally conceived, and would furthermore remain as such in the scripts and the original photography, until Lucas totally re-wrote it in post-production, as we will later examine.

One of the most significant changes in this revision that can be gathered, albeit indirectly, is that it appears Dooku was to survive until much later in the film—after all, the first recorded instance of him being killed at the film's beginning does not occur until *after* Lucas would totally revise the opening sequence in October, just after Lucas had re-thought the story in August. The original opening to the film, conceived of in April, had been a montage of Clone War battles on seven planets, as noted earlier. However, once Lucas began to work on the story in the summer and realised that he had to re-structure the film, this opening was done away with and replaced with a different one in which the Chancellor is kidnapped and rescued in a battle over Coruscant, which then also introduces Grievous and simultaneously kills off Dooku—Grievous had never been referenced by Lucas prior to this story change (to be specific, Grievous' first record of existence is November 8th, roughly a week after the new opening sequence was first introduced by Lucas,[22] and Lucas' approach here indicates that Grievous is a new idea that had occurred to him).

The killing of Dooku, of course, has more to it than just brushing aside a villain to introduce a new character to sell action figures—it is directly and indirectly tied to Anakin's turn into Darth Vader. Therefore it seems that Anakin's turn may have been the primary motivations to Lucas' rethinking of the structure of the film. It seems originally Dooku filled the role of Grievous—which should surprise no one, as the two characters are literally interchangeable—and perhaps a large part of the story was to surround the hunt for Dooku, not Grievous.

It was obvious where Lucas was going with Anakin and Dooku with regards to mirroring *Return of the Jedi*. In *Return of the Jedi*, Luke is being tempted to the dark side and his final defeat would come when Palpatine urges Luke to kill his apprentice—in that case, Vader—in order to become the new one, marking his final act to becoming a Sith Lord. Lucas clearly had in mind this type of mirror scenario in Episode III, even going as far as staging the scene on a set which was virtually identical to the Emperor's throne room from Episode VI, and perhaps Lucas had wanted these two scenes to parallel each other even closer,* with Anakin's murder of Dooku occurring in the latter half of the film and providing the final fall in his descent into darkness. The killing of Dooku could have also been persuaded by Palpatine to be done in the name of good, as it would end the war; Anakin states in the final film in order to justify his twisted ways, "I have brought peace, justice and security." As Lucas explains, most bad people think they are doing things for the right reasons[23]—but, with Anakin being more and more consumed by the dark side, this final act would push his soul past the point of no return as the dark side overtakes him. This fundamental philosophy, however, would eventually transform as well.

As it happens in the actual film, however, the above does not occur. In a plot move unusually structured for a *Star Wars* film, Dooku is killed at the very beginning of the film, and instead of marking the final act to christen Anakin into the dark side, it is the first act which begins his downward spiral in the film. Instead of mirroring *Return of the Jedi* in a more literal sense, the climax is moved to the head of the film, and it is as if we see what would happen had Luke made the other choice; both films progress to the same point, with the hero faced with killing the Sith apprentice, and then split in different directions: Luke chooses good, and so the film ends, but Anakin chooses evil, and so the film continues to chart his descent.

To answer why Dooku's death was moved from the middle to the beginning, if in fact this happened, we see the exact same problem that would prompt Lucas to change the structure yet again in post-production: the arc of Anakin's turn was too abrupt.

All of the events which detail Anakin's descent in Episode III stem from his killing of Dooku at the start of the story. Anakin kills a man in cold blood at Palpatine's urging and immediately feels guilt for the action, but Palpatine is able to manipulate Anakin by reminding him of the Tusken Raider massacre in order to normalise the brutal act. It is here that he first had his taste of the dark side, and it would be the start of his lust for power. Following this, Obi Wan is sent away to hunt Grievous, while Anakin, beginning to have terrible visions of Padme, is able to stay on Coruscant with Palpatine, becoming a sort of bodyguard, where he is slowly manipulated and coerced. At the same time, Anakin begins wanting more

---

* It is also noteworthy that in the rough draft of the script, Anakin finally overpowers and kills Dooku out of personal hatred—during Anakin's duel with Dooku, Palpatine tells him that Dooku admitted he was the one who arranged the Tusken Raiders to kidnap his mother, and Anakin becomes enraged.

power as he feels the Jedi excluding him from matters. Palpatine finally reveals his Sith identity in order to help Anakin by granting him the powers to save Padme from death and by arguing that the Jedi are plotting to take control of the Republic, which Anakin accepts. When the Jedi come to arrest Palpatine, Anakin is present, realising that the Sith Lord is right, and intervenes. This then results in his Sith knighthood after he helps kill Mace Windu, and his first act of initiation is to hunt down the Jedi. This was all possible because Anakin had struck down Dooku in the film's opening, freeing Anakin from being tied to this plot point, creating a more effective motivation in which Anakin's turn forces him to betray the Jedi, and providing a good jumping point for Anakin's transformation.

Moving the murder of Dooku to the last half of the film collapses the above plot structure, and with it the character's arc—as Lucas said, he had an emotional through-line to stick with.

We must first, however, understand the nature of Anakin's turn itself. The initial conception was that the dark side was corrupting and steadily turning Anakin, building in him a lust for power and control, slowly overtaking his mind, almost like a drug. The Tusken Raider massacre of Episode II was a pivotal plot point because it provided his first taste of the unrestrained power of the dark side and set up his gradual turn in Episode III, which was then paralleled with his conversion to Sith allegiance after Palpatine convinces him that the Jedi are overthrowing the Republic, for in the original edit Anakin truly believed the Jedi to be traitors.

For Anakin to switch from Jedi to Sith, he would also have to be with Palpatine for quite a bit to make it believable since their relationship was only minimal in the previous film,* and with Obi Wan off-world in search of Grievous, Palpatine is able to grab hold of Anakin and twist his mind. The actual act that causes Anakin to become a Sith would thus be made into a more believable *emotional* one where he saves Palpatine from assassination and betrays the Jedi, instead of the more abstract act of executing Dooku. Although Lucas' original plan was not bad or unbelievable per se and provided a satisfying *Return of the Jedi* parallel to mirror the two trilogies, as Lucas said himself, when it actually came to putting it on paper it simply did not work as well as the film needed it to. Furthermore, this would transform once again—the emotional angle, nearly absent from the pre-Grievous outline and now present in minor form, would eventually dominate the through-line of Anakin's character.

---

\* The only actual scene between them in *Attack of the Clones* was one added in pick-ups—it seems Lucas severely underestimated the relationship of these two characters.

As a result of his original structure not being convincing, Lucas had to find a way for Anakin to kill Dooku at the beginning of the film, in order to set the spark for Anakin's turn and give plenty of screen time to transition to the dark side. But in order to kill Dooku, Anakin needed to be solo and have Palpatine presiding over it in order to urge him to do the deed. Of course, it was also too early to reveal Palpatine's Sith identity, and so the scene would have to involve Palpatine in his chancellor visage. The film also had to open with an action-packed sequence of the Clone Wars. This presented quite a challenge, and could easily come off as contrived. Lucas came up with an ingenious solution: Coruscant is attacked and Palpatine is captured by the Separatists, which results in Coruscant deploying all of its resources in a spectacular battle over the planet. Obi Wan and Anakin are sent to rescue him, which results in Anakin confronting Dooku while the "captive" chancellor is present. Originally, Obi Wan had split off to find Grievous on the ship, but this was re-written, although he is conveniently knocked out so as to keep the true nature of Anakin's deed a secret.

With Dooku now eliminated, his role is replaced by a character who serves the exact same function, General Grievous. This allows Obi Wan to venture off-planet to destroy him, simultaneously giving a new villain and an exciting action sequence, but more importantly it allows Anakin to become Palpatine's bodyguard. This intensifies their relationship and his manipulation, and also allows the Grievous hunt to break up the more "talky" Coruscant scenes, while giving Anakin full breathing room to become Darth Vader now that his mentor is far from him.

This quick dealing-away-with of Dooku may have eliminated with it some of the plot bits left over from the other films, such as the mystery of "Sifo-Dyas." Boba Fett was confirmed by Lucas as being in Episode III,[24] although this was not the case in the final film—it was long rumoured that the bounty hunters helped the Emperor exterminate the Jedi, a plot point originating from Prince Valorum in the rough draft of *Star Wars*, but the seemingly-inevitable "Revenge of Boba Fett" went unseen in the film after being hinted at so strongly in his final shot in *Attack of the Clones*. "I had a lot of extraneous stories going on that I could have tied up," Lucas said,[25] but he chose instead to ignore them in favour of focussing on Anakin.

"The issue is that I've painted myself into a corner," Lucas reflected in *The Cinema of George Lucas*. "I have to get from there to here, and I have to connect these two things in a very precise way. When I started this I thought it was going to be the easiest one, but there are so many things to balance that I soon found it locked me in. Writing involves a lot of puzzle-solving, and there are more than usual in Episode III."[26]

The structuring presented a problem for Lucas from the outset. Since the prequels were never meant to made as films, and since Lucas had not given himself much breathing room with his re-alignment of the chronology with Episode I, roughly eighty percent of the story was still contained in Episode III. Lucas explained the pragmatic reality of constructing the prequels to *Static Multimedia*:

> I did run into the reality of the first film. Basically, he is a slave kid. He gets found by the Jedi and he becomes part of the Jedi order and that he loves his mother. You know, that's maybe a half hour movie. And so I did a kind of jazz riff on the rest of it and I said, 'Well, I'm just going to enjoy myself. I have this giant world to play in and I'm going to just move around and have fun with this because, you know, I have to get to the second part.' So, then I got to the second part, and it was kind of the same thing. They fall in love, they can't and they're not supposed to, and, you know, little bits of trivia in terms of, you know, setting up the empire and how all that stuff works.
>
> That's about another twenty percent of this story treatment. The first film is twenty percent, the second film is twenty percent and I then ended up with a third film. The problem was the third film was actually more like eighty percent of the story. So, I was sitting there with a lot more story to tell than I actually had time to tell it. It was the reverse of what I had in the first two films. I constantly had to cut it down and cut it down. I had a lot of extraneous stories going on that I could have tied up, but when you really got down to it, it was really Darth Vader's story. I focused in on Darth Vader and Darth Vader was the key element.
>
> So, Padme starting the rebel alliance. A lot of these other things with Obi-Wan and some of the other characters, Yoda and the Jedi council, all these other things had to go by the wayside and I just focused on everything that was Anakin related. When I did the first script, I ended up kind of where I was in Episode IV, which had way too much script. Instead of saying, "Well, I'm going to make these into other movies," I just started dropping stuff out and then brought it down to where it was a manageable film and it focused on the one character that we needed to focus on. And then I made that the movie.[27]

As Rinzler wrote: "Having toned down the other characters and the tempting tangents, Lucas can sum up the focus of the revised but still-evolving story in one word: '*Anakin*.'"[28] This epitomizes the shifting identity of the saga. The prequels were now a character study rather than a background piece, and with it came the shift of the original trilogy from a macro plot involving Han, Luke, Leia and the Rebel Alliance's fight against the Empire, to a micro story of Vader and his struggle, the culmination of the character study begun in the first three episodes. No longer were the prequels "*back*-story"—they were now, more than ever, simply "story," the first half of one narrative.

It appears that even Lucas himself did not intend for this personalised version of the saga, the character study of Anakin Skywalker, to take over with the extent that it eventually did. Even as late as the mid-'90s, Lucas remarked, "In the kind of movies I make, I tend to stress the plot side of things...usually the characters are archetypes to such a degree that it's not necessary to go into a lot of detail because I'm not dealing with psychological problems. My films are storytelling movies, not character movies."[29]

It is also interesting to trace how this ongoing transformation of the series seems to have occurred while Lucas was in the midst of making the films. Although Anakin was always the heart of the trilogy, his prominence as the singular focus of Episode III, at the expense of all other plot points, was unplanned. As the series went on, Lucas began placing more emphasis on him—Episode I is a macro-plot in the vein of the original trilogy which balances all the characters and stories, with Anakin being a relatively equal co-star with the other three or four characters (i.e. Qui Gon, Padme, Obi Wan, Jar Jar). Lucas makes the curious statement in 2005 that it wasn't until after *Phantom Menace* was written and shot that he consciously became aware of the new Anakin-biography form the series was taking on,[30] and hence began to then re-align the series in this manner. In fact, Lucas met with Episode I novelisation author Terry Brooks around this time (November 1997[31]) and admitted that he would have liked the story to revolve around Anakin more, and together they re-developed the Episode I novelisation to centre around the character. "George felt there should be more focus on Anakin Skywalker than what he was able to do in the movie," Brooks related to *Star Wars Insider*. "George provided a lot of the insights and a lot of the ideas for how that approach might take place."[32] With Episode II Anakin became a more central protagonist, but it wasn't until Episode III that the film would be told, essentially, from his point-of-view, with almost every non-Anakin scene eventually cut out of the film; it became a micro-plot, a character study on him, in opposition to Lucas' intentions expressed in the mid-90's.[33] The series was on its way to becoming dubbed the six-part "Tragedy of Darth Vader."

In the writing of Episode III, many of the characters would undergo significant changes in the story. Among the more notable ones was Obi Wan Kenobi. More and more, Obi Wan would turn out to be the trilogy's best example of a traditional hero—the one Jedi who kept his wits, did the right thing, and stayed loyal to both his friends and his moral code. Although Lucas would write in Kenobi lamenting "I have failed you,

Anakin, I have failed you," Kenobi is inevitably revealed as the incorruptible hero of the film, returning him to the immaculate do-gooder of 1977.

There would also be a change in Kenobi's motivation regarding confronting Anakin. Although in *Return of the Jedi* it is said that he once tried to turn Anakin back, here he does no such thing, and in the early drafts even *volunteers* to kill Anakin, though for the final film he would protest the assignment, explaining that he cannot kill his "brother."

Padme's character would undergo a metamorphosis as well. One of the complaints that the finished film received was that Padme essentially does nothing in the film except stand around pregnant and barefoot in the kitchen. This was due to the fact that "Mother Skywalker" had no place in Lucas' backstory, so she is essentially forced onto the sidelines and killed off. This is why Padme is prominent and downright *central* to the first two episodes—the episodes Lucas had to make from scratch and which only occupied a tiny percentage of his original treatment—but once we got the actual "meat" of the backstory in Episode III, she basically disappears from the story and dies, because she was never meant to be a part of it. Lucas would attempt to include her in the plot by involving her in the formation of the Rebellion but this would not survive the final cut, and she remains only to motivate Anakin's exploration of the dark side and give birth to the twins.

Padme's final fate was an element shrouded in mystery, for the only mention of her in the original trilogy was the ambiguous details of her death. Lucas never talked about the wife of Anakin Skywalker prior to the prequels, and by his own admission never developed her.[34] As covered earlier, Lucas' plan in the days of the original trilogy was that Mother Skywalker took Leia to Alderaan where she apparently lived her last days before dying when Leia was still a young child. In the final film, Padme dies of a broken heart, and this may be what Lucas had in mind all along—after the emotional devastation of watching her husband turn to evil and betray all that he cared about, with democracy crumbled to dictatorship and the Jedi exterminated, Padme retreated to the sanctuary of Alderaan with Bail Organa and his wife, where she lived her last years until finally giving out in emotional exhaustion. "She was kind, but sad," as Leia remembers.

In a passage in Rinzler's book, during a design meeting Padme is said to be last seen on Alderaan, but "for the first time" she is rumoured to die onscreen, presumably instead of the unchronicled years between trilogies. Rinzler reported, "For the first time, it is rumoured that Padme might die in this film. She may be seen last on Alderaan."[35] Deviating from the original backstory, however, if Mother Skywalker had indeed originally been conceived of dying of heartbreak, it was a slow, gradual one that occurred when Leia was a young girl, and not the instantaneous one of Episode III.

What Lucas had intended of Mother Skywalker in the initial pre-1978 configuration is a total mystery, and it seems Lucas never even developed her beyond giving birth to Luke and then somehow dying.

Of much significance is the fact that in the rough draft, Anakin's visions are not that Padme dies in childbirth—instead his vision is that she is engulfed in flames, perhaps a premonition of his own fate. This is then obviously a more metaphorical vision and not a truly literal precognitive dream as the final film is. According to Rinzler's book, on October 25th, 2002, Lucas confirmed the ending to the film will consist of "a thirty second wrap up," wherein Yoda will go to Dagobah, Obi Wan will go with the infant Luke to Tatooine, and Bail Organa will go to Alderaan with the infant Leia, implying indeed that Padme dies.[36]

That same day, Lucas also divulged that he had changed the opening of the film. It is described by Rinzler:

> [Lucas] has also altered the beginning of the film. Instead of starting with seven battles on seven planets, Episode III now opens with a huge space battle. Our heroes crash-land into a "bad guy ship," perhaps Neimoidian, where there will be lots of "cliffhangers, from one near-death experience to another—*Indiana Jones and the Temple of Doom* aboard a ship." The ship might be breaking apart. He asks the artists to work on a "grand control room and a grand office." The heroes will be trying to rescue a kidnapped character...He then reveals that Anakin and Count Dooku will have a huge duel aboard the ship. The entire opening sequence should last about twenty minutes.[37]

Slowly, Lucas drew out the plot of the film, and already it shows a surprising resemblance to the film, and Lucas had not even begun to write the script yet. Unlike the original trilogy, much of the story development was evolved in the art department—there is no paper trail of story changes for us to follow, nor are there story meetings to discharge the creative battles raging inside Lucas' head for us to view.

### Getting a Screenplay

By December 6th, Lucas admitted he still hadn't started the script; "Oh, god..." an exhausted Rick McCallum moaned.[38] According to Rinzler, by January, Boba Fett had been eliminated from the story,[39] while the first mentions of Grand Moff Tarkin are made, and a fairly major piece of news that a child version of Han Solo is to be seen on the Wookie planet of Kashyyyk.[40] Rinzler wrote:

> Lucas' rethink of the script is becoming manifest to the artists—though they have yet to read it—as more and more links are established between Episode III and IV. The bridge between the two is being buttressed, and the difficulty of writing that bridge is evident in many of Lucas' off-the-cuff-remarks...after his resuscitation, Vader is handed over to Governor Tarkin, who was played by the late Peter Cushing in Episode IV. Apparently there is some unused footage of the actor that can be cut into the new film.[41]

As more elements of the story congealed, Lucas drafted an outline of his new storyline, which was broken into acts with point-form lists of events in each act,[42] and then finally wrote a script—possibly at the urging of Rick McCallum, for it is for his eyes only. "We can't give the script to the department heads yet," McCallum said to Rinzler. "Instead, I interpret it for them, because I don't want them to go too far down the line. It has to stay ephemeral at this point. There has to be enough information so they know what's going on and can plan, but not enough information so they lock something down—because everything will change."[43] On January 31st, 2003, Lucas' completed rough draft was typed up.[44]

At 55 pages, it is only a temporary guide to the film, to be fleshed out and expanded into a full length script, and is titled *Revenge of the Sith*.

The rough draft reads like a simplified version of the final script, very nearly like an outline arranged in the format of a screenplay. It also contains a number of notable distinctions. Anakin's vision is slightly different from the film, as stated before. Rinzler's description is "Anakin is awakened by a nightmare in which Padme is consumed by flames."[45] After Anakin is placed on the Jedi Council, Yoda, who is attending the meeting by hologram due to his placement on Kashyyyk, speaks with the spirit of Qui Gon Jinn when the meeting is over, who says that the Force is out of balance (Qui Gon is never seen, only heard). A ten-year-old Han Solo then delivers to Yoda the tip of Grievous' whereabouts.

Mace confronts Palpatine alone after Grievous is killed by Kenobi, insisting that the war be stopped, but Palpatine attacks him with lightning bolts. At Palpatine's urging, Anakin, who is present for the encounter, cuts off Mace's lightsaber hand, and the Jedi master is engulfed by the bolts, finally falling to the ground dead (and not thrown out the window). It is described:

The tremendous effort needed to generate the sustained lightning has transformed PALPATINE's face into that of DARTH SIDIOUS.[46]

With Anakin standing by, Order 66[*] is given to the clone troopers, and various Jedi are cut down in montage, with Yoda and Obi Wan surviving their attacks as in the film.

Anakin's final seduction plays out much differently. From the *Making of Revenge of the Sith*:

On Coruscant, PALPATINE completes his seduction of ANAKIN, who at first refuses to go over to the dark side—until the Chancellor makes a startling confession:

DARTH SIDIOUS
I have waited all these years for you to fulfill your destiny [...] I arranged for your conception. I used the power of the force to will the midichlorians to start the cell divisions that created you.

ANAKIN
I don't believe you.

DARTH SIDIOUS
Ahhh, but you know it's true. When you clear your mind, you will sense the truth. You could almost think of me as your father.

ANAKIN
That's impossible!

DARTH SIDIOUS
Nevertheless, you must decide...

Thanks to promises of powers that would save PADME from death, ANAKIN gives in to temptation. OBI WAN and YODA return to Coruscant and the jedi temple, where they find a hologram that shows ANAKIN slaughtering the younglings. In the hologram, DARTH SIDIOUS enters, and ANAKIN kneels before him.

---

[*] There have been a few theories on what Order 66 means. The most obvious is that it's a variation on 666, the "number of the beast" in the Biblical book of Revelations that identifies the anti-Christ during Armageddon. Another theory states that it is meant to recall Executive Order 9066, which was the order that placed Japanese Americans in Internment camps during World War II.

DARTH SIDIOUS
You are a Jedi no more, Anakin Skywalker. That life is no more. Today you
begin your new life as Darth Vader, Lord of the Sith and bringer of peace and
justice to the galaxy.[47]

In this version, Obi Wan requests to go after Anakin, while Yoda
counsels patience and does not go off to confront the Emperor, instead
fleeing with Bail to Polis Massa. Obi Wan is to meet them there, but says
he will join them later and confronts Padme, asking where Anakin is, but
she won't tell him. Padme boards her ship, in this version with Captain
Typho and her handmaidens, to travel to Mustafar, where Anakin is
slaughtering the Separatists, as Rinzler describes:

PADME arrives—but her entourage is gunned down by clones. As they close
in on her, ANAKIN appears and calls them off. She pleads with ANAKIN, but
he says she is either with him or against him. Just then OBI WAN reveals
himself—having sneaked aboard her ship. ANAKIN is enraged, and, believing
PADME had betrayed him, Force-chokes her and then throws her against a
wall. OBI WAN and ANAKIN fight.

The old friends battle through Mustafar interiors and exteriors until,

Just as ANAKIN looks as if he has beaten OBI WAN, the Jedi makes a quick
move, cutting off ANAKIN's legs, and he tumbles down an embankment and
stops near the edge of the lava. Suddenly, the Sith Lord bursts into flames and
starts screaming.

OBI WAN picks up ANAKIN's lightsaber and walks away. There is no
dialog.[48]

The rest of the script follows the film, except the arrangement of the
final montage is slightly different, ending with Vader peering out the Star
Destroyer's bridge. Lucas tried this approach during *Attack of the Clones*
as well, ending the script with the clone troopers boarding the Republic
Cruisers as Palpatine presides over all, but this was switched with the
wedding ceremony to give a more hopeful, though still sombre, ending.

Lucas' first attempt at crafting Episode III is remarkably similar to the
final film, but a number of minor yet crucial differences are apparent, the
biggest being the details of Anakin's downfall.

The rough draft was a truncated version of a proper script, perhaps
better understood as an expanded treatment. As the story would become
more refined, so would Anakin's arc, and his character's transformation

would become more focused, consistent and drawn out as the production progressed. The biggest challenge Lucas had was realistically bringing Anakin into the dark side (the very issue that prompted his re-structuring of the story in 2002). This, it seems, was something of a struggle for Lucas, as he threw as many different incentives as he could at Anakin: the Jedi are taking over (as would become a more prominent point in the coming drafts), he can have unlimited power and bring peace to the galaxy, Palpatine is his father and Padme can be saved. However, most of these would eventually be eliminated, notably the admission that Palpatine is his father—this could also be seen as a ploy to get Anakin to join him, and would instead be dealt with more ambiguously in the Darth Plagueis tale added in the next draft.

Palpatine's transformation into Sidious is also given an approach that differs from Lucas' original conception. The popular theory to explain the Emperor's ravaged appearance in *Return of the Jedi* was that he was so consumed with the dark side that it was literally corrupting his body, similar to the way the dark side corrupts one's mind; this made its way into the novels and comics as well. Lucas appeared to be going down this route for the prequels, perhaps indicating that this story point stemmed from himself—Palpatine begins Episode I fairly healthy looking; when he becomes Supreme Chancellor, his growing power begins transforming him—he becomes older, more frail looking, with gaunt skin and liver spots, and actor Ian McDiarmid wore makeup to make him look more sickly. "Palpatine's face is showing signs of the Emperor's facial markings," Episode II concept artist Ian McCaig said in relation to that film. "The idea is that the evil inside him is corrupting his flesh. This is the missing link between [the prequel character] and the Emperor from the original films."[49] His office too was undergoing a similar metaphorical transformation, introducing black elements. Production designer Gavin Bocquet explained in *Mythmaking: Behind the Scenes of Attack of the Clones*:

> We went back and forth with George as to whether the office should have the same bloodred color that you see in Palpatine's apartment in *The Phantom Menace*...or whether it should have blacks and greys to suggest Palpatine's turning to the dark side. We finally suggested that we make the office half red and half monochromatic grays and blacks. Then, in Episode III, if we show Palpatine's room or office, we can lose the red and make it all black to indicate his complete turn to the dark side. It created a character arc through color.[50]

However, this was done away with for Episode III. His office remained as it was and not only was his withering physical progression ceased, but it was made backwards—he appears in the film younger and stronger than in Episode II, free of wrinkles or blemishes, and even manages some impressive physical action. "He seemed to have turned into action-man," McDiarmid said incredulously at his character's new portrayal.[51]

The transformation to the Emperor was then handled in a more instantaneous way; the gentle, grandfatherly exterior of Palpatine is stripped away once he exerts all of his power to destroy Mace, revealing the hideous monster beneath which he has been hiding for so many years. He then uses the physical transformation to frame the Jedi, accusing that they have scarred him (the final film would use this ploy to win Anakin as well, with some re-shot material in a more drawn-out version making it seem as if Palpatine's lightning is being deflected back at him and wounding him). We thus learn that his true appearance is a hideous form, one which lurked beneath the comforting mask of Palpatine, the personification of the monstrous evil of the dark side that can hide inside even the most unassuming of people. "George was very interesting when we started *The Phantom Menace*," McDiarmid recollected to *BBC Online*. "He told me I should think of my eyes as Palpatine's contact lenses, which was a great thing to say to an actor. So my face was actually Sidious' mask, and then when I put on the [Sidious monster makeup] mask I became him."[52] This method of instant "reveal" also allowed Lucas to portray Sidious more as a "frightening monster" than the "withered sorcerer" look of *Return of the Jedi*, adding to the vintage horror imagery of the film's last half.

Rinzler's summary of the rough draft does not specify that Padme dies of a broken heart, only that she dies on the operating table—in this script, and even in the final one, her attack by Anakin is more severe, with him throwing her against a wall, perhaps implying that she may also have died because of her injuries. In the final film, Anakin was to lift her off the ground with the Force and fling her to the floor but this was cut out, likely to emphasize her death-by-heartbreak.

Fleshing out the story, Lucas began readying a first draft. Rinzler reported a March, 2003 production meeting as Lucas describes his writing process:

> Sitting with others in his office, Lucas delivers a short 'state-of-the-script' report: "Well, I wrote a rough draft. It's really crude, but it basically gets the essence of the story down and the main beats of the film. I've also written about half of the first draft. Now I am going through, filling out and being more articulate. I still have elements, like Artoo-Detoo and Threepio, which I haven't really fit in everywhere. They're in one scene, but I haven't actually

filled in their reality yet, because the film doesn't centre on them. So I'm hoping to have the first draft done in two weeks. Then I'll start working on the second draft, and I'm hoping to get a third draft in before I have to go to Sydney—which means I'm going through a draft about every six weeks. Then I'll have it as best as I can—but I'm looking at the shooting very much as another draft."

When someone asks what his biggest challenge is going from rough draft to first draft, he responds, "What challenges me is what always challenges me...

"Inertia. [laughter] Procrastination. I sit there with that page in front me... I am very diligent about going to work at eight thirty every morning and leaving at six o' clock every night. But I can be chained to my desk and I still can't write it. I do it, you know, I do get it done; I actually write five pages a day. I force myself. It becomes agonizing to get those other four pages, otherwise—"

"You can't have dinner?"

"Well, I can't leave [laughter], so I do four pages and I get onto the fifth page, I rationalize it: I've done my five pages."[53]

On Thursday, April 10th, 2003, Lucas finally finished his all-important first draft. Ian McCaig remembered the day in *The Making of Revenge of the Sith*, as he travelled to Lucas' home for a storyboard discussion with Derek Thompson:

We drove up to a big white house surrounded by cypress trees...We drove through the double gates, past the main house, to an annex off to the right side. It's all beautiful redwood. You open the door and Lucas' office is like the deck of a ship, with what looks like a captain's poop deck at the end of a long room. That's his writing area. And today when Derek and I walked in with our boards, George was at the end of the room. His pencil was down and he was just sitting there with his head bowed. Then, looking calm and drained, he came down and said "I just wrote the end." He had just finished the first draft.[54]

The first draft is 56 pages longer than rough draft and is cleaner and more articulate, now resembling a proper script.

Notable revisions from the rough draft include Han Solo's elimination from the script. Instead, the location of Grievous is disclosed by Palpatine, where he also tells the tale of The Tragedy of Darth Plagueis "The Wise," as in the final film. Grievous is also now a four-armed lightsaber user; the animated *Clone Wars* micro-series would use this interpretation of Grievous, presenting him as something akin to a Terminator, but Lucas would revise the character in post-production to be a slimier, moustache-twirling, serial-style villain.* The Mace-Palpatine fight now resembles the one in the film, with Palpatine forced onto the defensive and Anakin intervening, and Mace is now sent out the window to his death.

After viewing the hologram at the Jedi temple, Yoda instructs Obi Wan to kill Anakin, to which Obi Wan now objects. Yoda now confronts Darth Sidious below the senate chamber. Rinzler described the climax differentiations as follows:

> On Mustafar, PADME and her entourage are attacked, but this time by droids, which ANAKIN destroys. PADME confronts ANAKIN with what OBI WAN told her—that he has gone over to the dark side—but ANAKIN claims to "have brought peace to the galaxy."
>
> PADME
> Obi-Wan was right. You've changed.
>
> ANAKIN
> For the better. I have become more powerful than any Jedi ever dreamed of being [...]Together we will rule the galaxy.
>
> On Coruscant, PALPATINE easily deflects YODA's attacks, and the latter barely escapes with the help of BAIL ORGANA.
>
> PADME dies on the operating table saying, this time, "He's not evil..." On Coruscant, after ANAKIN has become the mechanical Darth Vader, he asks where PADME is, and PALPATINE's line is new: "I'm afraid she was killed by a Jedi...she is no longer our concern."[55]

By June 13th, 2003, a 135-page revised second draft was completed, but with production drawing near, there wasn't much time to continue re-writing. This time Anakin and Obi Wan both take on Dooku, and the scene plays out as it does in the film. For the first time, Anakin's dream about Padme is that she dies in childbirth, not falling into a pit of flames—his arc now took on an ironic, *Macbeth*-like circle. New scenes also reveal the

---

* It is interesting that this new, serial-like conception of him is also similar to Darth Vader from the 1974 rough draft—slimy and vaguely cowardly, though still armed and dangerous, one who enjoys the frills of command and the spoils of war. Could General Grievous be a transformed General Darth Vader? The connections take another level, as physically he is similar to the final version of Vader, a cyborg, foreshadowing Anakin's mechanical transformation at the picture's end

Jedi's distrust of the Chancellor, and in a scene onboard a gunship with Obi Wan and Yoda, Mace expresses skepticism over Anakin's "Chosen One" status. Mace Windu is now accompanied by Jedi Eeth Koth, Kit Fisto and Saesee Tiin when he arrests Palpatine, and there is also dialogue now when Anakin is wounded by Obi Wan, as Rinzler describes:

> During his duel with OBI WAN, ANAKIN says, "This is the end for you, my friend. I wish it were otherwise. This is your last chance to join me." After OBI WAN cuts off ANAKIN's legs, his tune changes:
>
> ANAKIN
> Help me, Master.
>
> OBI WAN
> Don't ask me Anakin... you're evil. You bring nothing but pain and suffering. I can't help you.
>
> ANAKIN
> I hate you![56]

The medical droid also makes it clear now that Padme is dying of a broken heart, and Padme lives long enough to see her children. Darth Sidious informs Vader that he killed Padme in his anger, which causes Vader to break his bonds in anguish. Finally, the last shot is now the Lars and Luke on Tatooine.

A subplot of Anakin's jealousy of Obi Wan over Padme is present in these scripts, but it is downplayed in the finished film. Originally there were two scenes between Anakin and Palpatine where the latter manipulates the former's trust and tries to create a rift between the three of them. After crashing the Separatist cruiser, Palpatine walks with Anakin, telling him that Obi Wan was rumoured to fancy a certain senator and has been seen meeting with her, but says he doesn't know who she is. In another scene, after Padme secretly begins organising the Rebel Alliance, Palpatine mentions to Anakin that Padme is hiding something and should not be completely trusted. Finally, another scene occurred where Obi Wan visits Padme with concern that Anakin has been troubled lately; he also reveals that he knows Anakin is in love with Padme and wants to help them. The subsequent scene is the one shown in the film, where Anakin and Padme are in her apartment and Anakin states "Obi Wan's been here...," originally emphasizing Palpatine's manipulations.

A sort of triangle between Obi Wan, Anakin and Padme had been experimented with in the previous episodes but all but eliminated, and it was seemingly headed to this point, where Anakin's jealousies and insecurities lead him to the dark side. In the first draft of Episode I, it was strongly hinted that Padme had a crush on Obi Wan—when Kenobi argues with "Amidala" about Jar Jar on Naboo, Padme is said to be impressed that Obi-Wan was able to stand up to the "Queen," and as they enter Mos Espa, she "gives Obi-Wan a long, adoring look."[57] In Mos Espa, Padme watches Kenobi with interest and respect, making Kenobi very nervous. In Episode II Anakin accuses Obi Wan of being "jealous" of his power and deliberately holding him back.

On June 26th, 2003, a fourth draft had been written, just days before filming, clocking in at 129 pages, and includes, among other details, additional dialogue in Palpatine's Plagueis story, this time stating that his apprentice killed him, although it contains pieces not heard in the final film:

PALPATINE
...Plagueis never saw it coming. It's ironic he could save others from death, but not himself. According to the legend, it was a power his apprentice found no value in. So the ability to save loved ones was lost with Plagueis "the wise."[58]

The last part of his speech is especially notable. In the film, it is all but confirmed that Plagueis' insidious disciple is of course Palpatine himself, Darth Sidious, and that he—or perhaps his master, or perhaps both together—may have created Anakin. Yet, when Anakin finally pledges himself to Darth Sidious, Sidious says, "The power to cheat death is something only one has achieved, but if we work together I know we can discover the secret," implying that his master, and not he, knew of the ability (which is in fact stated in the above script excerpt). By eliminating the last two lines of his speech about Plagueis, Lucas enabled Palpatine to use the life-saving power as bait to lure Anakin, and it also allows Palpatine to keep Anakin there once he turns, with promises of "discovering its secret" in time (otherwise Anakin could have simply said "Okay, give me it now then"). This may also indicate that any implication of Palpatine's parentage may be a falsehood.

This fourth draft also has Kenobi's post-immolation "You were the chosen one!" speech as Anakin lays dismembered.

Lucas spoke to Jonathan Rinzler about scripting *Revenge of the Sith*:

As I write the next drafts...there'll be a lot of cutting and pasting. Certain sequences will be right, and I'll jump through them. The last thing that will be dealt with is the dialog, because that you can change on the set or even afterward—you know, I'm not known for my dialog. [laughs] I think of it as a sound effect, a rhythm, a vocal chorus in the overall soundtrack. Mostly, everything is visual.

What drove me to make these movies is that this is a really interesting story about how people go bad. In this particular case, the premise is: Nobody thinks they're bad. They simply have different points of view. This is about a kid that's really wonderful. He has some flaws—and those flaws ultimately do him in.

The core issue, ultimately, is greed, possessiveness—the inability to let go. Not only to hold on to material things, which is greed, but to hold on to life, to the people you love—to not accept the reality of life's passages and changes, which is to say things come, things go. Everything changes. Anakin becomes emotionally attached to things, his mother, his wife. That's why he falls—because he does not have the ability to let go.[59]

Finally, filming began on June 30th, 2003. Despite having more planets and locations than the previous two films combined, Episode III was photographed entirely in-studio. During what was from all accounts an enjoyable and satisfying shoot, the script also underwent further tweaking and re-writing.[60]

Lucas also hired an acting coach, Chris Neil, at the suggestion of Rick McCallum. "Rick brought in Chris," Natalie Portman said in Rinzler's *Making of*, "who was, I would say, a rehearsal arbiter. [laughs] We did end up rehearsing a lot more, which is really, really helpful, and we had a lot of conversations. This time, Anakin and I are supposed to have been married for several years. We've supposedly been living together and made a baby together, so you have to fill in those blanks."[61]

When shooting ended in September, however, the film was far from complete—more than anyone could have predicted.

### The Final Draft

Lucas has always claimed that he shapes his films as much in post-production as in pre-production and this was truer than ever in *Revenge of the Sith*, particularly in the area of major story and character points. He told Laurent Bouzereau:

The way I work is that I cut the movie together, I look at it and figure out what I'm missing. At that point, it's more about how the movie flows together rather than how the script flows together. I'm acknowledging more and more that a script and a movie are two different things.[62]

Just as had happened on *Attack of the Clones*, it seems the brief writing period (less than six months) forced Lucas to commit the material to film before it had been properly distilled in his mind; the result was that the editorial process of storytelling continued well after the film had been shot, as the story had not had adequate time to properly gestate.

The most significant re-write in *Revenge of the Sith* would thus occur in the post-production phase, when Lucas would totally alter Anakin's turn to the dark side and re-write the nature of his fall, ultimately adding a major, new aspect to his character and to the overall saga—all of this after the film had already been shot. Even while Episode III was filming Lucas had not set Vader's storyline in stone—the story was as fluid as it ever was, re-written in major ways up until the very end.

Seeking to gauge the film, Lucas showed the rough cut to a select group from ILM, then to Steven Spielberg and Jeff Nathanson, the screenwriter of Spielberg's latest film, *The Terminal*, in June of 2004. Lucas reported to Rinzler on the crucial event:

> I felt I needed to show it to Steven to figure out what the reality was, because we'd earlier had a rough-cut screening for ILM to test the film, and some of the people had strong opinions about things that were contrary to the way I was going. Some people were having a hard time with the reason Anakin goes bad. Somebody asked whether somebody could kill Anakin's best friend, so that he gets really angry. They wanted a real betrayal, such as "you tried to kill me so now I'm going to kill you." They didn't understand the fact that Anakin is simply greedy. There is no revenge. The revenge of the Sith is Palpatine. It doesn't have much to do with Darth Vader; he's a pawn in the whole scheme.
>
>    But then there were larger issues. So I had to ask myself, *What was I trying to say and didn't I say? Did it just get missed or is it not there?* I had to look at it very hard. I had to ask myself, *Is this how the audience is going to react?* Fortunately, Steven confirmed that most of everything was working. So, I may lose a certain demographic—maybe, maybe not. But I had to make a decision, and I decided that I'm not going to alter the film to make it more commercial or marketable. I have to be true to my vision, which is thirty years old, but I have to be true to it.[63]

However, Lucas would soon change his mind from his first reaction, which was to leave the film as it was. In the process of editing the film down further, Lucas dropped whatever scenes he could that weren't directly related to Anakin. This was a continuation from Lucas' decision in trying to first write the script in 2002, when he had to reorganize much of the plot so that it stressed mainly Anakin and his transition— now he was stressing it even more. What this did was unexpectedly shift focus towards the character's obsession with saving Padme, which Lucas then began to re-structure the film around, because, as he says, it seemed "poetic." Lucas explained in *The Making of Revenge of the Sith*:

> The first script I wrote had stories for everybody... and I cut it down and we had a script. But when we cut it together, there were still problems. Finally, I said, "Okay, let's be even more hard-nosed here and take out every scene that doesn't have anything to do with Anakin." But that causes you to juxtapose certain scenes that you were never contemplating juxtaposing before. And these scenes take on different qualities than before, because the scenes were never meant to be next to each other.
>
> In one case, there was supposed to be a scene with Padme and Bail Organa between two Anakin scenes, because we were following her story along with his. And when most of those scenes were cut out, suddenly all sorts of weird things started to happen that weren't intended in the script—but in some cases it worked much better.
>
> What happens then is that some of the themes grab hold of each other and really strengthen themselves in ways that are fascinating. You pull things together and suddenly a theme is drawn out because it's in three consecutive scenes instead of just one. Suddenly one theme is infinitely stronger than it was before, so we'll strengthen that theme because it seems poetic.[64]

Taking this one step further, Lucas began actively re-writing the film to reflect this story revision, accomplished mainly through additional scenes filmed later in the year. Although the Padme issue was always one of the main issues of Anakin's fall, here it now became *the* issue—and would subsequently alter Vader's motivations in the sequels. He would now turn to the dark side out of a quest to save a loved one. Much like the creation of Father Vader, here Lucas recognized elements already embedded in his story that could be made more resonant.

First, an additional vision of Padme's death would be added. Viewers who pay close attention will notice that this second vision is an edit trick used in post-production to focus Anakin's transformation—Obi Wan's dialogue of "hold on Padme" in the second vision in the film is taken from unused segments from the end of the film (which appear in the shooting script), and the vision itself is edited into a daytime scene between Padme and Anakin, rather than the prior scene in which Anakin had a literal nightmare. In the original filmed version Anakin is staring off, sensing that Obi Wan has visited Padme, but when the dream is inserted, suddenly the scene takes on a "waking vision" quality, and the need to save Padme through dark side powers emphasised, reminding the audience of Anakin's fears and motivation.

Among new scenes added was one between Anakin and Yoda, which emphasised Anakin's nightmares and his fear of losing Padme, in turn strengthening his motive for accepting the dark side. In this scene, Yoda refers to Anakin's visions as "premonitions," plural—the single nightmare originally scripted was not only reprised with the edit trick in Padme's apartment, but now reinforced by implying they are regular occurrences. Another scene to take place directly before Anakin's first nightmare showed Anakin and Padme basking in their love for one another and talking about plans for the baby, further stressing their relationship and Anakin's subsequent fear of losing this possible future.

Most significant was that the entire sequence of Anakin's turn was re-shot as a response to the new Padme-centric view of Anakin's downfall.

The following section of the film, as originally written and filmed, played out much differently:

Palpatine reveals his true nature to Anakin, telling him that the Jedi are planning to overtake the Republic and that the Sith and the dark side represent the only viable solution. Anakin is conflicted but distrusts the Jedi—his mind is being influenced by the dark side already and he chooses to stay with Palpatine, essentially accepting the Sith in this scene. Mace and the Jedi then enter Palpatine's office—with Anakin present beside Palpatine. Mace tells Anakin to get behind him but Anakin remains where he is. When the Jedi ignite their lightsabers to arrest him, Palpatine uses the Force to retrieve Anakin's lightsaber and the fight begins.[65] Anakin watches as his two mentors fight each other, and Palpatine unleashes his Force-lightning. Mace and Palpatine struggle, and Palpatine's face is drained of his visage in the effort to sustain the lightning. Finally, as the two masters are locked in a stand-still, Anakin cuts Mace's hand off, and Palpatine sends him out the window. Incredulous of it all, Anakin collapses in disbelief that the Jedi were indeed attempting to take over the Republic, and Sidious knights him, telling him to kill the rest of the Jedi before they retaliate.

This, the most pivotal section of the film, the one in which Anakin turns to the dark side, was given a major re-write in post-production, as can be seen from the much simpler original version summarized above. His goal to save Padme by dark side powers was originally a result of his mind being corrupted by the dark side and seeking any excuse to justify his embrace of power, eventually losing sight of the goal and being attracted to ruling the galaxy as he reveals to Padme later on Mustafar. "I want more, but I know I shouldn't," he says at one point, admitting his conflicting need for power and control, reflecting the original version of his motivation. But now his entire character was changing with the re-structuring of his turn, re-written to revolve around saving Padme because of his visions. No longer was it simple power lust but three-dimensional emotional motivation, a quest for a specific power to save his loved one, a power which *incidentally* happened to be found in the dark side; his sacrificial act of killing Mace Windu would become a spontaneous emotional reaction to save Padme through protecting Palpatine, instead of the previous version where he made a conscious decision to stop the Jedi coup.

As mentioned before, the original conception of the dark side was that it was like a drug, and once you had tasted its power it would be so alluring that you could not resist the temptation to use it again, eventually being consumed by it. As Yoda says in *Empire Strikes Back*, "If once you start down the dark path, forever will it dominate your destiny, consume you it will, as it did Obi Wan's apprentice." This is why the Emperor was so confident that Luke would fall to the dark side in *Return of the Jedi*, and why Luke's striking down of Vader was so dangerous—if he killed Vader in cold blood using the dark side, he would inevitably be drawn back to it, and slowly but surely he would be consumed by it. The Emperor had been so corrupted in mind that the power had even corrupted his flesh; but just as this was revised, so too was the psychological aspect of this concept.

The set-up to Anakin's turn was his massacre of the Tusken Raiders in Episode II—it gave him his first taste, and during his confession of the deed to Padme he makes his first vow to amass an ultimate power. This deed would also foreshadow his cold-blooded killing of the Jedi, killing even the women and children because he believed they deserved it. The original outline for Episode III was then based on this set-up—Anakin is already primed for the dark side, and Palpatine can manipulate him, slowly drawing him to the dark side and swaying Anakin to Sith allegiance by convincing Anakin that the Jedi are plotting to take control of the Republic, with his betrayal of Mace (or slaying of Dooku in the original conception) as his final defining act.

This "corruption" angle is even what was filmed, and it is still reflected in parts of the script. "Twisted by the dark side young Skywalker has become," Yoda observes at one point. "The boy you knew, gone he is, consumed by Darth Vader." Later Anakin laments to Obi Wan, "I should have known the Jedi were plotting to take over... from my point of view the Jedi are evil," and proposes to Padme that they rule the galaxy together, that he is becoming more powerful than any Jedi, to which she horrifically realises "Obi Wan was right—you've changed." This is all residual from the first version of the film, and perhaps even the entire series. All of these "corruption" motivations are intellectual ones— in order to make the film more engaging after viewing the rough cut, Lucas shifted the story by re-writing Anakin's arc so that his turn was entirely an emotional one. He came up with a cleverly ironic plot whereby Anakin embraces the Sith and the dark side because they hold the key to a power that can save Padme from the premonitions of death that he is having. Hence, he was not genuinely interested in the Sith or the dark side—he regretfully embraces both things because they allowed him access to the ability to save the love of his life. With this, Vader's entire character in the following three films is fundamentally altered.

The first major scene to be re-written in the sequence of his turn was the scene in which Palpatine reveals he is a Sith to Anakin, adding portions at the beginning in which Palpatine sympathises that it upsets him to see the Jedi not appreciating Anakin's talents, thus bringing Anakin further from the Jedi and closer to Palpatine. The ending of it was also reshot, with Palpatine revealing that the dark side holds the key to saving Padme from death—which begins the conflict in Anakin over which side to choose. Palpatine only reveals himself in order to offer Anakin the power to save his wife from dying, the one elusive power that Anakin has been seeking. Anakin remains good however, though undergoing a conflicted internal struggle, stating that he will discover the truth.

Not only would Anakin refuse Palpatine's initial offer, but he would stay loyal to the Jedi and turn him in, telling Mace Windu about Palpatine's secret, who then takes a squad of Jedi to arrest the chancellor. Finally, as he waits in the Jedi Council chamber for Mace to arrest Palpatine, Anakin and Padme tearfully watching each other across the city as an ominous storm gathers on the skyline, Anakin realises that he needs Palpatine to save her—"if the Jedi destroy me, any hope of saving her will be lost," echoes Palpatine's telepathic thoughts—and he barges in on the confrontation just as it appears Mace has beaten the Dark Lord. Palpatine begs for Anakin to help him, and as Mace and Palpatine struggle with the lightning, both of them call to Anakin for help. "You must chose," Palpatine begs as his face is distorted—in this version, apparently by the lightning Mace is deflecting back at him (though it may be interpreted as merely a manipulation used by Palpatine). "I have the power to save the one you love," Palpatine continues as he grows even frailer. Finally, Mace appears victorious, as Palpatine begs that he is too weak to carry on. "He must live," Anakin finally speaks up, "I need him!" But Mace refuses, and as he is about to do Palpatine in, Anakin saves him, and Palpatine fries Mace and sends him to his death. Anakin, horrified, cries out "What have I done?" and collapses, saying "Just help me save Padme's life…I can't live without her." Sidious then knights him and Anakin regretfully pledges himself to the Sith.

It is a radically different and much more complex arc for Anakin to go through. His motivation for finally giving in to the Sith is also made more specific, as it becomes entirely about Padme and being able to obtain a power to save her. Even though he realises that he was forced to put a stop to the Jedi coup, Anakin still momentarily expresses regret, and then reinforces that he is doing it for his wife. As the "depth commentary" on the *Revenge of the Sith* DVD informs:

> In the original script, Anakin is in disbelief not over his actions, but that the Jedi would attempt to take over the Republic. In pick ups, the dialog was changed to keep the subject on Anakin saving his wife.[66]

On the 2005 DVD, Lucas talked about the first of these scenes, in which Palpatine reveals his identity:

> Originally, this was written where Anakin was actually seduced in this scene and he became the Sith pretty much in this scene. At the end, in this [reshot version], when faced with the reality, he stays with the Jedi. And he says "I'll get to the bottom of this, I'm gonna turn you in." But originally, it wasn't like that, it was he kind of got more sucked in to the idea of becoming a Sith Lord and saving his wife. And it just didn't play that well, in terms of how fast he converted. So it seemed to make a lot more sense to have him stay loyal to the Jedi as long as possible, which meant later on in the scene with the fight with Mace we redid that scene. And at first there wasn't the part where the Emperor gives up [and] he says "Oh, you got me, you got me." It was basically the scene without that where it just gets more intense and then finally Anakin breaks down and saves him.[67]

With Mace Windu now informed of the fact that Palpatine is a Sith Lord, a whole new level of dramatic tension was added to their confrontation. Lucas stated on the 2005 DVD:

> Once I had Anakin say that he was going to go tell the Jedi I actually had to shoot a scene of him going and telling the Jedi. There was a lot of good factors that happened when I changed that. It strengthens the scene when Mace comes in, and it meant that when Mace entered the room with Palpatine he knew that he was a Sith Lord. It works actually much better that when he comes through that door he knows that he's going to arrest him. He knows that he's the bad guy.[68]

Lucas explained how he focused the primary motive behind Anakin's turn:

The real issue here is trying to save Padme. And that that's what [Anakin's] conflict is, and that's why he's emotionally going back and forth...but it wasn't until I cut it all together and looked at it that I said "okay, now this is— I can see what the problem is and how to solve it." Then I added this thing where he goes back to the Jedi temple and comes back to the office rather than staying there. I needed something that was just about [Anakin and Padme] and at this point, as I laid the movie out, it was very clear that we needed to be reminded why Anakin was turning; although it was put in there very strongly [already], it wasn't strong enough.[69]

The reworking of the Mace-Palpatine fight was the most significant addition to Anakin's character in the film, and because Anakin had refused Palpatine's earlier offer, the scene had to be even more drawn out in order to get Anakin to choose the dark side. Lucas commented in *The Making of Revenge of the Sith*:

The fight itself was fine...The problem was that the final confrontation between Mace and Palpatine wasn't specific enough in terms of Anakin, so we're working to make his story, his conflict sharper—I have what I call two sharp "right turns" in the movie... and they are very hard to deal with. For the audience, it's a real jerk, because you're going along and then somebody yanks you in a different direction. Anakin turning to the dark side and killing Mace is a very hard right, because we're dealing with things that aren't so obvious. The audience knows Anakin is going to turn to the dark side, but the things that he's struggling with are so subtle that it may be hard for people to understand why his obsession to hold on to Padme is so strong.[70]

Though this massive re-write does, however, raise a major curiosity (perhaps the other "hard turn" in the script) in that Anakin inexplicably agrees to kill his extended family, the Jedi, even when he was loyal to them moments before when he turns Palpatine over to Mace Windu. Now Anakin was no longer corrupted by the dark side and no longer believed the Jedi were evil and attempting a devious plot to take over the Republic. The first half of the film was entirely revised—but the second half was not. After Anakin pledges himself to Palpatine in order to save Padme, the film re-links to the original version—which is why he becomes at this point a twisted monster. The change-over in the two versions can be seen almost immediately; the last of the pickup shots of the knighting scene show Anakin looking away regretfully as Palpatine knights him as Darth Vader—and then seconds later he robotically states that he will kill all the Jedi, his brow furrowed evilly. Now, however, he wasn't twisted at all—he was playing along because he had become obsessed with Padme and only joined Palpatine to save her. He never cared for the Sith or the dark side, and didn't believe that the Jedi were evil.

Some of these inconsistencies can be alleviated with a bridge between the two versions (Padme versus corruption)—although he began with the intention of only exploring the dark side to discover the power to save Padme, it has soon corrupted him and he has begun to lose sight of his initial goal. This appears to be how Lucas himself justified the radical changes, judging by how he discusses the character on the *Revenge of the Sith* DVD commentary—though the strongest one, Anakin's slaughter of the Jedi, is still jarringly out of place considering his motivation at that point.

It may be argued that, given the enormous manner in which the film was broken apart, re-written and then stitched back together—after principle photography—it could not be totally re-assembled because it was originally written under a divergent conception of the plot and character. Lucas had re-written most of the first half of the film, but May 2005 was drawing closer and there was not enough time to coherently re-align the entire plot of the film.

Nonetheless, we see here just how evanescent the storyline was—even the very sequence that is arguably the heart of the entire trilogy. "The only scene I hadn't thought through enough is the [turn scene]," Lucas told Samuel L. Jackson and Ian McDiarmid during the 2004 re-shoots.[71] Lucas explained his new conception of the turn to Christensen the next day: "It's basically *Faust* in the end," Lucas says. "Where you make a pact with the devil. And that usually leads to the same end: You cannot change the inevitable. If you try, you're basically going against the cosmos or however you want to define that."[72]

### The Tragedy of Darth Vader

Before *Revenge of the Sith* was released, however, another significant entry in *Star Wars'* history occurred—the release of the original trilogy on DVD, with more revisions done to tie the two trilogies together. Lucas had initially hoped to wait until 2007, when the series would be finished and the original film celebrates its thirtieth anniversary, to release the series in one collection, but with the format replacing VHS he decided to release the original trilogy (only in the Special Edition version) on the Christmas of Episode III's release. The films were completely re-color-timed at Lucas' request and digitally cleaned up to remove scratches and dirt, reflecting the slicker and more high-contrast look of the prequels, and Lucas wanted to add more elements to the films, refining the initial Special Editions with the prequels in mind. With this, the "Special Edition" no longer was the "Special Edition"—it simply became *the* edition. The 2000 VHS release had removed all titling of "Special Edition" from the packaging, and now the films were taken a step further through more prequel tie-ins—the saga had shifted once again, now reflecting the new six-film Anakin Skywalker storyline even more. Naboo is seen during the end celebration in *Return of the Jedi*, Sebastian Shaw's face altered to more closely match what is seen in Episode III, and Hayden Christensen himself inserted into the final scene of the saga. A pivotal moment was also altered in *Empire Strikes Back*. On July 29th, 2003, during photography of *Revenge of the Sith*, Lucas filmed new shots of Ian McDiarmid to replace the original Emperor.[73] New dialogue was written for the scene:

DARTH VADER
What is thy bidding, my master?

EMPEROR
There is a great disturbance in the force.

DARTH VADER
I have felt it.

EMPEROR
We have a new enemy. The young Rebel who destroyed the Death Star. I have no doubt that this boy is the offspring of Anakin Skywalker.

DARTH VADER
How is that possible?

EMPEROR
Search your feelings, Lord Vader. You will know it to be true. He could destroy us.

DARTH VADER
He's just a boy. Obi Wan can no longer help him.

EMPEROR
The Force is strong with him. The son of Skywalker must not become a Jedi.

DARTH VADER
If he could be turned, he would be a powerful ally.

EMPEROR
Yes...yes...Can it be done?

DARTH VADER
He will join us or die, Master.

This addition was thought to dispel the previous notion that Vader learns of Luke's identity somewhere between Episodes IV and V, providing a more satisfying onscreen revelation. Of course, many reject this theory as it is incompatible with the film itself—Vader is obsessively searching for Luke before the film even begins, and says of the discovery of the Hoth base "I'm sure Skywalker is with them," implying that he has known all along that Luke is his son, or at least some kind of possible relative. Despite the fact that it seemed Lucas was trying to clarify the character arc with the revised scene, it is still obscure as to just what it is that he is clarifying.

The DVD trilogy instantly became one of the highest-selling items in the format's history, but was controversial for its denial of the original versions of the films. Lucas embarked on a sort of crusade to try to erase the originals from existence in order for the newer "Tragedy of Darth Vader" storyline to become the dominant *Star Wars* meme. "The other [version], it's on VHS, if anybody wants it,"[74] Lucas sardonically remarked, quite disturbing given the original film's pivotal place as a classic of cinema. In this act we see the same function as the "revisionist" history regarding the story's origins: it presents to the audience only the version of the story which Lucas wants presented, an especially paramount issue since there are multiple—and often contradictory—versions of the story itself in existence. "The Special Edition, that's the one I wanted out there," he said simply[75]—it was the only version designed to be fully compatible with the story of the newly forged "Saga."

Initially, Lucas had sought to design a series of prequels that filled-in the backstory of the original trilogy, but this slowly transformed to creating the first half of a new, six-part Anakin-centric series—now Lucas was pushing this transformation even more. Not content with simply molding the prequels to fit the originals, he was now molding those films to fit the prequels, jumping back and forth between the two sets and hammering out the dividing line between prequels and originals; out of this was forged a new series unto itself. With the term "Special Edition" obliterated and absorbed into the new story, what was initially referred to as a fun "experiment in learning new technology"[76] and "a nice little twentieth anniversary for the fans"[77] was transformed into a consummation of the post-prequel story, and now the designation of "prequels" had been obliterated, instead existing as the first half of a six-part story.

All of this would be the second major revision to the original trilogy—and perhaps a third one could be seen in the subsequent viewings post-Episode III. Now, Vader's menacing entry onboard the Blockade Runner in Episode IV was not that of a threatening villain, but the sad reveal of Anakin's long-term imprisonment. The appearance of Luke, Owen, Beru, the homestead and Obi Wan suddenly took on a new context, and even minor things like Luke's abandonment of his training to save his friends in *Empire Strikes Back* became much more ominous after seeing the repercussions of Anakin's fear of loss. Characters were revealed to have met each other earlier in time, and new personalities and histories brought a very different meaning to the later films. Lucas explained to Rinzler:

> If you see them in order it completely twists things about. A lot of the tricks of IV, V and VI no longer exist. The real struggle of the twins to save their father becomes apparent, whereas it didn't exist at all the first time [audiences saw Episodes IV, V and VI]. Now Darth Vader is a tragic character who's lost everything. He's basically a bitter old man in a suit. "I am your father" was a real shock. Now it's a real reward. Finally, the son knows what we already know.
>
> It's a very different suspense structure. Part of the fun for me was completely flipping upside down the dramatic track of the original movies. If you watch them the way it was released, IV, V, VI, I, II, III—you get one kind of movie. If you watch I through VI you get a completely different movie. One or two generations have seen it one way, and the next generations will see it in a completely different way.
>
> It's an extremely modern, almost interactive moviemaking. You take blocks and move them around, and you come out with different emotional states.[78]

The *Star Wars* series had irrevocably changed. No longer was it an adventurous trilogy about a Rebellion against an Empire, it was now a tragic saga of failure and redemption, no longer was the original film a simple swashbuckler about a dweeby farm boy saving the galaxy, but the darker tale of the Empire consolidating its control over the galaxy, the fourth episode in *The Tragedy of Darth Vader* wherein Obi Wan has been waiting for Luke to finally come of age so that he can be trained as a Jedi to confront and ultimately redeem his father. Most amazingly, the actual content of the film remained mostly as it was—the *plot* was the same, but the *story* had been altered by the changing of its context.

After the Special Editions were released—and especially after the original, unaltered versions had been discontinued—the complaint from many was that Lucas was changing the films. Not only would this "tinkering" continue, but it had been an ongoing process since May 25th, 1977. "I never arrived at a degree of satisfaction where I thought the screenplay was perfect," Lucas once said. "If I hadn't been forced to shoot the film, I would doubtless still be rewriting it now, as we speak."[79] The truth is that he very much was. In 1978 Mark Hamill remembered in an article for *Gossip Magazine*:

> The very night [*Star Wars*] opened, my phone rings at like 10 o'clock. This voice says, "Hiya, kid! You famous yet?" "Who's this?" "It's George. You famous yet? Think you can come in and loop a couple lines?" I say, "George, it's opening night! All over town! Wake up, big guy!" He says, "You don't understand. We're doing the monaural mix tonight. We're gonna clean up some of the dialogue. The monaural mix is gonna be even better than in stereo!" I mean, he is gonna fix up *Star Wars* after it's already opened! [laughs][80]

Years later, "Episode IV A New Hope" would be added to the opening crawl, further bringing the films towards a more serious "epic," and the expansion and elaboration offered by the Special Edition only further imbued this notion. In 1983's *Skywalking*, Lucas expresses concern over two Imperial officers who are shot on-camera,[81] which would eventually be corrected in 1997, and the sound was completely re-mixed at least five times since May 25th 1977.

Audiences fell in love with *Star Wars* in 1977, the self-contained adventure tale of a farmboy who becomes an intergalactic hero and topples an empire, and it was this film that garnered ten Academy Award nominations, including Best Picture, Best Screenplay, Best Director and Best Supporting Actor. It was this film that changed the face of Hollywood as much as *Godfather* and *Citizen Kane* combined, that became the most popular and profitable film in history, that defined the lives of hundreds of millions of fans over the course of at least two generations, and that ranks as an absolute cinema classic comparable with *Gone With the Wind* or *The Searchers*. But since it was unveiled in May of 1977 it has not been the same film. It has been one which has been constantly re-shaped and re-written. *Empire Strikes Back* irreversibly altered the story in countless significant ways, which were then embellished in *Return of the Jedi* as the series took its final shape in tracing Luke's growth as a Jedi while also creating a subplot concerning the redemption of his father. With each sequel, Lucas reached back to that 1977 film and altered the story by transforming one's perception of it. The prequels were natural extensions of this and further transformed the once-simple tale. As Episode III was finally completed, the new storyline became clear—a character-study of Anakin Skywalker, the tale of his fall and redemption, a story that was completely opposed to the intentions of the original film.

Lucas has long asserted that he would like to return to experimental filmmaking, without any product to show for it in the thirty-five years he has been making such statements. But his most on-going experiment is one which has been so subtle that the public did not even realise it in the three decades in which it had been occurring. *Star Wars* is Lucas' greatest experiment, an experiment in altering audience perception, not through the changing of content but by the changing of context. Lucas has created an entirely different and alternate film that belongs to an entirely different and alternate series, merely by adding material before and after which alters the meaning by changing audience perception.

### *A Last Hurrah*

As Episode III neared its release date, *Star Wars* mania began to slowly but surely build—it was, after all, the very last *Star Wars* film ever, as Lucas was quick to point out, dispelling the last hope of seeing the Sequel Trilogy. November 2004 kicked off the teaser trailer, which provided the first glimpse of a full-suited Darth Vader. As May 19th grew closer, *Star Wars* began to be seen more and more in places—in Burger King promotions, on magazine covers and television reports. This was the film that everyone was looking forward to—the return of Darth Vader and the end of the galaxy. A film that promised to be darker and more mature, simply by the nature of the story. Lucas spoke with *Wired*:

> Lucas: None of the films I've done was designed for a mass audience, except for *Indiana Jones*. Nobody in their right mind thought *American Graffiti* or *Star Wars* would work.
>
> Wired: But the second trilogy certainly had a built-in audience.
>
> Lucas: Yeah, everyone says the second trilogy was a slam dunk. But there was a lot of controversy around here about the fact that I wasn't doing the obvious —I wasn't doing the commercial version of what people expected. People expected *Episode III*, which is where Anakin turns into Darth Vader, to be *Episode I*. And then they expected *Episodes II* and *III* to be Darth Vader going

around cutting people's heads off and terrorizing the universe. But how did he get to be Darth Vader? You have to explore him in relationships, and you have to see where he started. He was a sweet kid, helpful, just like most people imagine themselves to be. Most people said, "This guy must have been a horrible little brat—a demon child." But the point is, he wasn't born that way—he became that way and thought he was doing the right thing. He eventually realizes he's going down the dark path, but he thinks it's justifiable. The idea is to see how a democracy becomes a dictatorship, and how a good person goes bad—and still, in the end, thinks he's doing the right thing.[82]

The movie would also be the most unsettling of all the films, with much dismemberment and evil acts abound, including Anakin's gruesome transformation. Although there were some upsetting images in the film, the story itself was dark and tragic, and perhaps because of that alone Lucas allowed the film to be branded with the PG-13 rating—a major step for the franchise, which had always been PG material. "My feeling is it'll probably be a PG-13, so it'll be the first *Star Wars* that's a PG-13," Lucas said to *60 Minutes* in March 2005. "[But] I would take a nine- or a ten-year-old to it, or an eleven. But I don't think I'd take a five- or a six-year-old to this, its way too strong. I could pull it back a little bit, but I don't really want to."[83]

Darth Vader's iconic image was everywhere (perhaps a bit misleading as he has only two brief scenes in the film) and after many were disappointed by the previous two films, there were high hopes for the long-awaited *Revenge of the Sith*.

Lucas seemed much more confident with the film than he had been with the others, and the growing buzz surrounding the film was good. *Wired* reported:

Those who have seen advance screenings of *Revenge of the Sith* say that the new film–which focuses on the transformation of the petulant and ambitious Anakin Skywalker into the malignant Darth Vader–is more emotionally engaging than the last two prequels, *The Phantom Menace* and *Attack of the Clones*. Lucas' friends observe that he seems happier with this film, which he's been showing off proudly for months in rough-cut form at the ranch. The invitation-only audiences have included many illustrious peers from his film school days, including the directors Steven Spielberg and Matthew Robbins, writer-producer Hal Barwood, and Walter Murch, winner of two Academy Awards in 1997 for film editing and sound on *The English Patient*.[84]

The film premiered by opening the prestigious Cannes Film Festival—not the most receptive group of critics for a *Star Wars* prequel. But amazingly, the film was well received. Critics were especially appreciative of the political subtext. After Michael Moore's *Fahrenheit 9/11* lit up controversy after debuting at the festival only a year earlier, the liberal Lucas caused his own spark of debate as many critics applauded the film's political statement, believing it to be a diatribe against President Bush and the much maligned contemporary political issues of the United States. Although the story was written to reflect the corruption of the '70s, with Vietnam and Watergate being the primary influences, Anakin's line "If you're not with me then you're my enemy," is a near-perfect citation of Bush's infamous speech following the September 11th attacks, and the imagery of the burning Jedi temple indicates a strong influence on the story from the post-9/11 political climate, manifest in the themes of restricting freedoms in the name of homeland security and justifying war. *The Associated Press* reported:

> Lucas said he patterned his story after historical transformations from freedom to fascism, never figuring when he started his prequel trilogy in the late 1990s that current events might parallel his space fantasy.
> "As you go through history, I didn't think it was going to get quite this close. So it's just one of those recurring things," Lucas said at a Cannes news conference. "I hope this doesn't come true in our country."
> "Maybe the film will waken people to the situation... When I wrote it, Iraq didn't exist," Lucas said, laughing. "We were just funding Saddam Hussein and giving him weapons of mass destruction. We didn't think of him as an enemy at that time. We were going after Iran and using him as our surrogate, just as we were doing in Vietnam...The parallels between what we did in Vietnam and what we're doing in Iraq now are unbelievable."[85]

The first review to be released was Todd McCarthy's in *Variety*, the industry trade-paper—and the news was good indeed:

> The Force returns with most of its original power regained in "Star Wars: Episode III - Revenge of the Sith." Concluding entry in George Lucas' second three-pack of space epics teems with action, drama and spectacle, and even supplies the odd surge of emotion, as young Anakin Skywalker goes over to the Dark Side and the stage is set for the generation of stories launched by the original "Star Wars" 28 years ago. Whatever one thought of the previous two installments, this dynamic picture irons out most of the problems, and emerges as the best in the overall series since "The Empire Strikes Back"... Entertaining from start to finish and even enthralling at times, "Sith" has some acting worth writing home about, specifically McDiarmid's dominant turn as the mastermind of the evil empire.[86]

Darth Vader adorned the cover of the May 9th edition of *Time*

Magazine, along with the headline "The Last Star Wars…Darker, Scarier, Better." Said the magazine:

> *Revenge of the Sith* shows Lucas storming back as a prime confecture of popular art. Again one feels the sure narrative footing of the first *Star Wars*, the sepulchral allure of *Empire*, the confident resolution of a dozen plotlines that made *Jedi* a satisfying capper to the original enterprise.[87]

Although the film once again had its share of detractors—for instance, the *New Yorker* and *Rolling Stone* did not give favourable reviews to the film—they were few and far between. The disappointment the previous two films had caused may have also aided the film's positive reception, as the atmosphere in the optimistic reactions seemed to be one of *relief*.

Michael Willmington in the *Chicago Tribune* gave it a perfect score and called it "a smashing success," while Michael Sragow in the *Baltimore Sun* called it "a pop masterpiece." Kirk Hunycut in the *Hollywood Reporter* wrote "the first two episodes of Lucas' second trilogy… caused more than a few fans of the original trilogy to wonder whether this prequel was worth it. The answer is a qualified yes. It did take a lot of weighty exposition, stiffly played scenes and less-than-magical creatures to get to 'Star Wars: Episode III—Revenge of the Sith.' But what a ride Lucas and Company have in store!" *The New York Times* even dared proclaim: "It's better than 'Star Wars.'"

The film was the highest-grossing movie of the year and earned nearly $400 million domestically, despite the fact that theatre attendance that year was at a record low.[88] The *Star Wars* saga ended on the highest of high notes, for once pleasing both critics and fans alike while taking in a handsome box office gross.

"I expected this to be one movie," Lucas said, reflecting on his life in 2005. "I expected to move on to other things. Especially in the storytelling sense, [*Star Wars*] was very stylised, very much in opposition to what my natural inclinations are. It was kind of a whim which turned into my life…I had mixed feelings about being George *Star Wars* Lucas. That was a hard thing, but I did finally accept the fact that there was probably nothing I was going to do with the rest of my life that was going to change that, that I might as well live with it. It's not the worst thing in the world."[89]

As Lucas disclosed on the Charlie Rose show, he also finally re-climbed to the position of wealth that had been swept away after his divorce:

> Lucas: That's what I've earned. That's what I've been struggling for all of

these years in the end, to be able to do what I want to do without a lot of corporate interference and craziness. And I felt strongly enough about it to where I dedicated myself to getting to a point where I could be independent enough to not have to go down the path of compromise for the sake of somebody who isn't really that interested in what you're doing anyways.

Charlie Rose: But are you saying you just got to that point?

Lucas: Pretty much. I've always had to invest everything in what I've been doing. So, like with all the *Star Wars* films, I took everything I made out of *Star Wars* and invested it in *Empire Strikes Back*. I took everything that I made in *Empire Strikes Back* and *Star Wars* and I put it into *Return of the Jedi*. When I finished all of that, unfortunately I got a divorce and that sort of set me back quite a ways. So then I had to kind of start over again. So then it took me six years to get back to point where I was financially even. And build my companies up. And then I started working again. And then I decided one of the reasons to go back to *Star Wars* was that it would hopefully make me financially secure enough to where I wouldn't have to go to a studio and beg for money. And so I took all the money that I had at that point and I invested it in *The Phantom Menace*, and then I did the other one [*Attack of the Clones*] and now I've got it all in this one [*Revenge of the Sith*].[90]

Everything had finally come full circle.

# Conclusion

WITH that, our story comes to an end. The saga was finally complete, and Anakin's tale finally told. It was one which was always changing, always moving and never stagnating, while simultaneously surviving more than thirty years of storage. So fluid was the writing of the *Star Wars* series that the tale finished was a completely different tale from the one began twenty-eight years earlier. For the first time, the story of *Star Wars* and Anakin Skywalker has been traced in its origins and charted—from his morph from the heroic Jedi Father to the evil Darth Vader, and from the evil Darth Vader to the redeemed Anakin Skywalker. Perhaps more than any example I can think of, it shows the true power of the creative process—spontaneous, organic; ideas combined, ideas done away with.

Creativity evolves. Things begin in one form, and are added to again and again, layer by layer, not unlike the way a sculptor builds up a clay model, as Lucas would sometimes compare. With each return to the world of *Star Wars*, Lucas pulled the story in a different direction and re-molded its essence. With this in mind, the continuing creation of the *Star Wars Saga* may be among the best examples of the storytelling process at work, of how a mythology is slowly grown.

It may be said that the creation of the *Star Wars Saga* was a process of discovery that was ongoing and fluid from its inception—beginning as a comic-book-like homage to action serials and science fiction pulp in its original rough drafts, Lucas finally found the completed film through a more fairy-tale-like adventure of a young farm boy. While *The Adventures of Luke Skywalker* was unveiled to the public, Lucas began discovering an even more interesting direction to take the story in through the merging of Darth Vader and Luke's father, building onto the original film a new context that was much more complex and serious in nature, intended as a generation-spanning epic of the galaxy's rise, fall and re-birth. Cut short after the third film, he ended up with a trilogy about the Rebels' defeat of an Empire, Luke's maturation into a Jedi knight, and the redemption of Darth Vader. When he finally returned to tell the backstory to this trilogy, he discovered the tragic and moving fall of Anakin Skywalker as a more captivating perspective to tell the story from, and began to rebuild the tale from the ground up. The series was changing once again, as Lucas began to recognize elements planted in his story that resonated even more powerfully to him, and thus the saga slowly was transformed into its final form which told the six-episode tale of Anakin Skywalker's rise, fall, and redemption, mirrored parallel to the galaxy itself as it undergoes upheaval, conflict and finally peace. While searching for the heart of his story Lucas continuously found a new one, pushing it further and further into the realm of emotional gravity and literary complexity, such that he had actually released three different storylines: stand-alone fairy tale *Star Wars*, the *Star Wars Trilogy*, and the six-episode *Star Wars Saga*.

Such story-searching is a normal part of the creative process, but Lucas was faced with the problem in that he had released each previous version of the story, in effect publishing the intermediate drafts, not realising that he would make drastic transformations in the future. With each previous version "published" in that it had been publically released in a completed form, he was thus bound by what he had written and filmed in the years prior, which facilitated the unique and backwards way in which new storylines were built over top of and within the existing ones.

With this of course came a parallel transformation in the way the story was presented through publicity, first advertised as the adventures of Luke and his friends but now presented as the saga of Anakin Skywalker. "In the [original] three films, it appeared the story is about Luke, but if you see all six films then you realise the story is about Darth Vader," Lucas said in 2004.[1]

There is also a lot of controversy, confusion and misinformation on the subject, which I hope I have finally cleared up. In the overwhelming hype that laid in the wake of *Star Wars*, the story was elevated to that of a modern myth, as it is commonly referred to even today, the greatest story ever told. And perhaps out of the inevitable insecurity this level of appraisal brought with it, the creator, George Lucas, covered up the true nature of his creation, preferring to tell that he had confidently set the tale in stone as far back as the early '70s, and presenting the material to reflect only the contemporary incarnation of the story. This is an unfortunate regret, as it represents a prime example of human creative ingenuity and demonstrates Lucas' innate instinct for terrific storytelling.

It also reveals a man whose material slipped beyond his own control as his cinematic fairy tale became a contemporary myth itself, and instead was compelled to satisfy public expectation that their revered story was in capable and knowing hands. But not even the creator himself knew just where the story would be headed, and any plans laid would prove to be only temporary, as personal and creative forces shaped the material in unexpected ways, for better or for worse.

The initial goal in setting out to write this work was to make known that Father Skywalker and Darth Vader were not the same character until well after the first *Star Wars* film was released, and to chart the origin and evolution of this fascinating character. I was not made aware of such a possibility until around 2002, when fellow fan Noah Henson brought up the fact that Darth Vader does not appear in any form in the earliest drafts of *Star Wars*, and therefore that the accepted notion that Anakin Skywalker was always the main part of the backstory must be inaccurate. This came as a result of the recent publication of *The Annotated Screenplays*, which provided synopses of Lucas' early drafts for the original trilogy, which I myself had not read at the time. This got me thinking, and as I read the actual early drafts of *Star Wars*, which have been available for years, I realised that this was true. Researching as many vintage George Lucas interviews as possible, it became obvious that Lucas clearly had in mind an entirely different series in 1977.

There is a clear evolution in the story—and backstory—of *Star Wars*, and intrinsically tied to it all, Darth Vader's story. It illuminates an utterly fascinating process of creation, and through it we can see the sheer ingenuity with which Lucas invented his saga, all the while keeping the public thinking he had it all figured out from the beginning.

The evolution of the *Star Wars* story is a subject without a dedicated volume (save for *The Annotated Screenplays*, which is limited in scope and lacks historical context or literary analysis), and when that history is referenced in other works it is almost always represented with inaccuracies from the changing history presented by Lucasfilm over the years. The history of the *Star Wars* story is fractured and elusive and I hope this book has mended those pieces into a cohesive whole. It is a preservation of not only a fantastic work of art but also a significant chapter in pop culture and in film history. I hope it has been as fascinating, illuminating and entertaining a discovery as it was for me.

# Appendix A: The Great Mystery of the Journal of the Whills

THE so-called "Journal of the Whills" is perhaps the most curious and mysterious item in the history of *Star Wars*, a thing so shrouded in legend and mystery that it has become a sort of Holy Grail, an elusive and mythic object that is said to exist but has never quite been substantiated by evidence.

What is the Journal of the Whills? What it is differs slightly from account to account, but the more consistent descriptions state that it is essentially a large chronicle that George Lucas compiled before he wrote any of the *Star Wars* scripts and which contains all of the background information on the galaxy, including the detailed pages on the prequel trilogy, that was later incorporated into the six films. Additional descriptions of it state that it was a chronicle of the galaxy that was so large that the stories which make up the *Star Wars* saga occupied only a small part of this book, which was written as if by gods, historians of the universe called "Whills."

This mysterious Journal of the Whills may seem a bit of an anomaly—one can clearly see Lucas began with *Flash Gordon*, adapted *Hidden Fortress* for his 1973 treatment and then developed the rough draft screenplay, which progressed until he arrived at the final draft in 1976, since re-titled as *A New Hope*; you may also recall that there is a brief two-page story outline with the title *Journal of the Whills* made before the thirteen-page treatment in 1973 (which, as we will later learn, is unrelated to the "history of the galaxy" Journal discussed here). It is a fairly linear and logical creative progression. So how does this Journal of the Whills fit in, and what is the history of our information of its existence?

Knowledge of its existence comes from Lucas, naturally, but more importantly, the early scripts of *Star Wars*. The first recorded instance of it comes from the second draft screenplay from 1975, which opens with a Bible-like passage:

> ... And in the time of greatest
> despair there shall come a savior,
> and he shall be known as: THE SON
> OF THE SUNS.
> Journal of the Whills, 3:127

This draft, however, was not available to the public, and so the fan introduction came in the form of the *Star Wars* novelisation from 1976. The passage in question was quoted earlier in this book, and describes in detail the history of the Republic's downfall. The two-page history in the novel was marked by an end notation which said "—From the Journal of the Whills." The novelisation was released in December of 1976 to much success, and for most fans this was their basis for knowledge of a "Journal of the Whills," which was apparently some kind of chronicle which contained the history of the Star Wars galaxy.

The final draft screenplay for *Star Wars*, which was released to the public through *The Art of Star Wars* book in 1979, was even titled "Star Wars...as taken from The Journal of the Whills." So now the rabbit hole went deeper—not only did the Journal of the Whills contain the background information on the galaxy, it contained the stories for the films, the scripts themselves. This was reinforced when it was revealed that Lucas had written stories for twelve films, as *Bantha Tracks* stated (Issues 2, May 1978, and 8, May 1980) and as Lucas said in Alan Arnold's book, "I have treatments on all nine films...I also have voluminous notes, histories and other material I've developed for various purposes."[1]

Many people hence believed that, although Lucas' indication that the scripts themselves were part of the Journal may perhaps be an exaggeration, the background information indeed was, as the 1976 novelisation proves since it is so similar to the political plot of the prequel trilogy, and that the Journal of the Whills existed as a sort of "History of the Galaxy" in synopsis form. Lucas claims that he wrote this Journal of the Whills before he even began a script, as he had to develop the history first, predating the earliest 1973 synopses.

*The Annotated Screenplays* even explicitly details how Lucas first developed the background information of his sprawling galaxy and collected it in this epic tome, stating "in compiling this information and these background details, Lucas created a reference book he called 'The Journal of the Whills,' which eventually became the starting point for the Star Wars saga."[2] We even have quotes from this document, and an accounting of its content in Dale Pollock's biography as well as *The Annotated Screenplays* and many other sources, giving it further legitimacy. Marcus Hearn, in his *The Cinema of George Lucas*, even explains that this *Journal of the Whills* was a massive tale which was so large that Lucas had to break it into thirds and adapted the first section into the first draft of *Star Wars*.

This is the great mystery that is the Journal of the Whills, a subject shrouded in much secrecy and confusion, but finally, after thirty years of obscurity, some light can be shed on it.

### *Solving a Puzzle*

The ten-page handwritten synopsis (which became fourteen pages when it was typed up) is dated as May, 1973, and was believed to be the earliest *Star Wars* story available, but when one accounts for the Journal of the Whills, Lucas must have been at work on the story long before May 1973.

In fact, *The Annotated Screenplays*, a reliable and accurate source on the *Star Wars* writings produced from first-hand analysis of the original documents as taken from the Lucasfilm archives, even accounts for this, stating that in 1973 Lucas handwrote a forty-page document entitled *Journal of Whills*, which was soon followed by the rest of the written material. So here we have pinpointed its birthdate.

But let's step back just a little. As stated, Lucas' first fourteen-page treatment entitled "The Star Wars" was written in late April, 1973 and completed in early May. Dale Pollock's 1983 book *Skywalking* talks about this 1973 synopsis and offers a summary consistent with the fourteen-page 1973 synopsis available. *The Annotated Screenplays* too includes this treatment in its account of *Star Wars*' development and runs commentary on the scenes, again consistent with Pollock's summary as well as the actual document itself.

But if the Journal of the Whills contained the background information, then it would have been written much earlier than the May 1973 treatment, but so far everyone has gotten any possible timeline wrong.

John Seabrook's January 6th, 1997 article in *The New Yorker* states "Lucas' first attempt at writing the story lasts from February, 1972, to May, 1973, during which he produced the thirteen-page plot summary." Other sources, such as Peter Biskind's monumental *Easy Riders, Raging Bulls*, as well as Ted Edward's *The Unauthorized Star Wars Compendium*, among many other examples, also cite 1972 as the start date, and most of these sources also state that it was begun after Lucas had filmed *American Graffiti*. This is incorrect however, as *American Graffiti* started filming in the summer of 1972, making it impossible for him to have begun the synopsis in February of that year, as *The New Yorker* claims, if he began writing it after filming. Is it possible Lucas started writing this Journal of the Whills at the same time he was writing *American Graffiti* in 1972, and then picked it up after filming was done? This seems highly unlikely, even though Lucas has said that he had the idea for a space opera as far back as the days of *THX 1138*. All other interviews from the '70s, plus Pollock's book and virtually any other source, very clearly state that Lucas started writing *Star Wars* after *Graffiti* was completed, including statements from Lucas himself, meaning it was written in spring 1973, which of course is consistent with the May 1973 date.

This is all cleared up in the 1977 *Star Wars* Souvenir program where Lucas states that he began work on the script in January 1973. The January 1973 start date is backed up by an interview in *Rolling Stone* in 1980, where Lucas describes how after the January 28th, 1973 preview screening of *American Graffiti*, he began work on his space opera (this fact is also repeated elsewhere). Jonathan Rinzler as well would later confirm this in *The Making of Star Wars*. The February 1972 date stems from Pollock, who inaccurately reports that this is when Lucas first began writing, and all subsequent reports of a 1972 date are merely due to people citing Pollock.

However, Pollock's 1983 book presents a curious anomaly—he writes that the May 1973 treatment tells "the story of Mace Windu, a revered Jedi-Bendu of Opuchi who was related to Usby C. J. Thape, a padawaan learner to the famed Jedi." Pollock also writes that this is the opening sentence of the "thirteen-page" May 1973 treatment. The full text in question, from *Skywalking*:

> As usual, George had difficulty getting his ideas on paper; he decided to write a story treatment (an expanded synopsis), rather than a complete screenplay. By May 1973, he had completed a bewildering thirteen-page plot summary. Handwritten on blue-lined paper, it tells "the story of Mace Windu, a revered Jedi-bendu of Opuchi who was related to Usby C.J. Thape, padawaan learner

to the famed Jedi." With that as its opening sentence, it is not surprising that *Star Wars* elicited little enthusiasm.[3]

This is *not* what the fourteen-page May 1973 treatment opens with, nor are any of these characters or information contained within it in any place. "Mace Windu" never is mentioned in the treatment or *any* of the drafts, nor is "Usby C.J. Thape," and the Jedi-Bendu are absent from the treatment. So just how does one explain this cryptic passage? Consulting the introduction of 1997's *The Annotated Screenplays* leads to yet another reference to this mysterious synopsis:

> It all began in 1973 when Lucas sat down and wrote a forty-page outline entitled "Journal of the Whills" about "Mace Windy, a revered Jedi Bendu of Opuchi," as told by "C.J. Thorpe, Padawaan learner of the famed Jedi." Following the outline was a list of characters.[4]

Now we have even more complications—the 1973 outline is said to be forty pages, not thirteen, and is also said to tell a story about "Mace Windy" and "C.J. Thorpe," called Journal of the Whills (also note the spelling differences). So now we have some kind of hint of the content of this Journal of the Whills.

Although today the origin and content of this document is revealed, prior to 2007 this "Mace Windu" or "Mace Windy" document was a source of much speculation. Here is where our detective work began: in Pollock's book, the outline that is spoken of above, the "Mace Windu" story, is summarised—and is consistent with the fourteen-page May 1973 synopsis that is available, which is also consistent with the summary in *The Annotated Screenplays*. Pollock's summary of this "Mace Windu" outline is of the story of "General Luke Skywalker" who escorts the princess across enemy territory, picking up two bumbling bureaucrats, eventually teaming up with a band of rebel boys, crashing on a jungle planet and rescuing the princess from the space fortress. It literally *is* the May 25th 1973 fourteen page synopsis. What makes this all very confusing is that, even though Pollock states that the thirteen-page outline was about "*Mace Windu*" who was a "*Jedi Bendu*" and related to "*Usby C.J. Thape*" the corresponding summary contains absolutely no mention of these characters, nor are Mace Windu and Usby C.J. Thape ever mentioned by Pollock ever again.

As related earlier, the introduction of *The Annotated Screenplays* also mentions the treatment of "Mace Windy" that was called "The Journal of the Whills,"—but very strangely it does not elaborate on its story. All that is said is the same opening passage that Pollock quotes. Furthermore, this is the only treatment that Laurent Bouzereau, author of *The Annotated Screenplays*, mentions when listing the initial drafts in the introduction, and yet the summary Bouzereau provides of "the treatment" in the rest of the book is again consistent with the fourteen-page May 1973 treatment, about General Luke Skywalker, who protects the princess across enemy territory with the two bureaucrats. "Mace Windy" and "C.J. Thorpe" are absent from Bouzereau's summation, and Bouzereau never again refers to these characters or to a Journal of the Whills—but he goes on to state that in developing the background notes "Lucas created a reference book he called 'The Journal of the Whills,' which eventually became the starting point for the Star Wars saga."[5]

Yet even more complications arose when one consulted the list of sources used for the *Star Wars* annotations in Bouzereau's book. The list begins:

Partial handwritten outline entitled "Journal of the Whills" (no date)
Handwritten list of characters (no date)
Handwritten list of planets (no date)
The Star Wars – synopsis (no date)
The Star Wars, May 1973 – treatment typed from original notes

Taken together, this all seemed to point to a historical tome by name of Journal of the Whills actually existing, as the *Star Wars* novelisation's intro implied—Bouzereau failed to point out that this *Journal of the Whills* which was written before May 1973 about "Mace Windy" is actually separate from the "history of the galaxy" concept.

Most confusing was that Bouzereau also states that it was a narrative story about a "Mace Windy"—which indicated it may have been something else altogether. But what was this document about? The fact that its summation provided by Pollock and Bouzereau reveals it to be identical to the May 25th, 1973 fourteen pager was a confounding inconsistency. Was it just a more detailed version of the fourteen pager with different names used (similar to the way the rough and first draft are the same but with different names)? If so, why was it many times longer? Or is it something completely different? Was there an entirely alternate *Star Wars* story that was hidden all that time? If so, why didn't Bouzereau make mention of this, which would be one of the most monumental discoveries in the origins of *Star Wars*?

Or did Bouzereau not even see this forty page Journal of the Whills? You will notice that his description, his *only* reference to it in the entire book, is a word-for-word quote from the small blurb in Pollock's book.

Perhaps that draft has been lost forever and he was forced to use Pollock's quote? If so, Bouzereau should have mentioned this startling fact, and if it was the same as the May 1973 version one would think this would be made explicit, as differences and similarities between everything else, even mundane details, are made explicit.

Other sources are no more helpful. John Baxter's *Mythmaker* summarises this "Mace Windu" treatment—but describes the fourteen-page May synopsis, complete with General Skywalker as the main character. Furthermore, the only description of this "lost synopsis" is the quote by Pollock: "The story of Mace Windu, a revered Jedi Bendu of Opuchi..." The answer to Baxter's account is thus revealed: he copied it from Pollock. Indeed, Pollock's short, inaccurate blurb was the only mention of this synopsis in any shape or form, anywhere—which is why the infamous opening line "The story of Mace Windu..." is all that was ever quoted. Marcus Hearn in his 2005 *The Cinema of George Lucas* tells a similar error-ridden tale, evidently basing his version off a combination of Pollock's and Bouzereau's—his states that Lucas first wrote a massive *Journal of the Whills* document in 1972, telling the tale of "Mace Windy" and "C.P. Thorpe" but then changed it for the May 1973 synopsis because the story was so large and not covered by the $3 million budget and was thus cut into a third, telling the story of Annikin and Kane Starkiller which Lucas then adapted into a first draft. Hearn also, unsurprisingly, quotes the single solitary line that Pollock first provided and that Bouzereau mis-copied.

Nothing about this Journal of the Whills draft seems to add up. The only explanation that addresses how these errors occurred is that Bouzereau never even saw this Journal of the Whills, and not only did he not see it, it appears he was not even aware of its existence. The two brief mentions of the Journal of the Whills, first in the introduction and then in the list of sources, are completely inconsistent with the rest of *Annotated Screenplays*—the main body of the book operates in ignorance to this document's existence. These references, then, are probably insertions. Pollock's single quote on the matter was plundered once again and slapped in the introduction. Hence, a forty-page "Journal of the Whills" which tells the tale of "Mace Windy" found its way into *The Annotated Screenplays*.

This detective work was all a bit of a wild goose chase—the "history of the galaxy" tome was nothing more than a literary device invented by George Lucas for the early screenplays, and did not really exist as an actual document; the mentioning of this non-existing document in the screenplays and novel are simply examples of the sort of throw-away references to a larger universe beyond the scope of the film, which were given additional credence by Lucas and Lucasfilm's claims of supposedly having written more story material than was actually the case. Combined with Pollock's inaccurate 1972 writing start-date and the mysterious "Mace Windy" document, it led many to believe that it actually existed. This last point is particularly important—the "Mace Windy" document, on the other hand, *does* exist, and is a two-page story synopsis, though this was not known until very recently. Furthermore, the statement about "compiling" a Journal of the Whills out of Lucas' notes in *The Annotated Screenplays* added yet more confusion, and seemed to confirm that this "history of the galaxy" tome was real—but this wasn't referring to the actual in-universe document referenced in the scripts and novels; it was merely a tongue-in-cheek nickname Lucas gave to his own collection of notes. Hence, all of these elements taken together persuaded fans to believe that such an actual document as indicated by the scripts and novels was real.

The Journal of the Whills, in the form of a massive tome which contained all the history of the *Star Wars* galaxy does not, and never did, exist. *Star Wars Insider* columnist and Episode III set diarist Pablo Hidalgo confessed in issue 79 of the magazine: "The whole saga is said to be taken from the Journal of the Whills. But ultimately that strange attribution is just meant to suggest that the Star Wars saga has been around for eons and has been adapted and interpreted from earlier works. There is no 'real' Journal of the Whills—George Lucas added that to spice things up a bit."[6]

But if the Journal of the Whills, in the concept presented by Lucasfilm, is non-existent, then what is the "Macy Windy" or "Mace Windu" document? As we will see, it is indeed one with the title of *Journal of the Whills*, though it is merely a rather simply two-page story synopsis.

### The Final Puzzle Piece

One extremely important fact remained unexplained: what is the "Mace Windu" quote Pollock provides and where did it come from? The quote is obviously genuine, as it contains many Lucas-isms, such as "Mace Windy" and "padawaan" and is even written in the same confusing and poor prose that plagued Lucas' early drafts, and there is no logical reason why this quote would be fabricated. Judging by the fact that Pollock's corresponding summation of the treatment which bears this supposed opening sentence does not contain these characters but the ones from the May 1973 synopsis, perhaps Pollock may have mixed up this "Mace Windu" synopsis with the May synopsis—in juggling all the information in his exhaustive book, Pollock's descriptions of the early drafts, the first-ever public reveal of such content, are fraught with minor yet significant inaccuracies. This summary is actually a confused fusion of both 1973 synopses, with additional elements from the rough draft thrown in.

My first hypothesis, based on this confusion, was that this Mace Windu document might have been the treatment made for the 1974 rough draft, and that Mace Windu and C.J. Thape were merely different names for Kane Starkiller and Annikin Starkiller that appeared in this hypothetical 1974 treatment, similar to the way those sets of names were then revised to Akira and Justin for the first draft. With only a single sentence to go off of, this was the best guess that could be made. However, a startling discovery was made in 2007 which ties together all of these confounding inconsistencies relating to the *Journal of the Whills*.

J.W. Rinzler, in researching his book *The Making of Star Wars*, brought forth news that he had discovered a *Star Wars* story that pre-dated the May 1973 *Hidden Fortress*-based synopsis. It is called *The Journal of the Whills* and tells the story of Mace Windy, a Jedi-Bendu or Jedi-Templer. This was a very important discovery that added a fairly significant revision of early *Star Wars* history. Indeed, it seems that Lucas *did* try out a space-opera story of his own before giving up in frustration. According to Rinzler, this treatment is less a treatment and more like a brief summary—it is a mere two pages long, written by hand. This is more or less consistent with what is reported in *The Annotated Screenplays*, except there it is incorrectly stated to be forty pages.

The first time this information was reported was in issue 92 of *Star Wars Insider* in the spring of 2007. An all-too-brief description of the plot was given, stating that Mace Windy is a Jedi-Templer and takes an apprentice, C.J. Thorpe, but is later expelled from the order. The plot ends in a serial-like cliffhanger, with the two Jedi dispatched by "the chairman" on a secret mission.

This also explains how Lucas began in January but didn't end up with the fourteen page synopsis until May. This *Journal of the Whills* story was so brief and inconsequential that Lucas has never referred to its existence (with the rare exception being the interviews Charles Lippincot conducted for his aborted making-of book, which eventually became Rinzler's 2007 book).

It is also interesting to note the spelling: indeed, Rinzler informs us that it is "Windy" and not "Windu,"[*] but also that Pollock's statement of "The story of Mace Windu...as related to Usby C.J Thape" is actually the result

---

[*] On a QWERTY keyboard, "Y" and "U" are next to each other, perhaps indicating a typo on Pollock's part

of a mis-reading of Lucas' messy printing. The sentence is actually "The story of Mace Windy...as related to us by C.J. Thorpe." Finally, Rinzler's book *The Making of Star Wars* gives a fairly lengthy explanation of this document, which is written in first-person narrative prose and divided into two parts, the first being Thorpe remembrance of his apprenticeship and the second being Thorpe's tale of his greatest mission.[7]

The last answer to be given is how, if Bouzereau was completely unaware of such a document and never saw it, did it end up being referenced in *The Annotated Screenplays*? It may be that it was not Rinzler who discovered it. A plausible explanation is that this was discovered at the last minute in 1997, after Bouzereau had turned in his manuscript, as *The Annotated Screenplays* was about to go to press; perhaps it was edited into the introduction and list of sources without Bouzereau's knowledge but there was no room to speak of its plot or to chart its development in the body of the book since the book was already on a release date. In any case, Bouzereau's book is otherwise written in ignorance to it.

So, there are actually two *Journal of the Whills*—the first is Lucas' ill-fated two-page attempt at creating a space opera and the second is an in-universe concept of a galactic history-book which the films themselves are contained within. The first version has never been publicly explained until 2007, and was a concept abandoned in early 1973; the second concept, however, was not abandoned, and so most knowledge relates to this version, which we will now finally turn to.

### Deconstructing the Origin

Still to be explained is where Lucas got the idea from, how it evolved and where it went. While the first concept of the two-page plot summary was abandoned immediately, the second concept—that of a galactic history book which contains the stories for the films—would remain as a part of Lucas' universe for quite a while.

Let's go back again to the first reference to a Journal of the Whills—draft two, from 1975, which opens with a Bible-like passage purportedly taken from the Journal.

The Journal of the Whills of course did not exist. But what was Lucas trying to accomplish with this opening passage? A very similar thing to what he was trying to accomplish with its replacement, the "A long time ago" opener: the Journal of the Whills reference places *Star Wars* in a larger narrative context. Just as the "A long time ago" passage connotes that of a storybook or a fairy tale about to be told, the "Journal of the

Whills" quote connotes that of a larger narrative unfolding which we only learn a piece of, very similar to what Lucas would attempt to do with his episode listing at the head of the film. "Journal of the Whills came from the fact that you 'will' things to happen," Lucas said of the subtitle in *The Making of Star Wars*. "The introduction was meant to emphasize that whatever story followed came from a book."[8]

In this second draft, the Journal is some sort of Holy book that exists within the *Star Wars* universe—the passage quoted in the film's opening foreshadows Luke's emergence, as it is in fact he who is the Son of the Suns, fulfilling the prophecy as a sort of saviour.

The opening passage was removed and replaced with the storybook-like opener, but the Journal of the Whills reference remained in the final script's title, which was:

> The Adventures of Luke Starkiller
> as taken from the Journal of the Whills
> Saga One
> The Star Wars

Here the Journal shifted somewhat—while before, in the second draft, it was a sort of Holy book, now the script title indicated that the story of the movie itself originated from this document, giving us the final conception where it is an ancient book by galactic history-keepers which contains the *Star Wars* stories. The use of the "A long time ago" opener starting in this draft further fosters this subtext. Lucas had an opportunity to create a prologue for the 1976 novelisation which told the history of the galaxy and was quick to used this "larger chronicle" portrayal once again, presenting the two-page history summation as if it was an excerpt from this ancient Journal.

Later, Lucas would collect all of his notes, prequel information, and character and planet lists and such, and place them all in a binder, which he jokingly nicknamed "The Journal of the Whills." This is likely the red binder seen in the first Episode I web doc, containing all of his background notes and which he also wrote the original *Star Wars* in, as well *American Graffiti*. So, it was kind of a tongue-in-cheek throwback to that idea. Lucas' private Journal of the Whills was the term he gave to his collected reference material. Lucas said in *Annotated Screenplays*:

> I eventually dropped this idea [of using the Journal of the Whills in the films], and... the Whills became part of this massive amount of notes, quotes, background information that I used for the scripts.[9]

Laurent Bouzereau states "in compiling this information and these background details, Lucas created a reference book he called 'The Journal of the Whills,' which eventually became the starting point for the Star Wars saga."[10] Some initially mis-read this as somehow proving that the Journal of the Whills literally exited.

The confusion regarding its existence was so far-reaching that even Mark Hamill made references to the Journal in interviews, further imbedding the misconception that it existed in a secret vault somewhere in Lucas' compound, covered in dust. This misconception became apparent two decades later in 1999, during an interview Lucas had with Johnny Vaughan:

> V: The way I imagine it is that George has this great big leather book, covered in dust, it's the Chronicles of Space and you've written the whole thing already and it's complete in your own mind. Is that right?
>
> GL: No, that's wrong.[11]

Others thought perhaps it was a rare novel Lucas published long ago, a confusion based on the fact that the *Star Wars* novelisation was published a half-year before the film was released and contained a supposed excerpt from the Journal. An even stranger theory was one that proposed that Yoda was a "Whill," since he is an ancient being whose species and origin are still unknown.

*Starlog* certainly knew enough to be able to pinpoint that Lucas had at one time presented this "Chronicles of Space" that Johnny Vaughan spoke of as the Journal of the Whills and questioned him about it during a convention Q&A in 1987. Lucas did not reveal that the Journal was fictional, and instead re-enforced this "larger narrative" view:

> Starlog: What is the *Journal of the Whills*?
>
> Lucas: I'm not sure I can explain that. It's where the *Star Wars* saga came from; it was a larger work that I had been working on, of which *Star Wars* was just a piece.[12]

Thus, the misconception was further imbued in fans, building the legend. Even in 1997, Lucas still maintained this in *The Annotated Screenplays*. "The stories were actually taken from the 'Journal of the Whills,'" he added after he explained that he originally was trying to portray *Star Wars* as being recounted in a larger chronicle.[13]

But where did Lucas get this idea from? Did he just think it up on his own or did he get inspiration from outside sources like he did for many of the early *Star Wars* ideas? Tolkien's *Silmarillion* is a possible influence. *The Silmarillion* was Tolkien's grandest work, one he had been working on for nearly fifty years and was published posthumously by his son, Christopher Tolkien. It told the ancient history of Middle-Earth, and was created as if it were a fictitious historical recordbook, recorded by god-like beings who had watched history unfold. The book was not published until 1977, although it had been known for some time since Tolkien had been working on it at the time of his death—1973, just as Lucas was writing *Star Wars*.

If not *The Silmarillion* itself, Tolkien's death might have also led Lucas to the popular *Lord of the Rings* story, which would have also been given renewed attention in light of the author's passing. The Red Book of Westmarch from the *Rings* trilogy is essentially the same thing as the Journal of the Whills. In the *Rings* saga, Bilbo and Frodo Baggins, protagonists of the prequel *The Hobbit* and the *Lord of the Rings* saga respectively, compile their adventures in a journal which is titled "The Lord of the Rings," and is later completed by Frodo's heir and best friend Samwise Gamgee—this book is later dubbed "The Red Book of Westmarch" since Bilbo bound it in red leather. In effect, it was portrayed that the events and story of Tolkien's *Lord of the Rings* are actually taken from a massive book *within the story itself*—"The Lord of the Rings"; in this light, Lord of the Rings/Red Book of Westmarch can be seen as The Journal of the Whills, and Bilbo, Frodo and Samwise as the Whills, the keepers and recorders of the journal. Tolkien also presented his Middle-Earth universe as a long-lost ancestral mythology of western Europe—in the first edition of *Fellowship of the Ring* (the first book of the Lord of the Rings trilogy), Tolkien wrote a foreword claiming that the Red Book of Westmarch had found its way into his hands, which he then translated to English from its original Westron language. The presentation of it as if from some long-lost grander narrative was a wonderful storytelling device.

So here—perhaps—we have traced the Earthly origins of Lucas' inspiration for his concept of the Journal.

So, now that we have established the original conception of the Journal, what exactly happened to the idea? Where did it go, and why? Fans familiar with the novel and comic adaptations as well as the script of *Revenge of the Sith* will be quick to point out that the Whills are referenced in a section that was deleted from the actual film. But let's trace how we got to that point.

Lucas' concept in the '70s was to present the film as if it was part of a huge tale, being told by beings wiser and older than anyone in the film. Like many of Lucas' namings, their name itself implies their function—"Whills," connotative of "will," as in destiny, fate, similar to the Greek gods who recount mortal stories themselves in many tales. Lucas mentions this in *The Annotated Screenplays*:

> Originally, I was trying to have the story be told by somebody else; there was somebody watching this whole story and recording it, somebody probably wiser than the mortal players in the actual events.[14]

This then is reflected in the titling of the movie, which was denoted as "From the Journal of the Whills." Mark Hamill obviously was familiar with this concept, as he reported in 1983:

> In fact my suggestion for the title was The Other Shoe Drops instead of *Revenge of the Jedi* which is a misnomer. It's really not right for Jedi to have revenge unless what we see in this part of the "Journal of the Whills" was recorded by non-Jedi.[15]

However, though the final draft of *Star Wars* bore the Journal of the Whills subtitle, it was not reprised for any of the sequels, nor was it widely publicised after the film became popular. But, the Journal of the Whills was not exactly dropped, but rather transformed into the more mystical view of the Force itself. The Journal was still used in the script and novel for *Star Wars*, however, so the concept had been diminished but not eliminated—*Empire Strikes Back* was to be silent of any mentions of the Journal or the Whills, and it is here that the view of the Force began to significantly shift.

Lucas explains of his Journal of the Whills concept: "I eventually dropped this idea, and the concepts behind the Whills turned into the Force."[16]

In the second draft of *Star Wars*, the Force is less mystical—it can help you focus and provide you with additional inner strength and a few nifty superpowers. But it had less to do with "god," less to do with the larger sentient-like outlook of the Force that we come to be familiar with in the sequels and prequels. The aspect to do with fate and destiny was provided by the Whills and their Journal—such as in the second draft, which opens with a prophecy from the book that a saviour will one day rise. But this was diminished as Lucas began the third draft and totally eliminated for *Empire Strikes Back*. The Whills would eventually become an aspect of the Force itself, as Lucas explains—the Will of the Force. This was all vague in the original trilogy but Lucas made it defined in the prequels. He explained in 1999's *The Making of Episode I*:

> The Force breaks into two sides: the living Force and a greater, cosmic Force. The living Force makes you sensitive to other living things, makes you intuitive, and allows you to read other people's minds, et cetera. But the greater Force has to do with destiny. In working with the Force, you can find your destiny and you can choose to either follow it, or not.[17]

The greater, cosmic Force is what the Whills became—the Will of the Force. This was all leading to a reinstatement of the Whills, in a slightly different form, accounting for this view.

The whole explanation behind why the Jedi of the original trilogy disappear when they die was said to be a major part of the prequels and that it would be explained, though it is only granted a brief mention at the very end of *Revenge of the Sith*, where Yoda explains that Qui Gon has somehow returned from the Netherworld and will teach Obi Wan to commune with him. But this was only a small portion of the original scene, which was cut for pacing reasons. It was included in the novelisation and comic. Below is a transcription of the scene based on the script:

222 INT. POLIS MASSA-OBSERVATION DOME-NIGHT

On the isolated asteroid of Polis Massa, YODA meditates.

YODA: Failed to stop the Sith Lord, I have. Still much to learn, there is ...

QUI-GON: (V.O.) Patience. You will have time. I did not. When I became one with the Force I made a great discovery. With my training, you will be able to merge with the Force at will. Your physical self will fade away, but you will still retain your consciousness. You will become more powerful than any Sith.

YODA: Eternal consciousness.

QUI-GON: (V.O.) The ability to defy oblivion can be achieved, but only for oneself. It was accomplished by a Shaman of the Whills. It is a state acquired through compassion, not greed.

YODA: ... to become one with the Force, and influence still have ... A power greater than all, it is.

QUI-GON: (V.O.) You will learn to let go of everything. No attachment, no thought of self. No physical self.

YODA: A great Jedi Master, you have become, Qui-Gon Jinn. Your apprentice I gratefully become.

YODA thinks about this for a minute, then BAIL ORGANA enters the room and breaks his meditation.

BAIL ORGANA: Excuse me, Master Yoda. Obi-Wan Kenobi has made contact.

Shortly after, this is explained in more detail to Obi Wan:

YODA: (continuing) Master Kenobi, wait a moment. In your solitude on Tatooine, training I have for you.

OBI-WAN: Training??

YODA: An old friend has learned the path to immortality.

OBI-WAN: Who?

YODA: One who has returned from the netherworld of the Force to train me . . . your old Master, Qui-Gon Jinn.

OBI-WAN: Qui-Gon? But, how could he accomplish this?

YODA: The secret of the Ancient Order of the Whills, he studied. How to commune with him. I will teach you.

OBI-WAN: I will be able to talk with him?

YODA: How to join the Force, he will train you. Your consciousness you will retain, when one with the Force. Even your physical self, perhaps.

So, Lucas brought back the Whills in a new form, melding the two concepts he had developed. They were related to the Force and eternity, but still retained some semblance of physicality as ancient beings who were wiser than the mortals participating in the story. The concept of the Whills is even vaguer in this version—were the Whills a race of beings, a race of gods, or some kind of collective? Who or what is a Shaman of the Whills, and how did the Whills, whatever they are, learn of immortality in the first place?

The majority of these references were deleted from the film to the extent that it is debatable if this version of the Whills should even be considered a canonical part of the *Star Wars* story.

Strangely, Lucas also returned to his first conception, remarking, somewhat jokingly, to Rob Coleman on the set of *Revenge of the Sith* that R2-D2 is the one who recounts the *Star Wars* story to the keeper of the Journal of the Whills one hundred years after the events of *Return of the Jedi*.[18] Obviously this is merely an off-the-cuff remark that was meant to be private and tongue-in-cheek, but it also shows that Lucas still was partial to his original conception of a *literal* Journal of the Whills.

(As a footnote, the messianic "Son of the Suns" referred to in the Journal of the Whills verse in the opening of the second draft of *Star Wars* has long been thought to have made it into the films. It has been believed that in the end celebrations of *Phantom Menace* and the *Return of the Jedi* Special Edition there can be heard the shouting of "The Son of Suns! The Son of Suns!" *Starwars.com* addressed this urban legend in its February 28th, 2007 Podcast Special. The original sound recording was dug up from the Skywalker Sound archives, revealing that it is merely jibberish Huttese and various crowd yellings).

## Appendix B: Of Heroines, Wookies and Little People
## The Legends of the Lost Draft Variations of Star Wars

EVEN less known than the *Journal of the Whills* myth are some very curious comments that demonstrate that there may indeed be some *Star Wars* writings yet to be discovered. By now most have come across comments from someone involved in the films discussing abandoned concepts from early drafts of *Star Wars*—how Luke's father was a main character in one and how Han Solo was a green alien in another. An examination of the scripts themselves reveals that indeed, the original drafts of *Star Wars* were telling a very different story than the one we ended up with. But even more obscure are a few comments by those involved in the production that describe variations unaccounted for.

Mark Hamill told *Starlog* in October 1980:

> Way back in the early days...I saw some preproduction sketches and was amazed. My character was cowering behind the Princess. Originally, she was the lead character, trying to save her brother, who was on the Death Star. Then they reversed the roles.

However, neither the rough, first, second, third nor the fourth draft of *Star Wars* contain a plot such as this. The second draft comes very close, with the protagonist's brother, Deak, being the one imprisoned and in need of rescuing—but in this draft the protagonist is male, Luke Starkiller. The only time this concept shows up is in rare verbal statements by Lucas or Hamill.

As *The Making of Star Wars* reveals, however, this concept never even made it to script form, hence accounting for its absence everywhere else. Lucas explains how in March 1975 he struck upon the concept:

> The second draft didn't really have any girls in it at all. I was very disturbed about that. I didn't want to make a movie without any women in it. So I struggled with that, and at one point Luke was a girl. I just changed the main character from a guy to a girl.[1]

As Hamill says, he did not come across this variation in a draft of the screenplay—rather it was concept artwork. Lucas was toying around with the idea and asked Ralph McQuarrie to reverse the gender, to see how it would play, resulting in artwork based off the second draft in which Luke appears female; Lucas returned to his original male concept when he reinstated the princess to the story in draft three. An interesting what-if, regardless. Lucas himself also tells of a draft similar to this, in a 1979 interview with Alan Arnold, again substituting characters regarding who is rescuing who. However, in this version, one brother enlists another brother to rescue their *father*:

> Originally, the story was about an older brother coming to find his younger brother, who's living on a farm, so that together they can rescue their father, an old Jedi. The older brother is a battle-hardened warrior. This character evolved into Han, the other side of Luke and an older brother figure. Ben Kenobi developed from the father figure into a friend of the father.[2]

Here Lucas is confusing his own drafts—he is describing the second draft. Sort of. In the second draft, brothers Deak and Clieg are on their way to Utapau (Tatooine) to contact their younger brother Luke—their father has summoned them to bring him the Kiber crystal. Their ship is boarded en route however, and Vader kills Clieg and imprisons Deak. Luke must then rescue Deak and return the Kiber crystal back to his father, The Starkiller as he is known. However, the father was never imprisoned. In draft one, though, General Skywalker—who is the Kenobi character and becomes a father-figure after Annikin's real father is killed early on— is imprisoned along with the rest of the heroes; perhaps this is the basis for Lucas' confusion about a "father" being captured.

Far more interesting than gender-reversals, Hamill tells of an even weirder variation in *Starburst* issue 24 in 1980. In this one, *Star Wars* is a storybook being read by a mother Wookie to her baby Wookie. As bizarre as this is, it is not unbelievable—Lucas was clearly trying to present the film as if a fairy tale, with his "A long time ago" opener, and he had also attempted to present the film as if a chapter of a grand book entitled *Journal of the Whills*. Hamill explained this variation to *Starburst* magazine:

> But I never thought of *Star Wars* as science fiction. I thought of it as a fairy tale. One of my favourite earlier versions of the *Star Wars* screenplay had a clever device to off-set the technology of the whole thing so that audiences wouldn't think that it was going to be another *2001* when they see the cruiser going overhead. It started with a helicopter shot of an enchanted forest and they push the camera through the window of a tree and you see a mother Wookiee trying to breast feed this squealing baby Wookiee. He keeps gesturing towards the bookshelf and there's all this Wookiee dialogue going on. She goes and points to one particular book and the baby gets all excited [Mark did a creditable imitation of what an excited baby Wookiee might sound like at this point]. She takes the book off the shelf and we see it's titled *Star Wars*. She opens the book and *that's* when the ship comes overhead and the film we know starts...Then, at the end, after we get our medals, we bow and it cuts back to the baby Wookiee asleep—hopefully not like the audience. And the mother closes the book and puts the baby to bed. And that would have got across that it was *intended* to be a fairy story.[3]

This variation is harder to debunk than the gender-reversal one. Hamill clearly states that it was a screenplay draft, and even describes camera movement from the intended scene. The scene even bears a striking resemblance to the *Star Wars Holiday Special*, a television special from 1978 which featured a family of Wookies who live in a tree-house, including a mother and a baby. Interestingly, that story itself was designed by Lucas.[4]

But once more, this draft variation is not accounted for anywhere, not in the drafts that are available, not in the authoritative and officially-licensed *Annotated Screenplays*, and not in the meticulously documented *Making of Star Wars*. The only recorded instance that this version is mentioned, as far as I am aware, is this one interview with Mark Hamill.

Again, I suspect that this was not an actual draft. Although Hamill refers to it as a screenplay, he does not state that he himself read it. Rather, it may be more likely that Lucas himself verbally described the scene to Hamill as one of the ideas he had been toying with but never committed to paper, just like the gender-reversal variation. Hamill naturally assumed that it was an actual early screenplay variation. Lucas' scripts never contained camera movement description, further indicating that Hamill's tale stems from Lucas verbally describing how the scene would have played. When

CBS approached Lucas a short time later about doing a television special, Lucas reused this idea as its basis, hence giving us the Wookie-oriented *Star Wars Holiday Special.*

Even more intriguing are revelations Hamill makes in *SF Movieland* magazine in 1978:

> George wanted to make *Star Wars* before *American Graffiti. Star Wars*, he told me, generated from the sequel to *THX-1138*. The part I play is Robert Duvall. But it evolved in a different way. At one time Luke Skywalker was a girl and the princess was her brother that she was rescuing. Gary Kurtz told me that for a couple of days George wanted Luke to be played by a midget and my aunt and uncle would be midgets so that when he goes to another world they're all giants. At one time he wanted to use all Japanese actors. It goes through a lot of changes.[5]

Lucas confirmed the little-people concept in 2004:

> There was a point where Luke Skywalker was going to be a midget. And all of the people on the farm and everything, the aunt and the uncle and that whole group were all going to be little people.[6]

J.W. Rinzler uncovers that this was brought up during the casting sessions in December 1975. "When I was in New York, I had done some screen tests for little people," Lucas said. "I think that idea was a little influenced by *Lord of the Rings*."[7]

It is easy to see that the "Little People" plot morphed into 1988's *Willow*, which is credited as "story by George Lucas." In *Willow*, the title character is a farmer in a small town of dwarves, who eventually must leave his home and embark on a quest to combat an evil sorceress, her henchman General Kael, and her dark forces; he reluctantly enlists the help of two bumbling "brownies" (even smaller people) as well as a washed-up warrior to help him make the journey to return a prophetic baby to her people, which the enemy is also vying for. It is not unlike a fusion of *Star Wars* with *Lord of the Rings*. Lucas revealed in 1987 that he had been working on the story of *Willow* for a decade—placing its birth precisely around the time he would have been contemplating the Little People version of *Star Wars*. Lucas told *Rolling Stone* in 1987:

> Ron Howard is directing *Willow*, an adventure-fantasy that takes place a long time ago in a mythical land...It's something I've been working on for about ten years; I've [finally] managed to get all the pieces put together.[8]

Hamill's earlier reference to Japan is also a very early idea of Lucas'—he initially wanted to film *THX 1138* in Japan with Japanese actors, but rejected it because of costs.[9] He briefly flirted with this idea for *Star Wars* as well, hoping to cast Toshiro Mifune as Obi Wan Kenobi (Kenobi's character is based off Mifune himself, General Mukabe of *The Hidden Fortress*), although here Hamill states that *all* the cast was to be Japanese. Rinzler backs this up in his book, stating "Lucas also considered doing the whole film in Japanese with subtitles,"[10] explaining that it would better communicate the exotic disorientation that Lucas was after and that he himself had first experienced when watching Kurosawa's films. Later this was scaled back to simply casting Kenobi as Japanese, which also would have meant that Princess Leia would be as well; had this been the case, Lucas had seriously inquired into casting a black actor for Han Solo (being particularly interested in Glynn Turman[11]), which would have led to an enormously different and ethnically diverse core cast. "There was talk at one point about having the princess and Ben Kenobi in Japanese," casting director Dianne Crittenden remembered in *Making of Star Wars*, "which led George into thinking Han Solo might be black."[12] Lucas confirmed this in the same book:

> This was actually when I was looking for Ben Kenobi...I was going to use Toshiro Mifune; we even made a preliminary inquiry. If I'd gotten Mifune, I would've also used a Japanese princess, and then I would have probably cast a black Han Solo. At the same time, I was investigating Alec Guinness."[13]

With all of these legend-like "Lost Drafts," they never were actually committed to paper, as far as evidence suggests, and rather were concepts toyed with.

## Appendix C: The Dark Father
## Darth Vader's Etymological and Paternal Origins

ONE aspect of this "secret history" of *Star Wars* that needs to be addressed in further detail is the "Dark Father" issue. In Lucas' 2005 interview with *Rolling Stone*, he reinforces his claim that Darth Vader was always Luke's father by asserting that "Darth Vader" is a variation of "Dark Father":

> Darth is a variation of dark. And Vader is a variation of father. So it's basically Dark Father.[1]

It has also come to light that "Darth Vader" is a direct translation of "Dark Father" in the Dutch language. Many people mistakenly have read this as evidence showing that Lucas must have always known that Darth Vader was Luke's father, and that his claims of writing the whole story all at once must be true, otherwise a coincidence like this could not be possible. But far too much is resting on far too little.

Darth Vader was not a Sith Lord in the first script, but rather a military General, a minor side character who gets blown up at the end of the film. Are we to believe then that this inconsequential General Darth Vader, who has only a handful of scenes and gets blown up on the space fortress, is supposed to be Luke's father and that his name is meant to cleverly suggest "Dark Father"? Aside from that, Luke's father, Kane, is already in that script as a major character and is training him to be a Jedi. Thus, if we are to believe that the name was originally not attached to Luke's father and had no inherent meaning but that, coincidentally, it ended up being attached to Luke's evil father in a later draft as a means of describing his character, then it is no stretch to say that this coincidental attachment in fact happened in 1978 and not 1975 (when Luke's father ceases to be a physical character in the script and thus when many assert that he must have become Darth Vader). The case really closes there. Since the name originated in a person verifiably separate from the father (1974's General Darth Vader), any eventual connection to the Dark Lord of the final film is a coincidence, whether it happened in 1975 or 1978, and thus this is not proof of anything. Aside from that, even when Darth Vader re-appears in the second draft no longer as a petty General but as a fearsome Sith Lord with a mechanical breathing suit, Luke's father is *still* a separate character who exists on-screen, thus we see how what might at first appear as deliberate design is simply a lucky coincidence.

The names in *Star Wars*—and in particular the early drafts—were not chosen for their symbolic meanings but more for their phonetic connotations. They were meant to sound exotic, alien, innocent, intimidating; whatever suited the character. They don't inherently carry any meaning other than being names that Lucas liked for their unusual and appropriate sounds. Take for instance the tale of the origin of "wookie"—radio DJ Terence McGovern, who did voice-over for *THX* and *Star Wars* and appeared in *Graffiti*, once stated as he drove with George Lucas, "I think I ran over a wookie back there." Lucas laughed and asked what a "wookie" was—"I don't know, I just made it up," McGovern replied, and Lucas jotted down the word for future use.[2] It was just a neat, alien-like word that popped into McGovern's head, and Lucas liked it because it lent an otherworldly quality to the language.[3] Later, during the sound mixing for *American Graffiti*, Walter Murch asked Lucas to grab "R2-D2"—reel two, dialog two—from the shelf. Again, Lucas liked the name and jotted it down for future use, and it ended up on the first page of his notes.[4]

In fact, *The Annotated Screenplays* literally says "The names in *Star Wars* were simply created phonetically."[5] Lucas elaborated in that book:

> As I was writing, I would say the names to myself and if I had a hard time dealing with a name phonetically, I would change it. It had to do with hearing the name a lot and whether I got used to it or not. [6]

In Rinzler's *Making of* book Lucas goes through most of the names and invariable the same answer comes back: phonetic quality.[7] On Han Solo: "It could have come from Solo [paper] cups." On Ben Kenobi: "A combination of a lot of words I put together." On Leia Organa: "I just picked that name." On Tarkin: "That was just a name made up out of nowhere." On Chewbacca: "I came up with a whole bunch of Wookie words, just changing words around, and I liked *Chewbacca* the best."

Now we come to Darth Vader. The character is described in the rough draft as a "tall, grim-looking general," who is basically Imperial Fodder along the lines of, say, Moff Jerjerrod. He is not a Sith, nor a cyborg, bearing neither a mask nor any sort of futuristic suit; he is merely an intimidating, large man. Nor is he anyone's father, being a two-dimensional tertiary character on the villains' side. The harsh, Germanic-sounding name "Vader" was merely an appropriate connotation for a "tall, grim-looking general," as was "Darth," with its Germanic allusions to "death" and "dark."

Lucas took many of his inspiration for names from other languages of the world, mixing and matching sounds and vowels and inventing his own to create a uniquely alien language that also seemed bizarrely plausible. "Taun," for instance, is "town" in Japanese, and Lucas evidently is fond of its phonetic sound since he devised both Tauntaun and Taune We from it. Jedi is of course derived from Jidai-Geki, a Japanese term meaning "period film," used, among other things, to describe some of the samurai films in which Lucas was inspired by. "Sith" is a word Edgar Rice Burroughs invented, as is "banths" ("banthas"), while "Coruscant" appears in E.E. Smith's Lensmen series (where it means shiny or glittering). Another example is Hoth—the inhospitable world with a similarly harsh-sounding name is also a Germanic word. Once again, there is no meaning in the word itself. Lucas may have come across it when reading about World War II—a famous General of the Third Reich was named Hermann Hoth. As mentioned elsewhere in this book, Lucas' scholarly research in preparation for the prequel trilogy was genuine, and that is reflected in the more mythologically-inspired aspects of that trilogy; for instance, the word Padme is part of the Buddhist mantra and means lotus, and its soft sound was also appropriate for a gentle and compassionate character. Conversely, "Vader" is harsh and aggressive sounding. The names of *Star Wars* above all else were derived through their purely aesthetic phonetic quality.[*]

A lot of the names are in fact regular names for human beings that you will find in real life, but ones that simply are not common, at least in Lucas' experience circa the mid-'70s. His very first brainstorming notes from 1973 were lists of names—such as Roland, Monroe, Kane, Owen, Wan, Crispin,

---

[*] A good example of Lucas' preference for similar phonetics can be observed in the similarities between "Bob Falfa" of *American Graffiti* and Boba Fett, for example

Hayden. All human first names, ones that were somewhat uncommon at the time and that appealed to Lucas for their unusual nature and phonetic quality—the last example is particularly ironic, since Lucas would cast Hayden Christensen as the star of his prequel films.

Lucas in the 1970s is much more straightforward, here showcasing the two-fold method described, that being real-life inspiration, and phonetic invention. He explains the origin of the name "Darth Vader":

> That's just another one of those things that came out of thin air. It sort of appeared in my head one day. I had lots of Darth this or Darth that, and Dark Lord of the Sith. The early name was actually *Dark Water*. Then I added lots of last names, Vaders and Wilsons and Smiths, and I just came up with the combination of *Darth* and *Vader*.[8]

The key to the secret of the name lies in that last bit—"Vaders and Wilson and Smiths." Darth Wilson, Darth Smith—it was a last name, as he explicitly states above, taken from people he had met.

The names of the characters in the final draft of *Star Wars* had eventually been settled on for associative reasons however, perhaps even chosen at an unconscious level, as the names draw strong connections to the characters' own defining traits, which is perhaps why many are inclined to believe the "dark father" theory:

> Han *Solo*: a loner who learns the value of friendship.
> Leia *Organa*: connoting "organic," a benign association for the leader of the good guys, in opposition to the cold and artificial world of the Empire.
> Luke *Skywalker*: With his head in the clouds, dreaming of greater things than his drab life on the farm—"daydreamer" in other words.
> *Obi Wan*: Connotes "Holy One."[*]
> *Darth Vader*: Connotes "Dark Invader."

If there is *any* meaning to be read into the name of Vader, it is that it is connotative of the negative and aggressive word *inVADER,* as some reviewers of the time even noted, similar to the way Sidious is meant to evoke *inSIDIOUS,* again making it suited for a villain, though even this

---

[*] Others have pointed out that "Obi Wan" may be "Obi *Juan*," since Lucas' notes describe the character as being like Carlos Castaneda's Don *Juan* mystic. On the other hand, Nikki White, in *Bantha Tracks* issue six, proposes that the name is meant to sound Japanese, which is also appropriate since Lucas' first choice for the role was Toshiro Mifune. Interpretation can be very subjective.

should be considered conjecture. "Darth" was also a suitable word to assign to a villain character since it clearly connotes both "death" and "dark," as Lucas has noted. Any connotation of "father" is completely absent from both the phonetic quality of the word "Vader" and the function and characterisation of the character within the context of the film itself.

Amongst the uncountable sums of *Star Wars'* alien names, many of them are related to, or literally are, words on earth. Given the vast amount of languages on the planet and the vast amount of *Star Wars* names, it is no surprise that once in a while, by sheer coincidence, a name's earthly meaning will coincide with its on-screen character in some way. In this we have the Dutch "Vader," or "father." But even more tenuously, the word "Vader" in Dutch is not pronounced "Vay-der" but "Vah-der," further undermining this connection to the original word. Additionally, "Darth" is not a word in the Dutch language at all. The connection came from foreign versions of the film where the character was called "Dark Vader," meaning the translation is not direct but a pick-and-choose mix of English and Dutch. Similarly, in France he was called "Dark Vador" and in Italy "Dart Fener."

What we have here is merely a coincidence which, conveniently for Lucas, happens to support a popular misconception about the writing of *Star Wars*. Lucas himself never made this Dutch connection claim (which was brought forth by Dutch fans), but merely states that "Darth *Vay-der*" connotes "Dark *Fah-ther*" on its own.

So where then did Lucas actually get the name "Vader" from? Did he just invent it on his own in 1974? As he pointed out earlier, it was intended as a surname and stemmed from human surnames, like Smith or Wilson; so where did he meet a Vader? A trip down memory lane provides us with an interesting revelation. Lucas was a scrawny boy, who liked science fiction and read comic books—when he was young, bullies would pick on him and his younger sister Wendy would chase them away. Lucas' Modesto school yearbook provides a roster of bulky, jock-looking boys who would have been prime candidates for the bullies that picked on the small Lucas. One name in particular stands out.

Gary Vader.

Lucas very likely got the name from a high school jock.

### *Lord or Darth?*

There is another less critical yet still common misconception regarding Vader's etymological origins and that is the misconception that "Darth" was synonymous with "Dark Lord of the Sith," or simply "Sith." Certainly that is the case today, but many have asserted that this was *always* the case, that back in the days of the original trilogy "Darth" was a Sith title or rank and that Darth Vader was akin to Baron Vader or General Vader. This is a genuine occurrence—many fans in the '80s and '90s, before Episode I introduced more "Darths," somehow got this impression. How and where did they glean this information? An interview with Lucas? No. Background information from publicity material? No. The novels? No. Then where? Nowhere, that's where.

The first instance of "Darth" Vader comes from the rough draft, and it is the name of a man who is not a Sith but merely a General—General Darth Vader. As stated earlier, the name Darth Vader was invented as a threatening-sounding name that suited the dangerous henchman of the Empire—Darth being his first name and Vader being his last name. This survived to the fourth draft, where the character was now a Sith. Darth Vader did not *become* Darth Vader—he simply *was* Darth Vader. It was his name, the name of a student of Obi Wan's who later turned to the dark side. As Kenobi states, "A young Jedi named Darth Vader..." Later, the two meet, and his student refers to his master as "Obi Wan," to which "Obi Wan" refers to his student as "Darth" twice. "Only a master of evil, Darth," and "You can't win, Darth." Luckily, all of these instances still work in light of the change from a name to a title—sort of (Kenobi's grammar seems a little strange, but not jarringly so). In the early drafts Prince Espa Valorum is also a Sith Lord—yet he uses his name. Drafts two and three introduces us to other Sith as well, who also are not named "Darth." An excerpt from a scene between Vader and another Sith in draft three:

1ST SITH
Darth, did you feel that?

Darth stands and stares at the crystal.

One should note the grammar here—"Darth stands"; had that word been intended as a rank or title the proper phrasing would be "The Darth stands," (for example, "The General stands," not "General stands"). Instead, the grammar treats it as a first name, perfectly consistent with the next draft where Kenobi says "a young Jedi named Darth Vader..." Equally consistent, in the third draft Kenobi says "The crystal Darth stole..."

But of course in early 1978 the story was changed: Father Skywalker *became* Darth Vader. Hence, we have extra meaning introduced into "Darth Vader" since it is no longer a birth-name but an *alias*. Was it here that the change in "Darth" from a name to a title came about? Probably not. There is nothing to suggest as much, and far from taking it on as a title, Father Skywalker apparently adopted a Sith *name*—Annikin Skywalker was no more. He was now Sith Lord "Darth Vader." In fact, this is precisely what happens in Episode III. Anakin adopts the Sith identity "Vader"; therefore it is no stretch at all to presume that he was originally to adopt the Sith identity "Darth Vader."

This is why there are no "Darths" in the *Star Wars* universe until 1999. But there were Sith characters well before that year. Exar Kun is a popular Sith Lord in the Expanded Universe, as is as his apprentice Ulic Qel-Droma, and many others introduced in the comics and novels. But they are not "Darths." True, they are not from the mind of George Lucas, but surely if Lucas had intended for "Darth" to be a Sith title he would have mandated that the Expanded Universe writers follow suit, and certainly if it was so clear in the films themselves that "Darth" was a Sith title the writers would have picked up on it. The entire *Tales of the Jedi* comic series endured since 1993 with many Sith characters, chronicling the entire Sith wars in the ancient Republic but with not a single "Darth."

Then in 1999, we are introduced to Darth Maul and Darth Sidious, establishing the concept that "Darth" is a Sith title. Suddenly, we see a slew of "Darths" in the Expanded Universe, from Darth Bane to Darth Bandon to Darth Malak. Lucas even explained this to MTV, stating that it wasn't until he wrote the prequels that he started calling all the Siths "Darth something":

> When I started out, it was Darth Vader... And then [in the prequels] I started calling everybody dark something or other.[9]

Where did fans get the idea before this that "Darth" was a title if it was never stated anywhere? The 1997 *Star Wars* internet FAQ even tried to explain it through the popular fan theory that "Darth" was created as an anagram—"DArk lord of the siTH." But how did this notion get in peoples heads?

The answer is rather simple, and that is that people simply made the assumption. "Darth" Vader and "Lord" Vader are used interchangeably in the films, and "Darth" being phonetically similar to "Dark Lord" (of the Sith) people naturally linked the two terms. Darth and Lord were portrayed as equal, and so the misconception began. But it was never meant as a title—similar to Luke Skywalker also being called Commander Skywalker, Darth Vader is also sometimes referred to as Lord Vader.

### *Did Lucas Develop Father Vader In Silence?*

Darth Vader was not made into Luke's father until the spring of 1978 when Lucas had to write the second draft of *Empire Strikes Back*. The amount of evidence backing this is virtually undeniable, and not only is the concept of "Father Vader" absent from everything prior, it is contradicted by practically every piece of writing, in addition to Lucas' own private conversations in which he explicitly conveys that Luke's father is dead, as it is related in the scripts. However, a curious incident from the third draft of *Star Wars* nonetheless is frequently cited in the erroneous theory that perhaps Lucas developed the concept of Father Vader in 1975 but either discarded it or was silent about the matter. The confusing incident occurs during the space battle in the third draft which was written in August of 1975. During the Death Star battle, Vader is trying to shoot down Luke and says the following cryptic line:

VADER
You're next, Blue Five...I have this feeling I know you. The Force is strong with you.

This has been a bone of contention for many. There is no reason at all to support this as evidence that hints that Vader is indeed Luke's father. It only appears to be an inconsistency when viewing the material with the preconceived notion that Lucas already intended for Vader to be Luke's father. There is a more rational reason as to why that line of Vader's is there, and it has nothing to do with fathering Luke. To understand what that line means we have to first understand a running theme throughout the script, which is Luke's growing relationship to the Force and the balance of the Ashla and Bogan (light side and dark side). Throughout the script, the Sith feel the Ashla's growing presence as Luke and Ben embark on their mission. When Ben Kenobi first explains the Force to Luke on Tatooine, the scene then cuts directly to the Sith on the Death Star—across the galaxy, no less—who stir, moved by Luke's newfound knowledge of the Force and Ben's return. At first they don't even know what to make of it, and one of them asks, "Darth, did you feel that?" They then debate that the presence may be an "omen" brought to them through the Force but eventually conclude that "something old has been awakened"—the Ashla Force (light side) is being used for the first time in some twenty years. The balance of the Force is shifting.

A similar scene occurs with Ben Kenobi, when he uses the Force on Alderaan and a Sith Lord detects the strange presence not felt for many years:

96 INT. ALDERAAN - CLASSROOM 96

Ben finds himself in a small conference room filled with about a dozen or so bureaucrats listening to an instructor who is explaining a type of technical philosophy. The class turns and stares at the old man. Ben raises his hands and all the bureaucrats, including the instructor, begin coughing and grabbing at their throats. They are unable to breather and eventually collapse on the floor.

97. INT. ALDERAAN - HALLWAY LEADING TO THE CRYSTAL CHAMBER

One of the Sith Lords stops in the hallway opposite the classroom door.

1ST LORD
What is it?

2ND LORD
Do you feel that?

1ST LORD
I don't feel anything.

2ND LORD
Maybe you're too young. It's the Force... If I didn't know better I'd say we were in the presence of a Jedi knight.

The first Sith Lord puts his hand to his ear as a message comes through on his helmet intercom.

1ST LORD
They're calling for us again on the prison level.

The two Dark Lords hurry off down the hallway and Old Ben silently exits the classroom.

The second aspect of Vader's line has to do with the Kiber crystal. In this version of the script, the Kiber crystal itself is the catalyst for Vader's abandonment of the Jedi and embrace of the dark side. Kenobi tells how Vader took the last crystal and turned on the Jedi long ago, driven to the dark side with its power. The crystal is stolen back by Kenobi on Alderaan however, and is possessed by Luke in his X-wing during the trench run, emitting power so great that it is illuminating his ship, magnifying his natural Force abilities multiple times. Vader finally meets this Force user, this presence, that he and his Sith peers have been feeling and pondering about for the length of the script.

In fact, the notion of Vader sensing the crystal is present and explicit in the previous draft. An excerpt from draft two, wherein Luke is given the Kiber crystal by his father, The Starkiller, to aid him in the final Death Star attack, alerting the Sith to his presence:

127. INT. IMPERIAL SPACE FORTRESS - MAIN CONTROL CENTER

Constant explosions rock the interior of the fortress. Troops scurry for safety in the panic-ridden control center. A Sith knight speaks to Lord Vader on the com-link.

SITH KNIGHT
Yes, my Lord, the Ashla Force is strong upon us. I can't hold the panic. How could it be?

VADER
I feel the influence of the Kiber Crystal. Perhaps the Starkiller is still alive. They must have brought it out of hiding at last. We must strain – counter the force. Their attack is organized; they're going for the poles. Concentrate there.

Also, it is important to acknowledge that Vader's line is not simply "I have this feeling I know you." It is "I have this feeling I know you. The Force is strong with you." The last part is key, explaining the line. When the scenes with the Sith feeling Luke's presence were cut out and the Kiber crystal eliminated entirely, the first part of Vader's line was also removed, further reinforcing the link. The line appears in the final film as simply "The Force is strong with this one."

The smoking gun in favour of tearing down the "Father Vader created in silence" theory appears in that very scene referenced above. Vader is listening in on the radio chatter of the Rebel pilots as he blasts them out of the air, and at one point is even playing cat and mouse with Luke. But most significantly he overhears "Blue Five" being called "Luke Starkiller"—to which Vader has not a single reaction. Rather, he merely continues trying to destroy Luke, sniping "Not yet my bold friend" and firing at him with a would-be fatal shot, before being foiled by Han's last-minute rescue. Thus, the notion that Vader is Luke's father is illogical within the confines of the script itself—Luke would hardly "feel familiar," as Vader has confirmation that Blue Five is indeed his son, to which he does not react, nor alter his behaviour. This, again, is because Vader's ambiguity about Luke's identity has nothing to do with any personal relationship but rather to identifying the source of the Force "omens" that the Sith have been feeling for the past while. Vader's line never implied any sort of personal or hereditary connection, only a connection through the Force, which is explained by the running theme of Luke and the Ashla Force's growing presence, magnified by the very crystal whose power drove Darth to evil, and which is present in the final film itself as a shortened version of that line, which is "The Force is strong with this one."

One of the five large engines on Blue Leader's fighter explodes. He careens wildly, leaving an erratic trail of smoke before eventually crashing into a solar panel. Luke can hear the sharp laugh of Vader over the com-link.

196. INT. VADER'S IMPERIAL TIE FIGHTER - COCKPIT – TRAVELING

Darth Vader laughs maniacally as he swings his craft around and starts after Luke's ship.

VADER
You're next, Blue Five... I have this feeling I know you. The Force is strong with you.

197. INT. LUKE'S STARSHIP - COCKPIT - TRAVELING
Luke's hand instinctively goes to the pocket that holds the Kiber Crystal. Its glow lights up the entire cabin.

LUKE (BLUE FIVE)
I am Luke Starkiller. Had we met earlier, you would not be here.
[...]

Luke (Blue Five) dives on the Death Star at an incredible speed. He soon realizes Vader is on his tail. He spins his ship to evade the pursuing Dark Lord, but Vader is still there. His ship rock and shudders under the nearby impact of Vader exploding laser bolts. Luke straightens his ship out and it skims across the surface of the fortress, creating a blur.

LUKE (BLUE FIVE)
Approaching target. I'm almost home.

VADER (V.O.)
Not yet, my bold friend.

In any case, the line was eliminated from the final film. Likely, Lucas realised it was vague, and with the Kiber crystal omitted from that version and the scene with the Sith feeling Luke's presence gone, the line no longer made any sense. Some defenders say it was Lucas toying with the idea of Vader being Luke's father but it simply isn't supported by any evidence. The fact that Vader lives at the end of this draft, and the final draft, is no more conclusive either—rather it is a throwback to the old serial films that *Star Wars* is based off. You can almost hear the 1930s voice-over proclaiming "The Rebels have won a victory, but the fight will continue...next week!" This is how Lucas explained the change in having Vader survive to Alan Dean Foster in late 1975: "Vader runs off in the end, shaking his fist: 'I'll get you yet!'"[10]

Additionally, Vader at this point had grown into a much more memorable scene-stealing villain that Lucas obviously wanted to keep around for sequels. In the outline for the third draft, Lucas even had Luke confront Vader face-to-face in a lightsaber duel onboard the Death Star, wherein Vader is killed once again; Lucas cut this out of the third draft screenplay because he felt it ruined the pacing of the final battle,[11] and thus he instead had Vader survive so that this face-to-face lightsaber duel could be included in the sequels, which it was.

Furthermore, when Lucas states that he had Vader in mind as the father all along he never, ever implies that he had ambiguously set up hints in an early draft but then eliminated them for the final screenplay some months later. Rather, his claims are that he wrote drafts where this concept was explicit, where the father was clearly identified and was a major story point, whether in his "Tragedy of Darth Vader" version of "the original big script" or his "*Star Wars-Empire-Jedi*" version of the "the original big script" where he claims he wrote the original trilogy as one massive document. This line from the third draft is never mentioned, hinted, implied or even of the same nature as the "proof" Lucas asserts exists.

So, this confusing line from the third draft turns out to be irrelevant to the matter after all. Is there any other reason to believe that Lucas silently created "Father Vader"? No—but this does not preclude such a possibility, of course.

If he had developed the idea before 1978 it would have to have been off-paper, and not hinted or hidden within the scripts—Lucas pursued the original orthodox storyline *instead* of one in which Vader was the father. While we can never presume with total certainty that Lucas had never dreamed of such a concept as making the villain the hero's father, we can at the very least state with absolute certainty that *Star Wars* was written with Vader and Father Skywalker as separate characters. Lucas may indeed have let his mind wander into such a possible story direction, but if it did then he had discarded it (although it would make for a fascinating explanation of where the 1978 story point originated). But, of course a fundamental method of analysis being overlooked here is: why are we asking such a question as a silent Father Vader? If there is no evidence at all that suggests Lucas had conceived of the concept before 1978 and if he continually wrote and spoke of them as separate, then, until there is reason to believe there was, we must assume the history I have laid out earlier is correct. Facts seem to suggest that Lucas was entirely ignorant to such a concept until after the film was released. Not only would the concept have to have been off-paper, but it would also have to be conspicuously absent from all of Lucas' private notes, which often speculated about such alternate possibilities. For example, Rinzler reports:

> Other notes for the second draft contain pieces of scenes and ideas that didn't make it into the actual script: "Jabba in prison cell"; the love relationship between Leia and Luke Starkiller is divided into "seven stages/crucial scenes," with her being crowned queen at the end; "Han Solo a wookie? Wookies talk to plants and animals."[12]

More notes present alternate ideas in previous and future drafts, often suffixed by question marks at the end of them, showing that Lucas was literally pouring his fleeting thoughts out on paper.

With Lucas notoriously careful about archiving and preserving his early notes, treatments and drafts (in fact, the first visual conception of the film is a doodle of the wookie planet that Lucas made on the back of a scrap of paper in early 1973 or 1974[13]), it is also extremely conspicuous that no such Father Vader note or story point was ever unearthed, even when Jonathan Rinzler meticulously combed through the entirety of the Lucasfilm archives and Lucas' private material for his making-of book. Rinzler also is the author of *The Making of Revenge of the Sith*, and thus was very aware of Lucas' *Tragedy of Darth Vader* claims, which Lucas makes in that book. Yet he could not turn up anything to reinforce or indicate this (see also: *Appendix G – Tales of Jonathan Rinzler*), and in fact the book should be noted for its considerable documentation of the orthodox storyline where Vader and Skywalker are separate. So, for someone who presumably was actually looking for evidence of what Lucas claims, or was at the very least expecting to find it, it is significant that he came out totally empty-handed, and not only that but with substantial proof of the opposite orthodox backstory being the only story point ever recorded. Thus, while it is reasonable to speculate that Lucas may have actually pondered about a

Father Vader, or even a broader Father Villain concept, the idea would have been so fleeting that it never even made it into note form, and was instantly dismissed in favour of the orthodox version of the story which the film was built with.

Noah Henson makes a similar argument, responding to some who argued that the notion of Father Vader pre-dating 1977 must have been a concept that Lucas kept in his head and did not pursue on paper until 1978:

> It is irrelevant that [Lucas] might have "thought about [Vader and Father Skywalker] in some other way [than what was presented in *Star Wars*]." In the process of creating a work of literature or film, an author will of course entertain any number of approaches, ideas and concepts that never make it onto paper. This is because *the author has dismissed those ephemeral notions and has instead proceeded with an entirely different set of approaches, ideas and concepts.* He or she now makes those ideas concrete by recording them onto quantifiable, verifiable and tangible documentary material, i.e. paper. The discarded thoughts are no longer applicable to any reasonable discussion as to origins, since they were *never entertained seriously enough to warrant being recorded.*[14]

If Lucas creatively pondered about merging the characters in 1974, 1975, 1976 or 1977, that concept was never taken with enough sincerity or worked out in a significant enough way to be jotted down on paper or listed as a future plot point, or integrated into a treatment or script.

There's also the very valid distinction that Lucas *did* record the "orthodox" history where they are separate, again and again, in written and verbal form, constantly throughout the entire four-year development period.

Additionally, the argument that the Father Vader idea was simply "in his head" has a serious flaw: while it is quite rational to speculate that Lucas may have toyed with that idea only in his mind earlier and then finally committed it to paper in 1978, this creative process is not professed by Lucas. If it were, it would lend believability to the notion that he came up with the Father Vader concept at some point in the writing of the first film but then dismissed it and proceeded with the opposite orthodox version, but later used the Father Vader idea in *Empire*. Yet Lucas himself insists on a totally different sequence of events. What he states is that *Star Wars* indeed *was* designed with this twist in mind, but it was simply kept secret from everyone (suggesting that he was engaging in an elaborate conspiracy to deceive not only the public but his own co-workers and collaborators, including Alan Dean Foster, the writer of the sequel in which this reveal would play in, for a movie without media interest or any need for secrecy); he claims that his only debate was whether to reveal the Father

Vader twist in film two or three (see *Annotated Screenplays*). But clearly this is not the case, as Lucas conceived, wrote, filmed, released and presented *Star Wars* with Vader and Skywalker being separate.

While it is reasonable to presume that if Lucas had developed the twist in advance that he would not reveal it in public, hence explaining why he speaks of the orthodox backstory in interviews throughout 1977, this argument itself is a circular, self-proving fallacy that operates on the presupposition that Father Vader was already in place, without firstly proving that this was actually the case. But, aside from this, secrecy would not figure into Lucas' personal notes, or his private conversations with his creative collaborators. These personal meetings between him and his collaborators were never intended for public release (and if any of the transcriptions were released contemporarously, the "secrets" would of course be omitted), and thus are exempt from theories of paranoia of the "secret" Father Vader twist leaking. One arguer stated that the absence of Father Vader being indicated—and the contradiction of the orthodox backstory being recorded again and again—is due to fear of the secret leaking; "Lucas never told anyone about Vader being Anakin because loose lips sink ships." My response was thusly:

> If that's the case—why did Lucas tell Alan Dean Foster the plots for the two sequels in a late 1975 meeting? One of the quotes I presented (elsewhere in the debate—see Rinzler, p. 107) that has him outlining how Skywalker was killed was a private meeting with Foster for the sequels that Foster himself was writing. If Lucas told Leigh Brackett "Vader is Luke's father" then that would be indisputable proof—but instead, Lucas tells his sequel-author Father Skywalker is a separate person. In private story meetings with authors and screenwriters of the very films being discussed, in transcripts that were never intended for publication, secrecy and story leakings do not enter the equation (otherwise how could he discuss anything?).
>
> Secondly, secrecy is not a factor in 1975 or 1976 when many of those comments were made. Lucas expected the film to be unsuccessful and soon forgotten, but more importantly the crew itself infamously cared little for the project, and hence Lucas would not expect any of the plot to be leaked. In the same way that there was no extra security measures taken during production—there were no blue photocopy-proof script pages for Obi Wan's death because no one knew who "Obi Wan Kenobi" was. So, a private creative meeting with the author of the sequels would not be conducive to misleadings and security, for the same reason that when Lucas met with Gary Kurtz around the same time he could openly discuss Obi Wan's death, for example. Secrecy doesn't extend to the people involved in the film. Lucas is upfront about every single other element in the film, even ones that would be considered "spoilers"

had they been leaked. So, when he tells Foster that Luke's father is dead, there is no reason to suspect any ulterior motive or secrecy at play.

This finally brings me back to a point I expressed earlier, that, while speculating about Lucas thinking about the Father Vader concept sometime before 1978 is not crazy, it must firstly be entertained only as unfounded speculation, and secondly, even if Lucas had thought about it he clearly dismissed it and pursued the alternate, orthodox version of the backstory instead, which is what the film was built on. But going beyond this, there simply isn't any indication or reason to believe that the Father Vader concept had occurred to him, and Lucas' profession of a much different and thoroughly implausible scenario gives credence to the lack-of-proof. I once expressed the process of analysis which we ought to scrutinize the issue with as follows:

> The issue with Darth "Father Skywalker" Vader is actually two issues. One is, was he considered and written as a separate character from Skywalker in *Star Wars*, and the second issue is, was the idea of having him be the father character an idea that originated before the final script and/or was at one time considered as a story direction? The answer to the second one is a little more complicated but the answer to the first issue is very simple: we know for certain, undeniably, that Vader was written and considered as a separate character in *Star Wars*. The fact that the early drafts portray them as such is quite substantial, but there is the crucial question of "did Lucas change his mind after draft three and combine them?" An analysis of that draft shows that no, he didn't, because a close inspection reveals the same separate-conception trajectory from draft two and one, and there are no hints of any connection (the few constantly raised are reading-in of preconception, as I have demonstrated). Then, the film itself says they are separate. The contention here is: was this a "red herring" intended to surprise the audience for the sequel? This is the essential linchpin that this entire first issue rests on. The only way to know for sure is if Lucas actually stated in explicit terms that it wasn't—and he does just this. He maps out the backstory to numerous individuals, in private, including the author of the speculated-sequels (Alan Dean Foster), and explicitly states how the actual, detailed backstory is what is given in the film, with Vader murdering Luke's father. Later on, he actually goes public with this, and then makes public his plans to show this in a prequel film, plans which he had been dreaming about since late 1975—as far back as that year he makes explicit that he wouldlike to film a movie about the backstory where Father Skywalker gets killed (see Rinzler, p. 107).
>
> So, Lucas shows beyond a shadow of a doubt that the story related in the film is not actually a red herring but a real, genuine commitment, and once you understand the complexity of that backstory—i.e. Kenobi and Father

Skywalker growing up on Tatooine—it makes it all the more clear that it was an integrated part of the characters and storyline.

Further backing this up of course is the fact that Lucas' sequel outline to Alan Dean Foster in 1975 has no such reveal of a Father Vader, and that Lucas' own 1977 treatment for *Empire* has no such reveal as a Father Vader.

Father Vader, whether an older idea that was initially rejected or a new idea stumbled upon, was a change of course in the story of the series and did not integrate until the second draft of *Empire Strikes Back* (in fact, in the first draft Father Skywalker's ghost is even a character; though we now get into the issue of whether or not Leigh Brackett added this element on her own, this is actually irrelevant since the larger point is that it is consistent in storyline with the final film of *Star Wars* and the conception that Lucas held of it at the time that it was written and which continued until the time of his *Empire* treatment which this very draft was based off).

So the real issue is, was the concept of Father Vader actually a rejected concept from *Star Wars*? The answer to that is not quite as definitive because we are now expected to prove a negative, and thus we cannot expect the luck of having as clear an answer as the first issue. The fundamental method of analysis when dealing with issues of unfalsifiability thus enters the question: what indication is there that this hypothesis has any merit for existence? The answer is: none. There's no indication it took place, which is significant, but what is even more significant is that Lucas continued to write down the opposite. The answer of "since it was a private creative conception, he may not have written it down" is quickly replied—but of course Lucas wrote down the private creative conception of the contrary orthodox version time and time again, and so too with virtually every other element in the film. There is a stunning absence—a total, complete void—of anything to indicate any process which held him speculating about combining them but then rejecting the idea and using it in a sequel in 1978. Thus, to the maximum degree that it is possible to prove a negative, we can state that there is no reasonable indication or implication that the two were ever at any point considered as a singular character. Perhaps one day persuasive evidence might come to light, but based on the wealth of information currently available, this does not seem likely.

Additional proofs also leverage this evidence, from the fact that once the 1978 debut of this Father Vader concept on paper takes place Lucas does talk about it in private, to the fact that such a story point is at odds to the style, tone and storyline of *Star Wars* (but not *Empire*), to the fact that Lucas' description of his actual early story material and scripts is often exaggerated or inaccurate to varying degrees, to the fact that Lucas has put a publicity spin on the behind-the-scenes history to reinforce the current story embodiment.

Thus, we should come to the conclusion that not only was Darth Vader written as and considered a separate character from Father Skywalker in *Star Wars*, but that the concept of them being amalgamated into a singular character was first arrived at around the time of the second draft of *Empire Strikes Back*. Sometimes the gap of late 1977 is proposed but again we return to the fundamental analysis of "why should we consider this?" He explicitly details in August of that year in *Rolling Stone* how Vader kills Skywalker, and then his November treatment is absent of a Father Vader. Here Father Skywalker is proposed to also have a twin child who is also training to be a Jedi—this story point being linked to the orthodox Father Skywalker concept and eliminated in April of 1978 once the second draft and the Father Vader concept was integrated. In fact, the controversial "Ghost of Father Skywalker" in draft one exists specifically to relay this information.

Thus, we can pinpoint the epiphany to have occurred sometime in the new year of 1978. Analysing things further, we can make an even more specific date of origin, plus a motivation that explains specifically how this wildly different and contradictory storyline was arrived at. Brackett turned in her draft in February of 1978, and Lucas, upon reading it, was displeased. Before anything could be done, Brackett died and Lucas was left alone with the pen now in his hand—he was forced into writing a draft himself. In considering how to make the story work now that he was writing it himself, he must have arrived at the concept that the character of Luke's father could be combined with Vader, a twist facilitated by the close link they already shared and the more complicated and serious style that *Empire* was heading down.

Thus, we can state definitively that Vader and Skywalker were separate in the final film of *Star Wars*, with a very high degree of certainty that the concept of their fusion was not arrived at or ever considered until after that film's release, with a reasonable degree of certainty that it occurred in early 1978, and with a high degree of likelihood that it was probably the result of Lucas' disappointment with Brackett's draft and the subsequent manner in which he was forced to come up with a script himself, by hand.

# Appendix D: The Legend of the Sequel Trilogy

THE so-called Sequel Trilogy to *Star Wars*—that is, Episodes VII, VIII and IX—is one of those urban legends of the series that has as much as myth about it as it does truth. Fans for years remember Lucas talking about making a third trilogy which took place years after *Return of the Jedi*, and Gary Kurtz has recently revealed the supposed plots for these films, as they existed during their initial conception in the late 1970s. Mark Hamill has even discussed how he was at one time supposed to return, playing an older version of Luke Skywalker. Further shrouding these three films in mystery, George Lucas himself now insists it was all a fabrication of the media and that there was never any story planned out. The appearance of a trilogy of novels in the early 1990s led many fans to believe that these stories by Timothy Zahn—*Heir to the Empire, Dark Force Rising* and *The Last Command*—were the novel adaptations of the Sequel Trilogy that never was.

But what was the Sequel Trilogy? And did it even exist at all?

The answer to the first question is pretty complicated but the answer to the second is an easy one: a resounding "Yes." The bizarre accusation of Lucas that the very basis for these films was a media invention is quite perplexing, simply due to the sheer volume of information Lucas has divulged on the subject. Even Steven Spielberg in 1999 remarked, "George always wanted to make nine. He wanted to make the first three, then he wanted to make the prequels to that, then he wanted to make the last three.

And that was something that was part of his concept."[1] Rick McCallum, producer of the prequels, even in 1999 still talked about the nine-episode plan: "Whether George only completes six of the nine-part series or he actually ever really ultimately completes the nine, it's really nine parts of one film. Its one big saga, a saga about a family that happens to live in a galaxy far, far away."[2]

The surfacing of Gary Kurtz in 1999 led to him revealing in interviews and at conventions the supposed plans that Lucas first drew up around 1978 or so. These plans revealed that the original plot for the series was not to be ended in *Return of the Jedi* but stretched out for another three films, forming a "hexology" for Luke's story, that is, a six-film continuous story. In Episode VI Darth Vader would be killed, in Episode VII Luke would continue his fight, now as a full Jedi, in Episode VIII Luke's twin Jedi sister would appear and in Episode IX the Emperor would finally be revealed and defeated, and the series finished. This led to the obvious conclusion that after the hardships of making *Empire Strikes Back*, Lucas basically compressed all of these story ideas into one film, ending the series with *Return of the Jedi*. However, this hypothesis is not correct. Its refutation has its own dedicated appendix and I have briefly been over the main tenets of its inaccuracy in the main body of this book but to put things simply, the storyline which Kurtz describes as being planned never existed at any given time, and his statements are a confused conflation of the ever-changing storylines from 1977-1980.

So, what were the *real* plans for these sequels? Well, that depends on what sequels you are talking about and at what date.

Let's go back to the beginning.

When *Star Wars* was first written it was meant to be a stand-alone film. The second draft ended with a teaser for a sequel which includes a "search for the Princess of Ondos," but, like the open-ended finale of the final film itself, this was probably not seriously expected to be made, and it is likely that Lucas only vaguely developed this story, if he had developed it at all. But Lucas began to realise that a number of spin-off stories *could* be made following the continuing adventures in this galaxy—the film was, after all, fashioned after the serial films. As early as 1974[3] Lucas expressed a desire to retain sequel rights, and by the time Lucas actually got to negotiating contracts he had Carrie Fisher and Mark Hamill signed for two sequels, just in case he felt like pursuing them.

Alan Dean Foster was then commissioned to not only write the *Star Wars* novelisation, but two sequel novels to the film which could be adapted into scripts and made on low budgets, as per Lucas' three-film Fox contract.[4] So whether the film was a failure or success, Lucas was planning on expanding the adventure in novels. As a film, *Star Wars* was designed to be self-contained since it was most likely that this would be the only cinematic entry in the series—Lucas added many embellishments to the final draft screenplay which reinforced its function as a stand-alone film, showing that he was leaning towards the notion that there would never be any sequels, such as the development that the destruction of the Death Star would lead to the fall of the Empire. But whether the film was successful or not, Lucas still had planned with Foster to at least do two follow-ups as novels. Before the first sequel novel was released, however, *Star Wars* became a hit; this initial story was then scrapped for the movie sequel and released in 1978 as the novel *Splinter of the Mind's Eye*.

With the film unexpectedly proving to be the most popular and successful motion picture in history, Lucas excitedly found himself with virtually unlimited funds and freedom, and was now allowed the ability to pursue the more epic and ambitious ideas he originally had wanted for *Star Wars*. Rather than merely a trilogy, Lucas decided that he would make the series into a franchise in the vein of James Bond; interviews from 1977 reveal that the series is to be a loosely-connected serial, with each chapter following different characters and time periods and containing different themes, as well as being made by different directors. The films apparently don't follow chronological sequence, as Lucas speculated that a possible sequel could be the early days of Obi Wan Kenobi, and Gary Kurtz has even indicated that a sequel was pondered which traced the formation of the ancient Jedi order. Mark Hamill compared the series to James Bond, and stated that he had been approached about doing more than his contracted three films.

Later that year, Lucas began working on the actual story material for *Star Wars II*, hiring Leigh Brackett as the screenwriter. The film was titled *Empire Strikes Back* and designated as Chapter II. After many story conferences a first draft was finally completed by February of 1978. The script itself is not wildly different from the actual film in terms of plot except Han is alive and well at the end and leaves to search for his Stepfather/mentor, Darth Vader is not Luke's father, and the ghost of Father Skywalker reveals Luke has a twin sister who is also undergoing Jedi training—in a future episode she would be seen.

Lucas revealed to the public around this very same time that the series was to be twelve films long, with the projected date of completion 2001. There are no apparent story ideas for future episodes other than what is set up in the first draft of *Empire Strikes Back*, although it is probable that Lucas had privately developed a few broad concepts.

Then Brackett dies, Lucas writes the second draft himself and makes the historic story change where he fuses Father Skywalker and Darth Vader into the same character. The script was still known as Episode II but this was soon revised to Episode V. The sister character was not reprised for obvious reasons.

On the set of *Empire Strikes Back*, Lucas reveals to Alan Arnold that the *Star Wars* series is divided into three trilogies which total nine films. Trilogy one is the prequel films which details Obi Wan and Father Skywalker's early days and the fall of the Republic, whereupon Father Skywalker turns to the dark side and becomes Darth Vader. Trilogy two is Luke's story, chronicling the Rebels versus Empire plot; the final film in this trilogy would have Luke and the Rebels finally defeating Vader and the Empire. The third trilogy he is much tighter-lipped about, but he says that there will be twenty years between each trilogy, making the whole series span over fifty years, and that each trilogy would feature different actors. Lucas said in 1979:

> There are essentially nine films in a series of three trilogies. The first trilogy is about the young Ben Kenobi and the early life of Luke's father when Luke was a little boy. This trilogy takes place some twenty years before the second trilogy which includes *Star Wars* and *Empire*. About a year or two passes between each story of the trilogy and about twenty years pass between the trilogies. The entire saga spans about fifty-five years... After the success of *Star Wars* I added another trilogy but stopped there, primarily because reality took over. After all, it takes three years to prepare and make a *Star Wars* picture. How many years are left? So I'm still left with three trilogies of nine films... The next chapter is called "Revenge of the Jedi." It's the end of this particular trilogy, the conclusion of the conflict begun in *Star Wars* between Luke and Darth Vader. It resolves the situation once and for all. I won't say who survives and who doesn't, but if we are ever able to link together all three you'd find the story progresses in a very logical fashion.[5]

Here is where the detective work begins. Much of the information regarding the Sequel Trilogy can be gathered from the reference to an "Other" by Yoda in *Empire Strikes Back*. Lucas claimed recently that he had no idea who Yoda was speaking of—it wasn't Leia and it wasn't a sister character; it was put in there to place Luke in more danger by making the audience think he could die and that the series could continue beyond him (which in fact was Lucas' plan at that time). But an examination of this famous line reveals that Lucas did indeed have some plan for sequels. The line in the initial drafts achieves what Lucas claims of it, and it first appears in the revised second draft. Yoda says "Now we must find another." In the third draft it is similar: "No…we must search for another." But in the fourth draft it undergoes a subtle yet highly significant change—"No, there is another." Implying that somebody is already out there, ready to step in and replace Luke.

Lucas was setting up the protagonist for the third trilogy. Who was this character? Lucas himself may not have known exactly, and had many avenues to take. Could it be another Jedi who escaped the purge like Obi Wan and Yoda and was in seclusion like them? If this is the case, he would be at least seventy years old by the time of the Sequel Trilogy, making this highly unlikely. The obvious answer then is that he was a Force-sensitive youngster, hidden at birth similar to the way Luke was, perhaps only being a child at the time of the middle trilogy. In the third trilogy he (or she) could become the protagonist. As Lucas said in 1981 to *Starlog*, no character would go through the entire series except perhaps the droids. He also mentions that the actors would all be different in the films, not surprising given that the actors of his current trilogy were only under contract for those three films. Thus, any characters from this trilogy that appeared in the third trilogy would be played by older actors. From 1981:

> Kerri O' Quinn: Is there going to be character continuity among all three trilogies?
>
> George Lucas: No—possibly the robots, but there weren't originally designed to go through the whole…nobody was designed to go through all three. I'd like to see the robots go through them, but I don't know whether they will.
>
> KOQ: What will provide the continuity then?
>
> GL: Well, the next trilogy—the first one—since it's about Ben Kenobi as a young man, is the same character, just a different actor. And it's the same thing with all the characters. Luke ends up in the third film of the first trilogy just three-and-a-half years old. There is continuity with the characters in other words, but not with the actors—and the look of the films will be different.[6]

The series at this point was no longer about Luke, as evident by the fact that the first and last thirds of the saga would not centre on him—which may be one reason why Lucas stopped referring to the series as *The Adventures of Luke Skywalker* in 1979, when this three-trilogy plan was revealed. It was three separate trilogies which told a chronological story when viewed together but followed different characters and had different styles and tones, although connected in various ways. The first trilogy was about Obi Wan. The second trilogy was about Luke. The third trilogy, then, may have followed this "Other," perhaps with Luke in the role of the mentor character (and played by someone other than Mark Hamill), similar to Obi Wan in the middle trilogy—the protagonist of the previous trilogy would step aside for the next one and make a cameo appearance; this is what connects the trilogies. "The sequel is about Jedi knighthood, justice, confrontation, and passing on what you have learned," Lucas would later say.[7]

Although Lucas would change some of these plans by the time he wrote *Return of the Jedi*, this natural arc of Luke taking an apprentice to continue the Jedi way after he is gone is still alluded to in that film when a dying Yoda intones "Pass on what you have learned…" That the sequels would involve Luke's successor seems like a given.

Would the rest of the middle trilogy characters be seen? Han, Leia, Chewie, Lando? Certainly audiences would want to find out what happened to them. But, there simply is not enough information to make anything more than assessments of probability; perhaps Lucas would make the films revolve around them, or perhaps Lucas would relegate them to background characters and instead prefer to introduce new ones. It's simply a matter of opinion.

So what about plot? There's not much known, and probably Lucas knew little more than we do. Denise Worrell writes in 1983 that Lucas has specific plots for the prequels, "but he has only a vague notion of what will happen in the three films of the sequel," also stating that he has only some notes on the films and not specific outlines.[8] In 1980 he revealed to *Time* magazine that the sequels would revolve around "the rebuilding of the Republic," and in 1983 stated that thematically it would be about "the necessity for moral choices and the wisdom needed to distinguish right from wrong," implying perhaps a more introspective tone, which is consistent with Lucas' implications that the three sets of films would all be stylistically different. The first trilogy is to be more Machiavellian and melodramatic, like a costume drama, as Lucas revealed in 1981, while the second is more action-packed and light-hearted, perhaps leaving the third to be more philosophical, addressing issues of ethical responsibility and moral ambiguity. "The third [trilogy will] deal with moral and philosophical problems," Lucas once said. "In *Star Wars*, there is a very clear line drawn between good and evil. Eventually you have to face the fact that good and evil aren't that clear-cut and the real issue is trying to understand the difference." §

Lucas may have had more ideas that he never revealed but they will regrettably be forever lost as he now denies the very existence of these films, let alone the original configuration of them.

The actual plot—beyond the premise of re-building the Republic and following the Jedi-in-training Other character—is anyone's guess, though a number of viable speculations can be made. The hardest accomplishment of the Sequel Trilogy is the introduction of a new threat and the creation of a central villain. Nothing could possibly match the effectiveness of Darth Vader and the Emperor, and creating any kind of central threat would inevitably lead to a re-tread of either the prequels or the middle trilogy, and with Vader and the Emperor both dead, anyone newly introduced may seem superfluous and unimpressive.

Perhaps a new menace would rise up in place of the Empire, threatening to consume or topple the struggling New Republic. Perhaps insidious evildoers would appear from within the New Republic itself, similar to the prequels, threatening to take over the democracy once again. Perhaps the remnants from the Galactic Empire itself have been taken over by a new leader and now are striking back as intergalactic terrorists in the ravaged post-war galaxy, similar to what Timothy Zahn would present in his own sequel trilogy. It could even be possible to bring back the Emperor himself—perhaps he somehow escaped the Death Star and his fate has been unknown but now resurfaces twenty years later to exact his revenge, as either a spirit or a corporeal being. Lucas himself okayed the use of returning the Emperor as a clone for *Dark Empire*.[10]

Moral ambiguity and the necessity for choices in the name of good, Jedi knighthood, and the passing on of knowledge will play key roles in the sequels, according to Lucas, and so perhaps Luke would wrestle with the dark side, exploring what it is, why his father fell and how he himself should avoid it—after all, he himself tasted it at the end of *Jedi*. This type of plot is similar to the *Dark Empire* comic, with Luke trying to destroy the dark side from within, which Lucas had some involvement with and apparently is quite fond of. With Luke taking on an apprentice, these issues would be all the more relevant. Those rebuilding the Republic would be

---

* These comments about moral ambiguity and responsibility were made in relation to the post-1980 revised "reunion" sequel but, although the character and story focus may have changed, I believe that the thematic and tonal qualities remained more or less the same

faced with a legacy of failure and the task of not repeating the mistakes of the past, which indeed would give the trilogy a reflective and philosophical tone.

But these are all just speculations on my part. The truth is that short of Lucas coming out and telling us, we will never know the details, other than the backdrop of the story was the rebuilding of the Republic, that it would thematically centre around choices of morality, and, through deduction, that it would follow Luke's young prodigy, likely with Luke and the middle trilogy characters briefly seen.

All of this story development is occurring in 1979, however. So, what happened to this trilogy?

Lucas never had a huge emotional investment in it. He revealed in the May 1980 issue of *Bantha Tracks* that his original story gave him the material for the first six films but that the third trilogy was only added after the success of *Star Wars*. "Originally, when I wrote *Star Wars*," he says, "[I] had material for six movies. After the success of *Star Wars* I added another trilogy."[11] The prequels were also more interesting and developed. Perhaps this is why by 1980 the plan is to film the prequels first and *then* the sequels—it gave him the option of backing out if he felt like it. He may have also been beginning to change his mind by then.

With the 1979 three-trilogy sequel plan in place, *Empire Strikes Back* goes into production. The complicated production does not go smoothly and is very stressful on everyone involved, and Lucas contemplates throwing away all the remaining episodes other than the third film in his original trilogy. His marriage was also falling apart, and his wife Marcia was pressuring him into settling down and starting a family; they had refused to do so thus far because Lucas knew his work on the *Star Wars* films would prevent him from properly raising a family. But now even he was beginning to tire of the films, as were the actors.

In any case, by 1981 he had decided to cancel the *Star Wars* saga, including his Sequel Trilogy. It was the most unnecessary and uninteresting of the films—*Revenge of the Jedi* stood poised to tie everything up nicely. With Vader and the Emperor dead, Luke and the Rebels victorious and the galaxy safe once again, what need was there to extend the story beyond this?

However, one point remained lingering: his set up of the Other. With no sequel trilogy to introduce the character with, it now needed to be resolved. He couldn't arbitrarily introduce a new character into the already-crowded plot, especially not another Jedi, and so Leia was written in as this Other, and her importance was justified by turning her into Luke's sister, bringing back the sister subplot that had been attached to draft one of

*Empire Strikes Back.* With the "Other" forced to be addressed in *Return of the Jedi* and made into Princess Leia, the Sequel Trilogy lost its key character and story link, and hence became even more unnecessary, which is perhaps what led to the shifting to a "reunion" type of story, set when the characters are in their sixties, which is what the majority of Lucas' comments pertaining to the "third trilogy" refer to. Lucas still spoke publically of the Sequel Trilogy and did not reveal that he had cancelled it, and with the Other now written out of the future stories he now began claiming that the sequels would follow a grey-haired Luke and company, perhaps with the original cast returning as their elder selves—this newly created plot point was first mentioned in *Time* Magazine in May, 1983. *Time* magazine wrote:

> Luke, who will then be the age Obi-Wan Kenobi is now, some place in his 60s, will reappear, and so will his friends, assuming that the creator decides to carry the epic further. Hamill and the others will get first crack at the roles—if they look old enough.[12]

Denise Worrell also reported in greater detail that same month:

> In the sequel Luke would be a sixty-year-old Jedi knight. Han Solo and Leia would be together, although Lucas says, "They might be married, or not. We have never actually discussed marriage in this galaxy. I don't even know if it exists yet. Who knows what relationship they will have? I mean, they're together, let's put it that way." The sequel focuses mainly on Luke, and Lucas says Mark Hamill will have first crack at the part if he is old enough. "If the first trilogy is social and political and talks about how society evolves," Lucas says, "*Star Wars* is more about personal growth and self-realisation, and the third deal with moral and philosophical problems. In *Star Wars*, there is a very clear line drawn between good and evil. Eventually you have to face the fact that good and evil aren't that clear-cut and the real issue is trying to understand the difference. The sequel is about Jedi knighthood, justice, confrontation, and passing on what you have learned."[13]

It appears that Lucas developed an alternate version of the Sequel Trilogy by this point, likely just in case he still felt like making it one day. This version also takes place much farther into the future, roughly forty years after *Return of the Jedi* as opposed to twenty (as evident by the fact that Luke is said to be in his 60s), and is more centred around the gimmick of re-uniting the aged original cast. However, it is possible that much of the thematic content of the original plan remained intact.

A June 1980 interview with *Rolling Stone* has him claiming he has twelve-page outlines for all *seven* remaining films. He also addresses the "Other" but his comments are so vague and ambiguous that it is impossible to precisely gather if it is indicating he had decided to write in Leia as the Other by this point:

*What is your deal with Fox?*

They have first refusal on every *Star Wars* film I want to make.

*How many is that?*

Seven left.

*Let's get back to* The Empire Strikes Back *for a moment. In the movie, Ben says Luke is the last hope and Yoda says no, there is another.*

Yes. [*Smiling*] There is another, and has been for a long time. You have to remember, we're starting in the middle of this whole story. There are six hours' worth of events before *Star Wars*, and in those six hours, the 'Other' becomes apparent, and after the third film, the 'Other' becomes apparent quite a bit.

*What will happen to Luke?*

I can't say. In the next film everything gets resolved one way or the other...

*Do you have story lines for the seven Star Wars movies left to be done?*

Yes, twelve-page outlines.[14]

Richard Marquand also has made some interesting statements, such as one particular quote from 1983 where he says that Lucas told him ideas for the sequels, apparently involving some kind of mastermind villain—however, the character he describes is clearly the Emperor, revealing that he may simply be confused on the complicated issue:

*Did George tell you the complete SW saga?*

Yes, all nine parts...if you follow the direction and project into the final trilogy, you realise you're going to meet the supreme intellect, and you think, how is it possible to create a man who has such profound cunning that he can not only control Darth Vader, but the fate of Luke Skywalker? Control the destiny of the whole galaxy? You'll be amazed![15]

It is also worthy to note that whatever he is referring to is not the original plan but the post-1980 version.

In any case, by 1983 Lucas is speaking of following the aged cast of the original trilogy in a Sequel Trilogy. But they are mostly empty promises—Lucas never had a strong desire to film these, perhaps explaining his comments that the Sequel Trilogy was never a serious consideration and more of a gimmicky reunion suggestion. It was merely left as an option for himself, one that was most likely going to be passed by.

In the 1990s the *Star Wars* renaissance gave Lucas enough wealth to make more films, conveniently coinciding with the digital revolution and the maturation of his kids. If he were to do any *Star Wars* films at all, they would be the prequels, which he had developed in fairly elaborate detail by that point and which held a strong personal interest to him; the sequels, on the other hand, remained vague and uninteresting—perhaps he might have had more conviction in his original 1979-era plan, but the notion of gathering the elderly cast of the originals for new films was never proposed with much enthusiasm.

In the mid-'80s, Lucas told *Starlog*, "No, no books. If I do [more *Star Wars* stories], I *will* do them as movies."[16] Yet by the '90s it became obvious to him that he would probably not get around to making these sequel films, and so it was allowed that authors could do ancillary material that took place after *Jedi* when such an idea was brought to Lucasfilm. The development of additional *Star Wars* novels was proposed in 1989 by publisher Bantam Spectra, and Lucas agreed—his first criteria for the books were that they take place a few years after *Return of the Jedi*. They were, in effect, replacements for the Sequel trilogy. Lucas said to *Wired*:

> The sequels were never really going to get made anyway, unlike 1, 2, and 3, where the stories have existed for 20 years. The idea of 7, 8, and 9 actually came from people asking me about sequels, and I said, "I don't know. Maybe someday." Then when the licensing people came and asked, "Can we do novels?" I said do sequels, because I'll probably never do sequels.[17]

Timothy Zahn's trilogy was finished in 1993, and each book was a *New York Times* best-seller, kick-starting the *Star Wars* renaissance of the early and mid '90s. It was here that Lucas finally decided that the prequels would be made, but with a significant shift, as the trilogies were not meant to be one narrative; they were stylistically and tonally different, but chronologically connected. When Lucas made Anakin the main character of the prequels and not Obi Wan the series thus shifted to being one which told Anakin's life story and thus became one large tale. With the overall series now charting Anakin's rise, fall and death, the third trilogy was rendered obsolete, the final nail in its coffin.

Interestingly, the themes of issues of morality and the ambiguity of good and evil that Lucas once said would be the focus of his Sequel Trilogy found their way quite prominently into the prequels (which again may indicate that these were in fact holdovers from the original 1979 plan, since they held such personal interest to him).

It is also interesting that Lucas did initially leave himself a window to still make the sequel films—his plans had the films set many decades after *Jedi*, while he mandated that the new sequel novels take place only a few years. This may be why one of his closest friends, Steven Spielberg, and his closest collaborator, Rick McCallum, continue to acknowledge the existence or possibility of sequels as late as 1999. However, at that same time, Lucas finally made a definitive decision on the matter of not doing them (perhaps explaining why it wasn't until this much later period that novels began to take place more than just a few years after *Jedi*).

Interviewers would still question Lucas about the Sequel Trilogy, but he was more hesitant and ambiguous than ever. Nevertheless, he did not definitively state that they would not be made, and would continue to make numerous references to having a nine-film series, finally stating in 1999 that the series would end with the prequels and making these plans very clear once *Revenge of the Sith* was released.

A plethora of examples follows. This is by no means a complete list—the sequels were talked about more frequently than even the prequels.

*Time* Magazine, May 19th, 1980:

> The second trilogy, which opened with Star Wars: Episode IV, centers on Luke Skywalker, who, will be seen as a child in Episode III. Empire continues the Skywalker story, and Episode VI, the next film to be made, which will be called Revenge of the Jedi, will end it, with either Luke or Darth Vader walking away from their final bout. The last three episodes involve the rebuilding of the Republic.
>
> Only two of the main characters will appear in all nine films, and they are the robots, Artoo Detoo and Threepio. Says Lucas: "In effect, the story will be told through their eyes."[18]

*Bantha Tracks*, issue 8, spring 1980:

> Revenge of the Jedi will complete the middle trilogy of the nine-part Star Wars epic. Following its completion, the first trilogy will be filmed, and then finally, the last trilogy.

Should production on the nine films continue at the same rate, we can expect to see the ninth film released in the spring of 2001.

## George Lucas, *Starlog*, July 1981

Starlog: Is there going to be character continuity among all three trilogies?

Lucas: No—possibly the robots, but they weren't originally designed to go through the whole...nobody was designed to go through all three. I'd like to see the robots go through them, but I don't know whether they will.

## George Lucas, 1982, as quoted in John Baxter's *Mythmaker*, p. 387:

I'm only doing [*Revenge of the Jedi*] because I started it and now I have to finish it. The next trilogy will be someone else's vision.

## *Time* Magazine, May 23rd, 1983:

The sequels, the three movies that would follow Jedi, are considerably vaguer. Their main theme will be the necessity for moral choices and the wisdom needed to distinguish right from wrong. There was never any doubt in the films already made; in those the lines were sharply drawn, comic-book-style. Luke, who will then be the age Obi-Wan Kenobi is now, some place in his 60s, will reappear, and so will his friends, assuming that the creator decides to carry the epic further. Hamill and the others will get first crack at the roles—if they look old enough.[19]

## Dale Pollock, *Skywalking: The Life and Films of George Lucas*, First Edition, 1983, p. 146, 1983:

He started anew with the middle story. It had the most action and starred Luke, the character with whom he felt the most secure. The first trilogy told the story of young Ben Kenobi and Luke's father and was set twenty years before Star Wars. The final three movies feature an adult Luke and the final confrontation between the rebels and the Empire. The entire saga spans more than fifty-five years; C-3P0 and R2-D2 are the only common element to all the films.

## George Lucas, *Press-Telegram*, May 18, 1983:

Now I've finished one book. And there may be two other books in my mind, but whether I start another book is not crucially important. The next book doesn't have anything to do with this book. Different sets, different actors. So it's not like I have to rush out and do another.

## George Lucas, *Starlog*, issue 127, February 1988:

Starlog: Will you return to the *Star Wars* universe?

Lucas: Hopefully, I will someday be doing the next three *Star Wars*, but I'm not sure when. The next three would take place 20 or 30 years before the films they're celebrating here today. I'll do the first trilogy first. There are nine [films] floating around there somewhere. I'll guarantee that the first three are pretty much organized in my head, but the other three are kind of out there somewhere.

Starlog: Why didn't you give Luke a girl?

Lucas: You haven't seen the last three yet.

## George Lucas, *Premiere*, September 1990:

Star Wars is a story, divided in three trilogies. It's a long movie of 18 hours, divided in nine parts. The next trilogy will be prequels, with events taking place some years before the current trilogy. The main characters will be, besides A Young Vader and a Young Ben Kenobi, completely new. The look will be different too.

## George Lucas, *Splinter of the Mind's Eye* second edition introduction, 1994:

It wasn't long after I began writing Star Wars that I realized the story was more than a single film could hold. As the saga of Skywalkers and Jedi Knights unfolded, I began to see it as a tale that would take at least nine films to tell - three trilogies – and I realised, in making my way through the back story and after story, that I was really setting out to write the middle story.

## George Lucas, *The Unauthorized Star Wars Compendium*, p. 13-14, January 1999:

The first film came out and was a giant hit, and the sequels became possible. Then people suggested we could do more than three, so I thought, "Gee, I can do these back stories, too." That's where the 'Chapter IV' came in. Then everyone said, "Well, are you going to do sequels to the first three?" But that was an afterthought. I don't have scripts on those stories. The only notion on that was, wouldn't it be fun to get all the actors to come back when they're sixty or seventy years old and make three more about them as old people. That's how far that has gone, but the first six will definitely get finished.

George Lucas, *Juice* magazine, May 1999:

No, no. [After Star Wars came out] somebody asked me if I was going to do a sequel. And I said, "I'm doing the other two parts to this one." And they said, "You're doing this trilogy-do you have any more?" And I said, "I've got a backstory, which I've got laid out. I could probably do that." And they said, "But are you going to do a sequel?" And I said, "I guess maybe I could do a sequel at some point." And that got turned into doing nine films. It's six films. It's really not nine films. It's extremely unlikely that I will go on and do any more.

George Lucas, *TV Guide*, November 19, 2001:

*What would it take for you to do a third trilogy, with episodes VII, VIII, and IX?*

Lucas: "Each time I do a trilogy it's 10 years out of my life. I'll finish 'Episode III' and I'll be 60. And the next 20 years after that I want to spend doing something other than 'Star Wars'. If at 80 I'm still lively and having a good time and think I can work hard for another 10 years between 80 and 90, I might consider it. But don't count on it. There's nothing written, and it's not like I'm completing something. I'd have to start from scratch. [The idea of episodes VII, VIII, and IX] was more of a media thing than it was me."

Mark Hamill also makes some interesting comments in 2004:

You know when I first did this, it was four trilogies. 12 movies! And out on the desert, any time between setups... lots of free time. And George was talking about this whole thing. I said, "Why are you starting with IV, V and VI? It's crazy." [Imitating Lucas grumble,] "It's the most commercial section of the movie." He said the first trilogy's darker, more serious. And the impression I got, he said, "Um, how'd you like to be in Episode IX?" This is 1976. "When is that going to be?" "2011." I defy anyone to add 36 years to their lives and not be stunned. Even an eight year old is like, "No, I'll never be 47." So I did the math and figured out how old I'd be. I said, "Well, what do you want me to do?" He said, "You'll just be like a cameo. You'll be like Obi Wan handing the lightsaber down to the next new hope."[20]

There have been many misconceptions about this Sequel Trilogy in the years since. The fact that Lucas now asserts that the very basis for these three sequel films were invented by the media is perhaps a reflection of the fact that after Lucas revised the sequel plans in 1980 he never seriously intended to make them, and mainly gave such statements to satisfy fan and media demand. He also likely believed that he could indeed one day make the revised "reunion" type trilogy some years down the road—if he felt up to it, that is. A quote from 2005 reveals the rather simple explanation for the post-1983 talk as merely boiling down to not anticipating the work involved:

> Somebody once asked me in an interview if I would be making sequels to the original trilogy…I said that it might be fun to come back and do sequels with all the characters in their eighties, and to ask Mark [Hamill] to come back when he's eighty. What I forgot, or didn't realise at the time, was that I'd be eighty too! So, no, I'm not going to make another *Star Wars* film at eighty.[21]

Rather than correcting the public that his original plans had been rendered obsolete, he continued to feed the press reports when they continued to ask, perhaps because he felt that maybe he truly could make such a film one day. "I sort of played into it," he admits today, "but I probably shouldn't have."[22]

# Appendix E: The Tales of Gary Kurtz

THE legendary Sequel Trilogy has been fuelled as of late with reports from a newly-resurfaced Gary Kurtz, who is now—or at least was—regularly appearing at fan conventions and conducting interviews after nearly two decades of silence (partially because of the rebirth of *Star Wars* in the late 1990s and partially because he had finally returned to the industry by producing an indie film entitled *5-25-77*, which has a plot which revolves around the opening day of *Star Wars*). He has shared many fascinating anecdotes and revealed a more candid side of the production of *Star Wars*. Among his most fascinating and popular revelations, however, is the supposed "secret history" regarding the Sequel Trilogy and *Return of the Jedi*.

Gary Kurtz, as interviewed by *IGN Filmforce* in 1999:

At that time [of *Empire Strikes Back*], [Lucas] always said that he had enough material for three earlier films and three later films, to make a total of nine, and there were outlined materials certainly for a later three that culminated with this big clash with the Emperor in *Episode IX*. So, we'll never see any of those, based on what he's said now... One of the reasons *Jedi* came out the way it did was because the story outline of how *Jedi* was going to be seemed to get tossed out, and one of the reasons I was really unhappy was the fact that all of the carefully constructed story structure of characters and things that we did in *Empire* was going to carry over into *Jedi*. The resolution of that film was going to be quite bittersweet, with Han Solo being killed, and the princess having to take over as queen of what remained of her people, leaving everybody else. In effect, Luke was left on his own. None of that happened, of course...Much, much less [of a happy ending]. It would have been quite sad, and poignant and upbeat at the same time, because they would have won a battle. But the idea of another attack on another Death Star wasn't there at all...it was a rehash of *Star Wars*, with better visual effects. And there were no Ewoks...it was just entirely different. It was much more adult and straightforward, the story.[1]

## Gary Kurtz, as interviewed by *Film Threat* in 2000:

So the story [for *Return of the Jedi*] was quite a bit more poignant and the ending was the coronation of Leia as the queen of what was left of her people, to take over the royal symbol. That meant she was then isolated from all of the rest and Luke went off then by himself. It was basically a kind of bittersweet ending. She's not his sister that dropped in to wrap up everything neatly. His sister was someone else way over on the other side of the galaxy and she wasn't going to show up until the next episode.[2]

## Second-hand report as given by Paul Ens, the current director of Lucas Online for Lucasfilm, for *TheForce.Net* in 1999:

Gary Kurtz, the producer of ANH and ESB, spoke at the Sci-Fi Expo in Plano, TX this weekend along with his daughters Tiffany and Melissa (as children they played Jawas in ANH). He shared with the crowd about meeting Lucas, leaving the Star Wars films and the original plans for the entire saga...When the time came to produce ROTJ, Kurtz was unhappy with the story direction Lucas was taking. He felt that it was too much of a rehash of the first films with no real challenges. At the same time, Jim Henson was inviting him to produce his experimental film, *Dark Crystal*, which he chose instead.

Kurtz gave TPM a mixed review as he was clouded by plans made for Episode 1 back in the early '70s. As someone involved with Star Wars from the initial concepts, Kurtz revealed the original intentions for the nine films as they were laid out BEFORE 1980. Very interesting.

- EPISODE 1: Was to focus on the origins of the Jedi Knights and how they are initiated and trained
- EPISODE 2: Introduction and development of Obi-Wan Kenobi
- EPISODE 3: Introduction and life of Vader
- EPISODE 4: There were seven different drafts of the film. At one point, they pursued buying the rights to *Hidden Fortress* because of the strong similarities. At one point, Luke was a female, Han was Luke's brother, Luke's father was the one in prison (interesting point for some debates) and the film featured 40 wookies
- EPISODE 5: Once written, the screenplay of Empire is almost exactly what is seen on screen. The only cut scenes were those involving

wampas in the rebel base (cut because of time and unsolved technical glitches) and about two minutes of Luke/Yoda Jedi training with no real dialog.

- EPISODE 6: Leia was to be elected "Queen of her people" leaving her isolated. Han was to die. Luke confronted Vader and went on with his life alone. Leia was not to be Luke's sister.
- EPISODE 7: Third trilogy was to focus on Luke's life as a Jedi, with very few details planned out.
- EPISODE 8: Luke's sister (not Leia) appears from another part of the galaxy.
- EPISODE 9: First appearance of the Emperor."[3]

These three blocks form the basis for the information of Gary Kurtz' version of the Sequel Trilogy. The main tenets of his version of the story are:

- The first three episodes would be a prequel trilogy detailing the Jedi history and Anakin's fall from grace (this is covered in the second half of this appendix)
- The story was not to end with *Return of the Jedi*, but continue until Episode IX
- The last six films of the nine episode saga would be Luke's tale, which would be a "hexology," that is, a six-film continuous series which went as follows:

- In Episode VI, Luke confronts Vader again, while Han is killed and Leia left alone as Queen of Alderaan. Vader dies and Luke leaves Leia to continue the battle
- The Rebel versus Empire plot is not resolved in Episode VI but instead continues for another three films.
- In Episode VII or VIII Luke's twin Jedi sister appears. This is apparently the "Other" that Yoda spoke of. Presumably, she and Luke team up to finally destroy the Emperor
- In Episode IX, the Emperor is finally revealed and killed and the story ends

All of this was scrapped once it came time to actually write the screenplay for Episode VI. The best conclusion that can be gathered from this information then is that all of the future story points were essentially combined into a final film, killing Vader and the Emperor and making Leia into the "Other" and Luke's sister. This was all presumably done because *Empire Strikes Back* had been a stressful and costly fiasco and because Lucas wanted to quickly wrap up the series and get on with his life.

This all makes perfect sense and is very logical. However, what Gary Kurtz has said does not appear to be the case.

The problem is that the *Star Wars* storyline changed so much that Kurtz couldn't keep up with it, and more than twenty-five years of time has blurred everything together.

Chapter V included a summary of the number of story changes prior to 1979. More would come after that, of course, but for the purposes of Gary Kurtz, this is all that is relevant. All told, there are four different storylines and series structures that occurred between 1976 and 1980. That is quite a lot of information to keep track of—especially when Kurtz' main duties were the supervision and management of the production of *Star Wars* and *Empire Strikes Back*, mammoth tasks in themselves, never mind trying to keep track of a complex and intricate storyline that changed four times (and possibly more off the record).

An examination of Kurtz' version of history reveals a curious fact: his story is impossible. It contains elements which were valid only at separate points in time and never co-existed together. For instance, take the "hexology" concept: the story could not be a hexology in which the Empire is not destroyed until Episode IX since Lucas revealed when *Empire Strikes Back* was still filming, in private no less, that not only was the series composed of three trilogies which took place twenty years apart from each other, but he also implied that the Rebel versus Empire plot would be wrapped up in Episode VI.[4]

Another example is the infamous Jedi sister—she was attached to draft one of *Empire Strikes Back* only, back when Father Skywalker was a separate character from Darth Vader. In story meetings it was decided she would appear in one of the sequels. However, this existed as part of the twelve-episode plan, and was not reprised for draft two. Once Vader became Luke's father, the storyline was overhauled and she was eliminated. The "Other" Yoda references is basically unknown, but definitely was not Luke's sister—the fact that the "Other" eventually was developed as his sister in *Return of the Jedi* is incidental. The concept of a continuous story for Luke into the last three episodes—rather than with a twenty year time-break—might come from the twelve-film stage, where the adventures might have continued in such a manner.

What it appears has happened is that Gary Kurtz has combined all the various plot threads which existed at various times in the story developments from 1976 to 1980 into a sort of Super-Storyline, though some of his comments regarding the original configuration of *Return of the Jedi* remain valid. The version which Gary Kurtz describes never existed at any point in time.

Let's examine the individual elements which comprise Gary Kurtz' version of the series and break down their origin.

*The series is nine episodes, composing a prequel trilogy and then a hexology for Luke, which is continuous, with Vader dying in VI and the Emperor not seen until IX.*

This stems from three sources. The first is the original 1977/78 plan—in this, the series is twelve episodes, with *Empire Strikes Back* as Episode II and the Emperor not seen until the end (1977 is included because although this plan was not revealed until March 1978 in *Time*, it was likely in place as early as late 1977). The second is the 1979 plan—this added three prequel films and a sequel trilogy, and had Vader dying in Episode VI.

The nine episode aspect stems from the 1979 plan, the prequel aspect stems from the 1979 plan, the hexology aspect Kurtz has probably developed out of the 1977/78 plan, the Emperor not battled until the final episode aspect seems to be common in every incarnation of the series, while Vader dying in Episode VI comes from the 1979 plan.

Kurtz remembers nine episodes as being the length, he remembers a prequel trilogy in place, he remembers Vader dying in Episode VI and he remembers Luke's story as being continuous and for more than just three films; therefore he has concluded that in order to fulfill the nine-episode structure, Luke's story must be six films long with the prequels occupying the first three, with the Emperor being faced at the end of the series (which, following this logic, would therefore be Episode IX) and Vader dying in Episode VI. But these elements are not all from the same version of the saga. Once the plan was made to make the saga three trilogies, Luke's immediate story was decided as being only three films, and it was also decided to kill Vader and the Empire at the end of that trilogy, rather than stretch it out for twelve films in a continuing storyline.

The sister is along similar lines.

*The "Other" appears in the sequels and is Luke's twin Jedi sister who helps him defeat the Empire*

Consistent with his belief that the series for Luke was to be a continuous six episode hexology, he also remembers the "Other" as being a prominent player in the last three films and a twin Jedi sister showing up, thus linking these two characters as the same.

This has two sources. The first is the twin Jedi sister plot from the 1977/78 plan—in this version the series was twelve episodes long; the first draft of *Empire Strikes Back* has Father Skywalker revealing that Luke has a twin Jedi sister, and it was decided in story meetings that she would appear in the sequels. One can imagine them teaming up to avenge their father's killer and defeating the Empire. This was not reprised for the second draft when Vader was made into the father, for obvious reasons. The second source is the 1979 plan, which was a nine-episode three-trilogy version. In this version there is an "Other" mentioned in *Empire Strikes Back* whom would appear prominently in the Sequel Trilogy.

So, Kurtz remembers the twin Jedi sister, who appears in later episodes, and he remembers an "Other" who would appear in the sequels. He combined them into the same person, as many fans have done themselves. But they are from two completely different versions of the film and are two different characters.

### *Han would die and Leia would be Queen of her people*

This is harder to say for sure but it appears to have been an alternate version of the *Return of the Jedi* storyline, created in the event that Harrison Ford refused to appear in the film and Han would have to be killed off. Lucas desperately wanted Han to live but if Ford refused he would have to be killed, leaving Leia by herself to take up the Alderaan crest. On the other hand, it is also plausible that Han was to be rescued but then killed off at the end, and that Lucas simply changed his mind in 1981 when he finally wrote the script. However, this is not conclusive.

Kurtz has taken bits and pieces from all the various revisions to the story and basically fused them together—inadvertently, most likely. Twenty years of time has only added to the confusion. Additionally, he may even be "selectively" remembering the aspects which he liked the most, which he believed, or had been led to believe, the series was still going with.

Kurtz' favouring of his "hexology" plot may be due to the fact that it he was he who first proposed that rather than three inter-connected trilogies, the series could be individual chapters of a single narrative, which the saga would ironically eventually become with Lucas' prequel developments in the 1990s. "If we ever got the first film off the ground," Kurtz remembered in a *Starlog* article, "I thought it would be nice to do several episodes that fit together into one giant story."[5]

In addition to the sequels, he has also commented on the original plans for the prequels.

Speaking to *IGN Film Force* in 1999:

Well a lot of the prequel ideas were very, very vague. It's really difficult to say. I can't remember much about that at all, except dealing with the Clone Wars and the formation of the Jedi Knights in the first place—that was supposed to be one of the keys of *Episode I*, was going to be how the Jedi Knights came to be. But all of those notes were abandoned completely.[6]

And *Film Threat* in 2000:

Well, I find it really difficult to have any kind of objectivity about [*Phantom Menace*] because I know I was around when we were talking about what the first three stories would be like and what he was thinking about. Some of the treatments had references to that and episode one was going to be about the origin of the Jedi and the killing off of the Sith Lords and much more kind of archetypal, political aspects. He's perfectly free to write and make what he wants to make, but because of all of that, I find seeing this film really difficult.[7]

And the report by Paul Ens, director of Lucas Online at Lucasfilm:

EPISODE 1: Was to focus on the origins of the Jedi Knights and how they are initiated and trained
EPISODE 2: Introduction and development of Obi-Wan Kenobi
EPISODE 3: Introduction and life of Vader[8]

His comments about the prequels are equally inaccurate. The fact that an entire film is supposedly dedicated to exploring the history of the Jedi is enough to dispel this—in his version, Anakin and Obi Wan are hardly in the storyline. The prequels were created specifically *because* of the Obi Wan-Anakin storyline—when Lucas merged Father Skywalker with Darth Vader in 1978, he created a dramatic and tragic backstory that was so interesting that *Empire Strikes Back* was moved from Episode II to Episode V.

So, what are the origins of Kurtz' bizarre comments? Likely, it is due to the initial post-release 1977 version of the series, wherein there was no main protagonist to the series and each film would explore different characters, aspects and even time periods. "One of the original ideas of doing a sequel [was] that if I put enough people in it and it was designed carefully enough I could make a sequel about anything," Lucas told *Rolling Stone* in August of 1977. "One of the sequels we are thinking of is the young days of Ben Kenobi. It would probably be all different actors." The films would not necessarily follow chronological sequence, and focus on different characters and storylines. As Alan Arnold wrote, "[Gary Kurtz] described [*Star Wars II*] as 'a new chapter in the *Star Wars* saga,' because the intention is never to refer to it as a sequel for the simple reason that future George Lucas stories do not have chronological sequence."[9] Likely one of these storylines bandied about was the history of the Jedi, taking place hundreds or even thousands of years before the events in *Star Wars*. Looking at the *TheForce.Net*'s report of Kurtz' information, this makes perfect sense—the plan he describes is obviously for the original 1977 version of the saga wherein Father Skywalker was his own character. One film details the ancient days of the Jedi. Another focuses on Obi Wan and Father Skywalker and their battles in the Clone Wars. Darth Vader did not enter the story until after the Clone Wars are complete, which is why he does not appear until the last prequel film, which details his betrayal and murder of Father Skywalker and the toppling of the Republic.

Once again, this was never part of the proper prequel trilogy, and Kurtz has simply combined it with the rest of the separate storylines. He remembers all of these story ideas as being planned for films which took place before *Star Wars*, and he remembers three prequels being decided on, so he combined the two.

Thus, we see that Gary Kurtz' statements on the Sequels and Prequels represent a confused amalgamation of virtually every single plot point from four different storylines (and possibly more) from 1976 to 1980.

# Appendix F: The Tales of Dale Pollock

IN the early '80s Dale Pollock was asked to write a biography on George Lucas, at the time the first ever such publication and the only time Lucas has ever collaborated with a journalist on a biography about himself. "I was asked by Crown Publishers to write an unauthorized biography, and my big coup was getting Lucas to agree. He has never made that mistake again," Pollock recollected to the *Washington Post*.[1] Pollock's finished book was highly detailed, balanced in opinion and mostly comprised of direct quotations and first hand knowledge. "I did more than 70 hours of interviews personally with Lucas, lived at Skywalker Ranch for two weeks, and spent time on the set of *Return of the Jedi*," Pollock remembered. "Additionally, I interviewed close to 100 other individuals who grew up with him, worked with him, or did business with him."[2] Lucas subsequently has denounced Pollock's book, saying it is inaccurate. "He hated it because it's honest, doesn't pull any punches, and was well-researched (i.e., does not rely on only George's version of life and the universe.)," Pollock stated. "I think it was upsetting to him to actually read what he said about people. The irony is that I was worried throughout the writing of the book that I was being way too nice to him, and that people would accuse me of kissing his butt. I was surprised by the vehemence of his reaction, because to me, twenty-one years later, the book is a very balanced portrait."[3]

Consequently, Pollock is the only member of the general public who spent any considerable time with Lucas during the creation of the original trilogy. He is also one of the few people who have had free access to Lucasfilm's archives and Lucas' original *Star Wars* documents, which at that time were a complete mystery to the public.

Dale Pollock has claimed in a recent interview that, probably sometime around 1981 or 1982, he was allowed to see brief synopses for plots for the Sequel Trilogy. He cannot reveal what they were, however, as he was only allowed to see them after signing a confidentiality agreement. He has also made the astounding statement that Lucas had developed story synopses for twelve films, and that each was roughly five to eight pages in length, with the most detailed ones covering the first six episodes, and even that Jar Jar or a similar character was part of one of them. These statements come from a transcript of an internet chat conducted through the *Washington Post* in May of 2005. The correspondences:

Alexandria, Va.: Jar Jar Binks is one of the most loathed characters in film history, and to many he represents what is 'wrong' with today's George Lucas. Why didn't someone step back and say, 'This character is too annoying for words?' Do you think Jar Jar's severely reduced role since Phantom Menace is evidence that Lucas is not completely immune to outside criticism?

Dale Pollock: I think Lucas is as immune to outside criticism as he has always been. He doesn't care what anyone else thinks other than a very small circle of close friends. But I think JAR JAR was only there for one film (I remember seeing the character mentioned in only one story outline that I read, provided by George)and just didn't fit into the other ones. Characters come and go in the STAR WARS films. We've barely seen a Wookie again until Episode III.

...

Denver, Colo.: Professor: How much of the prequel stories do you believe Lucas had in mind as he created the original Star Wars trilogy? Was it simply a very broad concept, or do you suppose he had quite a bit of details in mind, such the role of Qui Gon, Darth Maul, etc.?

Dale Pollock: He had very specific outlines, which each ran 5-8 pages. I read them for a total of 12 films, so at least that many were planned. The most detailed synopses were for Episodes I-VI. He says he has no more STAR WARS features planned, but I still think he could change his mind, because I know he worked out stories that followed the original 3 films.

...

Washington, D.C.: I feel that Lucas' claim that he wrote Episodes I through III before he wrote the old movies is bogus, self-serving tripe, and that he simply had a very rough outline of those stories before 1999. What do you think?

Dale Pollock: I never saw actual screenplays for Episodes I-III, but there were very detailed story outlines, with certain character names, but not all. I think he started in the middle because of the excruciating set-up we all witnessed in Episodes I and II. If he had started there, we wouldn't all be on this chat room now.

...

Arlington, Va.: Pray tell... can you summarize the plots of the three unmade Star Wars synopses you were able to read?

Dale Pollock: I had to sign a confidentiality agreement to read them, so I'm afraid I cannot.[4]

This seems to contradict every single quote Lucas has ever said, which have consistently stated that the entire trilogy-spanning outline was no more than twelve pages, hence explaining that Episodes I and II only occupied roughly twenty percent of it and that Lucas had to invent the rest of the plot. Pollock's comments here are inconsistent with everything else we know about the development of *Star Wars* and it can be reasonably suspected that these comments—made in 2005, almost twenty-five years after he supposedly read these treatments—are simply the exaggerated product of confusion. But, are we to write off such unorthodox and incredible statements so quickly? After all, Pollock was the only non-Lucasfilm employee allowed access to Lucas' archives and his writing; and he was the first and, to this day, one of the few people who has had some kind of direct contact with the once-mythical *Journal of the Whills* summary.

Furthermore, Pollock's statement that the story material covered up to twelve films is truly amazing—at the time Pollock began writing his famous book (circa 1981 or 1982), Lucas had reverted to the nine-film saga, and this is all Pollock has ever reported; the twelve-film saga was only seldom mentioned in a brief period much earlier, and is so obscure that most do not even remember these long-forgotten statements. Pollock himself was hired by his publisher to write the Lucas bio, and so he obviously was not following minute details of the *Star Wars* development beforehand. His report that the series had twelve stories developed for it seems to be not of a confused remembrance of information gleaned elsewhere—he seems to report the matter unaware that Lucasfilm announced these twelve films in 1978, and hence these statements must be accurate.

All of this also means that the story treatments Pollock read for the sequel trilogy were perhaps the earliest versions, seeing as Pollock also had access to the *sequel-sequel*-trilogy—episodes X-XII, which were only developed in early 1978 and existed for a few brief months, and would have been considered apocrypha by 1982 when the majority of Pollock's book was written.

First, I suspect that Pollock's memory of each film having its own five to eight page outline is erroneous. This is simply due to the fact that Lucas consistently—and against interest—reports that Episode I and II were faced with the problem in that they only contained a small section of his original seven to twelve page trilogy outline. Lucas describes the length of this trilogy outline as various amounts but I have placed it at the lower estimation of seven pages, which he has frequently stated. Therefore Pollock's statement that the individual films were averaging at seven pages or so each is likely a confusion based on the fact that the entire trilogy was merely represented by that number of pages ("with certain character names," as he reports). As for Jar Jar being a part of it, this can be explained that the first draft of 1974 contains a major character named "Bink" (he is Deak Starkiller in the rough draft), which is assuredly what he is actually remembering, consistent with the fact that Pollock remembers the character only being in one story. This shows that his recollections are not as accurate as they may first appear.

The twelve episode plan only existed for a brief period around early 1978 and was made obsolete by Lucas' second draft of *Empire* a few months later in April. Although a few vague notions of sequel ideas are bandied about in the story conferences for *Empire* in late 1977 (i.e. the twin sister), no actual story development was done between Lucas and Brackett. This would then indicate that Lucas may have gone off in private—perhaps in the period in which Brackett herself was writing the first draft, from December to February—and tried to flesh out some plot ideas for future episodes. It is hard to believe, however, that he created five to eight pages per film, especially since Lucas was already quite busy in that precise time period writing the treatment for *Raiders* and engaging in its story conferences.[5] If we are to take Pollock's quote literally, this would mean that Lucas at one time in early 1978 had written up to 96 pages (or more) of story treatments for his twelve-film saga. Rather, it is likely that these *Sequel-Sequel*-trilogy ideas were perhaps cumulatively only a couple pages, and very likely not even proper treatments but unordered hand-written notes, ideas and plot points, if in fact this is what Pollock actually saw, which is highly debatable.

Pollock also states that the story synopses for episodes I to VI were far more detailed than the sequels, which is consistent with what we know. This then means that if we have deduced that the prequel treatment was only about seven pages for the entire trilogy then the sequel trilogy outline was only three or four pages long. His notes on the sequel-sequel-trilogy, episodes X to XII, were likely even shorter, if they in fact existed at all. Pollock may very well have simply come across material which *indicated* that twelve films were being considered, not actual content created for these later films.

When all of these are combined with the story treatments Lucas had developed by that point for the original trilogy—complete *Star Wars*, *Empire* and *Jedi* synopses—the total amount of pages would easily exceed forty or fifty pages, which is an impressive amount of material, in addition to other notes Lucas had written, perhaps explaining why, twenty-five years later, Pollock remembers it as being much larger.

# Appendix G: The Tales of Jonathan Rinzler

IN May of 2007, celebrating the thirtieth anniversary of the film, Lucasfilm published Jonathan Rinzler's *The Making of Star Wars*, a mammoth book that meticulously detailed the production of the classic original. Aside from free access to Lucasfilm and its elaborate archives, this was accomplished mainly by the discovery of the so-called "Lost Interviews" which Charles Lippincott originally conducted from 1975-1978 for a making-of book that never was released, literally thousands of pages of interview transcriptions. This means that the book is based on the participants of the film reflecting and commenting on it either before or during its production and immediately thereafter, and is reinforced by other Lucasfilm documents from this period. As a result it is candid and refreshing in that it reflects the original perspective of the film, untainted by success or sequels. It also unveiled the hitherto private notes and story conferencing of George Lucas as he developed each of the drafts, revealing a remarkable insight into the creative process of that film.

An early draft of *The Secret History of Star Wars* was released online roughly a month before Rinzler's book, and I'm glad I wrote "the production of *Star Wars* has been covered by a plethora of other sources and need not be repeated here," because anything I could have said would be pretty redundant now. But the most pertinent issues are how does this book contradict or re-enforce my own conclusions? I was unsurprised—but also relieved—to discover that there were no major incompatibilities. Tons of information was provided that expanded and supplemented my own research, such as the third draft outline that I once wondered aloud about, as well an in-depth summary of the original *Journal of the Whills*—but there was no such fabled "Tragedy of Darth Vader" script unearthed, nor any personal note of Lucas' that pondered "make Vader Luke's father?" Indeed, this mammoth text may be the very indisputable proof against any Vader-centric story ambitions, for it details specifically and repeatedly how Lucas' story was Luke's and how Vader was inconsequential to it, showing that Lucas—unsurprisingly—regarded Vader exactly as he was written: a rather minor player in the story, a mere villain (and not the unrevealed key to some existing "Saga" plan).

There are, however, four instances where it may be surmised that contradictions crop up. One is where Lucas explains that Leia was always Luke's twin, for example, and another is where it is stated that Darth Vader's origin will be explored in a sequel. Some, no doubt, may uphold these as evidence that Lucas truly did have the basic saga figured out, at least in general terms—but these four instances are not what they appear to be. As I will explain, they themselves are either insertions from later sources—the Lost Interviews are not the only source Rinzler used—or are themselves explainable in other, simpler ways.

The first to be looked at is the one that is most explicit in its statement:

> Between the second and third drafts, Lucas wrote a six-page story synopsis. Dated May 1, 1975...Not long afterward Lucas, uncharacteristically, typed out a new outline...Lucas changed [Luke from a girl back into a boy], while at the same time resuscitating the princess. "It was at that moment," says the writer, "that I came up with the idea that Luke and the princess are twins. I simply divided the character in two."[1]

However, this quote is glaringly out of place in the context of the book. Aside from this statement, the overriding impression one gets is that Luke and Leia are unrelated—mainly because of the whole fairy tale motif where Luke is the naïve peasant who has to rescue the kidnapped princess, and despite this statement about Lucas deciding they are twins, they are still developed independently of one another, and there literally is no evidence of any linkage aside from this one isolated statement. But secondly, Lucas never once spoke of Leia as a twin before 1981, and this comment has a very retrospective tone—I find it hard to believe that this was something Lucas had said in the 1970s (and this is all aside from the fact that Lucas has implicitly admitted that the Sister Leia point was made up in 1981 with his admission that *Empire*'s "Other" line was not in reference to her but merely a suspense device). This may be cleared up when you look at Rinzler's interview sources—he spoke to Lucas three times in 2006. Undoubtedly these three interviews produced this statement.

These are generalised arguments but more specific ones better refute this statement. The biggest is the one I already spoke of in the main body of this work—Leia is explicitly described as being the specific age of sixteen. Luke, on the other hand, in the script is actually twenty: "LUKE STARKILLER, a farm boy with heroic aspirations who looks much younger than his twenty years," is how the revised fourth draft describes him, though this was somewhat give-and-take as the film was actually made; publicity material would later alternatively describe him as nineteen or eighteen—but clearly he is not to be sixteen like Leia. This is backed up in Rinzler's book by casting director Dianne Crittenden: "The princess was supposed to be about sixteen, Luke was about eighteen, and Han was in his early twenties."[2] For the practical purposes of shooting, however, Leia had to be over eighteen so that underage union laws would not slow down filming, and Harrison Ford's eventual casting led to Han being portrayed as someone in his late twenties rather than an early twenties "James Dean" type as it was written. Lucas also says that Leia has two younger brothers, age four and seven, on page 351.

The third contradiction of this comment is Lucas' own thoughts on sequels in December 1975. Practically the only specific ideas he speaks of for any sequels is that he wants Luke and Leia kissing in the second film! He describes it as a romance, *Gone With the Wind in Outer Space*, but with Han leaving and Leia and Luke getting together.[3] Alan Dean Foster would eventually implement this in his sequel *Splinter of the Mind's Eye*, which is rife with sexual tension between Luke and Leia. By the time Lucas got to *Empire Strikes Back* a few years later, however, he found the opportunity to take the story in slightly different directions, though in the treatment and first draft a plot point revolves around the fact that Luke is in love with Leia, and of course there is that notorious open-mouth kiss in the final film itself.

Lucas' statement does have some merit—Luke and Leia *are* twins, but metaphorical ones, not literal ones, in the same sense that Luke and Han are brothers of a sort. Han evolved out of Luke as a contrast to him, and Leia evolved in the same way. "All the characters came out of one composite—Luke," Lucas said in 1979. "Luke Skywalker might never have been; he might have been a heroine. Leia came out of Luke, so to speak, just as Han did, as the opposite of Luke. Han Solo evolved from my wanting to have a cynical foil for the innocent Luke. A lot of the characters came out of Luke because Luke had many aspects. So I took certain aspects of the composite Luke and put them into other characters."[4] Leia is like Luke in a lot of ways but is confident where he is unsure, active where is awkward. Han too is a closer twin to Luke—both start out as a nobody and become a hero, and one of the least emphasized arcs of the original film is Han's; he undergoes the exact same hero's journey as Luke, and it's no surprise that it is Luke and Han who stand side by side with medals at the conclusion, dressed in similar attire. Costume designer John Mollo told how this was intentional in Rinzler's book: "George said, 'No, I think [Luke] ought to look a bit more like Han [for the medal scene].' It was a very last minute thing, but we concocted an outfit like Han's in different colors."[5] Lucas even once stated, "Han Solo and Luke are like twin brothers, the spiritual brother and the warrior brother with the devil-may care attitude."[6] And of course, caught between them is a sort of sister figure if we think of the trio as functioning as a family unit that is a three-fold reflection of Lucas, with Leia bickering with the older brother Han and providing an example of leadership for the awkward younger brother Luke (though she still exists as a sort of outsider from the core Luke-Han duality, which also allows the subdued sexual rivalry for her).

The next quote has two parts to address. In this one Lucas hints at a Skywalker family drama and also hints at Vader's origins.

I want to have Luke kiss the princess in the second book. The second book will be *Gone With the Wind in Outer Space*. She likes Luke, but Han is Clarke Gable. Well, she may appear to get Luke, because in the end I want Han to leave. Han splits at the end of the second book and we learn who Darth Vader is...In the third book, I want the story to be just about the soap opera of the Skywalker family, which ends with the destruction of the Empire. Then someday I want to do the backstory of Kenobi as a young man—a story of the Jedi and how the Emperor eventually takes over and turns the whole thing from the Republic into an Empire, and tricks all the Jedi and kills them. The whole battle where Luke's father gets killed. That's impossible to do, but it's great to dream.[7]

This, however, is often viewed with the contemporary version of *Star Wars* in mind. Looking at it with simply the original film in mind, we get a different picture. Firstly, "we learn who Darth Vader is" should not necessarily be read as some kind of shocking father revelation; all Lucas is saying is that Vader's origins would be explored. These origins were that he was once a Jedi student of Kenobi's but betrayed the Jedi and killed Luke's father. With Luke having to confront him in the sequels, these issues would be natural to deal with and expand upon, and Lucas was even fantasizing about showing these events in a prequel-sequel. In fact, in practically the same breath as this statement Lucas goes on to explain how Luke's father is killed, and, as covered before, given that these were made in a private conference with Foster—who was writing the very sequels in which such a Father Vader revelation would have been made—for a movie that was thought to be unsuccessful and which no one held any interest in at that point, there's no reason why Lucas would be hiding anything; in fact he goes on to explain exactly what he means, stating how Luke's father was killed in battle. Lucas even spoils the ending for the sequel—Han may look like he will get Leia but Luke ends up with her.

Aside from that, it is worth seriously considering that Lucas planned on revealing Vader as the killer of Luke's father in that very sequel—after all, at the time Lucas made that statement, Luke's father was not killed by Vader, instead dying anonymously in battle. It is possible that "we learn who Darth Vader is" in the sequel would be this very reveal that Lucas had developed at that time in December of 1975. However, realising that he might only make the first film, Lucas felt that *Star Wars* would be better served by having this terrific addition included in that film rather than an up-in-the-air sequel that was currently only existing in the form of a novelisation from Foster. As pointed out before, the fourth draft had numerous changes to make it function better as a stand-alone film, probably because Lucas was growing pessimistic about the prospect of sequel films. Hence, a few months after Lucas made the comment about revealing Vader's further history in the sequel, it ended up being included in March's revised fourth draft.

Additionally, if Lucas was saving the "big Father Vader reveal" for the sequel, it is unbelievable that not only does *Splinter of the Mind's Eye* have no such element in it, but that Lucas' own treatment for *Empire*, made in late 1977, contains no such Father Vader reveal either, nor does Brackett's first draft. Why would Lucas not implement the main plot point in the trilogy when he finally got the chance to do so? The answer is because the big "reveal" was incorporated into *Star Wars* itself when Lucas changed his mind and decided that it would better suit that film since that was all he had (the sequels he discusses here are not films—they are books to be written by Foster; technically, Lucas had no movie sequels since the Fox contract would not be finalised until months later).

With this in mind, it may also give us further insight into the developments made in Vader throughout the third draft outline, third draft, and fourth draft. In the third draft outline Luke faced Darth in a lightsaber match and killed him, but because the scene ruined the pacing Lucas eliminated it for the third draft, but had Vader survive the film so that the scene might be reprised in a sequel. With Luke facing Darth in a lightsaber match in the second film, Vader could make the shocking revelation that it was he who in fact killed Luke's father, giving Luke not only a physical battle but an emotional wound as well—but then Lucas included this information in the revised fourth draft screenplay, so this development could not be used in the sequel confrontation. This may even lend further credence to Lucas' troubles when crafting *Empire*'s original climax; the face-to-face confrontation was originally saved with the revelation in mind, but when that revelation was moved into the first film, the Vader confrontation in *Star Wars II* had much less weight, as made obvious in Brackett's first draft, thus Lucas gave Vader a *different* revelation for Luke about his father. Speculatory perhaps, but interesting to ponder.

The second part of that statement is along similar lines—"soap opera of the Skywalker family." As covered in the main body of this book, a major part of Luke's story arc for the sequel would be the developing relationship between him and Vader, and that his destiny as a Jedi would be to avenge his father by finally slaying Darth, with the father's own lightsaber no less, a pretty operatic and mythic notion. Thus, the Skywalker family soap opera is more about Luke avenging Father Skywalker—there *is* a family soap opera at play in the film, and it has to do with the son's vengeance of the father ultimately symbolising his triumph as a Jedi, a triumph not culminating until the final film. The eventual sequels reinforce both of these things: in *Empire Strikes Back* draft one and *Splinter of the Mind's Eye*, Luke and Leia are in love, with Han leaving at the end of draft one (he is not even present for *Splinter*), and Luke battling Vader on behalf of his father is a major part of both as well, especially in draft one of *Empire* where the "soap opera of the Skywalker family" is given added weight by the fact that Father Skywalker himself returns in ghost form to induct Luke into Jedi Knighthood and take up the fight which he was killed in (though it's highly debatable if Lucas had this particular ghost-plot in mind at this time).

Finally, in that first *Empire* draft there was also the addition of a twin Skywalker sister who is also training to be a Jedi—this particular plot point was discussed by Lucas and Brackett in late 1977. It was also a concept that had been a major part of the early drafts of *Star Wars*. It may be wondered if Lucas had this aspect in mind at the time of making this 1975 statement; certainly that is a possibility, although there is nothing to suggest as much so we must take it with a grain of salt.

So to sum up, there was indeed a Skywalker family soap opera at play, and it's at play in *Star Wars* as well—Luke's father being a Jedi, being killed by Vader and then Luke taking up the sword and continuing the battle on his behalf. "I want to learn the ways of the Force and become a Jedi like my father." Family heritage is a major part of the story.

The final quote to be examined is one which looks to place The Duel, and the tragedy of Darth Vader being crippled, as being developed much earlier. In Chapter III we saw that the fourth draft of *Star Wars* is absent of any hints of The Duel, and that the concept of a volcano confrontation appears to have been developed somewhere between the fourth draft and the film's production, with the crippling aspect which necessitates the life-support-suit an aspect added in post-production—and Rinzler's book seems to reinforce this, as there is no hint of a duel story point being in place before the timeline I lay out. On page 111 Lucas states:

> The backstory is about Ben and Luke's father and Vader, when they are young Jedi Knights. Vader kills Luke's father, then Ben and Vader have a confrontation, just like they have in Star Wars, and Ben almost kills Vader. As a matter of fact, he falls into a volcanic pit and gets fried and is one destroyed being. That's why he has to wear the suit with a mask, because it's a breathing mask. It's like a walking iron lung. His face is all horrible inside. I was going to have a close-up of Vader where you could see the inside of his face, but then we said, "No, no, it would destroy the mystique of the whole thing."[8]

This, however, is a direct quote from Paul Scanlon's August 25th, 1977 interview with Lucas for *Rolling Stone*. Rinzler lists that interview as one of his sources, and he quotes from it in a few other places as well. So, there still is no evidence of it being in place before 1976; though Lucas maintains that it was in place all along, it was, in fact, developed in an evolutionary manner that only came to have the details noted above in post-production, not late 1975 as Rinzler places it. Rinzler's logic for placing it here is two-fold: Ben Kenobi ceases to be mechanical in the fourth draft, and so he surmises that Vader was turned into the mechanoid, while Lucas also states that he didn't develop Vader's character until the fourth draft. This last point, again, is in reference to his past, however—most of Vader's history, that is being a Jedi, being a student of Obi Wan's, and being a betrayer of the Jedi, was actually in place in the third draft, but the crucial plot point about him actually being the murderer of Luke's father and the all-purpose Sith-represerter does not occur until the revised fourth draft (or the fourth draft if Lucas had developed the murder plot point at that time but originally saved it for a sequel).

So, these apparent inconsistencies aren't really inconsistencies at all, they just take a little bit of research to better understand their meaning.

Aside from these three or four statements, Rinzler's book is honest, thoroughly researched, and expertly written.

# Appendix H: Script and Writing Sources

PRESENTED here is a list of all the currently known screenplays drafts, treatments and notes that were created by George Lucas, and on occasion in collaboration with a writing partner, for the series. *Annotated Screenplays* lists additional revisions omitted here, such as revisions to specific sequences (ie the Battle of Yavin for *Star Wars*) and script copies with handwritten annotations, and Rinzler also provides some additional copies of Episode III scripts with handwritten annotations. With regards to notes, I have included here only those accounted for with documentation or excerpting, which basically only extensively covers *Star Wars*, although I also include some surmised documents which are indicated as such.

- List of characters
  Undated. These are believed to have been written **circa January 1973**, just prior to beginning the *Journal of the Whills*, along with the list of planets. The first name listed is Emperor Ford Xerxes XII. Others include Thorpe, Lars, Kane, Hayden, Mace, Bail and Leila. Lucas then combined names and assigned them roles.

- List of planets
  Written during the same time as the list of characters, **circa January 1973**. Planets include Yavin, Yoshiro, Anchorhead, Starbuck and Kissel.

- *Journal of the Whills*
  **Undated, two-page handwritten plot summary** about C.J. Thorpe and his adventures with Mace Windy. Began **circa January, 1973**.

- *The Star Wars*
  **Treatment May, 1973**
  Ten-page handwritten document, typed into fourteen pages, begun in April and completed in early May, which is a remake of *Hidden Fortress*, telling the tale of General Skywalker's journey to protect "the princess" as they race through enemy territory

- Undated notes. Some detail plot and character, but many also sketch out the environment, developing the fascist Galactic Empire and its rebellion.

- *The Star Wars*
  **Rough draft May 1974**
  Lucas' first script, telling of the young Annikin Starkiller, as he is trained as a Jedi-bendu by his father, Kane Starkiller, and his mentor, General Luke Skywalker.

- *The Star Wars*
  **First draft July 1974**
  Same as above but with different names.

- Undated notes. Further ideas on plot and character.

- *Adventures of the Starkiller. Episode I: The Star Wars*
  **Second draft January 28th, 1975**
  Major revision of the previous story, simplifying the first quarter. The main character is now named Luke and is introduced on a farm. His father is an ancient guru named The Starkiller whom Luke must return the Kiber crystal to after rescuing his captured brother Deak.

- Notes, **January 30th, 1975**. *Annotated Screenplays* lists handwritten notes on this date. Whether these are the same as, or feed into, the ones described by Rinzler (here listed after the third draft outline) is unknown.

- *The Adventures of Luke Starkiller (episode one) "The Star Wars"*
  **Second draft synopsis May 1st, 1975**

Lucas typed up a six-page synopsis of the second draft to inform Fox executives on the current state of the script. Here the princess is re-instated, whom Luke must rescue.

- **Third draft outline circa May 1ˢᵗ, 1975**
  Around the same time as the above synopsis, Lucas also typed up an outline for his impending third draft. This outline contains the unique elements of a proto-Kenobi in the form of an "Old Man" on the side of the road who accompanies and instructs Luke along the way, as well as Luke facing Darth Vader in a lightsaber match at the very end.

- Undated notes. Most seem to explore developing Luke's character and arc.

- *The Star Wars: From the Adventures of the Starkiller*
  **Third Draft August 1ˢᵗ, 1975**
  Similar to the second draft except Princess Leia is reinstated and Ben Kenobi is introduced as the mentor figure.

- Undated notes.

- Around this time, the background notes that would help form the prequel story became more solidified. Among these would be the creation of Ben Kenobi, the development of Darth Vader as his failed student, and possibly more specific details surrounding the rise of Senator Palpatine in the old Republic. These would be added to when making the fourth draft, such as having Vader kill Skywalker, and after the fourth draft other details, such as the volcano duel, would also be added to the evolving story. The "prequel" treatment is not an actual treatment—rather it is an organized and unorganized collection of the background info, character outlines and plot trivia sketching out the film's history that Lucas had created by that point, totalling between 7 and 12 pages long, with the shorter estimation being the more likely one. Lucas also says that, sometime around the third or fourth draft, he also sketched out sequel plot points. My estimation is that it more likely occurred during the writing of the fourth draft.

- *The Adventures of Luke Starkiller as taken from the Journal of the Whills. Saga I: The Star Wars.*
  **Fourth Draft January 1ˢᵗ, 1976**

Notable additions include the elimination of the other Sith characters and Kiber crystal, the combination of the Death Star and Alderaan prison complex, and the death of Aunt Beru and Uncle Owen.

- *The Adventures of Luke Starkiller as taken from the Journal of the Whills. Saga I: The Star Wars.*
**Revised Fourth draft March 15<sup>th</sup>, 1976**
Willard and Gloria Huyck rewrite some of the dialogue and add some character bits. Lucas also continues to tweak it during shooting, changing Starkiller to Skywalker and killing off Ben Kenobi. In this draft Kenobi says Vader is the killer of Luke's father.

- *The Empire Strikes Back*
**Treatment November 28<sup>th</sup> 1977**
Nineteen pages, hand-written by George Lucas, resulting from the story conferences and apparently begun during their midst.

- **Story conferences** between Leigh Brackett and George Lucas **November 28<sup>th</sup>-December 2<sup>nd</sup>**
On the same date that the treatment bears, conferencing began with Leigh Brackett, lasting about a week. The film is designated as "Chapter II." The meetings were tape-recorded and transcribed.

- *Star Wars Sequel*
**First Draft February 23<sup>rd</sup>, 1978**
Leigh Brackett's draft. Amusingly, Brackett never even titled it, simply scrawling "star wars sequel" on the first page. There doesn't appear to be any numerical designation. Unique deviations include the ghost of Father Skywalker appearing to reveal that Luke has a sister and Han leaving the film to search for his long-lost father-figure.

- *Episode II: The Empire Strikes Back*
**Second Draft April 1978**
The "great divide" of *Star Wars* where Vader reveals he is Luke's father. Other additions include Han being frozen. This draft was written by Lucas.

- **Revised second draft April 1978**
No title is ascribed to this draft, according to *Annotated Screenplays*. Also written by Lucas.

- **Third draft April 1978**
  No title is ascribed to this draft, according to *Annotated Screenplays*.
  Once again, written by Lucas.

- **Story conferences** between Lawrence Kasdan, Irvin Kershner, Gary
  Kurtz and George Lucas **October 1978**
  These apparently were recorded, but *Annotated Screenplays* does not
  account for them. Pollock places them in November but since Kasdan
  completed a draft in late October they must have occurred in that
  month at the very latest. Here the film became more introspective and
  character-centred. Kurtz' presence seems to be more of a formality,
  though he did make his opinions and suggestions known, while
  according to Kershner he himself concentrated on character, Kasdan on
  dialogue and Lucas on plot.

- **Fourth draft October 1978**
  *Annotated Screenplays* strangely does not account for a fourth draft,
  but states that there are "fourth draft revisions dated **October 24th,
  1978**." This was the first draft that Lawrence Kasdan wrote.

- *Star Wars Episode V The Empire Strikes Back*
  **Fifth draft February 20th, 1979**
  This shooting script is credited to Kasdan and Brackett, although
  virtually none of Brackett's script contributions supposedly survive.
  The dialogue and scene blocking is also loose since Kershner changed
  and improvised some scenes. The version of this screenplay publically
  available omits many of the original scene configurations in favour for
  transcriptions of the revised (and, for at least one scene, reshot)
  versions as per the final edit of the film. A good example is the carbon
  freezing of Han Solo, which Alan Arnold's book details was originally
  scripted very differently.

- *Star Wars Episode VI: Revenge of the Jedi*
  **First draft February 20th, 1981**
  This draft, according to *Annotated Screenplays*, is handwritten. It is
  also not summarised in that book, but given that the "rough draft" was
  completed only days later it is reasonable to presume that it is merely
  a rougher version of that.

- *Star Wars Episode VI: Revenge of the Jedi*
  **Rough draft February 24th, 1981**
  This draft reads like a somewhat more straightforward version of the revision made later, with Vader in a more traditional villain role, competing with Jerjerrod and the Emperor for possession of Luke.

- *Star Wars Episode VI: Revenge of the Jedi*
  **Revised rough draft June 12th, 1981**
  In this major revision (a better way to think of the progression is the "first draft" as a rough draft, the "rough draft" as the revised version of that, and this as the real first draft) the story is told in parallel from Vader's perspective as he is turned into a sympathetic character.

- **Story conferences** between Lawrence Kasdan, Richard Marquand, Howard Kazanjian and George Lucas **July 13th-17th, 1981**
  As with *Empire*, these were recorded and transcribed. Again, the inclusion of the producer can be seen more as a formality rather than a creative collaboration.

- *Star Wars Episode VI: Revenge of the Jedi*
  **Second draft September 21st, 1981**
  This screenplay was written by Kasdan, and is credited as "story by George Lucas, screenplay by Lawrence Kasdan." Notable changes include the elimination of Had Abbadon, the return of Vader to a more villainous role and the instatement of Dagobah

- *Star Wars Episode VI: Return of the Jedi*
  **Revised Second draft November 1st, 1981**
  This version credits the screenplay to both Lucas and Kasdan. *The Annotated Screenplays* describes it as having handwritten notes with it, which resulted in *another* "Revised second draft" bearing the date of November 11th– with these drafts being titled *Return* of the Jedi.

- *Star Wars Episode VI: Return of the Jedi*
  **Third draft December 1st, 1981**
  Credited to Kasdan and Lucas once again.

- Notes, **December 15th, 1981**. Dubbed the "wookie doodle pad," these were miscellaneous handwritten notes made by Lawrence Kasdan, apparently with regards to Han Solo.

- *The Annotated Screenplays* also lists "Lucas **revisions** dated **January 4ᵗʰ, 1982**." Shooting occurred shortly thereafter.

- **Prequel expansion notes and outlines, circa 1993**
  Approximately around this time Lucas began the process of slowly developing elaborate notes on the detailed world and story he would build for the prequels, supplementing the many original notes he had accumulated by the completion of *Return of the Jedi* ten years earlier. By the next year they are collected in a red binder and organized by subject, such as Jedi, Empire and Outline. Just when this whole process occurred in somewhat unclear: he had preliminary interest in making the films since 1992, but wouldn't actually get around to writing the screenplay until 1994. 1993 is a good estimation for the surmised start of the bulk of this note expansion, which is also the year that the films were announced as going into production.

- *The Beginning*
  **Rough draft January 13ᵗʰ, 1995**
  Began on November 1ˢᵗ, 1994 and simply titled "The Beginning." Tells the tale of Obi Wan Kenobi, who is thrust into the invasion of Utapau and discovers slave child Anakin Skywalker on Tatooine, vowing to train him as a Jedi.

- *The Beginning*
  **Revised Rough draft January 13ᵗʰ, 1995**
  The revised rough draft is attributed to this date as well.

- *The Beginning*
  **First Draft January 13ᵗʰ, 1995**
  The typed first draft also is attributed to the same date. Presumably, these three are virtually identical.

- **Second draft 1995?**
  Notable for replacing Obi Wan's lead role with Qui Gon, demoting Kenobi to a student, as well as introducing elements such as midichlorians. Quotes from Lucas indicate that by late summer 1995 he still had not completed a second draft, but I estimate that a late 1995 date is appropriate for this. There may have been a revision made to this in early 1996; according to *The Making of Episode I*, the screenplay is "more or less" complete by 1996, when pre-production went into full-swing.

- **Third draft May 13ᵗʰ 1997**

- **Revised third draft June 6ᵗʰ, 1997**
  The shooting script. It is unknown when the change occurred to "Phantom Menace." It may well have been not until 1999, and the 1998 rough cut is still called The Beginning.

- **Additional scenes** were shot in **August 1998** and then in three more periods in the next seven months, including one where Palpatine notices young Anakin.

- *Episode II: Jar Jar's Great Adventure*
  **Rough draft March 13ᵗʰ, 2000**
  The title is meant to be a joke, since Lucas had not come up with one yet. Lucas says that although this was the first version typed up that, in accordance with his writing style, he had quickly completed many drafts before this; Doug Chiang remembers a draft in January. Among the more unique elements known about this is that the wedding of Anakin and Padme occurred mid-way through the story and was a larger focal point.

- **Story conferences** between George Lucas and Jonathan Hales **circa June**; these last roughly a day and a half, with most of it being Lucas explaining the story and his intentions.

- **First draft? (circa June 2000?)**
  Jonathan Hales supplements Lucas' draft while shooting is about to commence. After Lucas reads it he phones Hales with recommendations.

- **Second draft? (circa June 2000)**
  Hales makes additional changes as per Lucas' requests. Lucas then revised the final shooting script himself.

- **Third draft (circa June 2000?)**
  The shooting script by Lucas and Hales. According to Lucas it was completed roughly a week before the June 26ᵗʰ principal photography start.

- **Additional scenes** shot in **March and April and October and November 2001**, notably introducing the concept that Dooku was Qui Gon's master.

- Episode III preliminary outline
  **August 2002**
  Lucas begins outlining the film while on vacation in Canada, realising that his story is too full and that he has to reconfigure the film.

- List of planets
  **October 25ᵗʰ, 2002**
  Created more for the art department than anything, Lucas drew up a list of the thirteen planets planned to be seen in the film, with brief descriptions of them.

- Revised Episode III outline
  **Circa January 2003**
  Lucas re-writes a revised outline of the film, now with the structure that would be utilised in the screenplays. It is divided into three acts, with each act broken down into sections describing the major sequences and/or plot points and what happens in them.

- *Star Wars Episode III: Revenge of the Sith*
  **Rough draft January 31ˢᵗ, 2003**
  Reads like a highly simplified script or a very detailed outline, being only 55 pages.

- *Star Wars Episode III: Revenge of the Sith*
  **First draft April 10ᵗʰ, 2003**
  110 pages long first draft removes the child Han Solo as well as Sidious' claim that he is Anakin's father, adding the tale of Darth Plagueis and Yoda's confrontation with the Emperor.

- *Star Wars Episode III: Revenge of the Sith*
  **Second draft circa June 2003**

- *Star Wars Episode III: Revenge of the Sith*
  **Revised second draft June 13ᵗʰ, 2003**
  Notable for the change in Anakin's dream that Padme dies in childbirth.

- *Star Wars Episode III: Revenge of the Sith*
  **Third draft circa June 2003**

- *Star Wars Episode III: Revenge of the Sith*
  **Fourth draft June 26th, 2003**
  Completed days before filming, being 129 pages long. Adds additional dialogue bits, including Kenobi's "you were the chosen one!" monologue.

- **Principal photography** commences on **June 30th, 2003.** Lucas is revealed onset to have made additional revisions to the script, as in one documented video clip he reveals to Christensen that he rewrote the scene where he turns to the dark side to make it more drawn out. Other onset changes include the alteration of the Darth Plagueis tale from being staged in Palpatine's office to being staged in an opera house.

- In post-production, massive story changes are made, rewriting Anakin's character so that he stays loyal to the Jedi and is driven to the dark side out of his obsession for Padme. This was accomplished primarily through **additional scenes** shot in pick ups in **August 2004** and **January 2005.**

# Endnotes

## Introduction

[1] Lucas says he began writing the treatment on April 17th, 1973 in Starwars.com *Homing Beacon* # 223. This intro is somewhat inaccurate, however, but I use it more for dramatic effect: firstly, though in the first and second edition of the self-published online version of this book I attributed Lucas to living on Portola Drive, this is probably not true; he lived there while at USC but shortly before he was married, while writing *THX 1138* in late 1968, he and Marcia moved into a house somewhere in Mill Valley (as writes Marcus Hearn, on page 33 of *The Cinema of George Lucas*). The exact address of this location is still unknown to me, despite my best retroactive stalking efforts. In this edition I have changed the street name to Medway Avenue, the location of the home they bought just before *Grafitti* came out. However, the first home the Lucas' lived in 1968 until mid 1973, after Portola and before Medway, is still unknown, and wherever this was it would be where Lucas actually first wrote *Star Wars*. Secondly, though some—including myself—often speak of *Star Wars* beginning with this treatment, the truth is slightly more complicated, for Lucas had already taken a stab at it with the *Journal of the Whills*. However, since that was a somewhat unrelated piece that was discarded, *Star Wars* traces most of its direct origins to this treatment.

[2] "Religion of the Jedi Knights", *Museum of Hoaxes*, http://www.museumofhoaxes.com/jedi.html. The religion was later dismissed by officials due to the prank-like nature of the whole event—though a genuine faith called "Jediism" has also sprouted, vaguely New Age/Buddhist-like in beliefs. See http://www.thejediismway.org/

[3] *Star Wars* Definitive Edition Laserdisc interview, 1993

[4] *Once Upon A Galaxy: A Journal of the Making of The Empire Strikes Back* by Alan Arnold, 1980, p. 223

[5] BBC interview by Anwar Brett, May 18th, 2005, http://www.bbc.co.uk/films/2005/05/18/george_lucas_star_wars_episode_iii_interview.shtml

## Chapter I: The Beginning

[1] "Burden of Dreams: George Lucas" by Aljean Harmetz, *American Film*, June 1983

[2] *Skywalking: The Life and Films of George Lucas* by Dale Pollock, 1983, p. 12

[3] Pollock, p. 36

[4] Pollock, p. 36

[5] Pollock, p. 38

[6] "Luke Skywalker Goes Home" by Bernard Weinraub, *Playboy*, July 1997

[7] "I've Got to Get My Life Back Again" by Gerald Clarke, *Time*, May 23rd, 1983

[8] "I've Got to Get My Life Back Again" by Gerald Clarke, *Time*, May 23rd, 1983

[9] Arnold, p. 219

[10] Pollock, p. 19

[11] *Academy of Achievement* interview, June 19th, 1999, http://www.achievement.org/autodoc/page/luc0int-1

[12] "George Lucas Goes Far Out," by Stephen Zito, *American Film*, April 1977

[13] Arnold, p. 221

[14] *Icons: Intimate Portraits*, "The Dark Side of George Lucas" by Denise Worrell, 1989, p. 188

[15] "The George Lucas Saga" by Kerry O' Quinn, *Starlog*, July 1981

[16] Arnold, pp. 220-222

[17] "Star Wars Origins" by Kristen Brennan, 1999, http://www.jitterbug.com/origins/flash.html. This website has moved since this book was first published in 2007, though I will still attribute its original URL. It can now be found at http://moongadget.com/origins/index.html.

[18] "Star Wars Origins" by Kristen Brennan, 1999, http://www.jitterbug.com/origins/flash.html

[19] "Burden of Dreams: George Lucas" by Aljean Harmetz, *American Film*, June 1983

[20] *60 Minutes*, March 28th, 1999

[21] "The George Lucas Saga" by Kerry O' Quinn, *Starlog*, August 1981

[22] "George Lucas Interview" by Ty Burr, *The Boston Globe*, October 2005, http://www.boston.com/ae/movies/lucas_interview

[23] "Letter From Skywalker Ranch: Why is the Force Still With Us?" by John Seabrook, *The New Yorker*, January 6th, 1997

[24] Arnold, p. 188

[25] "Dialog: George Lucas" by Steve Galloway, *Hollywood Reporter*, June 9, 2005

[26] *The Cinema of George Lucas* by Marcus Hearn, 2005, p. 16

[27] "Life After Darth" by Steve Silberman, *Wired*, May 2005

[28] "Life After Darth" by Steve Silberman, *Wired*, May 2005

[29] Pollock, p. 35

[30] Hearn, p. 16

[31] Pollock, p. 41

[32] "The George Lucas Saga" by Kerry O' Quinn, *Starlog*, August 1981

[33] Pollock, p. 47

[34] Interview on *The Hidden Fortress* DVD, Criterion, 2001

[35] "The George Lucas Saga" by Kerry O' Quinn, *Starlog*, July 1981

[36] "The Filming of American Graffiti" by Larry Sturhahn, *Filmmakers Newsletter*, March 1974

[37] *Academy of Achievement*, June 19th 1999, http://www.achievement.org/autodoc/page/luc0int-1

[38] Pollock, p. 67

[39] Pollock, p. 59

[40] Hearn, p.22

[41] "The Empire Strikes Back and So Does Filmmaker George Lucas With His Sequel to Star Wars" by Jean Vallely, *Rolling Stone*, June 12th, 1980

[42] Pollock, p. 72

[43] Pollock, p. 72

[44] Hearn, p. 28

[45] "A Legacy of Filmmakers: The Early Years of American Zoetrope", *THX 1138* DVD, 2004

[46] "The Morning of the Magician: George Lucas and Star Wars" by Claire Clouzot, *Ecran*, September 15th, 1977

[47] *Mythmaker: The Life and Works of George Lucas* by John Baxter, 1999, pp. 84-85

[48] "The George Lucas Saga" by Kerry O' Quinn, *Starlog*, July 1981

[49] *Cinema By The Bay*, by Sheerly Avni, 2006, p. 220

[50] "A Legacy of Filmmakers: The Early Years of American Zoetrope", *THX 1138* DVD, 2004

[51] "A Legacy of Filmmakers: The Early Years of American Zoetrope", *THX 1138* DVD, 2004

[52] Avni, p. 30

[53] "A Legacy of Filmmakers: The Early Years of American Zoetrope", *THX 1138* DVD, 2004

[54] "A Legacy of Filmmakers: The Early Years of American Zoetrope", *THX 1138* DVD, 2004

[55] Avni, p. 31

[56] This is reported in Pollock, p. 73, and other sources, but John Baxter shows that, as inspiring a story as it is, it's inaccurate. See Baxter, p. 30

[57] *Easy Riders, Raging Bulls* by Peter Biskind, 1998, p. 22

[58] Biskind, p. 22

[59] Biskind, pp. 125-26

[60] "The Legacy of 2001," *2001* DVD, 2007

[61] Lucas even credits these two novels as being one of the few that impressed him (along with *Verne's 20, 000 Leagues Under the Sea*) on page 220 of Arnold's book

[62] "Artifact From The Future", *THX 1138* DVD, 2004

[63] Hearn, pp. 37-38

[64] "Artifact From The Future, *THX 1138* DVD, 2004

[65] Hearn, p. 37

[66] Hearn, p. 38

[67] Pollock, p. 66

[68] Pollock, p. 65

[69] *Biography: George Lucas*, A&E, 2001

[70] "George Lucas: The Stinky Kid Hits the Big Time" by Stephen Farber, *Film Quarterly*, vol. 27, no. 3, spring 1974

[71] "The George Lucas Saga" by Kerry O' Quinn, *Starlog*, July 1981

[72] "George Lucas" by David Sheff, *Rolling Stone*, November 5th, 1987

[73] *Bantha Tracks*, issue 1, May 1978

[74] "The George Lucas Saga" by Kerry O' Quinn, *Starlog*, July 1981

[75] "Star Wars Memories" by Kerry O' Quinn, *Starlog* 127, February 1988, p. 59, from *Phoenix Gazette*

[76] *The Making of Star Wars* by J.W. Rinzler, 2007, p. 2

[77] "George Lucas: The Well-Rounded Interview" by Well-Rounded Entertainment, http://www.well-rounded.com/movies/reviews/lucas_intv.html

[78] "The Empire Strikes Back and So Does Filmmaker George Lucas With His Sequel to Star Wars" by Jean Vallely, *Rolling Stone*, June 12th, 1980

[79] "The Empire Strikes Back and So Does Filmmaker George Lucas With His Sequel to Star Wars" by Jean Vallely, *Rolling Stone*, June 12th, 1980

[80] Baxter, p. 117

[81] "The Filming of American Graffiti" by Larry Sturhahn, *Filmmaker Newsletter*, March 1974

[82] Arnold, p. 196

[83] "The Empire Strikes Back and So Does Filmmaker George Lucas With His Sequel to Star Wars" by Jean Vallely, *Rolling Stone*, June 12th, 1980

[84] Biskind, p. 237

[85] Biskind, p. 237

[86] Hearn, pp. 61-62

[87] "The George Lucas Saga" by Kerry O' Quinn, *Starlog*, July 1981

[88] Pollock, p. 101

[89] Baxter, p. 66

[90] Pollock, p. 82

[91] Pollock, p. 83

[92] "George Lucas: The Stinky Kid Hits the Big Time" by Stephen Farber, *Film Quarterly*, vol. 27, no. 3, spring 1974

[93] "The George Lucas Saga" by Kerry O' Quinn, *Starlog*, July 1981

## Chapter II: The Star Wars

[1] "An Interview With Gary Kurtz", *IGN Film Force* online, November 11th, 2002, http://filmforce.ign.com/articles/376/376873p1.html

[2] Rinzler, *Making of Star Wars*, p. 6

[3] Rinzler, *Making of Star Wars*, p. 2

[4] Rinzler, *Making of Star Wars*, p. 4

[5] "A Long Time Ago: The Story of Star Wars," BBC Omnibus TV special, 1999

[6] "George Lucas Goes Far Out" by Stephen Zito, *American Film*, April 1977

[7] *Mediascene Prevue* , issue 42, 1980

[8] Rinzler, *Making of Star Wars*, p. 15

[9] "George Lucas: The Stinky Kid Hits The Big Time" by Stephen Farber, *Film Quarterly*, vol. 27, no. 3, spring 1974

[10] *Bantha Tracks*, issue 8, May 1980

[11] "The George Lucas Saga" by Kerry O' Quinn, *Starlog*, July 1981

[12] Biskind, p. 243

[13] "The Empire Strikes Back and So Does Filmmaker George Lucas With His Sequel to Star Wars" by Jean Valley, *Rolling Stone*, June 12th, 1980

[14] Rinzler, *Making of Star Wars*, p. 8

[15] Rinzler, *Making of Star Wars*, p. 8

[16] Baxter, p. 142

[17] Rinzler, *Making of Star Wars*, p. 97

[18] Baxter, p. 158

[19] Rinzler, *Making of Star Wars*, p. 9

[20] *The Warrior's Camera* by Stephen Prince, 1991, p. 36

[21] *Akira Kurosawa: It is Wonderful to Create*, 2002

[22] Starwars.com *Homing Beacon* #223, Thursday, April 17th, 2008. It reports that this info comes from a 1983 *Rolling Stone* interview with Lucas. In that interview Lucas also allegedly states that he completed it on May 20th—the *Homing Beacon* addresses the apparent contradiction in Rinzler's book. Their explanation is that the version submitted in the first week of May to UA might have been an earlier draft, and that Lucas continued writing it until the 20th. This may or may not be correct.

[23] As related in end-note 1, this timeline has been through a revision with information recently supplied by Jonathan Rinzler. The handwritten original merely states "May 1973" on its cover page, and the typed version begins with this date as well. However, it was thought that this treatment was actually dated to May 25th, 1973, since that date is suffixed in the bootlegged copy of the treatment. This, however, has turned out not to be the case—the typed version of this treatment was in existence as early as May 7th, 1973. This is revealed on page 11 of *The Making of Star Wars*, where Rinzler explains that United Artists VP David Chasman was given a copy of the fourteen-page typed treatment on that date. This treatment, then, comes from the very first week of May. However, given the info in the prior footenote—that Lucas alledges that it was May 20th that he actually completed it—it gives rise the theory that the May 25th date on the bootleg may be legitimate; perhaps the initial version was submitted in early May, but then the final version was not typed up by Lucas' secretary until the 25th (with Lucas' 1983 *Rolling Stone* quote regarding the 20th either being an approximation, a slight inaccuracy, or merely the date of completion of the handwritten original).

Its length is also clarified by Rinzler—he states on page 9 that the handwritten version was ten pages long, and clarifies that the typed version is fourteen pages, and not thirteen pages as is sometimes reported.

[24] "The Development of Star Wars as Seen Through the Scripts by George Lucas" by Jan Helander, 1997, http://www.starwarz.com/starkiller/writings/development_jan. htm

[25] "The Development of Star Wars as Seen Through the Scripts by George Lucas" by Jan Helander, 1997, http://www.starwarz.com/starkiller/writings/development_jan.

htm

[26] *The Films of Akira Kurosawa* by Donald Richie, 1965, pp. 134- 139

[27] Richie, p. 137

[28] Richie, p. 31

[29] Encyclopedia Brittanica

[30] Enclopedia Encarta, 2001edition

[31] *The Star Wars Souvenir Program*, 1977

[32] Arnold, p. 188

[33] "George Lucas: The Stinky Kid Hits the Big Time" by Stephen Farber, *Film Quarterly*, vol. 27, no. 3, spring 1974

[34] "George Lucas: The Stinky Kid Hits the Big Time" by Stephen Farber, *Film Quarterly*, vol. 27, no. 3, spring 1974

[35] "Star Wars The Years Best Movie", *Time*, May 30th, 1977

[36] *Star Wars* DVD commentary, 2004

[37] *The Making of Star Wars As Told By R2-D2 And C-3P0.* Lucasfilm, 1977

[38] *The Apocalypse Now Book* by Peter Crowie, 2001, p.1

[39] Rinzler, *Making of Star Wars*, p. 8

[40] Interestingly in the 1993 Definitive Edition Laserdisc commentary track for *Star Wars*, Ralph McQuarrie states that Lucas wanted him to initially base Chewbacca on an image he got of a lemur-like alien from some old magazine.

[41] *Chaplin* magazine, fall 1973

[42] In *The Cinema of George Lucas*, p. 80, Marcus Hearn states that the film was submitted to Universal in February—but this was before the fourteen-page treatment even existed. As Rinzler shows in *The Making of Star Wars*, it was actually in the summer, just before *Graffiti* was released.

[43] Rinzler, *Making of Star Wars*, p. 11

[44] Baxter, pp. 145-146

[45] Baxter, pp. 153-54

[46] Baxter, p. 51

[47] Rinzler, *Making of Star Wars*, pp. 24-25

[48] Baxter, p. 154

[49] Rinzler, *Making of Star Wars*, p. 14

[50] This is deduced from an interview published in *Filmmakers Newsletter* in March 1974, where Lucas states that he has been working on the screenplay for six months time

[51] *The Unauthorized Star Wars Compendium* introduction by Ted Edwards, 1999. Here Lucas says he was jotting down ideas while vacationing after *Graffiti* came out.

[52] Pollock, p. 144

[53] "The Morning of the Magician: George Lucas and Star Wars" by Claire Clouzot, *Ecran*, September 15th, 1977

[54] Rinzler, *Making of Star Wars*, p. 15

[55] *The Unauthorized Star Wars Compendium* introduction by Ted Edwards, 1999

[56] Pollock, pp. 141-42

[57] "The George Lucas Saga" by Kerry O' Quinn, *Starlog*, July 1981

[58] Rinzler, *Making of Star Wars*, p. 16

[59] Worrell, p. 182

[60] Worrell, p. 182

[61] Rinzler, *Making of Star Wars*, p. 18

[62] Rinzler, *Making of Star Wars*, p. 18

[63] Rinzler, *Making of Star Wars*, p. 16

[64] For additional discussion on this development, see the article "The Birth of Father Skywalker", http://secrethistoryofstarwars.com/birthoffatherskywalker.html

[65] Pollock, pp. 141-43

[66] Pollock, pp. 141-43

[67] Rinzler, *Making of Star Wars*, pp. 14-15

[68] Rinzler, *Making of Star Wars*, p. 16

[69] "The Development of Star Wars as Seen Through the Scripts by George Lucas" by Jan Helander, 1997, http://www.starwarz.com/starkiller/writings/development_jan.htm

[70] "George Lucas: Mapping the Mythology", CNN Online, May 8th 2002, http://archives.cnn.com/2002/SHOWBIZ/Movies/05/07/ca.s02.george.lucas/

[71] For example, his comments in an interview on the 1993 Definitive Edition Laserdisc, as well as his August 1977 interview with *Rolling Stone*, where he gives even greater detail. He repeats many of these throughout the commentary track on the 2004 *Return of the Jedi* DVD

[72] Worrell, p. 185

[73] "Mark Hamill", *Preview* magazine, 1983

[74] Rinzler, *Making of Star Wars*, p. 18

[75] "Life After Darth" by Steve Silberman, *Wired*, May 2005

[76] Rinzler, *Making of Star Wars*, p. 18. Here he says it is a deleted scene. However the same scene is excerpted by Marcus Hearn on page 33 of *The Cinema of George Lucas*, revealing it to be from the first draft. While it is possible that it appeared in the first draft, survived the final draft, was filmed but then deleted, it's far more likely that Rinzler was simply not entirely accurate in his description of it being "deleted" (ie it was in fact deleted after the first draft) and that he got this info from Hearn, whose book predates Rinzler's.

[77] "The Filming of American Graffiti" by Larry Sturhahn, *Filmmakers Newsletter*, March 1974

[78] "George Lucas: The Stinky Kid Hits The Big Time" by Stephen Farber, *Film Quarterly*, vol. 27, no. 3, Spring 1974

[79] Baxter, pp. 155-157

[80] Baxter, p. 157

[81] "A Long Time Ago: The Story of Star Wars," BBC Omnibus TV special, 1999

[82] Pollock, p. 147

[83] Rinzler, *Making of Star Wars*, p. 24

[84] Biskind, pp. 255-256

[85] Hearn, p. 78

[86] Pollock, p. 222

[87] Hearn, p. 78

[88] Hearn, p. 78

## Chapter III: Enter Luke Starkiller

[1] Rinzler, *Making of Star Wars*, p. 25

[2] Rinzler, *Making of Star Wars*, p. 9

[3] "Galactic Gasbag" by Stephen Hart, Salon.com, April 10th, 2002, http://www.salon.com/ent/movies/feature/2002/04/10/lucas

[4] "Star Wars Origins" by Kristen Brennan, 1999, http://www.jitterbug.com/origins/flash.html

[5] Rinzler, *Making of Star Wars*, p. 26

[6] Rinzler, *Making of Star Wars*, pp. 93-94

[7] Arnold, p. 226

[8] Rinzler, *Making of Star Wars*, pp. 25-26

[9] "The Development of Star Wars as Seen Through the Scripts by George Lucas" by Jan Helander, 1997, http://www.starwarz.com/starkiller/writings/development_jan.htm

[10] Pollock, pp. 146-147

[11] "George Lucas Goes Far Out" by Stephen Zito, *American Film*, April 1977

[12] Rinzler, *Making of Star Wars*, p. 15

[13] Rinzler, *Making of Star Wars*, p. 15

[14] Rinzler, *Making of Star Wars*, p. 15

[15] Rinzler, *Making of Star Wars*, p. 26

[16] Arnold, p. 223

[17] Rinzler, *Making of Star Wars*, p. 94

[18] *Mythmaking: Behind the Scenes of Attack of the Clones* by Jody Duncan, 2002, pp. 101-103

[19] "The Force Behind Star Wars" by Paul Scanlon, *Rolling Stone*, August 25th 1977

[20] *The Best of the Lucasfilm Archives* by Mark Cotta Vaz and Shinji Hatta, 1994, p. 14

[21] Rinzler, *Making of Star Wars*, p. 35

[22] *Star Wars Insider*, issue 50, July/August 2000, p. 63

[23] Pollock, p. 149

[24] Rinzler, *Making of Star Wars*, p. 34

[25] Pollock, p. 149 states that Lucas provided McQuarrie with comic books. In many interviews Lucas gave immediately following the release of *Star Wars* he would discuss contemporary comic books, being especially fond of the work of Moebius and Druillet, acclaimed illustrators of the *Heavy Metal* magazine (for example, see Arnold, p. 222). In fact, Moebius, Druillet and *Heavy Metal* (originally called *Metal Hurlant* in its native France) may have helped give Lucas the inspiration for his junky "used universe"—the stunning science fiction and fantasy illustrations of this magazine featured grimy, gritty, lived-in worlds, with tattered clothes, broken-down and rusted surfaces, fine detail and textures abound; this was the same source that also inspired Ridley Scott's similar art direction for *Alien* and *Blade Runner*.

[26] *Star Wars Insider*, issue 50, July/August 2000, p. 63

[27] Baxter, p. 158

[28] "George Lucas: The Stinky Kid Hits The Big Time" by Stephen Farber, *Film Quarterly*, vol. 27, no. 3, Spring 1974

[29] Rinzler, *Making of Star Wars*, p. 31

[30] Rinzler, *Making of Star Wars*, p. 31

[31] Baxter, p. 165

[32] "A Long Time Ago: The Story of Star Wars", BBC Omnibus documentary, 1999

[33] Worrell, p. 182

[34] Rinzler, *Making of Star Wars*, pp. 46-47

[35] Rinzler says this occurred in the last days of March, 1975. See Rinzler, *The Making of Star Wars*, p. 40

[36] Rinzler, *Making of Star Wars*, p. 40

[37] Pollock, p. 148. Rinzler corroborates this on page 42 of his *Making of.*

[38] Pollock, p. 148

[39] Pollock, p. 148

[40] *The Annotated Screenplays* by Laurent Bouzereau, 1997 , p. 3. Rinzler, *Making of Star Wars*, p. 47

[41] Rinzler, *Making of Star Wars*, p. 47

[42] Rinzler, *Making of Star Wars*, pp. 47-49

[43] Rinzler, *Making of Star Wars*, p. 58

[44] Rinzler, *Making of Star Wars*, p. 58

[45] Rinzler, *Making of Star Wars*, p. 59

[46] Rinzler, *Making of Star Wars*, p. 59

[47] Rinzler, *Making of Star Wars*, p. 63

[48] "The Development of Star Wars as Seen Through the Scripts by George Lucas" by Jan Helander, 1997, http://www.starwarz.com/starkiller/writings/development_jan.htm

[49] *Star Wars* Definitive Edition Laserdisc interview, 1993

[50] *The Big Breakfast*, July 16th, 1999

[51] Bouzereau, *Annotated Screenplays*, p. 120

[52] *Star Wars* DVD commentary, 2004

[53] Rinzler reports that, though Lucas had planned at this time to reserve his rights to sequels, with his lawyer Tom Pollock sending Fox a letter requesting this right as far back as September 1974 (p. 25), Fox was so stubborn that the contract was not begun formal negotiations until Februrary of 1976. It dragged on well into March, but by that time Lucas had written the revised fourth draft where the film became more self-contained.

[54] Rinzler, *Making of Star Wars*, p. 106

[55] Rinzler, *Making of Star Wars*, pp. 106-107

[56] Rinzler, *Making of Star Wars*, pp. 93-94

[57] Rinzler, *Making of Star Wars*, p. 106

[58] Bouzereau, *Annotated Screenplays*, p. 7

[59] Rinzler, *Making of Star Wars*, p. 132

[60] Rinzler, *Making of Star Wars*, p. 133

[61] Rinzler, *Making of Star Wars*, p. 169

[62] Baxter, p. 162

[63] Rinzler, *Making of Star Wars*, p. 155

[64] Rinzler, *Making of Star Wars*, p. 352

[65] *Star Wars* novelisation, by Alan Dean Foster, 1976, p. 80

[66] Rinzler, *Making of Star Wars*, p. 119

[67] Rinzler, *Making of Star Wars*, p. 352

[68] Rinzler, *Making of Star Wars*, p. 25

[69] Rinzler, *Making of Star Wars*, p. 352

[70] "Luke Skywalker is Alive and Well" by David Packer, *Starlog*, November 1980

[71] "The Force Behind Star Wars" by Paul Scanlon, *Rolling Stone*, August 25th, 1977

[72] *Empire Strikes Back* Definitive Edition Laserdisc Interview, 1993

[73] *Empire Strikes Back* Definitive Edition Laserdisc Interview, 1993

[74] *Star Wars Poster Monthly*, issue 4, Fall 1977

[75] Bouzereau, *Annotated Screenplays*, p. 14

[76] "The Morning of the Magician" by Clair Clouzqt, *Ecran*, September 15th, 1977

[77] "The George Lucas Saga" by Kerry O' Quinn, *Starlog*, July 1981

[78] Rinzler, *Making of Star Wars*, p. 94

[79] Rinzler, *Making of Star Wars*, p. 132

## Chapter IV: Purgatory and Beyond

[1] This is a slightly complicated issue: the contract was not completed until 1976, and though a memo deal had been closed in 1973 when Fox first bought the project, they would not concretely work out these rights until the actual contract years later. Nonetheless, Lucas made it clear at the time of writing the second draft that he was interesting in maintaining rights to any sequels and merchandising (for instance, Rinzler, p. 25). See *The Making of Star Wars* for a more detailed examination.

[2] Interview by Mr. Showbiz, www.mrshowbiz.go.com/interviews/299_3.html, January 31st, 1997

[3] For example, *Annotated Screenplays*, p. 120. Gary Kurtz also seems to vouch for post-*Star Wars* story material, although he may very well be referring to material made for the 1979 nine-film plan; see http://movies.ign.com/articles/376/376873p4.html.

[4] Worrell, p. 185

[5] Bouzereau, *Annotated Screenplays*, p. 120

[6] This is mentioned in the *Empire Strikes Back* DVD commentary, 2004. He also speaks of this in the 1993 Definitive Edition Laserdisc interview. In an interview with *Static Multimedia* in 2005 he also explains: "I do things. I kill Obi-Wan off and turn him into a ghost, but then I got stuck in the second film because I still had that character to deal with and so I created Yoda to sort of be the alternate Obi-Wan. If Obi-Wan had lived, that was his part." (http://www.staticmultimedia.com/film/features/feature_11156 43931)

[7] Rinzler, *Making of Star Wars*, p. 107

[8] Rinzler, *Making of Star Wars*, p. 59

[9] Rinzler, *Making of Star Wars*, p. 224

[10] Rinzler, *Making of Star Wars*, p. 107

[11] Hearn, p. 102

546

[12] Rinzler, pp. 84-85. These included more practical recycling of elements (ie extras from one scene re-used in another scene), the deletion of entire scenes, the scaling down of the Mos Eisely hanger, the deletion of the entire location of Alderaan (with that action moved onto the Death Star), moving the Rebel base from the jungle to the interior of a temple, and the scaling down of Ben's multi-leveled cave to a small hut.

[13] "Sith Strikes Again", *Entertainment Tonight Online*, May 30th, 2005, http://et.tv.yahoo.com/movies/11198. He says similarly: "I never intended for the back story to be told," in Static Multimedia's, "George Lucas Interview: The Greatest Story Ever Told," by R. Burke, September 10th, 2005, http://www.staticmultimedia.com/film/features/feature_111564 3931

[14] Bouzereau, *Annotated Screenplays*, p. 123

[15] *The Charlie Rose Show*, September 9th, 2004

[16] *Mediascene Prevue* , issue 42, 1980

[17] *Mediascene Prevue* , issue 42, 1980

[18] "*George Lucas*" article in *The Movie Brats* by Micahel Pye and Lynda Myles, 1979

[19] IMDB Studio Briefing, September 13th, 2004, http://www.imdb.com/news/sb/2004-09-13#film6

[20] Pollock, p. 155

[21] Some sources claim March 25th, but March 22nd is the actual date, as evident by the shooting schedule provided in *The Cinema of George Lucas*, p. 116. Rinzler confirms this.

[22] "The Force Behind Star Wars" by Paul Scanlon, *Rolling Stone*, August 25th 1977

[23] Rinzler, *The Making of Star Wars*, p. 85

[24] "The Force Behind Star Wars" by Paul Scanlon, *Rolling Stone*, August 25th 1977

[25] Biskind, p. 330

[26] Biskind, p. 334

[27] Pollock, p. 222

[28] Rinzler, *Making of Star Wars*, p. 107

[29] "Interview with Alan Dean Foster (Part One)" by T'Bone, starwarz.com, July 3, 2002, http://www.starwarz.com/tbone/interviews/alandeanfoster1.ht m

[30] see "Interview with Alan Dean Foster (Part One)" by T'Bone, starwarz.com, July 3, 2002, http://www.starwarz.com/tbone/interviews/alandeanfoster1.ht m

[31] "Starlog Salutes Star Wars", *Starlog*, July 1987, p. 42

[32] I have come across reports that *Splinter* came out in March. My 1994 reprinting says that the hardcover version was first published in February 1978, and the first paperback printing in April 1978.

[33] Rinzler, *Making of Star Wars*, p. 107

[34] Rinzler, Making of Star Wars, p. 133

[35] "The George Lucas Saga" by Kerry O' Quinn, *Starlog*, July 1981

[36] Biskind, p. 336

[37] Biskind, p. 336

[38] "The George Lucas Saga" by Kerry O' Quinn, *Starlog*, July 1981

[39] Rinzler, *Making of Star Wars*, p. 298

[40] Pollock, p. 182

[41] Pollock, p. 182

[42] Rinzler, *Making of Star Wars*, p. 300

[43] Rinzler, *Making of Star Wars*, p. 298

[44] Arnold, p. 183

[45] "Starlog Salutes Star Wars", *Starlog*, July 1987, p. 41

[46] Baxter, p. 254

[47] "An Interview with Gary Kurtz", Ken P., *IGN Film Force* online, November 11th, 2002, http://filmforce.ign.com/articles/376/376873p1.html

[48] *Revenge of the Sith* DVD featurette "The Chosen One", 2005

[49] Interview by Mr. Showbiz, www.mrshowbiz.go.com/interviews/299_3.html, January 31st, 1997

[50] "The Force Behind Star Wars" by Paul Scanlon, *Rolling Stone*, August 25th 1977

[51] "The Force Behind Star Wars" by Paul Scanlon, *Rolling Stone*, August 25th 1977

[52] "The Force Behind Star Wars" by Paul Scanlon, *Rolling Stone*, August 25th 1977

[53] "Empire Strikes Back and So Does Filmmaker George Lucas With His Sequel to Star Wars" by Jean Vallely, *Rolling Stone*, June 12th, 1980

[54] *The Making of Star Wars as Told by C-3P0 and R2-D2*, 1977

[55] *Science Fiction Magazine*, June 1978

[56] Arnold, p. 3

[57] "The Force Behind Star Wars" by Paul Scanlon, *Rolling Stone*, August 25th 1977

[58] *Gossip Magazine*, 1978

[59] "George Lucas' Galactic Empire", *Time*, March 6, 1978

[60] *Revenge of the Sith* DVD commentary, 2004
[61] *Bantha Tracks*, issue two, March 1978
[62] *Bantha Tracks*, issue three, May 1978
[63] *Bantha Tracks*, issue six, autumn 1979
[64] *Bantha Tracks*, issue eight, spring 1980
[65] Pollock, pp. 206-207
[66] Baxter, p. 273
[67] Arnold, p. 183
[68] "The Force Behind Star Wars" by Paul Scanlon, *Rolling Stone*, August 25th, 1977
[69] Baxter, p. 255
[70] Baxter, p. 255

## Chapter V: Revelations

[1] Personal correspondence with "Bad Radio"
[2] Bouzereau, *Annotated Screenplays*, pp. 127-128
[3] *The Complete Making of Indiana Jones*, by J.W. Rinzler, 2008, pp. 22-23
[4] Bouzereau, *Annotated Screenplays*, p. 173
[5] Bouzereau, *Annotated Screenplays*, p. 173
[6] *The Making of Revenge of the Sith* by J.W. Rinzler, 2005, p. 17
[7] Bouzereau, *Annotated Screenplays*, p. 167
[8] Bouzereau, *Annotated Screenplays*, p. 167
[9] Bouzereau, *Annotated Screenplays*, p. 181
[10] Bouzereau, *Annotated Screenplays*, p. 182
[11] Bouzereau, *Annotated Screenplays*, p. 127
[12] Bouzereau, *Annotated Screenplays*, p. 131
[13] Bouzereau, *Annotated Screenplays*, p. 196
[14] Bouzereau, *Annotated Screenplays*, p. 196
[15] Bouzereau, *Annotated Screenplays*, p. 196
[16] Bouzereau, *Annotated Screenplays*, p. 210
[17] Bouzereau, *Annotated Screenplays*, p. 214
[18] *The Vault*, by Steve Sansweet, 2007, p. 53
[19] These treatment excerpts come from Steve Sansweet's 2007 book *The Vault*, which had complete reproductions of Lucas' hand-written originals—unfortunately, only the first four pages, which is why I can only provide primary sources for the beginning sections
[20] Bouzereau, *Annotated Screenplays*, p. 176
[21] Bouzereau, *Annotated Screenplays*, p. 174
[22] Bouzereau, *Annotated Screenplays*, p. 226

[23] *Gone With The Wind* by Margaret Mitchell, 1936, p. 278. The version of the book I used is a free PDF version from Project Guttenburg Austrailia, http://gutenberg.net.au/ebooks02/0200161p.pdf. For a relative location of the passage in question, it comes from near the end of Chapter XIX. A sample:

> "Scarlett, you do like me, don't you?"
> That was more like what she was expecting.
> "Well, sometimes," she answered cautiously. "When you aren't acting like a varmint."
> He laughed again and held the palm of her hand against his hard cheek.
> "I think you like me because I am a varmint. You've known so few dyed-in-the-wool varmints in your sheltered life that my very difference holds a quaint charm for you."
> This was not the turn she had anticipated and she tried again without success to pull her hand free.
> "That's not true! I like nice men--men you can depend on to always be gentlemanly."

Elsewhere is an exchange that recalls the "I'd just as soon kiss a wookie!" moment (p. 253; Chapter XVII):

> "I'll bet you a box of bonbons against--" His dark eyes wandered to her lips. "Against a kiss."
> "I don't care for such personal conversation," she said coolly and managed a frown. "Besides, I'd just as soon kiss a pig."
> "There's no accounting for tastes and I've always heard the Irish were partial to pigs--kept them under their beds, in fact. But, Scarlett, you need kissing badly. That's what's wrong with you. All your beaux have respected you too much, though God knows why, or they have been too afraid of you to really do right by you. The result is that you are unendurably uppity. You should be kissed and by someone who knows how."

As Lucas said to Alan Dean Foster in 1975, book two would be *Gone with the Wind in Outer Space*. The theatrical poster of *Empire* would emulate the famous poster of *Gone with the Wind*, with Han and Leia in the same pose as Clark Gable and Vivien Leigh.

[24] *Bantha Tracks*, issue 5, summer 1979

[25] *Empire Strikes Back* novelisation by Donald F. Glut, 1980, p. 125

[26] *The World of Star Wars: A Compendium of Fact and Fantasy From Star Wars and The Empire Strikes Back*, 1981

[27] Rinzler, *Making of Star Wars*, p. 353

[28] *The Art of Attack of the Clones* by Mark Cotta Vaz, 2002, p. 74

[29] Bouzereau, *Annotated Screenplays*, p. 123

[30] Bouzereau, *Annotated Screenplays*, p. 125

[31] Arnold, p. 3

[32] Bouzereau, *Annotated Screenplays*, p. 144

[33] Baxter, p. 270. However, Baxter reports that her husband answered the phone—but Brackett's husband, sci-fi author Edmond Hamilton, died in 1977

[34] Bouzereau, *Annotated Screenplays*, p. 144

[35] Pollock, p. 206

[36] Bouzereau, *Annotated Screenplays*, p. 145

[37] Arnold, p. 144. In this passage he goes on to claim it took him three months to write, but he actually completed the second, revised second *and* the third drafts all in one month, April of 1978 (as per *Annotated Screenplays*). This unbelievably rapid progress is indicative of the success of his new storyline

[38] Hearn, p. 127. Unfortunately, Hearn only gives us a cropped photo highlighting this fragment. It appears that in this draft Luke is not defeated and wounded on the ledge, poised with death or surrender. Instead, Luke and Vader are battling constantly, with Vader taunting Luke throughout, finally, it seems, making a remark about Obi Wan and Luke's father, which causes Luke to shout "Enough! [Obi Wan] said you killed him," to which Vader makes the revelation.

[39] *Star Wars* Definitive Edition Laserdisc interview, 1993

[40] *Star Wars* novelisation by Alan Dean Foster, 1976, p. 80

[41] Rinzler, *Making of Star Wars*, p. 351

[42] Foster, p. 1-2

[43] Foster, p. 76-79

[44] This analysis is included in his profile page (as of the time of this writing) at Theforce.net's messageboards: http://boards.theforce.net/ASP/user.asp?usr=284138

[45] Rinzler, *Making of Star Wars*, p. 352

[46] Rinzler, *Making of Star Wars*, pp. 351-352

[47] Bouzereau, *Annotated Screenplays*, p. 173

[48] *Time* Magazine, May 19th, 1980

[49] Rinzler, *Making of Star Wars*, p. 352

[50] Rinzler, *Making of Star Wars*, p. 352

[51] "The George Lucas Saga" by Kerry O' Quinn, Starlog, July, 1981

[52] *Prevue* Magazine 1983

[53] Bouzereau, *Annotated Screenplays*, p. 217

[54] "The *Star Wars* Trilogy DVD Unveiled - Part 3!" by Scott Chitwood, *comingsoon.net*, September 17th, 2004, http://www.comingsoon.net/news/topnews.php?id=6418

[55] *Cinefantastique* Vol. 28, No. 28, February 1997

[56] Pollock, p. 208

[57] Pollock, p. 207

[58] "Lawrence Kasdan Screenwriter" by Scott Chernoff, *Star Wars Insider*, issue 49, May/June 2000, pp. 33-36

[59] Pollock, p. 209

[60] Pollock, p. 211

[61] Pollock, p. 211

[62] Pollock, p. 212

[63] Pollock, p. 210

[64] Baxter, p. 271

[65] Pollock, p. 211

[66] Pollock, p. 215

[67] *Baltimore Sun*, May 12th, 2002, http://www.baltimoresun.com/features/arts/bal-as.kasdan12may12.story

[68] *Star Wars Insider*, issue 49, May/June 2000, p. 27

[69] *Future Magazine*, April, 1978

[70] Bouzereau, *Annotated Screenplays*, p. 182

[71] Bouzereau, *Annotated Screenplays*, p. 200

[72] Arnold, p. 177

[73] Arnold, p. 177

[74] Arnold, p. 177

[75] Arnold, pp. 247-48

[76] see Appendix "Legend of the Sequel Trilogy"

[77] "I've Got to Get My Life Back" by Gerald Clarke, *Time* magazine, May 23rd, 1983

[78] Worrell, p. 186

[79] *The Art of The Empire Strikes Back* contains many examples. For instance, (my source is the 1997 reprinting), on page 13, the probot design, stamped with a 1978 copyright and dated as July 28th, is also stamped with the "Episode II: The Empire Strikes Back" logo. The "Episode II" stamp occurs on a design for a tauntaun armature on page 22, which is dated as July 20th, 1978, an Imperial Walker sketch from August 17th, 1978 on page 46, a blueprint of the Rebel hanger on pages 42-43 dated as September 22nd, 1978, and a snowspeeder blueprint on page 49 from August 18th, 1978, which also

prominently displays a heading which says "Star Wars Chapter II". The latest it occurs is on a snowspeeder cockpit design on page 48, dated as December 12th, 1978, an ion canon sketch from the same date on page 40, and a design of 2-1B from December 21st, 1978, displayed on page 32. When 1979 arrives and the final draft which now states "Episode V" appears in February of that year, artwork carries a new stamp which removes "Episode II" and simply says "Empire Strikes Back". This can be seen on page 51 (March 25th, 1979) and page 161 (June 8, 1979).

[80] The *Annotated Screenplays* first denotes "Episode V" in its title description of the fifth draft. This, however, is a bit of a concession—*Annotated Screenplays* carries *no listing at all* for a fourth draft screenplay! This is presumably an honest mistake in the listing of sources. Elsewhere, *Annotated Screenplays* even describes variations found in the fourth draft, and it also lists that there were revisions done to the fourth draft in its list of sources. It does indeed exist, but because it is not listed we cannot through official lines have a confirmation of its title.

As far as the office stamps referenced in the prior end-note, it is also allowable that the office would not be immediately caught up with the script title changes and therefore continued to use the old Episode II stamp for the two months remaining in the year (such a thing as an office stamp would be unimportant, especially when the final draft had not yet been agreed upon). Most significantly, even when Lucas *was* using Episode V after draft five was written in early 1979, there was no mention of Episode V in the revised stamp—perhaps this aspect was to be kept secret, so as to not alert office employees that three prequels were planned.

[81] Arnold, pp. 247-48

[82] Arnold, p. 177

[83] "An Interview with Gary Kurtz" by Ken P., IGN *Film Force*, November 11th, 2002, http://filmforce.ign.com/articles/376/376873p1/html. He also makes this statement in an interview with *Film Threat* online magazine: "Gary Kurtz Interview: The Original Star Wars Producer Speaks" by Chris Gore, *Film Threat*, March 5th, 2000, http://filmthreat.com/index.php?section=interviews&Id=8

[84] Arnold, p. 236

[85] *Time*, May 19th, 1980. Pollock also reports this on page 146 of his book.

[86] *Gossip Magazine*, 1978

[87] "I've Got to Get My Life Back" by Gerald Clarke, *Time*, May 23rd, 1983 and *Icons: Intimate Portraits* by Denise Worrell, 1989, p. 186

[88] For instance, Kerry O' Quinn's July 1981 *Starlog* interview, where it is said that the characters will be the same but the actors different. "There is continuity with the characters, in other words, but not with actors."

[89] "The George Lucas Saga" by Kerry O' Quinn, Starlog, July, 1981

[90] Arnold, pp. 247-8

[91] Arnold, p. 197

[92] "Behind the Scenes of The Empire Strikes Back", *American Cinematographer*, June 1980, p. 546

[93] Bouzereau, *Annotated Screenplays*, p. 217

[94] See "Star Wars: Episode III" by Anwar Brett, BBC online, May 18th, 2005, http://www.bbc.co.uk/films/2005/05/18/george_lucas_star_wars_episode_iii_interview.shtml, "Director George Lucas Takes A Look Back -- And Ahead" by William Arnold, *Seattle Post-Intelligencer*, May 12th, 2005, and his concluding comments on the *Revenge of the Sith* DVD commentary track, for example

[95] *Berliner Zeitung*, Number 114, Mai, 19, 2005

[96] Pollock, p. 195

[97] Rinzler, *Making of Star Wars*, pp. 107-108

[98] "A Long Time Ago: The Story of Star Wars", BBC Omnibus documentary, 1999

[99] "George Lucas: The Well-Rounded Interview" by Well-Rounded Entertainment, www.well-rounded.com/movies/reviews/lucas_intv.html)

[100] "Galactic Gasbag" by Steven Hart, salon.com April 10th, 2002, http://dir.salon.com/story/ent/movies/feature/2002/04/10/lucas/index.html

[101] "Galactic Gasbag" by Steven Hart, salon.com April 10th, 2002, http://dir.salon.com/story/ent/movies/feature/2002/04/10/lucas/index.html

[102] "George Lucas" by Michael Pye and Lynda Myles, *The Movie Brats*, 1979

[103] "George Lucas" by Michael Pye and Lynda Myles, *The Movie Brats*, 1979

[104] "George Lucas" by Michael Pye and Lynda Myles, *The Movie Brats*, 1979

[105] "George Lucas" by Michael Pye and Lynda Myles, *The Movie Brats*, 1979

[106] Arnold, p. 215

[107] *The Making of Star Wars As Told By C-3P0 and R2D2*, 1977

[108] *Empire of Dreams*, 2004

[109] "George Lucas: The Stinky Kid Hits the Big Time" by Stephen Farber, *Film Quarterly*, vol. 27, no. 3, spring 1974

[110] "Luke Skywalker Goes Home" by Bernard Weinraub, *Playboy*, July 1997

[111] "An Interview With Gary Kurtz", IGN *Film Force* online, November 11th, 2002, http://filmforce.ign.com/articles/376/376873p1.html

[112] Pollock, p. 2

[113] *Future Noir: The Making of Blade Runner*, by Paul M. Sammon, 1996, p. 27

[114] Pollock, p. 189

[115] "The George Lucas Saga" by Kerry O' Quinn, *Starlog*, July, 1981

[116] Pollock, p. 163

[117] *Starlog*, November 1980,

[118] *From Star Wars to Jedi*, 1983

[119] "Lights, Camera, Action! Lucas Takes The Film Industry By Storm" , http://www.evancarmichael.com/Famous-Entrepreneurs/538/Lights-Camera-Action-Lucas-Takes-the-Film-Industry-by-Storm.html

## Chapter VI: The Wreckage

[1] *Hearts of Darkness: A Filmmakers Apocalypse*, 1991

[2] Pollock, p. 217

[3] Arnold, pp. 131-147

[4] "Father Figure" by Michael Sragow, Salon.com, May 13th, 1999, http://www.salon.com/ent/col/srag/1999/05/13/kershner/index.html

[5] "The Empire Strikes Back Director: Irvin Kershner" by Joseph Krebs, *Sound and Vision* online supplement, October 2004, http://www.soundandvisionmag.com/article.asp?section_id=4&article_id=672&page_number=1

[6] Arnold, p. 178

[7] Pollock, p. 216

[8] "The Empire Strikes Back Director: Irvin Kershner" by Joseph Krebs, *Sound and Vision* online supplement, October 2004, http://www.soundandvisionmag.com/article.asp?section_id=4 &article_id=672&page_number=1

[9] *Star Wars Insider* issue 49, May/June 2000, p. 29

[10] "Farewell Luke Skywalker" by David Packer, *Starlog*, July 1983

[11] Pollock, p. 218

[12] Pollock, p. 218

[13] Pollock, p. 215

[14] Baxter, p. 287

[15] *Star Wars Insider* issue 49, May/June 2000, p. 29

[16] Pollock, p. 208

[17] Pollock, p. 208

[18] "An Interview With Gary Kurtz" by Ken P, *IGN Film Force*, November 11, 2002, http://filmforce.ign.com/articles/376/376873p2.html

[19] Pollock, p. 198

[20] Pollock, p. 251

[21] Pollock, pp. 217-18

[22] Pollock, p. 218

[23] Pollock, p. 218

[24] Pollock, p. 219

[25] Pollock, pp. 218-19

[26] Pollock, pp. 218-19

[27] Pollock, p. 221

[28] Pollock, p. 220

[29] Pollock, p. 215

[30] Pollock, p. 217

[31] Pollock, p. 217

[32] *Star Wars Insider*, issue 49, May/June 2000, p. 38

[33] "Darth Vader's Surprise Attack" by Gary Arnold, *Washington Post*, May 18th, 1980

[34] Pollock, p. 217

[35] Worrell, p. 175

[36] "Gary Kurtz Interview: The Original Star Wars Producer Speaks" by Chris Gore, *Film Threat* online magazine, March 5th, 2000

[37] "The Force Behind Star Wars" by Paul Scanlon, *Rolling Stone*, August 25th 1977

[38] "Gary Kurtz Interview: The Original Star Wars Producer Speaks" by Chris Gore, *Film Threat* online magazine, March 5th, 2000, http://www.filmthreat.com/index.php?section=interviews&Id=

8
[39] Baxter, p. 305
[40] Baxter, pp. 306-307
[41] Pollock, p. 220
[42] This is made explicit in a recollection in Baxter's book, p. 240. On page 83 of *Skywalking* she even expresses desire to start a family in 1969 but Lucas was afraid it would interfere with his work.
[43] "Hamill" by David Packer, *Starlog* 1980
[44] "Darth Vader's Surprise Attack" by Gary Arnold, *Washington Post*, May 18th, 1980

## Chapter VII: Demons and Angels

[1] "The Empire Strikes Back and So Does Filmmaker George Lucas With His Sequel to Star Wars" by Jean Vallely, *Rolling Stone*, June 12th 1980
[2] "Gary Kurtz Interview: The Original Star Wars Producer Speaks" by Chris Gore, *Film Threat* online, March 5th, 2000, http://www.filmthreat.com/index.php?section=interviews&Id=8
[3] Arnold, pp. 247-48
[4] *Bantha Tracks*, issue 8, May 1980
[5] "The George Lucas Saga" by Kerry O' Quinn, *Starlog*, July 1981
[6] Pollock, p. 230
[7] *Indiana Jones: Making the Trilogy*, *Indiana Jones* Trilogy DVD, 2003
[8] "An Interview with Gary Kurtz," by Ken P, *IGN Film Force*, November 11th, 2002, http://filmforce.ign.com/articles/376/376873p1.html
[9] Baxter, p. 274
[10] "An Interview with Gary Kurtz," by Ken P, *IGN Film Force*, November 11th, 2002, http://filmforce.ign.com/articles/376/376873p1.html
[11] Kurtz says of Lucas' *Empire* re-edit: "It was awful. It was chopped into tiny pieces, and everything was fast." (Baxter, p. 293)
[12] "The Empire Strikes Back and so Does Filmmaker George Lucas with his Sequel to Star Wars," by Jean Vallely, *Rolling Stone*, June 12, 1980
[13] "The Empire Strikes Back and so Does Filmmaker George Lucas with his Sequel to Star Wars," by Jean Vallely, *Rolling Stone*, June 12, 1980
[14] Pollock, p. 192

[15] Pollock, p. 192

[16] Arnold, pp. 178-179

[17] "The Empire Strikes Back and so Does Filmmaker George Lucas with his Sequel to Star Wars," by Jean Vallely, *Rolling Stone*, June 12, 1980

[18] Pollock, p. 242

[19] "The George Lucas Saga" by Kerry O' Quinn, *Starlog*, July 1981

[20] *Return of the Jedi* DVD commentary track, 2004. In this same statement, Lucas elaborates that the film represents the last third of his original, big trilogy script, whose main focus for the section represented by this film was the battle of primitives where wookies toppled the Empire and its Death Star. This, however, is extremely misleading and inaccurate: that 1974 rough draft was merely a more convoluted version of *Star Wars*, with those extra wookie scenes cut out

[21] "An Interview With Gary Kurtz" by Ken P., *IGN Film Force*, November 11th, 2002, http://filmforce.ign.com/articles/376/376873p1.html

[22] Worrell, p. 184

[23] *Prevue Magazine*, 1983

[24] Bouzereau, *Annotated Screenplays*, p. 269

[25] Bouzereau, *Annotated Screenplays*, p. 269

[26] "So Luke, Tell Me About Your Sister" by Douglas Hyde, CNN.com special, September 20th, 2004, http://www.cnn.com/2004/SHOWBIZ/Movies/09/20/sidebar.hamill/index.html

[27] Bouzereau, *Annotated Screenplays*, p. 281

[28] Bouzereau, *Annotated Screenplays*, p. 249

[29] *Starlog*, issue 127, February 1988, p. 48, as well as the *Return of the Jedi* novelisation by James Kahn, p. 135

[30] "Starlog Salutes Star Wars," *Starlog*, July 1987, p. 45

[31] Pollock, pp. 275-6

[32] "The Empire Strikes Back Director: Irvin Kershner" by Josef Krebs, *Sound and Vision*, October 2004, online exclusive, http://www.soundandvisionmag.com/article.asp?section_id=4&article_id=672&page_number=1

[33] *Lynch on Lynch* by Chris Rodley, revised edition, 2005, p. 113

[34] "Starlog Salutes Star Wars," *Starlog*, July 1987, p. 48

[35] "Producing and Directing Return of the Jedi" by Richard Patterson, *American Cinematographer*, June 1983, p. 110

[36] *The Making of Return of the Jedi*, by John Phillip Peecher, 1983, p. 69. This sentiment is also mentioned in "Producing and Directing Return of the Jedi" by Richard Patterson, *American Cinematographer*, June 1983, p. 113

[37] Peecher, p. 38

[38] "Filmforce: An interview with Gary Kurtz" by Ken P. , *IGN Film Force*, November 11, 2002, http://filmforce.ign.com/articles/376/376873p1.html

[39] "Producing and Directing Return of the Jedi" by Richard Patterson, *American Cinematographer*, June 1983, p. 112

[40] *Preview Magazine*, 1983

[41] Pollock, p. 7

[42] Bouzereau, *Annotated Screenplays*, p. 231

[43] *Star Wars Insider*, issue 49, May 2000, p. 36

[44] "Producing and Directing Return of the Jedi" by Richard Patterson, *American cinematographer*, June 1983, p. 113

[45] "Producing and Directing Return of the Jedi" by Richard Patterson, *American Cinematographer*, June 1983, p. 113

[46] Bouzereau, *Annotated Screenplays*, p. 268

[47] Bouzereau, *Annotated Screenplays*, p. 270

[48] Bouzereau, *Annotated Screenplays*, p. 269

[49] Bouzereau, *Annotated Screenplays*, pp. 290-91

[50] *Return of the Jedi* DVD commentary track, 2004

[51] Bouzereau, *Annotated Screenplays*, p. 270

[52] Bouzereau, *Annotated Screenplays*, p. 291

[53] *Empire of Dreams*, 2004

[54] Bouzereau, *Annotated Screenplays*, p. 314

[55] *Empire of Dreams*, 2004

[56] Bouzereau, *Annotated Screenplays*, p. 314

[57] Bouzereau, *Annotated Screenplays*, p. 314

[58] Bouzereau, *Annotated Screenplays*, p. 237

[59] Bouzereau, *Annotated Screenplays*, p. 297

[60] "Producing and Directing Return of the Jedi" by Richard Patterson, *American Cinematographer*, June 1983, p. 110

[61] *Return of the Jedi: Official Collectors Edition* souvenir book, 1983

[62] Bouzereau, *Annotated Screenplays*, p. 317

[63] "The Force Behind Star Wars" by Paul Scanlon, *Rolling Stone*, August 25th, 1977

[64] Bouzereau, *Annotated Screenplays*, p. 217

[65] Bouzereau, *Annotated Screenplays*, p. 165

[66] Bouzereau, *Annotated Screenplays*, pp. 316-17

[67] Peecher, p. 2

[68] Peecher, p. 7

[69] *From Star Wars to Jedi: The Making of a Saga*, 1983

[70] *Return of the Jedi* DVD commentary track, 2004

[71] Bouzereau, *Annotated Screenplays*, p. 319

[72] *Return of the Jedi* novelisation by James Kahn, 1983, p. 64

[73] Kahn, p. 175

[74] *Empire of Dreams*, 2004

[75] *Empire of Dreams*, 2004

[76] According to page 66 of *The Vault*, the media first reported the change on January 27th, 1983, though the first official piece displaying the new title did not arrive until much later.

[77] *Empire of Dreams*, 2004

[78] *Star Wars: The Magic and Mystery*, 1997

[79] Bouzereau, *Annotated Screenplays*, p. 234

[80] Arnold, pp. 247-48

[81] *Empire of Dreams*, 2004. Here Bloom says that he suggested they change the name of the film in order to avoid companies ripping them off with higher-than-normal costs whenever they had to rent or purchase equipment and material. This dovetailed into the increasing security needs that the production was encountering. Thus, *Blue Harvest* was created in the latter stages of production—it was only used while on location in California for the Endor sequences.

[82] Pollock, p. 276

[83] Sansweet, *The Vault*, p. 66

[84] This is reported in an archived Usenet post from net.movies.sw from June 20th, 1983. See http://groups.google.ca/group/net.movies.sw/browse_thread/th read/d31679569b39c865/ec5b91deb0644c63#ec5b91deb0644 c63. User CFV states "When I went to Octocon this year, Howard Kazanjian gave a film/slide presentation on 'Revenge of the Jedi'. He also got a lot of 'Jedi's don't belive in revenge' flack."

[85] Sansweet, *The Vault*, p. 67

## Chapter VIII: Endings

[1] Pollock, p. 274

[2] Pollock, pp. 274-75

[3] Baxter, p. 333

[4] "I've Got to Get My Life Back Again" by Gerald Clark, *Time*, May 23rd, 1983

[5] "The George Lucas Saga" by Kerry O' Quinn, *Starlog*, July, 1981

[6] Worrell, p. 175

[7] Pollock, p. 240

[8] Pollock, p. 267

[9] Pollock, p. 83. In 1977 Marcia reports that making a baby is their plan for the year. See "Off the Screen", *People*, July 14th, 1977, p. 64

[10] Biskind, p. 422

[11] *Empire of Dreams*, 2004

[12] Baxter, p. 335

[13] Baxter, pp. 333-334

[14] Biskind, p. 423

[15] Biskind, p. 422

[16] Pollock, p. 65

[17] Worrell, p. 192

[18] Pollock, p. 63

[19] Pollock, p. 147

[20] Pollock, p. 228

[21] Pollock, p. 84

[22] Baxter, p. 66

[23] Pollock, p. 228

[24] "Mark Hamill Walks Down Memory Lane With Film Freak Central" by Walter Chaw, *Filmfreakcentral.com*, March 20th, 2005, http://filmfreakcentral.net/notes/mhamillinterview.htm

[25] Biskind, p. 423

[26] This is made explicit in a recollection in Baxter's book, p. 240. On page 83 of *Skywalking* she even expresses desire to start a family in 1969 or so, but Lucas had the same reason for disagreeing.

[27] "Burden of Dreams: George Lucas" by Aljean Harmetz, *American Film*, June 1983

[28] Worrell, pp. 175-176

[29] Worrell, p. 192

[30] Biskind, p. 423

[31] Biskind, p. 423

[32] Biskind, p. 423

[33] Biskind, p. 423

[34] Pollock, p. 277

[35] Pollock, p. 240

[36] Biskind, p. 423

[37] Worrell, p. 195

[38] Baxter, p. 335

[39] Biskind, p. 423

[40] *60 Minutes*, March 28, 1999

[41] *60 Minutes*, March 28, 1999

[42] Pollock, p. 273

[43] "Skywalker Ranch: New 'Star Wars' Film to Debute In Two Weeks," CNN, May 7th, 2002, http://transcripts.cnn.com/TRANSCRIPTS/0205/07/lol.00.htm

l

[44] Biskind, p. 381

[45] Baxter, p. 70

[46] "Linda Rondstat: The US Interview" by Jonathan Schwartz, *US* magazine, December 25th, 2000. Schwartz writes "in the '80s she was engaged ('ring on the finger and all') to the writer, producer and director of the *Star Wars* films, George Lucas." A&E's 2001 *Biography* of Lucas says the relationship was four years long, which ends it at 1988—the same year Lucas adopted Katie.

[47] *60 Minutes*, March 28th, 1999

[48] Biskind, p. 423

[49] "Dialogue: George Lucas" by Stephen Galloway, *Hollywood Reporter*, June 9th, 2005

[50] Worrell, p. 174

[51] "I've Got to Get My Life Back Again" by Gerald Clarke, *Time*, May 23rd 1983

[52] "George Lucas" by David Sheff, *Rolling Stone*, November 5th, 1987

[53] "Starlog Salutes Star Wars," *Starlog*, July 1987, p. 51

[54] "The Grand Experiment", Starwars.com Homing Beacon #155, Feb. 16th, 2006

## Chapter IX: The Beginning…Again

[1] So says Zahn in Waldenbooks' newsletter, quote a few passages later. John Baxter, in *Mythmaker* gives a slightly different chronology, stating that Lou Aronica-Bantam Spectra contacted Lucasfilm initially in 1988, heard back a year later and then commissioned Zahn in 1990 (p. 388).

[2] Waldenbooks' "Hailing Frequencies: News and reviews from the worlds of Science Fiction and Fantasy", issue 1, 1992

[3] "Grand Illusion" by Paula Parisi, *Wired*, May 1999

[4] "I had a million different names for the home planet of the Empire, but Coruscant came out of publishing," Lucas says in *Annotated Screenplays*, p. 297

[5] "An Interview With Timothy Zahn, Author of Heir to the Empire", Totse.com, 1991, http://www.totse.com/en/ego/science_fiction/tzi.html,

[6] Waldenbooks' "Hailing Frequencies: News and reviews from the worlds of Science Fiction and Fantasy", issue 1, 1992, retrieved from http://www.totse.com/en/ego/science_fiction/tzi2.html

[7] "Star Wars Per-Zahn-ified" by Jeff Carter, *echostation.com*, December 19th, 1998, http://www.echostation.com/interview/zahn.htm,

[8] Baxter, p. 388

[9] See http://goodcomics.comicbookresources.com/2007/11/29/comic-book-urban-legends-revealed-131 for an explanation of its history at Marvel. Elsewhere, it is reported that *Dark Empire* was first proposed in 1989 and was to originally include an imposter of Darth Vader, a replacement that would don a copy of the Vader suit so that the Empire could say he was alive and continue to inspire fear in the galaxy. Lucas vetoed this—indicating that he was, much like on Zahn's books, involved with the direction of these early stories. *Dark Empire* writer Tom Veitch then suggested that the Emperor be brought back as a clone, which Lucas agreed to. Supposedly, *Dark Empire* is one of Lucas' favorite EU. See http://www.jazmaonline.com/interviews/interviews2007.asp?intID=432 and http://www.ugo.com/channels/comics/features/starwars for more info.

[10] Baxter, p. 389

[11] "The Greatest Story Ever Told" by R Burke, Static Multimedia, 2005, http://www.staticmultimedia.com/content/film/features/feature_1115643931?info=film

[12] "The Greatest Story Ever Told" by R Burke, Static Multimedia, 2005, http://www.staticmultimedia.com/content/film/features/feature_1115643931?info=film

[13] *Biography*, A&E, 2001

[14] "George Lucas: Past, Present and Future" by Ron Magid, *American Cinematographer*, February 1997

[15] Hearn, p. 172

[16] Hearn, p. 172

[17] Hearn, p. 182

[18] "Lucasvision" by Thomas R. King, *The Wall Street Journal*, March 21st 1994

[19] "George Lucas on Star Wars, Fahrenheit 9/11, and His Own Legacy" by Steve Silberman, *Wired* online exclusive, May 2005, http://wired.com/wired/archive/13.05/lucasqa.html

[20] *The Charlie Rose Show*, September 9th, 2004

[21] "George Lucas on Star Wars, Fahrenheit 9/11, and His Own Legacy" by Steve Silberman, *Wired* online exclusive, May 2005, http://wired.com/wired/archive/13.05/lucasqa.html

[22] *"Radioland Murders* Press Conference,"* transcribed by Sally Kline, appearing in *George Lucas Interviews*, edited by Sally Kline, 1999, p. 181

[23] *The Charlie Rose Show*, September 9th, 2004

[24] *Lucasfilm Fan Club Magazine*, issue 17, 1992, p. 5

[25] *Oprah*, February 1997

[26] Interview by Mr. Showbiz, 2000, http://mrshowbiz.go.com/interviews/299_2.html

[27] "An Expanded Universe," by Ron Magid, *American Cinematographer*, February 1997

[28] *ILM: Into the Digital Realm* by Mark Cotta Vaz, pp. 290-91

[29] See *ILM: Into the Digital Realm* by Mark Cotta Vaz, p. 294 as well as "An Expanded Universe," by Ron Magid, *American Cinematographer*, February 1997

[30] Hearn, p. 183

[31] *Starlog*, July 1987, p. 51

[32] *The Big Breakfast*, July 16th, 1999

[33] For example, Lucas remarks in 1992, as quoted in *Lucasfilm Fan Club* magazine issue 17, that not only was he committed to making the films but that they had already begun planning how the series would be shot (all three films at once); however, this is the only indication I can find that any work was being done at this early a time, therefore this 1992 development work would have been very preliminary. 1993 is the year Lucasfilm announced that the series had moved into official development, so it is likely that the preliminary plans expressed in 1992 were made more concrete and active work was commenced, and in this year Darabont says McCallum approached him about writing the scripts, indicating that Lucas had begun thinking in terms of story as well. Likely, this is when Lucas began fleshing out a more detailed treatment and set of notes, which can be seen to be quite thick by the next year when he commenced writing, as evident in the first Episode I web doc. McCallum mentions 1990 in an interview (http://www.scifi.com/sfw/issue446/interview2.html) quoted elsewhere in this book but I believe he is merely speaking in general terms or is simply mistaken (for starters—he wasn't even working with Lucas at that time).

[34] "The Phantom Redemption" by T'Bone, starwarz.com, May 8th, 2003, originally posted on creativescreenwriting.com, 2000, http://www.starwarz.com/tbone/index.php?categoryid=26&p2_articleid=168

[35] "Director George Lucas Takes a Look Back—And Ahead" by William Arnold, *Seattle Post-Intelligencer*, May 12th, 2005

[36] Worrell, p. 174

[37] *Lucasfilm Fan Club Magazine*, issue 17, 1992. Here he at least seems to have already decided the films would need to have stylistic continuity to fit as "one piece." (p. 6)

[38] *The Phantom Menace* DVD commentary track, 2001

[39] Bouzereau, *The Making of Episode I*, p. 4

[40] "Lucas: 'Star Wars' Isn't Iraq Wars" by Harlan Jacobson, USAToday.com, May 15th 2005, http://www.usatoday.com/life/movies/news/2005-05-15-cannes-lucas_x.htm

[41] "Of Myth and Men" by Bill Moyers, *Time*, April 26th, 1999

[42] "So, What's the Deal with Leia's Hair?" by Jess Cagle, *Time*, April 29th, 2002, http://www.time.com/time/covers/1101020429/qa.html

[43] *Episode I Insider's Guide* CD-ROM, 1999

[44] *The Art of Episode II* by Mark Cotta Vaz, 2002, p. 128

[45] Bouzereau, *The Making of Episode I*, pp. 23-24

[46] For instance Frank Oz tried to invent a history but Lucas told him it wasn't important, indicating he hadn't though through much of the character's background or had not committed to anything; see *Starlog*, issue 127, February 1988, p. 48. The *Return of the Jedi* novelisation only has vague answers as well, as the Emperor has a vague recollection that there was once a Jedi by the name of Yoda but doesn't seem to remember much about him (p. 135). Judging by the backstory info given by Kenobi in *Return of the Jedi*, and the character histories discussed in those meetings and elsewhere, Anakin's history only involves Kenobi (ie it is he who hides the twins, helps his wife escape, etc), and Yoda is never mentioned anywhere else in the backstory. Other than having trained Kenobi, it seems he had no background. In fact, it is probable that Dagobah had been envisioned as Yoda's dwelling all along, and not just a place of exile, with Kenobi having to seek him out just as Luke does—which ties in better with the "shaman on the remote island" motif Lucas was tapping into. This is what Leigh Brackett envisioned when she wrote that Kenobi and Father Skywalker used to train on Dagobah.

[47] Bouzereau, *The Making of Episode I*, p. 7

[48] "Lucas on Iraq War, 'Star Wars' " by Chris Burns, CNN.com, Monday, May 16, 2005, http://www.cnn.com/2005/SHOWBIZ/Movies/05/16/cannes.st arwars/

[49] *Episode I Insiders Guide* CD-ROM, 1999

[50] "Sith Strikes Again", Entertainment Tonight Online, May 30th, 2005, http://et.tv.yahoo.com/movies/11198

[51] "Director George Lucas Takes a Look Back -- and Ahead" by William Arnold, *Seattle Post-Intelligencer*, May 12th, 2005
[52] *Empire* Magazine, June 2005
[53] "The Greatest Story Ever Told" by R Burke, Static Multimedia, 2005, http://www.staticmultimedia.com/content/film/features/feature_1115643931?info=film
[54] Rinzler, *Making of Star Wars*, p. 224
[55] *Lucasfilm Fan Club Magazine*, issue 17, 1992, pp. 5-6
[56] *The Making of Episode I: The Phantom Menace* by Laurent Bouzereau, 1999, p. 11

## Chapter X: Returning Home

[1] *From Star Wars to Jedi: Making the Saga*, 1983
[2] *From Star Wars to Jedi: Making the Saga*, 1983
[3] *Star Wars Episode I webdoc I: All I Need is an Idea*, 1998
[4] *Star Wars Episode I webdoc I: All I Need is an Idea*, 1998
[5] *Star Wars Episode I webdoc I: All I Need is an Idea*, 1998
[6] Bouzereau, *The Making of Episode I*, pp. 3-4
[7] Bouzereau, *The Making of Episode I*, p. xii
[8] *Episode I Insiders Guide* CD-ROM, 1999
[9] *Star Wars Episode I webdoc I: All I Need is an Idea*, 1998. Note that this is the first draft, while the previous summation is the revised rough draft. However, Marcus Hearn provides the cover page of the handwritten original on page 190 of *The Cinema of George Lucas*—the handwritten rough draft is dated as January 13th, 1995. So the rough draft, the revised rough draft and the typed first draft were all completed on January 13th, 1995. Presumably, there are no major differences between them.
[10] Bouzereau, *The Making of Episode I*, p. 105
[11] *The Big Breakfast*, July 16th, 1999
[12] "Director George Lucas Takes a Look Back -- and Ahead" by William Arnold, *Seattle Post-Intelligencer*, May 12th, 2005; and *Empire* Magazine, June 2005; and "The Greatest Story Ever Told" by R Burke, Static Multimedia, 2005, http://www.staticmultimedia.com/content/film/features/feature_1115643931?info=film.
[13] *Echostation* interview, http://www.echostation.com/interview/gurney.htm
[14] "Star Wars and Dinotopia" by James Gurney, Dinotopia website November 23, 1999, http://www.dinotopia.com/statement.html
[15] *Star Wars Insider*, issue 26, summer 1995, p. 8

[16] *Star Wars Insider*, issue 26, summer 1995, p. 8

[17] *Star Wars Insider*, issue 26, summer 1995, p. 8

[18] *Star Wars Insider*, issue 26, summer 1995, p. 17

[19] McCallum says "until George completes the storylines", meaning that they were still in a state of flux. This is logical if the second draft had not been started yet—Lucas says "I'm writing [the scripts], at least the first drafts myself," which implies that not only does the second draft not yet exist but that he hadn't even finalized his plans on whether he himself would be writing the second draft or if he would bring in another writer. These interviews occurred in late April, 1995; likely, Lucas had been working on the concept art since the first draft that January. When he actually decided to go ahead and write the second draft is anyone's guess, but it could only have been summer 1995 at the earliest, and probably it was even later.

[20] *Star Wars Insider*, issue 26, summer 1995, p. 17

[21] "The Marketing of the Star Wars Trilogy," by Pamela Roller, *Star Wars Insider*, issue 27, 1995 pp. 16-18

[22] "The Marketing of the Star Wars Trilogy," by Pamela Roller, *Star Wars Insider*, issue 27, 1995 p. 18

[23] "The Phantom Redemption" by T'Bone, starwarz.com, May 8th, 2003, originally posted on creativescreenwriting.com, 2000, http://www.starwarz.com/tbone/index.php?categoryid=26&p2_articleid=168

[24] "The George Lucas Saga" by Kerry O' Quinn, *Starlog*, July, 1981

[25] as Lucas says in "Lucas Takes Manhattan" by Scott Chernoff and Kevin Fitzpatrick, *Star Wars Insider* issue 45, August 1999, p. 18

[26] Rinzler, *Making of Star Wars*, p. 353

[27] The *Episode I Insider's Guide* has no mention about a prophecy or virgin birth, nor any of the scenes related to the midichlorians (ie the blood test, Qui Gon explaining them) in its highly detailed summary of the rough draft, major issues which would have been referenced in the course of its summary. Instead, it says only that Anakin is gifted but his future clouded, and also that Anakin's existence was "foreseen". Thus, the Prophecy, the Chosen One, and the midichlorians came in the later drafts—logically in the second draft with Qui Gon's promotion.

[28] *Episode I Insider's Guide*, 1999. Warka is the modern name for ancient Mesoptamia's Uruk, the first city-state in human history.

[29] Bouzereau, *The Making of Episode I*, p. 8

[30] For further learning, see "The Influence and Imagery of Akira Kurosawa," by Michael Kaminski, april 10th, 2007, http://www.secrethistoryofstarwars.com/kurosawa1.html. Page 5 in particular has an example of this *Seven Samurai-Attack of the Clones* parallel.

[31] Bouzereau, *Annotated Screenplays*, p. 316

[32] Bouzereau, *Annotated Screenplays*, p. 316

[33] *Bantha Tracks*, issue 5, summer 1979

[34] *A Guide to the Star Wars Universe* by Bill Slavicsek, 1994, p. 95.

[35] Bouzereau, *The Making of Episode I*, p. 7

[36] Hearn, p. 197

[37] Even in the CD-ROM *Making Magic*, released in late 1996, Lucas stresses that he hasn't decided if he will direct any of the new *Star Wars* films—and adds that if he did do anyone of them he would only do one and not all three. The *Sarasota Herald-Tribune* reports on September 29, 1996 that the previous Wednesday (the 25th) Lucas announced through a spokesperson that he would be directing the first prequel. See "Lucas Returning to Film Directing", *Sarasota Herald-Tribune*, September 29th, 1996 and "Star Wars Prequels Draw Lucas Back" by Paula Parisi, *Contra Costa Times*, September 30th, 1996.

[38] Hearn, p. 194

[39] Bouzereau, *The Making of Episode I*, p. 44

[40] Bouzereau, *The Making of Episode I*, p. 44

[41] Bouzereau, *The Making of Episode I*, p. 48

[42] Bouzereau, *The Making of Episode I*, p. 45

[43] *Baltimore Sun*, May 12th, 2002, http://www.baltimoresun.com/features/arts/bal-as.kasdan12may12.stor

[44] *Eon Magazine*, September 1999, http://www.eonmagazine.com/archive/9909/features/big_pictur e/mumford_kasdan/features_frameset.htm

[45] " 'Star Wars' Juggernaut Began Slowly," by Glenn Lovell, *The Dallas Morning News*, Janurary 30th, 1997, as reported by *Augusta Chronicle* Online, http://chronicle.augusta.com/stories/013097/starwars_juggerna ut.html

[46] *Oprah*, February 1997

[47] *Oprah*, February 1997

## Chapter XI: The Madness

[1] "May the Boss Be With You" by Rob Lenihan, CNN Money, May 4th, 1999
http://money.cnn.com/1999/05/04/bizbuzz/starwars/

[2] For example, one of the most prominent pre-release reviews was *Ain't It Cool News*, who gave the film a mostly warm reception. These were posted on May 5th, among the first-ever reviews of the film. Overall the half-dozen reviewers say it is fun and imaginative, but nothing incredible; enjoyable if you don't carry big expectations. However, two days later, on May 9th, reviews from the press screening are released, from the most pre-eminent sources in journalism: *Rolling Stone*, *Time*, *Newsweek*, *New York Times*, *Variety*. They all trash the movie, among the most negative reviews Episode I received. Some days later, a mix of positive, negative, and mixed reviews appear, from papers like *USA Today*, media like BBC, and websites like *Film Threat*, which is basically the norm for the film's reception. Overall the film scores poor to so-so ratings—40% by *Rotten Tomatoes* for the few dozen major publications, and 64% overall for all reviews.

[3] "Ready, Set, Glow" by Richard Corliss, *Time*, April 26th, 1999

[4] "Full Force is Behind Effects, Not Story" by Roger Ebert, *Chicago Sun Times*, May 16th, 1999

[5] see prior notes. *Rolling Stone*, *Time*, *Newsweek*, *New York Times* and *Variety*, for example, were the first reviews released, and gave the film terrible ratings. A few days later it began to rebound with positive reviews like *Dailey News Los Angeles* and *USA Today*, but most that followed were overall mixed—by which I mean there were some negative, some positive and some lukewarm.

[6] As RottenTomatoes.com averages the film at 64% overall—okay, but nothing special. Though its "top critic" filter puts it at 40%—terrible.

[7] Their main concerns was Jar Jar's prancing and flighty nature and his effeminate voice. See "The Nelly Menace" by Richard Goldstein,
http://www.villagevoice.com/news/9923,goldstein,6325,1.html for an example of article's accusing this.
http://www.da.wvu.edu/archives/990707/news/990707,04,04.html details the Gay and Lesbian Alliance Against Defamation's criticism of the character.

[8] "Life After Darth" by Steve Silberman, *Wired*, May 2005

[9] *Top Gear*, series 8, episode 4, May 2006

[10] "The Phantom Redemption" by T'Bone, starwarz.com, May 8th, 2003, originally posted on creativescreenwriting.com, 2000, http://www.starwarz.com/tbone/index.php?categoryid=26&p2 _articleid=168

[11] Starwars.com *Homing Beacon* #165, July 6th, 2006

[12] Professor Michael Dyson of Columbia Univserity educates on African-American studies. He says, "[Jar Jar] seems to owe something to Disney characters. If you go back and look at cartoons from the 30's and 40's and 50's, they're full of racism. And it's deliberate. [For instance,] *Dumbo*, the black crows were meant to remind you of black people...Maybe this time around in reaching back to borrow from old movies, maybe Lucas or his people had trouble separating stereotypes." See "Jar Jar Jarring" by Michal Okwu, CNN online, June 14th, 1999, http://www.cnn.com/SHOWBIZ/Movies/9906/09/jar.jar/

[13] "Star Wars: Lucas Strikes Back", *Newsnite*, July 14th, 1999, http://news.bbc.co.uk/1/hi/entertainment/394542.stm

[14] "Star Wars: Lucas Strikes Back", *Newsnite*, July 14th, 1999, http://news.bbc.co.uk/1/hi/entertainment/394542.stm

[15] *Puppets to Pixels*, 2002

[16] "Critical Consensus: 'Star Wars' Prequels Actually Better Reviewed Than Originals" by Senh Duong, rottentomatoes.com, May 19, 2005, http://www.rottentomatoes.com/news/comments/?entryid=197 859

[17] Cannes Film Festival Press Conference, May 15th 2005, http://www.festival-cannes.fr/films/fiche_film.php?langue=6002&id_film=427801 9

[18] For example, in his 1997 review Roger Ebert opened by saying, "*Empire Strikes Back* is the best of the three Star Wars films, and the most thought-provoking," which seemed to be the general consensus among commentators on its re-release. *Empire* magazine's 1999 poll listed the film as the second-greatest film of all time (http://www.filmsite.org/empireuk100.html) , while Uk's Film Four listed it at number one. *TV Guide*'s 1998 Top 50 movies lists it at number 27, ahead of *Jaws, Graffiti, Raiders, On the Waterfront* and *Schindler's List* (http://www.filmsite.org/tvguide.html). *Return of the Jedi* is absent from these lists.

[19] Nontheless, one of the more infamous examples of the *Jedi* backlash that arose in the 90's as *Empire* underwent a converse re-appraisal is the humorous "50 Reasons Why Return of the Jedi Sucks" by Dan Vebber, which appeared in Ted Edwards' *Star Wars Compendium* in January 1999 and has been posted a million other places since then.

[20] "George Lucas Talks Future of Star Wars With Us" by Christopher Allen, *Cinescape* online, June 14th, 2002, http://www.cinescape.com/0/editorial.asp?aff_id=0&this_cat=Movies&action=page&type_id=&cat_id=270338&obj_id=34918

[21] "Coppola Sticks Up For Lucas," *Associated Press,* as reported by CNN online, May 20th, 1999, http://www.cnn.com/SHOWBIZ/News/9905/20/showbuzz/

[22] Respectively, these films score 78%, 74%, and 92% on the tomatometer, with the "top critics" selection essentially the same.

[23] "'Star Wars: Episode I The Phantom Menace'" by Kenneth Turan, *Los Angeles Times*, May 18th, 1999

[24] *The Beginning*, 2001

[25] "Neeson Says He'll Retire From Movie Acting", IMDB Studio Briefing, May 6th, 1999, http://www.imdb.com/news/sb/1999-05-06#film3

[26] *The Mercury News*, October 25th, 2000, http://www0.mercurycenter.com/premium/arts/docs/stamp26.htm

[27] "Declaring War," by Ian Spelling, *Starburst* special #40, summer 1999, http://www.visimag.com/starburst/s40_feature.htm

[28] *60 Minutes*, March 13th, 2005

[29] *The Beginning*, 2001

[30] *The Beginning*, 2001

[31] *Empire of Dreams*, 2004

[32] Worrell, p. 182

[33] *Screen Superstar* magazine, 1977

[34] "George Lucas Goes Far Out," by Stephen Zito, *American Film*, April 1977

[35] Rinzler, *Making of Star Wars*, p. 148

[36] "Life After Darth" by Steve Silberman, *Wired*, May 2005, http://www.wired.com/wired/archive/13.05/lucas.html

[37] "The Chosen One" featurette, *Revenge of the Sith* DVD, 2005

[38] Worrell, p. 182

## Chapter XII: Stitches

[1] Duncan, p. 11

[2] Duncan, p. 13

[3] Duncan, p. 12

[4] Duncan, p. 12

[5] Hearn, p. 219

[6] *The Art of Attack of the Clones* by Mark Cotta Vaz, p. 183

[7] "Prequel Update" by Dan Madsen, *Star Wars Insider* 39, August/September 1998, p. 10. Dan Madsen reports that Lucas had actually announced Fett's role earlier than when this interview takes place.

[8] *Time*, May 19th 1980

[9] Rinzler, *Making of Star Wars*, p. 352

[10] *Revenge of the Sith* DVD commentary track, 2005

[11] *The Art of Attack of the Clones* by Mark Cotta Vaz, pp. 110-116

[12] *The Art of Attack of the Clones* by Mark Cotta Vaz, p. 115

[13] *The Art of Attack of the Clones* by Mark Cotta Vaz, p. 119

[14] Bouzereau, *Annotated Screenplays*, p. 127

[15] Bouzereau, *Annotated Screenplays*, p. 297

[16] Bouzereau, *Annotated Screenplays*, p. 196. Bouzereau describes the description as stemming from Lucas' "notes"—probably, he is referring to the story treatment, which is written in note-form in places and has language similar to what Bouzereau describes

[17] "The Greatest Story Ever Told" by R Burke, Static Multimedia, 2005, http://www.staticmultimedia.com/content/film/features/feature_1115643931?info=film. Here Lucas says, that Anakin's romance, Palpatine's ascent (and the set-up of the Clone Wars) occupied the content of the original outline which would be contained in Episode II. He says, "So, then I got to the second [film], and it was kind of the same thing. They fall in love, they can't and they're not supposed to, and, you know, little bits of trivia in terms of, you know, setting up the empire and how all that stuff works. That's about another twenty percent of this story treatment."

[18] The situation is not quite as simple as I paint it. For example, Murnau, perhaps the most important individual in the German Expressionism movement, came to the US in 1926 and died in 1931, while influential Expressionist cinematographer Karl Freund had already immigrated to Hollywood in 1929. The most influential Expressionist to find a home in Hollywood after the Nazi crackdown is Fritz Lang.

In the 1940's, directors such as Alfred Hitchcock (*Shadow of a Doubt*), Otto Preminger (*Laura*) and Billy Wilder (*Double Indemnity*) would draw heavy inspiration from the German Expressionism movement.

[19] "L'attacco dei registi mutanti from outer space" by Davide Canavero, http://www.guerrestellari.net/athenaeum/stori_menuautore_ann i50.html, offers a good comparison of some examples

[20] Duncan, p. 89

[21] *Star Wars Insider*, issue 45, Aug/Sept 1999, p. 19

[22] Avni, p. 28

[23] Biskind, p. 421

[24] "Mark Hamill Walks Down Memory Lane with Film Freak Central" by Walter Chaw, *filmfreakcentral.com*, March 20th, 2005, http://filmfreakcentral.net/notes/mhamillinterview.htm

[25] Pollock, pp. 3-4

[26] "The Force Behind Star Wars" by Paul Scanlon, *Rolling Stone*, August 25th 1977

[27] "The George Lucas Saga" by Kerry O' Quinn, *Starlog*, July, 1981

[28] Duncan, p. 17

[29] *Star Wars Insider*, issue 48, Feb/ March 2000, p.11

[30] Duncan, p. 17

[31] "Confused? Lucas Planned Vader This Way All Along" by Terry Lawson, *Denver Post*, May 20th, 2005, http://www.denverpost.com/movies/ci_2744169

[32] "Prequel Update with Rick McCallum," *Star Wars Insider* 45, Aug/Sept. 1999, p. 63. The conversation took place two weeks before Episode I was released. He says: "George is about a quarter of the way through the script. He'll have the script done by September." Perhaps, he is simply reporting what Lucas had told him: on page 9 of Duncan's *Attack of the Clones* book, McCallum writes that Lucas is writing the Episode III script, but then adds, "at least that's what he tells me." In fact, he was not, as Rinzler's Episode III book shows (Duncan's book was released in mid-2002, while Lucas would only begin outlining Episode III that summer, with scripting not until the fall—identical to Episode II). Further confirming that Lucas didn't start scripting until September, Jody Duncan writes on page 11 of her book that Lucas took notes while on vacation in the summer of 1999, and that the script had not yet been written at that time.

McCallum makes similar statements in *Insider* issue 44 (though a typo on its cover states 39), p.10, which stem from sometime around April 1999: "George is writing the script [for

Episode II]...He's editing Episode I, but on weekends and the early mornings he works on the script." Again, as per the previous information, this does not seem to be the case. Perhaps when Lucas tells him he is "working on the script" he was exaggerating, or really only working on the outline (which, by some stretch, could be said to be an incarnation of "the script"). As Rinzler's Episode III book shows, Lucas' is very reluctant to start scripting, and puts it off to the last possible minute. Earlier, McCallum in issue 39, p. 11 says that Lucas won't begin scripting until summer. In issue 46, p. 10 McCallum says he will be making a trip to scout Italy in September or October (this issue was published in October, so this interview is likely from August) but that "we're now waiting on the script." Which seems to follow that if Lucas was ¼ through it in May he would be done it by August. This leads yet more credibility to Lucas' admission that he didn't actually begin until Septmeber and had a draft done by March (or a rough-rough draft by January, as per Chiang).

Giving a parallel situation, with the same pre-production schedule, on page 31of Rinzler's *Making of Revenge of the Script*, Lucas reveals that by November he still hadn't started writing Episode III even though he had told McCallum he had been long ago. "You said you've *been* writing," McCallum protests. "I've been *thinking* about it," Lucas admits. It would be over another month before he began.

[33] Duncan, p. 13. The art department was not assembled and working until this time as well, which, using *Revenge of the Sith* as a parallel, meant that indeed Lucas did not begin writing until September.

[34] Duncan, p. 23

[35] Duncan, p. 23

[36] Duncan, p. 23

[37] Rinzler, *The Making of Revenge of the Sith*, p. 27. Though McCallum here is referring to Episode III, the production is not only analogous, but Episode II's was even more constrained.

[38] Rinzler, *The Making of Revenge of the Sith*, p. 27. Though McCallum here is referring to Episode III, the production is not only analogous, but Episode II's was even more constrained.

[39] Hearn, p. 216. It should be admitted that the words "rough draft" are not written on it. However, Hearn always opens each chapter of his book with a photo of the hand-written rough draft of each script, so it is well within reason to make the assumption that this is, like every other handwritten original

displayed throughout the book, the coverpage to the rough draft. Amusingly, Lucas has it dated as "March 13, 1999", but then "1999" is crossed out in red pen and "2000" corrected over top of it. Perhaps this testifies to the state of hurriedness it was written under—Lucas was so busy he couldn't remember what year it was!

[40] *The Art of Attack of the Clones* by Mark Cotta Vaz, , p. 6

[41] Duncan, p. 13

[42] Hearn, p. 216

[43] Duncan, p. 17

[44] Hearn, p. 216

[45] Hearn, p. 216. For what it is worth, the shooting script leaked to the internet is also titled as the revised third draft. A title page addendum reads: "Last Revision: September 5, 2001", though what this last revision may be is not known. This could be a date when scenes were added for the second round of pick-up shooting (which was in October of 2001, as per Duncan, p. 207), but this script reflects the film in its original form at the time of production. Perhaps the title page is a mismatch to the actual body.

[46] Hearn, p. 224

[47] *The Art of Attack of the Clones* by Mark Cotta Vaz, , p. 100

[48] Hearn, p. 216

[49] "Special Announcement: Episode II Title", starwars.com, August 6th, 2001, http://www.starwars.com/episode-ii/release/promo/news20010806.html

[50] "McGregor: Star Wars 2 'Really Good' - But Title 'Not Good'", IMDB Studio Briefing, February 7th, 2002, http://www.imdb.com/news/wenn/2002-02-07#celeb7

[51] An overview of the reviews of the more pre-eminent critics (i.e. *Variety*, *Rolling Stone*, *New Yorker*, etc.) shows that it was actually received by them worse than *Phantom Menace*. Rotten Tomatoes.com's "top critics" filter rates *Phantom Menace* at 40% and *Attack of the Clones* at 37%. With fans, online sources, and other publications, however, it rated at 67%, compared to *Phantom Menace*'s 64%. In fan communities, however, while initially highly praised, its approval has rapidly dropped off.

[52] "Lucas Strikes Back: 'Star Wars' creator defends Jar Jar and says plot rules his universe" by Gary Dretzka, *San Francisco Gate*, May 13th, 2002, http://www.sfgate.com/cgi-bin/article.cgi?f=/c/a/2002/05/13/dd169158.dtl

## Chapter XIII: The Circle is Complete

[1] "As the *Star Wars: Episode III—Revenge of the Sith* DVD is Released, Producer Rick McCallum Turns to TV" by Melissa J. Perenson, *Science Fiction Weekly*, November 2005, http://www.scifi.com/sfw/issue446/interview2.html

[2] *Empire* magazine, August 1999

[3] "James Earl Jones To Speak At Hospital Fund Raiser" by Christopher Borrelli, *Toledo Blade*, March 18th, 2001

[4] Jones tells the same story as his quote to *Star Wars Insider* in issue 49, p. 58, from May 2000, where he reports that the meeting between him and Lucas in Idaho where the conversation took place actually occurred a few years *prior*—meaning it occurred sometime in the 90's.

[5] Rinzler, *The Making of Revenge of the Sith*, pp. 13-15

[6] Rinzler, *The Making of Revenge of the Sith*, p. 17

[7] Rinzler, *The Making of Revenge of the Sith*, p. 17

[8] *Starlog*, issue 300, July, 2002

[9] Rinzler, *The Making of Revenge of the Sith*, p. 28

[10] Rinzler, *The Making of Revenge of the Sith*, p. 28

[11] Rinzler, *The Making of Revenge of the Sith*, p. 23

[12] Rinzler, *The Making of Revenge of the Sith*, p. 24

[13] Rinzler, *The Making of Revenge of the Sith*, p. 29

[14] Rinzler, *The Making of Revenge of the Sith*, pp. 30-31

[15] Rinzler, *The Making of Revenge of the Sith*, p. 31

[16] Rinzler, *The Making of Revenge of the Sith*, p. 32

[17] Rinzler, *The Making of Revenge of the Sith*, p. 36

[18] Rinzler, *The Making of Revenge of the Sith*, p. 13

[19] For example on page 36 of Rinzler's book Lucas says that he had to "rethink" the plot, while on page 40 Rinzler describes it as the story being revised, and on page 39 describes it as a "rethink of the script".

[20] For example IMDB Studio Briefing Reports as far back as March 28th, 2002: " 'I told George I didn't mind dying,' Jackson told the *Calgary Sun*, 'I just didn't want to go out like some punk. George said that was fine and he'd see what he could do about a fitting death scene.' " This would be repeated many other sources. See http://www.imdb.com/news/sb/2002-03-28#film2

[21] Rinzler, *The Making of Revenge of the Sith*, p. 93

[22] Rinzler, *The Making of Revenge of the Sith*, p. 32

[23] "Lucas on Iraq War, 'Star Wars' " by Chris Burns, CNN.com, Monday, May 16, 2005, http://www.cnn.com/2005/SHOWBIZ/Movies/05/16/cannes.starwars/

[24] Rinzler, *The Making of Revenge of the Sith*, p. 13

[25] "The Greatest Story Ever Told" by R Burke, Static Multimedia, 2005, http://www.staticmultimedia.com/content/film/features/feature _1115643931?info=film

[26] Hearn, p. 240

[27] "The Greatest Story Ever Told" by R Burke, Static Multimedia, 2005, http://www.staticmultimedia.com/content/film/features/feature _1115643931?info=film

[28] Rinzler, p. 40

[29] Bouzereau, *Annotated Screenplays*, p. 168

[30] "Star Wars: The Last Battle" by Jim Windolf, *Vanity Fair*, February 2005, p. 167

[31] *Star Wars Insider* issue 39, August 1998, p. 33

[32] *Star Wars Insider* issue 39, August 1998, pp. 33-34,

[33] Bouzereau, *Annotated Screenplays*, p. 168

[34] Bouzereau, *Annotated Screenplays*, p. 291

[35] Rinzler, *The Making of Revenge of the Sith*, pp. 28-29

[36] Rinzler, *The Making of Revenge of the Sith*, p. 29

[37] Rinzler, *The Making of Revenge of the Sith*, p. 30

[38] Rinzler, *The Making of Revenge of the Sith*, p. 35. Lucas indicates a few days later that he has not yet completed a detailed outline of his still-evolving storyline (Rinzler, p. 36)

[39] Rinzler, *The Making of Revenge of the Sith*, p. 39

[40] Rinzler, *The Making of Revenge of the Sith*, p. 39

[41] Rinzler, *The Making of Revenge of the Sith*, p. 39

[42] Rinzler, *The Making of Revenge of the Sith*, p. 31. Also note that on page 36, Lucas states that he still did not have an outline yet—and this is on December 13th, 2002. Trisha Biggar asks for details of which costumes Padme will wear in each scene but Lucas protests, "It's too early. I have to get an outline together." He does seem to have a fairly specific conception of the plot by this point, as he follows this up by listing the sets she will appear in. This outline, then, is the product of late December, 2002, or early January, 2003.

[43] Rinzler, *The Making of Revenge of the Sith*, p. 40

[44] Rinzler, *The Making of Revenge of the Sith*, p. 40. When precisely he started writing is somewhat unclear, but early January seems a likely time. This is concluded because as late as December 13th, 2002, Lucas still had not yet put together an outline (Rinzler, p. 36). While it is possible that he began scripting in the final weeks of December, it seems highly unlikely that he would do this with the Christmas holidays looming (and with Lucas being a family man). More likely, he

would have perhaps drafted the outline in that time and then began the script once the holidays had concluded. It is January 31st when his rough draft is finally typed up (Rinzler, p. 40), and with it only being 55 pages long this seems more than adequate time, especially since he had developed the plot throughout the previous nine months.

[45] Rinzler, *The Making of Revenge of the Sith*, p. 41

[46] Rinzler, *The Making of Revenge of the Sith*, p. 41

[47] Rinzler, *The Making of Revenge of the Sith*, p. 42

[48] Rinzler, *The Making of Revenge of the Sith*, p. 42

[49] *The Art of Episode II* by Mark Cotta Vaz, 2002, p. 128

[50] Duncan, p. 39

[51] "Becoming Sidious" Episode III web doc, 2004

[52] "Ian McDiarmid" by Anwar Brett, BBC Online, May 2005, http://www.bbc.co.uk/films/2005/05/18/ian_mcdiarmid_star_w ars_episode_iii_interview.shtml

[53] Rinzler, *The Making of Revenge of the Sith*, pp. 47-48

[54] Rinzler, *The Making of Revenge of the Sith*, p. 51

[55] Rinzler, *The Making of Revenge of the Sith*, p. 53

[56] Rinzler, *The Making of Revenge of the Sith*, pp. 60-61

[57] *Episode I Insiders Guide* CD-ROM, 1999

[58] Rinzler, *The Making of Revenge of the Sith*, p. 62

[59] Rinzler, *The Making of Revenge of the Sith*, p. 53

[60] For example, on page 82 of Rinzler's book Lucas reveals to Christensen on shoot day six that he spent the weekend (this conversation occurs on a Monday) rewriting the scene where Anakin turns. "I've stretched it out and given you a little more to go on in terms of him pulling you in." On page 96 he also reveals that he changed the "Darth Plagueis" story to be set in an opera house instead of Palpatine's office after he realised he had already shot many scenes there.

[61] Rinzler, *The Making of Revenge of the Sith*, p. 95

[62] Bouzereau, *Annotated Screenplays*, p. 319

[63] Rinzler, *The Making of Revenge of the Sith*, p. 188

[64] Rinzler, *The Making of Revenge of the Sith*, p. 176

[65] *Homing Beacon*, issue 139, starwars.com, June 23rd, 2005

[66] *Revenge of the Sith* DVD "depth commentary", 2005

[67] *Revenge of the Sith* DVD commentary track, 2005

[68] *Revenge of the Sith* DVD commentary track, 2005

[69] *Revenge of the Sith* DVD commentary track, 2005

[70] Rinzler, *The Making of Revenge of the Sith*, pp. 204-205

[71] Rinzler, *The Making of Revenge of the Sith*, p. 205

[72] Rinzler, *The Making of Revenge of the Sith*, p. 206

[73] Rinzler, *The Making of Revenge of the Sith*, p. 109

[74] "Why Lucas Tinkered with 'Star Wars' ", *Associated Press*, September 20th, 2004, http://www.cnn.com/2004/SHOWBIZ/Movies/09/20/film.qa.george.lucas.ap/index.html

[75] "Why Lucas Tinkered with 'Star Wars' ", *Associated Press*, September 20th, 2004, http://www.cnn.com/2004/SHOWBIZ/Movies/09/20/film.qa.george.lucas.ap/index.html

[76] Hearn, p. 183

[77] *Oprah*, February 1997

[78] Rinzler, *The Making of Revenge of the Sith*, pp. 84-5

[79] "The Morning of the Magician" by Clair Clouzqt, *Ecran*, September 15th, 1977

[80] "Mark Hamill—One Minute Interview", *Gossip Magazine*, June 1978

[81] Pollock, p. 270

[82] "George Lucas on *Star Wars*, *Fahrenheit 9/11*, and his own legacy" By Steve Silberman, *Wired* Online Exclusive article, May 2005, http://www.wired.com/wired/archive/13.05/lucasqa_pr.html

[83] *60 Minutes*, March 13th, 2005

[84] "Life After Darth" by Steve Silberman, *Wired*, May 2005, http://www.wired.com/wired/archive/13.05/lucas.html

[85] "Cannes Embraces Political Message in Star Wars", *Associated Press*, May 16th, 2005, http://www.msnbc.msn.com/id/7873314

[86] "Star Wars: Episode III—Revenge of the Sith" by Todd McCarthy, *Variety*, May 5th, 2005

[87] *Time*, May 9th, 2005

[88] "Americans Prefer Watching Movies at Home" by Will Lester, *Associated Press,* June 17th, 2005. http://www.highbeam.com/doc/1P1-110055537.html. Lester says 2005 was estimated to be the worst year for theatre attendance in over a decade. This find is echoed in CNN Money's article from the same period, "Batman Attempts a Hollywood Rescue," by Krysten Crawford, who reports that it was the worst slump since 1985, http://money.cnn.com/2005/06/16/news/newsmakers/boxoffice_sales, and many other articles from this time.

[89] "A Look Back in Wonder," by Richard Schinkel, *Time*, May 9th, 2005

[90] *The Charlie Rose Show*, September 9th, 2004

# Conclusion

[1] *Return of the Jedi* DVD commentary, 2004

# Appendix A

[1] *Once Upon A Galaxy: A Journal of the Making of Empire Strikes Back* by Alan Arnold, p. 247
[2] *The Annotated Screenplays* by Laurent Bouzereau, p. viii
[3] *Skywalking: The Life and Films of George Lucas* by Dale Pollock, p. 134
[4] Bouzereau, p. viii
[5] Bouzereau, p. viii
[6] *Star Wars Insider*, issue 79, p. 55, November 2004
[7] *Making of Star Wars* by J.W. Rinzler, 2007, p. 8
[8] *Making of Star Wars*, Rinzler, p. 9
[9] Bouzereau, p. 6
[10] Bouzereau, p. viii
[11] *The Big Breakfast*, July 16th, 1999
[12] "George Lucas: Father of the Force" by Bill Warren, *Starlog*, issue 127, February 1988, p. 49
[13] Bouzereau, p. 6
[14] Bouzereau, p. 6
[15] *Bantha Tracks*, issue 18, November 1982
[16] Bouzereau, p. 6
[17] *Making of Star Wars Episode I* by Laurent Bouzereau and Jody Duncan, 1999, pp. 8-9
[18] *Making of Revenge of the Sith* by J. W. Rinzler, 2005, p. 72

# Appendix B

[1] *The Making of Star Wars* by J.W. Rinzler, 2007, p. 40
[2] *Once Upon a Galaxy* by Alan Arnold, 1980, p. 223
[3] *Starburst*, issue 24, 1980
[4] *Mythmaker: The Life and Work of George Lucas* by John Baxter, 1999, p. 264
[5] retrieved from http://www.stars.handshake.de/int70.htm
[6] Characters of Star Wars DVD featurette, 2004
[7] Rinzler, p. 102
[8] "George Lucas" by David Sheff, *Rolling Stone*, November 5th, 1987
[9] *Artifact From the Future: The Making of THX 1138*
[10] Rinzler, p. 69
[11] Rinzler, p. 124

580

[12] Rinzler, p.69
[13] Rinzler, p. 69

## Appendix C

[1] *Rolling Stone*, June 2, 2005
[2] Bantha Tracks issue 8, spring 1980; there are other variations on this story, such as that it was ad-libbed in the *THX* recording, but this earlier version to me seems more accurate due to its specification
[3] "The Force Behind Star Wars" by Paul Scanlon, *Rolling Stone*, August 25th, 1977
[4] *Skywalking: The Life and Films of George Lucas* by Dale Pollock, 1983, p. 141
[5] *The Annotated Screenplays* by Laurent Bouzereau, p. 10
[6] Bouzereau, p. 10
[7] *The Making of Star Wars*, J.W. Rinzler, p. 172
[8] *The Making of Star Wars*, J.W. Rinzler, p. 172
[9] "What Happened To Han And Leia? How About Jar Jar? 'Star Wars' Emperor Lucas Speaks" By Larry Carrol, MTV online, May 9th 2005, http://www.mtv.com/movies/movie/237059/news/articles/1501522/story.jhtml
[10] *The Making of Star Wars*, J.W. Rinzler, p. 107
[11] *The Making of Star Wars*, J.W. Rinzler, p. 59
[12] *The Making of Star Wars*, J.W. Rinzler, p. 26
[13] *The Making of Star Wars*, J.W. Rinzler, p. 22
[14] Personal correspondance

## Appendix D

[1] BBC Omnibus "A Long Time Ago: The Story of Star Wars", 1999
[2] BBC Omnibus "A Long Time Ago: The Story of Star Wars", 1999
[3] *The Making of Star Wars* by J.W Rinzler, p. 25
[4] *The Making of Star Wars* by J.W Rinzler, p. 107
[5] Arnold, pp. 247-48
[6] "The George Lucas Saga" by Kerri O' Quinn, *Starlog*, July 1981
[7] *Icons: Intimate Portraits* by Denise Worrell, 1989, p. 186
[8] Worrell, p. 185
[9] Worrell, p. 186

[10]
http://www.jazmaonline.com/interviews/interviews2007.asp?in
tID=432 and
http://www.ugo.com/channels/comics/features/starwars
[11] Arnold p. 247-8, 1980
[12] "I've Got to Get My Life Back" by Gerald Clarke, *Time* Magazine, May 23rd, 1983
[13] *Icons: Intimate Portraits* by Denise Worrell, 1989, p. 186
[14] "The Empire Strikes Back and So Does Filmmaker George Lucas With His Sequel To Star Wars" by Jean Vallely, *Rolling Stone*, June 12th, 1980
[15] *Prevue* Magazine, July 1983
[16] "Starlog Salutes Star Wars," *Starlog*, July 1987; the quoted comment was actually made earlier, being reprinted in this issue
[17] "Grand Illusion" by Paula Parisi, *Wired*, May 1999
[18] *Time*, May 19th, 1980
[19] "I've Got to Get My Life Back" by Gerald Clarke, *Time*, May 23rd, 1983
[20] "Mark Hamill Spills Some Dirt on Star Wars Episodes 7, 8 and 9" by John Champea, *The Movie Blog* September 10th, 2004, the movieblog.com,
http://www.themovieblog.com/archives/2004/09/mark_hamill_
spills_some_dirt_on_star_wars_episodes_7_8_and_9.html
[21] *The Cinema of George Lucas* by Marcus Hearn, 2005, pp. 240-242
[22] "What Happened to Han and Leia? What About Jar Jar? 'Star Wars' Emperor Lucas Speaks" by Larry Carroll, May 9th, 2005, MTV online,
http://www.mtv.com/movies/movie/237059/news/articles/1501
522/story.jhtml

## Appendix E

[1] "An Interview With Gary Kurtz" by Ken P., *IGN Film Force*, November 11th, 2002,
http://filmforce.ign.com/articles/376/376873p1.html
[2] "Gary Kurtz Interview: The Original Star Wars Producer Speaks" by Chris Gore, *Film Threat*, March 5th, 2000,
http://www.filmthreat.com/index.php?section=interviews&Id= 8
[3] "Gary Kurtz Reveals Original Plans For Episodes 1-9" by Paul Ens, *TheForce.Net*, May 26th, 1999,
http://www.theforce.net/latestnews/story/gary_kurtz_reveals_o
riginal_plans_for_episodes_19_80270.asp

[4] *Once Upon A Galaxy* by Alan Arnold, 1980, p. 177 and pp. 247-248

[5] *Starlog*, July 1987, p. 41

[6] "An Interview With Gary Kurtz" by Ken P., *IGN Film Force*, November 11th, 2002, http://filmforce.ign.com/articles/376/376873p1.html

[7] "Gary Kurtz Interview: The Original Star Wars Producer Speaks" by Chris Gore, *Film Threat*, March 5th, 2000, http://www.filmthreat.com/index.php?section=interviews&Id=8

[8] "Gary Kurtz Reveals Original Plans For Episodes 1-9" by Paul Ens, *TheForce.net*, May 26th, 1999, http://www.theforce.net/latestnews/story/gary_kurtz_reveals_original_plans_for_episodes_19_80270.asp

[9] Arnold, p. 3

# Appendix F

[1] "Star Wars: George Lucas' Vision" by Dale Pollock, *Washington Post* online, May 19th, 2005, http://www.washingtonpost.com/wp-dyn/content/discussion/2005/05/06/DI2005050600821.html

[2] "Star Wars: George Lucas' Vision" by Dale Pollock, *Washington Post* online, May 19th, 2005, http://www.washingtonpost.com/wp-dyn/content/discussion/2005/05/06/DI2005050600821.html

[3] "Star Wars: George Lucas' Vision" by Dale Pollock, *Washington Post* online, May 19th, 2005, http://www.washingtonpost.com/wp-dyn/content/discussion/2005/05/06/DI2005050600821.html

[4] "Star Wars: George Lucas' Vision" by Dale Pollock, *Washington Post* online, May 19th, 2005, http://www.washingtonpost.com/wp-dyn/content/discussion/2005/05/06/DI2005050600821.html

[5] *The Complete Making of Indiana Jones*, by J.W. Rinzler, 2008, pp. 22-23

# Appendix G

[1] *The Making of Star Wars*, by Jonathan Rinzler, 2007, p. 42

[2] *The Making of Star Wars*, by Jonathan Rinzler, 2007, p. 68

[3] *The Making of Star Wars*, by Jonathan Rinzler, 2007, p. 107

[4] *Once Upon a Galaxy: A Journal of the Making of Empire Strikes Back*, by Alan Arnold, 1980, pp. 222-223

[5] *The Making of Star Wars*, by Jonathan Rinzler, 2007, p. 192
[6] *Icons: Intimate Portraits* by Denise Worrell, 1989, p. 182
[7] *The Making of Star Wars*, by Jonathan Rinzler, 2007, p. 107
[8] *The Making of Star Wars*, by Jonathan Rinzler, 2007, p. 111

# Selected Bibliography

*60 Minutes*, March 28, 1999

*60 Minutes*, March 13, 2005

"George Lucas Interview", *Academy of Achievement*, June 19, 1999, http://www.achievement.org/autodoc/page/luc0int-1

*Akira Kurosawa: It is Wonderful to Create*. DVD. Toho, 2002

*All I Need is an Idea*, Episode I webdoc appearing on *Phantom Menace* DVD. Lucasfilm, 1998

Allen, Christopher. "George Lucas Talks Future of Star Wars With Us," *Cinescape* online, June 14, 2002, http://www.cinescape.com/0/editorial.asp?aff_id=0&this_cat=Movies&action=p age&type_id=&cat_id=270338&obj_id=34918

"Behind the Scenes of Star Wars", *American Cinematographer*, July 1977

"Behind the Scenes of The Empire Strikes Back", *American Cinematographer*, June 1980

Arnold, Alan. *Once Upon a Galaxy: A Journal of the Making of The Empire Strikes Back*. New York: Ballantine Books, 1980.

Arnold, Gary. "Darth Vader's Surprise Attack", *Washington Post*, May 18, 1980

Arnold, Gary. "Enough! May the Force Call it Quits!", *Washington Post*, May 22, 1983

Arnold, William. "Director George Lucas Takes a Look Back—And Ahead", *Seattle Post-Intelligencer*, May 12, 2005

*Attack of the Clones*, DVD commentary track. Lucasfilm, 2002

*Artifact from the Future*, appearing on *THX 1138* DVD. Warner Brothers Entertainment, 2004

*Associated Press*, "Cannes Embraces Political Message in Star Wars", May 16, 2005, http://www.msnbc.msn.com/id/7873314

Avni, Sheerly. *Cinema by the Bay*. San Francisco: George Lucas Books, 2006

*Baltimore Sun*, May 12, 2002, http://www.baltimoresun.com/features/arts/bal-as.kasdan12may12.story

*Bantha Tracks* (formerly titled *Newsletter of the Official Star Wars Fanclub*), issues 1-35, 1978-1987

Baxter, John. *Mythmaker: The Life and Work of George Lucas*. New York: Spike/Avon Books, 1999

*BBC Newsnite*, "Star Wars: Lucas Strikes Back", July 14, 1999, http://news.bbc.co.uk/1/hi/entertainment/394542.stm

*Becoming Sidious*, Episode III web doc appearing on *Revenge of the Sith* DVD. Lucasfilm, 2005

*The Beginning*, appearing on *Phantom Menace* DVD. Lucasfilm, 2001

*Berliner Zeitung*, Number 114, May 19, 2005. Translated from German by Alrik Fassbauer

*The Big Breakfast*, July 16, 1999

*Biography: George Lucas*, A&E, 2001

Biskind, Peter. *Easy Riders, Raging Bulls*. New York: Simon & Shuster, 1998

Bouzereau, Laurent. *The Annotated Screenplays*. New York: Ballantine Books, 1997

Bouzereau, Laurent. *The Making of Episode I: The Phantom Menace*. New York: Ballantine Books, 1999

Borrelli, Christopher. "James Earl Jones To Speak At Hospital Fund Raiser", *Toledo Blade*, March 18, 2001

Brennan, Kristen. "Star Wars Origins", 1999, http://www.jitterbug.com/origins/flash.html. This website has moved since this book was first self-published online in 2007. It can now be found at http://moongadget.com/origins/index.html.

Bresman, Jonathan. *The Art of Star Wars Episode I: The Phantom Menace*. New York: Ballantine, 1999

Brett, Anwar. "Ian McDiarmid", *BBC* Online, May 2005, http://www.bbc.co.uk/films/2005/05/18/ian_mcdiarmid_star_wars_episode_iii_i nterview.shtml

Brett, Anwar. "Star Wars: Episode III", *BBC* Online, May 18, 2005, http://www.bbc.co.uk/films/2005/05/18/george_lucas_star_wars_episode_iii_int erview.shtml

Brosnan, John. "The Making of Star Wars", *Starburst*, issue 1, January, 1978

Burke, R. "The Greatest Story Ever Told: An Interview with George Lucas," *Static Multimedia*, September 10, 2005, http://www.staticmultimedia.com/film/features/feature_1115643931

Burns, Chris. "Lucas on Iraq War, 'Star Wars' ", *CNN*, Monday, May 16, 2005, http://www.cnn.com/2005/SHOWBIZ/Movies/05/16/cannes.starwars/

Burns, James H. "Lawrence Kasdan", *Starlog*, September 1981

Burr, Ty. "George Lucas Interview", *The Boston Globe*, October 2005, http://www.boston.com/ae/movies/lucas_interview

Cagle, Jess. "So, What's the Deal with Leia's Hair?", *Time*, April 29, 2002, http://www.time.com/time/covers/1101020429/qa.html

Call, Deborah, et all. *The Art of The Empire Strikes Back*. New York: Ballantine, 1980 (reprinted in 1997)

Campbell, Joseph. *Hero With a Thousand Faces*. Princeton: Princeton University Press, 1949

Canavero, Davide. "L'attacco Dei Registi Mutanti From Outer Space", http://www.guerrestellari.net/athenaeum/stori_menuautore_anni50.html

Cannes Film Festival Press Conference, May 15, 2005, http://www.festival-cannes.fr/films/fiche_film.php?langue=6002&id_film=4278019

Carrol, Larry. "What Happened To Han And Leia? How About Jar Jar? 'Star Wars' Emperor Lucas Speaks", *MTV Online*, May 9, 2005, http://www.mtv.com/movies/movie/237059/news/articles/1501522/story.jhtml

Carter, Jeff. "Star Wars Per-Zahn-ified", *Echostation*, December 19, 1998, http://www.echostation.com/interview/zahn.htm

Champea, John. "Mark Hamill Spills Some Dirt on Star Wars Episodes 7, 8 and 9", *The Movie Blog*, September 10, 2004, http://www.themovieblog.com/archives/2004/09/mark_hamill_spills_some_dirt_on_star_wars_episodes_7_8_and_9.html

*Chaplin* magazine, fall 1973

*The Characters of Star Wars*, appearing on Star Wars trilogy DVD Bonus Material. Lucasfilm, 2004

*The Charlie Rose Show*, September 2004 (re-broadcast May 2005).

Chaw, Walter. "Mark Hamill Walks Down Memory Lane With Film Freak Central, *Film Freak Central*, March 20, 2005, http://filmfreakcentral.net/notes/mhamillinterview.htm

Chernoff, Scott, "Darth Vader: An Insider Exclusive Interview", *Star Wars Insider*, issue 49, May/June 2000

Chernoff, Scott. "Director Irvin Kershner", *Star Wars Insider*, issue 49, May/June 2000

Chernoff, Scott. "Lawrence Kasdan Screenwriter", *Star Wars Insider*, issue 49, May/June 2000

Chernoff, Scott. "Sword of the Jedi", *Star Wars Insider* issue 39, August 1998

Chernoff, Scott and Fitzpatrick, Kevin. "Lucas Takes Manhattan", *Star Wars Insider* issue 45, August 1999

Chernoff, Scott and Fitzpatrick, Kevin. "Prequel Update", *Star Wars Insider*, issue 45, Aug/Sept. 1999

Chitwood, Scott. "The *Star Wars* Trilogy DVD Unveiled - Part 3!", *Coming Soon*, September 17, 2004, http://www.comingsoon.net/news/topnews.php?id=6418

*The Chosen One*, appearing on *Revenge of the Sith* DVD. Lucasfilm, 2005

*Cinefantastique* Vol. 28, No. 28, February 1997

*Classic Creatures: Return of the Jedi*. Lucasfilm, 1983

Clarke, Gerald. "I've Got to Get My Life Back", *Time*, May 23, 1983

Cline, William C. *In the Nick of Time: Motion Picture Sound Serials*. Jefferson: McFarland and Company, 1997

Clouzot, Claire "The Morning of the Magician: George Lucas and Star Wars", *Ecran*, September 15th, 1977. Translated from French by Alisa Belanger.

*CNN* Online, "Coppola Sticks Up For Lucas", May 20, 1999, http://www.cnn.com/SHOWBIZ/News/9905/20/showbuzz/

*CNN* Online, "George Lucas: Mapping the Mythology", May 8, 2002, http://archives.cnn.com/2002/SHOWBIZ/Movies/05/07/ca.s02.george.lucas/

*CNN*, "Skywalker Ranch: New 'Star Wars' Film to Debute In Two Weeks," May 7, 2002, http://transcripts.cnn.com/TRANSCRIPTS/0205/07/lol.00.html

*CNN*, "Why Lucas Tinkered with 'Star Wars' ", September 20, 2004, http://www.cnn.com/2004/SHOWBIZ/Movies/09/20/film.qa.george.lucas.ap/index.html

Corliss, Richard. "Dark Side Rising", *Time*, May 9, 2005

Corliss, Richard. "Ready, Set, Glow", *Time*, April 26, 1999

Crawford, Krysten. "Batman Attempts a Hollywood Rescue", *CNN Money*, June 16, 2005, http://money.cnn.com/2005/06/16/news/newsmakers/boxoffice_sales

Crawley, Paul. "Harrison Ford: The Star Wars Star Going Solo", *Starbust*, issue 2, 1978

Cronin, Brian. "Comic Book Urban Legends Revealed #131", *Comic Book Resources*, November 29, 2007, http://goodcomics.comicbookresources.com/2007/11/29/comic-book-urban-legends-revealed-131

Crowie, Peter. *The Apocalypse Now Book*. New York: De Capo Press, 2001

*Deleted Magic*. Orange Cow Productions, 2005

Dolari, Jenn. "Draft Variations for The Empire Strikes Back," *Starkiller: The Jedi Bendu Script Site*, http://www.starwarz.com/starkiller/writings/draft_variations_esb.htm

Dolari, Jenn. "Draft Variations for Return of the Jedi," *Starkiller: The Jedi Bendu Script Site,*
http://www.starwarz.com/starkiller/writings/draft_variations_roj.htm

Duncan, Jody. *Mythmaking: Behind the Scenes of Attack of the Clones,* New York: Ballantine Books, 2002

Duong, Senh. "Critical Consensus: 'Star Wars' Prequels Actually Better Reviewed Than Originals", *Rotten Tomatoes,* May 19, 2005,
http://www.rottentomatoes.com/news/comments/?entryid=197859

Dretzka, Gary "Lucas Strikes Back: 'Star Wars' creator defends Jar Jar and says plot rules his universe", *San Francisco Gate,* May 13, 2002,
http://www.sfgate.com/cgi-bin/article.cgi?f=/c/a/2002/05/13/dd169158.dtl

Ebert, Roger. "Full Force is Behind Effects, Not Story", *Chicago Sun Times,* May 16, 1999

Edwards, Gavin. "The Cult of Darth Vader," *Rolling Stone,* June 2, 2005

Edwards, Ted. *The Unauthorized Star Wars Compendium.* New York: Little Brown and Company, 1999

*Empire* magazine, August, 1999

*Empire* magazine, May, 2005

*Empire* Magazine, June, 2005

*Empire of Dreams,* appearing on Star Wars Trilogy Bonus Material. Lucasfilm, 2004

*Empire Strikes Back,* Definitive Edition Laserdisc. Twntieth Century Fox, 1993

*Empire Strikes Back,* DVD commentary track. Lucasfilm, 2004

Ens, Paul "Gary Kurtz Reveals Original Plans For Episodes 1-9", *The Force.net,* May 26, 1999,
http://www.theforce.net/latestnews/story/gary_kurtz_reveals_original_plans_for_episodes_19_80270.asp

*Entertainment Tonight* Online, "Sith Strikes Again", May 30, 2005,
http://et.tv.yahoo.com/movies/11198

*Episode I Insider's Guide* CD-ROM. Lucasfilm,1999

*Eon Magazine*, September 1999,
http://www.eonmagazine.com/archive/9909/features/big_picture/mumford_kasda
n/features_frameset.htm

*Evan Carmichael*, "Lights, Camera, Action! Lucas Takes The Film Industry By
Storm", http://www.evancarmichael.com/Famous-Entrepreneurs/538/Lights-
Camera-Action-Lucas-Takes-the-Film-Industry-by-Storm.html

Farber, Stephen. "George Lucas: The Stinky Kid Hits the Big Time", *Film
Quarterly*, vol. 27, no. 3, spring 1974

Flynn, John L. "Origins of Star Wars: Evolution of a Space Saga," *Starkiller:
The Jedi Bendu Script Site*,
http://www.starwarz.com/starkiller/writings/origins.htm

Foley, Jack. "Star Wars Episode III—George Lucas Interview", *Indie London*,
2005, http://www.indielondon.co.uk/film/star_wars3_revenge_sith_lucas.html

Foster, Alan Dean. *Splinter of the Mind's Eye*, New York: Ballantine, 1978
(reprinted in 1994)

Foster, Alan Dean. *Star Wars*, New York: Ballantine, 1976 (reprinted in 1994)

Frayling, Christopher. *Sergio Leone: Something to do with Death*, London:
Faber and Faber Inc., 2000

*From Star Wars to Jedi: The Making of a Saga*. Lucasfilm, 1983

*Future Magazine*, April, 1978

Galloway, Stephen. "Dialogue: George Lucas", *Hollywood Reporter*, June 9,
2005,
http://www.hollywoodreporter.com/hr/search/article_display.jsp?vnu_content_id
=1000964422

Glut, Donald F. *Empire Strikes Back*, New York: Ballantine, 1980.

Goldstein, Richard. "The Nelly Menace", *Village Voice*, June 8, 1999,
http://www.villagevoice.com/news/9923,goldstein,6325,1.html

Gore, Chris. "Gary Kurtz Interview: The Original Star Wars Producer Speaks",
*Film Threat*, March 5, 2000,
http://filmthreat.com/index.php?section=interviews&Id=8

*Gossip Magazine*, 1978

*Gossip Magazine*, "Mark Hamill—One Minute Interview", June 1978

Gurney, James. "Star Wars and Dinotopia", *Dinotopia* website, November 23, 1999, http://www.dinotopia.com/statement.html

Harmetz, Aljean. "Burden of Dreams: George Lucas", *American Film*, June 1983

Hart, Stephen. "Galactic Gasbag", *Salon*, April 10, 2002, http://www.salon.com/ent/movies/feature/2002/04/10/lucas

Hearn, Marcus. *The Cinema of George Lucas*, New York: Harry N. Abrams, 2005

*Hearts of Darkness: A Filmmakers Apocalypse*, 1991

Helander, Jan. "The Development of Star Wars as Seen Through the Scripts by George Lucas", *Starkiller: The Jedi Bendu Script Site*, 1997, http://www.starwarz.com/starkiller/writings/development_jan.htm

Hidalgo, Pablo. "Ask the Master", *Star Wars Insider*, issue 79, January/February 2005

*The Hidden Fortress* DVD. Criterion, 2001

*Homing Beacon*, issue 223, *Starwars.com*, April 17, 2008

*Homing Beacon*, issue 139, *Starwars.com*, June 23, 2005

*Homing Beacon*, issue 165, *Starwars.com*, July 6, 2006

*Homing Beacon*, issue 155, *Starwars.com*, February 16, 2006

Houston, David. "Creating the Space-Fantasy Universe of Star Wars", *Starlog*, August, 1977

Hume, Alan, with Owen, Gareth. *A Life Through the Lens*, Jefferson: McFarland & Company, 2004

Hyde, Douglas. "So Luke, Tell Me About Your Sister", *CNN*.com special, September 20, 2004, http://www.cnn.com/2004/SHOWBIZ/Movies/09/20/sidebar.hamill/index.html

*IMDB Studio Briefing*, "Hamill Says Lucas Asked Him to Appear in Future 'Star Wars' Trilogy", September 13, 2004, http://www.imdb.com/news/sb/2004-09-13#film6

*IMDB Studio Briefing*, "Jackson on Episode III. A 'Spolier?' " March 28, 2002 http://www.imdb.com/news/sb/2002-03-28#film2

*IMDB Studio Briefing*, "McGregor: Star Wars 2 'Really Good' - But Title 'Not Good'", February 7, 2002, http://www.imdb.com/news/wenn/2002-02-07#celeb7

*IMDB Studio Briefing*, "Neeson Says He'll Retire From Movie Acting", May 6, 1999, http://www.imdb.com/news/sb/1999-05-06#film3

*Indiana Jones: Making the Trilogy*, appearing on *Indiana Jones* trilogy DVD. Paramount Studios, 2003

Jacobson, Harlan. "Lucas: 'Star Wars' Isn't Iraq Wars", *USA Today*, May 15, 2005, http://www.usatoday.com/life/movies/news/2005-05-15-cannes-lucas_x.htm

*Joseph Campbell and the Power of Myth*, PBS, 1988

*Juice* magazine, May, 1999

Kahn, James. *Return of the Jedi*, New York: Ballantine, 1983

Kasdan. *Empire Strikes Back*, fourth draft, October, 1978.

Kausch, Allan. "An Exclusive Interview with George Lucas", S*tar Wars Insider*, issue 26, summer 1995

King, Thomas R. "Lucasvision", *The Wall Street Journal*, March 21, 1994

Kline, Sally (ed). *George Lucas Interviews*, Jackson: University Press of Mississippi, 1999

Kline, Sally. *"Radioland Murders* Press Conference," appearing in *George Lucas Interviews*, 1999.

Krebs, Joseph. "The Empire Strikes Back Director: Irvin Kershner", *Sound and Vision* online supplement, October 2004, http://www.soundandvisionmag.com/article.asp?section_id=4&article_id=672&page_number=1

Lawson, Terry. "Confused? Lucas Planned Vader This Way All Along", *Denver Post*, May 20, 2005, http://www.denverpost.com/movies/ci_2744169

Lenihan, Rob. "May the Boss Be With You", *CNN Money*, May 4, 1999 http://money.cnn.com/1999/05/04/bizbuzz/starwars/

*The Legacy of 2001*, appearing on *2001* DVD. Warner Brothers Entertainment, 2007

*A Legacy of Filmmakers: The Early Years of American Zoetrope*, appearing on *THX 1138* DVD. Warner Entertainment, 2004

Lester, Will. "Americans Prefer Watching Movies at Home", *Associated Press*, June 17, 2005, http://www.highbeam.com/doc/1P1-110055537.html

Lofficier, Randy and Jean-Marc. "Star Wars Genesis", 1983 (according to http://www.starwarz.com/starkiller/writings/genesis.htm), http://www.lofficier.com/starwars.htm. Printed in *Starlog* issue 127, July 1987 as "The Primordial Star Wars."

*A Long Time Ago: The Story of Star Wars*, BBC Omnibus TV special, 1999

Longsdorf, Amy. "Creating The Galaxy: Myth Maker And Jedi Master George Lucas In His Own Words", *Merge Digital*, 2006, http://www.mergedigital.com/custom/archive/me-lucas0518,0,2920316.story?coll=me-archive-hed

Lovell, Glenn. " 'Star Wars' Juggernaut Began Slowly,", *The Dallas Morning News*, Janurary 30, 1997, as reported by *Augusta Chronicle* Online, http://chronicle.augusta.com/stories/013097/starwars_juggernaut.html

Lucas, George. *The Star Wars*, story synopsis, May, 1973

Lucas, George. *The Star Wars*, rough draft, May, 1974

Lucas, George. *The Star Wars*, revised first draft, July, 1974

Lucas, George. *Adventures of the Starkiller*. Episode One: *The Star Wars*, second draft, January 28, 1975.

Lucas, George. *The Star Wars: From the Adventures of Luke Starkiller*, third draft, August, 1975

Lucas, George. *The Adventures of Luke Starkiller* as taken from the "Journal of the Whills." *Saga I: The Star Wars*, revised fourth draft, March 15, 1976

Lucas, George. *The Empire Strikes Back*, story treatment, November 28, 1977

Lucas, George. *Star Wars* Episode VI: *Revenge of the Jedi*, revised rough draft, June 12, 1981

Lucas, George. *The Beginning*, revised third draft, June 6, 1997

Lucas, George and Hales, Jonathan. Episode II shooting script (title, draft number and date unavailable)

Madsen, Dan. "George Lucas: Future of the Force", *Lucasfilm Fan Club Magazine*, issue 17, 1992

Madsen, Dan. "Prequel Update", *Star Wars Insider*, issue 26, summer, 1995

Madsen, Dan. "Prequel Update", *Star Wars Insider*, issue 39, August/September 1998

Madsen, Dan. "Prequel Update", *Star Wars Insider*, issue 44, June/July 1999

Madsen, Dan. "Prequel Update", *Star Wars Insider*, issue 46, October/November 1999

Madsen, Dan. "Prequel Update", *Star Wars Insider*, issue 48, Feb/ March 2000

Magid, Ron. "George Lucas: Past, Present and Future", *American Cinematographer*, February, 1997

Magid, Ron. "An Expanded Universe", *American Cinematographer*, February, 1997

Magid, Ron. "Exploring a New Universe", *American Cinematographer*, September, 2002

*Making Magic* CD-ROM, 1996

*The Making of Star Wars as Told by R2-D2 and C-3P0*, 1977

McCarthy, Todd. "Star Wars: Episode III—Revenge of the Sith", *Variety*, May 5, 2005

*Mediascene Prevue* , issue 42, 1980

*The Mercury News*, October 25, 2000,
http://www0.mercurycenter.com/premium/arts/docs/stamp26.htm

Mitchell, Blake and Fergusen, James. "Lawrence Kasdan: Man of Many Words",
*Fantastic Films*, July 1980

Moyers, Bill. "Of Myth and Men", *Time*, April 26, 1999

*Mr. Showbiz*, Untitled George Lucas interview, January 31, 1997,
www.mrshowbiz.go.com/interviews/299_3.html

*Museum of Hoaxes*, "Religion of the Jedi Knights",
http://www.museumofhoaxes.com/jedi.html

*Mythology of Star Wars*, PBS, 2001

Nash, Eric. "Dark Father", *Star Wars Galaxy Magazine*, issue 11, May, 1997

Ness, Alex. "Star Wars Comics Group Interview", *UGO*,
http://www.ugo.com/channels/comics/features/starwars

Okwu, Michal. "Jar Jar Jarring", *CNN*, June 14, 1999,
http://www.cnn.com/SHOWBIZ/Movies/9906/09/jar.jar/

O' Quinn, Kerry. "The George Lucas Saga", *Starlog*, July, August, September
1981

O' Quinn, Kerry. "Star Wars Memories", *Starlog*, February, 1988

*Oprah*, February, 1997

P., Ken. "An Interview With Gary Kurtz", *IGN Film Force* online, November
11, 2002, http://filmforce.ign.com/articles/376/376873p1.html

Packer, David. "Farewell Luke Skywalker", *Starlog*, July, 1983

Packer, David. "Hamill", *Starlog*, 1980

Packer, David. "Luke Skywalker is Alive and Well", *Starlog*, November, 1980

Parisi, Paula. "Grand Illusion", *Wired*, May, 1999

Parisi, Paula. "Star Wars Prequels Draw Lucas Back", *Contra Costa Times*,
September 30, 1996

Patterson, Richard. "Producing and Directing Return of the Jedi", *American Cinematographer*, June, 1983

Peecher, John Phillip. *The Making of Return of the Jedi*, New York: Ballantine Books, 1983

*People*, "Off the Screen", July 14, 1977

*People*, "What's New with Linda Ronstadt? She's Singing her Love Songs to Star Wars Czar George Lucas," March 26, 1984

Perenson, Melissa J. "As the *Star Wars: Episode III—Revenge of the Sith* DVD is Released, Producer Rick McCallum Turns to TV", *Science Fiction Weekly*, November 2005, http://www.scifi.com/sfw/issue446/interview2.html

*The Phantom Menace*, DVD commentary track. Lucasfilm, 2001

Phillips, Loren. "Breathe Deep, Seek Peace", *Echostation*, June 6, 1999, http://www.echostation.com/interview/gurney.htm

Pollock, Dale. *Skywalking: The Life and Films of George Lucas*, New York: Harmony Books, 1983

*Premiere*, September 1990

*Press-Telegram*, May 18, 1983:

*Preview*, "Mark Hamill", 1983. Retrieved from http://www.stars.handshake.de/preview.htm

*Prevue*, June/July, 1983

Prince, Stephen. *The Warrior's Camera*, Princeton: Princeton University Press, 1991.

*Puppets to Pixels*, appearing on *Attack of the Clones* DVD. Lucasfilm, 2002

Pye, Michael and Myles, Lynda. *The Movie Brats*, New York: Henry Holt and company, 1979

*Return of the Jedi*, DVD commentary track. Lucasfilm, 2004

*Return of the Jedi: Official Collectors Edition* souvenir book, 1983

*Revenge of the Sith*, DVD commentary. Lucasfilm, 2005

*Revenge of the Sith*, DVD online "depth commentary". Lucasfilm, 2005

Richie, Donald. *The Films of Akira Kurosawa*, Berkeley: University of California Press, 1965, (1998 reprinting)

Rinzler, J.W. *The Art of Star Wars Episode III: Revenge of the Sith*, New York: Ballantine Books, 2005

Rinzler, J.W. *The Complete Making of Indiana Jones*, New York: Ballantine Books, 2008

Rinzler, J.W. *The Making of Star Wars*, expanded hardcover edition, New York: Ballantine Books, 2007

Rinzler, J.W. *The Making of Revenge of the Sith*, New York: Ballantine Books, 2005

Rinzler, J.W. "Unknown Origins", *Star Wars Insider*, issue 92, March/April 2007

Rodley, Chris. *Lynch on Lynch*, revised edition, London: Faber and Faber, 2005

Rogers, Michael. "LJ Talks to J.W. Rinzler", *Library Journal*, April 24, 2007, http://www.libraryjournal.com/article/CA6434292.html

Roller, Pamela. "The Marketing of the Star Wars Trilogy", *Star Wars Insider*, issue 27, 1995

Ross, Drew. "Stereotypes Abound in Summer Flicks", *The Dailey Athenaeum*, July 7, 1999, ttp://www.da.wvu.edu/archives/990707/news/990707,04,04.html

Rubin, Michael. *Droidmaker: George Lucas and the Digital Revolution*. Florida: Triad Publshing Company, 2005

Sammon, Paul M. *Future Noir: The Making of Blade Runner*, New York: Harper Prism, 1996

Sansweet, Steve. *The Vault*, New York: Harper Entertainment, 2007

*Sarasota Herald-Tribune*, "Lucas Returning to Film Directing", September 29, 1996

Scanlon, Paul. "The Force Behind Star Wars", *Rolling Stone*, August 25, 1977

*Science Fiction Magazine*, June, 1978

Schinkel, Richard. "A Look Back in Wonder", *Time*, May 9, 2005

Schwartz, Jonathan. "Linda Rondstat: The US Interview", *US* magazine, December 25, 2000

*Screen Superstar*, "The Making of Star Wars", *Star Wars* special 1, 1977

Seabrook, John. "Letter From Skywalker Ranch: Why is the Force Still With Us?", *The New Yorker*, January 6, 1997

Sheff, David. "George Lucas", *Rolling Stone*, November 5, 1987

Schickel, Richard. "A Look Back in Wonder", *Time*, May 9, 2005

Silberman, Steve. "George Lucas on Star Wars, Fahrenheit 9/11, and His Own Legacy", *Wired* online exclusive, May 2005, http://wired.com/wired/archive/13.05/lucasqa.html

Silberman, Steve. "Life After Darth", *Wired*, May, 2005

Slavicsek, Bill. *A Guide to the Star Wars Universe*, second edition, New York: Ballantine Books, 1994

Sragow, Michael. "Father Figure", *Salon*, May 13, 1999, http://www.salon.com/ent/col/srag/1999/05/13/kershner/index.html

*Starburst*, issue 24, 1980

*Starlog*, issue 300, July, 2002

*Starlog*, "Starlog Salutes Star Wars", July, 1987

Stone, Judy. "George Lucas," *The San Francisco Chronicle*, May 23, 1971

*Starwars.com*, "Special Announcement: Episode II Title", August 6, 2001, http://www.starwars.com/episode-ii/release/promo/news20010806.html

*Starwars.com Podcast Special*, February 28, 2007, http://www.starwars.com/welcome/about/news/news20070228.html

*Star Wars* Definitive Edition Laserdisc. Lucasfilm, 1993

*Star Wars* DVD commentary. Lucasfilm, 2004

*Star Wars Poster Monthly*, issue 4, Fall, 1977

*The Star Wars Souvenir Program*, 1977

*Star Wars: The Magic and Mystery*. Twentieth Century Fox, 1997

Sturhahn, Larry. "The Filming of American Graffiti", *Filmmakers Newsletter*, March 1974

Tambone, Lou (as "T'Bone"). "Interview with Alan Dean Foster", *starwarz.com*, July 03, 2002, http://www.starwarz.com/tbone/interviews/alandeanfoster1.htm

Tambone, Lou (as "T'Bone"). "The Phantom Redemption", *starwarz.com*, May 8, 2003, originally posted on creativescreenwriting.com, 2000, http://www.starwarz.com/tbone/index.php?categoryid=26&p2_articleid=168

*Time*, May 19, 1980

*Time*, "George Lucas' Galactic Empire", March 6, 1978

*Time*, "Star Wars: The Years Best Movie", May 30, 1977

Titelman, Carol. *The Art of Star Wars*, New York: Ballantine Books, 1979

"An Interview With Timothy Zahn, Author of Heir to the Empire", Totse.com, 1991, http://www.totse.com/en/ego/science_fiction/tzi.html

Turan, Kenneth. " 'Star Wars: Episode I The Phantom Menace' ", *Los Angeles Times*, May 18, 1999

*TV Guide*, November 19, 2001

Vallely, Jean. "The Empire Strikes Back and So Does Filmmaker George Lucas With His Sequel to Star Wars", *Rolling Stone*, June 12, 1980

Vasseur, Richard. "Tom Veitch", *Jazma Online,* February 4, 2007, ttp://www.jazmaonline.com/interviews/interviews2007.asp?intID=432

Vaz, Mark Cotta. *The Art of Star Wars Episode II: Attack of the Clones*, New York: Ballantine Books, 2002

Vaz, Marc Cotta. "Illusions of Grandeur," *Star Wars Galaxy Magazine*, issue 2, winter, 1995

Vaz, Mark Cotta. "Ralph McQuarrie & Doug Chiang", *Star Wars Insider*, issue 50, July/August, 2000

Vaz, Mark Cotta and Duignan, Patricia Rose. *ILM: Into the Digital Realm*, New York: Ballantine Books, 1996

Vaz, Mark Cotta and Hatta, Shinji. *From Star Wars to Indiana Jones: The Best of the Lucasfilm Archives*, San Francisco: Chronicle Books, 1994

Vincenzi, Lisa. "A Short Time Ago, On a Ranch Not So Far Away...", *Millimeter*, April, 1990

Vineyard, Jennifer. "George Lucas Declares 'Star Wars' Over After 'Revenge Of The Sith' " *MTV*.com, September 10, 2004

Von Gunden, Kenneth. *Postmodern Auteurs: Coppola, Lucas, De Palma, Spielberg and Scorsese*, 1991

Wahlberg, Björn. "The Connoisseur's Guide to the Scripts of the Star Wars Saga", http://www.starwarz.com/starkiller/writings/cguide.htm

Wahlberg, Brendon. "The Development of Star Wars: A New Hope", *Starkiller: The Jedi Bendu Script Site*, http://www.starwarz.com/starkiller/writings/development_brendon.htm

Wahlberg, Brendon. "Rough Draft Sourcebook", *Starkiller: The Jedi Bendu Script Site*, http://www.starwarz.com/starkiller/writings/rough_draft_sourcebook.htm

Wahlberg, Brendon. "Second Draft Sourcebook", *Starkiller: The Jedi Bendu Script Site*, http://www.starwarz.com/starkiller/writings/second_draft_sourcebook.htm

*Waldenbooks* newsletter. "Hailing Frequencies: News and reviews from the worlds of Science Fiction and Fantasy", issue 1, 1992

Warren, Bill. "George Lucas: Father of the Force", *Starlog*, issue 127, February, 1988

"Star Wars: George Lucas' Vision," *Washington Post*, May 19, 2005

Weiner, Rex. "Lucas the Loner Returns to Star Wars", *Weekly Variety*, June 5, 1995

Weinraub, Bernard. "Luke Skywalker Goes Home", *Playboy*, July, 1997

*Well-Rounded Entertainment*, "George Lucas: The Well-Rounded Interview", 1999, http://www.well-rounded.com/movies/reviews/lucas_intv.html

Windolf, Jim. "Star Wars: The Last Battle", *Vanity Fair*, February, 2005

*The World of Star Wars: A Compendium of Fact and Fantasy From Star Wars and The Empire Strikes Back*, 1981

Worrell, Denise. *Icons: Intimate Portraits*, New York: Atlantic Monthly Press, 1989.

Zito, Stephen. "George Lucas Goes Far Out," *American Film*, April, 1977

602

# Index

# About the Author

MICHAEL Kaminski was two years old or less when he first saw *Star Wars* and immediately was entranced by its magic spell; the event was significant in another major way in that it was the beginning of his fascination and passion for cinema in general. Many years later he found himself graduating from Vancouver Film School and immediately found work in Toronto in various forms in the camera department, from cinematography and camera operating to camera assisting. He is a member of the International Cinematographers Guild and has worked on productions such as *Degrassi: The Next Generation* and *The Incredible Hulk.*

In spite of a budding career, Kaminski still found time to write *The Secret History of Star Wars* between — and often on the set of — films, an effort that consumed three years. Originally released on the internet out of sheer passion for the subject matter, without a single advertisement the e-book became popular through word of mouth, and in a few months had been downloaded close to 100,000 times.

Currently, Kaminski is pursuing a degree in history from the University of Toronto, specializing in ancient near and middle-eastern civilizations.

# Also Available from Legacy Books Press

*A Funny Thing Happened on the Way to the Agora*
*Ancient Greek and Roman Humour*

By R. Drew Griffith and Robert B. Marks

ISBN: 978-0-9784652-0-9

Ancient Greece and Rome aren't usually remembered for their sense of humour. However, in reality the ancient Greeks and Romans often refused to take themselves seriously. Strange and outlandish activities abounded – including somebody accidentally exposing himself while dancing sideways at his wedding (those wearing bed sheets didn't wear underwear) and a group of drunk young men thinking their house is sinking at sea, and tossing all their furniture out the windows.

R. Drew Griffith and Robert B. Marks take you on a lively and funny journey through the more bizarre activities of the ancient world, ranging everywhere from moochers to quacks to shrews to willing suckers, and even revealing the most terrible thing you can do to anybody involving a radish.

# Coming in 2009

*The War that Changed the World*
*The Forgotten War that Set the Stage for the Global Conflicts of the 20th Century and Beyond*

By John-Allen Price

ISBN: 978-0-9784652-1-6

Between 1870 and 1871, the world changed forever.

The Franco-Prussian War is often a forgotten war, its significance lost amidst larger conflicts such as the Napoleonic Wars and World War I. But, while it lasted less than a year, its aftermath would shape the course of history for decades to come.

In this comprehensive and epic account, John-Allen Price explores how this short but far-reaching war came to be, bringing the men who shaped history to life. And he examines the aftermath of the war, and how its aftershocks led to a century of slaughter, a war to end all wars, and an even greater war after that.

Lightning Source UK Ltd.
Milton Keynes UK
UKHW02f0746160118
316235UK00008B/331/P